ECONOMICS
FOURTH EDITION
AS LEVEL

ALAIN ANDERTON

Causeway
Press

Credits

Original cover design by Susan and Andrew Allen, fourth edition by Tim Button

Cover drawing by Pete Turner, provided by Getty images

Cartoons by Brick

Graphics by Caroline Waring-Collins, Anneli Griffiths and Kevin O'Brien

Photography by Andrew Allen and Dave Gray

Edited by Dave Gray

Proofreading by Mike Kidson, Sue Oliver and Heather Doyle.

British Library Cataloguing in Publication Data

A catalogue record for this book is available from the British Library.

ISBN-10:1-902796-93-4
ISBN-13:978-1-902796-93-2

Pearson Education, Edinburgh Gate, Harlow, Essex, CM20 2JE
First edition 2000 (reprinted three times)
Fourth edition 2006, reprinted 2006
Third impression 2006

Typesetting by Caroline Waring-Collins and Anneli Griffiths (Waring Collins Limited), Ormskirk, L39 2YT.
Contribution © Alain Anderton
Printed in China
GCC/03

Contents

iii

Preface

Teachers and students of economics are critical groups of people. Constantly dissatisfied with the materials that they use, they face the problems of limited resources, a wide variety of needs and a constantly changing world. This book is intended to go some way to resolving this example of the basic economic problem.

The book has a number of distinctive features.

Comprehensive The book contains sufficient material to satisfy the demands of students taking a wide range of examinations including AS Level and Higher Grade economics.

Flexible unit structure The material is organised not into chapters but into shorter units. This reflects the organisation of a number of GCSE textbooks, and therefore students should be familiar with this style of presentation. The unit structure also allows the teacher greater freedom to devise a course. Economics teachers have a long tradition of using their main textbooks in a different order to that in which they are presented. So whilst there is a logical order to the book, it has been written on the assumption that teachers and students will piece the units together to suit their own teaching and learning needs. Cross referencing has been used on occasions to further aid flexibility. This approach also means that it is relatively easy to use the book for a growing number of courses which encompass part of an AS/A Level specification, such as professional courses with an economics input. To allow flexibility in course construction **Economics (Fourth Edition)** is also available. It is a complete coursebook for AS/A Level, higher Grade, higher education and professional courses.

Accessibility The book has been written in a clear and logical style which should make it accessible to all readers. Each unit is divided into short, easily manageable sections. Diagrams contain concise explanations which summarise or support the text.

A workbook The text is interspersed with a large number of questions. These are relatively short for the most part, and, whilst some could be used for extended writing work, most require relatively simple answers. They have been included to help teachers and students assess whether learning and understanding has taken place by providing immediate application of content and skills to given situations. I hope that many will be used as a basis for class discussion as well as being answered in written form. **Economics Teachers' Guide (Fourth Edition)** provides suggested answers to questions that appear in the book.

Applied economics as well as economic theory Many economics courses require teachers and students to have a book covering economic theory **and** an applied economic text. In this book, a systematic approach to applied economics has been included alongside economic theory. Each unit has an applied economics section and some units deal only with applied economics. It should be noted that many of the questions also contain applied economics material and, where sufficiently significant, this has been referred to in the index.

Use of data Modern technology has allowed much of the book to proceed from manuscript to book in a very short period. This has meant that we have been able to use statistics which were available in early 2006. Most statistical series therefore go up to 2004 or 2005, although some were only available for earlier years. At the same time, experience has shown that too many current stories quickly date a book. Materials have therefore been chosen, particularly for the macroeconomic section of the book, from throughout the post-war era, with particular emphasis on the turbulent times of the 1970s and 1980s, and the 1990s and 2000s. This approach will help candidates to answer questions which require knowledge of what has happened 'in recent years' or 'over the past decade'.

Study skills and assessment The last two units of this book provide guidance on effective study and the methods of assessment used in economics.

Key terms Many units contain a key terms section. Each section defines new concepts, which appear in capitals in the text of the unit. Taken together, they provide a comprehensive dictionary of economics.

Presentation Great care has been taken with how this book is presented. It is hoped that the layout of the book, the use of colour and the use of diagrams will make learning economics a rewarding experience.

Alain Anderton

Acknowledgments

The author and publishers wish to thank the following for permission to reproduce photographs and copyright material. Other copyright material is acknowledged at source.

Corel pp 3(t), 21, Digital Vision pp 2, 3(b), 7, 16(b), 67(t), 28(t), 100, 104, 283(t), Image 100 p 219, Photodisc pp 9, 65, 96, 113, 116, 121 (bc, br), 135, 146, 151, 263, 283(c), 291, 310, Rex Features pp 12, 130, 138, 157, 214, Stockbyte p 235, Stockdisc p 206, Topfoto pp 121(bl), 174, 238.

Office for National Statistics material is Crown Copyright, reproduced with the permission of the Controller of Her Majesty's Stationery Office.

Every effort has been made to locate the copyright owners of material used in this book. Any omissions brought to the notice of the publisher are regretted and will be credited in subsequent printings.

Thanks
I have many thanks to make. Mike Kidson, Sue Oliver and Heather Doyle carried out the unenviable task of proof reading. Waring Collins Limited designed the book with their usual flair and skill. Dave Gray has been a superb editor and, as always, has been an enormous pleasure to work with. Not least, I would like to thank my wife who has performed a variety of tasks, in particular putting up with the stresses and strains of the production of such a large volume. All mistakes in the book, however, remain my own responsibility.

Finally, I would like to thank all those who read this book. It is an enormous privilege to be able to explore the world of economics with you. Your comments are always welcome, whether critical or otherwise. I hope you find the subject as exciting, stimulating and rewarding as I have always found it.

Alain Anderton

the basic economic problem

Summary

1. Nearly all resources are scarce.
2. Human wants are infinite.
3. Scarce resources and infinite wants give rise to the basic economic problem - resources have to be allocated between competing uses.
4. Allocation involves choice and each choice has an opportunity cost.
5. The production possibility frontier (PPF) shows the maximum potential output of an economy.
6. Production at a point inside the PPF indicates an inefficient use of resources.
7. Growth in the economy will shift the PPF outwards.

Scarcity

It is often said that we live in a global village. The world's resources are finite; there are only limited amounts of land, water, oil, food and other resources on this planet. Economists therefore say that resources are SCARCE.

Scarcity means that economic agents, such as individuals, firms, governments and international agencies, can only obtain a limited amount of resources at any moment in time. For instance, a family has to live on a fixed budget; it cannot have everything it wants. A firm might want to build a new factory but not have the resources to be able to do so. A government might wish to build new hospitals or devote more resources to its foreign aid programme but not have the finance to make this possible. Resources which are scarce are called ECONOMIC GOODS.

Not all resources are scarce. There is more than enough air on this planet for everyone to be able to breathe as much as they want. Resources which are not scarce are called FREE GOODS. In the past many goods such as food, water and shelter have been free, but as the population of the planet has expanded and as production has increased, so the number of free goods has diminished. Recently, for instance, clean beaches in many parts of the UK have ceased to be a free good to society. Pollution has forced water companies and seaside local authorities to spend resources cleaning up their local environment. With the destruction of the world's rain forests and increasing atmospheric pollution, the air we breathe may no longer remain a free good. Factories may have to purify the air they take from the atmosphere, for instance. This air would then become an economic good.

Infinite wants

People have a limited number of NEEDS which must be satisfied if they are to survive as human beings. Some are material needs, such as food, liquid, heat, shelter and clothing. Others are psychological and emotional needs such as self-esteem and being loved. People's needs are finite. However, no one would choose to live at the level of basic human needs if they could enjoy a higher standard of living.

This is because human WANTS are unlimited. It doesn't matter whether the person is a farmer in Africa, a mystic in India, a manager in the UK or the richest individual in the world, there is always something which he or she wants more of. This can include more food, a bigger house, a longer holiday, a cleaner environment, more love, more friendship, better relationships, more self-esteem, greater fairness or justice, peace, or more time to listen to music, meditate or cultivate the arts.

The basic economic problem

Resources are scarce but wants are infinite. It is this which gives rise to the BASIC ECONOMIC PROBLEM and which forces economic agents to make choices. They have to allocate their scarce resources between competing uses.

Economics is the study of this allocation of resources - the choices that are made by economic agents. Every CHOICE involves a range of alternatives. For instance, should the

Question 1

Time was when people used to take their car out for a Sunday afternoon 'spin'. The novelty of owning a car and the freedom of the road made driving a pleasant leisure pursuit. Today, with 27 million cars registered in the UK, a Sunday afternoon tour could easily turn into a nightmare traffic jam.

Of course, many journeys are trouble free. Traffic is so light that cars do not slow each other down. But most rush hour journeys today occur along congested roads where each extra car on the road adds to the journey time of every other car. When London introduced a £5 a day 'congestion charge', a fee for cars to use roads in central London, the amount of traffic dropped by 17 per cent. This was enough to reduce journey times considerably.

Traffic congestion also greatly increases the amount of pollution created by cars. Our ecosystem can cope with low levels of emissions, but, as cities like Paris and Athens have discovered, high levels of traffic combined with the right weather conditions can lead to sharp increases in pollution levels. The car pollutes the environment anyway because cars emit greenhouse gases. One quarter of CO_2 emissions in the UK come from road transport.

Source: adapted from *Transport Statistics for Great Britain 2004*, Department for Transport; Office for National Statistics.

Explain whether roads are, in any sense, a 'free good' from an economic viewpoint.

Question 2

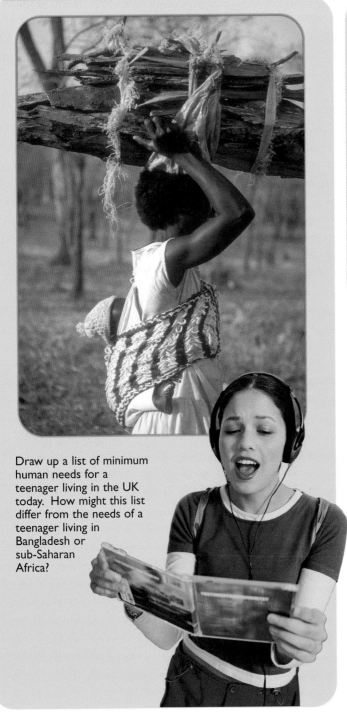

Draw up a list of minimum human needs for a teenager living in the UK today. How might this list differ from the needs of a teenager living in Bangladesh or sub-Saharan Africa?

Question 3

Over the past 10 years, university students have came under increasing financial pressure. For the previous 40 years, the government paid for all student tuition fees. It also gave a grant to students to cover their living expenses, although this grant was means tested according to the income of parents. In the 1990s, the government froze student grants and introduced a system of subsidised student loans to allow students to make up for the falling real value of the grants. In 1998, students for the first time were charged for part of their tuition fees. The amount they had to pay each year was set at £1 000. In 1999, maintenance grants were replaced completely by loans. From September 2006, students starting their university courses will be required to pay £3 000 a year towards tuition fees. The cost of going to university will then average over £7 000 a year to the student.

What might be the opportunity cost of the £7 000 in fees and maintenance:
(a) to parents if they pay them on behalf of their sons or daughters;
(b) to students if they have to borrow the money to pay them?

government spend £10 billion in tax revenues on nuclear weapons, better schools or greater care for the elderly? Will you choose to become an accountant, an engineer or a vicar?

These choices can be graded in terms of the benefits to be gained from each alternative. One choice will be the 'best' one and a rational economic agent will take that alternative. But all the other choices will then have to be given up. The benefit lost from the next best alternative is called the OPPORTUNITY COST of the choice. For instance, economics may have been your third choice at 'A' level. Your fourth choice, one which you didn't take up, might have been history. Then the opportunity cost of studying economics at 'A' level is studying history at 'A' level. Alternatively, you might have enough money to buy just one of your two favourite magazines - *totalDVD* or *DVD Monthly*. If you choose to buy *totalDVD*, then its opportunity cost is the benefit which would have been gained from consuming *DVD Monthly*.

Free goods have no opportunity cost. No resources need be sacrificed when someone, say, breathes air or swims in the sea.

Production possibility frontiers

Over a period of time, resources are scarce and therefore only a finite amount can be produced. For example, an economy might have enough resources at its disposal to be able to produce 30 units of manufactured goods and 30 units of non-manufactures. If it were now to produce more manufactured goods, it would have to give up some of its production of non-manufactured items. This is because the production of a manufactured item has an opportunity cost - in this case the production of non-manufactures. The more manufactures that are produced, the less non-manufactures can be produced.

This can be shown in Figure 1.1. The curved line is called the PRODUCTION POSSIBILITY FRONTIER (PPF) - other names for it include PRODUCTION POSSIBILITY CURVE or BOUNDARY, and TRANSFORMATION CURVE. The PPF shows the different combinations of economic goods which an economy is able to produce if all resources in the economy are fully and efficiently employed. The economy therefore could be:
- at the point C on its PPF, producing 30 units of manufactured goods and 30 units of non-manufactures;
- at the point D, producing 35 units of manufactured goods and 20 units of non-manufactures;
- at the point A, devoting all of its resources to the production of non-manufactured goods;
- at the points B or E or anywhere else along the line.

The production possibility frontier illustrates clearly the principle of opportunity cost. Assume that the economy is producing at the point C in Figure 1.1 and it is desired to move to the point D. This means that the output of

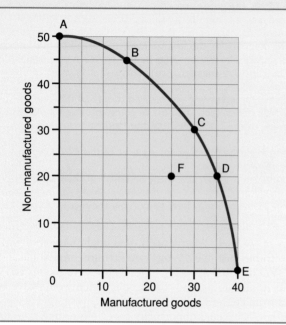

Figure 1.1 The production possibility frontier
ABCDE is a production possibility frontier. It shows the different combinations of goods which can be produced if all resources are fully and efficiently utilised. For instance, the economy can produce no manufactured goods and 50 units of non-manufactures, 30 units of manufactured goods and 30 units of non-manufactures, or 40 units of manufactured goods but no non-manufactures.

and efficiently employed. If there are unemployed workers or idle factories, or if production is inefficiently organised, then the economy cannot be producing on its PPF. It will produce within the boundary. In Figure 1.1 the economy could produce anywhere along the line AE. But because there is unemployment in the economy, production is at point F.

The economy cannot be at any point outside its existing PPF because the PPF, by definition, shows the maximum production level of the economy. However, it might be able to move to the right of its PPF in the future if there is **economic growth**. An increase in the productive potential of an economy is shown by a shift outwards of the PPF. In Figure 1.2 economic growth pushes the PPF from PP to QQ, allowing the economy to increase its maximum level of production say from A to B. Growth in the economy can happen if:

- the quantity of resources available for production increases; for instance there might be an increase in the number of workers in the economy, or new factories and offices might be built;
- there is an increase in the quality of resources; education will make workers more productive whilst technical progress will allow machines and production processes to produce more with the same amount of resources.

The production possibility frontiers in Figures 1.1. and 1.2 have been drawn concave to the origin (bowing outwards) rather than as straight lines or as convex lines. This is because it has been assumed that not all resources in the economy are as productive in one use compared to another.

Take, for instance, the production of wheat in the UK. Comparatively little wheat is grown in Wales because the soil and the climate are less suited to wheat production than in an area like East Anglia. Let us start from a position where no wheat is grown at all in the UK. Some farmers then decide to grow wheat. If production in the economy is to be maximised it should be grown on the land which is most suited to wheat production (i.e. where its opportunity cost is lowest). This will be in an area of the country like East Anglia. As wheat production expands, land has to be used which is less productive because land is a finite resource. More and more marginal land, such as that found in Wales, is used and output per acre falls. The land could have been used for another form of production, for instance sheep rearing. The more wheat is grown, the less is the output per acre and therefore the greater the cost in terms of sheep production.

manufactured goods will increase from 30 to 35 units. However, the opportunity cost of that (i.e. what has to be given up because of that choice) is the lost output of non-manufactures, falling from 30 to 20 units. The opportunity cost at C of increasing manufacturing production by 5 units is 10 units of non-manufactures.

The production possibility frontier for an economy is drawn on the assumption that all resources in the economy are fully

In Figure 1.3 only sheep and wheat are produced in the economy. If no wheat is produced the economy could produce OC of sheep. If there is one unit of wheat production only OB of sheep can be produced. Therefore the opportunity cost of the first unit of wheat is BC of sheep. The second unit of wheat has a much higher opportunity cost - AB. But if the economy produces wheat only, then the opportunity cost of the third unit of wheat rises to OA of sheep.

The PPF by itself gives no indication of which combination of goods will be produced in an economy. All it shows is the combination of goods which an economy could produce if output were maximised from a given fixed amount of resources. It shows a range of possibilities and much of economics is concerned with explaining why an economy, ranging from a household economy to the international economy, chooses to produce at one point either on or within its PPF rather than another.

Figure 1.2 Economic growth
Economic growth in the quantity or quality of the inputs to the production process means that an economy has increased its productive potential. This is shown by a shift to the right of the production possibility frontier from PP to QQ. It would enable the economy to move production, for instance, from point A to point B.

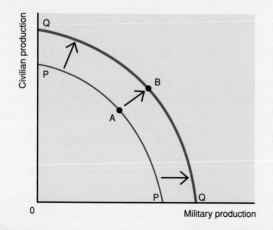

Figure 1.3 *Opportunity costs*
The production possibility frontier is concave, showing that the opportunity cost of production rises as more of a good is produced.

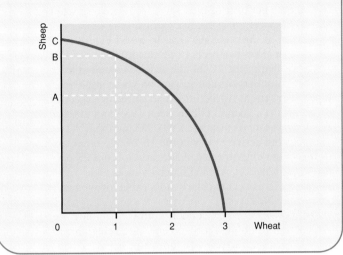

Question 4

Draw a production possibility frontier. The vertical axis shows the production of public sector goods and the horizontal axis shows production of private sector goods. The economy is currently producing at point A on the frontier where 50% of all production is devoted to public sector goods and 50% to private sector goods.

(a) Mark the following points on your drawing.
  (i) Point A.
  (ii) Point B which shows production following the election of a government which increases government spending on both education and the National Health Service.
  (iii) Point C where unemployment is present in the economy.
  (iv) Point D where the government takes over production of all goods and services in the economy.
(b) Draw another diagram putting on it the original production possibility frontier you drew for (a), labelling it AA.
  (i) Draw a new production possibility frontier on the diagram, labelling it PP, which shows the position after a devastating war has hit the economy.
  (ii) Draw another PPF labelling it QQ which shows an increase in productivity in the economy such that output from the same amount of resources increases by 50 per cent in the public sector but twice that amount in the private sector.

Key terms

Basic economic problem - resources have to be allocated between competing uses because wants are infinite whilst resources are scarce.
Choice - economic choices involve the alternative uses of scarce resources.
Economic goods - goods which are scarce because their use has an opportunity cost.
Free goods - goods which are unlimited in supply and which therefore have no opportunity cost.
Needs - the minimum which is necessary for a person to survive as a human being.
Opportunity cost - the benefits foregone of the next best alternative.

Production possibility frontier (also known as the production possibility curve or the production possibility boundary or the transformation curve) - a curve which shows the maximum potential level of output of one good given a level of output for all other goods in the economy.
Scarce resources - resources which are limited in supply so that choices have to be made about their use.
Wants - desires for the consumption of goods and services.

Applied economics

Work and Leisure

Time is a scarce resource. There are only 24 hours in a day and 365 days in a year. Average life expectancy for a UK male born in 2003 was 76 and 81 for a female. So people have to make choices about how to allocate their time.

One fundamental choice is how to divide time between work and leisure. Work can narrowly be defined as paid work. Table 1.1 shows that there has been a small reduction in the average number of hours worked per week over the past 20 years. On the other hand, holiday entitlements have shortened the working year. Most workers are now entitled to at least 3-4 weeks paid holiday each year plus bank holidays. In 1970, the average was only 2 weeks.

There has been a reduction in the average number of years worked by men. Figure 1.4 shows activity rates for men and women, comparing 1989 with 2004. The activity rate is the percentage of the population in work or seeking work (i.e. officially unemployed). For instance 96 per cent of men aged 25-34 were in work or seeking work in 1989. In contrast, only 69 per cent of women of the same age were in work. Figure 1.4 shows that there has been a significant fall in activity rates for men in the 18-24 age range, accounted for by growing numbers of men staying on and completing higher education. At the other end of the age spectrum, there has been a small fall between 1989 and 2004 in the activity rate of men aged 50+. Women, too, have seen reduced activity rates in the 16-24 age range due to higher staying on rates in education. From 25 onwards, however, women's activity rates have increased. This is particularly noticeable for women aged over 50.

People work for a variety of motives, including the satisfaction of doing a job and enjoying being part of a team. However, the primary motivator is pay. When workers retire, they might choose to undertake voluntary work, or do jobs about the house which previously they would have paid someone else to do. However, rarely will they put the time or the energy into these activities that they put into their previous paid job. Over time, the opportunity cost of not working has been rising because wages have been rising. Since 1945, earnings have roughly been doubling every 30 years in real terms (i.e. after inflation has been taken into account). Workers today can buy far more goods and services than their parents or grandparents at a similar age. If a 40 year old doesn't work today, he or she will have to forego the purchase of far more goods and services than, say, 30 years ago. This is arguably the most important reason why more and more women are choosing to stay in work rather than give up work to stay at home to bring up their families.

For those taking early retirement, the opportunity cost of leisure time is typically far less than for other workers. When they retire, they receive a pension. Hence, the money foregone is only the difference between what they would have earned and their pension. Tax, National Insurance contributions and work related payments like pension contributions or costs of commuting to work all help to reduce the monetary value of a wage. Hence, many workers taking early retirement find that their new retirement income is not that much below their old take home pay. The benefits of the extra leisure time they can gain by retiring far outweigh the losses in terms of the goods and services they could buy had they stayed in work.

Early retirement, however, is likely to become less common in the future. With rising life

Table 1.1 Average weekly hours of full-time employees		
	1986	2004
Males	41.8	39.2
Females	37.3	33.7

Source: adapted from *Annual Abstract of Statistics*, Office for National Statistics.

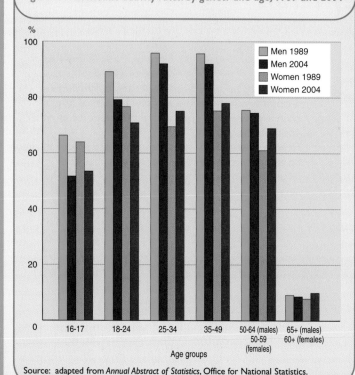

Figure 1.4 Economic activity rates: by gender and age, 1989 and 2004

Source: adapted from *Annual Abstract of Statistics*, Office for National Statistics.

expectancies, employers are finding it more expensive to provide pensions for workers. The public sector is reacting by trying to force up retirement ages and make it more difficult for workers to retire early. Private sector employers are tending to close down their existing pension schemes and replace them with far less generous schemes where workers have to save more to get the same pension. The result is that the opportunity cost of retiring early is likely to rise substantially. Workers will react by staying on in work longer.

Non-paid work

Paid work is not the only type of work undertaken by individuals. People also have to work at home, cooking, cleaning, maintaining equipment and property and looking after others, particularly children, the sick and the elderly. Table 1.2 shows that women tend to spend nearly twice as much time on housework and childcare than men. However, men tend to spend more time on employment and study. This could suggest that the traditional stereotype of men working whilst women do more housework and look after the children might still be the case, to some extent, even though more and more women are going out work.

Leisure

Individuals spend their leisure time in a variety of ways. Table 1.3 shows participation rates in the main home-based leisure activities and how they have changed over time. The most popular leisure activity is watching television. Nearly everybody had watched some television in the four weeks prior to being interviewed for the survey. Equally, seeing friends or relatives is a highly popular activity. Table 1.3 shows

that there are gender differences between leisure activities. Men are far more likely to do DIY and gardening, whilst women are more likely to do dressmaking, needlework and knitting. This time series shows that participation rates in most leisure activities have been rising over time. A greater proportion of the population, for example, read books, did DIY or did some gardening at the end of the twentieth century than they did in the 1970s. This greater variety of leisure activities has probably come about for a variety of reasons: increased incomes, allowing people to afford to engage in particular activities such as listening to CDs; better education, giving people access

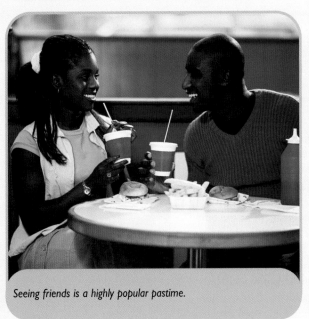

Seeing friends is a highly popular pastime.

Table 1.2 Time spent on main activities: by sex, 2000-2001

United Kingdom	Hours and minutes per day	
	Males	Females
Sleep	8:23	8:33
Leisure		
Watching TV and Video/DVD	2:41	2:17
Social life and entertainment	1:16	1:33
Reading and listening to radio and music	0:36	0:35
Hobbies and games	0:26	0:16
Sport	0:18	0:11
All leisure	5:17	4:52
Employment and study	4:17	2:42
Housework and childcare	2:17	4:03
Personal care	2:07	2:19
Travel	1:28	1:21
Other	0:09	0:10

Source: adapted from *Social Trends*, Office for National Statistics.

Table 1.3 Participation in home-based leisure activities: by sex

Great Britain			Percentages	
	1977	1986	1996	2002
Males				
Watching TV	97	98	99	99
Visiting/entertaining				
friends or relations	89	92	95	-
Listening to records/tapes/CDs	64	69	79	83
Reading books	52	52	58	58
DIY	51	54	58	-
Gardening	49	47	52	-
Dressmaking/needlework/knitting	2	3	3	-
Females				
Watching TV	97	98	99	99
Visiting/entertaining				
friends or relations	93	95	97	-
Listening to records/tapes/CDs	60	65	77	83
Reading books	57	64	71	72
DIY	22	27	30	-
Gardening	35	39	45	-
Dressmaking/needlework/knitting	51	48	37	-

Source: adapted from *Social Trends*, *General Household Survey*, Office for National Statistics.

to activities such as reading and less time spent at work giving more time for DIY or gardening.

Individuals have to allocate their scarce resources of time and money between different leisure pursuits. Children tend to be time rich but financially poor. 45 year olds tend to be the reverse: time poor but financially better off. Old age pensioners are time rich but less financially well off than when they were working. Their health may also preclude them from activities such as taking part in sport. These constraints could be represented on a production possibility frontier. For instance, a diagram could be drawn showing the trade off between home based leisure pursuits and leisure activities away from the home. The more time spent in the pub means that less time is available to watch television at home or gardening. Equally, a production possibility diagram could be used to illustrate the trade-off between work and leisure. The more time spent at work, the less leisure time is available. Ultimately, choices have to be made between work and leisure and individuals have to assume responsibility for the choices they make.

DataQuestion — Production possibility frontiers

The break up of Eastern Europe

When communism in Eastern Europe and the former Soviet Union was replaced by more democratic systems of government at the end of the 1980s, there was a move away from state control of the economy towards a market-led economy. Before, the state had often decided which factories were to produce what products, and would issue instructions about who was to buy the resulting output. In the new market-led system, factories had to find buyers for their products. The result was that many factories closed down. Consumers began buying foreign made goods, or found their incomes drastically slashed as they were made redundant from closing enterprises. Factories making goods for the defence industry were particularly badly affected as governments cut their spending on defence. Some attempted to transfer their skills to making civilian goods, but it often proved impossible to make the jump from the manufacture of fighter jets to the manufacture of washing machines. The total incomes and output of countries such as Russia and Bulgaria were actually lower in 2004 than they were in 1989. These countries have faced enormous problems in making the transition. Others, such as Hungary, have been more successful and have seen a rise in their total incomes and output.

Table 1.4 National income, selected countries in Eastern Europe and the former Soviet Union, 2004 as a % of 1989

	%
Albania	26.1
Belarus	12.2
Bulgaria	- 9.5
Croatia	- 4.2
Georgia	- 58.5
Hungary	23.4
Romania	- 2.7
Russia	- 18.4
Serbia and Montenegro	- 48.9

Source: adapted from United Nations, *Economic Survey of Europe.*

Former Yugoslavia

The collapse of communism in Eastern Europe was a mixed blessing for some. In Yugoslavia, it led to the break-up of the federation of states which formed the country. Serbia, which considered itself the most important part of the federation, strongly resisted the process. In 1992, it fought a war with Croatia and over-ran parts of that country which had majority Serb populations. Serbia then helped fuel a civil war in Bosnia-Herzegovina. In 1999, Serbian forces were accused of attempting to ethnically cleanse the majority Albanian population from its province of Kosovo. This resulted in intervention by US and European troops. Serbia paid a heavy price for its actions. Its economy shrank as infrastructure, such as houses and factories, were destroyed in fighting. Embargoes by the USA and the EU on trade with Serbia disrupted exports and imports. It was only from 2000 when peace was restored in the region that Serbia's economy began to grow again. Even then, as Table 1.5 shows, Serbia paid a heavy price for its aggression towards its neighbours. Croatia, which also engaged in war, was less badly affected because it had stopped fighting by the mid-1990s, allowing its economy to begin growing again.

Source: adapted from www.state.gov; www.washingtonpost.com.

Table 1.5 Croatia and Serbia, national income, 2004 as a % of 1989

	%
Croatia	- 4.2
Serbia and Montenegro	- 48.9

Source: adapted from United Nations, *Economic Survey of Europe.*

China

Since the mid-1970s, China has been growing dramatically. Over the period 1990 to 2005, it grew by nearly 10 per cent per annum. This means that output is doubling roughly every seven years. It is not difficult to understand why the Chinese economy has been so successful. By the mid-1970s, it already had a relatively well educated workforce. Much of its economy was inefficient and there was considerable scope for drawing in workers from rural areas into more productive work in towns and cities. There was a gradual easing of Communist control of the economy which allowed ordinary Chinese people to set up their own businesses in a more free market style economy. Finally, there was a considerable flow of investment money and technological know-how into China. Foreign investors were keen to take advantage of cheap labour and found the lure of what is likely to become the world's largest economy irresistible.

Third World debt crisis

In the 1970s and early 1980s, many Third World countries borrowed heavily from the West. The money was used for a combination of economic development, military spending and excessive consumption on the part of ruling elites. The borrowing, for the most part, stopped in 1982 when Mexico announced that it could no longer keep up with repayments on debts. Western banks, afraid that other countries would also default on their debts, stopped new lending to many countries. African countries were particularly badly affected. The money borrowed had been poorly used and they were faced with having to make considerable repayments each year. The result was deteriorating living standards. Governments cut back on social spending such as education and health care. Infrastructure such as roads and rail networks deteriorated.

Table 1.6 Average annual growth in real national income and population, selected developing countries, 1980-2003

		Percentage	
		1980-1990	1990-2003
Argentina	National income	- 0.4	2.3
	Population	2.5	1.3
Haiti	National income	- 0.2	- 0.8
	Population	3.6	2.0
Mozambique	National income	- 0.1	7.0
	Population	3.4	2.2
Niger	National income	- 0.1	2.7
	Population	6.0	3.3
Peru	National income	- 0.3	3.9
	Population	3.6	1.8

Source: adapted from World Bank, *World Development Report.*

In the first decade of the twenty first century, many countries were still living with the consequences of the 1980s debt crisis. Whilst forgiving debt would help these countries develop, it could not make up for the lost decades of development in the 1980s and 1990s when many countries, particularly in Africa, became poorer rather than richer. The situation has been made worse by often high increases in population. An economy may be growing, but average living standards can fall if population growth is higher than the growth in the productive potential of the economy.

1. What is a production possibility frontier for an economy?
2. Explain why a production possibility frontier might shift inwards or outwards. Illustrate your answer with examples from the data.
3. A peace group has put forward a proposal that the UK should halve its spending on defence, including giving up its nuclear capability. Using production possibility frontiers, evaluate the possible economic implications of this proposal.

Summary

1. An economy is a social organisation through which decisions about what, how and for whom to produce are made.
2. The factors of production - land, labour, capital and entrepreneurship - are combined together to create goods and services for consumption.
3. Specialisation and the division of labour give rise to large gains in productivity.
4. The economy is divided into three sectors, primary, secondary and tertiary.
5. Markets exist for buyers and sellers to exchange goods and services using barter or money.
6. The main actors in the economy, consumers, firms and government, have different objectives. Consumers, for instance, wish to maximise their welfare whilst firms might wish to maximise profit.

What is an economy?

Economic resources are scarce whilst human wants are infinite. An economy is a system which attempts to solve this basic economic problem. There are many different levels and types of economy. There is the household economy, the local economy, the national economy and the international economy. There are free market economies which attempt to solve the economic problem with the minimum intervention of government and command economies where the state makes most resource allocation decisions. Although these economies are different, they all face the same problem.

Economists distinguish three parts to the economic problem.

● **What** is to be produced? An economy can choose the mix of goods to produce. For instance, what proportion of total output should be spent on defence? What proportion should be spent on protecting the environment? What proportion should be invested for the future? What proportion should be manufactured goods and what proportion services?

● **How** is production to be organised? For instance, are hi-fi systems to be made in the UK, Japan or Taiwan? Should car bodies be made out of steel or fibreglass? Would it better to automate a production line or carry on using unskilled workers?

● **For whom** is production to take place? What proportion of output should go to workers? How much should pensioners get? What should be the balance between incomes in the UK and those in Bangladesh?

An economic system needs to provide answers to all these questions.

Question 1

Consider your household economy.
(a) What is produced by your household (e.g. cooking services, cleaning services, accommodation, products outside the home)?
(b) How is production organised (e.g. who does the cooking, what equipment is used, when is the cooking done)?
(c) For whom does production take place (e.g. for mother, for father)?
(d) Do you think your household economy should be organised in a different way? Justify your answer.

Economic resources

Economists commonly distinguish three types of resources available for use in the production process. They call these resources the FACTORS OF PRODUCTION.

LAND is not only land itself but all natural resources below the earth, on the earth, in the atmosphere and in the sea. Everything from gold deposits to rainwater and natural forests are examples of land.

NON-RENEWABLE RESOURCES, such as coal, oil, gold and copper, are land resources which once used will never be replaced. If we use them today, they are not available for use by our children or our children's children. RENEWABLE RESOURCES on the other hand can be used and replaced. Examples are fish stocks, forests, or water. Renewable resources can sometimes be over-exploited by man leading to their destruction.

LABOUR is the workforce of an economy - everybody from housepersons to doctors, vicars and cabinet ministers. Not all workers are the same. Each worker has a unique set of inherent characteristics including intelligence, manual dexterity and emotional stability. But workers are also the products of education and training. The value of a worker is called his or her HUMAN CAPITAL. Education and training will increase the value of that human capital, enabling the worker to be more productive.

CAPITAL is the manufactured stock of tools, machines, factories, offices, roads and other resources which is used in the production of goods and services. Capital is of two types. WORKING or CIRCULATING CAPITAL is stocks of raw materials, semi-manufactured and finished goods which are waiting to be sold. These stocks circulate through the production process till they are finally sold to a consumer. FIXED CAPITAL is the stock of factories, offices, plant and machinery. Fixed capital is fixed in the sense that it will not be transformed into a final product as working capital will. It is used to transform working capital into finished products.

Sometimes a fourth factor of production is distinguished. This is ENTREPRENEURSHIP. Entrepreneurs are individuals who:
- organise production - organise land, labour and capital in the production of goods and services;
- take risks - with their own money and the financial capital of others, they buy factors of production to produce goods and services in the hope that they will be able to make a profit but in the knowledge that at worst they could lose all their money and go bankrupt.

It is this element of risk taking which distinguishes entrepreneurs from ordinary workers.

Question 2

Table 2.1 *Factors of production: selected statistics*

	1989	2004
Production of coal (million tonnes)	98.2	25.1
Number of students gaining a degree qualification	74 953	258 560
Net investment in new physical fixed capital at 2001 constant prices (£ million)	43 572	58 478

Source: adapted from *Annual Abstract of Statistics*, Office for National Statistics, Higher Education Statistics Agency (HESA).

1. Net investment is 2003 figures.

(a) Explain what is meant by the 'factors of production'. Illustrate your answer from the data.

Specialisation

When he was alone on his desert island, Robinson Crusoe found that he had to perform all economic tasks by himself. When Man Friday came along he quickly abandoned this mode of production and specialised. SPECIALISATION is the production of a limited range of goods by an individual or firm or country in co-operation with others so that together a complete range of goods is produced.

Specialisation can occur between nations. For instance, a country like Honduras produces bananas and trades those for cars produced in the United States. **Globalisation** (☞ unit 40) is currently intensifying this process of specialisation between nations. Specialisation can also occur within economies. Regional economies specialise. In the UK, Stoke-on-Trent specialises in pottery whilst London specialises in services.

Specialisation by individuals is called THE DIVISION OF LABOUR. Adam Smith, in a passage in his famous book *An Enquiry into the Nature and Causes of the Wealth of Nations*

(1776), described the division of labour amongst pin workers. He wrote:

A workman not educated to this business ... could scarce ... make one pin in a day, and certainly could not make twenty. But in the way in which this business is now carried on, ... it is divided into a number of branches ... One man draws out the wire, another straightens it, a third cuts it, a fourth points, a fifth grinds it at the top for receiving the head; to make the head requires two or three distinct operations; to put it on is a peculiar business, to whiten the pins is another; it is even a trade by itself to put them into the paper.

He pointed out that one worker might be able to make 20 pins a day if he were to complete all the processes himself. But ten workers together specialising in a variety of tasks could, he estimated, make 48 000 pins.

This enormous increase in LABOUR PRODUCTIVITY (output per worker) arises from a variety of sources.
- Specialisation enables workers to gain skills in a narrow range of tasks. These skills enable individual workers to be far more productive than if they were jacks-of-all-trades. In a modern economy a person could not possibly hope to be able to take on every job which society requires.
- The division of labour makes it cost-effective to provide workers with specialist tools. For instance, it would not be profitable to provide every farm worker with a tractor. But it is possible to provide a group of workers with a tractor which they can then share.
- Time is saved because a worker is not constantly changing tasks, moving around from place to place and using different machinery and tools.
- Workers can specialise in those tasks to which they are best suited.

The division of labour has its limits. If jobs are divided up too much, the work can become tedious and monotonous. Workers feel alienated from their work. This will result in poorer quality of work and less output per person. Workers will do everything possible to avoid work - going to the toilet, lingering over breaks and reporting sick for instance. The size of the market too will limit the division of labour. A shop owner in a village might want to specialise in selling health foods but finds that in order to survive she has to sell other products as well.

Over-specialisation also has its disadvantages. For example, the north of England, Wales, Scotland and Northern Ireland suffered high unemployment in the 1960s, 1970s and 1980s as their traditional heavy industry, such as coal mining and shipbuilding, declined and were not replaced by enough new service sector jobs. Another problem with specialisation is that a breakdown in part of the chain of production can cause chaos within the system. Eighteen Toyota production plants in Japan were brought to a halt for two weeks in 1997 when the factory of the sole supplier of brake parts to Toyota in Japan was destroyed in a fire. Toyota had to work round the clock with new suppliers to get production going again. Equally, London businesses can be crippled by an Underground strike or a bus strike.

Sectors of the economy

Economies are structured into three main sectors. In the PRIMARY SECTOR of the economy, raw materials

Question 3

(a) Explain, with the help of the photograph, what is meant by 'specialisation'.
(b) What might be some of the (i) advantages to firms and (ii) disadvantages to workers of the division of labour shown in the photograph?

are extracted and food is grown. Examples of primary sector industries are agriculture, forestry, fishing, oil extraction and mining. In the SECONDARY or MANUFACTURING SECTOR, raw materials are transformed into goods. Examples of secondary sector industries are motor manufacturing, food processing, furniture making and steel production. The TERTIARY or SERVICE SECTOR produces services such as transport, sport and leisure, distribution, financial services, education and health.

Most firms tend to operate in just one of these sectors, specialising in producing raw materials, manufactured goods or services. Some very large firms, such as BP, operate across all three sectors, from the extraction of oil to its refining and sale to the public through petrol stations.

Money and exchange

Specialisation has enabled people to enjoy a standard of living which would be impossible to achieve through self-sufficiency. Specialisation, however, necessitates exchange. Workers can only specialise in refuse collecting, for instance, if they know that they will be able to exchange their services for other goods and services such as food, housing and transport.

Exchange for most of history has meant **barter** - swopping one good for another. But barter has many disadvantages and it would be impossible to run a modern sophisticated economy using barter as a means of exchange. It was the development of **money** that enabled trade and specialisation to transform economies into what we know today. Money is anything which is widely accepted as payment for goods received, services performed, or repayment of past debt. In a modern economy, it ranges from notes and coins to money in bank accounts and deposits in building society accounts.

Markets

There must be a buyer and a seller for exchange to take place. Buyers and sellers meet in the market place. For economists, markets are not just street markets.

Buying and selling can take place in newspapers and magazines, through mail order or over the telephone in financial deals in the City of London, or on industrial estates as well as in high street shopping centres. A MARKET is any convenient set of arrangements by which buyers and sellers communicate to exchange goods and services.

Economists group buyers and sellers together. For instance, there is an international market for oil where large companies and governments buy and sell oil. There are also national markets for oil. Not every company or government involved in the buying and selling of oil in the UK, say, will be involved in the US or the Malaysian oil markets. There are also regional and local markets for oil. In your area there will be a small number of petrol filling stations (sellers of petrol) where you (the buyers) are able to buy petrol. All these markets are inter-linked but they are also separate. A worldwide increase in the price of oil may or may not filter down to an increase in the price of petrol at the pumps in your local area. Equally, petrol prices in your area may increase when prices at a national and international level remain constant.

How buyers and sellers are grouped together and therefore how markets are defined depends upon what is being studied. We could study the tyre industry or we could consider the market for cars and car components which includes part but not all of the tyre industry. Alternatively, we might want to analyse the market for rubber, which would necessitate a study of rubber purchased by tyre producers.

Many Western economists argue that specialisation, exchange and the market lie at the heart of today's economic prosperity in the industrial world. Whilst it is likely that the market system is a powerful engine of prosperity, we shall see that it does not always lead to the most efficient allocation of resources (☞ units 15-23).

Question 4

Table 2.2 *Shops selling grocery items in Burscough*

	Number
Small independent grocers	2
Convenience store grocers	1
Supermarket grocers	1

Burscough is a town in Lancashire which has shops selling grocery items such as fresh vegetables, dairy products or tinned food.

(a) Who might be the buyers and sellers in the local Burscough market for grocery products?
(b) What is the relationship between this market and the market for (i) meat and (ii) petrol?

The objectives of economic actors

There are four main types of economic actors in a market economy - consumers, workers, firms and governments. It is important to understand what are the economic objectives of each of these sets of actors.

Consumers In economics, consumers are assumed to want to maximise their own **economic welfare**, sometimes referred to as UTILITY or **satisfaction**. They are faced with the problem of scarcity. They don't have enough income to be able to purchase all the goods or services that they would like. So they have to allocate their resources to achieve their objective. To do this, they consider the utility to be gained from consuming an extra unit of a product with its opportunity cost. If there is 30p to be spent, would it best be spent on a Mars Bar, a newspaper or a gift to a charity? If you could afford it, would you prefer to move to a larger but more expensive house, or spend the money on going out more to restaurants, or take more holidays abroad? Decisions are made at the margin. This means that consumers don't look at their overall spending every time they want to spend an extra 30p. They just consider the alternatives of that decision to spend 30p and what will give them the highest utility with that 30p.

Sometimes it is argued that economics portrays consumers as being purely selfish. This isn't true. Consumers do spend money on giving to charity. Parents spend money on their children when the money could be spent on themselves. Seventeen year old students buy presents for other people. What this shows, according to economists, is that the utility gained from giving money away or spending it on others can be higher than from spending it on oneself. However, individuals are more likely to spend money on those in their immediate family than others. This shows that the utility to be gained from paying for a holiday for your child is usually higher than paying for a holiday for a disabled person you do not know.

Workers Workers are assumed in economics to want to maximise their own welfare at work. Evidence suggests that the most important factor in determining welfare is the level of pay. So workers are assumed to want to maximise their earnings in a job. However, other factors are also important. Payment can come in the form of fringe benefits, like company cars. Satisfaction at work is also very important. Many workers could earn more elsewhere but choose to stay in their present employment because they enjoy the job and the workplace.

Firms The objectives of firms are often mixed. However, in the UK and the USA, the usual assumption is that firms are in business to maximise their PROFITS. This is because firms are owned by private individuals who want to maximise their return on ownership. This is usually achieved if the firm is making the highest level of profit possible. In Japan and continental Europe, there is much more of a tradition that the owners of firms are just one of the STAKEHOLDERS in a business. Workers, consumers and the local community should also have some say in how a business is run. Making profit would then only be one objective amongst many for firms.

Governments Governments have traditionally been assumed to want to maximise the welfare of the citizens of their country or locality. They act in the best interests of all. This can be very difficult because it is often not immediately obvious what are the costs and benefits of a decision. Nor is there often a consensus about what value to put on the gains and losses of different groups. For instance, in the 1990s the UK government brought the motorway building programme to a virtual halt following the growing feeling that motorways were destroying the environment and were therefore an economic 'bad' rather than a 'good'. However, many, particularly in industry, would argue that the environmental costs of new motorway building are vastly exaggerated and that the benefits of faster journey times more than outweigh any environmental costs.

Governments which act in the best interests of their citizens face a difficult task. However, it can also be argued that governments don't act to maximise the welfare of society. Governments are run by individuals and it could be that they act in their own interest. For instance, there is a tradition in government that bribery determines what decisions are made. Certain Third World countries have immense economic problems because their governments are not impartial, but are run for the monetary benefit of the few that can extort bribes from citizens. There is equally a long tradition of 'pork barrel politics'. This is where politicians try to stay in power by giving benefits to those groups who are important at election times. In the UK, it is expected that MPs (Members of Parliament) will fight for the interests of their constituents even if this clearly does not lead to an overall increase in welfare for the country as a whole.

So governments may have a variety of motives when making decisions. In an ideal world, governments should act impartially to maximise the welfare of society. In practice they may fall short of this.

Question 5

In April 2005, just weeks before a General Election, MG Rover, the last remaining UK owned mass car manufacturer, announced that it was going into receivership. The Labour government immediately announced a £150 million aid package. This included up to £50 million for training workers made redundant at MG Rover and its suppliers, over £40 million to cover redundancy payments and protective awards for Longbridge workers, £24 million to establish a loan fund to help otherwise viable businesses affected by MG Rover's collapse and £41.6 million for MG Rover suppliers who were left being owed large sums of money for products delivered but not paid for.

It could be argued that the aid package smacked of favouritism and 'election year politics'. MG Rover's main plant at Longbridge in Birmingham, where most of the company's 5 000 workers were employed, was in an area with several marginal constituencies. A swing to the Conservatives of just a few per cent of the voters would have turned those constituencies from being Labour held to Conservative held.

Many commentators pointed out that very few of the hundreds of thousands of workers made redundant each year across the UK received such generous help.

On the other hand, trade unions representing workers at Longbridge argued that the package was too small. There were calls for the government to provide a generous aid package to any buyer for MG Rover which would guarantee the safeguarding of its 5 000 jobs. It was pointed out that it was not just the MG Rover jobs which were at stake. It was also all the jobs at suppliers which would disappear if production ceased at Longbridge.

Source: adapted from www.manifest.co.uk.

(a) Suggest what might have been the motives of the UK government in offering a £150 million aid package for MG Rover.
(b) What might have motivated trade unions to call for government aid to help keep the Longbridge plant open?

Key terms

Division of labour - specialisation by workers.

Factors of production - the inputs to the production process: land, which is all natural resources; labour, which is the workforce; capital, which is the stock of man-made resources used in the production of goods and services; entrepreneurs, individuals who seek out profitable opportunities for production and take risks in attempting to exploit these.

Fixed capital - economic resources such as factories and hospitals which are used to transform working capital into goods and services.

Human capital - the value of the productive potential of an individual or group of workers. It is made up of the skills, talents, education and training of an individual or group and represents the value of future earnings and production.

Labour productivity - output per worker.

Market - any convenient set of arrangements by which buyers and sellers communicate to exchange goods and services.

Non-renewable resources - resources, such as coal or oil, which once exploited cannot be replaced.

Primary sector - extractive and agricultural industries.

Profits - the reward to the owners of a business. It is the difference between a firm's revenues and its costs.

Renewable resources - resources, such as fish stocks or forests, which can be exploited over and over again because they have the potential to renew themselves.

Secondary sector - production of goods, mainly manufactures.

Specialisation - a system of organisation where economic units such as households or nations are not self-sufficient but concentrate on producing certain goods and services and trading the surplus with others.

Stakeholders - groups of people which have an interest in a firm, such as shareholders, customers, suppliers, workers, the local community in which it operates and government.

Tertiary sector - production of services.

Utility - the satisfaction derived from consuming a good.

Working or circulating capital - resources which are in the production system waiting to be transformed into goods or other materials before being finally sold to the consumer.

Applied economics

Sport and Leisure

Different markets

The sport and leisure market is made up of many different markets. For instance, there is a market for travel and tourism, a market for football, a television entertainment market and a restaurant market. Some of these markets overlap. A Japanese visitor to the UK might eat in a restaurant in London and so the tourism and the 'eating out' markets overlap. Some markets are closely linked. Pubs near a football stadium are likely to benefit from increased trade on the day of matches.

Figure 2.1 gives data for one segment of this market, the market for visitor attractions, such as historic houses, theme parks and museums. The figures given are for the 3 295 most important attractions in the UK such as Alton Towers, the National Gallery and Edinburgh Castle. The data show, for example, that 18 per cent of attractions in 2002 were historic houses or castles, which accounted for 11 per cent of the 284.8 million visitors to these attractions.

Economic resources

Each market uses land, labour and capital to produce services. For instance, a visit to a National Trust property utilises land as a factor. There is likely to be a house built on land and the gardens too use land as their basic resource. Labour is needed for the upkeep of the property and to provide services to the visitor, including volunteers on the door and in the tea shop. Buildings on the property represent capital.

There are many examples of entrepreneurs in the market. Andrew Lloyd Webber, for instance, is an entrepreneur putting on musical shows for the mass market. Rich owners of football clubs are entrepreneurs too.

Objectives of participants in the market

In a market there are buyers and sellers. The objectives of consumers are to maximise their welfare or utility when buying sport and leisure services. They consider whether they will get more satisfaction per pound spent from going to a pub or going to a nightclub, for instance. They have to choose between spending on sport and leisure services and all other goods and services, like clothes or consumer durables. They also have to choose between different sport and leisure services.

There is a number of different types of suppliers to the market. First there are firms whose aim is to maximise profit. For example, Table 2.3 shows that 29 per cent of tourist attractions in the UK were either privately owned by an individual or group of individuals, or by a company with shareholders. Their aim is likely to be to make a profit from that attraction. Alton Towers, Blackpool Pleasure Beach, Chessington World of Adventures or Legoland at Windsor are not charities, but run for profit for the benefit of their owners.

Second, however, as Table 2.3 shows, there are many examples of charities and trusts in the market, making up 31 per cent of visitor attractions. The largest is The National Trust. Charities and trusts do not necessarily have the same objectives, but few are likely to have profit maximisation as their principle objective. The National Trust has as its primary aim to 'preserve places of historic interest and natural beauty permanently for the nation to enjoy'. Financially, it must break even over time to survive. But it is unlikely to see maximising profits or revenues as its priority. For instance, there are restrictions on the number of visitors to some properties that it owns because more visitors would lead to unacceptable levels of wear and tear.

Third, government is a major provider of services. If English Heritage, Historic Scotland and Cadw are included as part of government, Table 2.3 shows that 34 per cent of visitor attractions in the UK are owned by different government bodies. They include the British Museum, the Tower of London and London Zoo. The management of these tourist attractions want to maximise resources available to them, particularly by securing larger grants from government. However, government itself is often interested in minimising spending on such bodies because of conflicting objectives. Government may prefer to spend more money on the National Health Service than on museums. The arts and sport have tended to be subsidised by government. Concerning the arts, there is a belief that 'culture' is important to the health of the nation. Hence, the Royal Opera House is heavily subsidised, whilst an Andrew Lloyd Webber production like The Phantom of the Opera receives no subsidy. Some would argue that there is no difference between a Mozart opera like The Marriage of Figaro and The Phantom of the Opera. Indeed, The Phantom of the Opera might be a better case for subsidy because more foreign tourists are likely to see it than a Royal Opera House production. Tourism brings money into the country and creates prosperity.

The same arguments apply to sport. There is an argument that everyone should have access to sporting facilities. Traditionally, local authorities have subsidised swimming pools, leisure centres and sports facilities. Sometimes government is swayed by lobbying from a particular part of the country for spending on the arts or leisure. Local MPs fight for grants for new theatres or recreational facilities. So government is likely to be motivated by a variety of factors when deciding on spending on sport and leisure.

Table 2.3 UK distribution of attractions by ownership type, 2002

Ownership	Attraction	Visits
Sample	3,295	284.8m
	%	%
Government	5	17
English Heritage/Historic Scotland/Cadw	7	4
Local Authority	22	23
Privately owned	27	26
Public company/plc	2	3
The National Trust/National Trust for Scotland	10	6
Other trust/charity	21	14
Educational institution	2	1
Religious body	3	5
Other	2	1
UK	100	100

Source: adapted from UK Research Liaison Group, www.staruk.org.uk.

Figure 2.1 UK attractions by type and proportion of visitors

Source: adapted from UK Research Liaison Group, www.staruk.org.uk.

DataQuestion

The oil industry

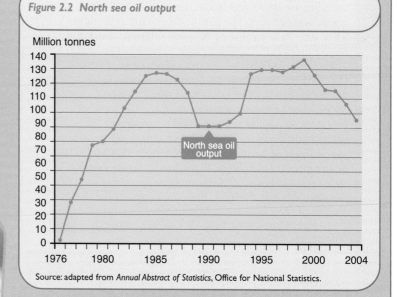

Figure 2.2 *North sea oil output*

Million tonnes

North sea oil output

Source: adapted from *Annual Abstract of Statistics*, Office for National Statistics.

Figure 2.3 *Oil prices*

Spot crude oil price, Arabian Light/Dubai, US $ per barrel

Oil prices

Source: adapted from *BP Statistical Survey of World Energy*.

Table 2.3 *Petroleum products by end use, 2004, thousand tonnes*

Butane and propane		3 939
Naphtha (LDF) and Middle Distillate Feedstock		2 115
Motor spirit		19 387
Kerosene	Aviation turbine fuel	11 765
	Burning oil	2 683
Gas/diesel oil	Derv fuel	19 117
	Other	4 927
Fuel oil		1 938
Bitumen		1 993
Lubricating oils		873
Total		73 880

Source: adapted from *Monthly Digest of Statistics*, Office for National Statistics.

1. Explain the following economic concepts in the context of the UK oil industry:
   (a) economic resources; (b) specialisation; (c) money and exchange; (d) markets.
2. North Sea oil companies face a problem about how to dispose of redundant oil rigs. Environmental groups are concerned that companies will opt for the cheapest solution possible without fully taking into account the environmental impact of their decisions. What do you think might be the objectives of the following groups in this situation: (a) oil companies with North Sea oil installations; (b) the UK government; (c) customers of the oil companies; (d) environmental pressure groups?

Summary

1. Economic data are collected not only to verify or refute economic models but to provide a basis for economic decision making.
2. Data may be expressed at nominal (or current) prices or at real (or constant) prices. Data expressed in real terms take into account the effects of inflation.
3. Indices are used to simplify statistics and to express averages.
4. Data can be presented in a variety of forms such as tables or graphs.
5. All data should be interpreted with care given that data can be selected and presented in a wide variety of ways.

The collection and reliability of data

Economists collect data for two main reasons.
- The scientific method requires that theories be tested. Data may be used to refute or support a theory. For instance, an economist might gather data to support or refute the hypothesis that 'Cuts in the marginal rate of income will increase the incentive to work', or that 'An increase in the real value of unemployment benefit will lead to an increase in the number of people unemployed'.
- Economists are often required to provide support for particular policies. Without economic data it is often difficult, if not impossible, to make policy recommendations. For instance, in his Budget each year the Chancellor of the Exchequer has to make a statement to the House of Commons outlining the state of the economy and the economic outlook for the next 12 months. Without a clear knowledge of where the economy is at the moment it is impossible to forecast how it might change in the future and to recommend policy changes to steer the economy in a more desirable direction.

Collecting economic data is usually very difficult and sometimes impossible. Some macro-economic data - such as the balance of payments figures or the value of national income - are collected from a wide variety of sources. The figures for the balance of payments on current account are compiled from returns made by every exporter and importer on every item exported and imported. Not surprisingly the information is inaccurate. Some exporters and importers will conceal transactions to avoid tax. Others will not want to be bothered with the paper work.

Other macro-economic data such as the Consumer Price Index (used to measure inflation) are based on surveys. Surveys are only reliable if there is accurate sampling and measuring and are rarely as accurate as a complete count.

Some macro-economic data are very reliable statistically but do not necessarily provide a good measure of the relevant economic variable. In the UK, the Claimant Count is calculated each month at benefit offices throughout the country. It is extremely accurate but no economist would argue that the figure produced is an accurate measure of unemployment. There is general agreement that some people who claim benefit for being unemployed are not unemployed and conversely there are many unemployed people who are not claiming benefit.

In micro-economics use is again made of survey data, with the limitations that this implies. Economists also make use of more experimental data, gathering evidence for case studies. For

Question 1

In November 1998, the Office for National Statistics (ONS) suspended publication of one of the most important economic series it compiles. The average earnings index was found to be giving inaccurate information. The average earnings index is a measure of how much earnings in the whole of the UK are rising. It is calculated monthly by taking data from thousands of returns from businesses. They report on whether or not they have given any pay rises during the previous month and if so, by how much.

Problems arose because of different ways of calculating the average. In October 1998, the ONS launched a new series for average earnings which used a different way of calculating the average than before. But as Figure 3.1 shows, this revised series gave very different figures than the original series used before. It also didn't fit in very well with what other economic indicators were showing at the time.

A government enquiry found that the revised series was based on inadequate statistical methods which gave too much importance to large changes in earnings by small businesses. In March 1999, a new series was published which followed more closely the old series.

(a) The three lines in Figure 3.1 should show the same data: the percentage change in average earnings. Give ONE time period when the original series showed an upward movement in earnings when the revised series showed a downward movement.
(b) Why do the three sets of statistics differ in their estimate of changes in average earnings?
(c) Explain TWO reasons why it is important for economic statistics, like growth in average earnings, to be measured accurately.

Figure 3.1 Estimates of growth in average earnings

Annual % change

Legend: Original series, Revised series, Proposed new series

Source: adapted from Office for National Statistics.

instance, an economist might want to look at the impact of different pricing policies on entry to sports centres. He or she might study a small number of sports centres in a local area. The evidence gathered would be unlikely decisively to refute or support a general hypothesis such as 'Cheap entry increases sports centre use'. But it would be possible to conclude that the evidence **tended** to support or refute the hypothesis.

In economics it is difficult to gather accurate data and, for that reason, academic economists mostly qualify their conclusions.

Real and nominal values

There are many different **measures** in use today such as tonnes, litres, kilograms and kilometres. Often, we want to be able to compare these different measures. For instance, an industrialist might wish to compare oil measured in litres, and coal measured in kilograms. One way of doing this is to convert oil and coal into therms using gross calorific values. In economics, by far the most important measure used is the value of an item measured in **monetary terms,** such as pounds sterling, US dollars or euros. One problem in using money as a measure is that inflation (the general change in prices in an economy) erodes the purchasing power of money.

For instance, in 1948 the value of output of the UK economy (measured by gross domestic product at market prices) was £11.9 billion. Fifty six years later, in 2004, it was £1 160.4 billion. It would seem that output had increased about 98 times - an enormous increase. In fact, output increased by only a fraction of that amount. This is because most of the measured increase was an increase not in output but in prices. Prices over the period rose about 24 times. Stripping the inflation element out of the increase leaves us with an increase in output of 4.1 times.

Values unadjusted for inflation are called NOMINAL VALUES. These values are expressed AT CURRENT PRICES (i.e. at the level of prices existing during the time period being measured).

If data are adjusted for inflation, then they are said to be at REAL VALUES or at CONSTANT PRICES. To do this in practice involves taking one period of time as the BASE PERIOD. Data are then adjusted assuming that prices were the same throughout as in the base period.

For instance, a basket of goods costs £100 in year 1 and £200 in year 10. Prices have therefore doubled. If you had £1 000 to spend in year 10, then that would have been equivalent to £500 at year 1 prices because both amounts would have bought 5 baskets of goods. On the other hand, if you had £1 000 to spend in year 1, that would be equivalent to £2 000 in year 10

prices because both would have bought you 10 baskets of goods.

Taking another example, the real value of UK output in 1948 at 1948 prices was the same as its nominal value (i.e. £11.9 billion). The real value of output in 2004 at 1948 prices was £48 billion. It is much lower than the nominal 2004 value because prices were much higher in 2004.

On the other hand, at 2004 prices, the real value of output in 1948 was £287.2 billion, much higher than the nominal value because prices in 2004 were much higher than in 1948. Further examples are given in Table 3.1.

UK government statistics expressed in real terms are adjusted to prices three or four years previously. So in 2005, real prices were expressed in 2002 prices.

Question 2

Table 3.2 Components of final demand at current prices

	2001=100	£ billion		
	Index of prices	Households' expenditure	Government expenditure	Fixed investment
2001	100	636	190	166
2002	101.3	666	209	172
2003	102.7	694	229	180
2004	104.0	726	247	196

Source: adapted from *Economic Trends*, Office for National Statistics; *Monthly Digest of Statistics*, Office for National Statistics.

Using a calculator or a spreadsheet, work out for the period 2001-2004 (a) at constant 2001 prices and (b) at constant 2004 prices the values of:
(i) households' expenditure;
(ii) government expenditure;
(iii) fixed investment.
Present your calculation in the form of two tables, one for 2001 prices and the other for 2004 prices.

Indices

It is often more important in economics to compare values than to know absolute values. For instance, we might want to compare the real value of output in the economy in 1994 and 2004. Knowing that the real value of output (GDP at market prices at 2001 prices) in 1994 was £808.1 billion and in 2004 was £1 066.5 billion is helpful, but the very large numbers make it difficult to see at a glance what, for instance, was the approximate percentage increase. Equally, many series of statistics are averages. The Retail Price Index (the measure of the cost of living) is calculated by working out what it would cost to buy a typical cross-section or 'basket' of goods. Comparing say £458.92 in one month with £475.13 the next is not easy.

So, many series are converted into INDEX NUMBER form. One time period is chosen as the base period and the rest of the statistics in the series are compared to the value in that base period. The value in the base period is usually 100. The figure 100 is chosen because it is easy to work with mathematically.

Table 3.1 Nominal and real values

Nominal value	Inflation between year 1 and 2	Real values	
		Value at year 1 prices	Value at year 2 prices
Example 1 £100 in year 1	10%	£100	£110
Example 2 £500 in year 1	50%	£500	£750
Example 3 £200 in year 2	20%	£166.66	£200
Example 4 £400 in year 2	5%	£380.95	£400

Note: £100 at year 1 prices is worth £100 x 1.1 (i.e. 1+10%) in year 2 prices.
£200 at year 2 prices is worth £200 ÷ 1.2 in year 1 prices.

Unit 3 *Economic data*

Table 3.3 Converting a series into index number form

	Consumption			
Year	£ millions	Index number if base year is:		
		year 1	year 2	year 3
1	500	100.0	83.3	62.5
2	600	120.0	100.0	75.0
3	800	160.0	133.3	100.0

Note: The index number for consumption in year 2, if year 1 is the base year, is (600 ÷ 500) x 100.

Taking the example of output again, if 1948 were taken as the base year, then the value of real output in 1948 would be 100, and the value of real output in 2004 would be 408.0. Alternatively if 2004 were taken as the base year, the value of output would be 100 in 2004 and 24.5 in 1948. Or with 2001 as the base year, the value of output in 1948 would be 26.3 whilst in 2004 it would be 107.3. Further examples are given in Table 3.3.

The interpretation of data

Data can be presented in many forms and be used both to inform and mislead the reader. To illustrate these points, consider inflation figures for the UK economy. Inflation is the general rise in prices in an economy. If there has been 2 per cent inflation over the past year, it means that prices on average have increased by 2 per cent. One way in which inflation figures can be presented is in **tabular form** as in Table 3.5.

The data could also be presented in **graphical form** as in Figure 3.2 (a). Graphs must be interpreted with some care. Figure 3.2 (b) gives a far more pessimistic view of inflation between 2001 and 2003 than Figure 3.2 (a) at first glance.

Question 3

Table 3.4 Consumers' expenditure

			£ billion
	Food and drink	Transport	Restaurants and hotels
2001	60.0	92.6	71.5
2002	61.2	94.9	76.7
2003	63.5	98.4	80.8
2004	65.6	101.5	85.4

Source: adapted from *Monthly Digest of Statistics*, Office for National Statistics.

Using a calculator or a spreadsheet, convert each category of expenditure into index number form using as the base year:
(a) 2001 and (b) 2004.
Present your calculations in the form of two tables, one for each base year.

Table 3.5 UK inflation (CPI)

Year	Inflation %
1990	7.0
1991	7.5
1992	4.2
1993	2.5
1994	2.0
1995	2.6
1996	2.5
1997	1.8
1998	1.6
1999	1.3
2000	0.8
2001	1.2
2002	1.3
2003	1.4
2004	1.3

Source: adapted from *Economic Trends*, Office for National Statistics.

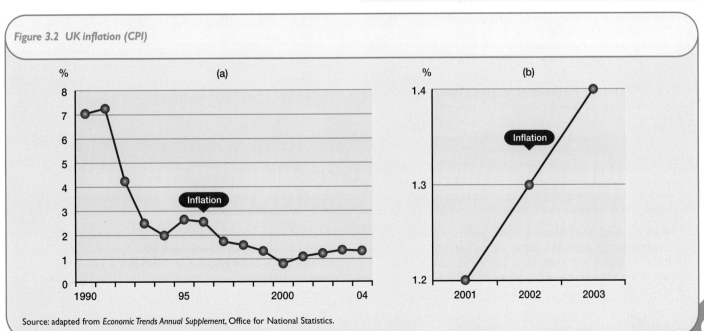

Figure 3.2 UK inflation (CPI)

Source: adapted from *Economic Trends Annual Supplement*, Office for National Statistics.

Question 4

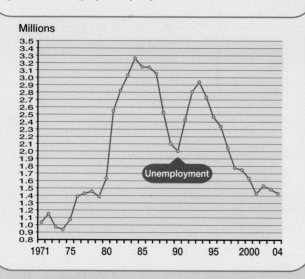

Figure 3.3 Unemployment (ILO), millions

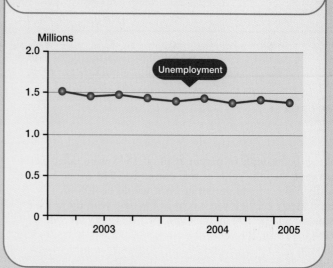

Figure 3.4 Unemployment (ILO), millions

Source: adapted from *Monthly Digest of Statistics*, Office for National Statistics.

Consider each graph in turn.
(a) What does each show?
(b) Explain why each seems to give a different picture of unemployment in the UK.

One reason is that Figure 3.2 (b) is taken out of the context of its surrounding years. Figure 3.2 (a) would suggest that inflation between 2001-2003 was relatively low for the whole period shown. Figure 3.2 (b) suggests the opposite, a dramatic increase in inflation. Another reason why Figure 3.2 (b) suggests a dramatic increase in inflation is because the line is drawn very steeply. This has been achieved through the scales used on the axes. The vertical axis in Figure 3.2 (b) only covers 1.0 to 1.5 per cent. In Figure 3.2 (a), in contrast, the vertical axis starts at zero and rises to 8 per cent over the same drawn height. The gradient of the line in Figure 3.2 (b) could have been even steeper if the length of the horizontal time axis had been drawn shorter.

Graphs are sometimes constructed using log scales for the vertical axis. This has the effect of gradually compressing values on the vertical axis as they increase. The vertical distance between 0 and 1, for instance, is larger per unit than between 999 and 1 000.

Data can also be expressed in **verbal form**. Figure 3.2 shows that inflation rose between 1990 and 1991, and then broadly fell to a low of 0.8 per cent in 2000 before fluctuating in the 1.2 to 1.4 per cent range between 2001 and 2004. When expressing data in verbal form, it can become very tedious to describe each individual change. For instance, it would be inappropriate to say 'Inflation in 1990 was 7 per cent. Then it rose to 7.5 per cent in 1991 before falling to 4.2 per cent in 1992. Then in 1993 it fell again to 2.5 per cent and again in 1994 to 2.0 per cent'. When describing data in verbal form, it is important to pick out the main trends and perhaps give a few key figures to illustrate these trends.

Key terms

Base period - the period, such as a year or a month, with which all other values in a series are compared.
Index number - an indicator showing the relative value of one number to another from a base of 100. It is often used to present an average of a number of statistics.

Nominal values - values unadjusted for the effects of inflation (i.e. values **at current prices**).
Real values - values adjusted for inflation (i.e. values at **constant prices**).

Applied economics

Tourism

Spending on tourism

Tourism is a major industry in the UK. Is it growing in size? There is a number of ways in which growth can be measured. Table 3.6 shows how total spending on tourism has grown between 1989 and 2003. It divides tourists into three categories - UK tourists who take a holiday within the country, foreign tourists who come to the UK and UK tourists who take holidays abroad. The figures in Table 3.6 are expressed at current prices. This means that inflation is not taken into account. If there had been very high inflation over the period 1989-2003, the volume of tourism could have declined given the data in Table 3.6. In fact, consumer prices over the 14 year period rose 57 per cent. So real growth in spending is anything which is above that 57 per cent rise.

Table 3.6 Spending on tourism at current prices, £ million

	£ millions at current prices		
	Spending on holidays by UK citizens in the UK	Spending in the UK by foreign visitors	Spending on foreign holidays by UK residents
1989	17 071[1]	6 945	9 357
1995	20 072	11 763	15 386
2003	26 482	11 855	28 550

1. Estimated

Source: adapted from *Annual Abstract of Statistics*, Office for National Statistics.

Table 3.7 shows the figures in Table 3.6 expressed at constant 2001 prices, i.e. after the inflation element has been stripped out and adjusted to the level of prices in 2001. Taking 2001 as the reference year for prices means that the 1989 and 1995 data at current prices increase as numbers when they become data at constant prices, whilst the 2003 numbers fall.

Table 3.8 shows the figures in Table 3.7 in index number form. This has the advantage that it is much

Table 3.7 Spending on tourism at constant 2001 prices, £ million

	£ millions at constant 2001 prices		
	Spending on holidays by UK citizens in the UK	Spending in the UK by foreign visitors	Spending on foreign holidays by UK residents
1989	25 677	10 446	14 047
1995	23 332	13 674	17 885
2003	25 308	11 329	27 284

Source: adapted from *Annual Abstract of Statistics*, Office for National Statistics.

easier to see which of the three areas of tourism has grown more quickly. At a glance, it can be seen that the value of domestic tourism fell by 1.4 per cent in real terms over the period 1989 to 2003. In contrast, spending on foreign holidays by UK citizens grew by 94.2 per cent. Foreign visitors to the UK spent 8.5 per cent more. Because these are index numbers, it is not possible to say how important is the 8.5 per cent rise in spending by foreign visitors to the total domestic tourist industry. For instance, if foreign tourists accounted for just 1 per cent of total spending, an 8.5 per cent rise would have almost no impact on tourism. This illustrates one of the disadvantages of using index numbers. To assess the relative impact of the increase in foreign tourists, we have to look back to Table 3.7. Total spending on tourism in the UK at constant 2001 prices rose from £36.1 billion to £36.6 billion, a 1.4 per cent increase, over the period 1989 to 2003. A 1.4 per cent change over 14 years is an insignificant change. What in fact has happened is that the 8.5 per cent rise in spending by foreign tourists has almost totally been cancelled out by a small drop in real spending by British tourists in the UK. British tourists account for more than twice the total spending of foreign tourists.

Employment in tourism

Spending on tourism within the UK fell by 1.4 per cent between 1989 and 2003. In contrast, employment in

Table 3.8 Spending on tourism at constant 2001 prices, 1989 = 100

			1989 = 100
	Spending on holidays by UK citizens in the UK	Spending in the UK by foreign visitors	Spending on foreign holidays by UK residents
1989	100.0	100.0	100.0
1995	90.7	130.9	127.3
2003	98.6	108.5	194.2

Source: adapted from *Annual Abstract of Statistics*, Office for National Statistics.

tourism related industries grew by 31.9 per cent as shown in Table 3.9. It is easier to see the increase in each sector by converting these figures into index number form as in Table 3.10.

The 94.2 per cent increase in the amount spent by UK citizens on holidays abroad is reflected in an 80.6 per cent rise in the number of workers amongst travel agents and tour operators. The 1.4 per cent real fall in spending on tourism over the period might suggest that employment in tourist jobs in the UK would be relatively stagnant. But employment in hotels and other tourist accommodation was up 31.3 per cent whilst spending in restaurants, cafes etc. was up 108.3 per cent. To understand why, it should be remembered that Tables 3.9 and 3.10 refer to tourism **related** industries. Much of the increase in employment in restaurants etc. will have come from an increase in non-tourist demand for meals out. Similarly, much of the employment in libraries, museums and culture, and sport and recreation will be non-tourist related.

Trips and prices

Data for UK domestic tourism, trips made by British citizens within Great Britain, reveal some very interesting aspects of tourism. Table 3.11 shows that the number of trips made increased by 41.4 million between 1989 and 2003. Each trip, though, was shorter. In 1989, the average number of nights spent was 4.0 but in 1998 had fallen to 3.2. Spending per trip at constant prices rose by 6.1 per cent, a relatively small increase given the 37.4 per cent increase in real spending by households on all goods and services over the same period.

Table 3.11 therefore shows that between 1989 and 2003, people went on more holidays in Britain, but they were shorter and spending on holidays per trip failed to keep up with increases in household spending on all other goods and services. Part of the reason for these trends is that 'short breaks' have now become far more popular. More people are now taking a weekend holiday for instance. These will be less expensive than longer holidays. The relatively low rise in spending per trip could also be an indication that the price of holidays has fallen relative to all other prices in the economy. Since 1989, there has been considerable expansion of chains of budget hotels such as Travel Inn or Travel Lodge. These have exercised downward pressure on the cost of hotel and other accommodation.

Table 3.9 Employment in tourism related industries, Great Britain, thousands at June in each year

							Thousands, not seasonally adjusted
	Hotels and other tourist accommodation	Restaurants, cafes etc	Bars, pubs clubs	Travel agents, tour operators	Libraries, museums, culture	Sport and other recreation	Total employment in tourist related industries
1989	299.2	283.4	428.2	64.9	82.8	294.7	1 644.2
1995	385.8	386.2	445.1	90.7	77.3	363.5	1 751.6
2003	392.7	590.4	568.2	117.2	86.7	412.9	2 168.1

Source: adapted from *Annual Abstract of Statistics*, Office for National Statistics.

Table 3.10 Employment in tourism related industries, Great Britain, 1989=100 at June in each year

							1989=100
	Hotels and other tourist accommodation	Restaurants, cafes etc	Bars, pubs clubs	Travel agents, tour operators	Libraries, museums, culture	Sport and other recreation	Total employment in tourist related industries
1989	100.0	100.0	100.0	100.0	100.0	100.0	100.0
1995	128.9	136.3	103.9	139.8	93.4	123.3	106.5
2003	131.3	208.3	132.7	180.6	104.7	140.1	131.9

Source: adapted from *Annual Abstract of Statistics*, Office for National Statistics.

Table 3.11 UK domestic tourism

	Number of trips, millions	Number of nights spent, millions	Average nights spent	Average expenditure per trip at current prices	Average expenditure per trip trip at constant 2001 prices
1989	109.6	443.2	4.0	99.1	149.1
1995	121.0	526.0	3.6	135.8	157.9
2003	151.0	490.5	3.2	175.4	167.6

Source: adapted from *Annual Abstract of Statistics*, Office for National Statistics.

Cinema data

Table 3.12 Cinema exhibitor statistics, GB, UK[1]

	Number of sites	Number of screens	Number of admissions, millions	at current prices			at constant 2001 prices		
				Gross box office takings, £ millions	Revenue per admission, £	Revenue per screen, £ 000	Gross box office takings, £ millions	Revenue per admission, £	Revenue per screen, £ 000
1987	492	1 035	66.8	123.8	1.85	118.7	210.6	3.15	201.9
1995	728	2 003	114.6	354.2	3.09	176.8	411.7	3.59	478.6
2004	773	3 475	171.3	769.6	4.49	221.4	726.3	4.24	685.5

Source: adapted from *Annual Abstract of Statistics, Monthly Digest of Statistics*, Office for National Statistics.

Table 3.13 Cinema exhibitor statistics, GB, UK[1]

1987=100

	Number of sites	Number of screens	Number of admissions	at current prices			at constant 2001 prices		
				Gross box office takings	Revenue per admission	Revenue per screen	Gross box office takings	Revenue per admission	Revenue per screen
1987	100.0	100.0	100.0	100.0	100.0	100.0	100.0	100.0	100.0
1995	148.0	193.5	171.6	286.1	167.0	148.9	195.5	114.0	237.0
2004	157.1	335.7	256.4	379.3	242.7	186.5	344.9	134.6	339.5

Source: adapted from *Annual Abstract of Statistics*, Office for National Statistics.
1. 1987 data are Great Britain. 1995 and 2004 data are UK.

1. Describe the main trends in cinema admissions shown in the data.
2. Explain the advantages and disadvantages of using index numbers to present data. Illustrate your answer from the data.
3. 'Revenues per admission and the number of screens cannot carry on rising.'
   (a) To what extent does this data support this statement for the period 1987-2004? (b) Discuss whether it is likely to be true in the future.

4 The demand curve

Summary

1. Demand for a good is the quantity of goods or services that will be bought over a period of time at any given price.
2. Demand for a good will rise or fall if there are changes in factors such as incomes, the price of other goods, tastes, and the size of the population.
3. A change in price is shown by a movement along the demand curve.
4. A change in any other variable affecting demand, such as income, is shown by a shift in the demand curve.
5. The market demand curve can be derived by horizontally summing all the individual demand curves in the market.

Demand

A market exists wherever there are buyers and sellers of a particular good (☞ unit 2). Buyers **demand** goods from the market whilst sellers **supply** goods on to the market. DEMAND has a particular meaning in economics. Demand is the quantity of goods or services that will be bought at any given price over a period of time. For instance, approximately 2 million new cars are bought each year in the UK today at an average price of, say, £8 000. Economists would say that the annual demand for cars at £8 000 would be 2 million units.

Demand and price

If everything else were to remain the same (this is known as the **ceteris paribus** condition ☞ unit 45), what would happen to the quantity demanded of a product as its price changed? If the average price of a car were to fall from £8 000 to £4 000, then it is not difficult to guess that the quantity demanded of cars would rise. On the other hand, if the average price were £35 000 very few cars would be sold.

This is shown in Table 4.1. As the price of cars rises, then ceteris paribus, the quantity of cars demanded will fall. Another way of expressing this is shown in Figure 4.1. Price is on the vertical axis and quantity demanded over time is on the horizontal axis. The curve is downward sloping showing that as price falls, quantity demanded rises. This DEMAND CURVE shows the quantity that is demanded at any given price. When price changes there is said to be a movement along the curve. For instance, there is a **movement along** the curve from the point A to the point B, a fall of 1 million cars a year, when the price of cars rises from £8 000 to £16 000.

It is important to remember that the demand curve shows

Table 4.1 The demand schedule for cars

Price (£)	Demand (million per year)
4 000	4.0
8 000	2.0
16 000	1.0
40 000	0.4

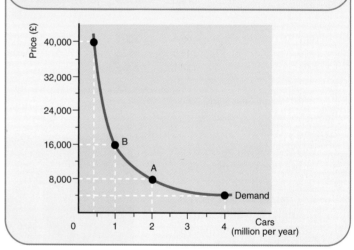

Figure 4.1 The demand curve
The demand curve is downward sloping, showing that the lower the price, the higher will be the quantity demanded of a good. In this example, only 0.4 million cars per year are demanded at a price of £40 000 each, but a reduction in price to £4 000 increases quantity demanded to 4 million units per year.

EFFECTIVE DEMAND. It shows how much would be bought (i.e. how much consumers can afford to buy and would buy) at any given price and not how much buyers would like to buy if they had unlimited resources.

Economists have found that the inverse relationship between price and quantity demanded - that as price rises, the quantity demanded falls - is true of nearly all goods. In unit 10 we shall consider the few examples of goods which might have upward sloping demand curves.

Demand and income

Price is not the only factor which determines the level of demand for a good. Another important factor is income. Demand for a normal good rises when income rises. For instance, a rise in income leads consumers to buy more cars. A few goods, known as inferior goods, fall in demand when incomes rise (☞ unit 10).

The effect of a rise in income on demand is shown in Figure 4.2. Buyers are purchasing OA of clothes at a price of OE. Incomes rise and buyers react by purchasing more clothes at the

Question 1

Stagecoach operates both bus and train services. It charges different prices to different passengers for the same journeys depending, for instance, on when they travel, their age, whether they are making a single or return journey or whether they have a season ticket. Using a demand curve diagram, explain what happens when:
(a) children are charged half price for a bus journey instead of being charged full price;
(b) senior citizens are given a free bus pass paid for by the local authority rather than having to pay the full fare;
(c) Stagecoach increases its prices on a route by 5 per cent;
(d) passengers can get a 60 per cent reduction by buying a day return if they travel after 9.30 compared to having to pay the full fare.

Figure 4.2 A change in income

An increase in income will raise demand for a normal good. At a price of OE, for instance, demand will rise from OA to OB. Similarly, at all other prices, an increase in income will result in a level of demand to the right of the existing demand curve. So the demand curve will shift from D_1 to D_2. A fall in income will result in less being demanded at any given price. Hence the demand curve will shift to the left, from D_1 to D_3.

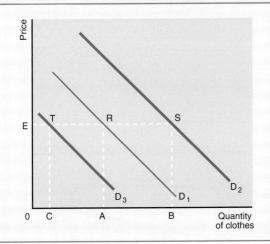

same price. At the higher level of income they buy, say, OB of clothes. A new demand curve now exists passing through the point S. It will be to the right of the original demand curve because at any given price more will be demanded at the new higher level of income.

Economists say that a rise in income will lead to an **increase in demand** for a normal good such as clothes. An increase in demand is shown by a SHIFT IN THE DEMAND CURVE. (Note that an **increase in quantity demanded** would refer to a change in quantity demanded resulting from a change in price and would be shown by a movement along the curve.) In Figure 4.2, the original demand curve D_1 shifts to the right to its new position D_2. Similarly, a fall in income will lead to a **fall in demand** for a normal good. This is shown by a **shift** to the left of the demand curve from D_1 to D_3. For instance, at a price of OE, demand will fall from OA to OC.

Two points need to be made. First, the demand curves in Figure 4.2 have been drawn as straight lines. These demand curves drawn show a hypothetical (or imaginary) position. They are drawn straight purely for convenience and do not imply that

actual demand curves for real products are straight. Second, the shifts in the demand curves are drawn as parallel shifts. Again this is done for convenience and neatness but it is most unlikely that a rise or fall in income for an actual product would produce a parallel shift in its demand curve.

Question 2

Table 4.2

Quantity demanded (million tyres)	Price(£)
10	20
20	16
30	12
40	8
50	4

Table 4.2 shows the demand curve facing a tyre manufacturer.
(a) Draw a demand curve for tyres from the above data.
(b) An increase in income results in an increase in quantity demanded of tyres of: (i) 5 million; (ii) 10 million; (iii) 15 million; (iv) 25 million. For each of these, draw a new demand curve on your diagram.
(c) Draw a demand curve for tyres which would show the effect of a fall in incomes on the original demand for tyres.
(d) Draw a demand curve for tyres which would show that no products were demanded when their price was £8.

The price of other goods

Another important factor which influences the demand for a good is the price of other goods. For instance, in the great drought of 1976 in the UK, the price of potatoes soared. Consumers reacted by buying fewer potatoes and replacing them in their diet by eating more bread, pasta and rice.

This can be shown on a demand diagram. The demand curve for pasta in Figure 4.3 is D_1. A rise in the price of potatoes leads

Figure 4.3 A rise in the price of other goods

A rise in the price of potatoes will lead to a rise in the demand for substitute goods. So the demand for pasta will increase, shown by a shift to the right in the demand curve for pasta from D_1 to D_2.

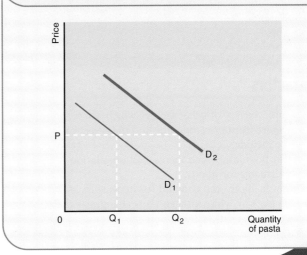

to a rise in the demand for pasta. This means that at any given price a greater quantity of pasta will be demanded. The new demand curve D₂ will therefore be to the right of the original demand curve.

Not all changes in prices will affect the demand for a particular good. A rise in the price of tennis balls is unlikely to have much impact on the demand for carrots for instance. Changes in the price of other goods as well may have either a positive or negative impact on demand for a good. A rise in the price of tennis rackets is likely to reduce the demand for tennis balls as some buyers decide that tennis is too expensive a sport. On the other hand, the demand for cinema places, alcoholic drink or whatever other form of entertainment consumers choose to buy instead of tennis equipment, will increase. The effect on the demand for one good of changes in price of other goods is considered in more detail in unit 7.

Question 3

Figure 4.4 *Brent crude oil price, 2005, $ per barrel*

In 2005, the price of Brent crude oil rose from $40 a barrel to over $60 a barrel. The price of oil was predicted to remain high for the foreseeable future because of growing demand for oil from emerging countries such as China. Explain, using diagrams, what effect you would expect this to have on the demand in the UK for:
(a) oil-fired central heating systems;
(b) luxury cars with low-mileage petrol consumption;
(c) rail travel;
(d) ice-cream;
(e) air travel.

Other factors

There is a wide variety of other factors which affect the demand for a good apart from price, income and the prices of other goods. These include:
- changes in population - an increase in population is likely to increase demand for goods;
- changes in fashion - the demand for items such as wigs or flared trousers or white kitchen units changes as these items go in or out of fashion;
- changes in legislation - the demand for seat belts, anti-

pollution equipment or places in residential homes has been affected in the past by changes in government legislation;
- advertising - a very powerful influence on consumer demand which seeks to influence consumer choice.

Question 4

New study shows yoghurt products are good for your health

(a) Explain the likely effect on demand for Activia of each of the four factors shown in the data. Use a separate demand diagram for each factor to illustrate your answer.

Figure 4.5 *Individual and market demand curves*
The market demand curve can be derived from the individual demand curves by adding up individual demand at each single price. In this example, for instance, the market demand at a price of £2 is calculated by adding the demand of firm A, B and C at this price.

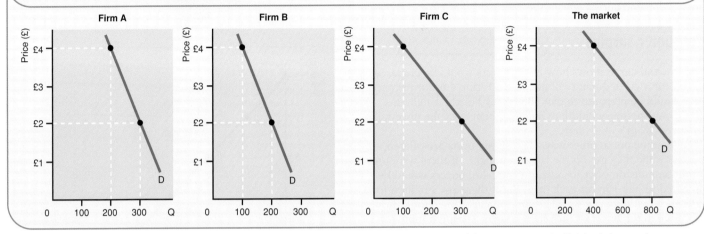

A summary

It is possible to express demand in the form of a **functional** relationship. The quantity demanded of good N (Q_n) varies according to (i.e. is a function of) the price of good N (P_n), income (Y), the price of all other goods ($P_1, ... P_{n-1}$) and all other factors (T). Mathematically, this is:

$$Q_n = f [P_n, Y, (P_1, ... P_{n-1}), T]$$

At this stage, this mathematical form of expressing the determinants of demand is a convenient shorthand but little else. The major tools for dealing with demand at this level are either the written word or graphs. At a far more advanced level, the algebraic formula for demand is often the most powerful and useful tool in analysing demand.

Individual and market demand curves

So far, it has been assumed that demand refers to demand for a product in a whole market (i.e. MARKET DEMAND).

Question 5

$$Q = 20 - \tfrac{1}{2} P$$

where Q is the monthly quantity demanded of compact discs (CDs) in millions and P is their price.
(a) Draw the demand curve given by this equation between CD prices of £1 and £20.
(b) A new format results in a fall in demand of CDs of 5 million per month at any given price. (i) What is the new formula for quantity demanded of CDs?
(ii) Plot the new demand curve on your diagram.
(c) A rise in consumer incomes results in consumers being less price sensitive than before when buying CDs. As a result, instead of monthly demand falling by half a million when price is increased by £1, monthly demand now falls only by 400 000. Assume that the original equation for demand is as in part (a) of this question. (i) What is the new formula for quantity demanded of CDs? (ii) Plot the new demand curve on your diagram.

However, it is possible to construct individual demand curves and derive market demand curves from them. An INDIVIDUAL DEMAND CURVE is the demand curve of an individual buyer. This could be a consumer, a firm or government.

The determinants of demand for an individual are no different from those of the market as a whole. When price rises, there is a fall in the quantity demanded of the product; when income rises, assuming that the product is a normal good, demand will increase, etc.

Figure 4.5 shows a situation where there are three and only three buyers in a market, firms A, B and C. At a price of £2, firm A will buy 300 units, firm B 200 units and firm C 300 units. So the total market demand at a price of £2 is 300 + 200 + 300 or 800 units. At a price of £4, total market demand will be 200 + 100 + 100 or 400 units. Similarly, all the other points

Question 6

Table 4.3

Price (£)	Quantity demanded of good Y (000 units)		
	Firm A	Firm B	Firm C
100	500	250	750
200	400	230	700
300	300	210	650
400	200	190	600
500	100	170	550

There are only three buyers of good Y, firms A, B and C.
(a) Draw the individual demand curves for each firm.
(b) Draw the market demand curve for good Y.
(c) A fourth business, firm D, enters the market. It will buy 500 at any price between £100 and £500. Show the effect of this by drawing a new market demand curve for good Y.
(d) Firm B goes out of business. Draw the new market demand curve with firms A, C and D buying in the market.

27

on the market demand curve can be derived by summing the individual demand curves. This is known as **horizontal summing** because the figures on the horizontal axis of the individual demand curves are added up to put on the market demand curve. But the figures on the vertical axis of both individual and market demand curves remain the same.

Consumer surplus

The demand curve shows how much buyers would be prepared to pay for a given quantity of goods. In Figure 4.6, for instance, they would be prepared to pay 10p if they bought 1 million items. At 8p, they would buy 2 million items. As the price falls, so buyers want to buy more.

This can be put another way. The more buyers are offered, the less value they put on the last one bought. If there were only 1 million units on offer for sale in Figure 4.6, buyers would be prepared to pay 10p for each one. But if there are 3 million for sale, they will only pay 6p. The demand curve, therefore, shows the value to the buyer of each item bought. The first unit bought is worth almost 12p to a buyer. The one millionth unit is worth 10p. The four millionth unit would be worth 4p.

The difference between the value to buyers and what they actually pay is called CONSUMER SURPLUS. Assume in Figure 4.6 that the price paid is 6p. The buyers who would have paid 10p for the millionth unit have gained a consumer surplus of 4p (10p - 6p). Those who would have paid 8p for the 2 millionth unit would gain 2p. So the total consumer surplus at a price of 6p is the shaded triangular area in Figure 4.6.

Adam Smith, writing in the 18th century, was puzzled why consumers paid high prices for goods such as diamonds which were unnecessary to human existence, whilst the price of necessities such as water was very low. Figure 4.6 explains this **paradox of value**. If there are few goods available to buy, as with diamonds, then consumers are prepared to pay a high price for them. If goods are plentiful, then consumers are only prepared to pay a low price. This doesn't mean to say that they don't place a high value on necessities when they are in short supply. In famine times, diamonds can be traded for small amounts of food. If diamonds were as common as water, buyers would not be prepared to pay much for the last diamond bought. Consumers enjoy large amounts of consumer surplus

on water because the price is low and large amounts are bought. Far less consumer surplus is enjoyed by consumers on diamonds because far fewer diamonds are bought.

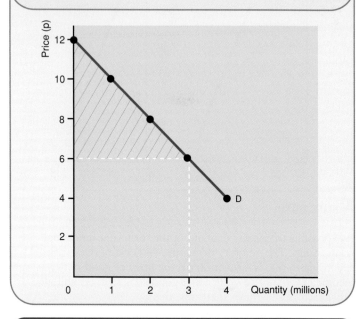

Figure 4.6 Consumer surplus
The demand curve shows the price that the buyer would be prepared to pay for each unit. Except on the last unit purchased, the price that the buyer is prepared to pay is above the market price that is paid. The difference between these two values is the consumer surplus. It is represented by the shaded area under the demand curve.

Question 7

Demand for a good is zero at £200. It then rises to 50 million units at £100 and 75 million at £50.
(a) Draw the demand curve for prices between 0 and £200.
(b) Shade the area of consumer surplus at a price of £60.
(c) Is consumer surplus larger or smaller at a price of £40 compared to £60? Explain your answer.

Key terms

Consumer surplus - the difference between how much buyers are prepared to pay for a good and what they actually pay.
Demand curve - the line on a price-quantity diagram which shows the level of effective demand at any given price.
Demand or effective demand - the quantity purchased of a good at any given price, given that other determinants of demand remain unchanged.

Individual demand curve - the demand curve for an individual consumer, firm or other economic unit.
Market demand curve - the sum of all individual demand curves.
Shift in the demand curve - a movement of the whole demand curve to the right or left of the original caused by a change in any variable affecting demand except price.

Applied economics

The demand for housing

Housing tenure

The housing market is not a single market because there are different forms of tenure in the market.

Owner-occupied housing Figure 4.7 shows that most homes today are owner-occupied. This means that they are owned by at least one of the people who live in the house.

Rented from local authorities The single largest group of landlords in the UK are local councils. Since the 1980s, their importance has declined as local authority housing has been sold off.

Rented from housing associations Housing associations are organisations set up to provide housing for rent. They have no shareholders and are not in business to make a profit. Their aim is to serve the needs of their customers. Much of their funding for building new houses comes from the government in the form of grants. Housing associations have grown in importance since the 1980s because the government has increasingly channelled grants for house building in the rented sector away from local authorities and towards housing associations.

Rented from private landlords Private landlords are in business to make a profit from renting property. The 1988 Housing Act (amended in 1996) revitalised the private renting sector. It allowed for new 'assured tenancies' where landlords could charge whatever rent they wished. For the first time in decades, landlords could charge the rent that the market would bear instead of having it capped, typically at a rent far below the market price. Landlords could also end tenancy agreements with an individual. This meant they could reclaim their property if they wanted to get rid of a difficult tenant, move back into the property or sell it without have a sitting tenant in place. The result has been an increase in the number of private properties for rent and a considerable improvement in the quality of housing for rent. In a competitive market where landlords are charging market rents, tenants can shop around not just for the cheapest rent but also for the best quality property at the price. In the housing boom of the early 2000s, 'buy-to-let', where individuals were buying properties with the intention of renting them out to earn a profit, became a significant component of demand for housing.

Factors affecting the demand for housing

There are many factors which determine the demand or quantity demanded of housing.

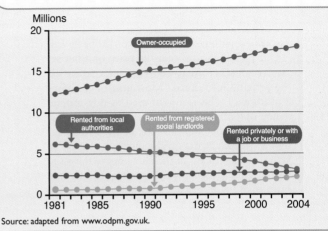

Figure 4.7 *Stock of dwellings by tenure, United Kingdom*

Source: adapted from www.odpm.gov.uk.

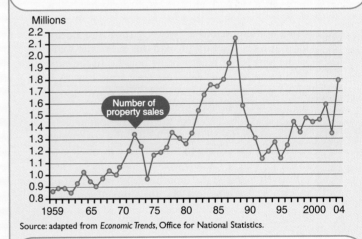

Figure 4.8 *Number of property sales: England and Wales (millions)*

Source: adapted from *Economic Trends*, Office for National Statistics.

Figure 4.9 *Average UK house prices, £ at current and constant 2005 prices*

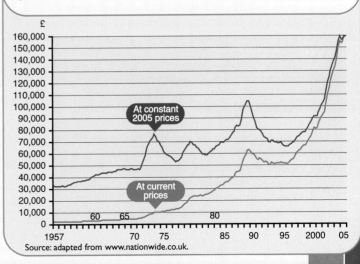

Source: adapted from www.nationwide.co.uk.

The price of owner-occupied housing Economic theory suggests that the higher the price, the less will be demanded of a good. In the owner-occupied market, rising house prices should lead to less demand and vice versa. However, Figures 4.8 and 4.9 show no evidence of this. In fact, rising house prices in the 1980s were associated with rising sales, whilst falling prices in the first half of the 1990s saw falling house sales. Equally, the house price boom of the early 2000s was also associated with rising numbers of property sales.

One explanation is that the price of a house is arguably the wrong price to consider when looking at the demand for homes. Most houses are bought with a **mortgage**. This is a loan used to buy property. When potential buyers look at the price of the transaction, they tend to look at the value of the monthly repayments on the mortgage rather than the actual house price. In the short term, the value of monthly repayments is more influenced by interest rates than house prices. If interest rates rise, mortgage repayments rise and vice versa. Figure 4.10 shows changes in bank base rates, which are the most important influence on banks and building societies when they set their own mortgage rates. For instance, between 1985 and 1987, interest rates were falling, making repayments lower. This was associated with rising house purchases. Between 1988 and 1990, interest rates rose sharply and this led to the sharp fall in the number of houses being bought. In the early 2000s, interest rates fell from over 5 per cent to a low of 3.5 per cent and this was associated with a rise in the number of house purchases.

Subsidies too can affect the monthly payments on a mortgage. In the 1970s and 1980s, the government subsidised borrowing to buy a house through giving tax relief on the interest paid on mortgages. This effectively reduced the monthly repayment cost of the mortgage. Starting in 1987, the value of mortgage tax relief was progressively reduced by the government and was finally abolished in 1999. This increased the cost of borrowing to buy a house and was one factor which dampened the demand for owner-occupied housing in the 1990s.

Even so, not all houses are purchased using a mortgage. Higher priced houses in particular tend to be bought outright or with mortgages which only account for a fraction of the buying price. So other factors must also be important in determining the demand for owner-occupied housing.

Incomes Real incomes (incomes after inflation has been taken into account) have been rising at an average of 2.5 per cent over the past 40 years in the UK. Figure 4.11 shows how the average real personal disposable income (income after income tax and National Insurance contributions have been deducted) of households has changed since 1971. Rising income has led to a rising demand for housing. When growth in income slowed or fell, as in the early 1980s and early 1990s, this was associated with slowdowns or

Figure 4.10 Interest rates: the base rate set by the Bank of England

Source: adapted from Bank of England website.

Figure 4.11 Real households' disposable income per head at 2001 prices

£ at 2001 prices

Real households' disposable income per head

Source: adapted from *Economics Trends*, Office for National Statistics.

Table 4.4 Population and number of households: UK

		Millions
	Population	Number of households
1961	52.8	16.3
1971	55.9	18.6
1981	56.4	20.2
1991	57.8	22.4
2001	59.1	23.8
2004	59.8	24.1

Source: adapted from *Social Trends*, Office for National Statistics; *Monthly Digest of Statistics*, Office for National Statistics.

falls in housing prices. In the early 2000s, moderate growth in average household income undoubtedly contributed to the housing boom.

The increase in owner-occupation compared to renting is also probably due to rising income. Households in the UK prefer to own their own homes rather than renting them. Rising incomes makes home ownership more affordable to more people. Equally, though, the growth in buy-to-let from the 1990s onwards has also increased demand for housing and contributed to rising house prices.

Population trends Population trends have also been important in increasing the demand for housing. As Table 4.4 shows, the population of the UK is growing over time. However, the number of households is growing at a much faster rate. A household is defined as a group of people living together in a dwelling. Households have been getting smaller over time. More people are living longer and pensioners tend to live on their own. Divorce rates have increased whilst there are more one parent families than before. Fewer young people want to live at home with their parents once they have left school. So the number of dwellings needed to accommodate households has been rising and is predicted to carry on rising to 2050.

Other factors Other factors may affect the demand for housing apart from prices, income and population trends. One factor which influenced house buying in the 1970s and 1980s, and from the late 1990s onwards, was speculation. Because house prices rose consistently during the 1950s and 1960s, many saw housing more as an investment rather than as a place to live. In the property booms of the early 1970s and late 1980s, higher house prices were encouraging people to buy houses in the hope that their value would go up even further. The 1990s saw far less speculative activity because house price increases remained relatively subdued, but speculation again took off from the late 1990s as house prices soared.

The end of the housing boom in the late 1980s saw a reverse effect to this. Millions of households in the early 1990s were caught in a **negative equity** trap. They bought houses at the top of the property boom in 1988 and 1989, borrowing almost all the money needed for the purchase. House prices fell in the early 1990s. This meant that many owed more money on their mortgage than their house was worth. Hence they had 'negative equity'. This discouraged people from buying houses because it was feared that house prices might fall even further, leading to equity losses. Moreover, due to very high interest rates and high unemployment, many fell behind with their mortgage payments and eventually saw their houses repossessed by their lenders. This experience discouraged households from overborrowing throughout much of the rest of the 1990s.

In the rented housing market, important legal changes led to changes in demand. In 1980, the government gave tenants of council houses the right to buy their homes at very low prices. Over the next two decades, more than one and half million council houses were sold to their tenants. So this legal change led to a rise in demand for owner-occupied housing.

Another important legal change occurred in 1988. The government introduced a new type of tenancy called an assured tenancy where rents were not regulated by the state and where landlords were able to repossess properties at the end of a period of time specified by the tenancy agreement. Existing laws dating from the 1960s had given tenants the right to ask council officials to fix a rent and effectively gave them the right to stay in the property for life. The result of the 1998 change was a rise in rents as landlords converted their tenancies wherever possible to the new assured tenancy agreements. This should have led to a fall in the quantity demanded for rented accommodation in the 1990s. However, two other factors more than outweighed this effect. First, some households decided to rent rather than buy because of the experience of negative equity. Second, more and better quality housing for rent came onto the market as a result of the 1988 changes. This again encouraged some households to rent rather than to buy. In 2005, with house prices at historically high levels, many could not afford to buy a property and therefore were forced into the rental market even though they would have preferred to buy.

The relative importance of different factors

In the long term, rising incomes and an increasing number of households are pushing up the demand for both owner-occupied and rented housing in the UK. In the short term, other factors have had a significant impact on the demand for housing, including property speculation, changes in the law, the ending of mortgage tax relief and changes in interest rates.

One measure which attempts to combine a variety of factors is the Nationwide Affordability Index shown in Figure 4.12. The Nationwide Building Society calculates the index based on average mortgage payments as a percentage of take home pay. Average mortgage payments depend on the size of the mortgage, and therefore for new house purchases the price of housing, and the rate of interest paid on the mortgage. If house prices fall, interest rates fall, or take home pay rises, then houses become more affordable and the index goes down. If house prices rise, interest rates rise, or take home pay falls, then houses become less affordable and the index rises. Figure 4.12 shows that houses were least affordable at the end of the 1980s due to a combination of relatively high prices and high interest rates. In the housing boom of the early 2000s, the affordability index rose sharply. Despite low interest rates and rising incomes, the size of mortgages was increasing rapidly because house prices were rising sharply. The surge in demand for housing which led to rising prices in the early

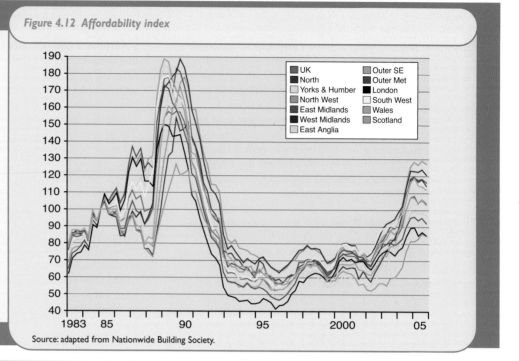

Figure 4.12 Affordability index

Legend:
UK, North, Yorks & Humber, North West, East Midlands, West Midlands, East Anglia, Outer SE, Outer Met, London, South West, Wales, Scotland

Source: adapted from Nationwide Building Society.

2000s can perhaps be partially explained by this combination of falling interest rates and rising incomes. However, the affordability index rose rapidly from around 70 in 2000 to over 100 by 2005. This partially explains the fall in demand for housing experienced in 2005. Even so, some commentators argued that housing in 2005 was not particularly expensive by historical standards and predicted continued strong demand for housing for the foreseeable future.

DataQuestion Admission charges for museums

In the 1990s, a number of national museums and galleries, such as the National History Museum and the V&A (Victoria and Albert Museum, London) introduced admission charges to increase their revenues. The government, which was responsible for running those museums, began relaxing those charges from April 1999. Free admission to children was introduced on 1 April 1999, for those over 60 on 1 April 2000, and then free admission for all was introduced from 1 December 2001. The result was a significant increase in admissions to these museums and galleries as can be seen from Table 4.5.

Another group of museums, which include the National Gallery and the British Museum, have always had free entrance. Their admissions also increased over the period 2000-2004 but not by nearly as much as those which had been charging before.

Table 4.5 Total visits to national museums and galleries

	2000	2001	2002	2003	Millions 2004
Museums and galleries which before December 2001 charged for admission	7.2	7.8	13.2	13.4	13.7
Museums and galleries which have never charged for admission	18.2	19.1	19.5	18.8	21.0
Total	25.4	26.9	32.7	32.2	34.7

Note: years are from December the previous year to November in that year, e.g. figures for 2000 are December 1999 to November 2000.

Source: adapted from www.culture.gov.uk.

Increasing admissions to national museums and galleries are being driven by a number of factors. The number of foreign tourists in the UK increased over the period and some of those would have visited museums and galleries. Increased numbers of short break holidays by UK citizens to London in particular also helped admission numbers. Culture Secretary Tessa Jowell would also like to think that the public's appetite for 'serious' culture is growing.

1. Using a demand curve diagram and the data, explain why abolishing admission charges led to an increase in the number of visits to national museums and galleries.

2. Suggest other factors, apart from price, that might have shifted the demand curve for admissions to national museums and galleries to the right.

3. Using a diagram, discuss the amount of consumer surplus that visitors to national museums and galleries might have received before and after the abolition of admission charges.

5 The supply curve

Summary

1. A rise in price leads to a rise in quantity supplied, shown by a movement along the supply curve.
2. A change in supply can be caused by factors such as a change in costs of production, technology and the price of other goods. This results in a shift in the supply curve.
3. The market supply curve in a perfectly competitive market is the sum of each firm's individual supply curves.

Supply

In any market there are buyers and sellers. Buyers **demand** goods whilst sellers **supply** goods. SUPPLY in economics is defined as the quantity of goods that sellers are prepared to sell at any given price over a period of time. For instance, in 2003 UK farmers sold 5.9 million tonnes of potatoes at an average price of £102 per tonne, so economists would say that the supply of potatoes at £102 per tonne over the 12 month period was 5.9 million tonnes.

Supply and price

If the price of a good increases, how will producers react? Assuming that no other factors have changed, they are likely to expand production to take advantage of the higher prices and the higher profits that they can now make. In general, quantity supplied will rise if the price of the good also rises, all other things being equal.

This can be shown on a diagram using a **supply curve**. A supply curve shows the quantity that will be supplied over a period of time at any given price. Consider Figure 5.1 which shows the supply curve for wheat. Wheat is priced at £110 per tonne. At this price only the most efficient farmers grow wheat. They supply 110 million tonnes per year. But if the price of wheat rose to £140 per tonne, farmers already growing wheat might increase their acreage of wheat, whilst other non-wheat growing farmers might start to grow wheat. Farmers would do this because at a price of £140 per tonne it is possible to make a profit on production even if costs are higher than at a production level of 110 million units.

A fall in price will lead to a **fall in quantity supplied**, shown by a **movement along** the supply curve. At a lower price, some firms will cut back on relatively unprofitable production whilst others will stop producing altogether. Some of the latter firms may even go bankrupt, unable to cover their costs of production from the price received.

An upward sloping supply curve assumes that:
- firms are motivated to produce by profit - so this model does not apply, for instance, to much of what is produced by government;
- the cost of producing a unit increases as output increases (a situation known as rising marginal cost) - this is not always

Figure 5.1 The supply curve

The supply curve is upward sloping, showing that firms increase production of a good as its price increases. This is because a higher price enables firms to make profit on the increased output whereas at the lower price they would have made a loss on it. Here, an increase in the price of wheat from £110 to £140 per tonne increases quantity supplied from 110 million tonnes to 150 million tonnes per year.

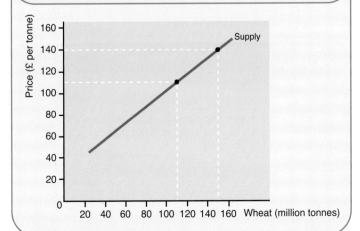

Question 1

Table 5.1

Price (£)	Quantity supplied (million units per year)
5	5
10	8
15	11
20	14
25	17

(a) Draw a supply curve from the above data.
(b) Draw new supply curves assuming that quantity supplied at any given price:
(i) increased by 10 units; (ii) increased by 50 per cent;
(iii) fell by 5 units; (iv) halved.

true but it is likely that the prices of factors of production to the firm will increase as firms bid for more land, labour and capital to increase their output, thus pushing up costs.

Costs of production

The supply curve is drawn on the assumption that the general costs of production in the economy remain constant (part of the **ceteris paribus** condition). If other things change, then the supply curve will shift. If the costs of production increase at any given level of output, firms will attempt to pass on these increases in the form of higher prices. If they cannot charge higher prices then profits will fall and firms will produce less of the good or might even stop producing it altogether. A rise in the costs of production will therefore lead to a decrease in supply.

This can be seen in Figure 5.3. The original supply curve is S₁. A rise in the costs of production means that at any given level of output firms will charge higher prices. At an output level of OA, firms will increase their prices from OB to OC. This increase in prices will be true for all points on the supply curve. So the supply curve will **shift** upwards and to the left to S_2 in Figure 5.3. There will have been a **fall in supply**. (Note that a fall in **quantity supplied** refers to a change in quantity supplied due to a change in price and would be shown by a movement along the supply curve.) Conversely a fall in the costs of production will lead to an increase in supply of a good. This is shown by a shift to the right in the supply curve.

Technology

Another factor which affects supply of a particular good is the state of technology. The supply curve is drawn on the

Figure 5.3 A rise in the costs of production
A rise in the costs of production for a firm will push its supply curve upwards and to the left, from S_1 to S_2. For any given quantity supplied, firms will now want a higher price to compensate them for the increase in their costs.

assumption that the state of technology remains unchanged. If new technology is introduced to the production process it should lead to a fall in the costs of production. This greater **productive efficiency** will encourage firms to produce more at the same price or produce the same amount at a lower price or some combination of the two. The supply curve will shift downwards and to the right. It would be unusual for firms to replace more efficient technology with less efficient technology. However, this can occur at times of war or natural disasters. If new technical equipment is destroyed, firms may have to fall back on less efficient means of production, reducing supply at any given price, resulting in a shift in the supply curve to the left.

The prices of other goods

Changes in the prices of some goods can affect the supply of a particular good. For instance, if the price of beef increases substantially there will be an increase in the quantity of beef supplied. More cows will be reared and slaughtered. As a result there will be an increase in the supply of hides for leather. At the same price, the quantity of leather supplied to the market will increase. An increase in the price of beef therefore leads to an increase in the supply of leather. On the other hand, an increase in cattle rearing is likely to be at the expense of production of wheat or sheep farming. So an increase in beef production is likely to lead to a fall in the supply of other agricultural products as farmers switch production to take advantage of higher profits in beef.

Question 2

Figure 5.2 Average percentage change in earnings over the previous 12 months

Change in average earnings

Source: adapted from *Economic Trends*, Office for National Statistics.

(a) Explain how a change in earnings can shift the supply curve of a product to the left.
(b) Discuss in which years the supply curves for goods made in the UK are likely to have shifted (i) furthest and (ii) least far to the left according to the data.

Question 3

Explain, using supply curves, why it cost £10 000 in 1970 for a machine that could do the same as a calculator which cost £100 in 1975 and £5 today.

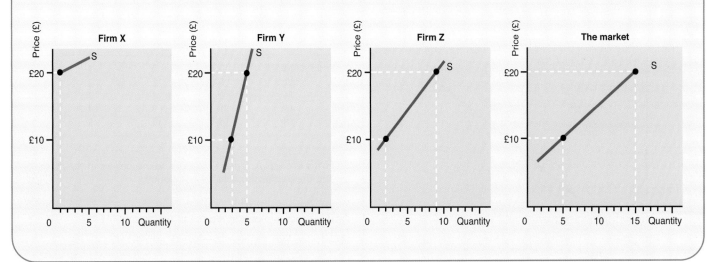

Figure 5.4 Individual and market supply curves
The market supply curve is calculated by summing the individual supply curves of producers in the market. Here the market supply at £20, for instance, is calculated by adding the supply of each individual firm at a price of £20.

Other factors

A number of other factors affect supply. These include:
- the goals of sellers - if for some reason there is a change in the profit levels which a seller expects to receive as a reward for production, then there will be a change in supply; for instance, if an industry such as the book retailing industry went from one made up of many small sellers more interested in selling books than making a profit to one where the industry was dominated by a few large profit-seeking companies, then supply would fall;
- government legislation - anti-pollution controls which raise the costs of production, the abolition of legal barriers to setting up business in an industry, or tax changes, are some examples of how government can change the level of supply in an industry;
- expectations of future events - if firms expect future prices to be much higher, they may restrict supplies and stockpile goods; if they expect disruptions to their future production because of a strike they may stockpile raw materials, paying

for them with borrowed money, thus increasing their costs and reducing supply;
- the weather - in agricultural markets, the weather plays a crucial role in determining supply, bad weather reducing supply, good weather producing bumper yields.

Individual and market supply curves

The MARKET SUPPLY CURVE can be derived from the INDIVIDUAL SUPPLY CURVES of sellers in the market (this assumes that supply is not affected by changes in the demand curve as would happen under monopoly or oligopoly). Consider Figure 5.4. For the sake of simplicity we will assume that there are only three sellers in the market. At a price of £10 per unit, Firm X is unwilling to supply any goods. Firm Y supplies 3 units whilst Firm Z supplies 2 units. So the market supply at a price of £10 is 5 units. At a price of £20, Firm X will supply 1 unit, Firm Y 5 units and Firm Z 9 units. So the market supply at a price of £20 is 15 units. The rest of the market supply curve can be derived by **horizontally summing** the level of output at all other price levels.

Producer surplus

The supply curve shows how much will be supplied at any given price. In Figure 5.5, firms will supply 10 million units at 10p whereas they will supply 25 million units at 20p. Assume that the price that firms receive is actually 20p. Some firms will then receive more than the lowest price at which they are prepared to supply. For instance, one firm was prepared to supply the 10 millionth unit at 10p. The firm receives 20p, which is 10p more. This 10p is PRODUCER SURPLUS. It is the difference between the market price which the firm receives and the price at which it is prepared to supply. The total amount of producer surplus earned by firms is shown by the area between the supply curve and horizontal line at the market price. It is the sum of the producer surplus earned at each level of output.

Explain, using diagrams, how you would expect supply of the following goods to be affected by the events stated, all other things being equal.
(a) Petrol 2004-2005. In 2004-2005, the price of crude oil rose from $25 a barrel to over $70 a barrel.
(b) Internet telephone calling from 2004. Since 2004, an increasing number of companies have been reducing the price of making a telephone call by offering Internet telephone services using new software which compete with traditional landline or mobile phone connections.
(c) Cotton 2005. In 2005, there was a record cotton crop in Pakistan, the world's fourth largest cotton producer after the USA, China and India, partly the result of good weather conditions and increased use of fertilisers.

Figure 5.5 Producer surplus

The supply curve shows how much will be supplied at any given price. Except on the last unit supplied, the supplier receives more for the good than the lowest price at which it is prepared to supply. This difference between the market price and lowest price at which a firm is prepared to supply is producer surplus. Total producer surplus is shown by the shaded area above the supply curve.

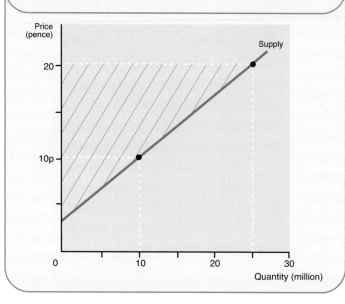

Question 5

Table 5.2

Quantity supplied (million units)			Price (£)
Firms in area A	Firms in area B	Firms in area C	
10	2	0	1
12	5	3	2
14	8	6	3
16	11	9	4
18	14	12	5

Firms in areas A, B and C are the sole suppliers in the market and the market is perfectly competitive.

(a) Draw the market supply curve.
(b) What is supply at a price of (i) £1 and (ii) £3.50?
(c) One firm in area A decides to increase production by 5 units at every given price. Draw the new market supply curve on your diagram.
(d) Explain what would happen to the market supply curve if new technology in the industry led to greater productive efficiency amongst individual firms.

Key terms

Individual supply curve - the supply curve of an individual producer.
Market supply curve - the supply curve of all producers within the market. In a perfectly competitive market it can be calculated by summing the supply curves of individual producers.

Producer surplus - the difference between the market price which firms receive and the price at which they are prepared to supply.
Supply - the quantity of goods that suppliers are willing to sell at any given price over a period of time.

Applied economics

The supply of housing

There is a number of different markets within the housing market, each of which has its own supply. Within the **owner-occupied** market, there is a market for buying and selling second hand dwellings. There is also a market for new housing. Within the rented sector, local authorities, housing associations and the private sector supply housing to the market. Supply has changed in different ways in these different markets in the UK, as can be seen from Figure 5.6. The broad trend has been for owner-occupation to increase whilst renting has declined.

The owner-occupied market

Figures 5.7 and 5.8 give two different measures of supply to the housing market. The first includes the total number of new houses built for sale to the private sector. The second shows the total number of property transactions per year. This includes both sale of the new houses and of existing houses which are sold

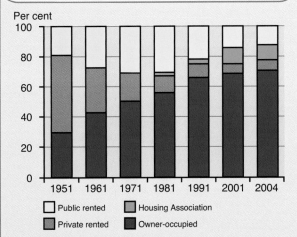

Figure 5.6 *Housing stock by tenure: 1951-2004*

Per cent

Public rented
Private rented
Housing Association
Owner-occupied

Source: adapted from Department of the Environment, *Transport and the Regions, Housing and Construction Statistics.*

Figure 5.8 *Number of property sales: England and Wales (millions)*

Millions

Number of property sales

Source: adapted from *Economic Trends Annual Supplement,* Office for National Statistics.

Figure 5.7 *Annual completions of new houses, Great Britain*

Thousands of dwellings

Total
Private
Housing association
Public sector

Source: adapted from Department of the Environment, *Transport and the Regions, Housing and Construction Statistics.*

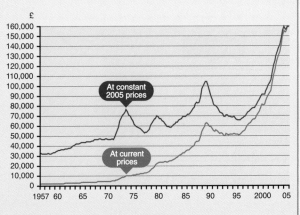

Figure 5.9 *Average UK house price, £ at current and constant values[1]*

£

At constant 2005 prices

At current prices

1. Average price of new dwellings with mortgages approved.
Source: adapted from *Economic Trends Annual Supplement,* Office for National Statistics.

second hand. Economic theory would suggest that the higher the price, the higher the quantity supplied. The experience of the past 30 years would tend to support this relationship in the housing market. Figure 5.9 shows that periods of high increases in house prices, as in 1972-73 and 1986-89 and the late 1990s to 2004, coincided with both high levels of new house completions and total number of property transactions. Slumps in property prices, as in 1990-93, occurred at the same time as falls in the number of sales of both new and existing houses.

Supply can also be influenced by other factors. One is cost. Increases in costs will push the supply curve upwards. The main cost in house building today in most areas of the UK is the cost of land. Typically, half the cost of a property represents the cost of the land on which it is built. The rest is made up of labour costs and materials. Figure 5.10, over the page,

shows how the price of land and the average hourly earnings of male manual workers in the construction industry increased between 1990 and 2004 and how they correlate with increases in prices of new housing during the same period.

Another factor which has been very important in influencing the supply of housing is government regulation. The government and local authorities have restricted the supply of new housing, particularly through green belt regulations. In order to build new houses, construction firms have to obtain planning permission from the local authority. When the housing market has been buoyant, as in the early 2000s, construction firms have wanted to build more new houses than local authorities have permitted. This has driven up the cost of building land as construction companies have competed to buy scarce sites. The higher cost of building land has then reduced the

Figure 5.10 *Housing land prices, average earnings in the construction industry and price of new houses*

Source: adapted from www.odpm.gov.uk and *Construction Statistics*, Department of Trade and Industry.

supply of new housing. This has been particularly true in areas like the South East of England where the population has been growing relatively fast.

There has also been a significant flow of houses into the owner-occupied sector from sales of council houses. In 1980, the government gave council house tenants the right to buy their homes at extremely advantageous prices. Figure 5.11 shows that over 3 million homes have become owner occupied since then as a result. Other factors have arguably not been significant in influencing the supply of houses in the UK. For instance, there have been no significant technological changes in building and the goals of building firms have not changed.

Renting from local authorities

The supply of local authority housing for rent is not determined by market forces but by political factors. In the 1950s, 1960s and 1970s, the government gave substantial grants to local authorities to build council houses. Each year, as Figure 5.7 shows, between 100 000 and 250 000 houses were completed.

However, the government of Margaret Thatcher, which came into power in 1979, was ideologically opposed to council housing. It wanted to create a 'nation of homeowners' and believed that local authorities were poor managers of their housing stocks. The government achieved its aims partly by introducing its right to buy legislation in 1980 which led to the sale of council houses to tenants shown in Figure 5.11. The stock of council housing was further reduced by sales of complete estates to housing associations by some councils. The other part of government policy was to cut off funding for new council house building. As Figure 5.7 shows, in 1978, 108 000 new council houses were built. In 1980, this had fallen to 86 000. By 1990, only 16 600 new council houses were built and in 2003 this was a mere 241.

With continued sales to tenants and insignificant new house building, the supply of council houses declined in the 1980s and 1990s as Figure 5.7 shows and is likely to continue to decline in the future.

Housing associations

Housing associations are organisations which exist to provide housing at affordable rents. Throughout the 1950s, 1960s and 1970s, with the help of government grants, they built between 1 000 and 15 000 houses a year, a relatively small addition to the total supply of housing in the UK. However, in the 1980s and 1990s, the government increasingly channelled grants away from local authorities and to housing associations for social housing. House building by housing associations peaked in the mid-1990s at around 40 000 houses a year and has since been declining. In 2003, housing associations built 18 098 houses.

Like council housing, the supply of homes from housing associations is determined mainly not by markets but by political decisions about where grants for house building should be given. It should be noted, looking at Figure 5.7. that housing associations are responsible only for a very small fraction of new housing and, from Figure 5.6, account for only a very small percentage of the total housing stock.

The private rented market

The supply of private rented accommodation fell in the 1950s, 1960s and 1970s. This was mainly because the rent or price that landlords received was too low and hence there was a movement down the supply curve. Increasing numbers either buying their own home or renting from a local authority put downward pressure on private rents. More important, though, from the mid 1960s there was legislation which gave tenants considerable rights including the right to a 'fair' or regulated rent. The legislation also made it very difficult for a landlord to evict a tenant if they wanted to stop renting the property. As a consequence, landlords withdrew from the housing market and the supply of private rented accommodation fell.

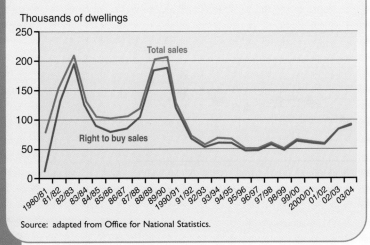

Figure 5.11 Sales of local authority dwellings for owner-occupation, Great Britain

Thousands of dwellings

Source: adapted from Office for National Statistics.

Table 5.3 Number of privately rented houses by type of tenancy, England

Millions of tenancies

	Assured	Assured shorthold	Regulated rent	Other	Total private rented
1990	0.36	0.14	0.59	0.70	1.79
1995/96	0.37	0.95	0.27	0.66	2.25
2003/04	0.22	1.48	0.14	0.53	2.37

Source: adapted from Department of Trade and Industry, www.odpm.gov.uk.

Table 5.4 Rents by type of tenancy, England

£ per week

	Assured	Assured shorthold	Regulated rent	Average of all private rented
1990	251	273	121	173
1995/96	285	395	170	301
2003/04	417	526	246	475

Source: adapted from Department of Trade and Industry, www.odpm.gov.uk.

Since 1988, however, the private rented sector has begun to expand again as Table 5.3 shows. This was because legislation passed in that year gave landlords the freedom to set their own rents and made it much simpler to evict tenants.

Rents on the new shorthold assured tenancy agreements were more than double those on traditional regulated rent properties as Table 5.4 shows. Not surprisingly, these new assured tenancy agreements quickly came to dominate the private rented market.

By the late 1990s, an increasing number of individuals were speculating in the housing market by buying properties with the specific intention of letting them out. This came to be called 'buy-to-let'. Often, such properties would be bought on mortgages. The hope was that the rent earned would cover the running costs of the property and the cost of the mortgage. The landlord would then be able to pocket the capital gain from rising house prices. The higher the increase in house prices, the more buy-to-let owners would make a profit on their property investment. However, if house prices stagnated or, worse still, fell, then many buy-to-let owners would find themselves losing money on their investment.

Buy-to-let has led to a healthy expansion of the private rented sector. Those wanting to rent properties now have more choice and the quality of rented accommodation has risen. However, the speculative element of buy-to-let means that any downturn in the housing market is likely to be amplified. A fall in house prices could bring new investment in buy-to-let to a halt and lead to some existing landlords selling their properties. This would increase the supply of houses for sale onto the market and depress demand. Inevitably this would lead to further falls in house prices.

DataQuestion

Cocoa beans

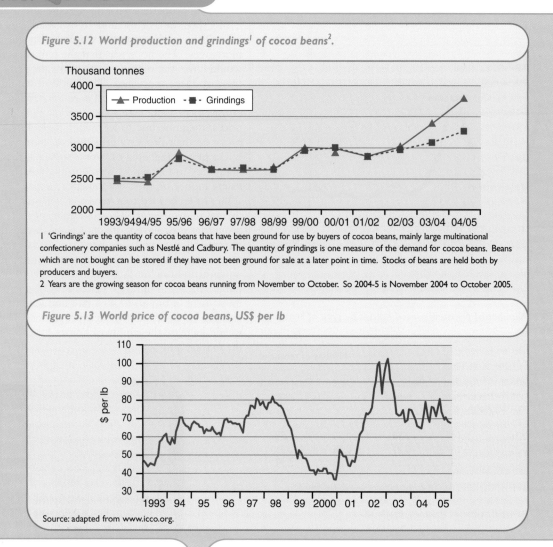

Figure 5.12 World production and grindings¹ of cocoa beans².

Thousand tonnes

1 'Grindings' are the quantity of cocoa beans that have been ground for use by buyers of cocoa beans, mainly large multinational confectionery companies such as Nestlé and Cadbury. The quantity of grindings is one measure of the demand for cocoa beans. Beans which are not bought can be stored if they have not been ground for sale at a later point in time. Stocks of beans are held both by producers and buyers.
2 Years are the growing season for cocoa beans running from November to October. So 2004-5 is November 2004 to October 2005.

Figure 5.13 World price of cocoa beans, US$ per lb

$ per lb

Source: adapted from www.icco.org.

The new millennium has brought good news for most cocoa farmers. Prices have risen substantially on the back of fears of poor harvests and growing demand for cocoa beans from the world's multinational confectionery companies. Farmers have responded by increasing their output.

However, not all cocoa growers have benefited. In 2003-04, for example, unfavourable climatic conditions and Witches' Broom disease, a disease which reduces yields, hit Brazilian production whilst drought in Indonesia cut their output at harvest time.

In the 18th century, Venezuela was the world's top supplier of cocoa beans. Today, it supplies just 0.5 per cent of the world's output. However, the Venezuelan government is keen to increase production. It is offering loans to cocoa farmers and to entrepreneurs who want to set up chocolate factories.

Venezuela has one big advantage over the world's two major producers, Cote d'Ivoire and Ghana which between them produce 75 per cent of the world's production: the advantage of quality. Cote d'Ivoire and Ghana produce a bean adequate for mass market chocolate. Venezuela, however, because of its soil and climate, produces premium beans which are suitable for high quality chocolate prized amongst connoisseurs. The country has also escaped Witches' Broom, a disease that affects cocoa trees and severely damaged last year's harvest in Brazil.

Source: adapted from the *Financial Times*, 27.9.2005.

1. Compare the trend in world production of cocoa beans with the demand for cocoa beans over the period 1993/94 to 2004/05.
2. Using a supply curve diagram, explain why the change in the price of cocoa beans between 2002 and 2005 led to an increase in world production.
3. Using a supply curve diagram, explain what effect Witches' Broom disease had on world supply of cocoa beans in 2004-05.
4. Using a supply curve diagram, discuss the impact that Venezuelan initiatives with regard to its cocoa industry are likely to have on (a) world supply of cocoa and (b) world supply of premium cocoa beans.

6 Price determination

Summary

1. The equilibrium or market clearing price is set where demand equals supply.
2. Changes in demand and supply will lead to new equilibrium prices being set.
3. A change in demand will lead to a shift in the demand curve, a movement along the supply curve and a new equilibrium price.
4. A change in supply will lead to a shift in the supply curve, a movement along the demand curve and a new equilibrium price.
5. Markets do not necessarily tend towards the equilibrium price.
6. The equilibrium price is not necessarily the price which will lead to the greatest economic efficiency or the greatest equity.

Equilibrium price

Buyers and sellers come together in a market. A price (sometimes called the **market price**) is struck and goods or services are exchanged. Consider Table 6.1. It shows the demand and supply schedule for a good at prices between £2 and £10.

Table 6.1

Price (£)	Quantity demanded (million units per month)	Quantity supplied (million units per month)
2	12	2
4	9	4
6	6	6
8	3	8
10	0	10

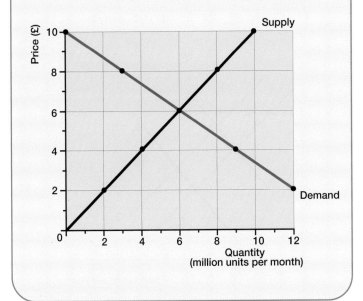

Figure 6.1 Equilibrium

At £6, the quantity demanded is equal to the quantity supplied. The market is said to be in equilibrium at this price.

- If the price is £2, demand will be 12 million units but only 2 million units will be supplied. Demand is greater than supply and there is therefore EXCESS DEMAND (i.e. too much demand in relation to supply) in the market. There will be a **shortage** of products on the market. Some buyers will be lucky and they will snap up the 2 million units being sold. But there will be a 10 million unit shortfall in supply for the rest of the unlucky buyers in the market. For instance, it is not possible to buy some luxury cars without being on a waiting list for several years because current demand is too great.
- If the price is £10, buyers will not buy any goods. Sellers on the other hand will wish to supply 10 million units. Supply is greater than demand and therefore there will be EXCESS SUPPLY. There will be a glut or surplus of products on the market. 10 million units will remain unsold. A sale in a shop is often evidence of excess supply in the past. Firms tried to sell the goods at a higher price and failed.
- There is only one price where demand equals supply. This is at a price of £6 where demand and supply are both 6 million units. This price is known as the EQUILIBRIUM PRICE. This is the only price where the planned demand of buyers equals the planned supply of sellers in the market. It is also known as the MARKET-CLEARING price because all the products supplied to the market are bought or cleared from the market, but no buyer is left frustrated in his or her wishes to buy goods.

An alternative way of expressing the data in Table 6.1 is shown in Figure 6.1. The equilibrium price is where demand equals supply. This happens where the two curves cross, at a price of £6 and a quantity of 6 million units. If the price is above £6, supply will be greater than demand and therefore excess supply will exist. If the price is below £6, demand is greater than supply and therefore there will be excess demand.

Changes in demand and supply

It was explained in units 4 and 5 that a change in price would lead to a change in quantity demanded or supplied, shown by a movement along the demand or supply curve. A change in any other variable, such as income or the costs of production, would lead to:

Question 1

Table 6.2

Price (£)	Quantity demanded (million units)	Quantity supplied (million units)
30	20	70
20	50	50
10	80	30

(a) Plot the demand and supply curves shown in Table 6.2 on a diagram.
(b) What is the equilibrium price?
(c) In what price range is there (i) excess demand and (ii) excess supply?
(d) Will there be a glut or a shortage in the market if the price is: (i) £10; (ii) £40; (iii) £22; (iv) £18; (v) £20?

- an **increase** or **decrease** in demand or supply and therefore
- a **shift** in the demand or supply curve.

Demand and supply diagrams provide a powerful and simple tool for analysing the effects of changes in demand and supply on equilibrium price and quantity.

Consider the effect of a rise in consumer incomes. This will lead to an increase in the demand for a normal good. In Figure 6.2(a) this will push the demand curve from D_1 to D_2. As can be seen from the diagram, the equilibrium price rises from P_1 to P_2. The quantity bought and sold in equilibrium rises from Q_1 to Q_2. The model of demand and supply predicts that an increase in incomes, all other things being equal (the **ceteris paribus** condition) will lead to an increase both in the price of the product and in the quantity sold. Note that the increase in income **shifts** the demand curve and this then leads to a **movement along** the supply curve.

Figure 6.2(b) shows the market for televisions in the early 2000s. In the early 2000s, many manufacturers introduced flat screen, slimline televisions. As a result, there was a boom in sales of these televisions and a slump in sales of older, more bulky sets. In economic terms the demand for older, bulky sets

---

Figure 6.2 *Shifts in the demand and supply curves*
Shifts in the demand or supply curves for a product will change the equilibrium price and the equilibrium quantity bought and sold.

Question 2

During the 1970s the price of metals such as nickel was historically high. This prompted nickel producers to invest in new production facilities which came on stream during the late 1970s and early 1980s. But the world economy went into deep recession during the early 1980s, prompting a collapse in the world price of nickel. Producers reacted by closing facilities. Between 1980 and 1986, the industry lost about 32 500 tonnes of annual capacity compared with an annual demand of between 400 000 and 500 000 tonnes.

The world economy started to recover from 1982 but it wasn't until 1987 that a sharp increase in demand from Japanese stainless steel producers, one of the major buyers in the industry, made prices rise. In the last quarter of 1987, nickel could be bought for $1.87 per lb. By March 1988, it had soared to over $9 per lb. This price proved unsustainable. Both the US and UK economies began to go into recession in 1989 and nickel prices fell to below $3 per lb by the end of 1989.

The invasion of Kuwait by Iraq in 1990 and the subsequent large military involvement of the USA and other countries in defeating Iraq led to a rise in most metal prices. The markets feared a long drawn out war with a possible increase in demand from armaments manufacturers and a possible fall in supply if any nickel producing countries decided to side with Iraq and suspend nickel sales onto the world market. However, the swift defeat of Iraq led to a sharp fall back in price. Recession in Europe and Japan produced further falls in price between 1991 and 1993 despite the beginning of recovery in the US economy, with the price falling below $2 per lb in the last quarter of 1993. The price would have been even lower but for cutbacks in output by major nickel producers over the period.

1994 saw a sharp rise in demand as all the major industrialised countries showed economic growth. By the start of 1995, nickel prices had risen to over $3 per lb. The next major price movement occurred in 1997. An increase in productive capacity led to oversupply and falling prices. But at the end of the year, this was compounded by the start of the Asian crisis. Several countries in East Asia, including South Korea and Thailand, experienced a financial crisis which led to a sharp fall in domestic production. Demand

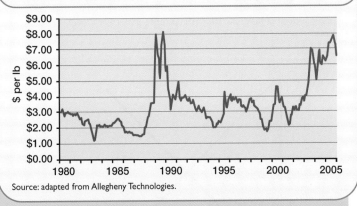

Figure 6.3 Nickel prices

Source: adapted from Allegheny Technologies.

for nickel from the Far East fell sharply, going below $2 per lb at the end of 1998 before recovering in price as East Asian economies bounced back in 1999 and 2000, reaching a high of nearly $5 per lb.

Fears of a recession in the world economy in 2000 and 2001 then led to a fall in the price of nickel back down to nearly $2 per lb at the end of 2002. However, growing demand from the Far East, particularly China, led to a surge in commodity prices from 2003, returning prices to levels not seen since the late 1980s.

Using demand and supply diagrams, explain why the price of nickel changed when:
(a) new production facilities came on stream in the late 1970s;
(b) there was a world recession in the early 1980s;
(c) the industry closed capacity during the early 1980s;
(d) Japanese stainless steel producers increased purchases in 1987;
(e) Iraq invaded Kuwait in 1990;
(f) all the major industrialised countries showed economic growth in 1994;
(g) the 1998 Asian crisis occurred;
(h) China, a country with the world's largest population, experienced fast economic growth between 2003 to 2005.

fell. This is shown by a shift to the left in the demand curve. The equilibrium level of sales in Figure 6.2(b) falls from OB to OA whilst equilibrium price falls from OF to OE. Note again that a shift in the demand curve leads to a movement along the supply curve.

Prices of many models of television set tended to fall in the 1970s and 1980s. The main reason for this was an increase in productive efficiency (☞ unit 16) due to the introduction of new technology, enabling costs of production to fall. A fall in costs of production is shown by the shift to the right in the supply curve in Figure 6.2(c). At any given quantity of output, firms will be prepared to supply more television sets to the market. The result is an increase in quantity bought and sold from OA to OB and a fall in price from OF to OE. Note that there is a shift in the supply curve which leads to a movement along the demand curve.

So far we have assumed that only one variable changes and that all other variables remain constant. But in the real world, it is likely that several factors affecting demand and supply will change at the same time. Demand and supply diagrams can be used to some extent to analyse several changes. For instance, in the 2000s the demand for flat screen and high

definition television sets increased due to rising real incomes (☞ unit 3 for a definition of 'real' values). At the same time, supply increased too because of an increase in productive efficiency. Overall, the price of television sets fell slightly. This is shown in Figure 6.2(d). Both the demand and supply curves shift to the right. This will lead to an increase in quantity bought and sold. In theory, depending upon the extent of the shifts in the two curves, there could be an increase in price, a fall in price or no change in the price. Figure 6.2(d) shows the middle of these three possibilities.

Do markets clear?

It is very easy to assume that the equilibrium price is either the current market price or the price towards which the market moves. Neither is correct. The market price could be at any level. There could be excess demand or excess supply at any point in time.

Nor will market prices necessarily tend to change to equilibrium prices over time. One of the most important controversies in economics today is the extent to which markets tend towards market-clearing prices.

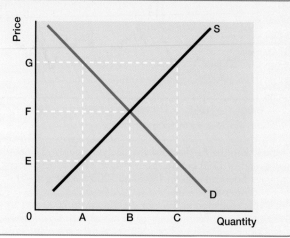

Figure 6.4 The operation of market forces in the coffee market
Market pressure will tend to force down coffee prices when there is excess supply, such as at price OG, but force up coffee prices when there is excess demand such as at price OE.

The argument put forward by neo-classical free market economists is that markets do tend to clear. Let us take the example of the coffee market. In this market, there are many producers (farmers, manufacturers, wholesalers and retailers) that are motivated by the desire to make as large a profit as possible. When there is excess demand for coffee (demand is greater than supply), coffee producers will be able to increase their prices and therefore their profits and still sell all they produce. If there is excess supply (supply is greater than

demand), some coffee will remain unsold. Producers then have a choice. Either they can offer coffee for sale at the existing price and risk not selling it or they can lower their price to the level where they will sell everything offered. If all producers choose not to lower their prices, there is likely to be even greater pressure to reduce prices in the future because there will be unsold stocks of coffee overhanging the market. Therefore when there is excess demand, prices will be driven upwards whilst prices will fall if there is excess supply.

This can be shown diagrammatically. In Figure 6.4, there is excess demand at a price of OE. Buyers want to purchase AC more of coffee than is being supplied. Shops, manufacturers and coffee growers will be able to increase their prices and their production and still sell everything they produce. If they wish to sell all their output, they can increase their prices to a maximum of OF and their output to a maximum OB, the market-clearing prices and production levels. This they will do because at higher prices and production levels they will be able to make more profit. If there is excess supply, coffee producers will be left with unsold stocks. At a price of OG, output left unsold will be AC. Producers in a free market cannot afford to build up stocks forever. Some producers will lower prices and the rest will be forced to follow. Production and prices will go on falling until equilibrium output and price is reached. This is usually referred to as a **stable equilibrium** position.

These pressures which force the market towards an equilibrium point are often called FREE MARKET FORCES. But critics of the market mechanism argue that free market forces can lead away from the equilibrium point in many cases. One example of **unstable equilibrium**, the Cobweb theory, is explained in unit 12. In other markets, it is argued that market forces are too weak to restore equilibrium. Many Keynesian economists cite the labour market as an example of this. In other markets, there are many forces such as government legislation, trade unions and multi-national monopolies which more than negate the power of the market.

Points to note

Equilibrium is a very powerful concept in economics but it is essential to remember that the equilibrium price is unlikely to be the most desirable price or 'right' price in the market. The most desirable price in the market will depend upon how one defines 'desirable'. It may be, for instance, the one which leads to the greatest economic efficiency, or it may be the one which leads to greatest equity. Alternatively it may be the one which best supports the defence of the country.

Demand can also equal supply without there being equilibrium. At any point in time, what is actually bought must equal what is actually sold. There can be no sellers without buyers. So actual demand (more often referred to as **realised** or **ex post** demand in economics) must always equal actual (or realised or ex post) supply. Equilibrium occurs at a price where there is no tendency to change. Price will not change if, at the current price, the quantity that consumers wish to buy (called **planned** or **desired** or **ex ante** demand) is equal to the quantity that suppliers wish to sell (called planned or desired or ex ante supply).

Therefore only in equilibrium will planned demand equal planned supply.

Question 3

The 1990s were a terrible time for the Australian wool industry. The problems started with the collapse of the Soviet Union. At the end of the 1980s, the Soviet Union bought about 19 per cent of Australian wool exports. By 2000, it bought nothing, unable to afford the product. Sales to the rest of the world stagnated in the 1990s, not helped by competition from synthetic fibres, and were badly affected by the Asian crisis of 1997-99. Asian countries such as Thailand, South Korea and Indonesia were rocked by a financial crisis which resulted in sharp falls in their purchasing power in world markets. Exports to these countries slumped, including wool. With stockpiles of wool hanging over the market throughout the decade, prices fell. For instance, as a result of the Asian crisis, prices fell from A$6 to A$3 between June 1997 and October 1998. Not surprisingly, there has been a sharp fall in production over the decade. Greasy wool production fell by nearly half in the 1990s and sheep numbers at about 120 million were back to their 1950s levels. The numbers of specialist wool producers fell by half.

Source: adapted from the *Financial Times*.

(a) Prices for Australian wool fell during the 1990s. Explain, using a diagram, whether this was associated with excess demand or excess supply for wool.
(b) Many Australian wool producers went bankrupt during the decade. Explain: (i) why this happened; and (ii) what was its impact on the supply of Australian wool.

Key terms

Equilibrium price - the price at which there is no tendency to change because planned (or desired or ex ante) purchases (i.e. demand) are equal to planned sales (i.e. supply).

Excess demand - where demand is greater than supply.

Excess supply - where supply is greater than demand.

Free market forces - forces in free markets which act to reduce prices when there is excess supply and raise prices when there is excess demand.

Market clearing price - the price at which there is neither excess demand nor excess supply but where everything offered for sale is purchased.

Applied economics

Demand and supply in the passenger transport market

The quantity demanded and supplied of passenger transport in the UK over the past 50 years has almost quadrupled, as Figure 6.5 shows. Almost all of this growth is accounted for by a rise in the demand for car travel. Rail travel (national rail plus the London Underground plus light rail systems) has grown by around one third since the mid-1990s, having been broadly constant over the previous 40 years. Bus and coach travel declined until the early 1980s when it broadly stabilised. Air travel has grown significantly from 0.2 billion passenger kilometres in 1952 to 9.8 billion passenger kilometres in 2004, but today only accounts for approximately 1 per cent of the total passenger miles travelled in the UK.

Demand and income

The main reason for the growth in demand for passenger transport has been rising incomes. As Table 6.3 shows, real personal households' disposable income (the average income per household after income tax and

inflation has been accounted for) has grown more than 2.5 times between 1965 and 2004. Consumers have tended to spend a relatively high proportion of increases in income on transport. As a result, spending on transport as a proportion of household expenditure has risen from 9.7 per cent in 1965 to 14.5 per cent in 2004. Spending on car transport has risen faster than spending on other types of passenger transport. In 1965, there were 7.7 million cars on the road as Table 6.4 shows. 41 per cent of households had the use of at least one car whilst spending on cars and their running costs accounted for three quarters of total household spending on transport. By 2003, there were 25.0 million cars on the roads. 74 per cent of households had use of at least one car and spending on motor transport accounted for 85.5 per cent of total transport spending.

Table 6.3 Disposable income and household expenditure on passenger transport

	Personal households' disposable income per head, £, at 2001 prices	Household expenditure on transport, £, average per week at 2001 prices	Household expenditure on transport as a percentage of total household expenditure %	Motoring expenditure as a percentage of all household expenditure on transport %
1965	4 640	30.90	9.7	74.5
1970	5 084	36.29	10.2	77.2
1975	5 873	37.78	13.8	80.2
1980	6 611	40.55	14.6	81.2
1985	7 147	44.25	15.2	84.4
1990	9 015	54.99	16.2	84.5
1995	9 978	50.16	15.1	85.7
2000	11 386	52.86	15.0	84.9
2004	12 491	54.99	14.5	85.5

1. Figures for expenditure for 1995 are 1994/5, for 2000 are 1999/2000 and for 2004 are 2003/4.
Source: adapted from *Economic Trends Annual Supplement*, Office for National Statistics; Department for the Environment, Transport and the Regions, *Transport Statistics*.

Figure 6.5 Passenger transport use

Billion passenger kilometres

Cars, vans and taxis

Rail

Buses and coaches

Source: adapted from *Transport Statistics*; www.dft.gov.uk.

Table 6.4 Car ownership

	Number of private cars licensed, millions	Households with regular use of car(s) %			
		no car	1 car	2 cars	3 or more
1965	7.7	59	36	5	-
1970	10.0	48	45	6	1
1975	12.5	44	45	10	1
1980	14.7	41	44	13	2
1985	16.5	38	45	15	3
1990	19.7	33	44	19	4
1995	20.5	30	45	21	4
2000	23.2	27	45	23	5
2003	25.0	26	44	25	5

Source: Department for the Environment, Transport and the Regions, *Transport Statistics*.

Table 6.5 National rail statistics

	National rail, passenger journeys (million)	National rail passenger kilometres (billion)
1946	1 266	47.0
1960	1 037	34.7
1985/86	686	30.4
1990/91	809	33.2
1995/6	761	30.0
2000/01	957	38.2
2004/05	1 088	42.4

Source: Department for the Environment, Transport and the Regions, *Transport Statistics*.

Table 6.6 Bus and coach travel

	Number of kilometres travelled by passengers on buses and coaches (bn)	Number of buses and coaches on UK roads (000)	Number of kilometres travelled by buses and coaches (bn)	Index of prices (1995=100) bus and coach fares	Index of all prices (RPI) 1995=100
1965	67	-	3.9	5.7	10.0
1970	60	-	3.6	8.0	12.4
1975	60	76.9	3.2	15.3	22.9
1980	52	69.9	3.5	36.5	44.9
1985	49	67.9	3.7	52.8	63.5
1990	46	71.9	4.6	73.8	84.6
1995	43	75.7	4.9	100.0	100.0
2000	47	79.2	5.2	119.6	114.2
2004	48	80.6	5.2	140.7	125.2

Source: adapted from Department for the Environment, *Transport and the Regions, Transport Statistics*.

Table 6.7 Passenger transport: consumer price indices (1995=100)

	Motor vehicles Total	of which net purchase	Rail	Bus and coach	All transport	All consumer expenditure (RPI)
1965	9.4	11.6	6.7	5.7	9.1	10.0
1970	12.0	13.6	8.5	8.0	11.7	12.4
1975	22.6	23.8	17.4	15.3	22.0	22.9
1980	47.1	55.4	39.6	36.5	45.8	44.9
1985	65.1	70.8	50.7	52.8	62.7	63.5
1990	79.4	87.8	72.3	73.8	84.6	84.6
1995	100.0	100.0	100.0	100.0	100.0	100.0
2000	119.0	94.7	116.5	119.6	114.2	114.2
2004	120.0	86.1	130.7	140.9	125.1	123.2

Source: adapted from *Economic Trends Annual Supplement*, Office for National Statistics; Department for the Environment, Transport and the Regions, *Transport Statistics*.

Rising income seems to have had little effect on overall rail travel. Between 1945 and 1985, the number of passenger journeys fell on the national rail network as shown in Table 6.5. Between the mid- 1980s and mid-1990s, the number of journeys made was roughly constant. Since then, the number of journeys and distances travelled has increased by roughly one third. There ia a number of possible reasons for this. One is that road congestion has become so bad that some motorists have abandoned their cars for the train. Another reason is the rail privatisation that took place in the mid-1990s. Before, the railways were owned by the government which tended to limit investment in the railways. When overcrowding became a problem on a particular line (i.e. there was excess demand), the response tended to be to put up prices. With privatisation, private rail companies such as Virgin have introduced much more sophisticated pricing policies. Such policies include reducing fares when this attracts more passengers onto the railways and raises the total revenue of the train companies. Investment on the railways has also increased, making rail travel more attractive. In the long term, privatisation has led to an increase in the supply of rail services.

As for bus and coach travel, Table 6.6 shows that the long term trend has been for bus and coach travel to fall. In 1952, 92 billion passenger kilometres were travelled. By 2004, this had fallen by approximately 50 per cent. With rising incomes over the period, it could be argued that passengers have deserted buses and coaches for cars.

Bus and coach travel would then be an inferior good. However, Table 6.6 shows that there has been a slight upturn in bus and coach travel since the late 1990s. This perhaps reflects improved services offered by bus and coach services, or increased congestion on the roads which have led to some motorists abandoning their cars for public transport. However, the increase at 9 per cent over the period 1995 to 2004 is relatively small.

Demand and prices

The average price of transport has risen broadly in line with the average increase in all prices in the economy, as can be seen from Table 6.7. However, Table 6.7 shows that the price of travelling by rail, bus and coach rose substantially faster than that of travelling by car in the 1980s and 1990s. The price of bus travel continued to increase above the rate of general inflation in the early 2000s. This broad trend can be explained mainly by a reduction in subsidies to bus and rail travel and the need for bus and rail companies to adopt a more commercial, profit-orientated approach to their operations. Bus and rail also suffered greater price competition from the car. In 2004, it was relatively cheaper to travel by car than by bus or train compared to 1965 or 1995. It is not surprising that demand for car travel has outstripped demand for bus or rail travel over the period.

For the past 15 years, the government's response to growing congestion on Britain's roads has been to talk about increasing the cost of motoring. Between 1993 and 2000, the government increased the tax on petrol above the rate of inflation in an attempt to discourage car use on both congestion and environmental grounds. The government was forced to abandon this policy when an alliance of farmers and truck drivers brought the country almost to a halt for a few days in protest against rising fuel prices. The congestion charge in London is another example of government using the price mechanism to reduce demand.

However, pricing motorists off the roads is a highly unpopular policy. Partly this is because the demand for motor transport is fairly unresponsive to increases in price (i.e. demand is fairly **inelastic** ☞ unit 8). It needs very substantial increases in price to discourage potential motorists from either owning a car or making fewer journeys. For many journeys, there is no suitable alternative to car transport. For many other journeys, public transport takes longer, is far less convenient and is more expensive. Table 6.7 shows that the cost of motoring actually went down compared to the increase in all prices in the economy over the period 1995 to 2004 despite increases in tax. Market forces are positively encouraging consumers to own cars and run them.

Other factors affecting the demand for transport

Demand for transport has grown for a number of other reasons apart from rising income. The population of the UK has increased. In 1951, it was 52.7 million; in 1971 it had increased to 55.9 million and in 2005 it was 60.1 million. Population-led increases in demand are set to continue with an estimated UK figure of 64.9 million by 2026.

Planning policies have led to a greater separation of housing and places of work. In Victorian England, workers tended to live within walking distance of their work. Planning regulations over the past 50 years, though, have created distinct zones within urban areas and, as a result, most people are no longer within walking distance of their place of work.

Improvements in infrastructure and advances in technology have created their own demands. Building a new motorway or bypass reduces journey times and encourages people to live further away from their place of work. Faster roads or rail links also encourage greater leisure travel. Equally, improvements in car design have made motoring more reliable and comfortable. One reason why railways failed to attract more passengers in the second half of the twentieth century was that there was not a similar increase in quality of service. For instance, the shortest journey

time from London to Birmingham was longer in 1999 than it was in 1979 and rolling stock had barely improved. Privatisation of the UK's railways in the mid-1990s, however, has led to increased investment in new rolling stock and shorter journey times. Since 2000, this has led to some increase in passenger numbers.

The supply of transport

There is no 'supply curve' for transport in general or for parts of the transport industry. For instance, there is no supply curve for motor vehicle transport because no single firm or industry provides this service. There are, though, supply curves for some of the components of the service such as petrol or servicing of cars. Nor is there a supply curve for rail travel. Until 1995, the rail industry was operated by a single company, British Rail, which was a monopoly (i.e. only) supplier and there is no supply curve under monopoly. Since 1995, the industry has been privatised but the key companies in the industry, such as Railtrack or Virgin, are still monopolies in their areas of service.

However, it could been argued that there has been a supply curve for bus and coach travel since 1980 (for coaches) and 1985 (for buses) when the industry was **deregulated** (☞ unit 18). Before deregulation, the government issued licences, and in general only one licence was offered on a route, establishing monopolies. After deregulation, any firm could set up and offer regular bus services in the UK. Table 6.6 shows that there was an increase in the number of buses on the roads during the 1980s and 1990s, travelling more kilometres. This was despite a fall in the number of kilometres travelled by passengers. The demand curve for bus transport has therefore probably been shifting to the left as more people switch to cars. The supply curve, however, has shifted to the right with new companies coming into the market and existing companies expanding their services. Opposing this rightward shift has been a fall in government subsidies to bus companies, which all other things being equal would have shifted the supply curve to the left.

Price determination

The supply and demand model cannot be used in industries where there is no supply curve in the market. In the rail industry, for instance, prices are fixed by the rail companies influenced by the actions of the rail regulator. In the bus industry, where arguably there is a supply curve, fares have risen by more than the general rate of inflation since the 1980s. As Table 6.7 shows, fares between 1980 and 2004 rose nearly four fold whilst prices in general only increased nearly three fold. Falls in demand for bus travel due to increased demand for car travel, and an increase in supply as evidenced by the increased number of bus companies and buses, should have led to a relative fall in bus fares. Instead they rose, almost certainly due to the cuts in government subsidies during the period.

DataQuestion

Copper

Figure 6.6 Copper price

Three-month forward ($ per tonne)

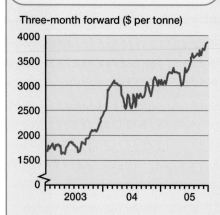

Figure 6.7 Copper: production minus demand

'000 tonnes

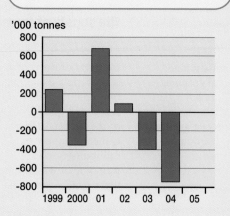

Figure 6.8 Copper usage

Copper usage
% of total world usage

■ China ■ US ☐ EU(15)

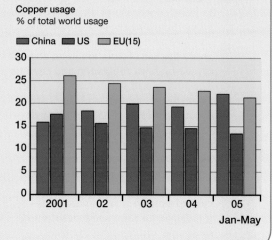

Jan-May

Source: adapted from Thomson Datastream; International Copper Study Group.

Copper prices rose to a record high yesterday. The metal has been the outstanding performer among base metal prices this year, with the benchmark three-month price hitting a record $3 885 a tonne on the London Metal Exchange, the world's largest metal trading exchange.

On the supply side, production has been hit this week by strikes in North America. In Zambia, there continue to be problems as some mines have had to halt production due to a lack of diesel fuel. Stocks of copper are also very low after three years when demand has outstripped production. Copper stockpiles have fallen almost 90 per cent over the period to about 116 000 tonnes today.

Demand remains strong. There seems to be no let up to demand from China's fast growing economy which has driven the price boom in commodities over the past few years. Latest figures show the US economy is healthier than previously expected and there is no sign of a slowdown in US demand. The world economy in general seems in pretty good shape with no indications that it will go into recession soon and cause a fall in demand for commodities such as copper.

Source: adapted from the *Financial Times*, 6.10.2005.

1. Explain (a) why the short term supply of copper in early October 2005 fell and (b) using a diagram, how this pushed up copper prices.
2. Explain (a) why demand for copper grew between 2002 and 2005 and (b) using a diagram, how this pushed up copper prices.
3. Analyse what might bring about a fall in copper prices in the long term.

Summary

1. Some goods are complements, in joint demand.
2. Other goods are substitutes for each other, in competitive demand.
3. Derived demand occurs when one good is demanded because it is needed for the production of other goods or services.
4. Composite demand and joint supply are two other ways in which markets are linked.

Partial and general models

A model of price determination was outlined in unit 6. It was explained that the price of a good was determined by the forces of demand and supply. This is an example of a **partial model**. A partial model is an explanation of reality which has relatively few variables (☞ unit 45). But a more **general model** or wider model of the market system can be constructed which shows how events in one market can lead to changes in other markets. In this unit we will consider how some markets are interrelated.

Complements

Some goods, known as COMPLEMENTS, are in JOINT DEMAND. This means that, in demanding one good, a consumer will also be likely to demand another good. Examples of complements are:
● tennis rackets and tennis balls;
● washing machines and soap powder;
● strawberries and cream;
● DVD disks and DVD recorders.

Economic theory suggests that a rise in the quantity demanded of one complement will lead to an increase in the demand for another, resulting in an increase in the price and quantity bought of the other complement. For instance, an increase in the quantity demanded of strawberries will lead to an increase in

demand for cream too, pushing up the price of cream. This can be shown on a demand and supply diagram. Assume that new technology reduces the cost of production of washing machines. This leads to an increase in supply of washing machines shown by a shift to the right of the supply curve in Figure 7.1 (a). As a result there is a fall in price and a rise in the quantity demanded of washing machines, shown by a movement along the demand curve. This in turn will increase the demand for automatic soap powder, shown by a shift to the right in the demand curve in Figure 7.1 (b). This leads to a rise in the quantity purchased of automatic soap powder and also an increase in its price.

Substitutes

A SUBSTITUTE is a good which can be replaced by another good. If two goods are substitutes for each other, they are said to be in COMPETITIVE DEMAND. Examples of substitutes are:
● beef and pork;
● Coca-cola and Pepsi-cola;
● fountain pens and biros;
● gas and oil (in the long term but not particularly in the short term).

Economic theory predicts that a rise in the price of one good will lead to an increase in demand and a rise in price of a substitute good.

Figure 7.2 shows a rise in the price of beef, due to a fall in its supply. This leads to a fall in the quantity demanded of beef as

Figure 7.1 Complements

An increase in supply and the consequent fall in price of washing machines will lead to a rise in the quantity of washing machines and a rise in demand (shown by a shift in the demand curve) for a complementary good such as automatic washing powder.

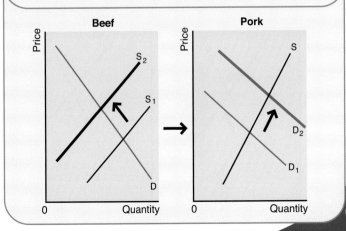

Figure 7.2 Substitutes

A fall in the supply of beef leading to a rise in its price will lead to a fall in the quantity demanded of beef and an increase in the demand for a substitute product such as pork.

the price of beef rises. In turn, there will be an increase in the demand for pork as consumers substitute pork for beef. The demand for pork will increase, shown by a shift to the right in the demand curve for pork. This leads to a rise in the price of pork and a rise in quantity purchased.

Many substitute goods are not clearly linked. For instance, a rise in the price of foreign holidays will lead some consumers to abandon taking a foreign holiday. They may substitute a UK holiday for it, but they may also decide to buy new curtains or a new carpet for their house, or buy a larger car than they had originally planned.

Question 1

(a) It could be argued that the following pairs of products are both complements **and** substitutes. Explain why.
  (i) Electricity and gas.
  (ii) Tea and milk.
  (iii) Bus journeys and train journeys.
  (iv) Chocolate bars and crisps.
(b) (i) For each pair of products, explain whether you think they are more likely to be complements or substitutes.
  (ii) Show on a demand and supply diagram the effect on the price of the first product of a rise in price of the second product.

Derived demand

Many goods are demanded only because they are needed for the production of other goods. The demand for these goods is said to be a DERIVED DEMAND.

For instance, the demand for steel is derived in part from the demand for cars and ships. The demand for flour is derived in part from the demand for cakes and bread. The demand for sugar is in part derived from demand for some beverages, confectionery and chocolate.

Figure 7.3 shows an increase in the demand for cars. This leads to an increase in quantity bought and sold. Car manufacturers will increase their demand for steel, shown by a rightward shift of the demand curve for steel. The price of steel will then increase as will the quantity bought and sold. Economic theory therefore predicts that an increase in demand

for a good will lead to an increase in price and quantity purchased of goods which are in derived demand from it.

Question 2

Milk sales have been in decline for 30 years, but one of the latest food fads has helped reverse the trend. About 35 million more litres of liquid milk were sold to consumers last year than the year before. This is not a big increase on 4.45 billion litres sold in the year to April 2004, but it represents welcome news for Britain's dairy farmers.

Liz Broadbent, director of market development at the Milk Development Council (MDC), said: 'The rise is down to an increase in the frequency of buying milk rather than people buying more during each shopping trip. The indications are that the extra milk is being used mainly in porridge, tea and coffee.'

Porridge consumption rose by 25 per cent last winter, according to TNS, which carried out market research for the MDC. Consumption of tea and coffee also improved by 17 per cent and 8 per cent respectively. According to Tesco, which saw its sales of porridge increased markedly over the year, an important factor in increased sales of porridge was the fashionability of the Glycemic or GI diet. This diet encouraged dieters to maintain their blood sugar at a steady level by having a healthy breakfast.

Gwyn Jones, chairman of the National Farmers' Union dairy board said that the increase in milk consumption 'is certainly a welcome development, even if it's only by a small amount. Eventually it ought to mean more money for farmers but there are lots of ifs and buts.'

Source: adapted from the *Financial Times* 20.5.2005.

(a) 'Milk is in derived demand from porridge.' Explain this statement.
(b) Analyse, with the help of diagrams, the effect of the change in demand for porridge on the demand for milk.
(c) Why might there be 'lots of ifs and buts' about whether the price of milk will go up due to the increase in demand for porridge?

Composite demand

A good is said to be in COMPOSITE DEMAND when it is demanded for two or more distinct uses. For instance, milk may be used for yoghurt, for cheese making, for butter or for

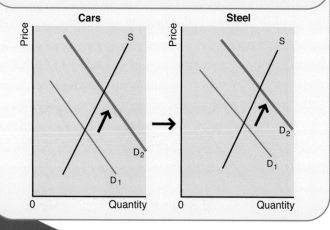

Figure 7.3 Derived demand

An increase in the demand for cars will lead to an increase in demand for steel. Steel is said to be in derived demand from cars.

Figure 7.4 Composite demand

An increase in the demand for oil from chemical producers will result in a fall in the supply of oil to the petrol market because oil is in composite demand.

drinking. Land may be demanded for residential, industrial or commercial use. Steel is demanded for car manufacturing and for shipbuilding.

Economic theory predicts that an increase in demand for one composite good will lead to a fall in supply for another. Figure 7.4 shows that an increase in the demand by the chemical industry for oil will push the demand curve to the right, increasing both the quantity sold and the price of oil. With an upward sloping supply for oil as a whole, an increase in supply of oil to the chemical industry will reduce the supply of oil for petrol. This is shown by a shift upwards in the supply curve in Figure 7.4. The price of oil for petrol will rise and the quantity demanded will fall.

Economic theory therefore predicts that an increase in demand for a good will lead to a rise in price and a fall in quantity demanded for a good with which it is in composite demand.

Joint supply

A good is in JOINT SUPPLY with another good when one good is supplied for two different purposes. For instance, cows are supplied for both beef and leather. An oil well may give both oil and gas.

Economic theory suggests that an increase in demand for one good in joint supply will lead to an increase in its price. This leads to an increase in the quantity supplied. The supply of the other good therefore increases, leading to a fall in its price. Figure 7.5 shows that an increase in demand for beef leads to an increase in both price and quantity bought and sold of beef. More beef production will lead, as a by-product, to greater

Question 3

At the start of 2000, most customers could withdraw cash from a cash machine free of charge. Since then there has been a dramatic expansion of new cash machines which charge customers a fee for withdrawing cash, typically £1.50 for any withdrawal. Fee-charging cash machines only handle an estimated 3 per cent of all transactions with most customers getting their money from cash machines inside or outside banks where there is no change. But fee-charging machines tend to be situated away from banks in locations like convenience stores, pubs, petrol stations and shopping centres and are becoming increasingly popular with customers.

Many fee-charging cash machines also have a facility for playing advertisements. So a cash machine can generate revenues and profits for its owners not just by charging customers for cash withdrawals but also by selling advertising space to companies.

Source: adapted from the *Financial Times*, 15.11.2004.

A cash machine can give two products: cash for bank customers and advertising. With the help of diagrams and the concept of joint supply, explain what impact an increase in demand by bank customers for withdrawals from fee-charging cash machines might have on the price of advertising space.

supply of leather. This is shown by a shift to the right in the supply curve for leather. The price of leather will then fall and quantity demanded, bought and sold will increase.

Key terms

Competitive demand - when two or more goods are substitutes for each other.
Complement - a good which is purchased with other goods to satisfy a want.
Composite demand - when a good is demanded for two or more distinct uses.
Derived demand - when the demand for one good is the result of or derived from the demand for another good.

Joint demand - when two or more complements are bought together.
Joint supply - when two or more goods are produced together, so that a change in supply of one good will necessarily change the supply of the other goods with which it is in joint supply.
Substitute - a good which can be replaced by another to satisfy a want.

Figure 7.5 Joint supply
An increase in the demand for beef, which leads to more beef being produced, results in an increase in the supply of leather. Beef and leather are said to be in joint supply.

Applied economics

Commercial transport

Derived demand

Commercial transport, the transporting of goods in the UK from factory to shop for instance, is a derived demand. It is ultimately derived from the purchase of consumer goods and services. The movement of coal from a coal pit to an electricity power station is part of the long chain of production in the eventual consumption of, say, a packet of cornflakes.

Demand for commercial transport

Demand for commercial transport has grown over time as consumer incomes have risen and more goods and services have been consumed. Table 7.1 shows, however, that the growth in tonnage of goods moved has been relatively small since the 1960s. Much of this is due to the fact that goods have got lighter and less bulky. Far more plastic and far less metal are used today, for instance. So whilst more consumer goods are purchased, the total weight and volume have only increased a little. In contrast, Table 7.2 shows that there has been a significant growth over the same period in the number of tonne kilometres travelled. Each tonne is travelling a longer distance today than 40 years ago. This is the result of greater specialisation between regions and firms. In turn, this has been encouraged by the growth of the motorway network in the UK, which has allowed much faster journey times.

Substitutes

Different modes of transport are substitutes for each other. Both Tables 7.1 and 7.2 and Figure 7.6 indicate that there has been a switch away from rail transport to other modes, particularly road transport. In the early 1950s, railways carried slightly more freight than

the roads. By the 1960s, rail had already lost much of its market share to road haulage and by the first decade of the 21st century accounted for just 7 per cent of freight transport by distance travelled and less than 5 per cent of total freight tonnage. Pipeline traffic has increased, mainly due to growth of gas consumption and North Sea oil production. The sudden increase in the share of water transport between 1976 and 1985 was entirely due to the growth of the North Sea oil industry.

Complements

The privatisation of British Rail led to an increase in the amount of rail freight carried. The private freight companies have proved more flexible than British Rail and have been able to drive down costs and win orders. However, the future of rail transport lies mainly as a complement to road transport. Lorries and vans will take goods to railway collection depots. The goods will then be transported by rail before being taken away again by lorry. Loading and unloading from one mode

Table 7.1 Goods: total transported in millions of tonnes

	Road	Rail	Water: coastwise oil	Water: other	Pipelines	Total
1961	1 295	249	57		6	1 607
1965	1 634	239	64		27	1 964
1970	1 610	209	58		39	1 916
1975	1 602	176	48		52	1 878
1980	1 383	154	54	83	83	1 757
1985	1 452	122	50	92	89	1 805
1990	1 749	152	44	108	121	2 163
1995	1 701	101	47	98	168	2 115
2000	1 689	95	40	97	151	2 072
2003	1 725	89	35	98	141	2 088
2004	1 831	102	na	na	158	na

Source: adapted from Department for the Environment, Transport and the Regions, *Transport Statistics*.

Table 7.2 Goods: distance transported, total tonne kilometres (billions)

	Road	Rail	Water: coastwise oil	Water: other	Pipelines	Total
1961	85.6	16.4	3.2	0.6	0.4	106.2
1965	108.0	15.8	3.7	0.6	1.8	129.8
1970	85.0	26.8	23.2	0.01	3.0	138.1
1975	95.3	23.5	18.3	0.1	5.9	143.1
1980	92.4	17.6	38.2	15.9	10.1	174.2
1985	103.2	15.3	38.9	18.7	11.2	187.3
1990	136.3	15.8	32.1	23.6	11.0	218.8
1995	149.6	13.3	31.4	11.1	11.1	226.6
2000	158.0	18.1	26.0	41.4	11.4	254.9
2003	159.3	18.9	23.3	37.6	10.5	249.6
2004	159.8	20.7	na	na	10.7	na

Source: adapted from Department for the Environment, Transport and the Regions, *Transport Statistics*.

Figure 7.6 Commercial transport: by mode, distance transported

Source: adapted from Department for the Environment, *Transport and the Regions, Transport Statistics*.

of transport to another is relatively expensive. Therefore rail transport has proved to be economic mainly when journeys of over 300-400 miles are made by rail or when a dedicated rail link can take goods door to door, for instance from a pit head to a power station. The number of dedicated rail links could decrease in the immediate future if the electricity industry burns more gas and imported coal and less domestic coal. The Channel Tunnel should have given a significant boost to rail freight. It is ideally suited, for example, for the transport of goods such as new cars being taken from manufacturing plants to dealers in other countries. However, inefficiencies in the rail system in the UK and even more so in Europe have meant that services using the Tunnel have been too unreliable and too slow to attract much extra traffic. Rail freight in general can only grow in future if journey times become faster and services are more reliable.

Composite demand

Roads are in composite demand with commercial transport and passenger transport. At present, there is no systematic pricing mechanism for the road system. Most roads are free from congestion at all times of day. A minority of roads suffer from congestion at certain times of the day. This is a problem of scarce resources. Some potential road users react by either not travelling or travelling by an alternative mode of transport. Commuters in the London area, for instance, may choose to travel by rail, underground or bus because the opportunity cost of travelling by car is too high. Some commuters arrive earlier or later to their place of work to avoid the rush hour. Other road users accept that their road journey times will be longer in the rush hour than at other times of the day.

The more cars on the road, the greater the potential for congestion and longer journey times for freight transport. Road pricing could help the freight industry if car users were discouraged from travelling. Road pricing is when cars and lorries are charged for the use of a road, as for instance with the London congestion charge or the toll on the M6 toll motorway. However, any road pricing system is likely to place charges on lorries as well as cars. Journey times for lorries might be reduced, lowering costs, but road tolls will increase freight costs. The experience of the M6 toll motorway shows the trade off between cost and time. Lorries have avoided using the toll motorway, opened in 2004, because of what they say are too high charges. Instead, most hauliers prefer to use the M6 through Birmingham, which is free, but they risk getting held up by congestion. For these hauliers, the cost of the toll motorway is greater than the possible loss of time through congestion of using the free motorway. Overall, British hauliers are estimated to lose up to £20 billion a year through congestion in increased journey times. Reducing journey times through applying tolls on all congested roads would reduce these costs but hauliers would inevitably have to pay tolls too, meaning that their gain would be far less than the £20 billion.

Imposing tolls on road freight transport could act as an incentive for firms to switch some freight from road to rail. Indeed, some environmentalists have argued that revenues from road tolls should be used to subsidise rail freight to create a large shift from road to rail.

DataQuestion

Land usage

The cost of planning restrictions

Planning restrictions have increased the price of housing land. The price of farming land, for instance, is often one-thirtieth or one-fortieth of what it is when housebuilding is allowed. Hence, there are plenty of farmers willing to sell their land for residential use. A 1994 study commissioned by the Department for the Environment, however, pointed out that this is a misleading comparison because the cost of preparing farming land for housing or industrial purposes is high. Instead, it estimated the opportunity cost of housing land by looking at prices of housing land in Barnsley, where at the time there was no shortage of housing land available for sale. The cost of planning restrictions could then be calculated. For instance, in Reigate, prime commuter country in Surrey in the South of England, land prices were 3.6 times their opportunity cost. In Beverley in Yorkshire, the ratio was 2.2.

Nimbyism

A 'Nimby' is someone who says 'not in my backyard'. The word came into fashion in the 1980s to describe people who were all in favour of better facilities, better roads, more housing and more places of work to reduce unemployment so long as none of this happened in their local area.

It has often been justified by high-sounding references to preserving rural England, maintaining local amenities and protecting areas of natural beauty. Every new bypass or road upgrade seems to run through a patch of land which is the habitat of some rare species of plant or animal. However, in practice, the vast majority of Nimbys are motivated solely by the losses that they might incur if development went ahead. For instance, building a new housing estate next door is unlikely to help the property prices of existing houses in the area.

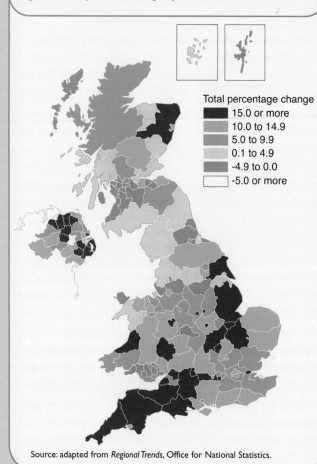

Figure 7.7 *Population change by area, 1982-2002*

Total percentage change
- 15.0 or more
- 10.0 to 14.9
- 5.0 to 9.9
- 0.1 to 4.9
- -4.9 to 0.0
- -5.0 or more

Source: adapted from *Regional Trends*, Office for National Statistics.

Table 7.3 *Changing population and number of households, England, millions*

	1971	1981	1991	2001	2004	2021 projected
Population	55.4	54.9	55.8	57.4	57.1	62.0
Number of households	18.6	20.2	22.4	23.8	24.1	28.0

Source: adapted from *Social Trends*, Office for National Statistics; *Regional Trends*, Office for National Statistics.

Greenbelt policies

Britain's greenbelts were established after the Second World War. They were intended to throw a cordon around urban areas to prevent their spread into the countryside. Within the greenbelt, planning restrictions are very strict about development. No new housing or industrial development is permitted. Greenbelt policies have severely restricted the supply of new land for housing and industry in the UK and contributed to the relatively high price of land in urban areas. This increases the costs of living for urban dwellers, the vast majority of people in the UK. Not only are house prices and rents much higher than they would otherwise be but the cost of services from supermarkets to cinemas is much higher. This is because high land prices paid by industry have to be paid for in the form of higher prices by consumers.

Households

The number of households in the UK is growing at a much faster rate than the slow growth in the overall population. The growth is coming partly from changes in society. The increase in divorce has created many one-person households and rising incomes mean that more young single people now have the choice between living at home with their parents or getting their own accommodation. Growth is also coming from demographic changes. There is an increasing number of elderly people who are living longer and living alone. The number of households with two parents and several children is declining.

New land for housing

New land for building houses comes from a variety of sources. 'Windfall sites' are those which come from homeowners selling part of their garden for development, or housebuilders buying a large old house, knocking it down and replacing it with a small estate of smaller houses. Another source is 'brownfield sites'. These are sites which have already been used for commercial or other urban purposes but now have a higher value as housing land. Third, and most controversially, new land can be found by small scale easing of greenbelt and other restrictions, usually amounting to just a few tens of acres in a specific locality.

1. Explain the following.
   (a) The demand for land is a derived demand.
   (b) Land is in composite demand.
   (c) Land is in joint supply.
   (d) Land is in joint demand with buildings.
2. Explain the economic relationships in the UK between land use and:
   (a) a growing population;
   (b) a shifting population geographically;
   (c) increasing affluence.
3. Do you think greenbelt regulations should be loosened to allow more house building in the UK? In your answer, consider the costs and benefits of such a change in policy. This will include an analysis of the effects on the price of houses, industrial property and agricultural land.

8 Price elasticity of demand

Summary

1. Elasticity is a measure of the extent to which quantity responds to a change in a variable which affects it, such as price or income.
2. Price elasticity of demand measures the proportionate response of quantity demanded to a proportionate change in price.
3. Price elasticity of demand varies from zero, or infinitely inelastic, to infinitely elastic.
4. The value of price elasticity of demand is determined by the availability of substitutes and by time.

The meaning of demand elasticity

The quantity demanded of a good is affected by changes in the price of the good, changes in price of other goods, changes in income and changes in other relevant factors. Elasticity is a measure of just how much the quantity demanded will be affected by a change in price or income etc.

Assume that the price of gas increases by 1 per cent. If quantity demanded consequently falls by 20 per cent, then there is a very large drop in quantity demanded in comparison to the change in price. The price elasticity of gas would be said to be very high. If quantity demanded falls by 0.01 per cent, then the change in quantity demanded is relatively insignificant compared to the large change in price and the price elasticity of gas would be said to be low.

Different elasticities of demand measure the proportionate response of quantity demanded to a proportionate change in the variables which affect demand. So price elasticity of demand measures the responsiveness of quantity demanded to changes in the price of the good. Income elasticity measures the responsiveness of quantity demanded to changes in consumer incomes. Cross elasticity measures the responsiveness of quantity demanded to changes in the price of another good. Economists could also measure population elasticity, tastes elasticity or elasticity for any other variable which might affect quantity demanded, although these measures are rarely calculated.

Price elasticity of demand

Economists choose to measure responsiveness in terms of proportionate or percentage changes. So PRICE ELASTICITY OF DEMAND - the responsiveness of changes in quantity demanded to changes in price - is calculated by using the formula:

$$\frac{\text{percentage change in quantity demanded}}{\text{percentage change in price}}$$

Sometimes, price elasticity of demand is called OWN PRICE ELASTICITY OF DEMAND to distinguish it from cross price elasticity of demand.

Table 8.1 shows a number of calculations of price elasticity. For instance, if an increase in price of 10 per cent leads to a fall in quantity demanded of 20 per cent, then the price elasticity of demand is 2. If an increase in price of 50 per cent leads to a fall

in quantity demanded of 25 per cent then price elasticity of demand is ½.

Elasticity is sometimes difficult to understand at first. It is essential to memorise the formulae for elasticity. Only then can they be used with ease and an appreciation gained of their significance.

Table 8.1

Percentage change in price	Percentage change in quantity demanded	Elasticity
10	20	2
50	25	½
7	28	4
9	3	⅓

Question 1

Table 8.2

	Percentage change in quantity demanded	Percentage change in price
(a)	10	5
(b)	60	20
(c)	4	8
(d)	1	9
(e)	5	7
(f)	8	11

Calculate the price elasticity of demand from the data in Table 8.2.

Alternative formulae

Data to calculate price elasticities are often not presented in the form of percentage changes. These have to be worked out. Calculating the percentage change is relatively easy. For instance, if a consumer has 10 apples and buys another 5, the percentage change in the total number of apples is of course 50 per cent. This answer is worked out by dividing the change in the number of apples she has (i.e. 5) by the original number of apples she possessed (i.e. 10) and multiplying by 100 to get a percentage figure. So the formula is:

$$\text{percentage change} = \frac{\text{absolute change}}{\text{original value}} \times 100\%$$

Price elasticity of demand is measured by dividing the percentage change in quantity demanded by the percentage change in price. Therefore an alternative way of expressing this is $\Delta Q/Q \times 100$ (the percentage change in quantity demanded Q) divided by $\Delta P/P \times 100$ (the percentage change in price P). The 100s cancel each other out, leaving a formula of:

$$\frac{\Delta Q}{Q} \div \frac{\Delta P}{P} \quad \text{or} \quad \frac{\Delta Q}{Q} \times \frac{\Delta P}{\Delta P}$$

This is mathematically equivalent to:

$$\frac{P}{Q} \times \frac{\Delta Q}{\Delta P}$$

Examples of calculations of elasticity using the above two formulae are given in Figure 8.1.

Question 2

Table 8.3

| | Original values | | New values | |
	Quantity demanded	Price (£)	Quantity demanded	Price (£)
(a)	100	5	120	3
(b)	20	8	25	7
(c)	12	3	16	0
(d)	150	12	200	10
(e)	45	6	45	8
(f)	32	24	40	2

Calculate the price elasticity of demand for the data in Table 8.3.

Elastic and inelastic demand

Different values of price elasticity of demand are given special names.

- Demand is price ELASTIC if the value of elasticity is greater than one. If demand for a good is price elastic then a percentage change in price will bring about an even larger percentage change in quantity demanded. For instance, if a 10 per cent rise in the price of tomatoes leads to a 20 per cent fall in the quantity demanded of tomatoes, then price elasticity is 20÷10 or 2. Therefore the demand for tomatoes is elastic. Demand is said to be **infinitely elastic** if the value of elasticity is infinity (i.e. a fall in price would lead to an infinite increase in quantity demanded whilst a rise in price would lead to the quantity demanded becoming zero).

Figure 8.1 Calculations of elasticity of demand

Example 1
Quantity demanded originally is 100 at a price of £2. There is a rise in price to £3 resulting in a fall in demand to 75. Therefore the change in quantity demanded is 25 and the change in price is £1.
The price elasticity of demand is:

$$\frac{\Delta Q}{Q} \div \frac{\Delta P}{P} = \frac{25}{100} \div \frac{1}{2} = \tfrac{1}{2}$$

Example 2
Quantity demanded originally is 20 units at a price of £5 000. There is a fall in price to £4 000 resulting in a rise in demand to 32 units.
Therefore the change in quantity demanded is 12 units resulting from the change in price of £1 000.
The price elasticity of demand is:

$$\frac{P}{Q} \times \frac{\Delta Q}{\Delta P} = \frac{5\,000}{20} \times \frac{12}{1\,000} = 3$$

- Demand is price INELASTIC if the value of elasticity is less than one. If demand for a good is price inelastic then a percentage change in price will bring about a smaller percentage change in quantity demanded. For instance, if a 10 per cent rise in the price of tube fares on London Underground resulted in a 1 per cent fall in journeys made, then price elasticity is 1÷10 or 0.1. Therefore the demand for tube travel is inelastic. Demand is said to be **infinitely inelastic** if the value of elasticity is zero (i.e. a change in price would have no effect on quantity demanded).
- Demand is of UNITARY ELASTICITY if the value of elasticity is exactly 1. This means that a percentage change in price will lead to an exact and opposite change in quantity demanded. For instance, a good would have unitary elasticity if a 10 per cent rise in price led to a 10 per cent fall in quantity demanded. (It will be shown in unit 9 that total revenue will remain constant at all quantities demanded if elasticity of demand is unity.)

This terminology is summarised in Table 8.4.

Question 3

Explain whether you think that the following goods would be elastic or inelastic in demand if their price increased by 10 per cent whilst all other factors remained constant: (a) petrol; (b) fresh tomatoes; (c) holidays offered by a major tour operator; (d) a Ford car; (e) a Mars Bar; (f) *GQ* magazine.

Graphical representations

Figure 8.2 shows a straight line graph. It is a common mistake to conclude that elasticity of a straight line demand curve is constant all along its length. In fact nearly all straight line demand curves vary in elasticity along the line.
- At the point A, price elasticity of demand is infinity. Here

Table 8.4 Elasticity: summary of key terms

	Verbal description of response to a change in price	Numerical measure of elasticity	Change in total outlay as price rises[1]
Perfectly inelastic	Quantity demanded does not change at all as price changes	Zero	Increases
Inelastic	Quantity demanded changes by a smaller percentage than does price	Between 0 and 1	Increases
Unitary elasticity	Quantity demanded changes by exactly the same percentage as does price	1	Constant
Elastic	Quantity demanded changes by a larger percentage than does price	Between 1 and infinity	Decreases
Perfectly elastic	Buyers are prepared to purchase all they can obtain at some given price but none at all at a higher price	Infinity	Decreases to zero

1. This is explained in unit 9.

quantity demanded is zero. Putting Q = 0 into the formula for elasticity:

$$\frac{\Delta Q}{Q} \div \frac{\Delta P}{P}$$

we see that zero is divided into ΔQ. Mathematically there is an infinite number of zeros in any number.

- At the point C, price elasticity of demand is zero. Here price is zero. Putting P = 0 into the formula for elasticity, we see that P is divided into ΔP giving an answer of infinity. Infinity is then divided into the fraction ΔQ÷Q. Infinity is so large that the answer will approximate to zero.

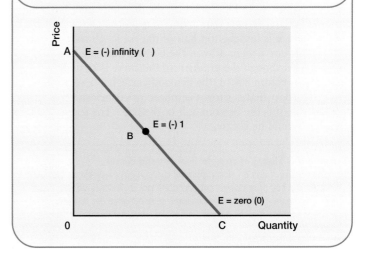

Figure 8.2 Price elasticity along a straight demand curve
Price elasticity varies along the length of a straight demand curve, moving from infinity, where it cuts the price axis, to half way along the line, to zero where it cuts the quantity axis.

- At the point B exactly half way along the line, price elasticity of demand is 1.

Worth noting is that the elasticity of demand at a point can be measured by dividing the distance from the point to the quantity axis by the distance from the point to the price axis, BC ÷ AB. In Figure 8.2, B is half way along the line AC and so BC = AB and the elasticity at the point B is 1.

Two straight line demand curves discussed earlier do not have the same elasticity all along their length.

Figure 8.3(a) shows a demand curve which is perfectly inelastic. Whatever the price, the same quantity will be demanded.

Figure 8.3(b) shows a perfectly elastic demand curve. Any amount can be demanded at one price or below it whilst nothing will be demanded at a higher price.

Figure 8.3(c) shows a demand curve with unitary elasticity. Mathematically it is a rectangular hyperbola. This means that

Figure 8.3 Perfectly elastic and inelastic demand curves and unitary elasticity
A vertical demand curve (a) is perfectly inelastic, whilst a horizontal demand curve (b) is perfectly elastic. A curve with unitary elasticity (c) is a rectangular hyperbola with the formula PQ = k where P is price, Q is quantity demanded and k is a constant value.

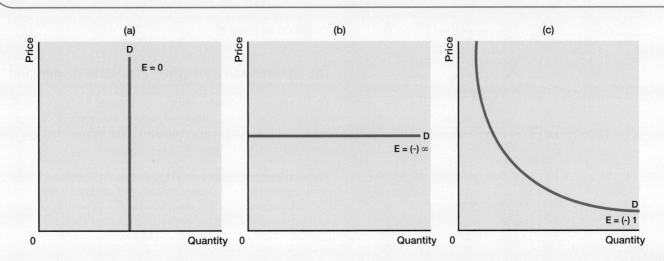

any percentage change in price is offset by an equal and opposite change in quantity demanded.

Another common mistake is to assume that steep demand curves are always inelastic and demand curves which have a shallow slope are always elastic. In Figure 8.4, two demand curves are drawn. In Figure 8.4(a), the demand curve has a very shallow slope. The part that is drawn is indeed elastic but this is only because it is just the top half of the curve which is drawn. If the whole curve were drawn, the bottom half would be inelastic even though the gradient of the curve is shallow. Similarly, in Figure 8.4(b), the demand curve has a very steep slope. The part that is shown is indeed price inelastic but this is only because it is the bottom half of the line. The top half of the steep line would be elastic.

> **Figure 8.4 Slopes of straight line demand curves**
> *Figures 8.4(a) shows an elastic demand curve but it is only elastic because it is the top half of the curve, not because it has a shallow gradient. Similarly, Figure 8.4(b) shows an inelastic demand curve but it is only inelastic because it is the bottom half of the curve, not because it has a steep gradient.*

Question 4

> **Figure 8.5 Demand**
>
>

Consider Figure 8.5.
(a) Between what prices is demand (i) elastic and
(ii) inelastic?
(b) At what price is demand (i) perfectly inelastic,
(ii) perfectly elastic and (iii) equal to 1?

Two technical points

So far we have written of price elasticity of demand as always being a positive number. In fact any downward sloping demand curve always has a negative elasticity. This is because a rise in one variable (price or quantity) is always matched by a fall in the other variable. A rise is positive but a fall is negative and a positive number divided by a negative one (or vice versa) is always negative. However, economists find it convenient to omit the minus sign in price elasticity of demand because it is easier to deal in positive numbers whilst accepting that the value is really negative.

A second point relates to the fact that elasticities over the same price range can differ. For example, at a price of £2, demand for a good is 20 units. At a price of £3, demand is 18 units. Price elasticity of demand for a rise in price from £2 to £3 is:

$$\frac{P}{Q} \times \frac{\Delta Q}{\Delta P} = \frac{2}{20} \times \frac{2}{1} = \frac{1}{5}$$

But price elasticity of demand for a fall in price from £3 to £2 is:

$$\frac{P}{Q} \times \frac{\Delta Q}{\Delta P} = \frac{3}{18} \times \frac{2}{1} = \frac{1}{3}$$

The price elasticity for a rise in price is therefore less than for a fall in price over the same range. This is not necessarily a problem so long as one is aware of it. One way of resolving this is to average out price and quantity. In the formulae, P becomes not the original price but the average price (i.e. the original price plus the new price divided by 2) and Q becomes the average quantity demanded (i.e. the original quantity demanded plus the new quantity demanded divided by 2). In the above example, the average price is £(2+3) ÷ 2 or £2½. The average quantity demanded is (20+18) ÷ 2 or 19. Price elasticity of demand is then:

$$\frac{P}{Q} \times \frac{\Delta Q}{\Delta P} = \frac{2\frac{1}{2}}{19} \times \frac{2}{1} = \frac{5}{19}$$

As you would expect, this value is in between the two price elasticities of ⅕ and ⅓.

The determinants of price elasticity of demand

The exact value of price elasticity of demand for a good is determined by a wide variety of factors. Economists, however, argue that two factors in particular can be singled out: the availability of substitutes and time.

The availability of substitutes The better the substitutes for a product, the higher the price elasticity of demand will tend to be. For instance, salt has few good substitutes. When the price of salt increases, the demand for salt will change little and therefore the price elasticity of salt is low. On the other hand, spaghetti has many good substitutes, from other types of pasta, to rice, potatoes, bread, and other foods. A rise in the price of spaghetti, all other food prices remaining constant, is likely to have a significant effect on the demand for spaghetti. Hence the elasticity of demand for spaghetti is likely to be higher than that for salt.

The more widely the product is defined, the fewer substitutes it is likely to have. Spaghetti has many substitutes, but food in general has none. Therefore the elasticity of demand for spaghetti is likely to be higher than that for food. Similarly the elasticity of demand for boiled sweets is likely to be higher than for confectionery in general. A 5 per cent increase in the price of boiled sweets, all other prices remaining constant, is likely to lead to a much larger fall in demand for boiled sweets than a 5 per cent increase in the price of all confectionery.

Time The longer the period of time, the more price elastic is the demand for a product. For instance, in 1973/74 when the price of oil quadrupled the demand for oil was initially little affected. In the short term the demand for oil was price inelastic. This is hardly surprising. People still needed to travel to work in cars and heat their houses whilst industry still needed to operate. Oil had few good substitutes. Motorists couldn't put gas into their petrol tanks whilst businesses could not change oil-fired systems to run on gas, electricity or coal. However, in the longer term motorists were able to and did buy cars which were more fuel efficient. Oil-fired central heating systems were replaced by gas and electric systems. Businesses converted or did not replace oil-fired equipment. The demand for oil fell from what it would otherwise have been. In the longer run, the demand for oil proved to be price elastic. It is argued that in the short term, buyers are often locked into spending patterns through habit, lack of information or because of durable goods that have

already been purchased. In the longer term, they have the time and opportunity to change those patterns.

It is sometimes argued that **necessities** have lower price elasticities than **luxuries**. Necessities by definition have to be bought whatever their price in order to stay alive. So an increase in the price of necessities will barely reduce the quantity demanded. Luxuries on the other hand are by definition goods which are not essential to existence. A rise in the price of luxuries should therefore produce a proportionately large fall in demand. There is no evidence, however, to suggest that this is true. Food, arguably a necessity, does not seem to have a lower elasticity than holidays or large cars, both arguably luxuries. Part of the reason for this is that it is very difficult to define necessities and luxuries empirically. Some food is a necessity but a significant proportion of what we eat is unnecessary for survival. It is not possible to distinguish between what food is consumed out of necessity and what is a luxury.

It is also sometimes argued that goods which form a relatively low proportion of total expenditure have lower elasticities than those which form a more significant proportion. A large car manufacturer, for instance, would continue to buy the same amount of paper clips even if the price of paper clips doubled because it is not worth its while to bother changing to an alternative. On the other hand, its demand for steel would be far more price elastic. There is no evidence to suggest that this is true. Examples given in textbooks, such as salt and matches, have low price elasticities because they have few good substitutes. In the case of paper clips, manufacturers of paper clips would long ago have raised prices substantially if they believed that price had little impact on the demand for their product.

Key terms

Elastic demand - where the price elasticity of demand is greater than 1. The responsiveness of demand is proportionally greater than the change in price. Demand is infinitely elastic if price elasticity of demand is infinity.

Inelastic demand - where the price elasticity of demand is less than 1. The responsiveness of demand is proportionally less than the change in price. Demand is infinitely inelastic if price elasticity of demand is zero.

Price elasticity of demand or own elasticity of demand - the proportionate response of changes in quantity demanded to a proportionate change in price, measured by the formula:

$$\frac{P}{Q} \times \frac{\Delta Q}{\Delta P}$$

Unitary elasticity - where the value of price elasticity of demand is 1. The responsiveness of demand is proportionally equal to the change in price.

Applied economics

The elasticity of demand for oil

Throughout the 1950s and 1960s oil was a cheap fuel. Indeed, the price of oil fell from approximately $1.70 a barrel in 1950 to $1.30 a barrel in 1970 as supply increased at a faster rate than demand. As Figure 8.6 shows the early 1970s saw a reversal of this trend. Demand increased more rapidly than supply as the world economy boomed and policy makers became increasingly convinced that oil would remain a cheap and an efficient energy source. By 1973, the price of a barrel of oil had risen to approximately $3.

In November 1973, politics in the Middle East was to catapult the oil market into the world headlines. The Egyptians launched an attack on Israel on the day of Yom Kippur, the Jewish equivalent to Christmas. Other Middle Eastern states, such as Saudi Arabia, gave support to their Arab neighbours by threatening to cut off oil supplies to any country which gave support to Israel. With an existing tight market, the result was an explosion in the price of oil. The war was soon over but its economic fall-out was not lost on OPEC, the Organisation for Petroleum Exporting Countries. OPEC, whose members at the time supplied over 60 per cent of world demand for oil, organised a system of quotas amongst themselves, fixing limits on how much each member could produce. By slightly cutting back on pre-1973 production levels, they were able to increase the average price of oil to $10.41 a barrel in 1974, as shown in Figure 8.6.

The reason why OPEC could engineer this massive price rise was because the demand for oil was price inelastic in the short run. Oil consumers had invested heavily in capital equipment such as oil-fired heating systems and petrol-driven cars. In the short term, there were no cheap alternative substitutes. Car owners, for instance, did not suddenly change their cars for more fuel efficient models because the price of petrol at the pumps increased. Hence the near quadrupling of the price of oil (a 300 per cent increase) only led to a 5 per cent fall in world demand for oil (i.e. the price elasticity of demand for oil in the short term was 0.016).

In the longer term, consumers were able to replace oil-powered equipment. Cars became far more fuel-efficient. Homeowners insulated their houses. In the UK, the bottom dropped out of the market for oil-fired heating systems. As a consequence, when the demand for oil began to grow again in 1976, it was at a slower rate than in the early 1970s.

In 1978, the Shah of Iran was toppled and was replaced by an Islamic fundamentalist government led by the Ayatollah Khomeini. Iran was a major oil producer and the Islamic revolution and subsequent war between Iran and Iraq severely disrupted supplies from these two countries. OPEC used this opportunity to tighten supply again. With highly inelastic demand, the price rose from $13.03 a barrel in 1978 to $35.69 a barrel in 1980. Total world demand, which peaked in 1979 at approximately 63 million barrels per day, fell to a low of 58 million barrels per day in 1982 before resuming its growth.

In August 1990, political events in the Middle East yet again rocked the world price of oil. Iraq invaded Kuwait and oil sanctions were immediately applied to the output of both countries by oil consuming countries. Other oil producing countries quickly increased production to fill the gap but the fear of a major shortage had driven oil prices up from $18 a barrel to $40. Prices fell back as it became clear that overall supply had not fallen. The successful counter attack by US and other forces in 1991 to retake Kuwait saw the price drop back to below $20 a barrel.

For much of the rest of the 1990s, the oil price fluctuated in the $15-$20 a barrel range. However, the short term inelasticity of demand for oil was shown again between 1997 to 2000. At the end of 1997, OPEC decided to expand its production. Prices in 1996 to 1997 had been relatively firm, touching $25 a barrel for a short period, and demand for oil had continued growing at a slow but steady rate. The move proved disastrous. The winter of 1997-98 proved to be relatively mild, dampening demand. The Asian crisis of 1998, when a number of Far Eastern countries experienced severe downturns in their economy, further reduced demand. The Japanese economy remained in recession. The result was that world demand grew by just 0.1 per cent compared to, for instance, 2.2 per cent in 1996 and 2.6 per cent in 1997. There followed a sharp fall in the price of oil. By the end of 1998, despite three successive cuts in production quotas by OPEC, oil prices fell below $10 a barrel. The market then pushed the price back up but it went beyond its 1990s long term range of $15-$20 a barrel. The episode shows how very small fluctuations in demand or supply can lead to large fluctuations in price because of the short term price inelasticity of demand for oil.

Figure 8.6 Oil prices

Spot crude oil price, Arabian Light/Dubai, US$ per barrel

Source: adapted from *BP Statistical Review of World Energy*.

The next significant movement in the price of oil occurred from 2002 onwards. The economies of some far Eastern countries, in particular China, had been growing for a number of years at a rate of between 5 and 10 per cent per annum. By the early 2000s, China, with a population greater than that of the EU, the USA and Japan combined, had become a major world economy. Its growing demand for oil and other commodities sparked a boom in commodity prices, including oil. A US invasion of Iraq in 2003 and subsequent occupation of the country unsettled markets. However, what became clear by 2004-05 was that, unlike in previous oil 'crises', the world oil industry no longer had any spare capacity to increase production. The world was consuming all the oil that could be produced from existing capacity. Inevitably, this led to sharp rises in prices because in the short term, the demand for oil is price inelastic. By 2005, prices were reaching over $60 a barrel.

At $60 a barrel, there was a major incentive for consumers and oil using businesses to change their buying habits just as there had been in the mid-1970s. If prices were to remain at this level for any length of time, demand would fall. As Figure 8.7 shows, there was a substantial fall in UK demand for oil from the mid-1970s to the early 1980s in response to the sharp rise in oil prices at the time. This period suggests that the long term price elasticity of demand for oil is greater than one. The fear today of some Middle Eastern oil

producers, including Saudi Arabia which has one fifth of the world's known reserves of oil, is that oil will be substituted for another fuel on a large scale. For example, the technology already exists for cars to be fuelled by hydrogen rather than oil. What prevents governments, car producers and consumers making the switch is the very large one-off cost of doing so. The higher the price, the greater the incentive. A long term price of over $60 a barrel is likely to lead to a significant long term fall in demand for oil.

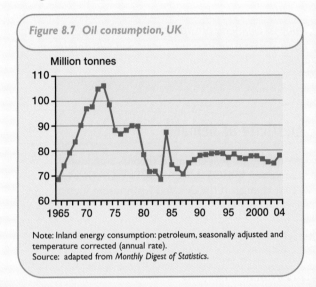

Figure 8.7 Oil consumption, UK

Million tonnes

Note: Inland energy consumption: petroleum, seasonally adjusted and temperature corrected (annual rate).
Source: adapted from *Monthly Digest of Statistics*.

DataQuestion

Congestion charges

In 2003, a congestion charge was introduced for the centre of London. Average traffic speeds in central London had remained the same since the days of the horse and cart in Victorian times at around 10 miles per hour. The congestion charge was designed to reduce the amount of traffic in central London, allowing journey speeds to increase.

The charge was initially fixed at £5 per day for vehicles wanting to travel within the zone during the day from Monday to Friday. Motorists could pay the £5 for one day, or they could pay a multiple for permission to travel within the zone for a week or a month. Motorists who travelled within the zone without having prepaid faced a substantial fine.

In its first year of operation, the congestion charge proved remarkably successful. Traffic was down 15 per cent. There was a 30 per cent reduction in congestion, showing that removing a relatively small percentage of traffic can have a dramatic impact on traffic speeds. Many of the negative effects that might have

occurred, such as increased congestion in the roads around the zone, or a breakdown in the public transport system as commuters swamped buses and the Underground, failed to materialise. However, retailers within the zone, which includes Oxford Street, claim that they have lost sales as a result of the charge. Fewer cars in the zone from Monday to Friday means reduced sales, they say.

In July 2005, the charge was raised to £8 per day. Ken Livingstone, the Mayor of London and main architect of the charge, predicted that there will be another significant fall in traffic and reduction in congestion. The lobby group, Transport for London, however, expected the reduction in traffic to be just 2 per cent. Critics of Ken Livingstone claim he is merely raising the charge to increase the amount of revenue gained from London motorists. On the other hand, the increased revenue will be ploughed back into better public transport.

Source: adapted from the *Financial Times*, 14.2.2004; *The Times*, 4.7.2005.

1 Using a diagram with axes labelled 'Congestion charge £' and 'Quantity of traffic' and a demand curve, explain what happened to demand for road space in central London between 2002 and 2005.
2 (a) Calculate the estimated price elasticity of demand

for 'traffic' in July 2005. (b) Suggest why demand to use roads in central London is so price inelastic.
3 To what extent are buses and rail (including underground services and metros) good substitutes for cars for the travelling public in the UK?

9 Elasticities

Summary

1. Income elasticity of demand measures the proportionate response of quantity demanded to a proportionate change in income.
2. Cross elasticity of demand measures the proportionate response of quantity demanded of one good to a proportionate change in price of another good.
3. Price elasticity of supply measures the proportionate response of quantity supplied to a proportionate change in price.
4. The value of elasticity of supply is determined by the availability of substitutes and by time factors.
5. The price elasticity of demand for a good will determine whether a change in the price of a good results in a change in expenditure on the good.

Income elasticity of demand

The demand for a good will change if there is a change in consumers' incomes. INCOME ELASTICITY OF DEMAND is a measure of that change. If the demand for housing increased by 20 per cent when incomes increased by 5 per cent, then the income elasticity of demand would be said to be positive and relatively high. If the demand for food were unchanged when income rose, then income elasticity would be zero. A fall in demand for a good when income rises gives a negative value to income elasticity of demand.

The formula for measuring income elasticity of demand is:

$$\frac{\text{percentage change in quantity demanded}}{\text{percentage change in income}}$$

So the numerical value of income elasticity of a 20 per cent rise in demand for housing when incomes rise by 5 per cent is +20/+5 or +4. The number is positive because both the 20 per cent and the 5 per cent are positive. On the other hand, a rise in income of 10 per cent which led to a fall in quantity demanded of a product of 5 per cent would have an income elasticity of -5/+10 or -½. The minus sign in -5 shows the fall in quantity demanded of the product. Examples of items with a high income elasticity of demand are holidays and recreational activities, whereas washing up liquid tends to have a low income elasticity of demand.

Just as with price elasticity, it is sometimes easier to use alternative formulae to calculate income elasticity of demand. The above formula is equivalent to:

$$\frac{\Delta Q}{Q} \div \frac{\Delta Y}{Y}$$

where is change, Q is quantity demanded and Y is income. Rearranging the formula gives another two alternatives:

$$\frac{Y}{Q} \times \frac{\Delta Q}{\Delta Y} \quad \text{or} \quad \frac{\Delta Q}{Q} \times \frac{Y}{\Delta Y}$$

Examples of the calculation of income elasticity of

Table 9.1 Calculation of income elasticity of demand

Original quantity demanded	New quantity demanded	Original income (£)	New income (£)	Income elasticity of demand		
				$\frac{\Delta Q}{Q} \div \frac{\Delta Y}{Y}$		Numerical value
20	25	16	18	5/20 ÷ 2/16		+2
100	200	20	25	100/100 ÷ 5/20		+4
50	40	25	30	-10/50 ÷ 5/25		-1
60	60	80	75	0/60 ÷ -5/80		0
60	40	27	30	-20/60 ÷ 3/27		-3

demand are given in Table 9.1. Some economists use the terms 'elastic' and 'inelastic' with reference to income elasticity. Demand is income inelastic if it lies between +1 and -1. If income elasticity of demand is greater than +1 or less than -1, then it is elastic.

Question 1

Table 9.2

	Original ||New		
	Quantity demanded	Income	Quantity demanded	Income
(a)	100	10	120	14
(b)	15	6	20	7
(c)	50	25	40	35
(d)	12	100	15	125
(e)	200	10	250	11
(f)	25	20	30	18

Calculate the income elasticity of demand from the data in Table 9.2.

Cross elasticity of demand

The quantity demanded of a particular good varies according to the price of other goods. In unit 8 it was argued that a rise in price of a good such as beef would increase the quantity demanded of a substitute such as pork. On the other hand, a rise in price of a good such as cheese would lead to a fall in the quantity demanded of a complement such as macaroni. CROSS ELASTICITY or CROSS PRICE ELASTICITY OF DEMAND measures the proportionate response of the quantity demanded of one good to the proportionate change in the price of another. For instance, it is a measure of the extent to which demand for pork increases when the price of beef goes up; or the extent to which the demand for macaroni falls when the price of cheese increases.

The formula for measuring cross elasticity of demand for good X is:

$$\frac{\text{percentage change in quantity demanded of good X}}{\text{percentage change in price of another good Y}}$$

Two goods which are substitutes will have a positive cross elasticity. An increase (positive) in the price of one good, such as gas, leads to an increase (positive) in the quantity demanded of a substitute such as electricity. Two goods which are complements will have a negative cross elasticity. An increase (positive) in the price of one good such as sand leads to a fall (negative) in demand of a complement such as cement. The cross elasticity of two goods which have little relationship to each other would be zero. For instance, a rise in the price of cars of 10 per cent is likely to have no effect (i.e. 0 per cent change) on the demand for Tipp-Ex.

As with price and income elasticity, it is sometimes more convenient to use alternative formulae for cross elasticity of demand. These are:

$$\text{Cross elasticity of good X} = \frac{\Delta Q_X}{Q_X} \div \frac{\Delta P_Y}{P_Y}$$

$$\text{or} \qquad \frac{P_Y}{Q_X} \times \frac{\Delta Q_X}{\Delta P_Y}$$

Some economists use the terms 'elastic' and 'inelastic' with reference to cross elasticity. Demand is cross elastic if it lies between +1 and -1. If cross elasticity of demand is greater than +1 or less than -1, then it is elastic.

Question 2

Explain what value you would put on the cross elasticity of demand of: (a) gas for electricity; (b) tennis shorts for tennis rackets; (c) luxury cars for petrol; (d) paper for socks; (e) CDs for MP3 downloads; (f) Sainsbury's own brand baked beans for Tesco's own brand baked beans; (g) Virgin Cola for Coca-Cola.

Price elasticity of supply

Price elasticity of demand measures the responsiveness of changes in quantity demanded to changes in price. Equally, the responsiveness of quantity supplied to changes in price can also be measured - this is called PRICE ELASTICITY OF SUPPLY. The formula for measuring the price elasticity of supply is:

$$\frac{\text{percentage change in quantity supplied}}{\text{percentage change in price}}$$

This is equivalent to:

$$\frac{\Delta Q}{Q} \div \frac{\Delta P}{P}$$

or

$$\frac{P}{Q} \times \frac{\Delta Q}{\Delta P}$$

where Q is quantity supplied and P is price.

The supply curve is upward sloping (i.e. an increase in price leads to an increase in quantity supplied and vice versa). Therefore price elasticity of supply will be positive because the top and bottom of the formula will be either both positive or both negative.

As with price elasticity of demand, different ranges of elasticity are given different names. Price elasticity of supply is:
- **perfectly inelastic** (zero) if there is no response in supply to a change in price;
- **inelastic** (between zero and one) if there is a less than proportionate response in supply to a change in price;
- **unitary** (one) if the percentage change in quantity supplied equals the percentage change in price;
- **elastic** (between one and infinity) if there is a more than proportionate response in supply to a change in price;
- **perfectly elastic** (infinite) if producers are prepared to supply any amount at a given price.

These various elasticities are shown in Figure 9.1.

It should be noted that any straight line supply curve passing through the origin has an elasticity of supply equal to 1. This is best understood if we take the formula:

$$\frac{P}{Q} \times \frac{\Delta Q}{\Delta P}$$

$\Delta Q/\Delta P$ is the inverse of (i.e. 1 divided by) the slope of the line, whilst P/Q, assuming that the line passes through the origin, is the slope of the line. The two multiplied together must always equal 1.

Determinants of elasticity of supply

As with price elasticity of demand, there are two factors which determine supply elasticity across a wide range of products.

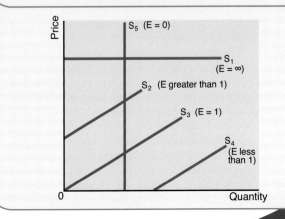

Figure 9.1 Elasticity of supply
The elasticity of supply of a straight line supply curve varies depending upon the gradient of the line and whether it passes through the origin.

Question 3

Figure 9.2 Supply

Calculate from Figure 9.2 the elasticity of supply of a change in price from: (a) £4 to £6; (b) £6 to £8; (c) £8 to £10; (d) £9 to £7; (e) £7 to £5.

Availability of substitutes Substitutes here are not consumer substitutes but producer substitutes. These are goods which a producer can easily produce as alternatives. For instance, one model of a car is a good producer substitute for another model in the same range because the car manufacturer can easily switch resources on its production line. On the other hand, carrots are not substitutes for cars. The farmer cannot easily switch from the production of carrots to the production of cars. If a product has many substitutes then producers can quickly and easily alter the pattern of production if its price rises or falls. Hence its elasticity will be relatively high. But if a product has few or no substitutes, then producers will find it difficult to respond flexibly to variations in price. If there is a fall in price, a producer may have no alternative but either to carry on producing much the same quantity as before or withdrawing from the market. Price elasticity of supply is therefore low.

Time The shorter the time period, the more difficult producers find it to switch from making one product to another. So the shorter the time period, the more inelastic is likely to be supply. There is a number of reasons why this is the case.

- Some items take a long time to make. For example, if there is a crop failure of a product like hazelnuts, it will take until the next growing season to increase supply again whatever price the market sets for hazelnuts in the short term.
- If there is no spare capacity to make more of a product, it will be difficult to increase supply very much even if prices rise sharply. The more spare capacity, the less constraint this places on increasing supply in response to price rises.
- With some products, it is easy and relatively cheap to hold stocks to supply onto the market when they are demanded. With others, it is impossible to hold stocks. For example, large stocks of wheat are kept around the world which can be released if prices rise, so keeping price elasticity of supply relatively high. But it is impossible in most cases to store electricity. So when there is a sharp rise in price of electricity in a free market, there is unlikely to be much response in terms of extra supply in the short term if the system is

working at full capacity. The longer the time period, the easier it is for the market to build up appropriate stocks or to build excess capacity if stocks are not possible. So price elasticity of supply is higher in the longer term.

- Price elasticity of supply will be higher the easier it is for a firm to switch production from one product to another or for firms to enter the market to make the product.

Price elasticity of demand and total expenditure

Price elasticity of demand and changes in total expenditure on a product are linked. Total expenditure can be calculated by multiplying price and quantity:

Total expenditure = quantity purchased x price

For instance, if you bought 5 apples at 10 pence each, your total expenditure would be 50 pence. If the price of apples went up, you might spend more, less, or the same on apples depending upon your price elasticity of demand for apples. Assume that the price of apples went up 40 per cent to 14p each. You might react by buying fewer apples. If you now buy 4 apples (i.e. a fall in demand of 20 per cent), the price elasticity of demand is 20 ÷ 40 or 0.5. Your expenditure on apples will also rise (from 50 pence to 56 pence). If you buy two apples (i.e. a fall in quantity demanded of 60 per cent), your elasticity of demand is 60 ÷ 40 or 1.5 and your expenditure on apples will fall (from 50 pence to 28 pence).

These relationships are what should be expected. If the percentage change in price is larger than the percentage change in quantity demanded (i.e. elasticity is less than 1, or inelastic), then expenditure will rise when prices rise. If the percentage change in price is smaller than the percentage change in quantity demanded (i.e. elasticity is greater than 1 or elastic), then spending will fall as prices rise. If the percentage change in price is the same as the change in quantity demanded (i.e. elasticity is unity), expenditure will remain unchanged because the percentage rise in price will be equal and opposite to the percentage fall in demand.

Key terms

Cross or cross-price elasticity of demand - a measure of the responsiveness of quantity demanded of one good to a change in price of another good. It is measured by dividing the percentage change in quantity demanded of one good by the percentage change in price of the other good.
Income elasticity of demand - a measure of the responsiveness of quantity demanded to a change in income. It is measured by dividing the percentage change in quantity demanded by the percentage change in income.
Price elasticity of supply - a measure of the responsiveness of quantity supplied to a change in price. It is measured by dividing the percentage change in quantity supplied by the percentage change in price.

Question 4

(a) Suggest reasons why the demand for some foods in Table 9.3 is more price elastic than the demand for others.

(b) An increase in the price of which foods would be most likely to lead to
 (i) the greatest and
 (ii) the least change in household expenditure?
 Explain your answer.

Table 9.3 Estimates of price elasticities of demand for selected household foods

	Price elasticity
Milk and cream	-0.36
of which	
Liquid wholemilk and skimmed milks	-0.17
Cheese	-0.35
Carcass meat	-0.69
Other meat and meat products	-0.52
Fresh fish	-0.80
Processed and shellfish	-0.17
Prepared fish	0.00
Frozen fish	-0.32
Eggs	-0.28
Fats	-0.75
Sugar and preserves	-0.79
Fresh potatoes	-0.12
Fresh green vegetables	-0.66
Other fresh vegetables	-0.33
Processed vegetables	-0.60
of which	
Frozen peas	-0.68
Frozen convenience potato products	-0.58
Fresh fruit	-0.29
of which	
Bananas	-0.32
Other fruit and fruit products	-0.81
of which	
Fruit juices	-0.55
Bread	-0.40
Other cereal and cereal products	-0.94
of which	
Cakes and pastries	-0.56
Frozen convenience cereal foods	-0.69
Beverages	-0.37

Source: adapted from *National Food Survey 2000*, Defra.

Applied economics

Cross elasticities of demand for food

Many foods are substitutes for each other. Eggs are a substitute for fish; fish is a substitute for meat. Economic theory would suggest that these goods would therefore have a positive cross elasticity of demand. An increase in the price of one good would lead to an increase in demand of the substitute good, whilst a fall in price of one good would lead to a fall in demand of another.

Evidence from the National Food Survey 2000 gives some evidence for this. Table 9.4 shows estimates of the cross elasticity of demand for three foods: carcass meat, fresh fish and eggs. In orange, going across diagonally, are the own-price elasticities of demand for each good. For example, the price elasticity of demand for carcass meat is - 0.69 (i.e. it is price inelastic). In black, reading across the rows, are the figures for cross elasticity of demand for a product with respect to the price of another. For example, the cross elasticity of demand of carcass meat with respect to the price of

fresh fish is + 0.15. The cross elasticity of demand of eggs with respect to the price of fresh fish is + 0.16.

These cross elasticities are relatively low suggesting, for example, that eggs are only a weak substitute for fresh fish or carcass meat. So a 10 per cent rise in the price of fresh fish, leading to a 8 per cent fall in demand for fresh fish (because the price elasticity of demand for fresh fish is - 0.8), is associated with only a 1.6 per cent rise in demand for eggs (because the cross price elasticity of eggs with respect to the price of fresh fish is + 0.16). Equally, a 10 per cent rise in the price of fresh fish is associated with only a 1.5 per cent rise in demand for carcass meat.

When cross elasticities are negative, it shows that goods might be complements to each other. Table 9.5 would suggest that milk and cream, eggs and fats are all complements. For example, the ingredients for pancakes, and some cakes include milk, eggs and fats. The National Food Survey estimates suggest that a

Table 9.4 *Estimates of price and cross elasticity of demand for carcass meat, fresh fish and eggs, 1988-2000*

	Elasticity with respect to the price of		
	Carcass meat	Fresh fish	Eggs
Carcass meat	-0.69	+0.15	+0.15
Fresh fish	+0.02	-0.8	+0.14
Eggs	+0.02	+0.16	-0.28

Source: adapted from HMSO, *Household Food Consumption and Expenditure*.

Table 9.5 *Estimates of price and cross elasticity of demand for milk and cream, eggs and fats, 1988-2000*

	Elasticity with respect to the price of		
	Milk & cream	Eggs	Fats
Milk and cream	-0.36	-0.40	-0.20
Eggs	-0.05	-0.28	-0.10
Fats	-0.04	-0.19	-0.75

Source: adapted from HMSO, *Household Food Consumption and Expenditure*.

10 per cent rise in the price of eggs leads to a 4 per cent fall in the quantity demanded of milk and cream. Interestingly, a 10 per cent rise in the price of milk and cream only leads to a fall of 0.4 per cent in the quantity demand of eggs. As with the data on

Table 9.6 *Estimates of price and cross elasticity of demand for eggs, non-fresh fruit and fruit products, and meat and meat products other than carcass meat, 1988-2000*

	Elasticity with respect to the price of		
	Eggs	Non-fresh fruit and fruit products	Meat and meat products other than carcass meat
Eggs	-0.28	0.00	0.00
Non-fresh fruit and fruit products	0.00	-0.81	-0.01
Meat and meat products other than carcass meat	+0.03	-0.04	-0.52

Source: adapted from HMSO, *Household Food Consumption and Expenditure*.

substitutes, the National Food Survey estimates suggest that where foods are compliments, they tend to be fairly weak compliments with numbers fairly near zero

Where changes in the price of one good have no effect on the quantity demanded of another good, the cross elasticity of demand is zero. Table 9.6, which shows data from the National Food Survey, would suggest that changes in the price of eggs, non-fresh fruit and fruit products, and meat and meat products other than carcass meat have little impact on demand for each other.

DataQuestion   Clothing, footwear and transport

Figure 9.3 *Expenditure on clothing and footwear as a percentage of total expenditure by gross income decile group*

Source: adapted from *Family Spending* 2003-04, Office for National Statistics.

Figure 9.4 *Expenditure on transport as a percentage of total expenditure by gross income decile group*

Source: adapted from *Family Spending* 2003-04, Office for National Statistics.

Decile groups

A population can be split into ten equal groups. These are called decile groups. In Table 9.8 the groups are households, which are split according to their gross income. So the first decile group is the tenth of households which have the lowest income. The fifth decile group is the tenth of households between 40 and 50 per cent of the total, whilst the tenth decile group is made up of the highest 10 per cent of households by gross income. In Table 9.8 data for the other 7 deciles groups is available but is not printed here in order to simplify the data.

Table 9.7 Clothing and footwear and transport as a percentage of total household expenditure, real household disposable income 1980 to 2003-2004

	Clothing and footwear %	Transport %	Real household disposable income 1980=100
1980	8.1	14.6	100.0
1992	6.0	15.8	120.0
2003-04	5.4	17.3	151.5

Source: adapted from *Family Spending 2003-04*, Office for National Statistics.

Table 9.8 Weekly household expenditure, £, on clothing and footwear and transport by gross income decile group 2003-2004

	Average weekly expenditure, £		
	First decile	Fifth decile	Tenth decile
Men's outer garments	0.70	3.30	12.50
Men's under garments	0.10	0.40	1.00
Women's outer garments	2.40	6.60	19.30
Women's under garments	0.50	0.90	2.70
Boys' outer garments (5-15)	0.20	0.70	1.60
Girls' outer garments (5-15)	0.30	1.00	2.50
Infants' outer garments (under 5)	0.30	0.50	1.30
Children's under garments (under 16)	0.20	0.30	0.70
Accessories	0.10	0.60	1.70
Haberdashery and clothing hire	0.10	0.30	0.40
Dry cleaners, laundry and dyeing	0.10	0.10	0.90
Footwear	1.70	3.70	9.20
Total clothing and footwear	**6.70**	**18.40**	**53.80**
Purchase of vehicles	5.20	21.50	74.20
Petrol, diesel and other motor oils	3.40	13.60	31.20
Other motoring costs	1.90	7.50	19.40
Rail and tube fares	0.30	0.80	6.70
Bus and coach fares	1.00	1.40	1.50
Combined fares	0.10	0.20	2.80
Other travel and transport	1.10	3.00	14.30
Total transport	**13.00**	**48.00**	**150.10**
Total household expenditure on all goods and services	**139.60**	**361.70**	**905.00**
Total household income	**0-123**	**351-444**	**1 092+**

Source: adapted from *Family Spending 2003-04*, Office for National Statistics.

Measuring income elasticity of demand

Income elasticity of demand is measured by dividing the percentage change in quantity demanded of a good or a basket of goods by the percentage change in income of consumers. Quantity demanded is a physical number, like 100 washing machines or 1 000 shirts. However, when data for quantity is not available, a good proxy variable is expenditure. This is quantity times price. If prices remain the same as expenditure changes, then the percentage change in quantity will be the same as the percentage change in expenditure.

1. Describe how spending on clothing and footwear and on transport (a) varies with income and (b) has changed over time.
2. Using the data, explain whether 'clothing and footwear' is likely to have a higher income elasticity of demand than transport.
3. Using Table 9.8, explain which components of clothing and footwear and transport are likely to have the highest income elasticities.
4. Using the data in Table 9.8 and the concept of income elasticity of demand, discuss whether bus and coach transport has a future in the UK.

10 Normal, inferior and Giffen goods

Summary

1. An increase in income will lead to an increase in demand for normal goods but a fall in demand for inferior goods.
2. Normal goods have a positive income elasticity whilst inferior goods have a negative elasticity.
3. A Giffen good is one where a rise in price leads to a rise in quantity demanded. This occurs because the positive substitution effect of the price change is outweighed by the negative income effect.
4. Upward sloping demand curves may occur if the good is a Giffen good, if it has snob or speculative appeal or if consumers judge quality by the price of a product.

Normal and inferior goods

The pattern of demand is likely to change when income changes. It would be reasonable to assume that consumers will increase their demand for most goods when their income increases. Goods for which this is the case are called NORMAL GOODS.

However, an increase in income will result in a fall in demand for other goods. These goods are called INFERIOR GOODS. There will be a fall in demand because consumers will react to an increase in their income by purchasing products which are perceived to be of better quality. Commonly quoted examples of inferior goods are:

- bread - consumers switch from this cheap, filling food to more expensive meat or convenience foods as their incomes increase;
- margarine - consumers switch from margarine to butter, although this has become less true recently with greater health awareness;
- bus transport - consumers switch from buses to their own cars when they can afford to buy their own car.

A good can be both a normal and an inferior good depending upon the level of income. Bread may be a normal good for people on low incomes (i.e. they buy more bread when their

income increases). But it may be an inferior good for higher income earners.

Normal and inferior goods are shown on Figure 10.1. D_1 is the demand curve for a normal good. It is upward sloping because demand increases as income increases. D_2 is the demand curve for an inferior good. It is downward sloping, showing that demand falls as income increases. D_3 is the demand curve for a good which is normal at low levels of income, but is inferior at higher levels of income.

Question 1

Table 10.1 Estimated household food consumption in Great Britain

	Grammes per person per week				
	1985	1990	1995	2000	2002/3
Sugar	238	171	136	105	111
Chicken	196	226	237	253	243
Bananas	80	125	176	206	208
Bread	878	797	756	720	756
Pickles and sauces	61	67	80	107	123
Butter	80	46	36	39	37

Source: adapted from Annual Abstract of Statistics, Office for National Statistics.

Household incomes rose between each of the years 1985, 1990, 1995, 2000 and 2002/3. Assuming that all other factors remained constant, which of the goods shown in Table 10.1 are normal goods and which are inferior goods?

Inferior goods and income elasticity

Inferior goods can be distinguished from normal goods by their income elasticity of demand. The formula for measuring income elasticity is:

$$\frac{\text{percentage change in quantity demanded}}{\text{percentage change in income}}$$

A normal good will always have a positive income elasticity because quantity demanded and income either both increase

Figure 10.1 Normal and inferior goods

On the quantity-income diagram, a normal good such as D_1 has an upward sloping curve, whilst an inferior good such as D_2 has a downward sloping curve. D_3 shows a good which is normal at low levels of income but is inferior at higher levels of income.

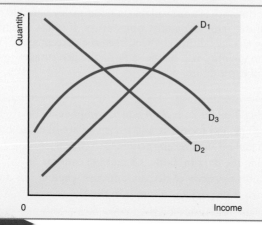

(giving a plus divided by a plus) or both decrease (giving a minus divided by a minus). An inferior good, however, will always have a negative elasticity because the signs on the top and bottom of the formula will always be opposite (a plus divided by a minus or a minus divided by a plus giving a minus answer in both cases).

For instance, if the demand for bread falls by 2 per cent when incomes rise by 10 per cent then it is an inferior good. Its income elasticity is -2/+10 or -0.2.

Giffen goods

A GIFFEN GOOD is a special sort of inferior good. Alfred Marshall (1842-1924), an eminent economist and author of a best selling textbook of his day, claimed that another eminent economist, Sir Robert Giffen (1837-1910), had observed that the consumption of bread increased as its price increased. The argument was that bread was a staple food for low income consumers. A rise in its price would not deter people from buying as much as before. But 'poor' people would now have so little extra money to spend on meat or other luxury foods that they would abandon their demand for these and instead buy more bread to fill up their stomachs. The result was that a rise in the price of bread led to a rise in the demand for bread. Another way of explaining this phenomenon is to use the concepts of INCOME and SUBSTITUTION effects. When a good changes in price, the quantity demanded will be changed by the sum of the substitution effect and the income effect.

- **Substitution effect.** If the price of a good rises, consumers will buy less of that good and more of others because it is now relatively more expensive than other goods. If the price of a good falls, consumers will buy more of that good and less of others. These changes in quantity demanded solely due to the relative change in prices are known as the substitution effect of a price change.
- **Income effect.** If the price of a good rises, the real income of consumers will fall. They will not be able to buy the same basket of goods and services as before. Consumers can react to this fall in real income in one of two ways. If the good is a normal good, they will buy less of the good. If the good is an inferior good, they will buy more of the good. These changes in quantity demanded caused by a change in real income are known as the income effect of the price change.

For a normal good the substitution effect and the income effect both work in the same direction. A rise in price leads to a fall in quantity demanded because the relative price of the good has risen. It also leads to a fall in quantity demanded because consumers' real incomes have now fallen. So a rise in price will always lead to a fall in quantity demanded, and vice versa.

For an inferior good, the substitution effect and income effect work in opposite directions. A rise in price leads to a fall in quantity demanded because the relative price of the good has risen. But it leads to a rise in quantity demanded because consumers' real incomes have fallen. However, the substitution effect outweighs the income effect because overall it is still true for an inferior good that a rise in price leads to an overall fall in quantity demanded.

A Giffen good is a special type of inferior good. A rise in price leads to a fall in quantity demanded because of the substitution effect but a rise in quantity demanded because of the income effect. However, the income effect outweighs the substitution effect, leading to rises in quantity demanded. For instance, if a 10p rise in the price of a standard loaf leads to a 4 per cent fall in

the demand for bread because of the substitution effect, but a 10 per cent rise in demand because of the income effect, then the net effect will be a 6 per cent rise in the demand for bread.

The relationship between normal, inferior and Giffen goods and their income and substitution effects is summarised in Table 10.2.

Giffen goods are an economic curiosity. In theory they could exist, but no economist has ever found an example of such a good in practice. There is no evidence even that Sir Robert Giffen ever claimed that bread had an upward sloping demand curve - it crept into textbooks via Alfred Marshall and has remained there ever since!

Table 10.2 Substitution and income effects on quantity demanded of a rise in price for normal, inferior and Giffen goods

Type of good	Effect on quantity demanded of a rise in price		
	Substitution effect	Income effect	Total effect
Normal good	Fall	Fall	Fall
Inferior good	Fall	Rise	Fall because substitution effect > income effect
Giffen good	Fall	Rise	Rise because substitution effect < income effect

Question 2

Table 10.3

Good	Change in price (pence per unit)	Change in quantity demanded as a result of	
		income effect	substitution effect
Bacon	+10	+5%	-8%
Bus rides	+15	+7%	-5%
Jeans	-100	+1%	+5%
Baked beans	-2	-1%	+4%
Compact discs	-150	+4%	+3%

An economist claims that she has observed the effects detailed in Table 10.3 resulting solely from a change in price of a product. Which of these products are normal goods, which are inferior and which are Giffen goods?

Necessities and luxuries

Some economists distinguish between **necessities** (or **basic goods**) and **luxuries** (or **superior goods**). They state that necessities have an income elasticity of less than +1 whilst luxury goods have an income elasticity of greater than +1. The problem with this distinction is that many products which have an income elasticity of less than +1 would hardly be classified as 'necessities' by most consumers. In

Table 10.4, for example, all the foods have an income elasticity of less than +1 and would therefore all be classified as necessities. Yet should a fruit juice be just as much a necessity as tea, milk or meat? Whilst it can be useful to discuss necessities and luxuries in theory, putting a precise value on these in terms of income elasticity of demand may not be particularly helpful.

Upward sloping demand curves

Demand curves are usually downward sloping. However, there are possible reasons why the demand curve for some goods may be upward sloping.

Giffen goods Giffen goods, a type of inferior good, have been discussed above.

Goods with snob appeal Some goods are bought mainly because they confer status on the buyer. Examples might be diamonds, fur coats or large cars. The argument is that these goods are demanded because few people can afford to buy them because their price is high. If large numbers of people could afford to buy them, then the demand (the quantity buyers would buy) would be low. This might be true for some individual consumers, but economists have not found any proof that it is true for markets as a whole. Whilst some might buy diamonds only because they are expensive, the majority of consumers would buy more diamonds if their price fell because they like diamonds. So there must be some doubt as to whether snob appeal does give rise to upward sloping demand curves.

Speculative goods Throughout most of 1987, stock markets worldwide boomed. Share prices were at an all time high and the demand for shares was high too. But in October 1987 share prices slumped on average between 20 and 30 per cent. Overnight the demand for shares fell. This could be taken as evidence of an upward sloping demand curve. The higher the price of shares, the higher the demand because buyers associate high share prices with large speculative gains in the future. However, most economists would argue that what is being seen is a shift in the demand curve. The demand curve is drawn on the assumption that expectations of future gain are constant. When share prices or the price of any speculative good fall, buyers revise their expectations downwards. At any given share price they are willing to buy fewer shares, which pushes the demand curve backwards to the left.

Quality goods Some consumers judge quality by price. They automatically assume that a higher priced good must be of better quality than a similar lower priced good. Hence, the higher the price the greater the quantity demanded. As with snob appeal goods, this may be true for some individuals but there is no evidence to suggest that this is true for consumers as a whole. There have been examples where goods that have been re-packaged, heavily advertised and increased in price have increased their sales. But this is an example of a shift to the right in the demand curve caused by advertising and repackaging rather than of an upward sloping demand curve.

In conclusion, it can be seen that there are various reasons why in theory demand curves might be upward sloping. But few, if any, such goods have been found in reality. The downward sloping demand curve seems to be true of nearly all goods.

Question 3

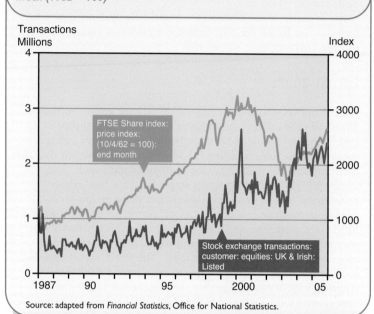

Figure 10.2 Number of Stock market transactions, FTSE all share price index (1962 = 100)

Source: adapted from *Financial Statistics*, Office for National Statistics.

In October 1987, prices on the London Stock Market crashed by around 25 per cent. The result was a sharp fall in the number of shares bought and sold. Similarly, in 2000, prices of 'dotcom' shares (shares in companies related to the Internet), having created a boom in share prices, fell sharply. By September 2002, the FTSE All Share Price Index stood at 1 802 compared to 3 242 in December 1999 at the height of the dotcom bubble. Equally, the number of shares traded per month fell from a high of 2.6 million in March 2000 to a low of 1.1 million in December 2002.

To what extent do the data support the existence of an upward sloping demand curve for shares?

Key terms

Giffen good - a special type of inferior good where demand increases when price increases.
Income effect - the impact on quantity demanded of a change in price due to a change in consumers' real income which results from this change in price.
Inferior good - a good where demand falls when income increases (i.e. it has a negative income elasticity of demand).
Normal good - a good where demand increases when income increases (i.e. it has a positive income elasticity of demand).
Substitution effect - the impact on quantity demanded due to a change in price, assuming that consumers' real incomes stay the same (i.e. the impact of a change in price excluding the income effect).

Applied economics

Income elasticities and inferior goods

Table 10.4 gives estimates of the income elasticity of demand for certain foods in the UK. The estimates have been calculated using data from the National Food Survey (which from 2001 was amalgamated with the Family Expenditure Survey to become the Expenditure and Food Survey) conducted by Defra (Department for the Environment, Food and Rural Affairs) and ONS (Office for National Statistics, the UK government statistical service).

The calculations pool data for the three year period 1998-2000. Sophisticated statistical techniques were used to take account of factors such as regional spending patterns and household size. The estimates are based on how food expenditure varies between households on different incomes.

Food itself, according to the data, has an income elasticity of demand of + 0.20. Hence, a 10 per cent increase in incomes leads to a 2 per cent increase in the quantity demanded of all foods. Incomes in the UK are growing at around 2.5 per cent per year on average. Growth in demand for food is increasing, therefore, at just one fifth of that amount, at around 0.5 per cent per year on average. An income elasticity of + 0.20 also means that spending on food is declining as a proportion of total household expenditure over time.

Most categories of food have a positive income elasticity of demand and are therefore normal goods. For example, cheese has an income elasticity of + 0.23, fish + 0.27 and fresh fruit + 0.30. Some foods, however, are inferior goods with negative income elasticities. In Table 10.4, these are liquid wholemilk, eggs, margarine, apples and tea. There is a variety of reasons why these particular foods have negative income elasticities.

● Some reflect growing awareness of what constitutes a healthy diet. So liquid wholemilk and margarine with their typically high fat content show a fall in demand as incomes increase. Higher income households tend to be more aware of health issues related to diet. They also have higher incomes to be able to afford to buy acceptable substitutes if these are more expensive.

● Some reflect changing tastes. Tea drinking is declining in the UK as consumers drink more coffee. Because coffee is more expensive than tea, this shift is arguably happening at a faster rate amongst higher income groups. Hence tea has a negative income elasticity of demand. Equally, - 0.02 is so small that, according to the National Food Survey report, it is 'not statistically different from zero', i.e. the evidence

would suggest that tea is on the borderline between being a normal and an inferior good.

● Others are more difficult to explain. Healthy eating campaigns should be encouraging consumers to eat apples and yet, according to the data, apples are an inferior good with an income elasticity of - 0.07. Perhaps as incomes increase, households are switching from apples to other fruit such as oranges and bananas, both of which have positive income elasticities.

The item with the highest income elasticity of demand in Table 10.4 is fruit juices with an income elasticity of + 0.45. Fruit juices tend to be purchased more by high income households than low income households. The high cost of fruit juices and their perceived health benefits might account for this.

Table 10.4 Estimated income elasticities of food products

	Income elasticity
Milk and cream	0.05
of which	
Liquid wholemilk	-0.17
Cheese	0.23
Carcass meat	0.20
Fish	0.27
Eggs	-0.01
Fats	0.08
of which	
Butter	0.20
Margarine	-0.37
Sugar and preserves	0.00
Fresh potatoes	0.09
Fresh green vegetables	0.27
Fresh fruit	0.30
of which	
Apples	-0.07
Oranges	0.23
Bananas	0.12
Fruit juices	0.45
Bread	0.12
Cakes and biscuits	0.13
Beverages	0.10
of which	
Tea	-0.02
Coffee	0.16
All foods	0.20

Source: National Food Survey 2000, Office for National Statistics.

DataQuestion

Tourism

Figure 10.3 Real household disposable income per head at 2001 prices, £

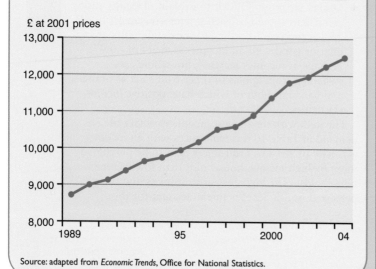

£ at 2001 prices

Source: adapted from *Economic Trends*, Office for National Statistics.

Figure 10.4 Domestic and international tourism by UK residents: number of trips taken in the UK and overseas by UK residents[1, 2]

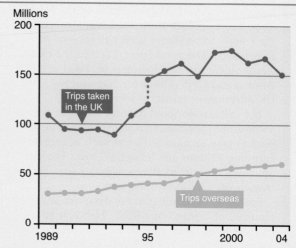

Millions

Trips taken in the UK

Trips overseas

1 Figures include business trips as well as holidays.
2 In 1995, there was a change in the way that domestic trips were calculated which led to an increase in the number of trips being recorded of 26.8 million trips.

Source: adapted from *Annual Abstract of Statistics*, Office for National Statistics.

Figure 10.5 Holidays abroad[1] by destination, percentages

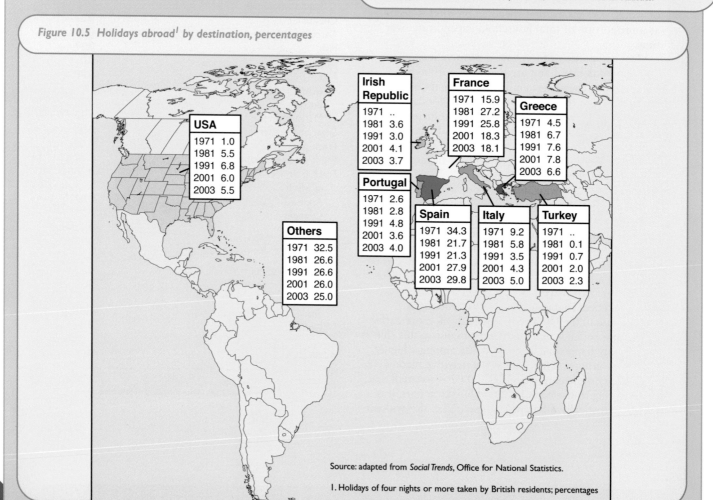

USA

1971	1.0
1981	5.5
1991	6.8
2001	6.0
2003	5.5

Irish Republic

1971	..
1981	3.6
1991	3.0
2001	4.1
2003	3.7

France

1971	15.9
1981	27.2
1991	25.8
2001	18.3
2003	18.1

Greece

1971	4.5
1981	6.7
1991	7.6
2001	7.8
2003	6.6

Portugal

1971	2.6
1981	2.8
1991	4.8
2001	3.6
2003	4.0

Spain

1971	34.3
1981	21.7
1991	21.3
2001	27.9
2003	29.8

Italy

1971	9.2
1981	5.8
1991	3.5
2001	4.3
2003	5.0

Turkey

1971	..
1981	0.1
1991	0.7
2001	2.0
2003	2.3

Others

1971	32.5
1981	26.6
1991	26.6
2001	26.0
2003	25.0

Source: adapted from *Social Trends*, Office for National Statistics.

1. Holidays of four nights or more taken by British residents; percentages

Table 10.5 *Visits to the most popular tourist attractions*

Great Britain							Millions
	1981	1991	2003		1981	1991	2003
Museums and galleries				**Historic houses**			
British Museum	2.6	5.1	4.6	**and monuments**			
National Gallery	2.7	4.3	4.4	Edinburgh Castle	0.8	1.0	1.2
Natural History Museum	3.7	1.6	2.9	Tower of London	2.1	1.9	2.0
Tate Gallery	0.9	1.8	4.4				
				Wildlife parks and zoos			
Theme parks				Chester Zoo	..	0.9	1.2
Blackpool Pleasure Beach	7.5	6.5	6.2				
Pleasure Beach, Great Yarmouth	..	2.5	1.5				

Source: adapted from *Social Trends*, Office for National Statistics; Star UK.

Table 10.6 *Holiday taking: by social grade*

Great Britain			Percentages[1]
	Holidays in Britain	Holidays abroad	No holiday
AB	44	59	18
C1	37	47	31
C2	38	32	38
DE	28	20	57

1. Percentage of people in each social grade taking holidays in each location. Percentages do not sum to 100 because some people take holidays in Britain and abroad.

AB = higher/middle management, administration and professional; C1 = junior management, supervisory or clerical; C2 = skilled manual; DE = semi and unskilled, lowest paid or unemployed.

Source: adapted from *Social Trends*, Office for National Statistics.

Figure 10.6 *Domestic holidays[1] taken by United Kingdom residents: by destination, 2002*

Millions
- 12.0 and over
- 8.0 - 11.9
- 4.0 - 7.9
- Under 4.0

1. Holidays of one night or more for holiday purposes by UK residents.

Source: adapted from *National Tourist Boards*.

1. Describe the main trends in tourism shown in the data.

2. Using Figure 10.3, explain what you would expect to have happened to the number of holidays taken by UK residents and visits to tourist destinations since 1989, assuming that tourism is a normal good.

3. What evidence is there in the data that some tourist destinations and attractions are inferior goods?

4. Firms associated with tourism in the Great Yarmouth area are concerned that they are losing out in the expansion of tourism in the UK and abroad. (a) Suggest THREE reasons why a tourist might prefer to go to places such as Scotland, Cornwall, Spain or Florida rather than Great Yarmouth. (b) Discuss THREE strategies which stakeholders in the tourist industry in the Great Yarmouth area could adopt to make the income elasticity of demand more favourable to themselves.

Indirect taxes and subsidies

Summary

1. Indirect taxes can be either ad valorem taxes or specific taxes.
2. The imposition of an indirect tax is likely to lead to a rise in the unit price of a good which is less than the unit value of the tax.
3. The incidence of indirect taxation is likely to fall on both consumer and producer.
4. The incidence of tax will fall wholly on the consumer if demand is perfectly inelastic or supply is perfectly elastic.
5. The incidence of tax will fall wholly on the producer if demand is perfectly elastic or supply is perfectly inelastic.

Indirect taxes and subsidies

An indirect tax is a tax on expenditure. The two major indirect taxes in the UK are VAT and excise duties.

VAT is an example of an AD VALOREM tax. The tax levied increases in proportion to the value of the tax base. In the case of VAT, the tax base is the price of the good. Most goods in the UK carry a 17.5 per cent VAT charge. Excise duties on the other hand are an example of a SPECIFIC or UNIT tax. The amount of tax levied does not change with the value of the goods but with the amount or volume of the goods purchased. So the excise duty on a bottle of wine is the same whether the bottle costs £5 or £500, but the VAT is 100 times more on the latter compared to the former. The main excise duties in the UK are on alcohol, tobacco and petrol. They should not be confused with customs duties which are levied on imports.

A SUBSIDY is a grant given by government to encourage the production or consumption of a particular good or service.

Subsidies, for instance, may be given on essential items such as housing or bread. Alternatively they may be given to firms that employ disadvantaged workers such as the long term unemployed or people with disabilities. Or they may be given to firms manufacturing domestically produced goods to help them be more competitive than imported goods.

The incidence of tax

Price theory can be used to analyse the impact of the imposition of an indirect tax on a good. Assume that a specific tax of £1 per bottle is imposed upon wine. This has the effect of reducing supply. Sellers of wine will now want to charge £1 extra per bottle sold. In Figure 11.1, this is shown by a vertical shift of £1 in the supply curve at every level of output. However many bottles are produced, sellers will want to charge £1 more per bottle and therefore there is a parallel shift upwards of the whole supply curve from S_1 to S_2.

The old equilibrium price was £3.30, at which price 60 million bottles were bought and sold. The introduction of the £1 tax

Question 1

The price of a litre of unleaded petrol at the pumps is made up as follows:

	pence
Petrol cost before tax	28.2
Excise duty	48.3
	76.5
VAT @ 17.5%	13.4
Price at the pumps	89.9

Calculate the new price of petrol if:
(a) an increase in the cost of crude oil pushed up the cost of petrol before tax from 28.2p to 31.3p;
(b) the government increased excise duty from 48.3 to 50.0p;
(c) VAT was reduced from 17.5 per cent to 15 per cent;
(d) the government removed both excise duties and VAT on petrol and instead introduced a subsidy of 2p a litre.
(For each part, assume that the price at the pumps is initially 89.9p.)

Figure 11.1 The incidence of a specific tax

The imposition of an indirect tax of £1 per unit on wine will push up the supply curve from S_1 to S_2. The vertical distance between the two supply curves at any given output is £1. As a consequence equilibrium price will rise from £3.30 to £4.00. The consumer therefore pays an extra 70p per bottle of wine. The other 30p of the tax is paid by the producer because the price it receives per bottle before tax falls from £3.30 to £3.00.

will raise price and reduce quantity demanded. The new equilibrium price is £4, at which price quantity demanded falls to 40 million bottles.

This result might seem surprising. The imposition of a £1 per bottle tax has only raised the price of a bottle by 70p and not the full £1 of the tax. This is because the INCIDENCE OF TAX is unlikely to fall totally on consumers. The incidence of tax measures the burden of tax upon the taxpayer. In this case the consumer has paid 70p of the tax. Therefore the other 30p which the government receives must have been paid by producers.

Question 2

Table 11.1

Price (£)	Quantity demanded	Quantity supplied
4	16	4
6	12	6
8	8	8
10	4	10
12	0	12

(a) Draw the demand and supply curves from the data in Table 11.1.
(b) What is the equilibrium quantity demanded and supplied?
The government now imposes a specific tax of £3 per unit.
(c) Show the effect of this on the diagram.
(d) What is the new equilibrium quantity demanded and supplied?
(e) What is the new equilibrium price?
(f) What is the incidence of tax per unit on (i) the consumer and (ii) the producer?
(g) What is (i) the tax per unit and (ii) total government revenue from the tax?
(h) By how much will the before tax revenue of producers change?

Tax revenues

Using Figure 11.1 we can also show the change in total expenditure before and after imposition of the tax as well as the amount of tax revenue gained by the government. The government will receive total tax revenue of £1 x 40 million (the tax per unit x the quantity sold); hence tax revenues will be £40 million. Consumers will pay 70p x 40 million of this, whilst producers will pay 30p x 40 million. Consumers will therefore pay £28 million of tax whilst producers will pay £12 million. Total spending on wine will fall from £198 million (£3.30 x 60 million) to £160 million (£4 x 40 million). Revenues received by producers will fall from £198 million (£3.30 x 60 million) to £120 million (£3 x 40 million).

Ad valorem taxes

The above analysis can be extended to deal with ad valorem taxes. The imposition of an ad valorem tax will lead to an upwards shift in the supply curve. However, the higher the price, the greater will be the amount of the tax. Hence the shift will

look as in Figure 11.2. Consumers will pay FG tax per unit whilst the incidence of tax on producers per unit will be HG.

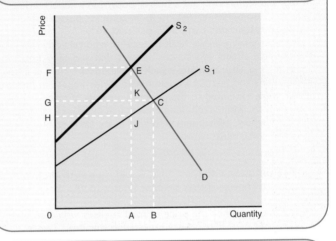

Figure 11.2 The incidence of an ad valorem tax
The imposition of an ad valorem tax will push the supply curve upwards from S₁ to S₂. The following gives the key facts about the change:
(a) original equilibrium price and quantity, OG and OB;
(b) new equilibrium price and quantity, OF and OA;
(c) incidence of tax per unit on consumers, GF;
(d) incidence of tax per unit on producers, HG;
(e) tax per unit in equilibrium, HF;
(f) total tax paid by consumers, GKEF;
(g) total tax paid by producers, GHJK;
(h) total tax revenue of government, FHJE;
(i) change in producers' revenue, OBCG - OAJH;
(j) change in consumers' expenditure, OBCG - OAEF.

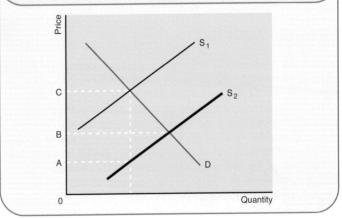

Figure 11.3 The effect of a subsidy on price
A subsidy of AC per unit will push the supply curve down from S₁ to S₂. The price to the consumer will fall by BC (i.e. less than the value of the subsidy per unit given).

Subsidies

A subsidy on a good will lead to an increase in supply, shifting the supply curve downwards and to the right. This is shown in Figure 11.3. It should be noted that a subsidy of AC will not lead to a fall in price of AC. Part of the subsidy, AB, will be appropriated by producers because of the higher unit cost of production of higher levels of output (shown by the upward sloping supply curve). Prices to consumers will only fall by BC.

Question 3

The Prime Minister's Strategy Unit has suggested that taxing unhealthy foods might be part of a wider strategy to combat rising levels of obesity. In a paper, *Personal Responsibility and Changing Behaviour*, it says: 'There might even be potential to consider fiscal measures - a 'fatty food tax' - applied to food not people - or different VAT treatment for food with poor nutritional standards. This would be a signal to producers as well as consumers and serve more broadly as a signal to society that nutritional content in food is important.'

Currently, VAT is levied at the full rate of 17.5 per cent on many foods most associated with obesity, such as crisps, fizzy drinks and ice cream. But a burger bought in a supermarket, like most foods, has no VAT on it. In contrast, burgers sold in fast food restaurants carry 17.5 per cent VAT.

Tom Marshall, a public health specialist who recently studied the possible effects of a fat tax, believes that adding VAT to foods high in saturated fats - such as full-fat milk, hard cheeses, butter, buns and biscuits - could have a major impact on health. If VAT were extended to the principal sources of dietary saturated fat, while exempting goods such as orange juice and low-fat yoghurt, consumers would be more likely to buy the cheaper, low-fat alternatives.

Source: adapted from *The Times*, 19.2.2004.

(a) Explain, using a diagram, what would happen to the supply of hard cheeses if they became subject to VAT at 17.5 per cent.

(b) Analyse whether the price of hard cheeses would go up by 17.5 per cent if VAT were imposed at this rate. Use a diagram to illustrate your analysis.

(c) Why might the imposition of VAT on hard cheeses have an impact on the demand for orange juice?

(d) 'A positive impact on health of the imposition of VAT would be most likely if demand for fatty foods were price elastic.' Using a diagram, explain this statement.

Taxes and elasticity

The extent to which the tax incidence falls on consumers rather than producers depends upon the elasticities of demand and supply. Figure 11.4 shows a situation where either the supply curve is perfectly elastic or the demand curve is perfectly inelastic. In both cases, the vertical shift in the supply curve, which shows the value of the tax per unit, is identical to the final price rise. Therefore, all of the tax will be paid by consumers.

Figure 11.5, on the other hand, shows two cases where the incidence of tax falls totally on the producer. Producers will find it impossible to shift any of the tax onto consumers if the demand curve is perfectly elastic. Consumers are not prepared to buy at any higher price than the existing price. If the supply curve is perfectly inelastic, then the supply curve after imposition of the tax will be the same as the one before. Equilibrium price will therefore remain the same and producers will have to bear the full burden of the tax.

Generalising from these extreme situations, we can conclude that the more elastic the demand curve or the more inelastic the supply curve, the greater will be the incidence of tax on producers and the less will be the incidence of tax on consumers. So far as the government is concerned,

Figure 11.4 *Where the incidence of tax falls wholly on the consumer*

If supply is perfectly elastic or demand perfectly inelastic, then it can be seen from the graphs that the incidence of tax will fall wholly on consumers.

Figure 11.5 *Where the incidence of tax falls wholly on the producer*

If supply is perfectly inelastic or demand perfectly elastic, then it can be seen from the graphs that the incidence of tax will fall wholly on producers.

Question 4

Table 11.2

	Price elasticity of demand
Food	- 0.52
Durables	- 0.89
Fuel and light	- 0.47
Services	- 1.02

Source: John Muellbauer, 'Testing the Barten Model of Household Composition Effects and the Cost of Children', *Economic Journal*.

The government wishes to raise VAT on selected goods, all these goods and services being zero-rated at present. Which categories of goods does the data suggest would yield (a) the most and (b) the least revenues? (Assume that at present the average price and the quantity demanded of goods in each category is identical.) Explain your reasoning carefully.

taxation revenue will be greater, all other things being equal, the more inelastic the demand for the product taxed. For instance, if demand were perfectly elastic, the imposition of an indirect tax would lead to quantity demanded falling to zero and tax revenue being zero. At the opposite extreme, if demand were perfectly inelastic, consumers would buy the same quantity after imposition of the tax as before. Hence revenue will be equal to the tax per unit times the quantity demanded before imposition. If the price elasticity of demand lies between these two extremes, the imposition of a tax will lead to a fall in quantity demanded. The higher the elasticity, the larger will be the fall in quantity demanded and hence the lower will be the tax revenue received by government. Hence, it is no coincidence that in the UK excise duties are placed on alcohol, tobacco and petrol, all of which are relatively price inelastic.

Key terms

Ad valorem tax - tax levied as a percentage of the value of the good.
Incidence of tax - the tax burden on the taxpayer.
Specific or unit tax - tax levied on volume.
Subsidy - a grant given which lowers the price of a good, usually designed to encourage production or consumption of a good.

Applied economics

Taxes, subsidies, congestion and the environment

The demand for transport keeps growing as Figure 11.6 shows. However, this growing demand is concentrated on motor transport. Other modes of transport, such as bus and rail, today are relatively insignificant. The increase in demand for motor transport poses two problems. One is that it is causing ever increasing congestion on the roads. The other is that it is causing a variety of environmental problems. The government, through taxes and subsidies, can tackle both problems but, as with so many complex economic issues, there are no easy and painless solutions.

Road congestion

Britain's roads are becoming ever more congested. In 1950, there was less than 2 million cars. Today, there are over 25 million. The Department for Transport projects that this will rise to 30 million by 2015 and 40 million by 2025. The demand for road space is therefore growing over time. The supply of road space in terms of the number of kilometres of road or the number of lanes on roads is hardly changing. Hence, key roads regularly become congested at certain times of day or certain days of the week. Figure 11.7 shows how average journey times in London have declined over time as a result of this increasing congestion.

The overall cost of motoring is one factor which limits the demand for road space. The fixed costs of owning a car, in terms of purchase, insurance, licensing and servicing, deter those on lower incomes from owning a car. However, the decision for a car owner about whether to use a particular road today is determined by the cost of fuel, the variable cost of motoring.

Raising taxes on motoring, such as raising taxes on petrol and diesel prices, is one way in which the government can price motorists off the road. However, this is a very crude way of doing this because there it gives no incentive for motorists to switch their journey

times to when roads are less congested. It also hits motorists, particularly in rural areas, who rarely face any congestion.

Reducing congestion through raising taxes on fuel is also likely to be politically impossible. In 2000, the country was brought to a halt by a relatively small group of protesters from the farming and road haulage lobby who wanted to the government to reduce the price of petrol through cutting taxes. Because the demand for motoring is relatively inelastic, there would have to be very large rises in tax on fuel to have an impact on congestion. Petrol would have to be, say, £5 a litre compared to less than £1 today, to force enough cars off the road at peak times to reduce congestion. Such prices would hit all motorists, not just those whose journeys create congestion in the first place.

Economists therefore favour taxing congestion directly. A start has already been made with the London Congestion Charge, where motorists have to pay £8 a day to enter central London. This has been highly effective at reducing congestion in central London and raising journey speeds. More broadly, the government has plans to introduce congestion charging across the whole country, currently by 2014. The hope is that all vehicles can be tracked via satellite and be charged when they travel in any zone where there is congestion. Trucks could be subject to charges as early as 2008. It might be politically acceptable to introduce such a charge if the revenues raised were used to reduce the tax on fuel. However, the technology is still unproven. It would also have to give significant benefits to motorists in terms of shorter journey times in congested areas.

In central London, the introduction of the Congestion Charge was accompanied by higher spending on and subsidies for public transport. In particular, bus services were expanded to offer an alternative to those who no longer wanted to bring their cars into Central London. Using part of the revenues from congestion charging throughout the country could prove less effective however. For example, where cars were priced off the motorway system, it might be difficult to offer satisfactory public transport alternatives. Equally, it would raise the overall cost of motoring since the cash raised from the congestion charges was not being recycled into lower fuel taxes or reduced vehicle licence fees. This might prove politically unpopular.

The environment

Motor vehicles are environmentally damaging. Roads eat into the countryside. Scarce natural resources are used up in the making and running of vehicles. There is noise pollution in the vicinity of roads. Engines run on carbon fuels and emit greenhouse gasses which contribute to global warming. Diesel engines emit particulates which can cause cancer.

One solution to reducing the damage done to the environment is simply to reduce the number and length of journeys made. Raising taxes on fuel would therefore be a good way of achieving this. In its April 1993 Budget, the government committed itself to such a rise in taxes on petrol by 3 per cent per year in real terms for the foreseeable future, a figure which it increased to 5 per cent in its December 1993 Budget. It justified this by pointing that petrol was cheaper in real terms in 1993 than it has been in the early 1980s. It was this policy which fuel protesters succeeded in getting the government to abandon in 2000. The vast majority of motorists put lower taxes on fuel ahead of any environmental concerns.

Another solution to at least some of the environmental problems associated with motoring is to modify vehicles themselves. Vehicles are slowly becoming more fuel efficient over time. Diesel engines emit fewer greenhouse gases than petrol cars. If everyone drove around in diesel powered minis, there would be considerable environmental gains. Figure 11.8 shows that over the period 1976 to 2004, there was some modest gains in efficiency. Distance travelled by all types of road vehicle increased 101 per cent whilst fuel consumption only increased by 67 per cent. The data also suggest that efficiency gains are increasing over time. Between 1997 and 2003, for example, distance travelled increased by 19 per cent but fuel consumption only increased by 3 per cent.

However, making incremental improvements in the efficiency of oil driven engines is unlikely to prevent the motor car from causing more damage to the environment in the future. This is because the number of motor cars worldwide will increase 5, 10 or 20 fold over the next few decades as developing economies such as China and India develop to the point where most households can afford at least one car. The only solution to this is to change the engine which powers the motor car. Electric cars driven by batteries or engines fuelled by hydrogen have been developed but both have so many drawbacks today that they are not being widely adopted. However, in 10 or 20 years' time, circumstances may have

changed and the petrol driven car with its damaging effects on the environment may have largely disappeared. It could be that the market mechanism will bring about this change. More likely, governments will intervene and through a combination of policies such as government regulations, taxes and subsidies, we will see less environmentally damaging vehicles on the roads.

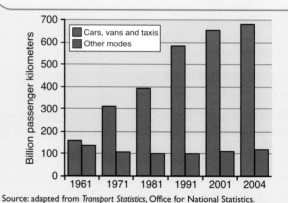

Figure 11.6 Passenger journeys by mode of transport

Source: adapted from *Transport Statistics*, Office for National Statistics.

Figure 11.7 Average traffic speeds in London, 1968-2003

Source: adapted from *Transport Statistics*, Office for National Statistics.

Figure 11.8 Distance travelled and fuel consumption: all transport UK

Source: adapted from *Annual Abstract of Statistics, Transport Statistics*, Office for National Statistics.

DataQuestion

SUVs

SUVs

SUVs, sports utility vehicles, are sometimes also called 'off-roaders'. They differ from ordinary cars in that they are taller, placing the driver in a higher position to other car drivers. They have 4x4 transmissions, meaning that power is directly taken to all four wheels rather than just two wheels on an ordinary car. This gives them much better grip for travelling across rough terrain such as fields or dirt tracks - hence the name 'off-roader'. They are designed to give the handling of a traditional work vehicle or utility vehicle like a farm Land Rover with the comfort of a modern car. According to a survey by YouGov, almost two thirds of the population want special taxes on sports utility vehicles. Londoners were even more strongly in favour of restrictions on 4x4s. Ken Livingstone, mayor of London, has described SUV drivers as 'complete idiots'.

Source: adapted from the *Financial Times*, 2.9.2004.

The Chelsea tractor

SUVs are sometimes known as 'Chelsea tractors'. They are used by the well heeled of one of the richest boroughs in London to do such exciting things as go to the local supermarket or pick up the children from school. They certainly would never be let out into the open countryside - that is just the fantasy which helps sell the car.

So what is the attraction for buyers? Women say they feel safer driving an SUV because they are higher up and so get better vision. But they are also a tremendous status symbol. They are a very large and prominent display of wealth and social standing. Not merely can you afford to buy it, but you can also afford the high running costs of the vehicle. A YouGov Survey found that a fifth of SUV owners bought them for 'pose value'. However, in the same survey, half of the respondents who didn't own an SUV believed that 'pose value' was the main reason for owners buying them.

Source: adapted from the *Financial Times*, 2.9.2004.

Demand for and supply of SUVs

Demand for SUVs has seen strong growth. In the past 10 years, sales have doubled with 80 000 sold in 2004 alone. They now account for 6 per cent of all new cars sold in the UK. Motor manufacturers have responded by developing new SUV models and all the major sellers in the UK market now have an SUV on offer. There is an added incentive for motor manufacturers in that the profit margins on SUVs are higher than on the average car. Customers seem to be less price sensitive, viewing their SUVs as luxuries for which they are prepared to pay extra.

Table 11.3 SUV price ranges, new, November 2005

Nissan X-trail	£15,000 - £25,000
Toyota Rav 4	£15,240 - £23,171
Mitsubishi Shogun	£9,999 - £28,511
Land Rover Discovery	£25,923 - £46,563
Suzuki Grand Vitara	£8,999 - £15,000

Source: adapted from BBC news website, 31.3.2005; autotrader at www.insuresupermarket.com.

Fuel consumption

SUVs tend to have very poor fuel consumption. Some petrol versions do as little as 13.4 miles to the gallon in a city and 25mpg on a motorway. The environmental lobby argues that few drivers of off-roaders ever need the 4x4 capability, but the extra weight of the complex system makes the vehicles less fuel-efficient. 'It is bound to be less efficient because it has the aerodynamics of a brick and the extra weight of a four-wheel-drive drivetrain' said John Wormaid, partner at Autopolis, the consultants.

Source: adapted from the *Financial Times*, 2.9.2004.

SUVs and safety

SUVs might make their drivers feel safer, but statistics tell us that they are a road hazard. US data suggest that SUVs are responsible for three times the number of road deaths compared with ordinary cars in accidents. Part of the problem is their height. When a child or an adult pedestrian is hit by an SUV, there is more impact from the high bonnet of an SUV than with an ordinary car with a much lower bonnet. Even worse is when SUVs are fitted with fashionable 'bull bars'. These were originally designed to protect the vehicle from impact with cows or sheep in country lanes. In an urban environment, they increase the impact on pedestrians. Although it is now illegal to sell new SUVs with bull bars, it is still permissible to buy them separately and have them fitted afterwards.

Source: adapted from *4x4s: A Programme for Change*, by Norman Baker MP.

At present, the government imposes VAT at 17.5 per cent on the purchase of all new cars. The government is now proposing to put an extra specific tax just on the purchase of new SUVs. This would be a flat sum, like £2 000 or £5 000, on each SUV regardless of the price of the vehicle.

1. Outline TWO reasons why the government might want to introduce a specific tax just on the purchase of SUVs.
2. Using a demand and supply diagram, explain how the price and quantity bought of SUVs might be affected by this specific tax.
3. Discuss, using the concept of elasticity, just how high the tax would need to be to bring about a significant reduction in purchases of SUVs by those who would never use their vehicles off-road.

12 Static and dynamic market models

Summary

1. The cobweb theorem is a dynamic model of price and output determination.
2. It assumes that suppliers base their output decisions on the price received in the previous time period.
3. Cobwebs can be divergent, convergent or stable.
4. The cobweb theorem predicts that markets do not necessarily converge to their long term equilibrium position.

Static market models

A static model is one where time is not a variable. Time is said to be an **exogenous variable**, a variable which is not determined within the model. The theory of demand, supply and price outlined in unit 6 is an example of a static model.

However it was pointed out that there is a tendency for people who use this model to make a hidden assumption: that there are market forces at work which will move the market from a point where demand does not equal supply to an equilibrium position where the two are equal. To make this assumption explicit would require a more complicated **dynamic** model of price determination, one where time was an **endogenous variable** (i.e. included in the model).

Economists have devised many dynamic models of the market, but in this unit we will consider only one such model, called the COBWEB THEORY.

The assumptions of the cobweb model

The cobweb theory was devised by an American economist, Mordecai Ezekial, in the 1930s. He used it to try to explain why there were price oscillations in the pig market in Chicago. He postulated that farmers based their supply decisions upon the price they received in the previous time period. Mathematically this can be expressed as:

$$Q_t = f(P_{t-1})$$

This says that the quantity supplied (Q_t) in time period t is a function of (i.e. varies with) the price received (P_{t-1}) in the previous time period $_{t-1}$.

Question 1

Supply is given by the following equation:

$$Q_t = 0.5 P_{t-1} - 10$$

where Q_t is quantity supplied in time period t, and P_{t-1} is price in time period t-1.

What would be the level of quantity supplied in 2000 if price in 2001 were:
(a) £60; (b) £100; (c) £300; (d) £250?

The cobweb diagram

The market for carrots can be used to illustrate the workings of the cobweb model. It takes time to plant and grow carrots for sale on the market. Because of this time lag, farmers are assumed within the model to base their decision as to how many carrots to grow this season on the price they received last season. So the supply in 2007 would be dependent upon the prices received by farmers in 2006.

In Figure 12.1, the market is in long run equilibrium at a price of P_0 and quantity Q_0. Assume that in year 1 a severe attack of carrot fly destroys much of the crop such that only Q_1 is available for sale. Consumers will pay a price of P_1 for Q_1 of carrots (remember the demand curve shows how much buyers will purchase at any given price). At the beginning of year 2 farmers have to decide how many carrots to grow. According to the cobweb theorem, they will base their decision on last year's prices. Hence, given that the price was P_1 last year and given that the supply curve remains unchanged, farmers in year 2 will decide to grow Q_2 of carrots. But when they come to sell them they will find that buyers are not prepared to buy Q_2 of carrots at a price of P_1. Farmers cannot store carrots for several years. They have to sell them within 12 months or destroy them. Therefore the price of carrots will have to fall to P_2 to clear the

Figure 12.1 A divergent cobweb
Output is based upon price received in the previous time period. So short term equilibrium, starting at the point A, moves to B, then to C and then to D, steadily moving away from the stable equilibrium price of P_0.

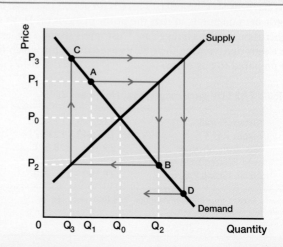

market of Q_2 carrots. At the beginning of year 3, farmers will base their planting decision on the very low price of P_2 obtained the previous year. They will therefore only plant Q_3 of carrots and be pleasantly surprised at the end of the year to receive a price of P_3 for them. In year 4, carrot planting will be higher than in any of the previous years and consequently prices will plummet at harvest time.

The path shown in Figure 11.1, from point A through to point D, shows a market which is moving further and further away from the long term equilibrium price of P_0 and quantity Q_0. This is called a **divergent cobweb**. However, cobwebs can also be either **convergent** or **stable**. A convergent cobweb is shown in Figure 12.2.

Here market forces do act to restore a market to its long run equilibrium position where demand and supply are equal. Figure 12.3 shows a stable cobweb. The market has regular cycles of high prices followed by low prices and there is no tendency for the market either to move nearer the point where demand and supply are equal or to move away from it.

Figure 12.2 *A convergent cobweb*

With a convergent cobweb, price and output move nearer and nearer to the long term equilibrium where demand equals supply. Starting at A, the market moves from B to C and so on.

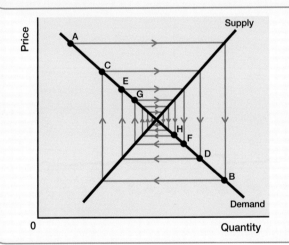

Figure 12.3 *A stable cobweb*

With a stable cobweb, the market neither converges towards equilibrium nor moves farther away from it over time.

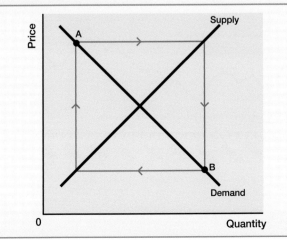

Question 2

Demand and supply are given by the equations:
$$D = 30 - 0.75 P_t$$
$$S = P_{t-1} - 10$$
where D is quantity demanded, S is quantity supplied, P is price and t is time period t.

(a) Draw the demand and supply curves within the quantity range 0 to 30 and the price range 0 to 40.
(b) Will these equations produce a convergent, divergent or stable cobweb?
(c) (i) Draw two new supply curves which would make the cobweb different to your answer in (b).
    (ii) What would be the equation for each of the new supply curves?

Realism of the model

The theory does not suggest that a convergent cobweb is any more likely to occur than a divergent or stable cobweb. However, empirical evidence suggests that divergent cobwebs are not common. Farmers operating in free markets do not base their planting decisions solely on the basis of last year's price. If they did, they would soon learn that it was an inaccurate predictor of current prices. They use more sophisticated techniques, using both past prices and estimates of future supplies from other farmers. Even so, these techniques are unlikely to lead to accurate predictions, especially given the vagaries of the weather and other factors which affect output. Cycles do seem to exist but they are for the most part either stable or convergent. Anyway, many agricultural product markets are regulated by the state in industrialised countries, from rice in Japan to wheat in the USA to beef in the European Union. Such regulation destroys any cobweb-type relationship that might have existed in these markets.

Apart from farming, cobweb-type cycles seem to occur most in highly capital intensive industries. These are industries such as chemicals, paper or semi-conductor manufacturing, where a significant part of the cost of production is plant and machinery rather than raw materials or labour. High prices lead to over-investment in new plant and machinery. This leads to over-production, falling prices and cutbacks in investment. Supply shortages as a result drive up prices leading to a rapid expansion in investment. The cycle then starts all over again.

Key terms

Cobweb theorem - a dynamic model of price determination which assumes that output decisions are based upon price received in the previous time period.

Applied economics

The oil tanker market

In the early 1970s, demand for oil was increasing at a rapid rate. The fuel was cheap and the world economy was expanding. The increase in demand meant that there was an increase in demand for ships to carry that oil. Ship technology was improving and the mid 1970s saw the introduction of VLCCs - very large cargo carriers - huge tankers which were able to cut the average cost of transporting oil because of their size.

At the end of 1973, however, oil prices shot up because of an Arab embargo on oil exports in support of a war by Egypt and Syria against Israel. The war was quickly over and oil exports resumed. But OPEC, the international oil cartel, learnt that it had immense power to push up short term prices to its benefit. By restricting output, it could maintain high prices. During the rest of the 1970s, demand for oil increased very little.

This had significant effects on the oil tanker market. Ship owners had placed large orders for new oil tankers in the early 1970s encouraged by buoyant freight rates for transporting oil. The oil crisis of 1973-74 led to freight rates falling as new tankers entered the market but demand for hiring tankers remained static. This is an example of part of cobweb in action. High prices lead to increased supply. But then oversupply leads to a fall in prices. In this case, the oversupply was made far worse by the political events of the mid-1970s.

Figure 12.4 shows how tanker rates changed in the 1980s, 1990s and early 2000s. For most of this period, ship owners were extremely cautious about ordering new tankers. During the 1980s, as Figure 12.5 shows, there was considerable overcapacity in the tanker market. By the end of the 1980s, this had been eliminated. (Note, there will always be some tankers laid up because of frictions in the market.) This led to some pick up in the shipbuilding market for new tankers. The increase in demand for new tankers was pushed further because old ships built during the boom years of the 1970s were being replaced. New safety requirements, that oil tankers should have a double hull - a hull within a hull - to avoid oil spillages

Figure 12.4 Oil shipping tanker rates

Thousand dollars per day

Tanker rates

Source: adapted from *Economic Outlook*, OECD.

Figure 12.2 Surplus capacity: oil tankers in lay-up, waiting for contract

Millions gross tonnes

Source: adapted from www.iea.org.

Figure 12.6 World-wide production of all types of ships, including oil tankers, million gross tonnes

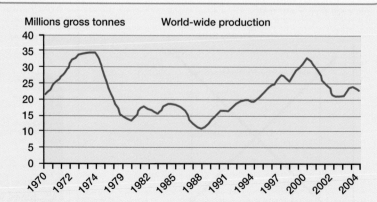

Millions gross tonnes   **World-wide production**

Source: adapted from ssa.org.uk.

if oil tankers run aground or are involved in another type of accident, also increased demand. By the early 2000s, shipyards were booming with new orders for all types of ships as Figure 12.6 shows. Demand for oil, and therefore its transportation, continued to increase. In the early 2000s, growth in demand was particularly strong from the emerging economies of East Asia such as China. The question was whether ship owners were being too optimistic. Were they behaving in the way the cobweb theory would predict, ordering too many tankers when prices for journeys were high, only for there to be too much capacity by 2010 to 2015?

DataQuestion

The pig cycle

Pig meat prices stuck in a trough

Pig prices are at a twenty year low. Factors outside the control of farmers are partly to blame. The Asian crisis of 1998 reduced exports from Europe to the region. The Russian financial crisis in the same year saw exports to Russia, which bought one third of all the EU's pig exports in 1997, collapse.

However, much of the problem can be laid at the door of farmers. In 1997 and the first part of 1998, pig herds expanded in the EU. In part this was a response to an outbreak of swine fever in the Netherlands. Competitors hoped to be able to take up the slack left by the fall in supply from that country.

The UK is also much more affected by trends in production in Europe and the USA than before. In 1998, the US pig market was in a trough, with farmers losing large amounts of money and cutting their herds. The slaughter of unwanted pigs increased the supply of pork in the US and therefore international markets, forcing prices down further. In future, hog cycles in Europe and the US are likely to move more in step than ever before. As a result, the hog cycle could be more volatile.

Source: adapted from the *Financial Times*.

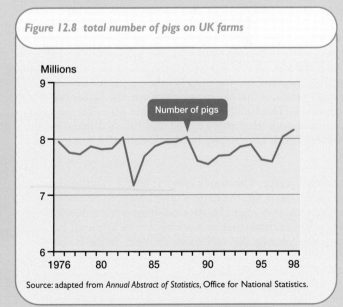

Figure 12.7 Pig prices

Source: adapted from *Annual Abstract of Statistics*, Office for National Statistics.

Figure 12.8 total number of pigs on UK farms

Source: adapted from *Annual Abstract of Statistics*, Office for National Statistics.

1. Explain (a) what is meant by 'the pig cycle' and (b) using diagrams, what might cause the cycle.
2. To what extent does the evidence in Figures 12.7 and 12.8 support the view expressed by the National Farmers' Union that a pig cycle exists in the UK?

3. As a farmer, how might a knowledge of the pig cycle affect your decisions about pig rearing?

Summary

1. In the labour market, the price of labour is the wage paid to workers. It is determined by the demand for and supply of workers.
2. In money markets, money is borrowed and lent. The price of money, the rate of interest, is determined by the demand for and supply of borrowed funds in a money market.
3. In foreign exchange markets, one currency is used to purchase another currency. The price of a currency, like the pound, euro or dollar, is determined by the demand for and supply of that currency at a point in time.

Different markets

In units 3-12, the demand and supply model has been used to explain the workings of goods markets. The term 'goods' in economics is used to describe both goods and services - everything from coal and steel to television sets to holidays and meals out. However, the demand and supply model can equally be used to explain the workings of other markets, such as factor markets, money markets and exchange rate markets.

Factor markets

The **factors of production** are land, labour, capital and entrepreneurship (☞ unit 2). These factors can either be bought and sold, or hired. Land, for instance, can be **rented**. Labour can be **hired** for a wage. The forces of demand and supply in these markets determine the equilibrium price. Take the labour market as an example.

The demand curve The demand curve for labour is downward sloping. This is because employers demand less labour as its price increases. One reason is that the higher the price of labour, the more incentive there is to substitute capital for labour. Another reason is that the higher the wage, the higher the cost of production. This is likely to lead to higher prices for the good being produced. Higher prices will lead to less demand for the good and hence less demand for the workers that produce the good.

The supply curve The supply curve of labour is upward sloping. The higher the wage, the more workers want to be employed. For instance, they might be attracted from other industries. They might currently not be working, but be attracted back into the labour force by the high wages on offer. In the longer term, new entrants to the labour force may train to work in that occupation, increasing supply.

Equilibrium The equilibrium wage is shown in Figure 13.1. When demand equals supply, the wage rate is OA and the level of employment is OB.

Excess demand and supply If the wage rate is different to this, then market forces act to return the market to equilibrium. For instance, assume that the wage rate is OF, above the equilibrium wage rate OG in Figure 13.2. There is then excess supply of labour to the market of

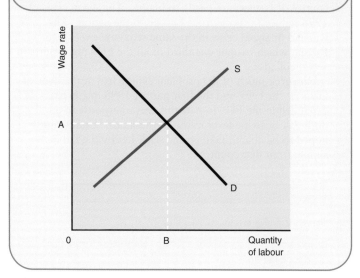

Figure 13.1 The demand for and supply of labour
The equilibrium wage rate of OA in a labour market is fixed by the forces of demand and supply. In equilibrium, OB labour will be demanded and supplied.

AB. Some workers, OA, have got jobs. But AB workers are not employed in this market and want a job. They may be unemployed or they could be working in another industry, for instance at a lower rate of pay. With AB workers wanting a job, employers will be able to offer lower wages and still attract workers to work for them. If, however, they cut wages below OG, there will then be excess demand. Employers will want to employ more workers than want to work at that wage rate. Only at OG does demand equal supply.

Shifts in the demand and supply curves The demand and supply curves for labour can shift. For instance, the demand curve for computer programmers has shifted to the right over the past 20 years as the computer industry has expanded. At any given wage rate, more computer programmers are now demanded. A substantial increase in the number of workers entering the workforce can shift the supply curve of labour to the right. In many Third World countries, very high birth rates have resulted in ever increasing numbers of young workers entering the workforce.

Elasticity The elasticity of demand and supply affects how shifts in demand and supply will change equilibrium wages and the

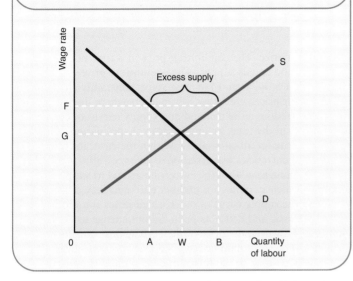

Figure 13.2 Disequilibrium in the labour market
If wages are OF, there is disequilibrium in the labour market because there is excess supply of labour. Wages will be bid down to the equilibrium wage of OG.

levels of employment. For instance, if the supply of labour is highly inelastic, then an increase in demand shown by a shift to the right in the demand curve will bring large increases in wages, but only a small increase in employment. If the demand for labour is highly elastic, an increase in the supply of labour will only decrease wages slightly but there will be a large increase in employment.

Market imperfections Most labour markets are not perfectly free markets. For instance, trade unions attempt to restrict the supply of labour, minimum wage legislation prevents firms from paying below a certain wage and some employers are the sole employers of certain types of workers. These can affect the ways in which the forces of demand and supply determine wages.

Money markets

Money can be borrowed and lent. The price of money is the rate of interest which is charged on the borrowing and lending. There is a large number of different money markets, each with its own rate of interest. For instance, there is the mortgage market where borrowers are individuals wanting to buy a home and lenders are banks and building societies.

The demand curve The demand curve for borrowed money is downward sloping. For instance, the higher the interest rate, the higher the cost of the monthly repayments on a mortgage. Higher interest rates therefore mean that some potential borrowers can no longer afford the repayments, whilst others choose not to borrow because they think the cost is now too high. This discourages some potential house buyers from the market, fewer houses are bought and sold and fewer mortgages are taken out.

The supply curve The supply curve for borrowed funds is upward sloping. For instance, the higher the rate of interest in the mortgage market, all other things being equal, the more profitable it is for lending institutions to lend to potential house buyers, rather than for business loans or personal loans.

The number of jobs for university leavers was up 11.3 per cent this summer on last year's total, according to the Association of Graduate Recruiters (AGR). Although the number of graduates is increasing, it still meant that the average number of applicants per vacancy fell from 37.6 to 32.9.

The Association for Graduate Recruiters represents some of the largest private and public sector employers. It found that the average starting salary for jobs with its employers had risen from £21 000 in 2004 to £22 000 in 2005, an above inflation increase of 4.8 per cent.

Some of the most undersubscribed vacancies are in accounting and professional services where there is international growth in demand for staff. It is in these sectors that there have been some of the fastest rises in graduate salaries.

Starting salaries are highest in London, with an average of £36 500. They are lowest in Northern Ireland at an average of £18 500. For the survey, conducted by the Association of Graduate Recruiters, 45 per cent of new graduate jobs were offered in London.

Source: adapted from the *Financial Times*, 17.7.2005.

(a) Using a demand and supply diagram, explain why the average starting salary for the graduates surveyed by AGR rose from £21 000 in 2004 to £22 000 in 2005.
(b) Explain why 'there have been some of the fastest rises in graduate salaries' in accounting and professional services.

Equilibrium price The equilibrium price or rate of interest is where demand equals supply at OA in Figure 13.3. If there is excess demand for mortgages, banks and building societies will switch funds from other money markets. New mortgage lenders will also be attracted into the market increasing the supply of

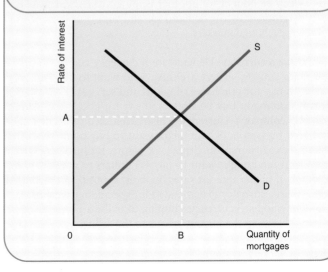

Figure 13.3 Money markets
The price of money is the rate of interest. In the market for mortgages, the equilibrium rate of interest is that which equals the demand for and supply of mortgages at OA.

Question 2

Mortgage lending picked up last month, fuelled by the quarter per cent cut in interest rates by the Bank of England. The value of new lending for home buying rose by 6 per cent to £12.5 billion. Adrian Coles, the director-general of the Building Societies Association, which also reported a pick-up in net advances and mortgage approvals, said: 'Lending has clearly stabilised....The prospect of a housing market crash now seems even more remote; the August interest rate reduction has helped to dispel any gloomy thoughts among homeowners.'

Source: adapted from the *Financial Times*, 21.9.2005.

(a) Explain, using a demand curve diagram, why mortgage lending might have 'picked up last month, fuelled by the quarter per cent cut in interest rates by the Bank of England'.
(b) If the Bank of England increased its interest rates, explain what you would expect to happen to mortgage lending.

funds. If there is excess supply, banks and building societies will switch funds out of the mortgage market to other money markets. Some mortgage lenders may leave the market because they can't do enough business at a profit.

Elasticities Elasticities vary from market to market. For instance, the supply of money to the mortgage market is relatively elastic. Banks and building societies can easily switch funds from other money markets into the mortgage market if they are able to earn higher rates of interest in the mortgage market. The elasticity of demand for mortgages is more difficult to estimate. However, if the elasticity of supply is elastic, large increases in mortgage lending will take place when there is a housing boom with relatively little effect on mortgage interest rates. The supply of mortgage finance is not a constraint to house buying.

Foreign exchange markets

Money can be bought and sold for other currencies (other forms of money). So dollars can be bought with yen, euros with pounds, and roubles with pesos. The price at which one currency can be bought for another is the EXCHANGE RATE. This is determined by the demand for and supply of currencies on foreign exchange markets.

Demand for a currency Demand for a currency comes from three major sources. There are those who want to buy currency in order to pay for purchases of goods and services. For instance, a British firm might buy US dollars to pay for goods it is buying from a US company. Currency is also demanded for saving and investment purposes. Nissan might want to buy pounds sterling to finance expansion of its British car plants, for instance. Or a UK pension fund might want to buy US dollars to take advantage of higher interest rates on bank deposits in the United States. Third, currency is demanded for speculative reasons. Traders buy and sell currencies hoping to make a profit on the difference between the buying price and the selling price.

The demand curve for a currency is downward sloping. The higher the price of a currency, the more expensive it becomes for foreigners to buy goods and services and hence less currency is demanded.

Supply of a currency The supply of a currency comes from those wanting to buy foreign goods and services, savers and investors wanting to invest abroad and currency speculators. The supply curve of a currency is upward sloping. The higher the price of a currency, the cheaper it becomes for businesses and individuals to buy goods from foreigners. Hence, more domestic currency is supplied.

Equilibrium price The equilibrium price of a currency occurs where demand equals supply. The equilibrium price of currencies such as the US dollar and Japanese yen is constantly changing because their prices are set by free markets where there is second by second trading. The demand and supply curves of currencies are shifting all the time, mainly because of speculation. However, this is not true for all currencies. Within the euro, for instance, the price of currencies was fixed on 1 January 1999. Central banks of countries within the euro zone agreed to supply any amount of their currency for another euro currency at a fixed price. So the supply curve of one euro currency for another was perfectly elastic and hence its price did not change as demand changed. However, the price of the euro against non-euro currencies like the pound or the US dollar was constantly changing according to the forces of demand and supply.

Question 3

The pound dropped to $1.76 yesterday, a 13-month low against the dollar, on concerns about falling interest rates and a weakening economy. The immediate trigger for the fall has been a change in expectations about what will happen to UK interest rates. The Bank of England is now expected to cut its 4.75 per cent official interest rate to 4.5 per cent this month. A fall in the Bank of England interest rate will then trigger a fall in a wide range of interest rates in the UK economy.

There are also concerns about the UK's growing trade deficit. Imports of goods are rising at a faster rate than exports. Despite a weakening economy, UK consumers and businesses have shown an increasing appetite for buying goods from abroad. In contrast, Europe, which is the UK's main trading partner, has experienced low growth for some time. Ian McCafferty, chief economist of the CBI employers' organisation, said that weak demand in Europe 'makes it difficult to sell into those markets'.

Source: adapted from the *Financial Times*, 5.7.2005.

(a) 'The exchange rate is a price.' Explain what this means, illustrating your answer from the data.
(b) Why might 'expectations about what will happen to UK interest rates' affect the value of the pound?
(c) Why might 'imports of goods ... rising at a faster rate than exports' lead to a fall in the value of the pound?

Key terms

Exchange rate - the price at which one currency is exchanged for another.

Applied economics

Female wages

Statistics show that women earn on average less than men. In research conducted by the London School of Economics published in 2000, women's earnings over a lifetime were compared with those of men. Table 13.1 shows that under different circumstances, the lifetime gap varied from £143 000 to £482 000. There is a number of different reasons why females earn less than males on average and most are to do with the traditional role of women as child carers.

One is that when women take time out of their career to bring up children, they lose training, skills and experience. What's more, this is at an age when workers tend to be most likely to gain promotion. When women come back to work, they often have to start off at the bottom in their chosen career. Even worse, they may be unable to get a job in their previous occupation and have to start again in another career. Losing skills and experience affects the demand for female workers. The greater the loss, the less employers are prepared to pay for a worker.

Another aspect of female employment is that child carers often take on part-time work. In Spring 2005,

there were 5.6 million female part time workers compared to just 1.7 million male part time workers.

Table 13.2 Employment by occupation, Great Britain, 2004

	Employees and self employed			
	Women		Men	
	millions	% of occupation	millions	% of occupation
Personal service	1.8	84	0.3	16
Administrative and secretarial	2.7	80	0.7	20
Sales and customer service	1.5	69	0.7	31
Associate professional & technical	1.8	48	2.0	52
Elementary	1.5	46	1.7	54
Professional	1.4	42	2.0	58
Managers & senior officials	1.3	33	2.7	67
Process, plant & machine operatives	0.3	15	1.7	85
Skilled trades	0.2	8	2.8	92
All occupations	12.5	46	14.5	54

Note: totals may not add up due to rounding.
Source: adapted from *Labour Force Survey*, Office for National Statistics.

Table 13.1 The pay divide

	Mrs Low-skill, left school with no qualifications, e.g. works as a shop assistant.	Mrs Mid-skill has GCSEs and works in a clerical job, e.g. as a secretary.	Mrs High-skill is a graduate and a professional, e.g. a teacher.
The female forfeit - how much less the woman would earn in a lifetime than a man with similar qualifications, even if she had no children.	£197 000	£241 000	£143 000
	Marries at 21 and has first child at 23 and second at 26. Takes nine years in all out of the labour market and works part-time for a further 26 years.	Marries at 26 and has first child at 28 and second at 31. Out of the labour market altogether for just two years and works part time for a further 12.	Marries at 28, has a first child at 30 and second at 33. Works part time for just a year, working full time for the rest of her working life.
The mother gap - how much less the woman would earn in a lifetime than a woman with similar qualifications but no children.	£285 000	£140 000	£19 000
The parent gap - how much less the woman would earn than a man with similar qualifications, i.e. the female forfeit and mother gap combined.	£482 000	£381 000	£162 000

Source: adapted from *The Guardian*.

Part time working accounted for 44 per cent of all female employment but only 11 per cent for males. Not only do women lose wages because they work part time rather than full time, but also part time jobs tend to be concentrated at the bottom of any occupational structure. This again is a demand side factor. Employers are unwilling to offer better jobs to part time workers because there is a perception that such jobs can only be done by full time workers.

A third problem facing women is that female employment is concentrated amongst low wage industries or occupations. For instance, nearly all secretaries are women, but secretaries are not particularly well paid on average. Table 13.2 shows how unevenly men and women are spread in many occupations. It

could be argued that this is a supply side factor. Women are attracted disproportionately into 'women's jobs' which happen to be less well paid than typical 'men's jobs'. On the other hand, it could be an example of discrimination. Employers offer lower wages for those jobs where they think most employees will be women.

Table 13.1 shows that low skilled women suffer a greater loss of earnings than more highly skilled women. High skilled women are less likely to be trapped in lower wage mainly female occupations. However, they still are likely to suffer some discrimination. Parenthood affects low skilled women the most because they are most likely to take time out to bring up children and are most likely then to become part time workers.

DataQuestion · Recruitment in different markets

The numbers in work have reached record highs whilst unemployment is down to levels not seen since the 1960s. Not surprisingly, skill shortages are reported in a number of industries. In construction, for example, order books are full with a heavy workload of public sector projects in new hospitals, schools and roads adding to strong private sector demand. Robert Leslie, business development director for Robertson Construction's east Scotland division, says: 'There are simply not enough tradesmen available to deliver these projects and we can't train sufficient young people in the short term to satisfy the requirement. Neither is it possible to recruit tradesmen from elsewhere in the UK, as the construction industry as a whole is suffering from the same problem.' In the City of London, there has been strong employment growth in the financial services sector. According to the Centre for Economic and Business Research, the think-tank, a rise in financial transactions, such as new issues and mergers, has prompted a recruitment drive.

Despite this, wage increases are on average relatively low, allowing for a low rate of increase in price of goods and

services across the economy. Mervyn King, governor of the Bank of England, has suggested that this might be due in part to the ability of employers to recruit from overseas. Last year, this was given added impetus by the accession of a number of Eastern European states such as Poland and Latvia to the European Union. Workers from these low wage countries have the automatic right under EU law to be able to work anywhere in the European Union, including the UK. British employers therefore potentially have an enormous labour market from which to draw. In London, the hospitality industry - hotels, restaurants, bars and cafes - has around half of its workforce comprised of non-UK citizens.

Recruiting from abroad has its limitations, though. It is relatively easy to find a Polish construction worker or an Estonian hotel cleaner. But employers like those in the City of London require highly skilled workers. These employers can expect to have to give above average pay rises to attract the right applicants for jobs.

Source: adapted from the *Financial Times*, 27.6.2005.

1. Using a demand and supply diagram, explain why (a) a boom in work and 'full order books' in the construction industry might lead to a rise in wage rates for construction workers; (b) recruitment from overseas might limit pay rises.

2. Analyse why pay rises in the construction industry might be lower than those in financial jobs in the City of London.

3. Discuss whether workers with UK citizenship might be better off or worse off because of the free flow of labour across the European Union.

14 International markets

Summary

1. If one country has lower costs of production for a good than another country, then it is said to have an absolute advantage in the production of that good.
2. International trade will take place even if a country has no absolute advantage in the production of any good. So long as it has a comparative advantage in the production of one good, international trade will be advantageous.
3. Transport costs will limit any welfare gain from international trade. However, economies of scale in production will increase the gains from trade.
4. The terms of trade (the ratio of export prices to import prices) will determine whether trade is advantageous for a country.
5. David Ricardo thought that comparative advantage existed because of differences in labour costs between countries. In the Heckscher-Ohlin model, comparative advantage is explained by differences in factor endowments.
6. The theory of comparative advantage argues that international trade takes place because of differences in the price of products. However, much world trade is the result of non-price competition between countries. Design, reliability, availability and image are some of the factors which determine purchases of foreign goods.
7. In the theory of preference similarity, it is argued that trade takes place because consumers demand more choice than can be provided by domestic producers.

International trade

Many goods and services are traded internationally. For instance, there are international markets in oil, motor vehicles and insurance. There is a number of reasons why international trade takes place.

Availability Some goods can only be produced in specific locations around the world. For instance, Saudi Arabia is oil rich whilst there are almost no known oil reserves in Japan. Fruits like bananas are tropical and so are not grown in the UK.

Price Some countries can produce goods at a relatively cheaper cost than other countries. This may be because of the availability of natural resources, the skills of the workforce or the quality of the physical capital in the economy. Much of the rest of this unit explains this in more detail.

Product differentiation Many traded goods are similar but not identical. For instance, a small hatchback car from one motor manufacturer is very much the same as another. It will, for instance, have four wheels, four seats and an engine. However, the differences mean that some consumers in one country will want to buy a car made in another country, even if domestically produced cars are available at exactly the same price. International trade allows consumers much wider choice about the product they buy. The same basic goods or service can differ in a wide variety of ways. Specifications might be slightly different. There may be different deals on finance available. Delivery times can vary. One product may be better quality than another. Much of world trade is driven by a combination of these factors.

Economists in the 18th and 19th century developed theories centred around why differences in costs led to international trade. These theories, which will now be considered, are as relevant today as they were then.

Absolute advantage

Adam Smith, in his famous example of a pin making factory, explained how specialisation enabled an industry to increase the production of pins from a given quantity of resources (☞ unit 2). In an economy, specialisation exists at every level, from the division of labour in households to production at international level.

Consider Table 14.1. Assume that there are only two countries in the world, England and Portugal. They produce only two commodities, wheat and wine. Labour is the only cost, measured in terms of worker hours to produce 1 unit of output. Table 14.1 shows that it costs more in worker hours to produce a unit of wine in England than in Portugal. Portugal is said to have an ABSOLUTE ADVANTAGE in the production of wine. It can produce both goods but is more efficient in the production of wine. On the other hand, it costs more in worker hours to produce wheat in Portugal than in England. So England has an absolute advantage in the production of wheat. It is clear that it will be mutually beneficial for England to specialise in the production of wheat and for Portugal to specialise in the production of wine and for the two countries to trade.

Table 14.1

| | Cost per unit in worker hours | |
	Wheat	Wine
England	10	15
Portugal	20	10

The same conclusion can be reached if we express relative costs in terms of absolute output. If Portugal could produce either 5 units of wheat or 10 units of wine, or some combination of the two, the relative cost of wheat to wine would be 2:1 as in Table 14.1. If England could produce either 9 units of wheat or 6 units of wine, the relative cost would be 3:2 as in Table 14.1. Hence, Portugal could produce wine more cheaply and England wheat more cheaply.

Question 1

Table 14.2

	UK			France	
	Cars	Computers		Cars	Computers
(a)	10 OR	100		9 OR	108
(b)	5 OR	10		4 OR	12
(c)	20 OR	80		25 OR	75
(d)	5 OR	25		4 OR	30
(e)	6 OR	18		8 OR	16

Two countries with identical resources, UK and France, using all these resources, can produce either cars or computers or some combination of the two as shown above. Assuming constant returns to scale, state which country has an absolute advantage in the production of (i) cars and (ii) computers in each of (a) to (e) above.

Comparative advantage

David Ricardo, working in the early part of the 19th century, realised that absolute advantage was a limited case of a more general theory. Consider Table 14.3. It can be seen that Portugal can produce both wheat and wine more cheaply than England (i.e. it has an absolute advantage in both commodities). What David Ricardo saw was that it could still be mutually beneficial for both countries to specialise and trade.

Table 14.3

	Cost per unit in worker hours	
	Wheat	Wine
England	15	30
Portugal	10	15

In Table 14.3, a unit of wine in England costs the same amount to produce as 2 units of wheat. Production of an extra unit of wine means forgoing production of 2 units of wheat (i.e. the opportunity cost of a unit of wine is 2 units of wheat). In Portugal, a unit of wine costs 1½ units of wheat to produce (i.e. the **opportunity** cost of a unit of wine is 1½ units of wheat in Portugal). Because relative or comparative costs differ, it will still be mutually advantageous for both countries to trade even though Portugal has an absolute advantage in both commodities.

Table 14.4

	Production before trade		Production after trade	
	Wheat	Wine	Wheat	Wine
England (270 worker hours)	8	5	18	0
Portugal (180 worker hours)	9	6	0	12
Total	17	11	18	12

Portugal is relatively better at producing wine than wheat: so Portugal is said to have a COMPARATIVE ADVANTAGE in the production of wine. England is relatively better at producing wheat than wine: so England is said to have a comparative advantage in the production of wheat.

Table 14.4 shows how trade might be advantageous. Costs of production are as set out in Table 14.3. England is assumed to have 270 worker hours available for production. Before trade takes place it produces and consumes 8 units of wheat and 5 units of wine. Portugal has fewer labour resources with 180 worker hours of labour available for production. Before trade takes place it produces and consumes 9 units of wheat and 6 units of wine. Total production between the two economies is 17 units of wheat and 11 units of wine.

If both countries now specialise, Portugal producing only wine and England producing only wheat, total production is 18 units of wheat and 12 units of wine. Specialisation has enabled the world economy to increase production by 1 unit of wheat and 1 unit of wine. The theory of comparative advantage does not say how these gains will be distributed between the two countries. This depends upon the wheat/wine exchange rate, a point discussed below.

The THEORY OF COMPARATIVE ADVANTAGE states that countries will find it mutually advantageous to trade if comparative costs of production differ. If, however, comparative costs are identical, there can be no gains from trade. Table 14.5 shows the maximum output of two countries, A and B of two

Table 14.5

	Output		
	Good X		Good Y
Country A	20	OR	40
Country B	50	OR	100

Question 2

Table 14.6

	Cost per unit in worker hours	
	Meat	Bread
UK	5	10
France	3	4

(a) Which country has comparative advantage in the production of (i) meat and (ii) bread?
(b) The UK has a total of 300 worker hours available for production whilst France has a total of 200. Before any trade took place, the UK produced and consumed 38 units of meat and 11 units of bread. France produced and consumed 20 units of meat and 35 units of bread. How much more could the two countries produce between them if each specialised and then traded?
(c) How would the answer to (a) be different, if at all, if the cost of meat and bread in France were: (i) 4 and 4; (ii) 3 and 7; (iii) 3 and 6; (iv) 6 and 12; (v) 6 and 15; (vi) 1 and 3?

products, X and Y. The Table shows that country A, for instance, can either produce 20 units of good X or 40 units of good Y or some combination of both. The comparative costs or the opportunity cost of production is identical in both countries: one unit of X costs two units of Y. Hence there can be no gains from trade.

The assumptions of the theory of comparative advantage

The simple theory of comparative advantage outlined above makes a number of important assumptions.
● There are no transport costs. In reality, transport costs always exist and they will reduce and sometimes eliminate any comparative cost advantages. In general, the higher the proportion of transport costs in the final price to the consumer, the less likely it is that the good will be traded internationally.
● Costs are constant and there are no economies of scale. This assumption helps make our examples easy to understand. However, the existence of economies of scale will tend to reinforce the benefits of international specialisation. In Table 14.4 the gains from trade will be more than 1 unit of wheat and 1 unit of wine if England can lower the cost of production of wheat by producing more and similarly for Portugal.
● There are only two economies producing two goods. Again this assumption was made to simplify the explanation. But the theory of comparative advantage applies equally to a world with many economies producing a large number of traded goods. Table 14.7 shows that Chile has no absolute advantage in any product. However, it has a comparative advantage in the production of copper. Portugal has a clear comparative advantage in the production of wine whilst England has a comparative advantage in the production of apples. Exactly what and how much will be traded depends upon consumption patterns in all three countries. For instance, if neither Portugal or Chile consume apples, England will not be able to export apples to these countries.
● The theory assumes that traded goods are homogeneous (i.e. identical). Commodities such as steel, copper or wheat are bought on price. But a Toyota car is different from a Ford car and so it is far more difficult to conclude that, for instance, the Japanese have a comparative advantage in the production of cars.
● Factors of production are assumed to be perfectly mobile. If they were not, trade might lead to a lowering of living standards in a country. For instance, assume the UK manufactured steel but then lost its comparative advantage in steel making to Korea. UK steel making plants are closed down. If the factors of production employed in UK steel making are not redeployed, then the UK will be at less than

full employment. It might have been to the UK's advantage to have kept the steel industry operating (for instance by introducing quotas) and producing something rather than producing nothing with the resources.
● There are no tariffs or other trade barriers (☞ unit 40).
● There is perfect knowledge, so that all buyers and sellers know where the cheapest goods can be found internationally.

The terms of trade

In Table 14.4 it was shown that England and Portugal could benefit from trade. Whether trade takes place will depend upon the TERMS OF TRADE between the two countries. From the cost data in Table 14.3, England could produce 2 units of wheat for every 1 unit of wine. It will only trade if it receives more than a unit of wine for every 2 units of wheat. Portugal on the other hand can produce 2 units of wheat for every 1⅓ units of wine. It will only trade if it can give England less than 1⅓ units of wine for 2 units of wheat. Hence trade will only take place if the terms of trade are between 2 units of wheat for 1 unit of wine and 2 units of wheat and 1⅓ units of wine (i.e. between 2:1 and 2:1⅓).

This is shown in Figure 14.1. The cost ratios of wine for two units of wheat are drawn. England will only gain from trade if the international price of wine for wheat is to the right of its existing domestic cost line. Portugal on the other hand will only gain if the international price is to the left of its domestic cost line. Hence trade will only be mutually advantageous if the terms of trade are somewhere between the two lines, the area shaded on the graph.

The terms of trade is defined as the ratio between export prices and import prices:

$$\text{Index of terms of trade} = \frac{\text{Index of export prices}}{\text{Index of import prices}} \times 100$$

It is an **index** (☞ unit 3) because it is calculated from the weighted average of thousands of different export and import prices.

Question 3

Table 14.8

| | Cost per unit in worker hours | | | |
	DVDs	Sweaters	Beefburgers	Chocolate
England	20	10	8	20
Portugal	30	8	12	30
Chile	40	8	4	25

(a) Which country has an absolute advantage in the production of (i) DVDs; (ii) sweaters; (iii) beefburgers; (iv) chocolates?
(b) Which country has a comparative advantage in the production of (i) DVDs; (ii) sweaters; (iii) beefburgers; (iv) chocolates?

Table 14.7

| | Cost per unit in worker hours | | | |
	Apples	Wine	Wheat	Copper
England	10	15	20	50
Portugal	15	10	30	60
Chile	20	20	50	70

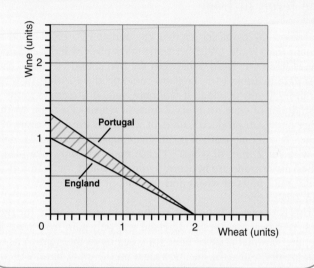

Figure 14.1 The terms of trade
England will find it advantageous to trade only if its terms of trade are at least 1 unit of wine for every 2 units of wheat exported. Portugal will only trade if it can receive at least 2 units of wheat for every 1⅓ units of wine exported. Therefore the terms of trade between the two countries will lie somewhere in the shaded area on the graph.

Why comparative advantage exists

David Ricardo believed that all costs ultimately could be reduced to labour costs. This belief is known as the **labour theory of value**. Hence the price of a good could accurately be measured in terms of worker hours of production. Following on from this, he argued that differences in comparative costs reflected differences in the productivity of labour.

There is an element of truth in this idea. The theory suggests that high labour productivity countries would have a comparative advantage in the production of sophisticated high technology goods whilst low labour productivity countries would have a comparative advantage in the production of low technology goods. Looking at the pattern of world trade, it is true for instance that developing countries export low technology textiles whilst developed countries export high technology computer equipment.

However, neo-classical price theory suggests that labour is not the only source of differing opportunity costs of production. For instance, the price of a piece of agricultural land can increase several times overnight if planning permission is given for residential building. This increase in value has little to do with worker hours of production. Prices and costs are, of course, linked to quantities of labour inputs, but they are also linked to forces of scarcity which can drive prices up or down.

Heckscher and Ohlin, two Swedish economists working in the inter-war period, suggested that different costs were the result not just of different labour endowments between countries but also of different capital and land endowments. If an economy, such as India, has a large quantity of unskilled labour but little capital, then the price of capital relative to labour will be high. If, on the other hand, an economy like the USA has a large stock of capital relative to labour, then capital will be relatively cheap. Hence India will have a comparative advantage in the production of goods which can be made using unskilled labour. The USA will have a comparative advantage in the production of goods which require a relatively high capital input. Saudi Arabia is much more richly endowed with oil than France. France, on the other hand, has a rich abundance of skilled labour and capital equipment in the defence industry. Hence the theory would suggest that Saudi Arabia will specialise in producing oil, France in producing defence equipment and that the two countries will trade one product for the other.

Non-price theories of trade

The theory of comparative advantage provides a good explanation of world trade in commodities such as oil, wheat or copper. Countries with relatively rich endowments of raw materials or agricultural land specialise in the production of those commodities. It also provides a good explanation of the pattern of trade between First and Third World countries. Third World countries tend to export commodities and simple manufactured goods whilst importing more technologically sophisticated manufactures and services from the First World. However, the theory does not account for much of that half of world trade which occurs between the rich developed economies of the world.

Commodities are **homogeneous** products. There is nothing to choose between one grade of copper from Chile and the same grade from Zambia. Therefore the main determinant of demand is price. Manufactured goods and services tend to be **non-homogeneous**. Each product is slightly different. So when a consumer buys a car, price is only one amongst many factors that are considered. Reliability, availability, image, colour, shape and driving performance are just as important, if not more so. There is a wide variety of cars to choose from on the market, some produced domestically but many produced abroad. **Preference similarity theory** suggests that many manufactured goods are imported not because they are relatively cheaper than domestic goods but because some consumers want greater choice than that provided by domestic manufacturers alone. Domestic manufacturers, however, should have a competitive edge because they should be more aware of the needs of their domestic customers. This limits the extent to which foreign manufacturers can penetrate the home market.

Question 4

Look again at the data in Table 14.6.
(a) Show on a graph the price ratios of meat for bread in the two countries before trade.
(b) Would both countries find it mutually advantageous to trade if the international trade price ratio were 1 unit of meat for: (i) 4 units of bread; (ii) 3 units of bread; (iii) 1½ units of bread; (iv) 1 unit of bread; (v) ½ unit of bread; (vi) 2 units of bread; (vii) 1⅓ units of bread?

Question 5

For much of the first half of the 1990s, European alcoholic drinks producers saw their domestic markets as mature markets, producing little or no growth in sales. They looked to exports to grow in size. Developing a brand across international markets is a costly business. There need to be good distribution links established so that the product is available when the customer wants to buy it. Advertising, too, is essential to make customers aware of the value of the brand. Individual products are sold at premium prices. Cutting prices in times of difficulty would devalue the brand in the eyes of customers. After all, those buying Johnnie Walker whisky, Martell cognac or Pernod do so partly because they wish to show that they can afford the best drinks on the market.

In the second half of the 1990s, international drinks manufacturers were hard hit by the Asian crisis, caused by major problems in the financial systems of countries like South Korea and which led to sharp falls in GDP. For instance, Diageo saw its sales fall 40 per cent in the region. The economic rebound in 1999 and 2000 saw a sharp rise in sales, however.

Source: adapted from the *Financial Times*.

(a) Suggest why there is a market for expensive imported alcoholic drinks in countries such as Thailand, South Korea or India when there are locally produced substitutes sold at a fraction of the price.
(b) When sales fell during the Asian crisis, suggest why European drinks producers didn't respond by severely cutting prices.

Key terms

Absolute advantage - exists when a country is able to produce a good more cheaply in absolute terms than another country.
Comparative advantage - exists when a country is able to produce a good more cheaply relative to other goods produced domestically than another country.

Terms of trade - the ratio of export prices to import prices.
Theory of comparative advantage - countries will find it mutually advantageous to trade if the opportunity cost of production of goods differs.

Applied economics

UK trade flows

Table 14.9 UK exports and imports of traded goods and services, national income

£ billion

	Exports		Imports		GVA[1]
	Goods	Services	Goods	Services	
1955	3.1	1.0	3.4	1.0	17.6
1965	5.0	1.6	5.2	1.7	32.8
1975	19.5	7.4	22.7	6.0	99.3
1985	78.2	23.8	81.7	17.0	320.5
1990	102.3	31.6	121.0	27.2	501.4
1995	153.6	49.9	165.6	41.5	639.1
2000	187.9	79.4	220.9	65.7	841.5
2004	190.9	99.1	249.5	78.9	1 033.3

1. Gross value added at factor cost, a measure of national income.
Source: adapted from *Economic Trends*, Office for National Statistics.

Total exports and imports

The UK trades in both goods and services. Table 14.9 shows that both exports and imports of goods have accounted for between approximately three quarters and two thirds of total exports since 1955, whilst exports and imports of services have accounted for a quarter to a third. Foreign trade has increased at a slightly faster rate than that of national income. In 1955, total exports accounted for 24 per cent of national income. By 2004, this had risen to 28.1 per cent.

Visible trade

Although the proportion of trade in goods to services has remained broadly the same in the post-war era, there

Table 14.10 Exports and imports by commodity (% of total value)

		1955	1975	1985	1995	2004
Food, beverages	Exports	6.0	7.1	6.3	7.3	5.5
and tobacco	Imports	36.9	18.0	10.6	9.4	8.9
Basic materials	Exports	3.9	2.7	2.7	1.9	2.0
	Imports	29.0	8.4	6.0	3.9	2.6
Fuels	Exports	4.9	4.2	21.5	6.5	9.4
	Imports	10.6	17.5	12.8	3.7	6.6
Total food and	Exports	14.8	14.0	30.5	15.7	16.9
raw materials	Imports	76.5	43.9	29.4	17.0	18.1
Semi-	Exports	36.9	31.2	25.6	28.3	29.6
manufactured	Imports	17.9	23.9	24.8	27.3	24.1
Finished	Exports	43.5	51.0	41.2	54.8	53.1
manufactured	Imports	5.3	29.9	44.0	54.7	57.1
Total	Exports	80.4	82.2	66.8	83.1	82.7
manufactures	Imports	23.2	53.8	68.8	82.0	81.2
Unclassified	Exports	4.8	3.8	2.7	1.2	0.4
	Imports	0.3	2.7	1.8	1.0	0.7

Source: adapted from *Annual Abstract of Statistics*, *Monthly Digest of Statistics*, Office for National Statistics.

have been some significant shifts in the composition of trade in goods. Table 14.10 gives a breakdown of visible trade (trade in goods) by commodity.

- Exports of fuel, nearly all of which is oil and related products, grew from less than 5 per cent in 1975 to 21.5 per cent of total visible exports by 1985. This was due to North Sea oil which first came on stream in 1976. The importance of oil exports declined from the mid-1980s. Partly this was because volumes of oil extracted from the North Sea remained relatively static whilst other export volumes have been growing at over 3 per cent per year. Partly it was because real oil prices fell. Finally, there was considerable downstream investment in new refineries which meant that more North Sea oil was bought and sold in the UK. This had the effect of reducing North Sea oil exports and also reducing imports of crude oil. However, the jump in the value of fuel exports and imports in 2004 was caused by the commodity price boom which started in 2002-2003. Oil prices shot up and caused a major shift in the relative importance of fuel to both exports and imports. High oil prices should stimulate oil exploration and development in the North Sea and may increase oil production and exports in the future.
- Imports of food and raw materials declined from 76.5 per cent of the total in 1955 to 18.1 per cent in 2004. In the Victorian age, Britain was known as the 'workshop of the world', importing raw materials and exporting manufactured goods. This fall would suggest that the UK has lost comparative advantage in the production of manufactured goods.
- This loss of comparative advantage in manufactured goods is clear from import figures for manufactures. In 1955, manufacturers accounted for only 23.2 per cent of imports. By 2004, this had risen to 81.2 per

cent.

The decline of British manufacturing industry relative to its industrial competitors goes back 100 years. At the turn of the 20th century, many commentators were pointing out how French, German and US manufacturers were overtaking UK firms on both price and quality. In the 1960s and 1970s, industries such as the motor cycle industry and electrical goods were decimated by competition from Japan. Britain's textile industry, once one of the country's most important exporters, has shrunk due to competition, first from Europe and then from Third World countries. In contrast, there have been some success stories such as pharmaceuticals. Inward investment in the 1970s, 1980s and 1990s also transformed the competitiveness of industries such as motor manufacturing and electrical goods.

The theory of comparative advantage is often expressed in terms of relative costs of production. Whilst it is clear that the UK's loss of competitiveness in industries such as textiles has been due to higher relative costs, this is less obvious in industrials such as motor manufacturing. Here, poor quality, unreliability, poor design and long delivery dates were key to the destruction of the industry in the 1970s and 1980s. Equally, high quality, reliability and good design were an essential part of the story of the revival of the British motor manufacturing industry in the 1990s and 2000s.

The loss of UK competitiveness in manufactured goods could be argued to be unimportant if manufactures can be replaced by services. However, as Table 14.9 shows, growth in trade in services in the post-war period has been roughly the same as growth in trade in goods. Table 14.9 also shows that for every 1 per cent fall in exports in goods, services exports need to grow by 2-3 per cent to fill the gap. This would be very difficult to achieve over a period of time. So exports of goods, particularly manufactures, are the most important way in which imports are financed and are likely to remain so.

Table 14.11 Trade in services

				£ billion
	1975	1985	1995	2004
Exports				
Transport	3.4	6.1	10.2	15.4
Travel	1.2	5.4	13.0	15.4
Financial and insurance			7.9	22.0
	2.9	12.1		
Other			18.8	46.3
Total	7.5	23.6	49.9	99.1
Imports				
Transport	3.3	6.4	10.7	18.6
Travel	0.9	4.9	15.8	30.9
Financial and insurance			1.6	4.2
	1.5	4.6		
Other			13.4	25.2
Total	5.7	15.9	41.5	78.9

Source: adapted from the Blue Book, *National Income Accounts Quarterly*, Office for National Statistics; the Pink Book, *United Kingdom Balance of Payments*, Office for National Statistics.

Table 14.12 Income and current transfers

		1955	1975	1985	1995	2004
Income	Credits	0.5	6.5	51.4	88.1	139.7
	Debits	0.4	6.1	52.4	85.9	113.5
Current transfers	Credits	0.2	0.8	4.7	12.6	12.8
	Debits	0.1	1.1	7.6	20.1	23.5

Source: adapted from the Pink Book, *United Kingdom Balance of Payments*.

Trade in services

Table 14.11 shows the composition and change in trade in services since 1975. In 2004, the UK ran a deficit on transport and tourism. For instance, UK citizens spent more on foreign holidays than foreigners taking a holiday in the UK. However, the UK has a significant comparative advantage in financial services and insurance. London is arguably the most important financial centre in the world and provides a wide range of services to foreign customers. Its comparative advantage, despite fierce competition from centres such as New York, Tokyo or Frankfurt, would seem to have grown in recent years, with financial services and insurance taking an increasing proportion of total service exports.

Income and current transfers

There is a third type of flow which forms part of the current account of the balance of payments. This is income and current transfers.

● Income is interest, profits and dividends on overseas assets. Foreigners own assets in the UK and take out income from the UK. This is a debit on the current account. Equally, UK firms and individuals own assets abroad and bring back income to the UK. This is a credit on the current account. Assets include financial assets, such as loans or shareholdings, or physical assets such as property or factories.

● Current transfers are transfers of income. This is made up of payments and receipts between the UK government and other bodies and the European Union (EU). For instance, all customs duties collected in the UK are paid to the EU. On the other hand, the EU pays large subsidies to UK farmers. The EU Social Fund gives grants to deprived regions of the UK.

Table 14.12 shows the UK has tended to receive more in income and current transfers than it has paid out. Income is in fact vitally important for the UK and in the 2000s has been the single most important contributor to the financing of the large deficit in the trade in goods that the UK tends to record. In 2004, income was one third of the value of all credits on the current account (i.e. the value of traded exports of goods and services, income and current transfers) and 24 per cent of all debits as Figure 14.3 shows. It is as if a household paid 24 per cent of its income in mortgage repayments whilst receiving one third of its income from interest on money saved.

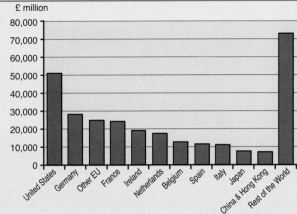

Figure 14.2 The UK's main trading partners, exports 2004

Source: adapted from *Annual Abstract of Statistics*, Office for National Statistics.

Figure 14.3 Credits and debits on the current account, 2004

Source: adapted from the Pink Book, *United Kingdom Balance of Payments*, Office for National Statistics.

Table 14.13 Trade[1] by area

		Percentage of total			
		1955	1975	1995	2004
Europe	Exports	31.9	51.3	60.5	58.3
	Imports	31.0	53.8	63.3	63.4
of which EU[2]	Exports	26.8	41.1	49.5	52.0
	Imports	25.9	45.1	51.0	55.6
North America	Exports	11.3	12.1	15.6	19.8
	Imports	19.8	13.5	15.3	12.7
Other developed countries[3]	Exports	15.3	9.6	5.8	5.6
	Imports	12.4	8.0	7.0	5.5
of which Japan	Exports	0.5	1.6	3.0	2.6
	Imports	0.6	2.8	5.0	2.9
Rest of the World	Exports	41.5	27.0	18.1	16.3
	Imports	36.8	24.7	14.4	18.4
of which China	Exports	-	-	0.5	1.2
	Imports	-	-	1.0	3.3

Source: adapted from *Annual Abstract of Statistics*, *Monthly Digest of Statistics*, the Pink Book, *United Kingdom Balance of Payments*, Office for National Statistics.

1 1955 and 1975 data are trade in goods only. 1995 and 2004 data are trade in goods and services.
2 Includes all 1995 EU countries in 1955 and 1975 percentages; 2004 data are for EU 25 members in that year.
3 Australia, New Zealand, Japan, South Africa

The direction of trade in goods

Table 14.13. shows how the direction of trade in goods has changed over time. In 1955, the UK was still to a great extent following trading patterns established during the Victorian era, buying raw materials from developing countries and selling them manufactured goods. By 2004, UK trade had shifted dramatically. Over half of exports and imports were now with EU countries. Markets in the Third World were relatively unimportant. It has been argued by Eurosceptics that the UK could withdraw from the EU and rely more on its US trading connections. The UK would become the equivalent of Hong Kong or Singapore, a free trading nation benefiting from its geographical location. The problem with this idea, as Figure 14.2 and Table 14.13, show is that the USA is a relatively unimportant trading partner with the UK. Assume that the UK left the EU and as a result the EU imposed higher tariffs and quotas on the UK. If Britain lost just 10 per cent of its exports to the EU as a result, it would have to increase exports by one third to the United States to compensate for this. It is most unlikely that UK exporters have such a comparative advantage that they could achieve this. Certainly from a trade viewpoint, Europe is vital to UK economic interests and is likely, if anything, to increase in importance over time.

DataQuestion

UK manufacturing

Mass production in Britain and other developed countries is over, according to a report published today by the EEF engineering organisation. Cheap labour costs and low cost of transport mean that countries such as China and Thailand can undercut prices for easy to produce, large volume products. However, manufacturing can still thrive in the UK. Successful manufacturing companies have turned to making specialist products for narrow market niches, where volumes are often small but design and quality are high and competition is low.

Source: adapted from the *Financial Times* 13.12.2004.

Peter Weidenbaum is moving his water filter manufacturing operation in Thailand back to his headquarters in Radcliffe, Manchester. His company, Trumeter, has been manufacturing, measuring and monitoring equipment in north west England since 1937. The move back to England is the result of a £1.5 million investment in new machinery following a five year order from a German company. Automation of processes will cut the number of people required on the assembly line from 67 to 5. Peter Weidenbaum says: 'We have been able to move because there is now such a small labour component to the product. Our customer also feels comfortable with this because we don't have the quality assurance issues we sometimes experienced in south east Asia.'

Source: adapted from the *Financial Times*, 6.7.2004.

Halifax Fan makes 1 800 fans a year, most of them different selling from between £200 to £200 000 each. 'Virtually all of them require some special engineering design to fit the product to the requirement of the customer' says Malcolm Staff, managing director. About 70 per cent of the company's fans are exported directly or indirectly.

Source: adapted from the *Financial Times*, 13.12.2004.

Sovrin Plastics is a company in Slough which makes plastic parts for industries such as medical equipment and electronics. With annual sales of £7 million and a workforce of 135, it has found the trading environment tough in recent years. The main problem has been that many of the company's products can be made in countries such as Poland where labour costs are a quarter of those in the UK. 'In the past few years, we have lost a lot of work, both potential and actual orders, to low-cost countries' according to Mr Joiner, Sovrin's managing director. Sovrin's answer has been to move into making more customised parts that are particularly hard to produce and are manufactured in small volumes. It has also invested £600 000 in new machinery.

Source: adapted from the *Financial Times* 10.3.2005.

1. Using the concept of comparative advantage, explain why much production of mass produced manufactured goods has moved to countries such as China or Poland, whilst production of specialised low volume products has remained in countries such as the UK.
2. As countries such as China become more developed, discuss whether the UK could retain any comparative advantage in manufacturing.

Summary

1. The market is a mechanism for the allocation of resources.
2. In a free market, consumers, producers and owners of the factors of production interact, each seeking to maximise their returns.
3. Prices have three main functions in allocating resources. These are the rationing, signalling and incentive functions.
4. If firms cannot make enough profit from the production of a good, the resources they use will be reallocated to more profitable uses.

The role of the market

Adam Smith, in his book *An Enquiry into the Nature and Causes of the Wealth of Nations*, attacked the economic system of his day. It was a system founded upon protectionism, economic restrictions and numerous legal barriers. He presented a powerful case for a free market system in which the 'invisible hand' of the market would allocate resources to everyone's advantage. There are three main types of actor or agent in the market system. Consumers and producers interact in the **goods markets** of the economy. Producers and the owners of the factors of production (land, labour and capital) interact in the **factor markets** of the economy.

The main actors in the market

The consumer In a pure free market system it is the consumer who is all powerful. Consumers are free to spend their money however they want and the market offers a wide choice of products. It is assumed that consumers will allocate their scarce resources so as to maximise their welfare, satisfaction or utility.

The firm In a pure free market, firms are servants of the consumer. They are motivated by making as high a profit as possible. This means maximising the difference between revenues and costs.

- **Revenues.** If they fail to produce goods which consumers wish to buy, they won't be able to sell them. Consumers will buy from companies which produce the goods they want. Successful companies will have high revenues; unsuccessful ones will have low or zero revenues.
- **Costs.** If firms fail to minimise costs, then they will fail to make a profit. Other more efficient firms will be able to take their market away from them by selling at a lower price.

The price of failure - making insufficient profit to retain resources and prevent factor owners from allocating their resources in more profitable ways - will be the exit of the firm from its industry. On the other hand, in the long run firms cannot make higher than average levels of profit. If they did, new competitors would enter the industry attracted by the high profits, driving down prices and profits and increasing output.

Owners of the factors of production Owners of land, labour and capital - rentiers, workers and capitalists - are motivated by the desire to maximise their returns. Landowners wish to rent their land at the highest possible price. Workers wish to hire

themselves out at the highest possible wage, all other things being equal. Capitalists wish to receive the highest rate of return on capital. These owners will search in the market place for the highest possible reward and only when they have found it will they offer their factor for employment. Firms, on the other hand, will be seeking to minimise cost. They will only be prepared to pay the owner the value of the factor in the production process.

Question 1

(a) 'In a free market, consumers have no choice about what they can buy. Firms simply impose their wishes on the consumer.' Use the photograph to explain why this is incorrect.

The function of prices in the market

In a market, there are buyers who demand goods and sellers who supply goods. The interactions of demand and supply fix the price at which exchange takes place. Price has three important functions in a market.

Rationing Consumer wants are infinite, but we live in a world of scarce resources (☞ unit 1). Somehow, those scarce resources need to be allocated between competing uses. One function of price in a market is to allocate and ration those resources. If many consumers demand a good, but its supply is relatively scarce, then prices will be high. Limited supply will be rationed to those buyers prepared to pay a high enough price. If demand is relatively low, but supply is very high, then prices will be low. The low price ensures that high numbers of goods will be bought, reflecting the lack of scarcity of the good.

Signalling The price of a good is a key piece of information to both buyers and sellers in the market. Prices come about because of the transactions of buyers and sellers. They reflect market conditions and therefore acts as a signal to those in the market. Decisions about buying and selling are based on those signals.

Incentive Prices act as an incentive for buyers and sellers. Low prices encourage buyers to purchase more goods. For consumers, this is because the amount of satisfaction or utility gained per pound spent increases relative to other goods. Higher prices discourage buying because consumers get fewer goods per pound spent. On the supply side, higher prices encourage suppliers to sell more to the market. Firms may have to take on more workers and invest in new capital equipment to achieve this. Low prices discourage production. A prolonged fall in prices may drive some firms out of the market because it is no longer profitable for them to supply.

To illustrate how these functions help allocate resources, consider two examples.

Example 1 Assume that lobbying from animal welfare groups changes consumers' tastes. In the market for fur coats, fewer fur coats will be purchased. In the short run, companies are likely to cut prices to boost demand. The fall in price is a signal that market conditions have changed. It also acts as a disincentive to production. At the new low prices, profits fall. So in the long run, some firms will leave the industry, reducing supply. When the price is in long run equilibrium, it will ration supply amongst those customers prepared to pay the new price. Factors markets too will be affected. The demand by firms in the fur industry for workers, equipment and animals will fall. So wages of fur workers may fall. This fall in wages, the price of labour, acts as a signal to workers. The incentive to work in the industry will have fallen so fewer workers will want jobs in the fur trade. Some workers will now leave the industry and get jobs elsewhere in the economy. This is the operation of the rationing function. Meanwhile, consumers will have increased their spending on other goods, for instance on imitation furs. In the short term, the price of imitation furs may rise. This acts as a signal and an incentive for existing firms to expand output and new firms to enter the market. With increased supply, there will be an increase in resources used in the production of imitation furs, an example of the rationing function of prices.

Example 2 There is a large increase in the number of young workers in the population. This increased supply of young workers will force their wages, the price of labour, down. The wage fall acts as a signal to firms that labour is now cheaper. It also acts as an incentive to employ more young workers because they are cheaper. Thus, the allocation of resources changes. Lower wage costs should reduce the costs of firms, which in turn may be passed on to the consumer in the form of lower prices. These lower prices will act as a signal to consumers and provide an incentive for them to increase purchases of goods, again altering the allocation of resources.

Maximising behaviour

In the market mechanism, everyone is assumed to be motivated by self interest. Consumers are motivated by the desire to maximise their welfare or utility. Producers wish to maximise profits. Workers, rentiers and capitalists seek to maximise the returns from the factor that they own. This maximising behaviour determines the way in which resources are allocated.

Consumers, for instance, will spend to maximise their satisfaction or utility. They cast spending 'votes' between different products and different firms. If consumer tastes change so that they want more ice cream and fewer hot dogs, then they will spend more on ice cream

and less on hot dogs. Ice cream manufacturers will collect more money from the sale of ice cream which they will use to expand production. Manufacturers of hot dogs will be forced to lay off staff, buy fewer raw materials and in the long term shut factories.

Profit and not revenue is the signal to firms to change levels of production. When consumers demand more ice cream, firms will expand production only if it is profitable to do so. Hot dog manufacturers will shut down manufacturing plant only if these resources could be used at higher profit levels elsewhere. In a free market, changes in consumer demand are met by changes in patterns of production by firms because of their desire to maximise profit.

Question 2

Pioneer, the Japanese electronics manufacturer, is to close about one-quarter of its global manufacturing facilities. It will consolidate its 40 manufacturing facilities into 30 and reduce its workforce by 5 per cent, or 2 000 jobs, mostly outside Japan.

The move is in response to sharp falls in price in its main markets for plasma display panels (one type of flat screen television) and DVD recorders. Pioneer forecasts demand for plasma display panels to grow from 2.4 million in the year to the end of March 2005 to 11 million by March 2009. However, prices have recently fallen by 40 per cent. This has been due to an aggressive expansion of supply by manufacturers worldwide who have acted on predictions that flat screen televisions will replace traditional television sets. But the falls in price have led most flat screen television manufacturers to make losses on every set they now produce. Like Pioneer, they have a choice: they either have to cut their costs of manufacturing to be able to make a profit on each set sold, or they must leave the market.

Source: adapted from the *Financial Times*, 24.3.2005.

Explain how prices for flat screen televisions have:
(a) acted as signals to the market;
(b) provided incentives to consumers and firms to allocate their resources.

Judging the market

Markets are one way of allocating resources. There are alternatives. For instance, the government could allocate resources as it does with defence, education or the police. Economists are interested in knowing how to judge whether markets are the best way of allocating resources. There are two main ways in which they do this.

First, they consider whether markets are **efficient** (☞ unit 16) ways of allocating resources. By this, we mean whether firms produce at lowest cost and are responsive to the needs of consumers as in the ice cream and hot dog example above. Second, they consider issues of **equity** (☞ units 16 and 20). Efficiency takes income distribution for granted. But is income and wealth in society distributed in an acceptable way?

If resources are allocated inefficiently and inequitably, then there may be a case for governments to intervene, either by altering conditions in the market or by removing production from the market mechanism altogether. Units 16-22 consider these complex issues.

Question 3

Samsung Electronics, the South Korean manufacturer, has come from nowhere to become a global force in products such as memory chips, flat panel displays and mobile phones. Last week, the company held an unusual news conference dedicated to its new MP3 players, declaring it would increase its share of the mini hard disk-drive music player market from just 7.7 per cent now to become the world's top producer, unseating Apple which controls 70 per cent, by 2007.

Apple's iPod has proved an unexpected and spectacular success. Easy to use and with a 'cool', 'must have' image amongst its young buyers, it has transformed the fortunes of Apple. The company quadrupled its first quarter profits this year compared to last year's figures on the back of sales of the iPod.

Samsung hopes young people will be lured to its multi-functional MP3 players with a built-in voice recorder, camera and radio tuners, which will allow users to play electronic games, watch music videos and movies and take digital photographs. Technologically, the company has a strong technological

advantage over Apple because it is the world's largest producer of flash memory chips, a key component of MP3 players. Samsung's global brand power and sales network are also expected to help it increase market share in the US. This year, the company plans to spend $40 million on marketing for its MP3 players.

Analysts warn, though, that Samsung's strategy may not work, as many consumers still prefer simple products with user-friendly interfaces, which is the strength of iPod. 'Cool' is also very difficult to capture in a copycat product. Yet it is the 'cool' factor which allows products such as Nike shoes and BMW cars to be sold at higher prices than competing products and generates large profits for their owners.

Source: adapted from the *Financial Times*, 30.3.2005.

(a) Explain, using Samsung as an example, the role of profit in allocating resources.

Applied economics

Motor cars

The history of the UK motor car industry in recent decades is a good example of how markets allocate resources. In the 1950s and 1960s, the British market was insulated to a great extent from foreign competition. The British motorist bought cars made in British factories, even if some of these factories were owned by foreign companies such as Ford. It was largely a sellers' market, with demand constrained by the ability of consumers to obtain credit for the purchase of cars.

However, the car industry suffered two major weaknesses at the time. First, it failed to address problems of quality. In a sellers' market, firms were under no pressure to manufacture world beating cars. Second, there was underinvestment by the industry. This was perhaps not surprising given the poor profitability of some companies. For instance, the original Mini car, first produced in 1959, failed to make a profit in its first five years of production because its price was set too low. Poor profitability led to rationalisation, with companies being taken over by others, and production was streamlined. However, the necessary investment in new production processes and facilities lagged behind the UK's main overseas competitors.

The weakness of the British motor industry became apparent in the 1970s and 1980s as shown in Figures 15.1 and 15.2. Imports soared, whilst exports declined. Domestic production fell from a peak of 1.9 million cars per year in 1972 to 0.9 million by 1984.

What happened was that UK consumers increasingly wanted to buy foreign cars because they were better built, more reliable and, in the case of Japanese cars, more keenly priced. Equally, foreign customers turned away from British cars, reducing exports to a third of their 1960s levels. British car manufacturers responded by closing factories, laying off workers and reducing orders for components. The reduction in demand for British made cars resulted in a fall in demand for the factors of production used to manufacture those cars.

The mid-1980s was a turning point for British motor manufacturing. Arguably the most important factor in forcing change was the arrival of Japanese manufacturers in the UK. Honda established a working partnership with Rover and also built an engine plant in Swindon. Nissan built a new car plant in the North East of England, followed by Toyota which set up in Derby. They came to the UK because they wanted to sell more cars in Europe. At the time, they were prevented from selling as many cars as they wanted because European countries had fixed limits on Japanese imports to protect their own car manufacturers from competition. England was in the European Union and so there would be unlimited access into Europe for Japanese cars built in the UK. Japanese car producers lifted car production numbers in the UK simply by establishing plants here. But they also had an important effect on US and European car manufacturers. Japanese cars were increasingly popular with customers across the globe. Companies like General Motors and Ford could see that unless they could produce cars to the same quality and price as Japanese competitors, they would be driven out of the market. They responded by changing the way in which they designed and built cars. They adopted Japanese production methods such as just-in-time deliveries of components to factories. Workers were given far greater skills. New investment and new models were given to car plants which could show that they had high levels of productivity. British factories in particular were given a choice. Either they adopted new ways of working or they would be starved of investment and eventually closed. If British factories could not supply the right goods, the market would force them to shut down.

Market forces also played a part in the decision by the Japanese to come to the UK. In the first half of the 1980s, the government of Margaret Thatcher pursued **supply side policies** (☞ unit 38) which attracted foreign investment. Trade union power was curbed. Taxes on company profits were cut. Higher rates of tax paid by company executives were slashed. Finally, taxes paid by employers on their workers fell. The poor performance of the UK economy in the 1960s and 1970s relative to other European countries also

meant that wages in the UK were now often lower than in Germany or France. Low taxes and low wages acted as powerful incentives for the Japanese and other foreign countries to set up in the UK.

In the 1990s, as Figures 15.1 and 15.2 show, the UK car industry made a substantial recovery. Domestic production increased from 1.3 million cars in 1990 to 1.8 million cars in 1999, an increase of nearly 40 per cent. Over the same period, exports rose 73 per cent whilst imports only rose 49 per cent. The market was signalling that UK car plants could be as competitive, if not more competitive, than foreign car plants. The market was also providing an incentive for car manufacturing firms to invest in their UK car plants because they could be as profitable, if not more profitable, than car plants abroad.

The highly competitive nature of the car industry if anything intensified in the 2000s. For example, countries in Eastern Europe which joined the EU in 2004, with their low wage labour force and low taxes, saw significant investment by multinationals. As a result, a boom in car sales in the UK, rising from 2.3 million cars a year in 2000 to 2.6 million cars a year in 2004, was supplied entirely by imports rather than an increase in domestic production. Another example of the fierce nature of competition in the market was the collapse in 2004 of Rover, the UK's only remaining UK-owned mass car manufacturer.

Despite this competition, the long term future of the UK car industry looks secure. UK car plants, for the most part, are competitive. Nissan's car plant in Sunderland has the highest labour productivity in Europe and is also Nissan's most productive plant worldwide. This shows that British car plants can be world class units if managed effectively and if their owners continue to invest in them.

Figure 15.1 Annual production and sales of cars, UK (millions)

Source: adapted from *Economic Trends Annual Supplement*, Office for National Statistics.

Figure 15.2 Annual exports and imports of cars, UK (millions)

Source: adapted from *Economic Trends Annual Supplement*, Office for National Statistics.

DataQuestion   The market for mobile phones

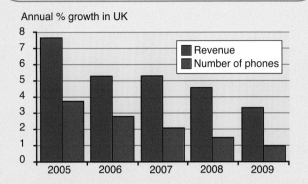

Figure 15.3 Growth in revenues and physical number of mobile phones, UK, forecast 2005-2009

Source: adapted from Ovum.

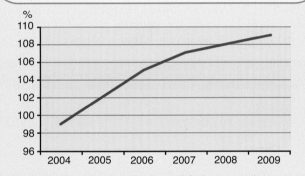

Figure 15.4 Mobile phone penetration: number of phones as a percentage of the population¹

1. More than 100 per cent shows that some mobile phone owners have two or more phones.

Source: adapted from Ovum.

The UK mobile phone market is now so competitive that it could force one of the major players out of the market within the next twelve months, according to Peter Erskine, the chief executive of O_2. There are four established networks in the UK - Vodafone, Orange, T-Mobile and O_2. A newcomer to the market, 3 UK, has quickly gained market share by undercutting the prices of the established networks. They are also facing competition from so-called 'virtual operators'. These are companies which don't own any of the infrastructure for mobile telephony, such as masts and cables. Instead, they rent capacity from companies such as Vodafone which do have physical infrastructure. The most successful of the virtual operators has been Virgin Mobile which now has 5 million customers after just five years. But virtual operators such as BT (British Telecom) and Tesco may prove strong competitors too.

Source: adapted from the *Financial Times*, 23.3.2005.

Relatively new entrants to the UK mobile phone market have tended to gain market share by undercutting their more established rivals in price. Virgin Mobile, for example, has targeted the pre-pay market, where customers don't have an annual contract but simply buy phone minutes up-front. These customers typically spend just £10 a month compared with the average contract customer for one of the main networks that spends more than £500 a year. 3, the latest entrant to the market to have its own infrastructure, has undercut its more established rivals on price in the contract market. It is also in the forefront of offering the latest generation 3-G technology. 3-G will allow a wide range of new services to be offered to customers including Internet connection and video and music downloads. These new services will be offered at premium prices, earning companies high profits. The winning companies will be those that offer the right mix of 'must have' services at the right price.

Source: adapted from the *Financial Times*, 23.3.2005.

1. Describe the forecast trends shown in Figures 15.3 and 15.4 in the mobile phone market.
2. Explain how prices function to ration, signal and provide incentives in the mobile phone market.
3. 'The UK mobile phone market is now so competitive that it could force one of the major players out of the market within the next twelve months.' Discuss how profits allocate resources within a market, using the mobile phone market as an example.

Summary

1. Static efficiency refers to efficiency at a point in time. Dynamic efficiency concerns how resources are allocated over time so as to promote technical progress and economic growth.
2. Productive efficiency exists when production is achieved at lowest cost.
3. Allocative efficiency is concerned with whether resources are used to produce the goods and services that consumers wish to buy.
4. All points on an economy's production possibility frontier are both productively and allocatively efficient.
5. Free markets tend to lead to efficiency.
6. Market failure occurs when markets do not function efficiently. Sources of market failure include lack of competition in a market, externalities and missing markets.

Efficiency

The market mechanism allocates resources, but how well does it do this? One way of judging this is to consider how **efficiently** it resolves the three fundamental questions in economics of how, what and for whom production should take place (☞ unit 2). Efficiency is concerned with how well resources, such as time, talents or materials, are used to produce an end result. In economic terms, it is concerned with the relationship between scarce inputs and outputs. There are a number of different forms of efficiency which need to be considered.

Static vs dynamic efficiency

STATIC EFFICIENCY exists at a point in time. An example of static efficiency would be whether a firm could produce 1 million cars a year more cheaply by using more labour and less capital. Another example would be whether a country could produce more if it cut its unemployment rate. Productive and allocative efficiency (discussed below) are static concepts of efficiency. Economists use them to discuss whether more could be produced now if resources were allocated in a different way. These concepts can be used, for instance, to discuss whether industries dominated by a monopoly producer might produce at lower cost if competition were introduced into the industry (☞ unit 18). Or they might be used to discuss whether a firm should be allowed to pollute the environment (☞ unit 19).

DYNAMIC EFFICIENCY is concerned with how resources are allocated **over a period of time**. For instance, would there be greater efficiency if a firm distributed less profit over time to its shareholders and used the money to finance more investment? Would there be greater efficiency in the economy if more resources were devoted to investment rather than consumption over time (☞ unit 27)? Would an industry invest more and create more new products over time if it were a monopoly than if there were perfect competition (☞ unit 18)?

Productive efficiency

PRODUCTIVE EFFICIENCY exists when production is achieved at lowest cost. There is productive inefficiency when the cost of production is above the

minimum possible given the state of knowledge. For instance, a firm which produces 1 million units at a cost of £10 000 would be productively inefficient if it could have produced that output at a cost of £8 000.

Productive efficiency will only exist if there is TECHNICAL EFFICIENCY. Technical efficiency exists if a given quantity of output is produced with the minimum number of inputs (or alternatively, if the maximum output is produced with a given

Question 1

Table 16.1

Output	Minimum input levels	Units
	Labour	Capital
10	4	1
20	8	2
30	11	3
40	14	4
50	16	5

(a) Firm A uses 21 units of labour and 6 units of capital to produce 60 units of output. A competing firm uses 19 units of labour and 6 units of capital to produce the same output. Explain whether Firm A is more technically efficient than the competing firm.

(b) Firm B uses 24 units of labour and 7 units of capital to produce 70 units of output. Firm B pays £10 000 to employ these factors. A competing firm employs the same number of factors to produce the same level of output but only pays £8 000 for them. Explain whether Firm B is more productively efficient.

(c) Now look at Table 16.1. From the table, which of the following combinations are: (i) technically efficient and (ii) productively efficient if the minimum cost of a unit of labour is £100 and of a unit of capital is £500?
(1) 8 units of labour and 2 units of capital to produce 20 units of output at a cost of £1 800. (2) 15 units of labour and 4 units of capital to produce an output of 40 units at a cost of £3 500. (3) 4 units of labour and 1 unit of capital to produce 10 units of output at a cost of £1 000.

number of units). For instance, if a firm produces 1 000 units of output using 10 workers when it could have used 9 workers, then it would be technically inefficient. However, not all technically efficient outputs are productively efficient. For instance, it might be possible to produce 1 000 units of output using 9 workers. But it might be cheaper to buy a machine and employ only 2 workers.

Equally, Firm A might be using a machine and two workers to produce a given output. However, if it is paying £100 000 a year for this, whilst a competing business is paying only £80 000 a year for the same factor inputs, then Firm A is productively inefficient.

Allocative efficiency

ALLOCATIVE or ECONOMIC EFFICIENCY is concerned with whether resources are used to produce the goods and services that consumers wish to buy. For instance, if a consumer wants to buy a pair of shoes, are the shoes available in the shops? If a consumer wants schooling for her child, is education available?

There are many examples of where allocative efficiency is not present. In the Second World War, a system of rationing in the UK limited what consumers could buy. They were not free to buy more food and less clothing because both food and clothing could only be bought using coupons issued by the government. In the Soviet Union (now Russia), there were constant chronic shortages of consumer goods. What was available was often distributed via queuing mechanisms. Consumers did not have the power to choose between shoes and food because shoes might be unavailable in the shops at the time.

Allocative efficiency occurs when no-one could be made better off without making someone else worse off. In the Second World War, for instance, some people would have preferred to buy more clothes and consume less food. Others wanted more food and fewer clothes. Allocative efficiency would have been greater if people had been allowed to trade their clothes coupons for food coupons because both groups would have gained.

Efficiency and the production possibility frontier

The various concepts of efficiency can be illustrated using a **production possibility frontier** or **PPF** (☞ unit 1). A production possibility frontier shows combinations of goods which could be produced if all resources were fully used (i.e. the economy were at full employment).

There is productive efficiency in an economy only if it is operating on the PPF. To understand why, consider an economy where all industries except the shoe industry are productively efficient. This means that the shoe industry is not operating at lowest cost and is using more resources than is necessary for its current level of output (i.e. it is technically inefficient). If the shoe industry became technically efficient, it could produce more shoes without reducing the output of the rest of the economy. Once the shoe industry is productively efficient, all industries are productively efficient and output cannot be increased in one industry without reducing it in another industry. But this is true about any point on the PPF. In Figure 16.1, the economy is initially at B, within the PPF. The shoe industry is productively inefficient because YZ more shoes could be produced without affecting the output, OX, of the rest of the economy. At A, the shoe industry cannot produce any more shoes without taking away resources from other industries and causing their output to fall. Hence the shoe industry must be productively efficient at A.

All points on the PPF are productively efficient because at any point, production must be taking place using the least amount of resources. All points are also allocatively efficient. Points to the right of the PPF are not obtainable. If production takes place within the PPF, it is possible to gain both more shoes and more of all other goods which can be distributed to consumers. So consumers don't have to give up shoes in order to get more of all other goods. On the frontier, a trade-off has to be made. So at any point on the frontier, a movement to another point would involve giving up one good for another. It is not possible to say which point is the most socially desirable because we would need information about social preferences to make this judgment.

Question 2

In some areas of the country, some state schools are over-subscribed. This means that there are more children wanting to come to the school than there are places available. In such circumstances schools have to choose their children according to admission rules. Typically, these are based on catchment areas. Children who live close to the school get in. Those who live further away do not. This might not be the most efficient way of allocating places. Some economists have advocated giving each child in the country a voucher worth £x which is handed over to their school and then cashed in to pay for the expenses of running the school. Oversubscribed schools could charge fees over and above the value of the voucher. The size of the fee would be fixed to limit the number of entrants to the school to the number of places offered. Just as in, say, the market for second hand cars, if some cars are more popular than others then car sellers can charge higher prices, so would be the case in the education market. Resources will thus be efficiently allocated.

(a) Why might it be argued that there is allocative inefficiency in areas where some schools are oversubscribed?
(b) What might be the advantages and disadvantages to introducing a voucher and fee system in education?

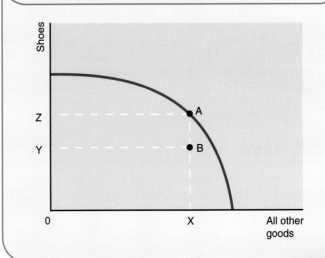

Figure 16.1 *Efficiency and the production possibility frontier*
At B, the economy is productively inefficient because more shoes could be produced without affecting the amount of all other goods available. All points on the PPF are productively efficient and allocatively efficient.

Question 3

Privatisation (the transfer of ownerships of assets from the government to the private sector) in the UK in the 1980s and 1990s led to a considerable reduction in the number of workers employed in the industries that were privatised. In electricity, gas, the railways and water, fewer workers were employed after privatisation to produce the same amount of goods and services. In the case of coal, the output of coal and the number of miners employed declined substantially after privatisation as coal mines found that demand for UK coal fell. The main customer for coal, the electricity industry, switched to gas fired power stations and also increased its imports of cheaper foreign coal.

(a) Using a production possibility diagram, explain the effect of privatisation on productive efficiency in the UK.
(b) Using a production possibility diagram and labelling the axes 'coal' and 'all other goods', explain how privatisation coincided with a change in allocative efficiency.

The market and economic efficiency

Markets often lead to an efficient allocation of resources. In a market where there are many buyers and sellers, competition forces producers to produce at lowest cost. If they fail to do so, buyers will purchase their goods from lower cost firms. So competitive markets tend to lead to productive efficiency. Markets also tend towards allocative efficiency. Customers are able to cast their spending 'votes' in the market. This determines what is produced. If consumers want to buy more shoes and fewer garden chairs, then shoe firms will expand production, whilst manufacturers of garden chairs will cut back on their production. Free markets allow this transfer of productive resources from one use to another.

Market failure

Markets, though, do not necessarily lead to economic efficiency. MARKET FAILURE, where markets lead to economic inefficiency, can occur for a number of reasons. These will be considered in detail in units 18 to 22. However, market failure occurs for a number of reasons.

Lack of competition in a market (☞ unit 18) Economic efficiency is likely to be present in a market where there are many buyers and sellers. But in many markets, there are either only a few buyers or a fewer sellers. In the rail transport industry, for instance, most travellers have no choice about which company to use on a particular journey. In the water industry, households are forced to buy their water from one company. In the UK soap powder market, two firms dominate sales. In the defence industry, the UK government is the only UK buyer of goods. Trade unions would like to be in a position where only union members work in a place of work. Where there is **imperfect competition**, there is likely to be market failure. Firms which dominate their markets, for instance, will attempt to charge high prices in order to make greater profit. But they can only do this by restricting supply to the market, denying customers the ability to buy as much as they would have done if the market had been competitive. This leads to allocative inefficiency. Trade unions can push up costs to firms if they are successful in getting higher wages for their members than the market rate. This leads to productive inefficiency.

Externalities (☞ unit 19) Prices and profits should be accurate signals, allowing the actors in the market mechanism to allocate resources efficiently. In reality, prices and profits can be very misleading. This is because actual prices and profits may not reflect the true prices and profits to society of different economic activities. For instance, in Brazil it makes commercial sense to cut down the rain forest to provide grazing land for cattle sold to the West as meat for hamburgers. But this could lead to economic catastrophe in the long term because of the effects of global warming. The market is putting out the wrong signals and leading to economic inefficiency and a misallocation of resources.

Missing markets (☞ unit 20) The market, for a variety of reasons, may fail to provide certain goods and services. Some goods such as defence (called **public goods**) will not be provided by the market. Other goods, called **merit goods**, will be underprovided. Health care and education are two examples of merit goods. Part of the reason for underprovision is that the market mechanism can be poor at dealing with risk and providing information to agents in the market.

Information failure In an efficient market, both buyers and sellers have good knowledge of the product. Sometimes, though, information is imperfect (☞ unit 20). For example, a consumer buying a soft drink is likely to have tried out a variety of drinks before. The beer being bought is likely to be something the consumer likes and so the consumer has good information about the product. But what about the purchase of a washing machine which the consumer might only make every 8 years? In this case, the consumer might have imperfect information and make the wrong choice. Other examples relate to situations where the consumer is most unlikely ever to have greater information than the seller. If a dentist recommends a treatment when the patient is not in any pain, how does the patient know that the treatment is really in his or her best interest? Could it be that the dentist is more interested in gaining a fee than treating the patient?

Factor immobility Factors of production (land, labour and capital, ☞ unit 2) may be immobile. This means that they are difficult to transfer from one use to another. For instance, a train once built is only useful as a train. It cannot be changed into a car or a plane. As for labour, workers can be immobile.

A coal miner made redundant might have few skills to offer in other types of work. So he or she may find it difficult to get a job. An unemployed worker in a high unemployment area might be unable or not be willing to move to a job in a low unemployment area. For instance, it may be impossible to find housing at an affordable rent or price in the low unemployment area. Or the worker might not want to leave family and friends in the local area. The greater the immobility of factors, the more time it will take for markets to clear when there is a shock to the economic system. Factor immobility was one of the reasons why the North of England, Wales, Scotland and Northern Ireland suffered above average unemployment rates during the 1960s, 1970s and 1980s. Traditional heavy primary and manufacturing industries were concentrated in these areas. As they declined, workers were made redundant. However, new industry with new capital was not created in sufficient volume to compensate for the decline of old industries. Unemployed workers found it hard, if not impossible, to get jobs. But neither were sufficient workers prepared to leave these regions to find employment in low unemployment areas of the UK.

Inequality Market failure is not just caused by economic inefficiency. It can also be caused by **inequality** in the economy. In a market economy, the ability of individuals to consume goods depends upon the income of the household in which they live. Household income comes from a variety of sources.

- Wages are paid to those who work outside the household. In the labour market, different wages are paid to different workers depending on factors such as education, training, skill and location.
- Interest, rent and dividends are earned from the wealth of the household. Wealth may include money in bank and building society accounts, stocks and shares, and property.
- Private pensions are another type of unearned income. Private pensions represent income from a pension fund which can be valued and is a form of wealth.

- Other income includes state benefits such as unemployment benefit, child benefit and state pensions.

The market mechanism may lead to a distribution of income which is undesirable or unacceptable. For instance, income levels may be so low that a household is unable to afford basic **necessities** (☞ unit 1) such as food, shelter or clothing. If healthcare is only provided by the private sector, a household may not be able to afford medical care. The state may then need to intervene, either to provide income in the form of benefits, or goods and services such as healthcare to increase consumption levels.

Key terms

Allocative or economic efficiency - occurs when resources are distributed in such a way that no consumers could be made better off without other consumers becoming worse off.
Dynamic efficiency - occurs when resources are allocated efficiently over time.
Market failure - where resources are inefficiently allocated due to imperfections in the working of the market mechanism.
Productive efficiency - is achieved when production is achieved at lowest cost.
Static efficiency - occurs when resources are allocated efficiently at a point in time.
Technical efficiency - is achieved when a given quantity of output is produced with the minimum number of inputs.

Applied economics

The Common Agricultural Policy (CAP)

When the European Union (EU), formerly the European Community, was first formed there was a commitment to free trade between member countries. This found its first major expression in 1962 in the Common Agricultural Policy, a Community-wide policy which aimed to harmonise the agricultural policies of the original six member countries (☞ unit 21). One of the implicit aims of CAP was to increase efficiency in the market for agricultural products. To what extent has this been achieved?

Productive efficiency has certainly increased. Table 16.3 shows that the number of small, relatively inefficient, farms has declined over time whilst the number of large farms over 50 hectares with lower overall costs has increased. There has been a substantial fall in employment in the agricultural sector

as Table 16.4 shows. At the same time, due to more intensive farming methods, more use of fertilizers and machinery and higher yielding crop and animal strains, output has risen.

However, European agriculture is not fully productively efficient. There are still far too many small farmers producing on marginal land, such as in Wales or the French Alps. In 2000, considering the 25 EU member countries that had joined by 2004, the average size of a farm ranged from 1.3 hectares in Malta, to 23.7 hectares in Belgium, 45.8 hectares in France and 84.6 hectares in the UK. Small farmers are unable to exploit the economies of scale enjoyed by large farms and consequently their costs of production are much higher.

But it could be argued that the difference in

productivity between farms in Europe is not as important an issue as the difference in the cost of production between the EU and the rest of the world. World prices for many agricultural commodities, such as wheat or butter, have been considerably below those maintained by the complex system of tariffs, quotas and intervention prices in the EU.

Consumers lose out because of these high domestic prices. Their loss can be calculated by multiplying the amount they purchase by the difference between domestic and world farm gate prices.

However, farmers worldwide also tend to be supported by the taxpayer. Figure 16.2 shows the extent of the subsidies paid to farmers throughout the world. In the EU, for instance, farmers in 2004 received in subsidies an average 33 per cent of the market value of what they produced.

The agricultural market is not just productively inefficient. It is arguably allocatively inefficient. The fact that taxpayers throughout the developed world are having to subsidise farmers means that the marginal cost of production far exceeds the price consumers are prepared to pay. Allocative efficiency could therefore be increased by shifting resources out of agriculture into other industries.

Over the past 20 years, there has been an increasing awareness of the costs of CAP and other agricultural support systems. In the latest Doha round of trade talks, many Third World countries along with agricultural exporting countries such as Australia and New Zealand were fighting to get trade in agricultural products liberalised. In practice, this means both the EU and the USA dismantling their support regimes for agriculture. In the EU, there is strong resistance to a reduction in subsidies to farmers from certain countries, particularly those which benefit the most from CAP, such as France.

The abolition of CAP would produce losers as well as gainers. Land prices would plummet because prices for produce would fall substantially. Marginal farmers too would lose because their land would not be

productive enough to support them in business. The experience of New Zealand, which almost abolished farm subsidies in the 1980s, suggests, however, that farm profits would remain roughly constant. There would be lower prices and less state handouts. But equally, the costs of production, particularly rents on farms, would fall too leaving most farmers on good farming land with broadly similar incomes.

Table 16.4 Employment in agriculture, hunting, forestry and fishing

					Millions
	1970	1980	1990	2000	2003
Greece	1.3	1.0	0.9	0.7	0.6
Spain	3.7	2.2	1.5	1.0	0.9
France	2.8	1.8	1.4	1.0	1.0
Germany	2.3	1.4	1.1	1.0	0.9
UK	-	0.6	0.6	0.4	0.3
EU12	-	11.9	8.9	6.4	6.1
EU15	-	12.7	9.5	7.2	6.8
EU25	-	-	-	11.2	10.4

Source: European Commission, *The Agricultural Situation in the European Union 1997*; European Commission, *Agricultural Statistics Pocketbook*.

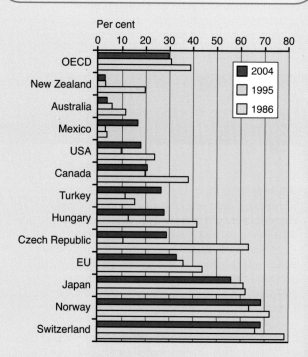

Figure 16.2 Farming subsidies: producer subsidies as a percentage of total farm incomes[1]

Per cent

OECD
New Zealand
Australia
Mexico
USA
Canada
Turkey
Hungary
Czech Republic
EU
Japan
Norway
Switzerland

■ 2004
□ 1995
□ 1986

1 Farm incomes = market value of farm production + producer subsidies.
Source: adapted from www.oecd.org.

Table 16.3 Number of holdings by size, millions

	Total	0-5ha	5-20ha	20-50ha	>50+ha
EUR-10					
1970	7.67	4.26	2.36	0.85	0.20
1987	5.00	2.32	1.53	0.78	0.37
EUR-12					
1987	6.92	3.40	2.10	0.95	0.47
1993	7.23	4.23	1.68	0.78	0.53
2000	5.18	2.65	1.33	0.64	0.56
EU-25					
2000	4.38	2.26	0.86	0.64	0.62

Note: ha = hectares.
Source: adapted from European Commission, *European Economy, EC Agricultural Policy for the 21st Century*, Number 4, 1994; European Commission, *The Agricultural Situation in the European Union 1997*; European Commission, *Agricultural Statistics Pocketbook*.

DataQuestion

Car rental pricing

Avis Europe was a brand leader in the car rental market during the 1990s. During that period, it charged high, premium prices and earned high profits, showing its ability to dominate its market.

Today, the company is suffering. Its market has been transformed by the Internet and increased competition from smaller more nimble rivals. The Internet made prices far more transparent, with customers able to compare the high prices charged by Avis with lower prices charged by new rivals. Lower prices led to rapid growth in the market, with far more car rentals being bought. For example, online holiday companies saw an explosion of car rental deals which they sold alongside package holidays. The problem for Avis Europe was that its share of the market shrank and revenues fell.

Source: adapted from the *Financial Times*, 17.6.2005.

Faced with increased competition, Avis has found it hard to achieve the price reductions it needs to survive. The company's strategy to return to profitability mainly concentrates on improving its revenues. However, the company recognises that it also needs to cut costs. For example, in its 2004 *Annual Report*, the company stated that: 'To support the Group's recovery strategy, the IT function has been significantly reduced in size and restructured to focus on lower costs and faster implementation of solutions to support core operations and the development of sales channels.' It also stated that the commission would no longer be paid to travel agencies and on-line agencies on corporate contracted rentals.

Source: adapted from Avis Europe, *Company Report and Accounts*, 2004.

Table 16.5 Avis Europe, revenue and profit¹

							Euros (millions)
	1998	1999	2000	2001	2002	2003	2004
Revenue	854	997	1 205	1 255	1 189	1 169	1 177
Profit¹	147	172	143	144	106	-43	-19

1 Profit before taxation and goodwill amortisation, after exceptional charges.

Source: adapted from Avis Europe, *Company Report and Accounts* 2002 and 2004.

1. Distinguish between productive and allocative efficiency. Use examples from the data to illustrate your answer.
2. Discuss whether (a) a lack of competition in the car rental market in the 1990s led to market failure and (b) the Internet has since reduced market failure in this market.

17 Competition and efficiency

Summary

1. Competitive markets tend to be characterised by a number of different firms, none of which is able to control the market, producing homogeneous or weakly branded goods, in a market where there are low barriers to entry and there is perfect knowledge.
2. Firms in competitive markets are likely only to earn normal profit in the long run. In a perfectly competitive industry, firms will operate where their average costs are at a minimum.
3. Firms in perfectly competitive markets are likely to be economically efficient in that they produce at lowest cost and are unable to earn abnormal profits in the long run. In an imperfectly competitive market, prices are likely to be higher because firms are unlikely to produce at the lowest average cost possible and may be able to earn abnormal profits.

Market structure

No two markets are the same. The market for sports shoes is different from the market for steel or holidays abroad. This is because the MARKET STRUCTURE is different in each market. The market structure is those characteristics of the market which influence the way in which firms in the market behave. A **competitive market** has a number of different characteristics.

A number of different firms in the industry In a competitive industry there are at least two firms in the industry. In the most competitive industries, where there is PERFECT COMPETITION, there is a large number of firms, none of which is large enough to have any economic power over the industry. In farming, for instance, there are large numbers of farms. Even the largest farm in the UK still produces only a very small fraction of total farming output. In other industries, there is IMPERFECT COMPETITION, i.e. there is not full competition in the market. In some imperfectly competitive industries, there are large numbers of small firms. In most, though, a few firms tend to dominate the industry. In the grocery retailing industry in the UK, for instance, the largest four supermarket chains sell over 50 per cent of all goods (i.e. their MARKET SHARE is more than 50 per cent). In the soap powder industry, two firms have over 80 per cent of the market.

Entry to the industry New firms are constantly being set up. Existing firms may expand their product range and enter new markets. In some markets, it is easier to set up and enter than in others. The obstacles to setting up are called BARRIERS TO ENTRY. There are many types of barrier to entry (☞ unit 18 for a more detailed discussion). For instance, it may be so costly to set up that only very large firms could consider entering the industry. Car manufacturing is an example. On the other hand, it is relatively cheap to set up in business as a grocery store. The law may be another barrier to entry. For instance, to set up a pharmacy in the UK, you have to have a licence. When setting up as a book publisher, you cannot print any books where the copyright is owned by another publisher. No firm in the UK is legally allowed to enter the drugs trade. Costs of production might be another barrier to entry. In industries like car manufacturing or bulk chemical production it is

very expensive to produce in small quantities. Producing in large quantities drives down the average cost. In these industries there are considerable **economies of scale** (☞ unit 18). In a perfectly competitive industry, barriers to entry are very low. It is very easy, for instance, to enter the retail industry. In some imperfectly competitive industries, barriers to entry are low too, but in others they can be very high. This would then be a reason why competition was imperfect, because high barriers reduce competition in the market.

Product homogeneity and branding For there to be perfect competition, customers must be able to have a wide choice of supplier, all of whom are selling the same product. This means the goods being sold must be HOMOGENEOUS. In farming, for instance, carrots are a standard product. No farmer can claim that his or her carrots are different from those of another farmer. The same is true for products such as steel, oil, basic chemicals and copper.

In an imperfectly competitive market, however, the product of one firm is different from that of another. Persil washing powder is different from Ariel. A Vauxhall Vectra is different from a Ford Escort. Firms are then said to BRAND their products.

Knowledge In a perfectly competitive industry, there is PERFECT KNOWLEDGE. This means that all firms have access to the same information. They can all find out what is the current market price. There are no trade secrets. All firms have access to the same information about production techniques. In an imperfectly competitive industry, there might be perfect knowledge or knowledge may be imperfect when firms have secret formulations which make their products unique. The formula for Coca-Cola, for instance, is known only to a few at Coca-Cola itself. Firms may keep knowledge about methods of production to themselves, not allowing rivals to see how a good is manufactured.

Prices, profits and costs in competitive markets

In perfectly competitive markets, like farming or copper mining:
- there are large numbers of small firms in the industry;
- there is freedom of entry to the market;

Question 1

The dry cleaning market is shrinking. According to estimates by Mintel, the market research company, revenues have fallen by 10 per cent since 1999. It estimates that there are now about 4 500 dry cleaning outlets in the UK, compared to almost 5 300 in 2000.

Some factors behind the trend are positive. The number of high income, AB socio-economic group, adults is rising as is the number of households where both adults are out at work and thus have less time for domestic chores. Other factors, though, outweigh these positive trends. People are dressing more casually. Fewer men wear suits to the office for example. Equally, the price of formal wear, such as suits, is coming down. A growing number of people don't bother to dry clean a cheap £80 suit when the cost of cleaning is £20. Instead, they prefer to go out and buy another cheap suit.

The dry cleaning businesses which have the best chance of survival are those which provide a high quality service and whose customers buy up market, expensive, designer label clothes. New legislation will also add to dry cleaners' costs. The European Directive on solvent emissions means that dry cleaners will have to use less chemicals per item to reduce workers' exposure to dangerous fumes. Dry cleaners could face a bill of about £200 a year from their local authority just to cover the administration costs of the relevant licences. In some cases, a company will need to upgrade its cleaning machines, costing about £25 000 each. Some estimates suggest that about one quarter of the industry will disappear as a result of the new legislation.

The industry is highly fragmented. An estimated 64 per cent of the market is supplied by small independent firms. The largest player in the market is Johnson Service Group with 638 outlets nationwide but it still only has 24 per cent of the market. Supermarket groups such as Asda and Tesco are also expanding their share of the market. However, convenience, being able to pop into a shop near where you live, is still a key competitive advantage for the small independent dry cleaner.

Source: adapted from the *Financial Times*, 5.7.2005.

Figure 17.1 UK retail dry cleaning market, number of outlets

Source: adapted from Mintel.

(a) Describe the market structure of the UK dry cleaning industry.
(b) To what extent is the UK dry cleaning industry competitive?
(c) Discuss whether the dry cleaning industry might become more competitive in future if supermarket groups such as Tesco expand further in the dry cleaning market.

● firms produce identical or homogeneous goods;
● perfect knowledge exists throughout the industry.

This market structure affects the way in which firms behave. Because there is freedom of entry to a market where firms produce identical goods, all firms will charge the same price in equilibrium. To understand why, consider what would happen if a firm charged a higher price than other firms. Customers would then switch their demand to other firms because other firms are offering identical products. The firm charging the higher price will lose all its sales and go out of business. If a firm charged a lower price than all other firms, then buyers would switch away from other firms and they would all lose their customers. So they would have to cut their prices to stay in the industry.

Competition will not drive prices down to zero. In the long term, firms will only supply a good if they can make a profit. The minimum profit that a firm must make to prevent it from moving its economic resources to production of another good is called NORMAL PROFIT. If firms in a perfectly competitive industry are able to make ABNORMAL PROFITS, profit which is greater than normal profit, then new firms will be attracted into the industry. They will want to take advantage of being able to earn higher than normal profit. However, their entry will increase supply and drive prices down. The long run equilibrium price will be the one where prices are just high enough for firms to make normal profits, so no firms are being forced out of the industry, but equally no firms are being attracted into the industry.

Firms in a perfectly competitive industry will also produce at lowest average cost. Assume that one firm was a higher cost producer than other firms in the industry. It would have to charge the same price as other firms or risk losing all its customers. But then its profits would be lower than those of other firms because its costs were higher. Since all other firms are only earning normal profit, it would be making less than normal profit, the minimum profit needed to persuade the owners of the firm to keep their resources in that industry. So this firm would leave the industry because it was not sufficiently profitable.

On the other hand, assume that a firm could produce at lower cost than other firms and was making abnormal profit. Then other firms would be able to find out why this firm had lower costs because there is perfect knowledge in the industry. If it is because the firm has adopted new production methods, then these production methods will be taken up by other firms. If it is because the firm has a particularly productive factor of production, other firms will attempt to buy it, raising its price and hence its cost. For instance, if success is due to a very successful managing director, then other firms will attempt to employ him or her by offering a higher salary. In the long term, costs will become the same across the industry. They will be the minimum cost possible.

In imperfectly competitive industries:
● there may be many small firms in the industry or it could be dominated by just a few firms;
● there might be relatively free entry to the industry or there might be barriers to entry;
● firms produce branded goods;
● there may or may not be perfect knowledge.

This market structure limits competition. Because each firm is producing a slightly different branded product, it

Question 2

The great British sandwich is alive and well, even if 30 per cent of the market is made up of 'innovative' or 'exotic' products. These are products such as chicken ciabatta, or Italian chicken with sun dried tomato in focaccia, which are increasing favourites with customers tired of cheese and tomato or egg mayonnaise.

The sandwich market is highly competitive. According to the British Sandwich Association, the industry trade body, there are about 5 000 independently owned sandwich shops compared with 700 chain outlets. The chain outlets include highly successful companies such as Subway and Pret A Manger. The chain outlets bring high quality standardised products. The independent outlets offer everything from convenience on the local parade of shops to unique product offerings and a flexibility to change their offerings from week to week to satisfy local demand and tastes in Glasgow, Birmingham or London.

Since the 1990s, sales of sandwiches have steadily soared as high-income, time-pressed consumers identify the sandwich as a health alternative to fast food. Last year 1.8 billion sandwiches were sold for £3.5 billion, an increase of 5 per cent on the year before. New businesses continue to come into the market, including McDonald's, which recently added a range of toasted deli sandwiches to its menu, while Burger King now offers fresh backed baguettes. Equally, there has been no shortage of new local independent shops opening up to exploit the growing market.

Source: adapted from the *Financial Times*, 20.6.2005.

(a) Why are new entrants to the UK sandwich market unlikely to earn abnormal profit despite a growing market?

is able to some extent to decide on what price it will charge. If other firms charge lower prices, it is likely to still keep some of its customers who will remain loyal to buying its branded good. Market power will increase the fewer the number of competitors and the higher the barriers to entry. If entry barriers are very high, firms will be able to charge higher prices without worrying that new entrants will come in and take away market share. So in imperfect competition it could be that competitive pressures are strong enough to force profits down to a normal level in the long run. However, it is more likely that firms will be charging high enough prices to earn abnormal profit.

Competition and efficiency

Perfect competition is likely to lead to economic efficiency (☞ unit 16). First, firms in a perfectly competitive industry will, in the long run, be productively efficient. As explained above, competitive pressures will ensure that firms produce at lowest average cost. If they fail to do so, they will be driven out of the industry. Second, firms in a perfectly competitive industry are likely to be allocatively efficient (☞ unit 16). Customers will be able to buy at the lowest price that is possible because firms are only able to make normal profit.

In contrast, firms in imperfectly competitive industries are likely to be neither productively or allocatively efficient. There is no pressure to produce at lowest average cost because firms produce branded goods. This gives them some control over how much they wish to sell, i.e. it gives them some control over where on the demand curve they sell. Firms will choose to sell where profit is maximised and this is unlikely to be the minimum average cost point. Hence, imperfectly competitive firms are unlikely to be productively efficient.

They are unlikely to be allocatively efficient either. Production would be greater and prices lower if the industry were perfectly competitive. Firms in imperfect competition are likely to earn

Question 3

Sending freight across France by rail should be straightforward. But the freight division of SNCF, France's national railway company, is dominated by powerful local divisions and poor co-ordination between them often disrupts long-distance trains. The result is high prices, long journey times and unreliable service. France is not unique. European railways have long suffered from a lack of competition leading to disorganisation and inefficiency.

This is all about to change. Since March 15, 2003, any company has the right to compete with traditional operators on cross-border rail freight on the main trans-European routes. All they need are an operating certificate and safety clearances. The law is the first stage of a drive to introduce competition on Europe's railways. In the long term, the vision is that any company will be able to offer freight services across Europe's rail tracks, however long or short the journey.

Competition has already been introduced within national railways in some countries like the UK and Germany. In the Netherlands, Ewout Sandker, policy manager for the European Shippers' Council, an industry group, says the service of Railion Nederland, the Dutch traditional rail freight operation, was transformed after it lost some contracts to private operators. 'Users saw an immediate change in the traditional railway company's behaviour, its service orientation', Mr Sandker says.

In France, SNCF is due to restructure its operations. It is also planning to invest €500 million in new locomotives to speed up journey times and increase reliability.

Matthias Raith, managing director of Rail4Chem, a new freight operator, says traditional railways have long overcharged certain customers. His company, he says, offers a cheaper, more responsive alternative. That should force traditional railways to charge more realistic prices.

Source: adapted from the *Financial Times*, 22.9.2004.

(a) How might increased competition in the European rail freight market lead to greater efficiencies in the market?

abnormal profits. If they earned only normal profit, they would have to cut prices and expand their production. Hence, in imperfect competition, firms restrict supply in order to exploit the customer for abnormal profit. Even where firms earn only normal profit, output is still likely to be lower and prices higher than if the industry were perfectly competitive. This is because firms will choose to produce where profit is maximised, in this case where they are earning just normal profit, and not where average costs are lowest.

Productive and allocative efficiency are aspects of static efficiency (efficiency at a point in time ☞ unit 16). Perfect competition is likely to lead to productive and allocative efficiency, whilst imperfect competition is not. Therefore perfect competition is likely to lead to static efficiency, whilst imperfect competition is not. However, perfect competition may not lead to greater **dynamic efficiency**. There is no incentive to innovate over time in a perfectly competitive industry. Because there is perfect knowledge in the industry, discoveries and inventions by one firm will become quickly available for use by all other firms. There is therefore no point in spending large amounts on research and development. In imperfect competition where firms can protect innovation, for instance through patents and copyrights, they have an incentive to be innovative. If they can develop a new product which customers like, they can sell it at a high price and earn abnormal profit on it.

Key terms

Abnormal profit - the profit over and above normal profit.
Barriers to entry - factors which make it difficult or impossible for firms to enter an industry and compete with existing producers.
Branded good - a named good which in the perception of its buyers is different from other similar goods on the market.
Homogeneous goods - goods which are identical.
Imperfect competition - a market structure where there are several firms in the industry, each of which has the ability to control the price that it sets for its products.

Market share - the proportion of sales in market taken by a firm or a group of firms.
Market structure - the characteristics of a market which determine the behaviour of firms within the market.
Normal profit - the profit that the firm could make by using its resources in their next best use. Normal profit is an economic cost.
Perfect knowledge or information - exists if all buyers in a market are fully informed of prices and quantities for sale, whilst producers have equal access to information about production techniques.

Applied economics

The DIY and builders' merchants market

Figure 17.2 Market share of DIY market

Others 47%
B&Q 15%
Travis Perkins 10%
GUS 7%
Wolseley 7%
St. Gobain 7%
Grafton 4%
Focus 3%

Source: adapted from www.travisperkins.co.uk.

In 2004, the value of sales in the DIY and builders' merchants market was approximately £28 billion. Sales were split between individuals doing DIY, such as painting a room or installing a new toilet, to professional tradespeople and building companies doing building and repair work for customers.

Figure 17.2 shows how these sales were divided between businesses. The business with the highest market share was B&Q, with 15 per cent of the market. Travis Perkins, which owns Wickes, had 10 per cent. 47 per cent of the market was divided up between relatively small businesses, like a builders' merchant or a hardware store in a local town or a local high street.

Barriers to entry to the industry are relatively low and are mainly financial. Setting up a small builders' merchant might cost several hundred thousand pounds. Knowledge of running the business successfully can be gained through working for another builders' merchants or being in the building trade.

Companies like B&Q and Wickes are well known brands in their own right. However, these market leaders would probably argue that this gives them little power over their markets. Customers come to a particular store because it is convenient and local, stocks the products the customer wants and offers competitive prices. The product they offer, the service of a retailer, is not homogeneous, but equally the service of one business is a fairly good substitute for the service of another business. Their branding power is relatively weak.

The competitive nature of the market was illustrated by an event in 2005. The housing market, for the first time in nearly 10 years, had performed poorly. Prices had hardly changed. The number of sales, both of second hand houses and new houses, was considerably down on previous years. Consumer confidence was also lower than in previous years. Interest rate rises in 2003-2005 had increased the cost of mortgage repayments. Soaring oil prices in 2004-2005 had led to increased motoring costs and costs of domestic heating. All this had cut into the amount that consumers had to spend on other items. They responded by being more cautious about how they spent their money and how much new debt they took out.

The DIY and builders' merchants market was badly affected. In November 2005, Travis Perkins announced that its sales were down. Geoff Cooper, chief executive of Travis, said that consumers were reluctant to splash out on big-ticket investments such as a new kitchen or bathroom and were keeping any spare cash for Christmas. On the builders' merchant side, he said that jobbing builders and small housebuilders were also admitting that they had less work. Sales to trade customers, such as builders, were down 0.4 per cent in the previous 4 months. Sales at Wickes, where customers were more likely to be DIY householders, had fallen 9 per cent. The showroom business at Wickes, selling kitchens, bathrooms and conservatories,

was down 21.1 per cent over the same period.

In a competitive market, less demand is likely to lead to lower prices. Some competitors, such as B&Q, were cutting prices in 2005 in an attempt to maintain sales. Travis Perkins attempted to maintain profits per unit sold by cutting costs and by tempting customers into stores with selected promotional discounts on some items. However, it was losing market share as a result. Customers were switching to competitors with lower prices.

The competition in the market meant that businesses were unlikely to be earning any normal profit. Indeed, some businesses were making losses even before the fall in sales in 2005. MFI, which was part of the market because it sold kitchens, had struggled for a number of years to make a profit. It could therefore be argued that competition in the market meant that businesses were allocatively efficient, selling at prices which were equal to cost plus normal profit. Equally, many businesses were also productively efficient, producing at lowest cost. Companies like B&Q had forced many local hardware stores and builders merchants to close because their costs were too high and they couldn't compete. It could also be argued that there was some dynamic efficiency in the market. The large companies, like B&Q and Travis Perkins, were innovative in a number of ways. For example, B&Q introduced very large stores to the market for the first time. These stores, because of the range of products they could offer, were very popular with customers. Equally, the large businesses in the market expanded own brand sales in areas such as paint.

It can be argued that the DIY and builders' merchant market is competitive. This competition benefits customers because businesses within the market tend to be efficient. However, as 2005 showed, intense competition can lead to businesses seeing lower profits when demand falls across the market.

Source: adapted from the *Financial Times* 12.11.2005; Travis Perkins plc, Interim Results 2005.

DataQuestion — The market for flowers

Sales of flowers have trebled in the past decade to more than £1.3 billion. The UK is now the 10th biggest nation for flower sales, still behind Switzerland, Norway and the Netherlands, the world leaders, but ahead of France, Japan and the US.

Rising sales have been driven by the marketing power of a range of big name retailers, including Tesco, Clinton Cards and Next. However, the fortunes of the UK's 6 800 independent florists have been mixed. Whilst overall their sales have risen, their market share has halved over the period. Prices are also falling because of the fierce competition from supermarkets.

Independent retailers who have stuck mainly to selling flowers to passers by have been most affected by the increased competition. Despite low wages in the industry, overheads such as rent are often high. It doesn't take much of a fall in sales for a traditional florist to be in the red and out of business.

The more successful independent florists, however, have responded by going upmarket, giving added value or cutting costs.

Judy MacDevitt, who runs The Flowerstalk in Reading, Berkshire, says: 'You have florists that say the supermarkets are putting us out of business. But these companies are also responsible for making more people buy flowers for themselves, which has to be good for the market.' She has developed a service where she uses e-mail to send customers digital pictures of the arrangements they have ordered. This service has proved very popular, particularly among people sending flowers from abroad.

Miraflores, based in a former railway station between Dorking and Leatherhead, Surrey, has made the Internet its main sales channel for similar reasons. The company, which sells about 150 arrangements a day, and expects to turn over just under £1 million this year, uses a courier company to guarantee next-day delivery. 'If somebody asks for 500 boxes of tulips, many florists could not do it. But that is exactly what we have done' says Andrew Franklin, a manager at the company.

Some of the newer florists, who have graduated from floristry courses at college work, from home, selling either to other florists or over the Internet. This can cut out the main overhead cost of a florist, the premises from which they operate.

The challenge for independent florists is to differentiate themselves from the store chains in a way that their larger rivals cannot copy. Whether this is focusing on demand for complicated floral arrangements, selling rare but popular breeds of plant, providing added value services or simply providing the best service in a local area, it is the only way they will survive in the long term.

Source: adapted from the *Financial Times*, 12.5.2005.

Figure 17.3 Sales of flowers

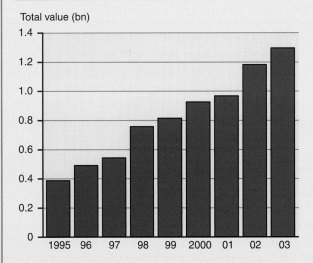

Source: adapted from The Flowers and Plants Association/TNS.

Figure 17.4 Florists: market share of independents and supermarkets

Source: adapted from The Flowers and Plants Association/TNS.

1. Describe the trends shown in Figures 17.3 and 17.4.
2. Explain the market structure of the UK flower market.
3. To what extent has increased competition in the UK flower market led to economic efficiency?

18 Monopoly and efficiency

Summary

1. Monopolies exist because of legal and resource barriers to entry to an industry, natural cost advantages and uncompetitive practices.
2. Natural monopolies exist because of large scale economies in an industry. Economies of scale include purchasing economies, marketing economies, technical economies, managerial economies and financial economies.
3. Monopolies tend to earn abnormal profit by choosing a price higher than would be the case if the industry were competitive.
4. Monopolies are productively efficient if they are natural monopolies exploiting economies of scale and dynamically efficient if their existence leads to technological innovation.
5. Monopolies are allocatively inefficient if they exploit customers by charging higher prices than would be the case under competition.
6. Governments can intervene to correct market failure caused by monopoly activity through taxes and subsidies, prices controls, nationalisation and privatisation, deregulation, breaking up the monopolist or reducing entry barriers.

Monopoly

A MONOPOLY exists where there is only one firm or supplier in an industry. For instance, Transco has a monopoly on UK gas pipelines whilst Railtrack has a monopoly on UK rail infrastructure. In practice, firms which have a dominant share of the market tend to be referred to as monopolists as well. For instance, Microsoft, with 90 per cent of the world's PC operating systems market, could be seen as a monopolist.

Firms gain monopoly powers in the long run because of **barriers to entry** (☞ unit 17) to the industry. There are various barriers to entry which can create monopolies.

Legal barriers The government can create monopolies through the legal system. It can make competition illegal in an industry. For instance, in the UK only pharmacies can sell prescription drugs by law. The government has granted GNER a monopoly to run train services on the East Coast Main Line railway.

Resource barriers In some industries, a monopolist may be able to buy or otherwise acquire the key resources needed to produce a good. For instance, an airline may be able to buy up the sole rights to fly from one airport to another. A supermarket chain may be able to buy the only plot of land available for development for a large supermarket in a small town. An electricity company may buy out all the other competing electricity companies in a country. Customers would then be faced with a sole supplier for the product.

Unfair competition Once created, a monopolist may defend itself through unfair competitive practices. For instance, an airline with a monopoly on a route may slash prices below cost if a new entrant comes into the market. When the new entrant is forced out, the monopolist then puts back up its fares. Or the monopolist may refuse to supply customers with other goods if it buys one good from a new entrant into the market.

Natural cost advantages Some firms are NATURAL MONOPOLIES. They become monopolies because not even a single firm in the industry is large enough to

reduce average costs to their minimum. Size can reduce average costs because of the existence of ECONOMIES OF SCALE. These are factors which cause average costs to fall as the scale of production is increased. There is a number of different sources of economies of scale.

- Purchasing economies. The greater the quantities bought of raw materials and other supplies, the lower is likely to be the average cost. Large buyers are able to negotiate larger

Question 1

Intel has a stranglehold on the world market for personal computer chips. It supplies 80 per cent of all chips put into personal computers (PCs). Last year it made a net profit of $7.5 billion and it makes an average 41 per cent profit over costs on every microprocessor sold. It would argue that its dominance in the market is due to superior products, backed by patents, sold at a competitive price. It would also point out that it has a strong record of bringing new products to market based on considerable research and development spending.

AMD (Advance Micro Devices) would disagree. It has around 10 per cent of the market for PC chips and has just launched a legal claim in US courts against Intel of running an illegal conspiracy to restrict AMD's share of the market. AMD claims that Intel is doing this through a system of rebates and other financial incentives. For example, AMD alleges that: 'In return for payments, (Dixons, the UK high street retailer) has agreed to keep AMD's share of its business below 10%'. Toshiba, once an important AMD customer, has also stopped buying its processors. Four times a year, Toshiba allegedly receives 'market development funds' worth $25-$30 million from Intel. This money is allegedly given on the understanding that Toshiba will not use any AMD microprocessors in its PCs.

Source: adapted from *The Sunday Times*, 3.7.2005.

(a) Explain why Intel, in practice, has a monopoly on production of microprocessors for personal computers.
(b) How might Intel have maintained its monopoly powers over the market?

discounts because they have more market power. It is also usually cheaper to sell large quantities. For instance, transport costs might be lower if a given quantity is delivered to one customer rather than ten as bulk orders might save on packaging.

● Marketing economies. Marketing costs, such as advertising or the cost of promotional leaflets, are often lower per unit sold the greater the volume of sales. The cost of an advertisement, for instance, is the same however many sales it generates. If a catalogue is sent out to customers, again the cost remains the same whatever the response.

● Technical economies. Larger scale machinery or plant can often be more efficient than smaller scale plant. For instance, a boat which is twice the length, breadth and depth of another boat can carry 8 times as much cargo. But it likely to cost less than four times as much to build. A large supermarket costs much less to build per square metre than a small supermarket. What's more, the larger the scale of production, the more likely it is that resources will be fully utilised. A small building firm, for instance, might own a truck which it uses only for a few hours a week to transport materials. A large firm might be able to use the truck far more intensively because it has more jobs on at any one time.

● Managerial economies. **Specialisation** (☞ unit 2) is an important source of greater efficiency. In a small firm, the owner might be part time salesperson, accountant, receptionist and manager. Employing specialist staff is likely to lead to greater efficiency and therefore lower costs.

● Financial economies. Small firms often find it difficult and expensive to raise finance for new investment. When loans are given, small firms are charged at relatively high rates of interest because banks know that small firms are far more at risk from liquidation than large firms. Large firms have a much greater choice of finance and it is likely to be much cheaper to raise than for small firms.

Examples of natural monopolies include transport systems, such as pipeline networks, rail tracks and electricity power grids. If these are underutilised, which they usually are, then it is possible to lower average costs by increasing throughput in the system. This would be an example of a technical economy of scale.

Prices and profits under monopoly

Monopolists, in the absence of government regulations, can set whatever price they choose to customers. They can choose, for instance, whether to charge £10 per item or £2. It should be remembered, though, that the higher the price they set, the lower will be the demand for the product, i.e. monopolists face a downward sloping demand curve.

The highest price is not necessarily the profit maximising price. If the price is set too high, they could lose profit. This is because the profit gained from sales at a high price could be less than the profit lost from even more sales at a lower price. For instance, a firm might charge £20 for an item costing £12 for which sales are 1 million units. It then makes a profit of £8 per item or a total of £8 million (£8 x 1 million). But it might be able to sell 2 million units if it reduced its price to £17. Its profit per unit would then only be £5, but its total profit would be £10 million (£5 x 2 million).

The profit earned is likely to be **abnormal profit** (☞ unit 17). It is higher than the minimum amount needed to keep resources

employed in that industry, i.e. it is higher than normal profit. The profit is therefore higher than would be earned by the industry if it were **perfectly competitive** (☞ unit 17). In a perfectly competitive industry, fierce competition between many small firms drives the price down to the point where firms are making just enough profit to stay in the industry, i.e. to the point where firms only make normal profit. If there is **imperfect competition** (☞ unit 17), firms may be able to charge higher prices than under perfect competition and earn abnormal profit. Whether the price will be as high as under monopoly, or whether the total industry profits will be as high, depends on how little price competition there is between the firms.

Monopoly, efficiency and market failure

A natural monopoly will be producing at the lowest average cost possible for the level of total demand in the industry. Breaking a natural monopoly up into several smaller firms would only result in increased average costs. Hence, natural monopolies are productively efficient, i.e. production is at lowest

Question 2

Tesco is the largest supermarket chain in the UK. In 2005, it announced record profits of £2 billion. In 2005, it had a market share within the grocery market of approximately 33 per cent and sold an astonishing 12.5 per cent by value of everything that is sold in Britain's shops.

Tesco, along with other supermarkets, has however come in for fierce criticism for 'ripping off the consumer' and 'ripping off suppliers'. The supermarkets counter these criticisms by pointing out that supermarkets are in intense competition with each other. But this is not always the case because in many areas, particularly rural areas, a supermarket chain may enjoy a local monopoly. The UK Competition Commission, the government monopoly watchdog, published a report in 2000 which found that Safeway, Sainsbury and Tesco had policies of 'varying prices in different geographical areas in the light of local competition'. Where a supermarket chain enjoyed a local monopoly, prices tended to be higher than in areas where customers had a range of stores within easy travelling distance.

Source: adapted from www.gnn.gov.uk, http://news.bbc.co.uk.

(a) Suggest what might be meant by a supermarket having a 'local monopoly'.
(b) Why might supermarkets increase their prices in areas where they have a local monopoly compared to areas where they are in competition from other supermarkets?
(c) Tesco claims that it charges very low prices to its customers compared to its competitors. Explain why it doesn't raise prices to earn even more profit than the £2 billion it earned in 2004-2005.

cost (☞ unit 16) compared to a more competitive industry.

However, if the monopoly is not a natural monopoly, then the effect of a break up is more complex. If the industry becomes perfectly competitive, costs will be driven down to a minimum and hence productive efficiency will be achieved. By comparison, monopoly is productively inefficient. If the industry became imperfectly competitive, it is not possible to say whether prices or total profits would fall. Hence, it is impossible to make a comparison about productive efficiency.

As for **allocative efficiency** (☞ unit 16), a natural monopoly is allocatively inefficient in that the firm will have driven up prices and reduced output to earn abnormal profit. But splitting up the industry is unlikely to result in allocative efficiency because prices are likely to be even higher. This is because average costs of production will be higher with several firms in the industry rather than just one.

Allocative efficiency will be achieved if the firm is not a natural monopolist and it is split up into a number of perfectly competitive firms. Perfect competition will ensure that prices to customers are as low as possible and that firms are only able to earn normal profit. The reduction in price from competition will expand demand and output in the industry, again benefiting customers.

However, if a monopolist is split up but only imperfect competition results, then there may be no improvement in allocative efficiency. Prices may not fall because the new firms may still earn just as much abnormal profit, and hence output may not increase.

Productive and allocative efficiency are types of **static efficiency** (☞ unit 16). However, there is also **dynamic efficiency** to consider. This looks at whether efficiency occurs over a period of time rather than at a point in time. It can be argued that monopoly is dynamically efficient, whilst perfect competition is not. In perfect competition, there is no incentive for individual firms to spend on research and development. This is because there is perfect knowledge in a perfectly competitive industry. Any innovation will quickly become known throughout the industry and if it gives the firm a competitive advantage it will be copied.

With a monopoly, the benefits of any research and development can be exploited by the monopolist. If it develops a new drug, or a new machine, it can exploit that invention and earn abnormal profits. Hence, the ability to keep abnormal profits acts as an incentive for innovation.

What's more, it can be argued that the existence of monopolies and abnormal profits encourages those outside the industry to destroy monopolies by leapfrogging the technology used in the industry. This is called the **process of creative destruction**. For instance, the monopoly of the canals was destroyed by the invention of railways. Telephone and postal monopolies are being destroyed by e-mails and the Internet.

However, it can equally be argued that a monopolist could easily become complacent and lazy, sheltering behind high barriers to entry. Lack of competition reduces the incentive to innovate. Spending on research and development is always risky and the monopolist may choose to become extremely risk adverse, preferring profits now to the possibility of higher profits in the future. What's more, the monopolist may not even attempt to profit maximise. Its management may aim to make enough profit to satisfy the shareholders (profit satisficing), and then run the firm for its own benefit. This is unlikely to involve aggressive attempts to innovate.

Government intervention

Governments are able to use a number of different policies to attempt to correct the market failure caused by monopolies.

Taxes Monopolies are likely to earn abnormal profits. Governments could tax away these abnormal profits, but this is unlikely to increase efficiency. There would be no incentive for the monopolist to reduce its prices as a result. Hence, there would still be allocative inefficiency. Productive inefficiency could even increase because the monopolist would have no

Question 3

Land based telephone companies have traditionally been monopolies in Europe. Usually state owned, they have had a stranglehold on voice communication. Today, those monopolies face two threats. First, their legal monopolies have been taken away as they have been privatised and their markets opened up to competition from other firms. Second, they face at the extreme the loss of most of their market to a new technology: the mobile telephone, which has only been in existence since the 1980s.

Land based phone networks are, in fact, most unlikely to disappear. They possess cost advantages for large volumes of traffic over mobile phone networks. There is no limit to the

number of lines that can be laid, whereas there is a limit to the number of calls that can be made on frequencies allocated to mobile phone networks. Established land line networks also represent a 'sunk' cost - a cost that has already been paid for - and so today's cost of using the system is much lower than if the whole system had to be replaced.

Privatisation and competition have led to falling land line telephone charges in real terms. This has benefited customers as has mobile phone technology which allows customers to call from anywhere.

(a) Why might mobile phone technology represent an example of creative destruction in the telephone industry?
(b) Explain how customers have benefited from the breakdown of the monopoly of land line telephone companies.

incentive to reduce costs. After all, any reduction in costs which led to higher profit would simply be taxed away. It would also reduce any incentive to innovate since any abnormal profits earned from innovation would be taxed. In practice, there would also be the problem of how to set the tax. It is very difficult to estimate the level of abnormal profit made by a firm in a real life situation. If the government set the tax too high, it would discourage the monopolist from even making essential routine investment and the quality and quantity of the good or service produced could deteriorate increasing rather than reducing market failure. The most important advantage of a tax on monopoly profits is that it redistributes income away from the owners of monopoly firms to the rest of the society, arguably improving **equity** in the economy.

Subsidies Monopolists are likely to be allocatively inefficient because they increase prices and reduce output compared to the situation which would occur if the industry were perfectly competitive. A way of reducing prices and increasing supply is to give subsidies to the monopolist to cut its prices and produce more. Whilst this might seem a possible solution, in practice it would be difficult to implement. It would be difficult for the government to know what would be the price and level of output which would lead to allocative efficiency. Hence, it is almost impossible to know what level of subsidy would maximise efficiency. Moreover, subsidising monopolists already earning abnormal profits would be politically unacceptable. Citizens would question why taxpayers' money was being used to increase the profits of already highly profitable firms.

Price controls If a monopolist sets its prices too high to be allocatively efficient, then the government could impose price controls, limiting the prices that the monopolist can set. This is the policy currently adopted to control UK monopoly utilities such as water, telephones and railways. It has the added advantage that there is an incentive for monopolists to increase productive efficiency. If the monopolist faces a fixed price set by the government, it can still earn higher profit if it can drive down its costs. The major drawback of price controls is that it is difficult for the government to know what price to set to maximise efficiency. The monopolist will always argue that it needs higher prices to justify investment which will lead to dynamic efficiency. For instance, the UK water industry always argues that if prices are set too low, it will have to cut back on investment to improve water quality and preserve the environment.

Nationalisation If the monopoly is a private sector company, a solution to lack of efficiency would be to NATIONALISE the firm, i.e. turn it into a state owned company. The government could then force it to set its prices to ensure allocative efficiency. Nationalisation was a very common policy throughout the world from the 1940s onwards. However, nationalised industries came to face two major problems. First, there was no incentive for these firms to reduce costs and hence, over time, they became increasingly productively inefficient. PRIVATISATION (i.e. the transfer of ownership from the public sector back to the private sector) of industries in the 1980s and 1990s has led to considerable reductions in costs and improvements in productive efficiency. Second, governments tended to starve nationalised industries of funds for investment. This damaged dynamic efficiency. Again, privatisation has usually led to considerable increases in investment, to the benefit of customers.

Privatisation and deregulation Many monopolies in the past have been nationalised industries. As already argued, the prices they set might be nearer those needed to ensure allocative efficiency than a private sector monopolist would have set. However, they tended to be productively and dynamically inefficient. So privatising them might increase overall efficiency. To prevent them exploiting the consumer by raising prices, the government could combine privatisation with price controls. Alternatively, it could attempt to bring competition into the industry. Either it could split the monopolist up at privatisation into a number of competing companies. Or it could DEREGULATE the industry by allowing competitors to set up in an industry previously protected by legal barriers to entry. Competition would then hopefully drive prices down towards the level at which allocative efficiency would be achieved.

Breaking up the monopolist The government could order the break up of a monopoly. This won't necessarily lead to any increase in efficiency if the monopoly is a natural monopoly, or if the new firms are in imperfect competition with each other. It is most likely to lead to an increase in efficiency if the new firms are in perfect competition with each other. This could be very difficult to achieve. For instance, it would be impossible if the monopolist produced branded goods.

Reducing entry barriers The government could try to reduce barriers to entry to the industry. This policy would be most easy to implement if the entry barriers were legal. For instance, a way of introducing competition in the UK gas delivery service would be to abolish Centrica's legal monopoly on ownership of the UK's gas pipeline network. However, there is no guarantee that competition would develop, especially if the monopoly is also a natural monopoly. Even if there were competition, the industry might become imperfectly competitive and there might be few efficiency gains as a result.

Question 4

Royal Mail currently has a monopoly on the collection and delivery of letters, although it faces fierce competition in the parcels market. But from 1 January 2006, any licensed company will be able to deliver mail to business and residential customers. For a number of years, the postal market has been regulated by Postcomm. It has set prices that Royal Mail can charge for its letter service. It will continue to regulate Royal Mail prices for the foreseeable future and will be responsible for licensing companies that want to enter the market. Royal Mail will continue to have to provide a universal service, collecting mail from post boxes throughout the UK and delivering to every address. Rival companies will not have this universal obligation and will be free to set their own charges.

The reason why Postcomm will continue to regulate the market is that Royal Mail's monopoly is unlikely to be broken very fast. In the two countries in the world that have introduced competition into their postal markets - New Zealand five years ago and Sweden 12 years ago - the original monopoly supplier still has at least 90 per cent of the market.

Source: adapted from http://news.bbc.co.uk, 18 February 2005.

(a) What might be the advantages to customers of Postcomm's regulation of Royal Mail?
(b) Why might introducing competition into a market, when Royal Mail had a monopoly, benefit customers?

Key terms

Deregulation - the process of removing government controls from markets.

Economies of scale - a fall in the long run average costs of production as output rises.

Monopoly - a market structure where one firm supplies all output in the industry without facing competition because of high barriers to entry to the industry.

Nationalisation - the transfer of firms or assets from private sector ownership to state ownership.

Natural monopoly - where economies of scale are so large relative to market demand that the dominant producer in the industry will always enjoy lower costs of production than any other potential competitor.

Privatisation - the opposite of nationalisation, the transfer of organisations or assets from state ownership to private sector ownership.

Applied economics

DVD Technology formats

In the 1970s, the audio cassette, developed by Philips, revolutionised home recording. In the 1980s, the audio CD was launched onto the market delivering high quality sound. In the same decade, the video recorder proved a smash hit. In the early 2000s, DVDs took off. All these technologies were only successful because a variety of manufacturers supported the new technology and were prepared to share out the profits to be made from the sale of equipment and from the sale of films and music. Over the same period, there was a large number of formats which failed. Digital Audio Tape, for example, provided CD quality listening but was a tape in a cassette rather than a round CD shaped disk. Despite the fact customers could buy blank tapes on which to record, the format never took off. Customers were happy to use audio cassettes to do their recordings and listen to pre-recorded music on their CD players.

In the mid-2000s, a new format battle geared up between Sony and Toshiba. It was over high-definition DVDs. The new product would enable viewers to buy films on DVD but view them in high definition format. Relatively few televisions in people's homes today have high definition. But the assumption is that over the next ten years, more and more televisions sold will be high definition, giving better viewing quality. Part of the incentive for customers to buy the new televisions would be that they had widely available high definition DVDs to play on them. High definition DVDs, because they carry much more information than existing DVDs, would also be ideal to use in games consoles where there is ever increasing demand for more sophisticated games which need more and more memory space.

Sony and Toshiba have each produced a new high-definition DVD format, but they are incompatible with one another. Sony's Blue Ray disk technology cannot be used on Toshiba's HD-DVD machines and vice versa. Sony claims that its product is technologically superior because its disk can hold almost twice the amount of information as its rival. Toshiba points out that its disks are cheaper to make and can be made in factories making today's DVDs. Blue Ray disks would need totally new equipment to manufacture them.

For Sony and Toshiba, what is at stake is the ability to create a monopoly protected by patents. Both companies would license their technology to other manufacturers. Equally, both companies would license the format to the film studios for them to issue their films in the format. However, whoever owns the licence would get a royalty fee. Equally, they would be in charge of the technology which would give them a competitive advantage as they made small incremental improvements to the technology. In the short term, whoever owns the technology could probably get their products out into the market first and be able to charge high prices to customers wanting to have the technology immediately. The abnormal profits that the first mover could make would eventually be competed away by other manufacturers. But overall, their profits would have been higher over the life cycle of the product than their rivals.

For Sony, the stakes are high because it also owns one of the major US film companies with a vast back list of films. If it loses the battle, it will have to pay Toshiba to put its films onto Toshiba's HD-DVD format. If it wins, it will save this cost and gain licence fees from other film studios.

Format wars are a mixed blessing for consumers. On the one hand, new formats are an example of dynamic efficiency in action. Over the past 50 years, the world of audio and visual communication has been revolutionised by the audio cassette, the CD, the video recorder and the DVD. On the other hand, there is no guarantee that the best format wins out. Many argue, for example, that the video recorder format, VHS, which eventually came to dominate the market was inferior technologically to its main rival, Sony's Betamax format.

In the short term, the existence of patents and copyright over the format may lead to higher prices than would be the case if there were no barriers to entry to the market. However, the productive and allocative inefficiency that result from this are unlikely to be great in the case of the new generation of DVDs. One reason why Sony lost its video recorder war with VHS was that it was reluctant to license the technology to other manufacturers. It learnt its lesson from this and Sony today positively wants to license its Blue Ray technology to gain its quick adoption.

The worst scenario for both manufacturers and customers is that both formats are launched and a winner only emerges after a few years. Companies will experience either higher costs or lost sales, whilst those customers who have bought into the losing format will eventually have to write off their equipment and disks to move over to the new format. Equally, if there is no agreement, there is a danger that a new technology will

make the format redundant. The very fast progress in computer technology could result in consumers by-passing the new generation of DVD players in favour of something superior. This example of creative destruction would leave Sony and Toshiba unable to recoup the development costs of the high definition DVD technologies and prevent them from earning profits from sales of hardware and software.

DataQuestion

Artificial sweeteners

Tate&Lyle

In its 2005 *Annual Report and Accounts*, Tate&Lyle described itself in the following way.

'Tate&Lyle is a world leading manufacturer of renewable food and industrial ingredients. Through the use of innovative technology, we transform corn, wheat and sugar into value added ingredients for customers in the food, beverage, pharmaceutical, cosmetic, paper, packaging and building industries. We work hard to understand our customers' needs and help meet the demands of consumers for tasty, nutritious, healthy and innovative products. We are a leader in cereal sweeteners and starches, sugar refining, value added food and industrial ingredients and citric acid. We are the world number one in industrial starches and the sole manufacturers of SPLENDA ® Sucralose.'

Nutrasweet

Until the 1990s, the US company Nutrasweet held a monopoly over the world's most widely-used sweetener: aspartame. Before Nutrasweet's patents expired, it could sell a pound of aspartame for $100, and $75 of that was profit. When its patents expired at the end of the 1990s, the price of aspartame collapsed to around $9 a pound as competitors entered the market with identical generic products. In spite of strong competition, Nutrasweet has maintained a large share of the $566m aspartame market, which is still twice the size of the market for sucralose. What is more, the amount of profit made from $100 worth of sales is still a healthy $15. Nutrasweet, after a period of closing down and mothballing factories after its patents expired, is now increasing output again because of growing demand.

Splenda

Tate&Lyle owns the monopoly patent rights to sucralose, better known in the UK by its brand name Splenda. 20 per cent of the profits of the company are now derived from the product. What is more, global sales are expanding faster than the industry average. Last year, sales grew 63 per cent compared to 8 per cent growth in the broader artificial sweetener market. Tate&Lyle can't keep up with demand and is currently rationing supplies to customers whilst it builds new plant to triple production by 2007.

So profitable is sucralose that competitors are constantly trying to find ways around the patents rights to produce it legally themselves. One competitor, the US company Nutrasweet, announced this week that it is talking to potential partners in China and India about possible techniques to produce sucralose without violating patents. Tate&Lyle believes that its patents are strong enough to prevent competition until patents expire in 2020. But with several Chinese companies already producing small quantities of the sweetener, many analysts doubt that Tate&Lyle will hold out that long.

Innovation

Artificial sweeteners have traditionally been used by food manufacturers to create 'low calorie' products which appeal to customers who don't want the high calorie content of a product made with natural sugar.

Sucralose currently leads the artificial sweeteners market on taste. It the most 'natural' sweetener being made from sugar and many consumers find that it tastes the most like sugar.

However, taste is not everything in this market. Nutrasweet, the US sweetener company, has recently launched Neotame. This is so sweet and cheap to produce that $1 of Neotame can be used to replace $10 of refined sugar in a product. Some soft drink manufacturers are now mixing Neotame with natural sugar in their drinks to cut costs of production. Sales of Neotame quadrupled last year.

The holy grail of the industry, however, is to produce a truly organic, plant-based sugar substitute that would taste exactly like sugar but have minimal calories. The company which comes up with this product is set to make a fortune if it can ring fence the product with patents.

Source: adapted from the *Financial Times*, 28.9.2005, Tate&Lyle, *Annual Report and Accounts*, 2005.

1. Explain the link between a 'patent' and a 'monopoly'.
2. Using examples from the data, explain why firms take out patents.
3. Discuss whether patents in the artificial sweeteners market lead to market efficiency or market failure.

Externalities

Summary

1. Externalities are created when social costs and benefits differ from private costs and benefits.
2. The greater the externality, the greater the likely market failure.
3. Governments can use regulation, the extension of property rights, taxation and permits to reduce the market failure caused by externalities.

Private and social costs and benefits

A chemical plant may dump waste into a river in order to minimise its costs. Further down the river, a water company has to treat the water to remove dangerous chemicals before supplying drinking water to its customers. Its customers have to pay higher prices because of the pollution.

This is a classic example of EXTERNALITIES or SPILLOVER EFFECTS. Externalities arise when private costs and benefits are different from social costs and benefits. A PRIVATE COST is the cost of an activity to an individual economic unit, such as a consumer or a firm. For instance, a chemical company will have to pay for workers, raw materials and plant and machinery when it produces chemicals. A SOCIAL COST is the cost of an activity not just to the individual economic unit which creates the cost, but to the rest of society as well. It therefore includes all private costs, but may also include other costs. The chemical manufacturer may make little or no payment for the pollution it generates. The difference between private cost and social cost is the externality or spillover effect. If social cost is greater than private cost, then a NEGATIVE EXTERNALITY or EXTERNAL COST is said to exist.

However, not all externalities are negative. A company may put up a building which is not just functional but also beautiful.

The value of the pleasure which the building gives to society over its lifetime (the SOCIAL BENEFIT) may well far exceed the benefit of the building received by the company (the PRIVATE BENEFIT). Hence, if social benefit is greater than private benefit, a positive externality or EXTERNAL BENEFIT is said to exist.

This is often the case with health care provision (an example of a merit good ☞ unit 20). Although one individual will benefit from inoculation against illness, the social benefit resulting from the reduced risk of other members of society contracting the illness will be even greater. Positive externalities could also result from education and training. An individual may benefit in the form of a better job and a higher salary but society may gain even more from the benefits of a better trained workforce.

Activities where social benefit exceeds private benefit are often inadequately provided by a market system. In many cases this results in either state provision or a government subsidy to encourage private provision.

Market failure

The price mechanism allocates resources. Prices and profits are the signals which determine this allocation. However, a misallocation of resources will occur if market prices and profits

Question I

(a) Why might each of the examples in the photographs give rise to positive and negative externalities?

do not accurately reflect the costs and benefits to society of economic activities.

For instance, in the case of the chemical plant above, the price of chemicals does not accurately reflect their true cost to society. The private cost of production to the manufacturer is lower than the social cost to society as a whole. Because the price of chemicals is lower than that which reflects social cost, the quantity demanded of chemicals and therefore consumption of chemicals will be greater than if the full social cost were charged. On the other hand, if the water company is pricing water to consumers, it will have to charge higher prices to consumers than would have been the case without the chemical pollution. Demand for water and consumption of water will therefore be less than it would otherwise have been without the externality.

The greater the externality, the greater the market failure and the less market prices and profits provide accurate signals for the optimal allocation of resources.

Government policy

The government has a wide range of policies that it could use to bring about an efficient allocation of resources where externalities exist.

Regulation Regulation is a method which is widely used in the UK and throughout the world to control externalities. The government could lay down maximum pollution levels or might even ban pollution creating activities altogether. For instance, in the UK, the Environmental Protection Act 1989 laid down minimum environmental standards for emissions from over 3 500 factories involved in chemical processes, waste incineration and oil refining. There are limits on harmful emissions from car exhausts. Cars that do not meet these standards fail their MOT tests. Forty years before these MOT regulations came into force, the government banned the burning of ordinary coal in urban areas.

Regulation is easy to understand and relatively cheap to enforce. However, it is a rather crude policy. First, it is often difficult for government to fix the right level of regulation to ensure efficiency. Regulations might be too lax or too tight. The correct level would be where the economic benefit arising from a reduction in externality equalled the economic cost imposed by the regulation. For instance, if firms had to spend £30 million fitting anti-pollution devices to plant and machinery, but the fall in pollution was only worth £20 million, then the regulation would have been too tight. If the fall in pollution was worth £40 million, it implies that it would be worth industry spending even more on anti-pollution measures to further reduce pollution and thus further increase the £40 million worth of benefits.

Moreover, regulations tend not to discriminate between different costs of reducing externalities. For instance, two firms might have to reduce pollution emissions by the same amount. Firm A could reduce its emissions at a cost of £3 million whilst it might cost Firm B £10 million to do the same. However, Firm A could double the reduction in its pollution levels at a cost of £7 million. Regulations which set equal limits for all firms will mean that the cost to society of reducing pollution in this case is £13 million (£3 million for Firm A and £10 million for Firm B). But it would be cheaper for society if the reduction could be achieved by Firm A alone at a cost of £7 million.

Extending property rights If a chemical company lorry destroyed your home, you would expect the chemical company to pay compensation. If the chemical

Question 2

Small to medium sized businesses are responsible for 80 per cent of environmental crimes. Yet, according to a report by the House of Commons environmental audit committee, almost all offences fail to be detected or prosecuted by the relevant legal authorities. For example, since 2001 when businesses have had to pay to use waste tips, fly-tipping has increased by 40 per cent. This is the illegal dumping of waste by the roadside, or on waste land. The cost of dealing with fly-tipping is estimated at between £100 million and £150 million per year.

Fly-posting is another major problem, but local authorities will soon be able to recover the cost of removing fly-posting and graffiti from offending companies under the provisions of the Clean Neighbourhoods and Environment Bill. Fly-posting has been regularly used by clubs and concert promoters wishing to advertise particular events. The local area is deluged with posters strapped to lamp posts but not taken down afterwards. Local authorities then have to pay their workers to remove the posters.

The House of Commons Report said that 'unless there is a real threat of being detected, the offender will continue to offend'. The Department for Environment, Food and Rural Affairs believes that, even when prosecutions do reach the court, many companies receive unreasonably small fines for polluting.

Source: adapted from the *Financial Times*, 9.2.2005.

(a) Explain how fly-tipping creates an externality.
(b) From an economic viewpoint, why do lack of detection and small fines for environmental crimes limit the effectiveness of regulation as a way of dealing with environmental problems?
(c) Explain why matching fines to the environmental damage caused might be a better way of dealing with environmental crimes than simply levying fixed penalties.

company polluted the atmosphere so that the trees in your garden died, it would be unlikely that you would gain compensation, particularly if the chemical plant were in the UK and the dead trees were in Germany.

Externalities often arise because property rights are not fully allocated. Nobody owns the atmosphere or the oceans, for instance. An alternative to regulation is for government to extend property rights. It can give water companies the right to charge companies which dump waste into rivers or the sea. It can give workers the right to sue for compensation if they have suffered injury or death as a result of working for a company. It can give local residents the right to claim compensation if pollution levels are more than a certain amount.

Extending property rights is a way of **internalising the externality** - eliminating the externality by bringing it back into the framework of the market mechanism. Fifty years ago, asbestos was not seen as a dangerous material. Today, asbestos companies around the world are having to pay compensation to workers suffering from asbestosis. They have also had to tighten up considerably on safety in the workplace where asbestos is used. Workers have been given property rights which enable them to sue asbestos companies for compensation.

One advantage of extending property rights is that the government does not have to assess the cost of pollution. It is generally assumed that property owners will have a far better knowledge of the value of property than the government. There should also be a direct transfer of resources from those who create pollution to those who suffer. With regulation, in contrast, the losers are not compensated whilst polluters are free to pollute up to the limit despite the fact that the pollution is imposing costs on society.

There are problems though. One is that a government may not have the ability to extend property rights. This occurs, for instance, when the cause of the externality arises in another country. How do Western governments prevent countries like Brazil from logging huge areas of forest, leading to global warming, which imposes costs on them? One way around this is to pay the agents causing the externality to stop their economic activity. So Western countries could pay countries like Brazil not to log their forests.

Another problem is that extending property rights can be very difficult in many cases. Asbestos companies, for instance, will not pay claims to asbestos workers unless it can definitely be proved that their medical condition was caused by working with asbestos. The compensation process can take years, and many ex-workers die before their cases are settled. They receive no compensation and the asbestos company has not had to include payment in its costs. This would tend to lead to a continuing overproduction of asbestos.

A final problem is that it is often very difficult even for the owners of property rights to assess the value of those rights. For instance, one homeowner might put a far higher value on trees in his or her garden than another homeowner. If a cable company lays cable in the road, cutting the roots of trees in front gardens, should the homeowner who places a high value on trees be compensated more than the homeowner who is fairly indifferent when trees die? What happens if the homeowner wanted to get rid of the trees anyway?

Taxes Another solution, much favoured by economists, is the use of taxes. The government needs to assess the cost to society of a particular negative externality. It then sets tax rates on those externalities equal to the value of the externality. This increases costs to customers by shifting the supply curve to the left. The result is a fall in demand and output and thus fewer externalities are created.

For example, the government might put a tax on petrol for cars because emissions from cars contribute to global warming. The tax should be set at the level where the tax revenues equal the cost to society of the emissions. This **internalises** the externality, as explained above, making the polluter pay the cost of pollution.

Taxes, like extending property rights, have the advantage that they allow the market mechanism to decide how resources should best be allocated. Those creating the highest levels of negative externalities have a greater incentive to reduce those externalities than those creating fewer externalities.

However, it is often very difficult for government to place a monetary value on negative externalities and therefore decide what should be the optimal tax rate. With global warming, for instance, there is considerable disagreement about its likely economic impact. Some environmentalists would argue that the potential economic costs are so large that cars should be virtually priced off the roads. At the opposite extreme, some argue that global warming, if it occurs at all, will bring net economic benefits. For instance, slightly higher temperatures will increase the amount of food that can be produced and make it easier to feed the world's growing population. There is therefore no need for taxes on petrol designed to reduce emissions.

Question 3

The death of the drinks can is now a distinct possibility in environmentally conscious Germany. Since January, a new refundable deposit of between 25 and 50 cents has been levied on most recyclable cans and bottles. The deposit in effect doubles the retail price of the drinks. Consumers can get their deposit back by returning the empty can to the retailer who sold them the can. But this is so much trouble for most consumers (and impossible if bought from most vending machines) that sales of drinks in cans have slumped. Can manufacturers estimate that sales of cans in Germany fell by about 50 per cent in the first half of this year.

The new measures have been introduced not just to encourage recycling of cans but also to encourage consumers to move more towards using refillable bottles. Refillable bottles are used in the UK by door step milk delivery companies where empty milk bottles are returned to the dairy to be reused. The deposit though was too successful this year. In June, both Coca-Cola and the German Brewers' League ran out of refillable bottles and launched advertising campaigns to stop buyers hoarding them or throwing them away.

Source: adapted from the *Financial Times*, 9.7.2003.

(a) Why might cans and bottles create an externality?
(b) The German scheme is an example of extending property rights. Explain why.
(c) How will the scheme reduce externalities?

Where positive externalities occur, governments should offer subsidies. It can be argued, for instance, that parks, libraries, art galleries, concert halls and opera houses create positive externalities. Therefore they should be subsidised. As with taxes and negative externalities, the level of subsidy should equal the positive externality created.

Permits A variation on regulating negative externalities through direct controls is the idea of issuing permits. Assume that the government wishes to control emissions of sulphur into the atmosphere. It issues permits to pollute, the total of which equals the maximum amount of sulphur it wishes to see emitted over a period of time like a year. The government then allocates permits to individual firms or other polluters. This could be done, for instance, on the basis of current levels of emissions by firms or on output of goods giving rise to sulphur emissions in production. The permits are then tradable for money between polluters. Firms which succeed in reducing their sulphur levels below their permit levels can sell their permits to other producers who are exceeding their limits.

The main advantage of permits over simple regulation is that costs in the industry and therefore to society should be lower than with regulation. Each firm in the industry will consider whether it is possible to reduce emissions and at what cost. Assume that Firm A, with just enough permits to meet its emissions, can reduce emissions by 500 tonnes at a cost of £10 million. Firm B is a high polluter and needs 500 tonnes worth of permits to meet regulations. It calculates that it would need to spend £25 million to cut emissions by this amount.

If there was simple regulation, the anti-pollution costs to the industry, and therefore to society, would be £25 million. Firm B would have to conform to its pollution limit whilst there would be no incentive for Firm A to

Question 4

Smoking is widely accepted to be a killer. But so too is passive smoking, the taking in of smoke fumes in a room when another person is smoking. A leaked Report from the Scientific Committee on Tobacco and Health indicated that second-hand smoke increased the risk of heart disease by an estimated 25 per cent.

The UK is about to implement the 2003 European Union Tobacco Advertising and Sponsorship Directive which orders member states to outlaw advertising in the press and other forms of media by 2005. The UK has chosen to allow tobacco companies to advertise at the point of sale so long as posters are no larger than a single A5 sheet.

The tobacco industry has long argued that advertising doesn't attract new users or increase the quantity of cigarette smoking. Instead, it shifts customer preferences between brands. It is arguing the implementation of the new ban on advertising will not hurt them. However, there is evidence that overall sales do decline with increases in taxes on tobacco. In Germany, the government over the past 18 months has increased taxes on tobacco, raising the price of a packet of cigarettes from €3.00 to €3.80 (£2.00 to £2.63). Volumes of cigarettes sold have decreased 13 per cent over the period, and are expected to fall further.

Source: adapted from the *Financial Times*, 19.10.2004.

(a) Explain why cigarette smoking causes externalities.
(b) Discuss whether the market failure caused by the sale of cigarettes is best tackled by bans on advertising **or** rising taxes. Use demand and supply diagrams and the concept of price elasticity of demand in the analysis to your answer.

Question 5

Industry reacted with fury yesterday when the government announced plans to further reduce emissions of greenhouse gases. Under the Kyoto Protocol, signed in 1997, the UK agreed to reduce emissions by 12.5 per cent from their 1990 levels. But government ministers yesterday announced a two-stage plan to cut emissions by 20 per cent from 1990 levels by 2010.

The burden will fall disproportionately on a few heavy industries, such as electricity generation, oil refining, and steel, cement, glass and paper production, which currently account for half of the UK's CO_2 emissions. These industries will have to cut their emissions quite dramatically under a new EU-wide emissions trading scheme starting in 2005. Transport and domestic emissions will not be covered. Individual industrial sites will be allocated a set number of 'emission permits'. For each tonne of CO_2 they produce over their allocation, they will have to buy extra permits from those sites which have produced less CO_2 than they are allowed to.

Business organisations warned that the effect of the scheme would be to increase electricity prices and force production offshore to countries that did not recognise the Kyoto Protocol.

Source: adapted from *The Independent*, 20.1.2004.

(a) Explain what is meant by an 'emission permit'.
(b) How can a system of tradable permits lead to a more efficient way of reducing pollution than simple regulation?
(c) Discuss whether UK producers are being put under an unfair competitive disadvantage because of the Kyoto Protocol.

cut pollution.

With permits, Firm A could sell 500 tonnes of permits to Firm B. The cost to society of then reducing pollution would only be £10 million, the cost that Firm A would incur, and not £25 million as with regulation. It might cost Firm B more than £10 million to buy the permits. It would be prepared to spend anything up to £25 million to acquire them. Say Firm A drove a hard bargain and sold the permits to Firm B for £22 million. Society would save £15 million (£25 million - £10 million), distributed between a paper profit of £12 million for Firm A and a fall in costs from what otherwise would have been the case for Firm B of £3 million.

Key terms

Externality or spillover effect - the difference between social costs and benefits and private costs and benefits. If net social cost (social cost minus social benefit) is greater than net private cost (private cost minus private benefit), then a **negative externality** or **external cost** exists. If net social benefit is greater than net private benefit, a **positive externality** or **external benefit** exists.

Private cost and benefit - the cost or benefit of an activity to an individual economic unit such as a consumer or a firm.
Social cost and benefit - the cost or benefit of an activity to society as a whole.

Applied economics

Global warming

The environmental problem

During the 1980s, there was a growing awareness that levels of greenhouse gases in the atmosphere were rising and that this might pose a serious problem for the future of the planet. Global warming, a rise in world temperatures, comes about because greenhouse gases act as a blanket, trapping heat within the earth's atmosphere.

A rise of a few degrees in world temperatures sounds very little. However, it would be enough to cause major shifts in the desert zones of the world. Many of the major wheat producing areas, such as the American plains, would become deserts. Old deserts, such as the Sahara, would become fertile in time. The transition costs to the world economy would be substantial. Figure 19.1 shows by how much world temperatures and those in Central England have deviated from the average of 1961-1990 since 1772. It is clear that average temperatures rose during the twentieth century compared to the nineteenth century. It is also clear that average temperatures since 1990 have been rising compared to the historical average. Four of the five warmest years since 1772 in Central England have been since 1990.

A second problem associated with global warming is rising sea levels. Higher world temperatures would lead to some melting of the polar icecaps, releasing large volumes of water in the oceans. With a 3 degree centigrade rise in world temperatures, there could be an increase in sea levels of 30cm. This would be enough to flood areas such as the east coast of England, the Bangladesh delta and the Maldive Islands. Sea defences and dykes could and probably would be built, but the cost to the world economy would be considerable. Figure 19.2 shows sea level rises that have already taken place at selected sites around the UK between 1850 and 2003.

Figure 19.1 Average surface temperature, world and Central England, 1772-2004

Difference between actual temperature and 1961-1990 average, degrees centigrade

Source: adapted from Defra, *Environment in your pocket.*

Figure 19.2 Sea level rise at selected UK sites, 1850-2003

Difference between actual sea level and 1920 level (cm)

Source: adapted from Defra, *Environment in your pocket.*

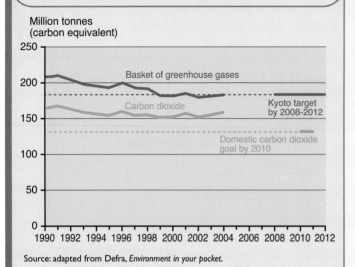

Figure 19.3 UK emissions of greenhouse gases, 1990-2004

Source: adapted from Defra, *Environment in your pocket.*

Figure 19.4 UK air pollutants: emissions of selected gases and GDP, 1990=100

Source: adapted from *Sustainable Consumption and Production Indicators*, Defra; *Annual Abstract of Statistics*, Office for National Statistics.

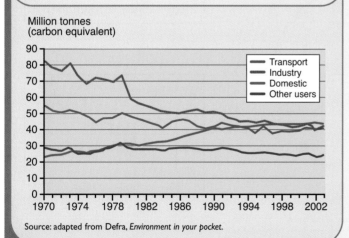

Figure 19.5 Carbon dioxide emissions, by end users: 1970-2003

Source: adapted from Defra, *Environment in your pocket.*

Sources of greenhouse gas emissions

Figure 19.3 shows that around 80 per cent of greenhouse gas emissions come from carbon dioxide. Almost all the rest is split roughly equally between methane and nitrous oxide.

In terms of who creates these emissions, roughly 90 per cent of carbon dioxide emissions are split equally between the transport, industry and domestic sectors. Petrol and diesel fuels account for almost all transport CO_2 emissions. Industry uses power generated by burning gas, coal and oil, as well as a variety of industrial processes which in themselves release CO_2 into the atmosphere. Equally, homes use gas, electricity and oil for heating and other uses. Agriculture creates roughly half the methane and nitrous oxide emissions. Nitrous oxide comes from fertilisers that farmers put onto the land, whilst methane comes from sheep and cattle.

Reducing greenhouse gas emissions

It is easy to assume that there is a direct link between growth in the economy and pollution: the higher the income of a country, for example, the higher its pollution levels. However, the evidence does not bear this out. Figure 19.4 shows how certain emissions have fallen over a period when real income (GDP) increased by 36 per cent. There are two main reasons why higher growth may lead to less rather than more pollution. First, industry may, by itself, move over to less polluting forms of technology. So coal fired power stations have become more efficient, producing more electricity from a tonne of coal. Steel manufacturing uses less energy per tonne of steel produced than 30 years ago. In the case of the UK, economic growth over the past 30 years has been almost entirely in the tertiary sector of the economy. Offices, shops, schools and hospitals produce fewer greenhouse gas emissions than aluminium plants or coal mines.

Second, government has been implementing policies to reduce the amount of pollution. Some of these policies have come about because of agreed action on an international scale. For example, the Montreal Protocol signed in 1987 committed 93 countries, including the major industrialised nations of the world, to phasing out the use of CFCs which were destroying the earth's ozone layer. The Rio Summit of 1992, which was followed by the Kyoto Protocol of 1997, led to industrialised nations, excluding the USA, to agree to reducing greenhouse gas emissions to 12.5 per cent less than their 1990 levels.

Figure 19.5 shows how greenhouse gas emissions by end user have changed since 1970. Carbon emissions of the electricity generation industry have been divided up according to who consumes the electricity. Figure 19.5 shows that industry has been the most successful end user in reducing carbon emissions. Reduction in domestic emissions have come almost entirely from less carbon polluting forms of electricity generation. Transport in the 1990s and early 2000s saw a small increase in carbon emissions. 'Other users' is mainly agriculture, which has made a small but not particularly significant contribution to reductions in carbon emissions.

UK policies

In signing the 1997 Kyoto Protocol, the UK government agreed to reduce its greenhouse gas emissions to 12.5 per cent less than their 1990 levels by 2010. In 2004, it went further, announcing that it would reduce emissions to 20 per cent less than their 1990 levels by 2010. The government has adopted a piecemeal approach to ensuring that it meets its greenhouse gas emission targets.

One major source of greenhouse gas emissions is industry, including the power generation industry. In 2005, the government in conjunction with other EU countries, introduced an emissions trading scheme. Existing industrial users were given carbon permits for each site they operated. If the company created more carbon than its total permits allowed, it would have to buy permits on the open market from other companies which created less carbon than their total permits allowed. Over time, companies will be given fewer permits, giving them an incentive to reduce their carbon emissions.

Industrial users include electricity generation companies. In the 1980s and 1990s, major reductions in carbon emissions were achieved by the shrinkage of the coal industry and a shift towards more carbon efficient electricity power stations powered by gas. However, the government now faces a dilemma because of nuclear power. In 2005, around 20 per cent of UK electricity was generated by nuclear power stations. These, however, are nearing the end of their operational life. They could be replaced by building new nuclear power stations, but this would be vigourously opposed by the environmental lobby on safety grounds. Equally, they could be replaced by 'renewable' energy sources such as wind power. However, renewable energy sources are still relatively expensive. There are environmental concerns about building large numbers of 'wind farms' which 'spoil' the landscape where they are situated. Finally, there are doubts about whether renewables can provide energy security at all times of the year given that there are times when the wind doesn't blow or the sun doesn't shine and so no electricity is generated. The third alternative is to build more gas or coal fired stations, but this would lead to a significant increase in

greenhouse gas emissions which would make achieving the Kyoto targets impossible.

Transport, too, poses problems for government policy. Increasing numbers of road journeys have led carbon emissions from transport to increase over time. In 1993, the Chancellor announced that the duty on fuel would be increased by 3 per cent per year above the rate of inflation to curb growth in journeys. In 1998, this was increased to 6 per cent. But this policy was effectively abandoned in 2000 when a blockade of oil refineries by a mix of farmers and road hauliers angry at high fuel prices brought the country almost to a standstill. It is also doubtful whether higher petrol prices would lead to much reduction in the number of car journeys made because fuel is highly price inelastic. Government policy with regard to road transport is now mainly targeted at reducing congestion rather than fuel emissions. Road transport is likely to add to carbon emissions over the next decade rather than reduce them.

Growth in air transport poses even more problems for the government (see the Data Question). With air traffic growing at 3-5 per cent per annum, it is likely that the aviation industry will contribute to higher carbon emissions in future. As with road transport, the main focus of government policy is concentrated on how to accommodate the growth of air transport rather than curbing it to achieve lower carbon emissions over time.

The government has a large number of small scale initiatives to curb carbon emissions by households. These range from encouraging householders to lag their lofts, to getting householders to turn down their central heating, to getting builders to build new houses which are more energy efficient. Agriculture is also a major contributor to greenhouse gas emissions. Through encouraging 'greener', less intensive, farming methods, the government is hoping to have some impact on emissions. However, the government does not expect significant reductions in greenhouse gas emissions from either households or agriculture.

Most environmental groups argue that the government is unlikely to achieve its Kyoto Protocol targets by 2010. With households and agriculture only making at best very small contributions to the target, and with emissions from transport likely to grow, it is industry including power generation that will have to make the reduction needed. This would be very challenging at the best of times. But if nuclear power is replaced, mainly by gas or coal fired power stations, it will be impossible. The choice about how to generate electricity over the next 20 years will probably be key to whether greenhouse gas emissions rise or fall in the UK.

DataQuestion — Aviation and global warming

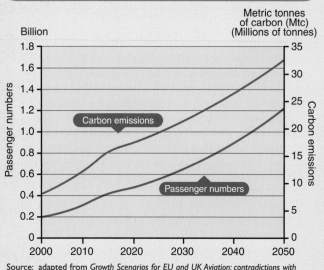

Figure 19.6 Forecast passenger numbers, carbon emissions, UK airline traffic

Source: adapted from *Growth Scenarios for EU and UK Aviation: contradictions with climate policy*, Tyndall Centre for Climate Change and research, a report commissioned by Friends of the Earth.

Air passenger traffic in the UK increased by an average 6.4 per cent a year between 1993 and 2001. However, the volume of emissions per passenger has gone down. Manufacturers have incorporated fuel efficiency measures into the design of their aircraft. Over the past 40 years, better airframes, larger aircraft and improved engine technology have reduced emissions by 70 per cent per passenger per kilometre.

Source: adapted from the *Financial Times*, 9.6.2005.

The UK can't make a sizeable difference to the problem of aircraft pollution on its own. Any attempt to impose taxes or other restrictions on flights into and out of the UK would simply lead to a massive diversion of air traffic out of UK space into continental Europe. What is more, the UK is only a small part of a worldwide problem. Collective action is needed.

Matters are being discussed at a European level, both within the European Parliament and the European Commission. Critics of the growth of the aviation industry point out that airlines pay no tax on the aviation fuel used to power aircraft. In contrast, most of the cost of petrol used by motorists is made up of taxes. Some European politicians are convinced that imposing a tax on the distance an aircraft travels and its engine performance would be the simplest method of tackling soaring emissions. These ideas are strongly opposed by most European airlines. They want to see an emissions trading scheme, where companies that achieved deeper emission cuts than expected would be able to sell surplus permits to companies that exceeded their allocated emissions. One reason why European airlines favour an emissions trading scheme is that it would probably only add a few pounds to the price of a return ticket within Europe. This would not be enough to influence demand or stimulate improvements in efficiency. In the longer term, growing demand for carbon permits from the aviation industry could send the price of tradable carbon permits sky high. This would impact on all industries which needed to buy carbon permits on the open market.

Source: adapted from the *Financial Times*, 23.9.2004.

Airline passenger numbers are forecast to grow by 3-4 per cent a year in the UK. More and more people are taking a break abroad, lured by low prices from budget airlines such as easyJet or Ryanair. But the increase is causing an environmental headache. The UK, along with most of the world's rich nations, is committed by the Kyoto agreement to reduce CO_2 emissions to their 1990 levels by 2010. Yet the growing number of flights is hampering the

UK's achievement of that target. The severity of the problem was underlined last week when the Prime Minister said that aviation was likely to make up a quarter of the UK's contribution to global warming by 2030. The European Commission said: 'Aviation sector emissions have grown by 40 per cent since 1990. I think everyone accepts that it is a sector that something needs to be done about.'

Source: adapted from the *Financial Times*, 23.9.2004.

1. Describe the trends in air travel and carbon emissions from aviation between 2000 and 2050.
2. Explain why air travel may cause externalities.
3. Analyse THREE ways in which governments or international bodies such as the EU could reduce carbon emissions from aviation in the future.

4. Discuss whether governments should intervene at all in the aviation industry to reduce carbon emissions and, if so, how much airlines should be forced to pay on their emissions.

20 Public and merit goods

Summary

1. There will inevitably be market failure in a pure free market economy because it will fail to provide public goods.
2. Public goods must be provided by the state because of the free rider problem.
3. Merit goods are goods which are underprovided by the market mechanism, for instance because there are significant positive externalities in consumption.
4. Governments can intervene to ensure provision of public and merit goods through direct provision, subsidies or regulation.
5. Government failure can be caused by inadequate information, conflicting objectives, administrative costs and creation of market distortions.
6. Public choice theory suggests that governments may not always act to maximise the welfare of society because politicians may act to maximise their own welfare.

Markets and market failure

Markets may lead to an efficient allocation of resources. However, there are some goods and services which economists recognise are unlikely to be best produced in free markets. These may include defence, the judiciary and the criminal justice system, the police service, roads, the fire service and education. More controversially, some believe that the free market is poor at producing health care and housing for the less well off. There are different reasons why there might be market failure in the production of these goods.

Public goods

Nearly all goods are **private goods** (not to be confused with goods produced in the private sector of the economy). A private good is one where consumption by one person results in the good not being available for consumption by another. For instance, if you eat a bowl of muesli, then your friend can't eat it; if a firm builds a plant on a piece of land, that land is not available for use by local farmers.
A few goods, however, are PUBLIC GOODS. These are goods which possesses two characteristics:
- **non-rivalry** - consumption of the good by one person does not reduce the amount available for consumption by another person;
- **non-excludability** - once provided, no person can be excluded from benefiting (or indeed suffering in the case of a public good like pollution).
 There are relatively few examples of pure public goods, although many goods contain a public good element. Clean air is a public good. If you breathe clean air, it does not diminish the ability of others to breathe clean air. Moreover, others cannot prevent you from breathing clean air. Defence is another example. An increase in the population of the UK does not lead to a reduction in the defence protection accorded to the existing population. A person in Manchester cannot be excluded from benefiting even if she were to object to current defence policy, prefer to see all defence abolished, and refuse to pay to finance defence.
 Goods which can be argued to be public goods are:
- defence;
- the judiciary and prison service;
- the police service;

- street lighting.
 Many other goods, such as education and health, contain a small public good element.

The free rider problem

If the provision of public goods were left to the market mechanism, there would be market failure. This is because of the FREE RIDER problem. A public good is one where it is impossible to prevent people from receiving the benefits of the good once it has been provided. So there is very little incentive for people to pay for consumption of the good. A free rider is someone who receives the benefit but allows others to pay for it. For instance, citizens receive benefits from defence expenditure. But individual citizens could increase their economic welfare by not paying for it.

Question I

(a) Explain why lamp posts might be classed as a public good.

In a free market, national defence is unlikely to be provided. A firm attempting to provide defence services would have difficulty charging for the product since it could not be sold to benefit individual citizens. The result would be that no one would pay for defence and therefore the market would not provide it. The only way around this problem is for the state to provide defence and force everyone to contribute to its cost through taxation.

Merit and demerit goods

Even the most fervent advocates of free market economics agree that public goods are an example of market failure and that the government should provide these public goods. However, more controversial are merit and demerit goods.

A MERIT GOOD is one which is underprovided by the market mechanism (i.e. one which some people think should be provided in greater quantities). One reason for underprovision is that individuals lack perfect information and find it difficult to make rational decisions when costs occur today but the benefits received only come in, say, thirty years time. Another reason is because there are significant positive externalities (☞ unit 19) present.

Health, education and insurance are the main merit goods provided today by government in the UK. Health and insurance are two examples where consumers find it difficult to make rational choices because of time. If left totally to market forces, the evidence suggests that individuals would not give themselves sufficient health cover or cover against sickness, unemployment and old age. Young people tend to be healthy and in work. Many find it difficult to appreciate that one day they will be ill and out of work. However, the cost of health care and pensions is so great that young people can only afford them if they save for the future. If they don't, they find when they are older that they do not have sufficient resources to pay for medical services, or the insurance needed to cover them against loss of earnings due to illness or retirement. Therefore it makes sense for the state to intervene and to force young people in particular to make provision against sickness, unemployment and old age.

In the case of education, the main beneficiary (the child or student) is unlikely to be the person paying for the education. Therefore there could be a conflict of interest. It could be in the interest of the parents to pay as little as possible for the child's education but in the interest of the child to receive as high quality an education as possible. Others in society also have an interest. Children who, for instance, cannot read or write are an economic liability in the UK today. They are more likely than not to have to receive support from others rather than contribute to the nation's welfare. There are many other examples of goods with a merit good element. Lack of industrial training, for instance, is seen as a major problem in the UK. Individual firms have an incentive not to train workers, not only because it is so costly but also because their trained workers can then be poached by competitors. Rather, they go into the market place and recruit workers who have been trained at other firms' expense. This is an example again of the free rider problem. It is partly countered by the government providing funding for organisations which organise training in local areas.

A DEMERIT GOOD is one which is overprovided by the market mechanism. The clearest examples of demerit goods are drugs - everything from hard drugs such as LSD to alcohol and tobacco. Consumption of these goods produces large negative **externalities**. Crime increases, health costs rise, valuable human economic resources are destroyed, and

friends and relatives suffer distress. Moreover, individuals themselves suffer and are unable to stop consuming because drugs are addictive. Therefore it can be argued that consumers of drugs are not the best judges of their own interests.

Governments intervene to correct this market failure. They have three main weapons at their disposal: they can ban consumption as with hard drugs; they can use the price system to reduce demand by placing taxes on drugs; or they can try to persuade consumers to stop using drugs, for instance through advertising campaigns.

Equity

It would be extremely improbable that a free market system would lead to a distribution of resources which every individual would see as equitable. It is therefore argued by some economists that the state has a duty to reallocate resources.

In the UK today, for instance, there is some consensus that British citizens should not die for lack of food, or be refused urgent medical treatment for lack of money.

In the UK, over 30 per cent of all public spending is devoted

Question 2

(a) Suggest reasons why education might be considered a merit good.

Cost of school places to rise

to social security payments. Some of these payments come from the National Insurance fund and therefore could be seen as merit goods. But benefits such as family credit are an explicit attempt to redistribute income to those in need. It could also be argued that the free provision of services such as health and education leads to a more equitable distribution of resources.

Government intervention

Markets are likely to underprovide public and merit goods. This leads to **allocative inefficiency** because consumers are not able to spend their money in a way which will maximise their utility (their welfare or satisfaction). For instance, households in a city would be prepared to pay a few pounds a year to have street lighting throughout the city. But, because of the free rider problem, they are reluctant to make any contribution either because they hope everyone else will pay or because they don't want to make large payments because few others are paying. It then makes sense for government to force everyone to pay through a system of taxes.

Merit goods are more controversial, partly because they contain a private good element. The main beneficiaries of health care and education, for instance, are patients and students. Governments can attempt to increase the provision of merit goods in a variety of ways.

Direct provision Governments can supply public and merit goods directly to consumers free of charge. In the UK, primary school education, visits to the doctor and roads are provided in this way. The government may choose to produce the good or service itself, as with primary school education. Or it may buy in the services of firms in the private sector. General practitioners, for instance, work for themselves and the government buys their services.

Subsidised provision The government may pay for part of the good or service (a **subsidy**) but expect consumers to pay the rest. Prescriptions or dental care are subsidised in this way in the UK.

Regulation The government may leave provision to the private sector but force consumers to purchase a merit good or producers to provide a merit good. For instance, motorists are forced to buy car insurance by law. There is an ongoing debate in industrialised countries about whether workers should be forced to pay into private pensions. Motorway service stations are forced to provide toilet facilities free of charge to motorists whether or not they purchase anything.

There is a number of advantages and disadvantages to each of these solutions. The advantage of direct provision is that the government directly controls the supply of goods and services. It determines the number of hospital beds in the system because it provides them. It decides how many soldiers there are because it pays them directly. However, direct provision has disadvantages. It may be productively inefficient, particularly if the government produces the good itself. Employees of the state, whether providing the good or buying it in, may have no incentive to cut costs to a minimum. It may be allocatively inefficient, especially if the goods are provided free of charge to taxpayers. The government may provide too many soldiers and too few hospital beds, for instance. Markets, in contrast, give consumers the opportunity to buy those goods which give the greatest satisfaction. In a market, if producers supplied too many

soldiers, they would be left unsold. Firms would then move resources out of the production of defence and into the production of a good which consumers were prepared to buy.

Subsidies are a way of working through the market mechanism to increase the consumption of a good. So subsidising dental care, for instance, increases the amount of dental care provided, hopefully to a level which maximises economic welfare. Subsidies can also help those on low incomes to afford to buy goods. One problem with subsidies is that decisions about the level of subsidies can become 'captured' by producers. Subsidies then become too large to maximise welfare. For instance, it can be argued that farmers in Europe have to some extent 'captured' the Common Agricultural Policy. Instead of government ministers deciding what level of farm subsidy will maximise economic welfare, they bow to the pressure of the farming lobby. Farming subsidies then become far too large. The resultant welfare gains to farmers are far less than the welfare loss to consumers and taxpayers.

Regulation has the advantage that it requires little or no taxpayer's money to provide the good. Consumers are also likely to be able to shop around in the free market for a product which gives them good value, ensuring productive and allocative efficiency. However, regulations can impose heavy costs on the poor in society. How many poor families, for instance, could afford to pay for private health care insurance if it was a requirement for them to do so? Regulations can also be ignored. Not all motorists have insurance, for instance. If parents had a legal obligation to pay for their children to go to school, some parents would defy the law and not give their children an education. The more likely citizens are to evade regulations, the less efficient they are as a way of ensuring the provision of public and merit goods.

Government failure

Markets can fail, but so too can governments. GOVERNMENT FAILURE occurs when it intervenes in the market but this intervention leads to a loss of economic welfare rather than a gain. There is a number of reasons why government failure may occur.

Inadequate information Governments, like any economic agents, rarely possess complete information on which to base a decision. In some cases, the information available is positively misleading. It is not surprising, then, that governments may make the wrong policy response to a problem. For instance,

Question 3

There is a variety of ways in which the government could ensure that all households have access to dental services.

(a) It could provide the service directly, making it free to all users, and raise the required finance through taxes.

(b) It could subsidise some dental treatment considered to be essential, but not subsidise other treatment. This is the present system in the UK.

(c) It could make it a legal obligation that all households take out dental insurance to cover the cost of essential dental treatment.

Discuss the relative merits of each of these options.

governments have to make decisions about whether to fund a selective school system or a comprehensive school system. In Germany, the school system is selective. In the USA, it is comprehensive. In the UK, it is mainly comprehensive, but a significant minority of local authorities fund selective schools. The issue is important because education is a key determinant of the long term competitiveness of the UK. It also affects every individual child. However, the evidence about which is the most effective form of education is conflicting. In the 1960s and 1970s, the UK government supported the change from a mainly selective system to a mainly comprehensive system. In the 1980s and 1990s, the Conservative government favoured selective schools. In the 2000s the Labour government was pushing for a variety of provision and specialist schools.

Conflicting objectives Governments often face conflicting objectives. For instance, they may want to cut taxes but increase spending on defence. Every decision made by the government has an opportunity cost. Sometimes, a decision is made where the welfare gain from the alternative foregone would have been even higher. In the case of education, assume that those receiving a selective education in grammar schools receive a better education than if they were in a comprehensive school. In contrast, assume that those who fail to get into a selective school achieve less than if they were in a comprehensive school. There is now a conflict of objectives about which system to implement. Are the needs of those who would be selected for grammar schools more important than those of the rest of the school population, or vice versa? Governments may make the wrong policy decision when there are such conflicts of objective, choosing the option which gives lower economic welfare rather than higher economic welfare. They may do this because of lack of information. Or they may deliberately choose this option because they wish to reward their supporters in the electorate who voted for them (☞ below).

Administrative costs Sometimes, the administrative cost of correcting market failure is so large that it outweighs the welfare benefit from the correction of market failure. For instance, the government may put into place a scheme to help the unemployed back into work. During a year, 100 000 pass through the scheme. Of those, 50 000 would have found jobs anyway but simply use the scheme because it is advantageous for them or their employer to do so. 10 000 find a job who would otherwise not have done so. 40 000 remain unemployed. It may cost £3 000 per person per year on the scheme, giving a total cost of £300 million. This means that the cost per worker who would otherwise not have got a job is £300 million ÷ 10 000 or £30 000 per worker. This is an enormous cost for the benefit likely to be gained by the 10 000 workers. Indeed, they almost certainly would have preferred to have been given the £30 000 rather than gain a job. Another example would be the payment of welfare benefits. If it costs £1 to pay out a £3 benefit, is this likely to improve economic welfare?

Market distortions In some cases, government intervention to correct one market failure leads to the creation of far more serious market failures. One example is government intervention in agricultural markets such as the Common Agricultural Policy. Here, governments offer farmers financial support, partly to raise farm incomes which can be low and second to even out fluctuations in income from year to year arising from changes in the size of crops.

However, financial support typically leads to increases in the supply of food which may not be matched by increases in demand. The result is an over-supply of farm produce. Countries may choose to dump this over-supply on world markets at low prices. This leads to lower farm incomes for world farmers outside the European Union, destroying the markets for their produce. Higher farm incomes in Europe may be gained at the expense of lower farm incomes in Egypt or New Zealand. Agricultural markets within the EU may also be distorted. For instance, the price of beef is artificially high in the EU because of CAP support but pig prices receive no subsidy. The result is that EU consumers buy less beef and more pork than they would otherwise do if there were no government intervention. Another market distortion may occur with respect to the environment. The CAP encourages over-production of food. Marginal land is brought into production when it might otherwise be left wild. Too much pesticide and fertiliser may be used to raise yields because CAP offers too high prices to farmers. Lower prices might lead to less intensive modes of production and less destruction to wildlife.

There are many examples of market distortions in the labour market. For instance, the government may want to raise income levels for the poor by setting a high minimum wage. But this may be so high that employers shed low paid workers, putting out of work large numbers of people whom the government wanted to protect. Similarly, the government may raise unemployment benefit to help the unemployed. But this may discourage them from looking for work since more are now better off on the dole than working. This increases the numbers of unemployed.

Public choice theory

It is generally assumed that governments act in a way which they believe will maximise economic welfare. They may not succeed in this because of lack of information, conflicting objectives, etc. However, PUBLIC CHOICE THEORY suggests that governments

---

Question 4

In 1861, Mrs Beeton, then the authority on cookery and household management and the Victorian equivalent of Delia Smith, wrote that her readers should always make their own vinegar. This was because shop bought vinegar of the day tended to consist of diluted sulphuric acid.

Today, food manufacturers and retailers are so strictly controlled by government regulations that this could not happen. Some argue, though, that such regulations are excessive. Government red tape restricts the opening and running of new businesses. Consumers have to pay higher prices for their food because it costs firms money to conform to government regulations. For instance, in 1999, the costs of production to UK pig farmers went up because they could no longer rear pigs in stalls. Animal welfare activists would like to see battery hen production stopped and all chickens reared in free range conditions, but why shouldn't consumers have the choice about whether or not they buy cheaper battery produced eggs and chickens?

(a) Explain why markets fail according to the data.
(b) Discuss whether, in the examples given in the data, government intervention leads to government failure.

may not attempt to maximise economic welfare at all.

Public choice theory analyses how and why public spending and taxation decisions are made. 'Consumers' or 'customers' are voters in the system. They vote for politicians and political parties who are the 'producers' in the system. Producers make decisions about how public money should be spent, about taxes and about laws. The decisions have to be 'sold' by politicians to voters.

The voters want to maximise the net benefits they get from the state. For instance, all other things being equal, voters would like the state to provide large quantities of goods and services but with minimal levels of taxation.

Politicians want to maximise their welfare too. In the simplest models, politicians are assumed to want to maximise their votes, so that they can get into power and remain in power. In more complicated models, more sophisticated assumptions can be made, such as that politicians want to get posts in government, or use their political connections to maximise their own earnings.

If politicians want to maximise their votes, then the most obvious thing to do is to appeal to the centre ground. Consider Figure 20.1 which shows a normal distribution of votes. A right wing politician is facing a left wing politician who has pitched his policies so that they will attract votes to the left of OA. The obvious stance to take is for the right wing politician to pitch his policies just to the right of B, as near as possible to the middle ground whilst remaining to the right of the political spectrum. On the other hand, if the left wing politician were rational, he too would move to the centre ground to try and maximise his vote.

In practice, democracies tend to throw up governments which do veer towards the centre. It is for this reason that governments like those of Margaret Thatcher's in the 1980s were so unusual. Due to Britain's first past the post voting system, a UK party can get a majority in Parliament with as little as 40 per cent of the votes cast. With a 75 per cent turnout on polling day (i.e. 25 per cent of eligible voters don't vote), this means that a British government only has to gain the vote of 30 per cent of all voters. Not surprisingly, this sometimes allows a right wing party which itself has voted in a right wing leader to gain office. The same would of course be true for a left wing party in the UK which had a left wing leader.

In much of economic theory, there is a hidden assumption that governments act so as to maximise the welfare of society as a whole. Public choice theory can help explain why governments often fail to do this.

Local interests Assume that an MP has a large textile mill in her constituency which employs 1 000 workers. The company owning the mill lobbies the MP to support the imposition of higher tariffs (taxes on imports) on textiles, arguing that the mill will have to close unless foreign competition is reduced. Economic theory would probably suggest that the mill should be allowed to close and the resources released be used to produce something which the UK is better at producing (the **theory of comparative advantage** ☞ unit 14). However, the MP may be frightened that losing 1 000 jobs could mean losing 1 000 votes. Therefore, she could well put pressure on the government to impose higher tariffs even if she knows that the nation's welfare would be lessened as a result.

Favouring minorities Assume that a political party can get elected with considerably less than 50 per cent of the votes, because of the nature of the voting system and because not all

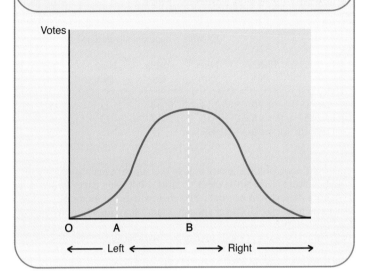

Figure 20.1 *Voting behaviour of electors.*
Politicians will tend to maximise their votes by moving to the centre ground in politics.

voters turn out on polling day. In UK national elections, as argued above, a party could get a majority with the support of just 30 per cent of voters. In a local election, where the turnout is often only 30-50 per cent, a party can get a majority with far less. Assume that those who do vote tend to possess similar characteristics. For instance, in the UK, middle class voters are more likely to vote than working class voters. In a local election, voters from one ethnic group may be far more likely to vote than voters from another ethnic group. In these situations, it is clear that politicians wishing to maximise their share of the vote will want to appeal to a minority, not the majority, because it is the minority who cast votes. A government might, for instance, introduce government spending and tax changes which leave 30 per cent of the population better off and 70 per cent worse off. This would be rational behaviour if the 30 per cent of the population better off tended to vote for that party in a first past the post system with a 75 per cent turnout. However, it is arguable as to whether the nation's welfare would be maximised as a result.

Conflicting personal interests Politicians, parties and governments may be prone to corruption. Assume that politicians are not just interested in winning votes and retaining power, but also in gaining personal economic wealth. There may then be a conflict of interest between maximising the nation's welfare and maximising the welfare of the individual politician. Assume, for instance, that a Third World political leader can remain in power by giving massive bribes to electors at election time. Between elections, he accepts bribes from electors for granting political favours. In the process, the country fails to develop because decisions are made on the basis of maximising the wealth of the individual politician rather than that of the country. The individual politician is far better off as a rich head of a poor country than as a leader who has lost power in a fast growing country.

Short-termism In the UK, there has to be a general election at least every five years. Assume that a government wants a high growth, low inflation economy. Unfortunately, the current state of the economy at the time is one of

Question 5

Table 20.1 Shares of disposable income				Percentages
Quintile groups of individuals				
Bottom fifth	Next fifth	Middle fifth	Next fifth	Top fifth
Year 0	10	14	18	23	35
Year 5	8	12	17	23	36
Year 10	6	11	17	23	43

Table 20.1 Shares of disposable income — Percentages

	Bottom fifth	Next fifth	Middle fifth	Next fifth	Top fifth
Year 0	10	14	18	23	35
Year 5	8	12	17	23	36
Year 10	6	11	17	23	43

A right wing political party enjoys the support mainly of above average income voters. It faces a left wing party which gains a majority of its votes from below average income supporters. The electoral system is such that a party only needs 40 per cent of the vote to secure a majority in Parliament, whilst a 45 per cent vote would give it a massive majority. On average, 75 per cent of the electorate vote, but the higher the income of the individual, the more likely they are to turn out to vote. The top 20 per cent of income earners have a turnout rate of 90 per cent.

The right wing party wins an election in year 0 committed to 'increasing incentives for individuals to earn money and create wealth for the nation'. It wins two further elections in year 5 and year 10.

(a) (i) Would Table 20.1 suggest that the nation's welfare has been maximised?
  (ii) What additional information would you need to support your conclusion?
(b) Explain why the party can win elections when the relative income position of most individuals is worsening over time.

high inflation and low growth. If the government pursues anti-inflationary policies, these will need to be long term policies if they are to be successful. But they are also likely to push up unemployment and lead to a tough tax and low government spending regime. A government coming up to re-election has two choices. It can cut taxes, increase public spending, and cut interest rates to stimulate spending and make voters 'feel good'. Or it can pursue austere policies which might keep the economy on course but leave voters feeling they are not particularly well off. Assume that the austere policies are the ones which will maximise welfare in the long term, but would mean the government losing the election. It is obvious that the government will go for the reflationary policies if that means it can win the election, even though it knows this will damage welfare.

Regulatory capture Governments are responsible for regulating many areas, such as monopolies or the environment. 'Regulatory capture' means that groups such as monopolists earning abnormal profit or polluters damaging the environment can strongly influence the way they are being regulated to their own advantage. Take, for instance, a utility which is about to be privatised. The board of the utility will want to make sure that it is as easy as possible after privatisation for it to make high profits to satisfy its shareholders and maximise the pay of members of the board. It will lobby hard to have as weak powers as possible given to the regulatory body which will supervise it after privatisation. National welfare would probably be maximised if the regulatory body were given strong powers to keep consumer prices as low as possible.

However, in the short term, the government is far more likely to be wanting to maximise its own short term electoral advantage from having a successful sale of the shares and by allowing small investors (probably its own voters) to make quick gains on the share price. This requires weak regulation. Once the company has been privatised, it will want to dominate the regulator. It will do this by supplying only the information which is favourable to its case. For instance, it will tend to underestimate revenues and overestimate costs in order to make it seem that future profits will be low. The regulator, with little evidence apart from that supplied by the utility, will constantly make decisions which are in the utility's interest.

Evidence from the UK since 1984, when the first regulator was appointed, suggests that the individual appointed to head the regulatory team can be crucial in determining whether or not the regulatory body is captured. A regulator who wants to minimise confrontation with a utility (i.e. have a quiet life) will allow him- or herself to be captured.

In economic theory, it is often assumed that market failure should be corrected by government. If a monopolist is exploiting the consumer, then the government should regulate or abolish the monopoly. If a polluter is damaging the environment, then the government should act to limit the actions of those responsible. Public choice theory suggests that government may fail to act in these cases because politicians are more interested in maximising their own rewards (such as votes to stay in power) than in maximising the nation's welfare. Indeed, in some cases, politicians maximising their own rewards may lead to an even greater loss of economic welfare than if market failure had been left unregulated. At one extreme, some economists argue that governments should intervene as little as possible in the economy because their interventions are likely to be more damaging than the problems they are trying to solve. On the other hand, it is argued that politicians are not all out to maximise their own self-interest. Some politicians do act in the public interest even when this does not accord with their own self-interest. A left wing MP, for instance, who votes for higher income tax rates on higher income earners is likely to pay more in tax as a result. This doesn't mean to say that he or she won't vote in favour. The more a political system can encourage its politicians to act in the public interest, the more it will accord with the traditional view that government acts as an impartial actor in the economic system, intervening to maximise national welfare.

Key terms

Free rider - a person or organisation which receives benefits that others have paid for without making any contribution themselves.
Government failure - occurs when government intervention leads to a net welfare loss compared to the free market solution.
Merit good - a good which is underprovided by the market mechanism. A demerit good is one which is overprovided by the market mechanism.

Public choice theory - theories about how and why public spending and taxation decisions are made.
Public good - a good where consumption by one person does not reduce the amount available for consumption by another person and where once provided, all individuals benefit or suffer whether they wish to or not.

Applied economics

Lighthouses

Public goods are goods which possess the two properties of non-excludability (once provided, it is impossible to prevent others from benefiting) and non-rivalry (benefit by one does not diminish the amount by which others can benefit). Lighthouses possess both these characteristics. Once the lighthouse is working, it is impossible to prevent any ship in the area benefiting. The fact that one ship sees the lighthouse doesn't prevent other ships from seeing it as well.

Economists from Adam Smith onwards have then argued that public goods need to be provided by the public sector because there is no economic incentive for the private sector to provide them. Non-excludability would mean that there would be large numbers of free-riders - individuals or firms which benefited but did not pay. For instance, how could ships be made to pay for lighthouses?

In the UK, government doesn't provide lighthouses. They are provided by Trinity House, a private corporation. However, the government has given it the right to build lighthouses. In return, the government allows it to charge each ship which visits a British port a 'light charge'. This is collected by Revenue and Customs, part of the government. Trinity House has to submit its budget to both the government and representatives of the shipping industry each year, where it has to justify the scale of its

charges. So in this case, whilst the government doesn't provide the public good, it is involved at every stage and crucially in forcing ships to pay charges for the upkeep of lighthouses.

It is in fact difficult to think of any public good for which the government doesn't provide or regulate its private provision. However, the example of lighthouses shows that a public good is not necessarily one directly provided by the government.

Housing since 1945

Housing was identified as one of the key elements of a Welfare State in the Beveridge Report of 1942. Since 1945, the government has played a key role in the housing market. In the 1950s and 1960s, government, through local authorities, built millions of houses for rent to overcome the problem of a lack of accommodation fit for human habitation at an affordable rent. It was generally felt that the private sector would not provide sufficient new housing or of the right quality to satisfy the needs of the post-war population. In the early 1960s, a series of scandals highlighted the high rents, poor quality accommodation and lack of security offered by some private landlords. As a result, the private rented sector became subject to controls through the imposition of maximum rents and the introduction of strong rights of tenure for tenants. Again, from the 1960s, a strong financial incentive to buy houses was introduced through the scrapping of a tax on the notional rent on owner occupied houses and the introduction of tax relief on mortgage payments.

1979 saw the beginnings of a marked shift in government policy. Owner occupation was given a more important priority, with government talking of the creation of a 'property owning democracy'. Council tenants were given the right to buy their rented homes at a price below the true market price of the property. Financial deregulation increased the willingness of banks and building societies to give mortgages to individuals. A severe squeeze was put on local authority spending on building of new council houses in the belief that local authorities were inefficient bureaucracies which mismanaged their housing stock and which failed to give their tenants sufficient choice and control over their dwellings. At the same time, the government channelled much larger grants to Housing Associations, charity-type bodies which had a long history of building and renting out houses at affordable rents. Central government forced local authorities to increase rents, although much of the cost of this was born by central government which then had to give larger housing benefits to individuals whose income was too low to be able to afford to pay the rent. Homelessness increased as the stock of affordable rented property declined whilst social changes, such as increased divorce rates, increased the numbers of households needing to be housed.

Tax relief was effectively a subsidy given to anyone buying a house using a mortgage. It reduced the cost of mortgage repayments once the relief was given and so allowed house buyers to afford higher mortgage repayments, and therefore to buy more expensive houses. It was justified in terms of making home ownership more affordable to a wider range of income groups.

In the late 1980s, there were further significant policy changes. First, the government began the process of phasing out income tax relief on mortgages. Removing the subsidy increased the cost of mortgage repayments to homebuyers and so increased the cost of home ownership to those with mortgages. One justification was that the subsidy mainly went to better off households. Another was that, with a highly inelastic price elasticity of supply of houses, the subsidy didn't make housing more affordable. Instead, it just pushed up the prices of houses.

The second significant change at the end of the 1980s was the passing of the Housing Act 1988. This created a new form of tenure for private letting of houses, the assured tenancy. Under the Act, private landlords could now set whatever rent they wanted and could evict tenants at relatively short notice if they agreed an assured tenancy agreement with the renter of the property. Very rapidly, assured tenancy agreements became the norm in the private rented market. This effectively swept away the rent controls imposed by government in the 1960s.

In the 1990s and the 2000s, the effects of these changes had significant effects on the housing market. The stock of council housing fell from 5.2 million in 1990 to 3.1 million in 2003. Partly this reflected sales of council houses partly to their tenants and partly to Housing Associations.

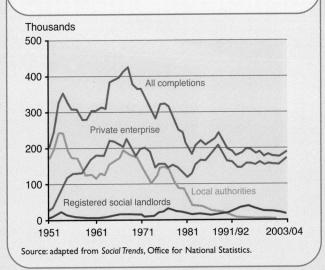

Figure 20.2 *Housebuilding completions by sector: number of new homes built*

Source: adapted from *Social Trends*, Office for National Statistics.

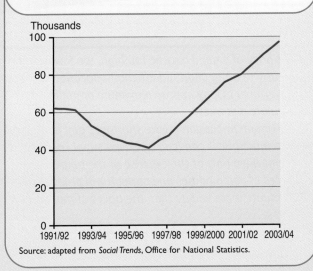

Figure 20.3 *Homeless households in temporary accommodation*

Source: adapted from *Social Trends*, Office for National Statistics.

Table 20.2 *Percentage of households by gross yearly income (£) of main householder and partner in different types of household tenure, 2003-2004*

	Gross income of the head of household and partner (£ per year)				
	Under £10 000	£10 000-£15 000	£15 000-£30 000	£30 000 and over	All income groups
Owner occupied	15%	13%	32%	41%	100%
Rented from private landlord	31%	16%	30%	24%	100%
Rented from housing association	53%	21%	21%	5%	100%
Rented from council	55%	23%	18%	3%	100%

Source: adapted from www.odpm.gov.uk.

Homeless families from across the country will deliver a 60 000 strong public petition to the home of the Chancellor of the Exchequer this Wednesday as part of a campaign to end Britain's housing crisis. The families, and the housing charity Shelter, are urging the Chancellor to commit to building 60 000 extra social rented homes between 2008 and 2011 on top of the 90 000 which have been planned for by government. The charity warns that without these homes, the government will fail to tackle the housing crisis facing Britain today. The call comes as part of Shelter's Million Children Campaign. This, last year, revealed that more than one million children in Britain are homeless, trapped in temporary house, or living in unfit or overcrowded homes. These conditions are ruining their health, education and future prospects in life. The campaign is calling on the government to end bad housing for the next generation of children.

Source: adapted from *Press Release*, Shelter, 30.11.2005.

Lower income households have far more problems affording a home than they did 25 years ago. The fall in the income share of the poorest sections of the population is far sharper after housing costs are taken into account.

Although the severity and prevalence of overcrowding has diminished, the inequality of space has increased considerably over the 30 years to 2001, with owner-occupiers gaining most and social sector tenants (local authority and Housing Associations) gaining least.

Source: adapted from *Press Release*, Shelter, 25.7.2005.

1. Outline the main changes in the housing market shown in the data.
2. To what extent can housing be seen as a merit good? Give examples from the data to support your arguments.
3. Assess whether economic welfare would be increased if government either (a) reintroduced subsidies on buying a house or (b) reduced rents for those in social housing (mainly for tenants of councils or Housing Associations).

Summary

1. The price of a good may be too high, too low or fluctuate too greatly to bring about an efficient allocation of resources.
2. Governments may impose maximum or minimum prices to regulate a market.
3. Maximum prices can create shortages and black markets.
4. Minimum prices can lead to excess supply and tend to be maintained only at the expense of the taxpayer.
5. Prices of commodities and agricultural products tend to fluctuate more widely than the prices of manufactured goods and services.
6. Buffer stock schemes attempt to even out fluctuations in price by buying produce when prices are low and selling when prices are high.

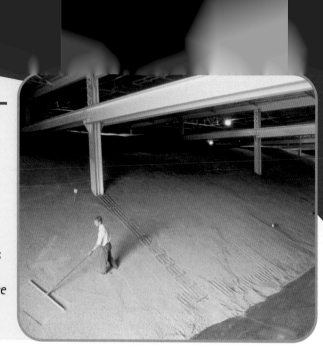

Prices and market failure

The market mechanism establishes equilibrium prices for each good or service in the economy. However, this price or the way in which it has been set may not lead to an efficient allocation of resources. The price may fluctuate too greatly in the short term, or it may be too high or too low.

Large fluctuations in price In some markets, particularly agricultural and commodity markets, there can be large fluctuations in price over a short space of time. Prices act as signals and incentives to producers. Large fluctuations in price mean that these signals can give a very confusing picture to producers and result in over or under production in the short term, and over or under investment in the longer term. This in turn can lead to a less than optimal allocation of resources.

Too high a price The price of a good may be too high. It may be an essential item, such as bread, rice or housing, which poor households are unable to afford to buy in sufficient amounts. The government may judge these items as **merit goods** (☞ unit 20), or it may want to reduce inequalities in society and hence want to reduce their prices. Alternatively, there could be significant positive **externalities** (☞ unit 19) in consumption. Too high a market price would lead to a less than optimal level of demand for the good.

Too low a price The free market price of goods like cigarettes may be too low because their consumption gives rise to significant negative externalities. Alternatively, the government may judge that too low a price is having a negative economic impact on producers. For instance, it may judge that farmers' incomes need to be raised because otherwise they would leave the land and there would be rural depopulation.

Governments can intervene in markets and change prices. For instance, they can impose indirect taxes or give subsidies (☞ unit 11). They can set maximum or minimum prices or they can establish buffer stock schemes to stabilise prices.

Prices and revenues

Governments can have other motives for market intervention other than to correct market failure. Sometimes, they intervene in markets in order to change price for their own benefit or the benefit of their own citizens. For example, OPEC, the Organisation of the Petroleum Exporting Countries, is a group of countries which attempts to maximise its long term revenues from the sale of oil. In doing so, it switches income from oil consumers, particularly in rich industrialised countries, to the countries of its own members. In theory, this should raise the living standards of their citizens at the expense of citizens living in countries which purchase the oil. It also tends to enrich ruling elites in member OPEC countries.

Maximum prices

The government can fix a maximum price for a good in a market. In Figure 21.1, the free market price is P_1 and Q_1 is bought and sold. Assume that this is the market for rented accommodation. At a price of P_1 the poorest in society are unable to afford to rent houses and there is therefore a problem of homelessness. The government intervenes by fixing a maximum price for accommodation of P_2. In the very short term, this may well seem to alleviate the problem. Landlords will continue to offer Q_1 of housing whilst the poorest in society will be more able to afford the new lower cost housing. But in the longer term, economic theory predicts that new problems will arise. At a price of P_2, demand will be higher than at P_1, whilst supply will be lower. There will in fact be an excess demand of Q_2Q_3. At the lower price, consumers will demand more housing. On the other hand, landlords will reduce their supply, for instance by selling off their properties for owner occupation, not buying new properties to rent out, or living in their own properties instead of renting them out.

Permanent rent controls will thus reduce the supply of privately rented accommodation to the market whilst increasing its demand. The market may react in a number of ways. In a law abiding society, queues or waiting lists may develop. It may be a matter of luck rather than money whether one is able to get

Figure 21.1 *Maximum prices*

OP_1 is the free market price. If the government sets a maximum price of OP_2 in the market, demand will increase to OQ_3 whilst supply will fall to OQ_2. The result will be excess demand in the market of Q_2Q_3.

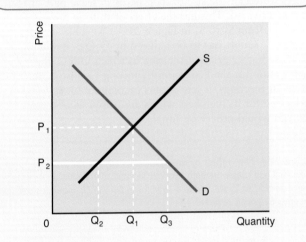

maximum prices may benefit some consumers - those able to obtain the goods which are controlled in price - but will disadvantage those who are prepared to pay a higher price for the good but are unable to obtain it because of a shortage of supply.

If the maximum price were set at P_3, there would be no effect on the market. P_1, the free market price, is below the maximum price and therefore nothing will happen following the introduction of maximum price controls.

Minimum prices

Minimum prices are usually set to help producers increase their incomes. Consider Figure 21.2, which shows the market for wheat. The free market price is P_1. The government decides that this is too low a price for farmers to receive and sets a minimum price of P_2. As a result, farmers will now grow Q_1Q_3 more wheat. Consumers will react to the new higher prices by reducing their demand by Q_1Q_2. Total excess supply of Q_2Q_3 will result.

This poses a problem for the government. With maximum prices, the government did not need to intervene when excess demand appeared. The excess demand could remain in the market forever if need be. But this is not true of excess supply. If consumers only buy Q_2 of wheat then farmers can only sell Q_2 of wheat. Q_2Q_3 will remain unbought. Unless the government takes action, there will be strong pressure for farmers to sell this at below the minimum price. Average prices will fall until the market is cleared. The resulting price structure is likely to be very complex, some wheat being sold at the official minimum price of P_2 whilst the rest is sold at a variety of prices, the lowest of which is likely to be below the free market clearing price of P_1. Government action will have been frustrated.

So an effective minimum price structure must be accompanied by other measures. There are two main ways of dealing with this problem. The first is for the government to buy up the wheat that consumers refuse to buy (i.e. buy up the excess supply Q_2Q_3). This in turn creates problems because the government has to do something with the wheat it buys. This has been the classic problem with the Common Agricultural Policy in the

rented accommodation. The state may devise systems to allocate rented accommodation on the basis of greatest need. Landlords may develop a variety of ways in which they can get round the price controls. A black market may develop, illegal and uncontrolled, where rents are fixed at, or greater than, the free market price of P_1. Economic theory therefore predicts that

Question 1

In the 1960s, the government introduced a system of maximum rents for privately rented properties in the UK. Typically, these 'registered' rents were below the free market rent. In the late 1980s, the government reversed its policy by introducing a new type of private tenancy agreement, assured tenancies, which allowed private landlords to set whatever rent they wished. By 2005, there were very few rented properties left with registered rent contracts.

Table 21.1 *Number of privately rented properties, UK*

Number of properties rented privately or with a job or business	
	millions
1961	5.0
1971	3.7
1981	2.4
1991	2.2
2001	2.4
2004	2.5

Source: adapted from *Housing Statistics*, Office for National Statistics.

(a) What happened to the stock of privately rented properties between 1961 and 1991?
(b) Using a demand and supply diagram, explain why the introduction of registered rents in the 1960s might have caused (i) a fall in the supply of rented property and (ii) excess demand for private rented property.
(c) Using a demand and supply diagram, explain why the introduction of assured tenancies led to a change in the quantity demanded for and supply of privately rented housing.

Figure 21.2 *Minimum prices*

OP_1 is the free market price. If the government sets a minimum price of OP_3 in the market, supply will increase to OQ_3 whilst demand will fall to OQ_2. The result will be excess supply in the market of Q_2Q_3.

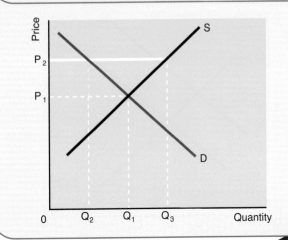

Question 2

A bumper cereals harvest across Eastern Europe has forced the European Commission to intervene, buying up and moving large amounts of surplus stocks to prevent a European-wide fall in prices. EU cereal stocks are now at their highest for a decade after EU countries produced 290 million tons in 2004, an increase of one quarter compared from 2003. The main problem has been an increase of 40 per cent in production from the ten new member states in Eastern Europe. For example, Hungarian farmers increased their production by 89 per cent whilst farmers in the Czech Republic increased their harvest by 54 per cent.

Storage is now a major problem with the EU already committed to buying up 13.5 million tons as intervention stocks. There simply isn't enough storage capacity in the new Eastern European member states to store all this grain. The Hungarian Ministry of Agriculture has requested the use of storage facilities in Belgium and Germany to help solve its storage crisis.

To reduce intervention stocks, the EU has begun offering export subsidies for the first time since 2003. Last week, it increased the payment to farmers for each ton of grain they sold for export to €10. In addition, it has offered to subsidise the transport of some grain from landlocked Eastern European countries to the nearest ports for export.

Source: adapted from www.nutraingredients.com and www.farmersjournal.

(a) Using demand and supply diagrams, explain (i) why 'EU cereal stocks are now at their highest for a decade';
(ii) how giving subsidies for grain exports can reduce EU cereal stocks.
(b) How did EU grain farmers benefit and EU taxpayers lose out from the bumper grain harvest of 2004?

European Union. A variety of solutions, from selling wheat mountains to Third World countries at rock bottom prices, selling it back to farmers to feed to animals, or offering it at reduced prices to those in need in the EU, or simply destroying the produce, have been adopted. All have one drawback - they cost the taxpayer money because the price paid to farmers is inevitably higher than the price received from the sale of the surplus.

The second solution to the problem of excess supply is to restrict production. Governments can either force, or pay, farmers to reduce the size of their herds or leave part of their land uncultivated. This has the effect of shifting the supply curve to the left, from S_1 to S_2 in Figure 21.3. To achieve a minimum price of P_2, supply has to be reduced by Q_2Q_3. Reducing output to achieve higher prices is the way in which OPEC, the Organisation for the Petroleum Exporting Countries, operates. At regular meetings, it sets quotas (maximum limits) on production for its members which are below what these countries would otherwise supply.

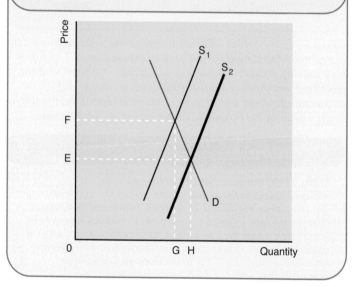

Figure 21.4 The effect of an increase in supply on price
If demand and supply are both relatively inelastic, then a small increase in supply from S_1 to S_2 will lead to a large fall in price of FE. Incomes will therefore be greatly reduced.

Buffer stock schemes

The free market price of **primary products** (commodities such as gold and tin, and agricultural products such as wheat and beef) tends to fluctuate much more than the price of either manufactured goods or services.

This is mainly due to supply side influences. The demand for canned tomatoes or fresh tomatoes is likely to remain broadly constant over a twelve month period. However, the supply of these two products will differ. Canned tomatoes can be stored. Therefore the supply too will remain broadly the same over a twelve month period. But the supply of fresh tomatoes varies greatly. In the summer months, supply is plentiful and the price of tomatoes is therefore low. In winter, supply is low and prices are high.

On a year to year basis, the supply of raw agricultural commodities can vary greatly according to crop yields. A bumper crop will depress prices whilst crop failure will lead to high prices. Bumper crops can be disastrous for farmers. In Figure 21.4, if the demand for a product is price inelastic, a large fall in price is needed to sell a little extra produce. This will greatly reduce farmers' revenues.

Equally, a poor crop can be disastrous for individual farmers.

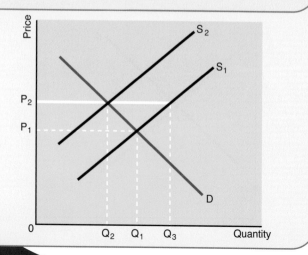

Figure 21.3 Achieving minimum prices through reducing supply
OP_1 is the free market price. If a government or organisation wishes to set a minimum price of OP_2, it may be able to force producers to reduce their supply, shifting the supply curve to the left from S_1 to S_2.

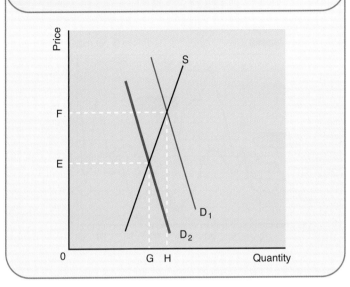

Figure 21.5 The effect of a fall in demand on price
If demand and supply are both relatively inelastic, then a small fall in demand from D_1 to D_2 will lead to a large fall in price of FE.

fluctuations for commodities. In manufacturing and services, producers devote much effort and money to stabilising demand through branding, advertising and other marketing techniques. However, Zambian copper is little different from Chilean copper. Buyers are free to buy from the cheapest source so demand fluctuates more greatly. In the short term, supply is relatively inelastic. Countries have invested in mines, oil wells and other commodity producing plant and need, often for foreign exchange purposes, to maximise output and sales. Small changes in demand, as shown in Figure 21.5, can produce large changes in price. Any slowdown in the world economy is likely to have a larger impact on commodities than on manufactured goods. Manufacturers may react to a small fall in their sales by cutting their stock levels and perhaps delaying the buying of stock by a few months. This results in a large, if temporary, fall in the price of raw materials. Whilst the slowdown persists, prices are likely to remain low. The converse is also true - in a boom, commodity prices go up far faster than those of manufactures or services.

Demand and supply influences combine to bring about large fluctuations in the price of commodities. Governments and other bodies have often reacted to this situation by intervening in the market place. One way to do this is to set up a BUFFER STOCK SCHEME which combines elements of both minimum and maximum pricing. In theory it is designed to even out price fluctuations for producers. An intervention price is set, shown as P_1 in Figure 21.6. If the free market price is the same as the intervention price, as in Figure 21.6(a), then the scheme doesn't need to intervene in the market. If the free market price is below the intervention price, as in Figure 21.6(b), then the buffer stock agency buys up enough supply to restore prices to the minimum price. In Figure 21.6(b), it increases demand by buying up Q_2Q_3. In contrast, if the free market price is above the intervention price, as in Figure 21.6(c), it can sell stocks it has accumulated. In Figure 21.6(c) it increases supply by selling Q_2Q_3, forcing the price down to the intervention level. In effect, the buffer stock shifts the demand curve for the product to the

Although farm income overall will be higher than average, only farmers who have crops to sell will benefit. Farmers whose crops have been mostly or completely destroyed will receive little or no income.

Manufactures and services also contain greater value added than primary products. The cost of a can of tomatoes is made up not only of the cost of tomatoes themselves but also of the canning process and the can. If fresh tomatoes only account for 20 per cent of the cost of a can of tomatoes, then a doubling in the price of fresh tomatoes will only increase the price of a can by just over 7 per cent.

Demand side influences can, however, also be a source of price

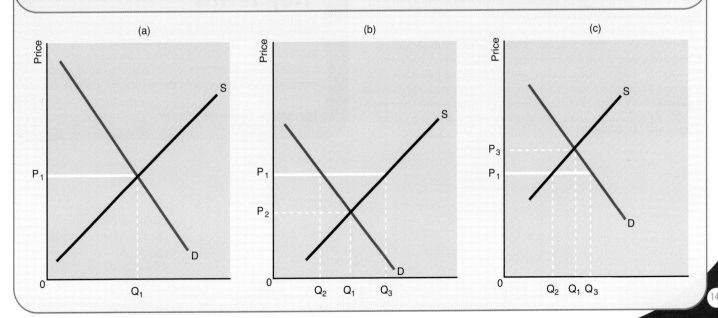

Figure 21.6 Buffer stock interventions
In (a), the free market price of P_1 is the same as the intervention price set by the buffer stock scheme and so it does not need to intervene in the market. In (b), the free market price, P_2, is below the intervention price and so it has to buy up Q_2Q_3 to bring prices back up to P_1. In (c), the free market price, P_3, is above the intervention price. So the buffer stock scheme can sell up to Q_2Q_3 from its stocks without bringing prices down below the intervention level.

Question 3

The world tin industry has commodity agreements going back to 1921. The International Tin Council (ITC) came into being in 1956. It was able to support the price of tin during periods of low prices by buying tin for its buffer stockpile and selling tin when prices were high. During the 1970s, its stockpile of tin was not sufficiently large to prevent serious price rises in the commodity. However, the world recession of 1981-82 hit world tin consumption. The ITC was able to avoid sharp declines in tin prices by buying in the open market. However, it was only able to afford the cost of its increasing stockpile by extensive borrowing from banks and metal trading firms. In late 1985, it reached its credit limits and its supporters, such as the UK, refused to extend further credit. The International Tin Council was disbanded and its stocks sold off over a four year period. Prices did not recover their early 1980 levels until 2004 when sharp increases in demand from the booming countries of East Asia, particularly China, fuelled a commodity price boom.

Source: adapted from http://minerals.er.usgs.gov/minerals/pubs/commodity/tin/.

(a) Explain, using a demand and supply diagram, how the International Tin Council (ITC) affected the price of tin in the market.
(b) According to the data, how well did the ITC succeed in fixing prices in the 1970s and 1980s?
(c) Explain why the price of tin was low in the 1990s compared to the late 1970s and early 1980s.

Figure 21.7 Prices and world production of tin

Source: adapted from *Historical Statistics for Mineral Commodities in the United States, Metal prices in the United States through 1998,* United States Geological Survey

right when free market prices are below the intervention price, and shifts the supply curve to the right when free market prices are above the intervention price.

Buffer stock schemes are not common. One major reason for this is that a considerable amount of capital is needed to set them up. Money is required to buy produce when prices are too low. There are also the costs of administration and storage of produce purchased. But in theory, the overall running costs of the scheme should be low. Indeed, with skilful buying and selling the scheme may make an operational profit. This is because the scheme buys produce at or below the intervention price but sells at a price above the intervention price.

Buffer stock schemes also have a mixed record of success. Pressure to set up these schemes tends to come from producers who have a vested interest in setting the intervention price above the average market price. If they succeed in doing this, their revenues in the short term are likely to be larger than they would otherwise have been. But the buffer stock scheme will have been buying more produce than it sold. Eventually it will run out of money, the scheme will collapse, and prices will plummet

because the accumulated stocks will be sold to pay the debts of the scheme. The glut of produce on the market will result in producers receiving below average prices for some time to come. Successful buffer stock schemes are those which correctly guess the average price and resist attempts by producers to set the intervention price above it.

Key terms

Buffer stock scheme - a scheme whereby an organisation buys and sells in the open market so as to maintain a minimum price in the market for a product.

Applied economics

The Common Agricultural Policy (CAP)

One of the most important steps taken by the European Union (formerly the European Community) in its early years was to create the Common Agricultural Policy in 1958. Article 39 of the Treaty of Rome cites 5 objectives of agricultural policy:

- to increase agricultural productivity;
- to ensure a fair standard of living for farmers;
- to stabilise markets;
- to guarantee availability of supplies;
- to ensure fair prices for consumers.

It was hoped that CAP would achieve this through regulation of the agricultural industry in the Union. For many products, an intervention price was established. Farmers could then choose to sell their produce on the open market or to the EU at this minimum fixed price. The EU guaranteed to buy up any amount at the intervention price. Farmers were protected from overseas competition through a complex system of tariffs (taxes on imported goods) and quotas (physical limits on the amount that could be imported). Tariffs and quotas effectively raised the price of imported agricultural produce to EU consumers. With high enough tariffs and quotas, agricultural produce from outside the EU could be kept out, allowing EU farmers to sell their own produce into their domestic markets at much higher prices than they would otherwise have been able to do.

CAP proved to be far more favourable to farmers than to consumers. The farming community in the EU became very good at lobbying their individual governments to vote for high intervention prices at the annual price fixing negotiations in Brussels. Consumers lost out in two ways. First, they had to pay directly for food which was much higher in price than it would otherwise have been if it had been bought on world markets. Second, as taxpayers, they had to pay for the heavy costs of running the CAP.

In theory, the CAP should have been fairly inexpensive to run. If there was a glut of produce on the market in one season, the EU would buy some of it at the intervention price and store it. The next season, when there was perhaps a shortage, the EU could take the produce out of storage and sell it. Prices would not fluctuate by as much as under a market system and the sale of produce would ensure that the major cost of the system would be administration and storage.

In practice, the cost of the CAP rose year after year. High intervention prices led to increased production, as economic theory would predict. Supply then began to outstrip demand. Instead of selling produce taken into storage to European consumers at a later date, mountains and lakes of produce developed, as shown in Figure 21.8. This produce then had to be sold, often at a fraction of the cost of production, to the former USSR, Third World countries, and to EU farmers for

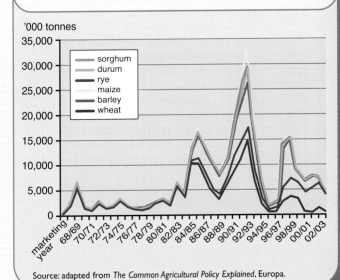

Figure 21.8 EU intervention stocks, cereal crops

Source: adapted from *The Common Agricultural Policy Explained*, Europa.

use as animal feed. Some was even destroyed.

EU reform

Reform of CAP has been a long standing issue. As early as 1968, the Mansholt Plan recommended that farm size should increase to enable farmers to enjoy economies of scale and thus be better able to provide food at world market prices. By the early 1980s, political pressure was building to limit the growth of the CAP budget. In 1984, a quota system (see below) was introduced for milk production to limit production and therefore subsidies to dairy farmers. In 1988, a ceiling was introduced on the CAP budget.

However, the first fundamental changes to CAP were the MacSharry reforms of 1992. Ray MacSharry was the European Commissioner for Agriculture at the time. There were two major ways in which agriculture was affected. One was through a set-aside scheme (see below) where farmers received payments for leaving ground uncultivated rather than growing crops on it. The second was limiting the amount of financial support to selected crops and animals and replacing them by direct grants to farmers for a variety of schemes not linked to production. Giving grants to farmers which are not linked to their production levels is known as **decoupling**.

In 2003, EU farm ministers agreed a more radical scheme to decouple farm subsidies. Between 2005 and 2012, it was agreed that EU member states would change their farm subsidy regime to eliminate most production subsidies and replace them with direct grants to farmers. The total EU agricultural budget was fixed up to 2012 and included changes needed to accommodate new Eastern European entrants to the European Union.

Economic effects of different schemes

Agricultural policy in the EU distorts free markets in a variety of ways.

External trade barriers Putting tariffs (i.e. taxes) on agricultural produce entering the EU keeps out cheap food produced outside the EU. EU farmers benefit because the market price inside the EU is higher as a result. EU consumers lose out because they have to pay higher prices for their food. There are many other types of trade barrier than tariffs. The EU, for example, has been accused of using safety and welfare standards to keep imports out of the EU area.

Intervention prices Intervention prices were minimum prices set for some (but not all) agriculture products in the EU. They were effectively minimum prices which were often above the free market price. They raised farmers' incomes. Consumers paid not just higher prices for those agricultural products but also taxes to buy up surplus produce which would then have to be disposed of in some way at less than the buying price.

Quotas Quotas on milk production were introduced in 1984. Each member country of the EU was given a milk quota, a maximum amount of milk that could be produced. This was then divided up between farmers, originally depending on how much milk they produced before quotas were introduced. Quotas were

Table 21.2 EU farm support, EU 15

| | Yearly average | |
	1986-88	2002-2004
Transfers from consumers (€ millions)	82 142	55 343
Transfers from taxpayers (€ millions)	25 747	58 960
Budget revenues (€ millions)	-1 517	-903
Total support estimate (€ millions)	106 372	113 401
EU population (million)	363	380
Total support cost per head (€)	293	298
Total support estimate as percentage of GDP	2.82	1.20

Source: adapted from *Agricultural policies in OECD countries: monitoring and evaluation 2005*, OECD.

transferable. A farmer owning a quota could sell all or part it to another farmer. Quotas were set at levels which would reduce the production of milk. In terms of demand and supply, quotas shifted the supply curve of milk to the left, reducing the equilibrium level of production but raising the equilibrium price compared to the free market price. This benefited farmers but consumers had to pay higher prices for their milk and milk-based products. The quota system was cheap to run for the EU taxpayer because dairy farmers did not receive subsidies for production of milk.

Set-aside Set-aside was introduced in 1992 for cereal farmers. They were paid for setting aside (i.e. not using) a certain proportion of their land. The land set aside had to be rotated from year to year to prevent farmers simply setting aside their least productive land. By reducing the amount of land available for production, the supply of cereals is reduced, thus raising their price. Farmers received a payment from the EU for each acre set-aside. Hence, not only did EU consumers pay higher prices for cereals than they would otherwise, but EU taxpayers had to pay a direct subsidy to farmers.

Decoupling Decoupling subsidies from production in theory should reduce, if not eliminate, production distortions. Farmers will receive a grant according to the number of acres they own, not how much they produce. Prices for agricultural products will be set by the forces of demand and supply in a free market. Consumers will therefore not pay higher prices for agricultural products as they would, say, with a system of intervention prices, set aside or quotas. In a rational world, marginal farmers who find it difficult to make a reasonable profit from agricultural activities will simply not produce. Instead, they will do nothing and collect their subsidy on their acreage. In practice, farmers are likely to be less rational. With a basic income given by the subsidy, they will be prepared to work for lower returns than they would otherwise. Hence, production is likely to be higher than if there were no subsidies at all.

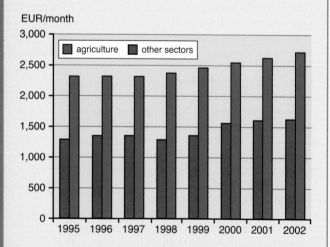

Figure 21.9 Farm incomes - development of average gross monthly wages in the economy and gross monthly agricultural income

EUR/month

agriculture   other sectors

Source: adapted from *The Common Agricultural Policy Explained*, Europa.

Figure 21.10 Main beneficiaries of CAP

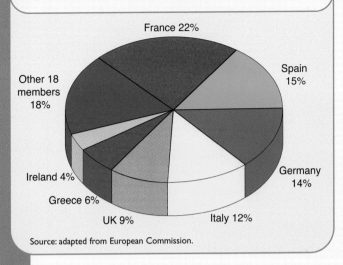

France 22%

Spain 15%

Other 18 members 18%

Germany 14%

Ireland 4%

Greece 6%

UK 9%

Italy 12%

Source: adapted from European Commission.

Advantages and disadvantages of the Common Agricultural Policy

The Common Agricultural Policy is highly controversial. It can be judged in a variety of ways.

Maintaining farmers' incomes One key argument for CAP is that it transfers income from the richer non-farming community to the poorer farming community. Figure 21.9 shows that farm incomes on average are below those in the non-farm sector. However, there are no other industries in the EU where income transfers are made on an industrial basis. Average wages in the EU tourist industry, for example, are below those in all other industries but there is no call to subsidise the whole of the tourist industry as a result. Critics would argue that application of the general system of taxes and welfare benefits to the poorer workers in farming would be a fairer way of dealing with rural poverty than CAP. They also point out that 80 per cent of total spending on CAP goes to 20 per cent of the EU's largest farmers and agricultural corporations. In the UK, the largest beneficiary of CAP was the sugar company Tate and Lyle which received £127 million in subsidies.

Cost The cost of the CAP to EU citizens has been substantial. In the past, they have not only had to pay for subsidies to the farming community through their taxes, but they have also had to pay higher prices for the food they buy because it was available at lower prices on world markets. Table 21.2 gives a breakdown of the cost of that support, comparing the yearly average for 1986-88 and 2002-2004 for the EU 15 countries. What it shows is that the balance of support has shifted. In 1986-88, by far the largest cost of farm support was from consumers having to pay higher prices for the food they purchased. By 2002-04, the cost of higher prices was roughly

matched by subsidies given to farmers by the EU. In 2002-04, the cost of CAP per head in the EU was €298, roughly equivalent to £200. A family of four people living in the UK was therefore subsidising EU farming by roughly £800 per year.

The EU budget In the 1970s, expenditure on CAP was over 70 per cent of the EU budget. By 2005, this was approximately 50 per cent. Supporters of CAP argue that agriculture is a key industry within the EU. Critics would point out that agriculture now accounts for only 2 per cent of EU GDP. Agriculture is of little importance to the EU economy. The opportunity cost of spending so much of the EU budget on agriculture is considerable. It would be better spent on areas such as regional assistance.

Government failure Support for reform of CAP varies between countries across the EU. The countries which are most resistant to change tend to be those countries which most benefit from CAP. Figure 21.10 shows that France is the single largest beneficiary from the CAP. For both Ireland and Greece, although they receive relatively small percentages of the total, CAP is especially important. On average, countries receive CAP support of around 0.5 per cent of GDP. For Ireland and Greece, this is three times as large at 1.5 per cent of GDP. Critics of the CAP argue that the support of countries like France for CAP has little to do with economic efficiency or the economic welfare of the EU. They support CAP and resist change simply because they are the major beneficiaries of the policy.

Self sufficiency Supporters of the CAP point out that it has created a Europe which is broadly self sufficient in food. In times when a country was at war, food self sufficiency was a strategic objective. However, critics point out that in no other commodity does the EU attempt to be self sufficient. There are no objectives, for example, for the EU to be self sufficient in the production of television sets, microchips, clothes or foreign holidays. In an era of globalisation, self sufficiency in food could be argued to be an outdated goal.

Food quality and animal welfare Supporters of CAP argue that EU farmers provide high quality food with minimum guaranteed levels of animal welfare. By implication, some food that is imported to the EU is below acceptable standards and comes from unacceptable farming practices. Critics would argue that the quality of food produced in the EU is on average no better than that produced elsewhere in the world. To be sold in the EU, imported food has to conform to certain standards anyway. Some animal rearing practices outside the EU do not conform to EU standards. However, the EU can and does impose a wide variety of conditions upon meat imported to the EU and has the power to prohibit imports if there are good reasons to do so under its trading obligations with the World Trade Organisation (WTO).

The environment Supporters of CAP argue that it is a key factor in supporting the rural environment. Farmers look after the countryside, ensuring that it is protected for future generations. Critics of CAP point out that the agricultural sector is a major polluter of the environment. Animals are the major source of methane gas, a key contributor to global warming. Farmers, through the use of fertilisers and pesticides, pollute the environment. In southern European countries, their overuse of scarce water resources for irrigation is causing major problems to the environment. Little of the rural environment, anyway, is 'natural' in any sense. It has been created over thousands of years by farmers to suit the needs of production.

Supporting the rural economy Supporters of CAP argue that it is needed to maintain an appropriate economic environment in rural areas. Without CAP, some rural areas would become completely depopulated because there would be no jobs or income in the area. Other areas would suffer considerable depopulation as residents left to find jobs in towns and cities. There would be pressure on the urban environment which would have to expand to accommodate these migrants. Critics of CAP argue that urban dwellers have no duty to support financially those living in the countryside: the countryside should not be seen as a charity. There is no benefit overall to having a thriving rural economy in a locality as opposed to seeing it completely depopulated. Urban areas have been expanding to take in people from rural areas for centuries. If towns and cities created large costs for their inhabitants, people would not have migrated to them from rural areas in the first place.

Impact on poorer countries in the world Supporters of CAP argue that the EU is a major importer of food from countries round the world, including poorer developing countries. The EU has helped millions of poor farmers establish markets for their products.

Critics accuse the EU of damaging farming markets round the globe. First, through its system of protection for its farmers, the EU has denied access to farmers outside the EU to EU markets. Second, the EU has dumped large amounts of food onto world markets at low prices to get rid of the surpluses that its farming regime has created. This has hurt non-EU farmers because it has denied them the opportunity to sell into those markets. Critics of the EU argue that the CAP has increased world poverty over the past fifty years.

CAP is already being radically reformed Supporters of CAP point to the radical reforms which have already been implemented and will be implemented over the next ten years. They argue that any further quickening of pace of reform will have serious consequences for the farming sector and the rural economy. Critics argue that the pace of reform is too slow and that the reforms are too timid. They point out that there are some areas of CAP, such as the dairy sector, wine, fruit and vegetables, where there are no current plans for reform. Export subsidies and tariffs on imported food remain too high. Agriculture remains a major source of inefficiency within the EU even with the current reform programme.

DataQuestion

Rubber

The International Natural Rubber Organisation (INRO) is to break up following the withdrawal of two of the world's largest rubber producers, Thailand and Malaysia. The buffer stock scheme, set up in 1980, buys up rubber when prices fall and sells when prices rise. Members include the six leading rubber producing countries as well as the biggest consuming countries such as the US, Japan and China.

Thailand and Malaysia have become dissatisfied with the low price of rubber in world markets in recent years. They have accused INRO of failing to intervene to stop the price of rubber falling. For instance, at the start of 1998, rubber was 230 Malaysian cents a kilo. By 1999, this had fallen to 150 cents. They also accuse INRO of pursuing policies which favour member countries with low volumes of production and failing to pay sufficient attention to the interests of the three countries which account for nearly three quarter of world production. Thailand, for instance, paid around 40 per cent of the total yearly contributions which financed INRO, but was only responsible for 30 per cent of output.

Source: adapted from the *Financial Times*, 6.10.1999

In August 2002, Malaysia, Indonesia and Thailand, the world's three largest producers of natural rubber, controlling around two thirds of world production, set up the International Rubber Consortium (IRCo). The Consortium was established to co-ordinate production and exports of the three countries. In April 2004, IRCo was officially registered with a capital of US$225 million. Its objectives are to achieve a long term price trend that is stabilised, sustainable and remunerative to farmers, and to maintain a supply-demand balance to ensure adequate supply of natural rubber in the market at fair prices.

Source: adapted from International Rubber Consortium, www.irco.biz

The collapse of the International Natural Rubber Organisation could have spelt disaster for rubber prices as stocks built up were offloaded onto the market. As it was, growing demand allowed prices to remain relatively stable, although prices fell to an all time low at the end of 2001. Since then, growing demand, especially from the booming economies of East Asia and particularly China, has driven up prices. Without this increased demand, rubber prices could easily have collapsed.

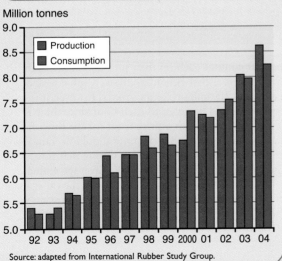

Figure 21.11 World natural rubber production and consumption

Million tonnes

Source: adapted from International Rubber Study Group.

Figure 21.12 Rubber prices

Singapore cents per kilogram

Source: adapted from Singapore Commodity Exchange.

1. **Explain, using INRO as an example, what is meant by a buffer stock scheme.**
2. **Why had INRO built up stocks of rubber by 1999?**

3. **To what extent could IRCo be seen as having been responsible for substantially increasing the price of rubber in the early 2000s?**

22 Cost-benefit analysis

Summary

1. Cost-benefit analysis is a technique which attempts to evaluate the social costs and benefits of an economic decision.
2. Social costs and benefits may differ from private costs and benefits.
3. It is often difficult and sometimes impossible to place a price on externalities.
4. Cost-benefit analysis is often used to assess public sector investment projects.

Market failure

In a free market, decisions are based upon the calculation of **private costs and benefits**. However, there are many markets where significant **externalities** exist (☞ unit 19). This means that there are significant costs or benefits which are unlikely to be taken account of by the private economic decision maker.

COST-BENEFIT ANALYSIS is a procedure which takes into account all costs and all benefits (i.e **social costs and benefits**). Its purpose is to give guidance in economic decision making. It is used particularly by governments to evaluate important investment projects.

Costs and benefits

It is relatively easy to place a value on private costs and benefits. For instance, the government may want a toll motorway to be built round Birmingham. The company which builds and operates the motorway will be able to calculate the financial cost of constructing the road. This is the private cost to the operating company. It will also be able to calculate the revenues to be earned from tolls. These will be its private benefits. If the private benefits exceed private costs the motorway will be profitable and the operating company will be prepared to build the road.

However, there will be other costs and benefits associated with the project. These are the externalities of the road. For instance, residents near the motorway will suffer from pollution, including noise pollution. The motorway may generate more traffic on some roads joining the motorway, again increasing pollution to local residents. The motorway may go through areas of outstanding natural beauty or take away areas which have been used by local people for recreational activities such as walking. Habitats of rare species may be destroyed. Sites of historical interest may be lost. On the other hand, jobs and wealth may be created locally as industry is attracted to the area by the new motorway. Car and lorry drivers may save time using the new motorway. Traffic may be taken off some local roads, relieving congestion.

These externalities are very important costs and benefits which could be completely ignored by the operating company if it operated in a pure free market. In a cost-benefit analysis the company would attempt to place a value on these externalities in order to calculate the social cost and social benefit of the project and proceed only if social benefit exceeded social cost.

Problems with placing a value on externalities

The value of many externalities is difficult to estimate. For instance, assume that, as a result of the building of the motorway, 5 million travellers every year save on

Question 1

The Aberdeen Western Peripheral Route is a proposed 30 km long bypass of the city on its western side. Its building cost is currently put at between £210 million and £405 million. Local industry is supporting the building of the bypass. It claims that it will reduce congestion and journey times. It will also help attract new businesses and jobs to the area because of the improved transport links.

Opponents of the scheme, including Friends of the Earth, argue that it will have minimal impact on congestion in the centre of Aberdeen. It will encourage motorists to use their cars more and public transport less, so increasing congestion problems. The bypass will open up new development land, concreting over more of Scotland's natural land. New development will increase congestion too. Increased numbers of road journeys encouraged by the building of the new bypass will increase air pollution and reduce air quality. More car journeys will also increase greenhouse gas emissions at a time when the UK is committed to reducing them.

Source: adapted from www.foe-scotland.org.uk, March 2005.

(a) What are the main social costs and benefits of building the Aberdeen Western Peripheral Route?
(b) Which of these would be private costs and benefits to the Scottish Executive, and Aberdeen and Aberdeenshire Council, which are the two government bodies which will fund the bypass?

average 30 minutes each on their journey times around Birmingham. In a cost-benefit analysis, a value would need to be placed on the 2.5 million hours saved. However, it is unclear what value should be given to each hour since there is no obvious market in which a price is set for the time. A high cost estimate would assume that the time should be valued as if the travellers could have earned money during that time. This might give an estimate of £10 per hour at an average annual wage for the typical motorway user of £20 000. On the other hand, it could be assumed that the traveller places almost no value on the time saved. It could be just 50p per hour. Comparing these two estimates, we get a high estimate of £25 million and a low estimate of £1.25 million.

Even more difficult is how to place a value on a human life. Assume that the motorway takes traffic off other roads and as a result 5 fewer people are killed in road accidents each year. The value of a life today in a court case involving accidents is mainly determined by the expected earnings of the deceased. For instance, if a company director earning £500 000 per annum were killed in a road crash, together with her chauffeur earning £10 000 per year, then all other things being equal (age, family circumstances etc.) the family of the company director would receive far more compensation than the family of the chauffeur. These values, however, are open to much debate.

Other intangibles, such as pollution and illness, are very difficult to value in money terms. Even the values placed on private costs and benefits may be difficult to estimate. For instance, the operating company may charge £2 for a journey from one end of the motorway to the other. But that may not necessarily reflect the cost to the operating company of the journey. It may include a large element of monopoly profit, or it may be subsidised by the government to encourage people to use the motorway. It may therefore be necessary for the cost-benefit analysis to estimate a **shadow price** for the journey - a price which more accurately reflects the cost to the operating company of providing the service.

Question 2

Next time you eat some junk food, just remember it might cost you more than the price you paid in the supermarket or the fast food restaurant. Obesity is a growing problem worldwide, fuelled by the falling cost of food in relation to income and changing diets. In the UK today, over 20 per cent of the adult population is now obese (defined as having a body mass index over 30), up from 7 per cent in 1980. The costs of obesity are many, ranging from increased illness, to lost days at work, to premature death. The incidence of diabetes and high blood pressure is rising, with heart disease, a major killer in the western world, also up. All can be caused by being overweight.

Source: adapted from the *Financial Times*, 31.8.2004.

(a) You buy a super sized burger and fries meal in a fast food restaurant for £4.99. What might for you be (i) the private cost and (ii) the externalities of the meal?
(b) Why might an economist, calculating the costs of overeating and poor diets, put a shadow price on the lower life expectancy that results from obesity?

Costs and benefits across time

Calculations are further complicated by the fact that costs and benefits will occur at different points in time. A Channel Tunnel rail link, for instance, could still be carrying passengers in the year 2100 and beyond. Many of our major rail links today in the UK were first built over 100 years ago.

A value has to be given to future costs and benefits. Economic theory suggests that £1 of benefit in 20 years' time is worth considerably less than £1 of benefit today. This is because £1 today could be saved or invested. Each year that passes it should be worth more. For instance, if the rate of interest (or rate of return, or rate of discount) is 10 per cent per annum then £1 today is worth £1.10 in one year's time, £1.21 in two years' time, £1.33 in three years' time, £10.83 in 25 years' time and £117.39 in 50 years' time (these figures are calculated using compound interest). It must therefore be true that a benefit of £117.39 available in 50 years' time is only worth £1 today if the rate of return is 10 per cent per annum.

So in cost-benefit analysis, all future costs and benefits need to be revalued using a rate of discount. There are two ways of doing this. Either a rate of discount is assumed and all costs and benefits are calculated as if they occurred today. This is known as calculating present values. Saying that £117.39 available in 50 years' time is worth £1 today is an example of this technique.

Question 3

A rail link could be built to last either 25 years or 50 years. It has been estimated that it would cost £100 million to build it for 25 years and £200 million for 50 years. In 25 years' time the cost of upgrading it to make it last another 25 years would be £900 million.

(a) If the rate of discount (or rate of interest or rate of return) were 10 per cent, would it be cheaper to build it to last for 25 years and repair it, or build it to last for 50 years?
(b) Would your answer be different if the rate of discount was 5 per cent? Explain why.

Alternatively the internal rate of return on the project can be calculated. So if we knew that £1 had been invested today and the one and only benefit were £117.39 which would be paid in 50 years' time, then we would know that the rate of return on the project would be 10 per cent per annum.

A critique of cost-benefit analysis

Cost-benefit analysis is a procedure where:
- all costs and benefits, both private and social, are identified;
- then a value is placed on those costs and benefits, wherever possible in monetary terms.

The technique is used mainly where it is assumed that market failure is present. Calculating all costs and benefits would seem to be a more rational way of evaluating an important investment project than relying upon projections of private profit or even having no facts and figures to consider.

However, cost-benefit analysis can be a very imprecise procedure. It is difficult to place a value on certain important costs and benefits and the results depend crucially upon the rate of discount of future costs and benefits used.

So the results of cost-benefit analysis should be used with caution. The assumptions made in the analysis should be explicit. Ideally a range of results should be calculated showing what would happen to costs and benefits if different assumptions were made. Social costs and benefits which cannot be valued in monetary terms should be clearly stated.

If this is done, cost-benefit analysis can be a useful tool in the evaluation of investment projects. But it should be recognised that it is only one piece of evidence amongst many and it could well be that other considerations, such as political considerations, prove ultimately to be more important.

Key terms

Cost-benefit analysis - a procedure, particularly used by governments to evaluate investment projects, which takes into account social cost and benefits.
Rate of return or rate of discount - the rate of interest or rate of profit earned on an investment project over time. The rate of discount can be used to calculate the present value of future income.

Cost-benefit analysis of smoking

Background

In January 2005, the government published the results of a cost-benefit analysis of a smoking ban in all workplaces and public places. Since the 1960s, it has become generally accepted that smoking is a major cause of ill health and death. Smokers reduce their life expectancy, whilst non-smokers too can be negatively affected if they live, work or recreate in environments where others smoke.

The benefits of a ban

The report identified a number of benefits from a ban, summarised in Table 22.1.

- Active smokers and passive smokers suffer from greater incidence of certain illnesses such as asthma and chronic bronchitis. As a result, they are forced to take days off work which is a cost to the economy. More days in work for passive smokers would benefit the economy by an estimated £70-£140 million. More days in work for smokers would give a benefit of £340-680 million.
- Health benefits were calculated in terms of greater life expectancy. The authors of the report calculated the probability of reduced life expectancy for passive smokers and active smokers. Amongst active smokers, probabilities were assigned to a ban encouraging less smoking and giving up all together. An assumption was made that the value of a life was £1 million if an individual died at 43 with a life expectancy of a further 35 years. This figure was taken from the Department of Transport, which uses it to assess the impact of a death in a road accident. Using these figures, a small benefit was gained by non-smokers by banning smoking in workplaces. Smokers who cut down their smoking and so increased their life expectancy would benefit by £550 million. Smokers who quit altogether as a result would be benefit by £1 600 million.
- There would be a variety of safety benefits, for example from fewer fires caused by smokers.

The costs of a ban

What costs would arise from a ban?

- Some smokers would not give up and continue to smoke at work by taking unofficial breaks which non-smokers would not take. Smokers would therefore be less productive than non-smokers. It was assumed that smokers would on average lose 14 minutes working time a day, with a loss of output to the UK economy of £430 million.

- Smokers gain pleasure (or 'utility' or 'welfare') from smoking. If they are forced to smoke less or give up by a ban in the workplace, this pleasure will be lost. Smokers have to pay for cigarettes and will be able to use the money to buy other products. So the loss to society is only the difference between the total pleasure gained and the opportunity cost of smoking (the pleasure or benefits lost from the next best product that could be bought). This difference is the consumer surplus on cigarettes. The report estimated that a total of £1 850 million of consumer surplus would be lost. This was broken down into three components. Continuing smokers who smoked less would lose £155 million in consumer surplus. Those who quit would lose £550 million. In addition, these two groups would lose a further £1 145 million in consumer surplus, but this is currently taxed away by the government. So the government and ultimately other taxpayers would lose out from this.

Net benefit

The total net benefit, taking costs away from benefits, was found to be between £505 million and

Table 22.1 *Banning smoking in the workplace: costs and benefits for employers and employees*

	£ million per year
Benefits	
Fewer days lost through illness at work:	
passive smokers	70-140
smokers	340-680
Higher life expectancy	
passive smokers	21
smokers who reduce their smoking	550
smokers who give up altogether	1 600
Safety benefits	64
Cost savings to NHS	-
Other benefits	140
Total benefits	**2 785-3 195**
Costs	
Lost output through smoking breaks	430
Consumer surplus lost	
smokers who reduce their smoking	155
smokers who give up altogether	550
taxes that would have been paid	1 145
Total costs	**2 280**
Total net benefit	**505-915**

£915 million a year. This is a substantial net benefit. It would therefore suggest that the government should go ahead with banning smoking in all workplaces and public places.

Assumptions and problems

The report itself identifies a number of issues which might affect the validity of its findings. These include the following.

- The value of a life aged 43 is put at £1 million. This, though, could be questioned.
- Assumptions are made about the probability of smokers giving up or cutting down if there is a ban. These assumptions are based on the experience of other countries, but these might not be replicated in the UK.
- No estimate is given for savings to the NHS because of the difficulty of calculating these. The problem arises because on the one hand smokers and passive smokers cost the NHS in extra treatments, but on the other hand this cost is offset by their greater chance of an early death and so fewer treatments in later life. The report was unwilling to quantify these costs and benefits.
- The consumer surplus calculation is based on an estimate of price elasticity of demand for cigarettes: what would be the responsiveness of quantity demanded to a rise in price. The price elasticity of demand of any product, though, is difficult to estimate accurately.
- The report chose not to include the consumer surplus figures in its final calculation of net benefits. This considerably increased the net benefit of a ban. The authors did this because they argued that smoking was addictive. Therefore the economic consumer choice model, where consumers are 'freely choosing, fully informed ' and 'are the best judges of their own welfare' does not apply. Table 22.1, however does include these costs.
- No value is put on the reduced quality of life that smokers and their families experience as a result of smoking related illnesses. For example, no value has been put on the suffering that takes place when a smoker dies of lung cancer.

Despite these and other problems, it is likely that banning smoking in workplaces and public spaces would give a positive net benefit. Smokers, however, could argue that ultimately the issue is not about monetary net benefits but about freedom. Government should not limit the freedom of its citizens to engage in an activity unless there are very important reasons for doing so. A cost benefit analysis which shows a possible yearly benefit of a couple of billion pounds is not sufficient reason to deprive individuals of their freedom to smoke. This type of argument shows that cost-benefit analysis can play an important part in decision making, but ultimately other considerations can be more important when the final decision is made.

DataQuestion   Switching off analogue transmissions

The government is proposing to switch off the analogue signal for television transmissions by 2012. Analogue television signals have been used since television first started in the 1920s. Digital signals have only been used since the 1990s, first by Sky Television and then by a variety of broadcasters including the BBC. To receive digital television, viewers either need a television equipped to received digital signals, or a traditional television attached to a set top digital box, such as a 'Freeview' box. Many viewers will also need to upgrade their aerial to boost signal strength.

The digital changeover is fraught with difficulties. An increasing number of households now have digital television. However, this might only be for one television in the house. The average household now owns three television sets and will face a cost in upgrading all these. Some households will not have any form of digital television at the point of changeover. They will then either have to buy new equipment or lose their ability to watch television. A large proportion of these households are likely to be either on low incomes or be pensioner households. Estimates of the cost of transition per customer range from £80 to £570. The cost is not just made up of buying digital equipment or replacing aerials. It is also technical advice costs and time costs of buying equipment and setting it up. Elderly people are most likely to have difficulties setting up and then using the new equipment.

There are two major benefits to the switch-over. Households will receive better quality pictures and sound. Digital signals will allow the move into even better quality with 'high definition TV'. The other benefit is that digital signals don't take up the bandwidth of analogue signals. Switching off the analogue signal will release bandwidth which the government will probably auction off. When the government auctioned off bandwidth allocated for mobile phones a few years ago, it raised £22 billion. It is unlikely to repeat this, especially since the released bandwidth is likely to be used for more television channels. However, a cost-benefit analysis of the change-over commissioned by the government put the value of the released bandwidth at around £2 billion a year.

The cost-benefit study found that there were considerable net benefits to the switch-over. It also argued that the net benefits of the switch-over would be greater, the sooner it was achieved. This was because the longer in the future the net benefits were realised, the lower the value of those benefits (the Net Present Value) today.

Table 22.2 Cost benefit appraisal of switch-over to digital television

| | £ billions at 2004 prices Year of completion of switch-over | |
	2010	2015
Benefits		
Consumer benefit in areas which are not currently able to receive digital television	3.2	2.0
Consumer benefit from released spectrum	2.0	1.2
Other benefits	2.1	1.6
Total benefits	**7.2**	**4.8**
Costs		
Consumer purchase of equipment	2.5	2.0
Other costs	2.5	1.7
Total costs	5.0	3.7
Total net benefit	**2.2**	**1.1**

Source: adapted from the *Financial Times*, 16.9.2005; *Cost Benefit Analysis of Digital Switch-over, 2005*, Department for Trade and Industry.

1. Assess the costs and benefits of the proposed switch-over to digital television. In your answer, outline the problems of putting a value on particular costs and benefits. Also explain briefly why delaying the switch-over from 2010 to 2015 could lead to lower net benefits today.

Applied economics

The leisure industry is a significant part of the UK economy. Spending on leisure goods and services, for instance, in 2004-05, accounted for £81.00 per week per household out of total spending of £432.90. The leisure industry is highly diversified, from book publishers to travel agents to football clubs. In this unit, we will consider four markets within the leisure industry: package holidays, air travel, spectator sports and television broadcasting.

Package holidays

The package tour holiday industry in the UK in 2006 was dominated by four large firms. These firms, MyTravel, First Choice, Thomas Cook and TUI, accounted for over three quarters of sales. The industry would therefore seem to be oligopolistic because a few firms dominate it.

In a traditional oligopolistic industry, economic theory would assume that there were high barriers to entry. This would enable firms in the industry to keep out new entrants. The firms could then charge high prices and earn abnormal profit due to lack of competition. The competition between the firms would tend to be non-price competition, such as advertising or other forms of promotion. Competing on price would drive prices down, reducing profits for all firms in the industry. This would be in none of their interests, although it would benefit the customer.

The package tour industry does not fit neatly into this oligopolistic model. Barriers to entry are relatively low. It is easy for a firm to set up. There are thousands of small package tour holiday companies, many offering specialist holidays such as adventure holidays in Africa, pilgrimages to Rome or bus tours of the Rhine. There are also thousands of independent travel agents. This is significant because all the four largest package tour operators own chains of travel agents. One reason for low barriers to entry is that the financial cost of entry is relatively small. A company can be run from a single room office with a telephone and a computer. A key to success is marketing and again the four largest companies cannot control this aspect of the market. Small companies are free to advertise their brochures in newspapers and magazines, or use independent travel agents. The Internet is also opening up further opportunities for small firms to communicate with potential customers.

Unable to control entry, the largest firms have been created over the past twenty years through a series of takeovers and mergers. Firms have competed on price

and occasionally there have been price wars which have plunged the industry into losses. The aim of price wars has been to expand market share.

In terms of efficiency, the package tour industry can be argued to be productively efficient. The largest operators have enough size to be able to exploit economies of scale to their maximum. Smaller operators tend to cater for niche markets, where volumes are much lower. It can also be argued that the industry is allocatively efficient. Consumers have wide choice whilst firms usually do not earn abnormal profits.

The industry has been investigated on a number of occasions by the government through what is now the Competition Commission and on the whole found not be acting against the interests of consumers. The largest firms would, no doubt, like to extend their market power to raise profitability at the expense of consumers. In a 1997 report, the Competition Commission found, for instance, that travel agents operated by the package tour operators were offering customers discounts on holidays if they bought travel insurance at the same time. The problem was that the travel insurance was so expensive that customers would usually have been better off not having the discount on the holiday and buying the travel insurance independently. However, this type of market abuse is limited. It would be more worrying in the long term for efficiency if independent travel agents were squeezed out of the market. If the large tour operators responded by deciding only to sell their holidays in their own chains of travel agents, then consumer choice would be restricted and firms might be able to raise prices.

The market for air travel

The air travel market is expanding as Figure 23.1 shows. In 1993, there was a total of 40 million passengers flying in and out of the UK. By 2004, this had grown to 70 million. The fastest growing sector was the leisure section: individuals using the plane to take a holiday.

The market for air travel is an example of what the competition authorities in the UK would call a 'complex monopoly'. Airline companies would argue that the industry is subject to fierce competition. In practice, competition is limited for two main reasons.

First, governments restrict which airlines can fly in and out of their countries. Traditionally, this was part of a deliberate attempt to stop free trade in airline

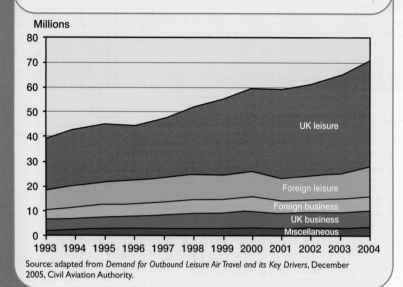

Figure 23.1 *International visits by air to and from UK airports*

Millions

Source: adapted from *Demand for Outbound Leisure Air Travel and its Key Drivers*, December 2005, Civil Aviation Authority.

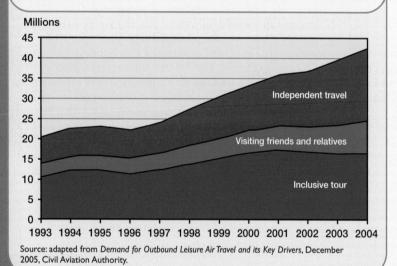

Figure 23.2 *UK resident's international air travel by type of leisure travel*

Millions

Source: adapted from *Demand for Outbound Leisure Air Travel and its Key Drivers*, December 2005, Civil Aviation Authority.

and rail connections. However, it operates at 100 per cent capacity during the day. Slots are allocated on a historical basis. If an airline received a slot in 1955, it will still have it today unless it has voluntarily given it up. So there are no landing or take off slots available for new entrants. This means that a carrier like British Airways has a dominant position at Heathrow because it has more slots than any other single airline. It also means that competition on routes tends to be restricted.

The result of these restrictions is that competition is limited. On the North Atlantic routes, for instance, there are only four airlines operating out of Heathrow, two UK carriers (BA and Virgin Atlantic) and two US carriers. Partly this is because of international agreements where the US, for instance, would not allow another UK carrier to fly to the US without the UK agreeing to allow another US carrier to fly into Heathrow. Partly it is because the existing four airlines would have to give up some of their slots to new competitors. They wouldn't do this voluntarily.

There are parts of the industry where there is relatively free competition. In the United States, for instance, any US airline can set up internal scheduled services. In Europe, governments have opened up routes between EU member countries. This has led to the entry of a number of low cost budget airlines such as EasyJet and Ryanair. They tend to fly from smaller, regional airports such as Newcastle, Luton or Stansted, reflecting the scarcity of landing slots at airports such as Heathrow. These low cost airlines could be said to be operating in a perfectly competitive market, with relatively low entry costs, where customers have no preference for which airline they fly and where they buy on price. The entry of low cost carriers has arguably been the main reason why independent leisure travel numbers have grown so fast in recent years, as shown by Figure 23.2.

Low cost airlines have driven some high cost, inefficient established carriers out of the market. Other established airlines, however, have survived by concentrating on their core customers.

First, there are package tour customers who are provided with their ticket as part of the cost of the holiday. They make no decision about which airline they fly with. Bookings are made by the package tour operators, who often charter whole airlines for flights.

Second, there are individuals who wish to fly a particular route, such as Birmingham to Lyons. They are relatively price inelastic customers, prepared to pay a premium price for a particular service. Such routes are often natural monopolies - where costs per

services to benefit national carriers. So the United States, for instance, would allow international flights to the USA by US airlines but restrict flights by other airlines. No foreign airline is allowed to operate internal flights in the USA. Agreements about which airline can fly where are negotiated through international treaties. Many would prefer to see an 'open skies' policy where governments were not involved in decision making.

Second, airlines are restricted by which airports they can use. In the UK, most carriers would prefer to use Heathrow rather than any of the other airports in the South East. This is because Heathrow is the largest airport in the UK and acts as a 'hub'. Some passengers want to be able to transfer from one flight to another. Flying from Luton or Stansted is unlikely to provide this connection. Moreover, Heathrow has good road passenger are considerably lower if there is only one producer in the market. Airlines can therefore develop monopolies on these routes.

Third, there are business customers. The most important characteristic of business customers is that they are unlikely to be paying for the flight personally. It will be their employer who pays the bill. Business customers are likely to want the best service possible. Hence, advertisements for flights often talk about leg room, meals or frequent flyer incentive schemes. Business flyers have perfect price inelasticity. Since they aren't paying, they don't care what price is the ticket. Their employers tend to be price inelastic. Typically, they want their employees to be able to work throughout the trip and return as home as soon as possible. Hence, they don't want their workers wasting time saving a few pounds flying between inconvenient airports. They don't want their workers to be exhausted by travelling in uncomfortable conditions. Flying can also be seen as a perk, rewarding an employee for working long hours during a trip. Airlines exploit this market by offering business class services. These offer better facilities than standard 'tourist' services and customers can choose the time of day they wish to travel. However, the price is often several times higher. On flights to New York, for instance, the lowest return fare available might be a few hundred pounds. Business class tickets might cost £3 000.

Firms should be able to earn abnormal profit when there is a complex monopoly. In practice, many airlines from the 1960s onwards have made substantial losses. This was mainly because lack of competition led to high levels of inefficiency. For instance, unionised airline staff have often been paid far more than the free market wage. What's more, many airlines were national carriers owned by their governments. They failed to put sufficient pressure on their airlines to become profitable. The opening up to competition on many routes and the privatisation of many national carriers such as BA has transformed the productive efficiency of many airlines and enabled them to return to profitability.

Whether the airline industry as a whole makes abnormal profits is more debatable. On some routes where there is little competition and where there is a

high volume of traffic, airlines almost certainly do make abnormal profit. On other routes where there is more competition and where average seat capacity is low, profits are likely only to be normal. Competition, then, tends to reduce profits and prices. It also usually increases the number of services available to passengers. As such, competition in the airline industry tends to lead to allocative efficiency.

Spectator sports

The market for spectator sports, like the airline market, is a complex monopoly. The main spectator sport in the UK is football. Others include rugby, cricket and boxing. The product supplied is non-homogeneous i.e. it is different from competing products. A Manchester United game, for instance, is different from a Newcastle or Oxford United game. This is reflected in the willingness of fans to view the game. Manchester United can attract far more fans to one of its games and charge a higher price than Oxford United. Loyalty by fans to a club acts as barrier to entry to the market. Other barriers to entry include the high financial cost of running a top football club and the possible losses to be incurred of owning a lower division club. Location is also a barrier to entry. A larger proportion of the population of Newcastle are Newcastle United fans than in, say, Birmingham or London.

Successful football clubs exploit their monopolies in a number of different ways.

Tickets Successful football clubs tend to charge higher prices for tickets than lower division clubs. The prices of Premiership football tickets increase each year, although some prices are raised more than others. Football clubs price discriminate, charging different prices for different types of matches, for different positions in the ground, to different age groups and for different purchase times, for instance. Table 23.1 shows some different ticket prices at Liverpool FC. Season ticket holders often pay a lower average price per match than those who buy tickets for a single game. Corporate customers who sponsor the club in return for 'free' tickets may pay higher prices for those tickets than individual fans.

Merchandise Clubs raise revenue by selling merchandise to fans. Sales of merchandise are a major source of revenue for Premiership clubs. Their monopoly in this area is weaker than in tickets because there are better substitutes. For example, clothing is in competition with other forms of fashion accessory.

Advertising, sponsorship and broadcasting rights Clubs also gain revenue from advertising, sponsorship and broadcasting rights. The last are another form of legal

Table 23.1 Liverpool FC, season ticket prices, 2005-06

Stadium position	Before 22nd June 05	After 22nd June 05
Anfield Road Stand		
Adult	£550	£600
Child	£275	£300
Over 65	£413	£450
Kop Grandstand		
Adult	£520	£565
Child	£260	£283
Over 65	£390	£424

Source: adapted from www.liverpoolfc.tv.

monopoly power. Over the past fifteen years, the Premiership has been able to increase considerably its revenues by negotiating deals with Sky television. Manchester United and Chelsea have launched their own television channel. Pay-per-view television has further potential to increase club revenues. If the most important football matches were only shown on a pay-per-view basis, fans could be charged on a one-off basis. In economic terms, football clubs are attempting to gain some of the consumer surplus (☞ unit 4) at present enjoyed by fans.

At the other end of the scale, clubs in lower divisions are likely to continue to struggle. Opportunities for non-ticket revenues are limited. Whilst a few fans may be loyal, many others in a local area will support one of the large premier division clubs.

All clubs, though, face one major problem: escalating players' wages. Football players have become increasingly able to appropriate the profit of football clubs by bargaining in a free market. The success of a football club ultimately depends on its players. The top European clubs have risen to the top by being able to afford to buy the best players. In theory, clubs are prepared to pay up to the amount of extra profit that a player will generate for the club. If there were a large supply of the best footballers, the clubs could drive wages down. In practice, there are relatively few good footballers. Supply is price inelastic, in that increasing wages will not lead to a large increase in supply. Hence, wages have been driven up. The more revenues the clubs can generate from new sources, like pay-per-view, the more they can afford to pay higher wages to attract the best players.

Television broadcasting

Television broadcasting in the UK is another example of a complex monopoly. Television is currently delivered through four main vehicles.

Terrestrial analogue television There are five analogue terrestrial channels. Two are provided by the BBC and paid for through a tax on all television users, the licence fee. Three, ITV, Channel 4 and Channel 5, are provided by commercial television companies. Their main source of revenue is television advertising.

Cable television A number of commercial companies supply cable television. Each company has been granted a monopoly on cable provision in a local area by the government to encourage them to make the very heavy financial investment in laying cable lines. Viewers have to pay a monthly fee to subscribe to cable television. Cable television also receives revenue from advertising.

Digital television A number of companies offer digital television. BSkyB uses satellites to broadcast its signals. In the UK, the alternative to BSkyB is Freeview. This is broadcast, as with analogue television, from terrestrial transmitters. Freeview is jointly owned by the BBC, National Grid Wireless, Channel 4, ITV and BSkyB. On Freeview, customers can receive the five analogue terrestrial channels as well as a number of other television and radio channels offered by the main broadcasters. BSkyB is financed through a mixture of advertising revenue and customer subscriptions. The BBC channels on Freeview are financed through the licence fee, a tax on every household owning a television in the UK. Other channels on Freeview are financed mainly through advertising.

The UK government is committed to switching off the analogue signal, possibly by 2012. This would release bandwidth which could be used either to broadcast more channels or be sold off for other uses, such as for mobile phones.

Terrestrial commercial television stations have tended to be highly profitable. This is because lack of competition has enabled them to charge high prices to their advertising customers. However, the audience share of ITV, Channel 4 and Channel 5 has been falling in recent years due to migration of customers to new digital channels. Some of these digital channels are owned by these television companies and so there is less pressure on advertising revenue as their audience share for their main channels declines. However, some customers have moved to BSkyB and other digital providers on Freeview. Moreover, growth of the number of channels puts pressure on costs because each extra channel costs money to run. Most programmes put out by channels outside the main five are made up of repeats, cheap imports from the USA, or new programmes which will be shown on the five main channels at a later date. The cost of content is therefore low but is not zero.

Cable television companies have been less financially successful than BSkyB. They have failed to attract enough subscribers to become significantly profitable after their heavy investment in infrastructure. Lack of success has been compounded by a failure to earn sufficient advertising revenue. Advertisers, after all, are only prepared to place adverts or pay high prices for them if there are large audiences. BSkyB has been more successful. Its greatest success has been in attracting young male subscribers through its strategy of outbidding other television channels for exclusive television rights to the Premiership. Its children's channels have also particularly attracted subscribers. It is due to lose its monopoly on football rights to the Premiership in 2008, whilst its children's channels now face competition from those on Freeview. The danger for the company is that it will consequently lose subscribers and therefore revenues.

The future of broadcasting is uncertain. However, one factor that will change is the amount of choice. Digital broadcasting will lead to a far greater number of channels available for viewers to watch. In economics, greater choice is usually seen as contributing to consumer welfare. But this might not be the case in television. Assume that the amount of money available from advertising and all other revenues is fixed. Then the amount of money that can be spent per channel on programming declines as the number of television channels increases. If the number of channels doubles, the amount available per channel halves. The less money spent on programming, the poorer the quality of each programme. The USA is often cited as an example of this. In the USA, viewers have plenty of choice but most of what is produced is of poor quality, constrained by lack of funds. Hence, choice may lead to allocative efficiency if consumers would prefer to have less choice but higher quality programming.

In practice, the amount of money available is not fixed. Television, for instance, can increase advertising revenues by competing more effectively with other advertising media such as newspapers or magazines. Cable and satellite companies can increase the number of subscribers, or increase subscription rates. The government could lower taxes and other payments made by television companies. However, revenues are unlikely to increase in proportion to the number of television channels. So extra channels are likely to be low budget, low quality channels. The danger is that money will be taken away from high cost, high quality channels to fund new channels. Quality will then suffer.

There is also pressure from commercial television for the BBC licence fee to be scrapped or at least reduced. The BBC provides considerable competition for all forms of commercial television. If the BBC could have its funding reduced, it would be forced to offer lower quality programmes. Audiences would then shrink and commercial television would gain viewers. This would enable them to charge more to their advertisers or make their subscriptions more attractive to viewers. Again, this might not benefit viewers if viewers have to pay more for worse programming. Even if programming improves, consumers could still be worse off. For instance, until the early 1990s, viewers could watch any live football matches on the BBC. Then Sky outbid the BBC for the rights to show live Premiership matches. The result was that only subscribers to Sky Sports could now watch this live football. Sky would argue that Sky Sports provides a better service than the BBC because it broadcasts more matches. On the other hand, the service is restricted. Those who do subscribe are funding the profits of Sky and a large increase in the rights paid to Premiership clubs. Is restricted access compensated by better programming?

DataQuestion The London Olympic Games, 2012

In 2005, London won the bid to stage the summer 2012 Olympic games. The games will be hosted mainly in North East London in the Lower Lea Valley, one of the most deprived and undeveloped parts of the Capital.

The government commissioned a study in 2005 to assess the impact of the games on the UK economy. It found that there would be an £8.5 billion positive impact on total spending (measured by GDP) in the economy between 2005 and 2016. Part of this benefit would come from the building of new infrastructure such as an Olympic stadium and an Olympic hockey stadium. The projected costs of this infrastructure are shown in Table 23.2. Tourism would also receive a substantial boost, as shown in Table 23.3.

By siting the games in a deprived area of London, the government hopes that there will be positive regeneration benefits for the local economy. Apart from the new sports buildings in the area, 3 600 new homes will be built to form the Olympic Village. Construction

itself will bring jobs and businesses into the area, some of which should survive after 2012. Training opportunities and skill development for the local workforce should improve its competitiveness in the long term.

Bringing the Olympics to the UK it is hoped will have a significant impact on physical health. Over 20 per cent of adults in the UK are now obese. The Olympics should provide encouragement for everyone to take more physical exercise. In terms of the environment, the Lower Lea Valley is an area which has relatively poor infrastructure and quantities of abandoned derelict land. The government report states that environmental benefits will occur in terms of 'remediation of contaminated sites, redevelopment of brownfield land, restoration of river corridors, improvements to water quality, investment in low carbon energy infrastructure, undergrounding of electricity pylons, creation of a major urban green space and upgrading of other amenity areas'.

Critics of the London Olympics fear that there will be considerable cost overruns and shortfalls in revenues from those predicted in Table 23.4. Someone, whether London Council Tax payers or UK tax payers, would then have to pick up the bill.

Table 23.2 London Olympics: estimated infrastructure costs (£ million at 2004 prices)

| | Estimated cost | | |
	Low	Central	High
Olympic stadium	200	325	360
Press centre and broadcast centre	50	75	95
Olympic sports halls	42	55	84
Olympic aquatic centre	60	67	90
Greenwich sports hall	20	22	56
Olympic hockey stadium	15	16	21
Velodrome	22	26	30
Training venues	10	15	25
Other	32	41	47
Total[1]	553	642	731

[1] The totals of the low and high probability estimates are not the sums of their components because they are derived through a statistical technique called 'systematic sensitivity analysis'.

Table 23.3 Expected impact on tourism (£ million)

		During the Olympics 2012	After the Olympics 2013-2016	Total 2005-2016
UK	Domestic	-2	454	518
	Foreign	66		
London	Domestic	1	162	244
	Foreign	81		

Table 23.4 London Organising Committee for the Olympic Games: estimated revenues and costs (£ million at 2004 prices)

| | Estimated cost | | |
	Low	Central	High
Revenues			
Local sponsorship	240	411	590
Ticket sales	205	301	230
Transport	30	40	50
Asset sales	34	70	110
Catering	7	9	10
TV rights	410	455	500
TOP sponsorship	98	109	120
Total[1]	1 164	1 395	1 627
Operating costs			
Sports events - furniture, fixtures and equipment	23	30	46
Sports events- other costs	162	171	184
Technology	240	260	300
Olympic village	42	100	144
Administration	210	250	300
Security	16	18	27
Transport	50	52	60
Culture	30	51	60
Advertising and promotion	70	78	90
Total[1]	931	1 010	1 089

[1] The totals of the low and high probability estimates are not the sums of their components because they are derived through a statistical technique called 'systematic sensitivity analysis'.

Source: adapted from *Olympic Games Impact Study*, Department for Culture, Media and Sport, *The Economic Impact of the London 2012 Olympics*, Adam Blake, Nottingham Business School, www.nottingham.ac.uk and www. culture.gov.uk.

1. Explain, using demand and supply diagrams, the likely impact of the London 2012 Olympic games on the price of:
   (a) hiring a hotel room in London during the Olympics;
   (b) land in the Lower Lea Valley before 2012;
   (c) hiring casual labour in the construction industry in London before 2012.
2. How might the London Olympics help correct market failure (a) in the Lower Lea Valley; (b) throughout the UK?
3. Critics of the London Olympics argue that the cost of staging the event will be far more than predicted, there will be few benefits outside of North East London and the UK taxpayer will end up with a massive bill. Evaluate the circumstances that would have to occur for this to be correct.

24 National economic performance

Summary

1. Macroeconomics is concerned with the economy as a whole whilst microeconomics is the study of individual markets within the economy.
2. National economic performance can be measured in a number of different ways. Four key macroeconomic variables are the economic growth rate, unemployment, inflation and the current account balance.

Microeconomics and macroeconomics

Units 4-23 were concerned with MICROECONOMICS. This is the study of individual markets within an economy. For instance, microeconomics is concerned with individual markets for goods or the market for labour. Housing, transport, sport and leisure are all mainly microeconomic topics because they concern the study of individual markets.

In contrast, MACROECONOMICS is concerned with the study of the economy as a whole. For instance, macroeconomics considers the total quantity produced of goods and services in an economy. The price level of the whole economy is studied. Total levels of employment and unemployment are examined. Housing becomes a macroeconomic issue when, for instance, rises in house prices significantly affect the average level of all prices in the economy.

National economic performance

One of the reasons why macroeconomics is useful is because it tells us something about the performance of an economy. In particular, it allows economists to compare the economy today with the past. Is the economy doing better or worse than it was, say, ten years ago? It also allows economists to compare different economies. Is the Japanese economy doing better than the US economy? How does the UK compare with the average in Europe?

An economy is a system which attempts to resolve the basic economy problem (☞ unit 2) of scarce resources in a world of infinite wants. An economic system is a mechanism for deciding what is to be produced, how production is to take place and who is to receive the benefit of that production. When judging the performance of an economy, one of the criteria is to consider how much is being produced. The more that is produced, the better is usually considered the economic performance. Another criterion is whether resources are being fully utilised. If there are high levels of unemployment, for instance, the economy cannot be producing at its potential level of output. Unemployment also brings poverty to those out of work and therefore affects the living standards of individuals. The rate at which prices rise is important too. High rates of price rises disrupt the workings of an economy. A national economy must also live within its means. So over a long period of time, the value of what it buys from other economies must roughly equal what it sells. In this, it is no different from a household which cannot forever overspend and accumulate debts.

Economic growth

One of the key measures of national economic performance is the rate of change of output. This is known as economic growth

(☞ unit 26). If an economy grows by 2.5 per cent per annum, output will double roughly every 30 years. If it grows by 7 per cent per annum, output will approximately double every 10 years. At growth rates of 10 per cent per annum, output will double every 7 years.

There is a standard definition of output based on a United Nations measure which is used by countries around the world to calculate their output. Using a standard definition allows output to be compared between countries and over time. This measure of output is called **gross domestic product** or **GDP** (☞ unit 25). So growth of 3 per cent in GDP in one year means that the output of the economy has increased by 3 per cent over a 12 month period.

Economic growth is generally considered to be desirable because individuals prefer to consume more rather than fewer goods and services. This is based on the assumption that wants are infinite. Higher economic growth is therefore better than lower economic growth. Periods when the economy fails to grow at all, or output shrinks as in a RECESSION or DEPRESSION, are periods when the economy is performing

Question 1

Table 24.1 *Economic growth rates*

				Average yearly changes, %	
	1961-73	1974-1979	1980-1989	1990-1999	2000-2004
United States	3.9	2.5	2.5	2.7	2.8
Japan	9.6	3.6	4.0	1.5	1.3
Germany	4.3	2.4	2.0	2.4	1.0
France	5.4	2.8	2.3	1.8	2.0
Italy	5.3	3.7	2.4	1.3	1.3
Mexico	6.6	6.1	2.0	3.0	2.6
United Kingdom	3.1	1.5	2.4	1.8	2.7

Source: adapted from OECD, *Historical Statistics, Economic Outlook*.

(a) Which country had the highest average yearly growth rate between (i) 1961 and 1973; (ii) 1974 and 1979; (iii) 1980 and 1989; (iv) 1990 and 1999; (v) 2000 and 2004?

(b) 'Mexico enjoyed a better economic performance than Germany over the period 1961 to 2004'. Does the evidence support this statement?

(c) In 1961, the UK enjoyed one of the highest living standards in Europe. By the mid-1990s, as measured by GDP, it lagged behind countries such as France and Germany. By 2004, the UK had caught up again with its main European competitors. Explain how the data show this story of the UK's poor relative economic performance over the period 1961 to the mid-1990s and its subsequent improvement.

Question 2

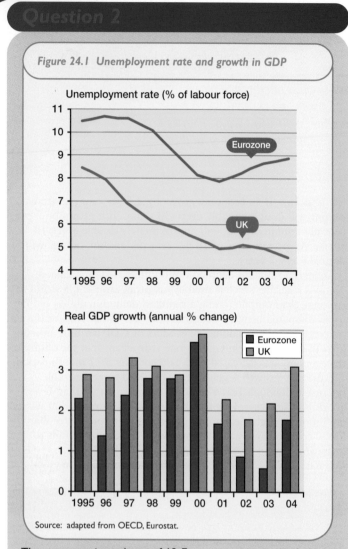

Figure 24.1 Unemployment rate and growth in GDP

Unemployment rate (% of labour force)

Eurozone

UK

Real GDP growth (annual % change)

Eurozone
UK

Source: adapted from OECD, Eurostat.

The eurozone is made up of 12 European countries, including France and Germany, which agreed to join the European Monetary Union in 1999, leading to the creation of a single European currency. The UK decided not to join and in 2005 was still not a member.
(a) Compare the economic performance of the UK with countries in the eurozone.
(b) Suggest why the UK's unemployment record between 1995 and 2004 was better than that for the eurozone.

poorly. The depression years of the 1930s in Europe and the Americas, for instance, were years when poverty increased and unemployment brought misery to millions of households.

Unemployment

Unemployment is a major problem in society because it represents a waste of scarce resources (☞ unit 29). Output could be higher if the unemployed were in work. It also leads to poverty for those who are out of work. So high unemployment is an indicator of poor national economic performance. Conversely, low unemployment is an indicator of good national economic performance.

Economic growth and unemployment tend to be linked. Fast growing economies tend to have low unemployment. This is because more workers are needed to produce more goods and services. Low levels of economic growth tend to be associated with rising levels of unemployment. Over time, technological change allows an economy to produce more with fewer workers. If there is little or no economic growth, workers are made unemployed through technological progress but fail to find new jobs in expanding industries. If growth is negative and the economy goes into recession, firms will lay off workers and unemployment will rise.

Fast economic growth, then, will tend to lead to net job creation. More jobs will be created than are lost through the changing structure of the economy. So another way of judging the performance of an economy is to consider its rate of job creation.

Inflation

Inflation is the rate of change of average prices in an economy (☞ unit 28). Low inflation is generally considered to be better than high inflation. This is because inflation has a number of adverse effects (see unit 28). For instance, rising prices mean that the value of what savings can buy falls. If a person had £50 in savings and the price of CDs went up from £10 to £25, then they would be worse off because their savings could only now buy 2 CDs compared to 5 before. Another problem with inflation is that it disrupts knowledge of prices in a market. If there is very high inflation, with prices changing by the month, consumers often don't know what is a reasonable price for an item when they come to buy it.

Today, inflation of a few per cent is considered to be acceptable. When inflation starts to climb through the 5 per cent barrier, economists begin to worry that inflation is too high. Inflation was a major problem for many countries including the UK in the 1970s and 1980s. In the UK, inflation reached 24.1 per cent in 1975 for instance. However, these levels of inflation are nothing compared to the **hyperinflation** (☞ unit 28) experienced by countries such as Argentina and Brazil in the 1980s. Prices were increasing by up to 1 000 per cent per year.

The current balance

A household must pay its way in the world. If it spends more than it earns and takes on debt, then at some point in the future it must repay that debt. Failure to repay debt can lead to seizure of assets by bailiffs and the household being barred from future borrowing. The same is true of a national economy. A nation's spending on foreign goods and services is called **imports**. It earns money to pay for those imports by selling goods and services, known as **exports**, to foreigners. If imports are greater than exports then this must be financed, either through borrowing or running down savings held abroad. The economic performance of a country is sound if, over a period of time, its exports are either greater than or approximately equal to its imports. However, if its imports are significantly greater than exports, then it could face difficulties.

Where exports of goods and services are greater than imports, there is said to be a **current account surplus** (☞ unit 30). Where imports exceed exports, there is a current account deficit. Deficits become a problem when foreign banks and other lenders refuse to lend any more money. A 'credit crunch' like this occurred, for instance, to Mexico in 1982 and Thailand in 1998. Countries have to respond to restore confidence. This is likely to involve cutting domestic spending, which leads to less demand for imports. Cutting domestic spending, though, also leads to reduced economic growth and rising unemployment. So the current account position of a country is an important indicator of performance.

Question 3

In July 2005, four terrorists planted bombs on London's underground and buses, killing 52 people and injuring many more. London is a major tourist destination and inevitably there was a wave of cancellations for London hotels in the aftermath of the bomb.

The World Travel and Tourism Council (WTTC) made an immediate impact assessment of the likely effects of the bombings on UK tourism. It predicted that in 2005 there would be nearly 600 000 fewer visitors to the UK, down from 31 million visitors. The contribution of travel and tourism to UK GDP would fall by £927 million, a 2 per cent fall in this contribution. UK Tourism contributes £185 billion to GDP and represents 4 per cent of the total. It directly and indirectly creates 2.8 million jobs.

The WTTC's conclusion was that the effects of the bombings on UK tourism would continue to be felt through to 2007. Jean-Claude Baumgarten, President of the WTTC, said the day after the bombings: 'This assumes that UK authorities undertake at least similarly strong measures of reassurance and encouragement to regain and rebuild visitor confidence and that no further events take place in the meantime.'

Source: adapted from www.wttc.org.

(a) What impact might the 2005 London bombings have had on the performance of the UK economy (a) in the short term; (b) in the long term?

Key terms

Depression - a period when there is a particularly deep and long fall in output.
Macroeconomics - the study of the economy as a whole, including inflation, growth and unemployment.
Microeconomics - the study of the behaviour of individuals or groups within an economy, typically within a market context.
Recession - a period when growth in output falls or becomes negative. The technical definition now used by governments is that a recession occurs when growth in output is negative for two successive quarters (i.e. two periods of three months).

Applied economics

A tale of four economies

The USA, Germany, Japan and the UK are four of the largest economies in the world. They form part of the G7 group (the other three being France, Italy and Canada) which meets regularly to discuss common economic problems. For much of the post-war period, Japan and Germany were seen as highly successful. They had high economic growth, low inflation, low unemployment and a persistent current account surplus. The USA was less successful mainly because its growth rate seemed low in comparison with Japan and much of continental Europe. As for the UK, it seemed to have a disappointing economic performance with slow growth and persistent inflation and balance of payment problems.

The 1990s, though, saw a reversal of fortunes as Figures 24.2 to 24.5 show. Japan's growth rate at the start of the decade was not untypical of what it had achieved during the previous four decades. However, it became bogged down in a series of recessions interspersed with short periods of positive economic growth. Over the period 1991-2004, it only averaged economic growth of 1.3 per cent per annum, compared to the 4-10 per cent range of its 'economic miracle' years of the 1950s to 1980s. Inflation reflected depressed

demand. In 1995, prices fell and this was followed by four years of price falls between 1999 and 2003. In the 1990s, unemployment remained low, but by the end of the decade was beginning to rise as years of low economic growth resulted in a shake out of jobs from Japanese industry. By 2004, unemployment was more than double what it had been in 1991.

The period 1991-2004 was difficult for Germany too. Part of its problems arose from the cost of reunification of East Germany with West Germany in 1990. East Germany had been a **command economy** (☞ unit 41) within the Soviet sphere of influence since 1945. By 1990, East Germany was a relatively inefficient economy where output per head was far below that of its highly successful western neighbour. Reunification resulted in a transfer of resources from West Germany to East Germany. Despite this, the East Germany economy remained a drag on the performance of the German economy as a whole. Growth for the reunited German economy was relatively slow after 1991. By the late 1990s, the failure of the German economy to pick up after reunification began to be blamed on its 'social' economic model which it shared with low growth countries, such as France and Italy. 'Social Europe' was

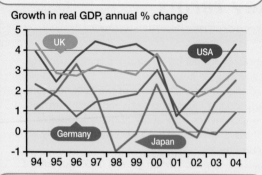

Figure 24.2 Economic growth

Growth in real GDP, annual % change

Figure 24.3 Inflation

Inflation, consumer prices, annual % change

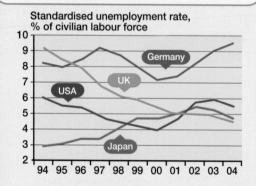

Figure 24.4 Unemployment

Standardised unemployment rate, % of civilian labour force

Figure 24.5 The current balance as a percentage of GDP

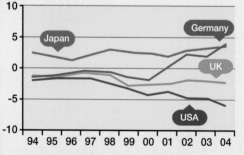

Current account balance, % of GDP

Source: adapted from OECD, *Economic Outlook*.

growing slowly because it lacked flexibility in its markets. Government red tape, high taxes on labour, difficulties in sacking workers and other **supply side** constraints (☞ unit 38) were discouraging firms from investing and taking on workers. The result was low growth and high unemployment. By 2004, German unemployment was at more than twice its 1991 level and was still rising. Inflation, which rose at the start of the 1990s following reunification, fell back quickly to below 2 per cent, partly a reflection of low economic growth and lack of demand.

The story for the USA and the UK was the reverse for that of Germany and Japan. Both the USA and the UK, after decades of relatively low economic growth, saw their position transformed into relatively high economic growth countries. Between 1960 and 1990, the US's long term growth rate had been around 2.5 per cent per year. However, from 1992, economic growth averaged over 3 per cent. One of the consequences was that unemployment fell despite strong growth in the number of workers with jobs in the US economy. Strong economic growth was also combined with subdued inflation.

In the UK, after a deep recession in the early 1990s, the economy bounced back and enjoyed average growth of 3 per cent between 1993 and 2004. This compared to a 2.6 per cent average for the period 1950-1990 and 2.3 per cent for 1970-1990. Unemployment nearly halved between 1991 and 2004 and inflation fell.

The performance of the four economies on the current account of the balance of payments can be interpreted in two ways. One is to argue that the persistent current account deficits of the UK and the USA will drag down future growth of these economies. If the deficits have been financed through borrowing to pay for current spending, the money will one day have to be repaid with interest. Just as heavy borrowing now by a household means lower consumption in the future when the debt has to be repaid, so it could be with both the UK and the USA. On this argument, Japan, which has run a persistent surplus, will benefit in the future. On the other hand, if the current account deficits have been caused by inflows of investment capital, where foreigners are investing in UK and US businesses, then the economies of the UK and the USA have been strengthened, not weakened over the period. If, for example, Japan is using part of its current account surplus to invest in new car plants in the UK, the British economy is likely to benefit in the long term. Economists are divided about whether the current account deficits and surpluses of the UK, USA, Germany and Japan have had and will have an effect on economic performance.

It could be argued that the performance of the UK and the US economies has barely changed since the 1970s and 1980s. An increase in the average economic growth rate of around half a percent looks fairly insignificant. However, it should be taken in the context of the fall in the long term growth rate of countries like Germany and Japan. In the 1970s and 1980s, Japan and Germany were growing at up to twice the rate of the UK and the USA. Since 1991, the growth rates of Japan and Germany have been half that of the UK and the USA. This turnaround has been used to argue that the 'Anglo-Saxon economic model' associated with free markets and globalisation is superior to the 'social economic model' of countries like Germany associated with more controlled markets and protectionism. By 2004, the UK's economic performance looked extremely good compared to that of Germany. The USA was outperforming its long term economic rival, Japan. The only worrying feature of the performance of the UK and the USA was their persistent current account deficits.

DataQuestion — Ireland and The Czech Republic

Ireland

Ireland joined the European Union at the same time as the UK in 1973. When it joined, it was one of the poorer EU members and consequently attracted a considerable amount of EU regional aid as well as benefiting from agricultural subsidies from the EU Common Agricultural Policy (CAP).

Successive Irish governments pursued two sets of policies which were, arguably, to prove crucial in its economics success. One was to spend generously on education so that by the 1990s, the workforce of Ireland was as richly endowed with human capital as its economic rivals. The other was, for example through grants and tax breaks, to attract foreign companies to set up in Ireland. Not only did these directly and indirectly create jobs, but they encouraged Irish companies to come up to world class standards.

With many low wage countries in Central and Eastern Europe joining the EU in 2004, and more to come later in the decade, Ireland faced the same problem as other Western European EU members: can they compete successfully or will they see jobs drain away to the East? For Ireland, was this the end of its economic boom time and would its growth rate fall to the Western European average of little more than 2 per cent per annum?

The Czech Republic

Until 1990, the Czech Republic was a command economy and part of the Eastern Bloc. Relatively poor by Western standards, its trade was orientated towards other Eastern Bloc countries such as Poland, East Germany and the Soviet Union.

From 1990, it began a transition to democracy and a free market economy. Much of industry owned by the state was privatised (i.e. sold off to the private sector). Trade was re-orientated towards Western Europe. But the transition was painful. Inefficient firms closed down. Other enterprises had to scale back their production. Increases in GDP in some sectors of the economy were offset by decreases in other sectors. Czech consumers and producers showed a preference for imported goods over Czech made products. In 2004, the Czech Republic joined the European Union. It looked to the success of economies such as Ireland and Portugal following their accession to the European Union as a model for its own future development.

1. Compare the economic performance of the Czech Republic and Ireland over the period 1994 to 2004.
2. What problems may the Czech Republic and Ireland face in the future and how might these problems impact on the future economic performance of these two countries?

Economic indicators

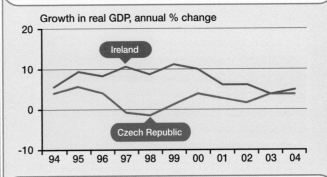

Figure 24.6 Economic growth

Growth in real GDP, annual % change

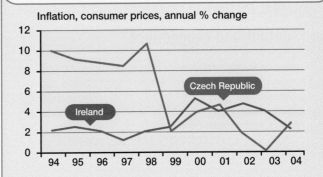

Figure 24.7 Inflation

Inflation, consumer prices, annual % change

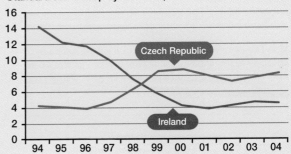

Figure 24.8 Unemployment

Standardised unemployment rate, % of civilian labour force

Figure 24.9 The current balance as a percentage of GDP

Current account balance, % of GDP

Source: adapted from OECD, *Economic Outlook*.

Summary

1. National income can be measured in three ways: as national output, national expenditure or national income.
2. The most commonly used measure of national income is Gross Domestic Product (GDP). Other measures include Gross National Product (GNP) and Net National Product (NNP). All these measures can be at market prices or factor cost.
3. National income statistics are used by academics to formulate and test hypotheses. They are used by policy makers to formulate economic policy both on a micro-economic and macro-economic level. They are often used as a proxy measure for the standards of living and to compare living standards between countries and within a country over time.
4. National income statistics can be inaccurate because of statistical errors, the existence of the black economy, of non-traded sectors, and difficulties with valuing public sector output.
5. Problems occur when comparing national income over time because of inflation, the accuracy and presentation of statistics, changes in population, the quality of goods and services and changes in income distribution.
6. Further problems occur when comparing national income between countries. In particular, an exchange rate has to be constructed which accurately reflects different purchasing power parities.

Income, output and expenditure

Macroeconomics is concerned with the economy as a whole. A key macroeconomic variable is the level of total output in an economy, often called NATIONAL INCOME. There are three ways in which national income can be calculated. To understand why, consider a very simple model of the economy where there is no foreign trade (a CLOSED ECONOMY as opposed to an OPEN ECONOMY where there is foreign trade) and no government. In this economy, there are only households and firms which spend all their income and revenues.

- Households own the wealth of the nation. They own the land, labour and capital used to produce goods and services. They supply these factors to firms in return for rents, wages, interest and profits - the rewards to the factor of production.

Figure 25.1 *The circular flow of income in a simple economy*
Households supply factors of production to firms in return for rent, wages, interest and profit. Households spend their money on goods and services supplied by firms.

They then use this money to buy goods and services.
- Firms produce goods and services. They hire factors of production from households and use these to produce goods and services for sale back to households.

The flow from households to firms is shown in Figure 25.1. The flow of money around the economy is shown in red. Households receive payments for hiring their land, labour and capital. They spend all that money on the goods and services produced by firms (consumption). An alternative way of putting this is to express these money payments in real terms, taking into account changes in prices (unit 3 explains the distinction between real and monetary values). The real flow of products and factor services is shown in black. Households supply land, labour and capital in return for goods and services. The CIRCULAR FLOW OF INCOME MODEL can be used to show that there are three ways of measuring the level of economic activity.

National output (O) This is the value of the flow of goods and services from firms to households. It is the black line on the right of the diagram.

National expenditure (E) This is the value of spending by households on goods and services. It is the red line on the right of the diagram.

National income (Y) This is the value of income paid by firms to households in return for land, labour and capital. It is the blue line on the left of the diagram.

So income, expenditure and output are three ways of measuring the same flow. To show that they must be identical and not just equal, we use the '=' sign.

$$O = E = Y$$

Measures of national income

Economies are not as simple as that shown in Figure 25.1. Calculating national income in practice involves a complex system of accounts. The standard used in most countries today

Question 1

Table 25.1

	£bn
Rent	5
Wages	75
Interest and profit	20

The figures in Table 25.1 represent the only income payments received by households. There are no savings, investment, government expenditure and taxes or foreign trade in the economy.

(a) Draw a circular flow of income diagram. Label it at the appropriate place with the value of: (i) income, (ii) output and (iii) expenditure.
(b) How would your answer be different if wages were £100 billion?

is based on the System of National Accounts (SNA) first published in 1953 by the United Nations. This system of accounts has subsequently been developed and modified. The system currently in use in the UK is based on the European System of Accounts last modified in 1995 (ESA 1995).

The key measure of national income used in the UK is GROSS DOMESTIC PRODUCT (GDP). This is at market prices, which means it is a measure of national income that includes the value of **indirect taxes** (taxes on expenditure) like VAT. Indirect taxes are not part of the output of the economy, so this measure inflates the actual value of national income. GDP also includes the value of exports and imports and is therefore a more complex measure of national income than in the simple circular flow model described earlier. There are other measures of national income.

Gross value added (GVA) at basic cost This is GDP minus indirect taxes plus subsidies on goods. Indirect taxes minus subsidies is called the basic price adjustment.

Gross national income (GNP) at market prices GROSS NATIONAL INCOME (GNP) is GDP plus income earned abroad on investments and other assets owned overseas minus income paid to foreigners on their investments in the UK.

Net national income at market prices Each year, the existing capital stock or physical wealth of the country depreciates in value because of use. This is like depreciation on a car as it gets older. If individuals run down their savings to finance spending, their actual income must be their spending minus how much they have used from their savings. Similarly with a country, its true value of income is gross (i.e. before depreciation has been taken into account) national income minus depreciation. This is net national income.

GDP at market prices is the main headline figure used for national income because the data to calculate it is most quickly available. When comparing over time and between countries, movements in GDP at market prices are broadly similar to movements in other measures of national income. So it is a good guide to what is happening in the economy and can be used to judge the performance of the economy.

Question 2

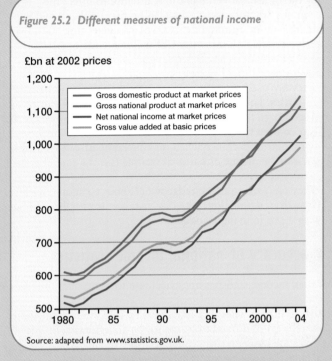

Figure 25.2 Different measures of national income

£bn at 2002 prices

Gross domestic product at market prices
Gross national product at market prices
Net national income at market prices
Gross value added at basic prices

Source: adapted from www.statistics.gov.uk.

(a) Briefly explain the difference between each measure of national income shown on the graph.
(b) 'Changes in GDP at market prices broadly reflect changes in other measures of national income over time.' To what extent do the data support this?

Transfer payments

Not all types of income are included in the final calculation of national income. Some incomes are received without there being any corresponding output in the economy. For instance:
- the government pays National Insurance and social security benefits to individuals, but the recipients produce nothing in return;
- students receive student grants from government, but again produce nothing which can be sold;
- children receive pocket money and allowances from their parents;
- an individual selling a second hand car receives money, but no new car is created.

These incomes, called TRANSFER PAYMENTS, are excluded from final calculations of national income. For instance, government spending in national income is **public expenditure** minus spending on benefits and grants.

Why is national income measured?

National income is a measure of the output, expenditure and income of an economy. National income statistics provide not only figures for these totals but also a breakdown of the totals. They are used in a number of different ways.
- Academic economists use them to test hypotheses and build models of the economy. This increases

our understanding of how an economy works.

- Government, firms and economists use the figures to forecast changes in the economy. These forecasts are then used to plan for the future. Government may attempt to direct the economy (☞ for instance unit 36 on fiscal policy), making changes in its spending or its taxes at budget time. Groups such as trade unions or the CBI will make their own recommendations about what policies they think the government should pursue.
- They are used to make comparisons over time and between countries. For instance, national income statistics can be used to compare the income of the UK in 1950 and 2007. Or they can be used to compare France's income with UK income. Of particular importance when making comparisons over time is the rate of change of national income (i.e. the rate of economic growth).
- They are used to make judgements about economic welfare. Growth in national income, for instance, is usually equated with a rise in living standards.

The accuracy of national income statistics

National income statistics are inaccurate for a number of reasons.

Statistical inaccuracies National income statistics are calculated from millions of different returns to the government. Inevitably mistakes are made: returns are inaccurate or simply not completed. The statistics are constantly being revised in the light of fresh evidence. Although revisions tend to become smaller over time, national income statistics are still being revised ten years after first publication.

The hidden economy Taxes such as VAT, income tax and National Insurance contributions, and government regulations such as health and safety laws, impose a burden on workers and businesses. Some are tempted to evade taxes and they are then said to work in the BLACK, HIDDEN OR INFORMAL ECONOMY. In the building industry, for instance, it is common for workers to be self-employed and to under-declare or not declare their income at all to the tax authorities. Transactions in the black economy are in the form of cash. Cheques, credit cards, etc. could all be traced by the tax authorities. Tax evasion is the dominant motive for working in the hidden economy but a few also claim welfare benefits to which they are not entitled. The size of the hidden economy is difficult to estimate, but in the UK estimates have varied from 7 to 15 per cent of GDP (i.e. national income statistics underestimate the true size of national income by at least 7 per cent).

Home produced services In the poorest developing countries in the world, GNP per person is valued at less than £100 per year. It would be impossible to survive on this amount if this were the

Question 3

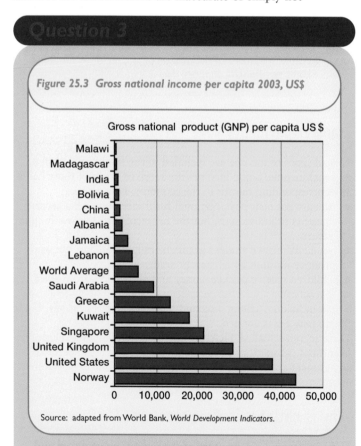

Figure 25.3 Gross national income per capita 2003, US$

Source: adapted from World Bank, *World Development Indicators*.

(a) What statistics do governments need to collect in order to be able to calculate GNP per capita?
(b) How might (i) an economist and (ii) a government use these statistics?

Question 4

Researchers from the University of Cyprus have estimated the size of the hidden economy in the UK to be at least 10.6 per cent of GDP. They looked at the incomes of the self-employed and compared them to their expenditure using the Family Expenditure Survey compiled by the Office for National Statistics (FES). They compared this with the incomes and expenditure of employed workers such as civil servants who were unlikely to have any hidden income. They estimated that households where the head of the household was a blue collar worker and self-employed reported only 46 per cent of their income to the tax authorities. Households whose self-employed head was in a white-collar occupation on average reported only 61 per cent of their income. Given that reported self-employment income is around 12.3 per cent of GDP, this means that self-employment related black economy activities in the UK amount to 10.6 per cent of GDP.

Workers who are employed may also have undeclared part-time jobs which would increase the size of the black economy. Their ability to avoid tax, however, is limited because their employers deduct their tax from their pay packet through the PAYE (Pay As You Earn) scheme. In 2004, there were 3.6 million self-employed workers and 24.6 million employees.

Source: adapted from 'Estimates of the black economy based on consumer demand approaches', P.Lyssiotou, P.Pashardes and T.Stengos, *Economic Journal*, July 2004 and *Monthly Digest of Statistics*, Office for National Statistics.

(a) Explain why there is an incentive for workers to work in the 'hidden economy'.
(b) UK tax authorities estimate that painters and decorators, cleaners, taxi drivers and gardeners tend to evade tax. Suggest why these workers, rather than teachers or civil servants, are more likely to work in the 'hidden economy'.
(c) The UK government is currently aiming to create a more flexible workforce, with a greater proportion of part-time, casual and self-employed workers. What are the implications of this for the size of the hidden economy?

true value of output in the economy. However, a large part of the production of the agricultural sector is not traded and therefore does not appear in national income statistics. People are engaged in subsistence agriculture, consuming what they themselves produce. Hence the value of national output is in reality much higher. In the UK, the output of the services of housewives and househusbands is equally not recorded. Nor is the large number of DIY jobs completed each year. The more DIY activity, the greater will be the under-recording of national output by national income statistics.

The public sector Valuing the output of much of the public sector is difficult because it is not bought and sold. This problem is circumvented by valuing non-marketed output at its cost of production. For instance, the value of the output of a state school is the cost of running the school. This method of valuation can yield some surprising results. Assume that through more efficient staffing, the number of nurses on a hospital ward is reduced from 10 to 8 and the service is improved. National income accounts will still show a fall in output (measured by a drop in the two nurses' incomes). In general, increased productivity in the public sector is shown by a fall in the value of output. It looks as though less is being produced when in fact output remains unchanged.

Comparing national income over time

Comparing the national income of the UK today with national income in the past presents problems.

Prices Prices have tended to increase over time. So an increase in national income over the period does not necessarily indicate that there has been an increase in the number of goods and services produced in the economy. Only if the rate of increase of national income measured in money terms (the nominal rate of economic growth) has been greater than the increase in prices (the inflation rate) can there be said to have been an increase in output. So when comparing over time, it is essential to consider real and not **nominal** changes in income (☞ unit 3).

The accuracy and presentation of statistics National income statistics are inaccurate and therefore it is impossible to give a precise figure for the change in income over time. Moreover, the change in real income over time will also be affected by the inflation rate. The inevitable errors made in the calculation of the inflation rate compound the problems of inaccuracy. The method of calculating national income and the rate of inflation can also change over time. It is important to attempt to eliminate the effect of changes in definitions.

Changes in population National income statistics are often used to compare living standards over time. If they are to be used in this way, it is essential to compare national income per capita (i.e. per person). For instance, if the population doubles whilst national income quadruples, people are likely to be nearer twice as well off than four times.

Quality of goods and services The quality of goods may improve over time due to advances in technology but they may also fall in price. For instance, cars today are far better than cars 80 years ago and yet are far cheaper. National income would show this fall in price by a fall in national income, wrongly implying that living standards had fallen. On the other hand,

pay in the public sector tends to increase at about 2 per cent per annum faster than the increase in inflation. This is because pay across the economy tends to increase in line with the rate of economic growth rather than the rate of inflation. Increased pay would be reflected in both higher nominal and real national income but there may well be no extra goods or services being produced.

Defence and related expenditures The GDP of the UK was higher during the Second World War than in the 1930s, but much of GDP between 1940 and 1945 was devoted to defence expenditure. It would be difficult to argue that people enjoyed a higher standard of living during the war years than in the pre-war years. So the proportion of national income devoted to defence, or for instance to the police, must be taken into account when considering the standard of living of the population.

Consumption and investment It is possible to increase standards of living today by reducing investment and increasing consumption. However, reducing investment is likely to reduce standards of living from what they might otherwise have been in the future. As with defence, the proportion of national income being devoted to investment will affect the standard of living of the population both now and in the future.

Externalities National income statistics take no account of **externalities** (☞ unit 19) produced by the economy. National income statistics may show that national income has doubled roughly every 25 years since 1945. But if the value of externalities has more than doubled over that time period, then the rate of growth of the standard of living has less than doubled.

Income distribution When comparing national income over time, it is important to remember that an increased national

Table 25.2 GDP, prices and population

	Nominal GDP at market prices (£bn)	Index of Retail Prices (2004 = 100)	Population (millions)
1948	11.9	4.2	48.7
1958	22.8	6.5	51.7
1968	43.5	8.8	55.2
1978	167.8	26.8	56.2
1988	468.4	57.2	56.9
1998	860.5	87.3	58.5
2004	1 163.9	100.0	59.8

Source: adapted from *Economic Trends Annual Supplement, Monthly Digest of Statistics, Annual Abstract of Statistics,* Office for National Statistics.

(a) For each year, calculate the value of: (i) nominal GDP per head of the population; (ii) real GDP per head of the population at 2004 prices.
(b) To what extent is it possible to judge from the data whether living standards increased over the period 1948-2004?

income for the economy as a whole may not mean that individuals have seen their income increase. Income distribution is likely to change over time, which may or may not lead to a more desirable state of affairs.

Comparing national income between countries

Comparing national income between economies is fraught with difficulties too. Income distributions may be different. Populations will be different and therefore it is important to compare per capita income figures. National income accounts will have varying degrees of inaccuracy, caused, for instance, by different sizes of the informal economy in each country. National income accounting conventions will differ.

There is also the problem of what rate of exchange to use when comparing one country's national income with another. The day to day market exchange rate can bear little relation to relative prices in different countries. So prices in some countries, like Switzerland or West Germany, can be much higher at official exchange rates than in France or Italy. Therefore if national income statistics are to be used to compare living standards between countries it is important to use an exchange rate which compares the cost of living in each country. These exchange rates are known as PURCHASING POWER PARITIES. For instance, if a typical basket of goods costs 10 francs in France and £1 in the UK, then national income should be converted at an exchange rate of 10 francs to the £1, even if the market exchange rate gives a very different figure.

Even this is not accurate enough. In some countries, consumers have to purchase goods which in others are free. For instance, Sweden spends a greater proportion of its national income than Italy on fuel for heating because of its colder climate. But this extra expenditure does not give the Swedes a higher standard of living. Again, countries are different geographically and one country might have higher transport costs per unit of output than another because of congestion or having to transport goods long distances. In practice, it is almost impossible to adjust national income figures for these sorts of differences.

Question 6

Table 25.3 *GNP, exchange rates and population, 2003*

Country	Currency units per £		GNP, value in local currency	Population millions
	Market exchange rates	Purchasing power parity exchange rates		
France	1.4456	1.3021	€1345.7 bn	59.8
Germany	1.4456	1.2939	€1842.3 bn	82.5
Italy	1.4456	1.1368	€1099.5 bn	57.6
Japan	189.34	222.49	505123 bn yen	127.6
Spain	1.4456	1.0882	619.5 bn	41.1
Switzerland	2.197	2.7015	401.9 bn Swiss francs	7.4
UK	1.0000	1.0000	£1027.8 bn	59.3
USA	1.6346	1.6036	US$11013 bn	290.8

Source: adapted from *World Development Indicators*, World Bank; *Economic Trends*, Office for National Statistics.

(a) Rank in order the countries in the table according to (i) GNP and (ii) GNP per head. Do this by converting GNP and GNP per head into pounds sterling using the purchasing power parity exchange rate.

(b) Would your rank order have been different if you had coverted GNP at market exchange rates rather than purchasing power parity exchange rates? If so, explain why.

Key terms

Circular flow of income - a model of the economy which shows the flow of goods, services and factors and their payments around the economy.

Closed economy - an economy where there is no foreign trade.

Gross domestic product (GDP) and gross national product (GNP) - measures of national income which exclude and include respectively net income from investments abroad, but do not include an allowance for depreciation of the nation's capital stock.

Hidden, black or informal economy - economic activity where trade and exchange take place, but which goes unreported to the tax authorities and those collecting national income statistics. Workers in the hidden economy are usually motivated by the desire to evade paying taxes.

National income - the value of the output, expenditure or income of an economy over a period of time.

Open economy - an economy where there is trade with other countries.

Purchasing power parities - an exchange rate of one currency for another which compares how much a typical basket of goods in one country costs compared to that of another country.

Transfer payments - income for which there is no corresponding output, such as unemployment benefits or pension payments.

Applied economics

France and the United Kingdom

France has a lower GNP than the UK. In 2003, French GNP was €1345.7 bn compared to £1027.8 bn for the UK. At an exchange rate of €1.4456 to the pound, this meant than the French economy produced 10 per cent less than the UK economy.

Crude national income statistics like these don't say very much when making inter-country comparisons. For a start, populations may be vastly different. In this case France and the UK have almost identical populations of approximately 59 million, with the UK having a slightly smaller population than that of France (59.3 million compared to 59.9 million). So GNP per capita gives little extra information compared to total GNP when making comparisons. Purchasing power parities (PPPs) do, however, differ substantially from market exchange rates. In 2003, market exchange rates undervalued the franc in comparison with PPPs. French GNP, when converted into pounds using PPPs in 2003 was £1 033 bn. This was almost identical to UK GNP measured at PPP rates of £1 027.8 bn. The conclusion must be that France and the UK had broadly similar GNPs when measured in purchasing power parity values, but the UK had a slightly higher GNP per head because of its slightly smaller population. The difference in GNP per head at PPP rates was 1 per cent.

In making comparisons about living standards, national income is only one among many factors to be taken into account. One such factor is the distribution of income. Table 25.4 shows that income in the UK in the second half of the 1990s was less evenly distributed than that in France. Average incomes of the poorest 20 per cent in the UK were lower than in France whilst average incomes of the highest 20 per cent were higher.

Another group of factors which are important relates to how national income is distributed between different types of expenditure. Table 25.5 shows that in 2003, 24 per cent of GDP in France was accounted for by general government consumption on items such as education and environmental services, compared to 21 per cent in the UK. Spending on investment was higher too in France, partly accounted for by higher government investment in infrastructure such as roads, railways and school buildings. However, higher spending in the UK was partly the result of a current account deficit on the balance of payments. France ran a 2 per cent surplus on current account compared to a 3 per cent deficit for the UK. If the UK financed this deficit by borrowing, it was spending now but would have to repay the debt at some time in the future. Government spending on defence was broadly similar in both countries at 2.5 per cent of GNP in 2003. Spending on health was higher in France in 2002, with approximately 10 per cent of GDP being spent on public and private health care compared to 8 per cent in the UK. British households were able to spend a larger proportion of GDP than the French. Private consumption accounted for 66 per cent of GNP in the UK in 2003 compared to 55 per cent in France, a significant difference. However, many in the UK who bought a house over the previous five years would have seen much, if not all, of that difference eroded by the cost of their mortgages on houses which were considerably more expensive than in France.

Quality of life is difficult to measure. The French are less urbanised than their UK counterparts. In 2003, 76 per cent of French people lived in towns and cities compared to 90 per cent in the UK. Important too is the fact that France is over twice the size of the UK and hence population density is much lower in France. Certainly, French roads are, on average, far less congested than those in the UK and lower population densities and a more dispersed industry and population mean that air pollution is less in France than in the UK.

Many other factors need to be taken into account before deciding whether the British have a higher standard of living than the French or vice versa. The relative position of the two countries also changes over time. Forty years ago, the British probably enjoyed a higher standard of living than the French. By the 1990s, the French, because of higher economic growth over the subsequent decades, arguably had reversed this position. But the end of the 1990s, the French economy was stagnating compared to the UK economy. So by 2002-2004, the two economies were delivering roughly equal average incomes at purchasing power parities to their citizens. If recent trends continued for the next decade, the British would easily outstrip the French in purchasing power parity terms by 2010-2015.

Table 25.4 Income distribution

| | Percentage share of income | | | | |
	Lowest 20%	Next 20%	Middle 20%	Next 20%	Highest 20%
France (1995)	7.2	12.6	17.2	22.8	40.2
UK (1999)	6.1	11.4	16.0	22.5	44.0

Source: adapted from World Bank, *World Development Indicators*.

Table 25.5 Structure of demand, 2003

| | | | | % of GDP |
	Private consumption	Government consumption	Gross domestic investment	Exports minus imports
France	55	24	19	2
UK	66	21	16	-3

Source: adapted from World Bank, *World Development Indicators*.

DataQuestion

Living standards

Table 25.6 National income indicators, 2003

	Gross national income ($ million)	Gross national income per capita ($)	PPP estimates of gross national income per capita ($)
Ethiopia	6.4	90	710
Ghana	6.5	320	2 190
Indonesia	173.5	810	3 210
Pakistan	77.6	1 110	4 690
Colombia	10.1	630	6 410
Russian Federation	374.8	2 610	8 950
Czech Republic	72.9	7 150	15 600
New Zealand	62.2	15 530	21 350
UK	1 680.1	28 320	27 690
USA	11 012.6	37 870	37 750

Table 25.7 Income distribution

	Lowest 20%	Next 20%	Middle 20%	Next 20%	Highest 20%
Ethiopia (1999-2000)	9.1	13.2	16.8	21.5	39.4
Ghana (1998-99)	5.6	10.1	14.9	22.9	46.6
Indonesia (2002)	8.4	11.9	15.4	21.0	43.3
Pakistan (1998-99)	8.8	12.5	15.9	20.6	42.3
Colombia (1999)	2.7	6.6	10.8	18.0	61.8
Russian Federation (2002)	8.2	12.7	16.9	23.0	39.3
Czech Republic (1996)	10.3	14.5	17.7	21.7	35.9
New Zealand (1997)	6.4	11.4	15.8	22.6	43.8
UK (1999)	6.1	11.4	16	22.5	44
USA (2000)	5.4	10.7	15.7	22.4	45.8

Table 25.8 Population

	Population growth, average annual % growth 1990-2003	% of population aged 0-14, 2003	% of population aged 65+, 2003	Urban population % of total, 2003
Ethiopia	2.3	45.4	2.8	17
Ghana	2.3	41.9	4.4	37
Indonesia	1.4	29.7	4.9	44
Pakistan	2.4	40.1	3.4	34
Colombia	1.9	31.8	4.8	76
Russian Federation	- 0.3	16.3	13.2	73
Czech Republic	- 0.1	15.5	13.9	75
New Zealand	1.2	21.9	11.7	86
UK	0.2	18.2	16.0	90
USA	1.2	21.0	12.4	78

Table 25.9 Health indicators

	Life expectancy at birth, years, 2003	Under-five mortality rate, per thousand of the population 2003	Prevalance of child malnutrition % of children underweight 1995-2003	Access to safe water, % of population 2002	Access to sanitation facilities, % of population 2002	Public expenditure on health, % of GDP, 2002
Ethiopia	42	169	47.2	22	6	2.6
Ghana	54	95	22.1	79	58	2.3
Indonesia	67	41	27.3	78	52	1.2
Pakistan	64	98	35.0	90	54	1.1
Colombia	72	21	6.7	92	86	6.7
Russian Federation	66	21	5.5	96	87	3.5
Czech Republic	75	5	n.a.	100	100	6.4
New Zealand	79	6	n.a.	100	100	6.6
UK	78	7	n.a.	100	100	6.4
USA	77	8	n.a.	100	100	6.6

Table 25.10 Energy and the environment

	Energy use per capita (Kg of oil equivalent) 2002	Carbon dioxide emissions per capita, metric tons 2000	Average annual deforestation, %, 1990-2000	Nationally protected areas as % of total land area 2003
Ethiopia	297	0.1	0.8	16.9
Ghana	411	0.3	1.7	5.6
Indonesia	737	1.3	1.2	20.6
Pakistan	454	0.8	1.5	4.9
Colombia	625	1.4	0.4	10.2
Russian Federation	4 288	9.9	0.0	7.8
Czech Republic	4 090	11.6	0.0	16.1
New Zealand	4 573	8.3	- 0.5	29.6
UK	3 824	9.6	- 0.6	20.9
USA	7 943	19.8	- 0.2	25.9

Table 25.11 Education

	Public expenditure on education, % of GDP, 2002	Adult literacy, % of people aged 15 and older, 2002		Net enrolment ratio, % of relevant age group, 2002-03		Children in the labour force, % of age group, 2003
		Male	Female	Primary	Secondary	
Ethiopia	4.6	49	34	47	15	40
Ghana	n.a.	82	66	63	33	11
Indonesia	1.3	92	83	92	n.a.	7
Pakistan	1.8	n.a.	n.a.	59	n.a.	14
Colombia	5.2	92	92	87	54	6
Russian Federation	3.1	100	99	n.a.	n.a.	0
Czech Republic	4.2	n.a.	n.a.	88	89	0
New Zealand	6.7	n.a.	n.a.	100	93	0
UK	4.7	n.a.	n.a.	100	96	0
USA	5.7	n.a.	n.a.	93	85	0

Table 25.12 Communications

	Paved roads, % of total, 1997-2002	Telephone mainlines per 1 000 people, 2003	Mobile phones per 1 000 people, 2003	Televisions per 1 000 people, 2003	Personal computers per 1 000 people, 2003	Internet users per 1 000 people 2003
Ethiopia	12.0	6	1	6	2.2	1
Ghana	18.4	13	36	53	3.8	8
Indonesia	58.0	39	87	153	11.9	38
Pakistan	59.0	27	18	150	4.2	10
Colombia	14.4	179	141	319	49.3	53
Russian Federation	67.4	242	249	n.a.	88.7	n.a.
Czech Republic	100.0	360	965	538	177.4	308
New Zealand	64.0	448	648	574	413.8	526
UK	100.0	591	841	938	658.9	551
USA	58.8	621	543	n.a.	110.1	119

Table 25.13 Distribution of GDP by sector and by demand

	Distribution of GDP by sector, %			Structure of demand, % of GDP[1]		
	Agriculture	Industry	Services	Private consumption	Government consumption	Gross domestic investment
Ethiopia	42	11	47	75	24	21
Ghana	36	25	39	77	12	23
Indonesia	17	44	40	69	9	16
Pakistan	23	23	53	73	12	16
Colombia	12	29	58	65	21	15
Russian Federation	5	34	61	53	16	20
Czech Republic	3	39	57	51	24	28
New Zealand	7	28	65	60	18	21
UK	1	27	72	71	15	16
USA	2	23	75	71	15	18

Source: adapted from World Bank, *World Development Indicators*.

1 Figures do not necessarily add up to 100. This is because the balance shows net resource flows from foreign countries. For example, Ethiopia spent 120 per cent of GDP on consumption and investment and financed this by a net 20 per cent inflow of funds from abroad.

1. You have been asked to write an article for a magazine of no more than 1 000 words. The editor wants you to compare the standard of living of 10 countries using national income statistics. Using the data provided, in your article: (a) make such a comparison; (b) discuss the limitations of using national income statistics to compare living standards between countries, giving examples of how different economic indicators might provide an additional or perhaps even better basis for making a comparison.

Summary

1. Economic growth is the change in potential output of the economy shown by a shift to the right of the production possibility frontier. Economic growth is usually measured by the change in real national income.
2. Economic growth is caused by increases in the quantity or quality of land, labour and capital and by technological progress.
3. It is sometimes argued that growth is unsustainable because of the law of diminishing returns. Because land in particular is fixed in supply, diminishing returns will set in. However, most natural resources are not in fixed supply and historical evidence suggests that all factors are variable over time.

Economic growth

Economies change over time. Part of this change involves changes in productive capacity - the ability to produce goods and services. Increases in productive capacity are known as ECONOMIC GROWTH. Most economies today experience positive economic growth over time. However, economic disruption caused by war as in parts of Africa, or severe economic dislocation because of changing economic systems as in Russia, can lead to negative economic growth.

It is not possible to measure the productive capacity of an economy directly because there is no way of producing a single monetary figure for the value of variables such as machinery, workers and technology. Instead, economists use changes in GDP, the value of output, as a proxy measure.

The output gap

Using GDP has its problems, particularly in the short term. This is because the economy can operate below or indeed above its productive potential over a period of time. For instance, if the economy falls into a **recession** (☞ unit 24), unemployment rises and therefore it fails to produce at its potential level of output. In a boom, the economy may operate beyond its productive potential. For instance, workers may be prepared for a short time to work excessively long hours. In the long term, they would refuse to work these hours and so the economy is operating beyond its potential output. The same could be true of an individual firm. Workers may be prepared to work large amounts of overtime to get out an important and urgent order, but they wouldn't want to work those hours every week.

Figure 26.1 shows this OUTPUT GAP. The straight line is the trend rate of growth in GDP over a long period of time. It is assumed that this shows the level of GDP associated with the productive potential of the economy. The actual level of GDP may vary from this. When the economy is in recession and there is high unemployment, the actual level of GDP can be below the trend line and a NEGATIVE OUTPUT GAP is said to exist. Sometimes, the actual level of GDP is above the trend line and a POSITIVE OUTPUT GAP exists. These

Figure 26.1 The output gap
The trend rate of growth of GDP approximates the growth in productive potential of the economy. When actual GDP falls below this or rises above it, there is said to be an output gap. When actual GDP growth falls below this, there is a negative output gap. When actual GDP growth rises above it, there is a positive output gap.

fluctuations in the actual level of GDP around the trend rate of growth are known as the BUSINESS CYCLE or TRADE CYCLE or ECONOMIC CYCLE.

The production possibility frontier

Production possibility frontiers (PPFs) can be used to discuss economic growth. The PPF shows the maximum or **potential** output of an economy (☞ unit 1). When the economy grows, the PPF will move outward as in Figure 26.2. A movement from A to C would be classified as economic growth. However, there may be unemployment in the economy. With a PPF passing through C, a movement from B (where there is unemployment) to C (full employment) would be classified as ECONOMIC RECOVERY rather than economic growth. Hence, an increase in national income does not necessarily mean that there has been economic growth. In practice it is difficult to know exactly the location of an economy's PPF and therefore economists tend to treat all increases in GNP as economic growth.

Figure 26.2 can also be used to show the conflict between investment and consumption. One major source of economic growth is investment. All other things being equal, the greater the level of investment the higher will be the rate of growth in the future. However, increased production of investment goods can only be achieved by a reduction in the production of consumption goods if the economy is at full employment. So there is a trade off to be made between consumption now and consumption in the future. The lower the level of consumption today relative to the level of investment, the higher will be the level of consumption in the future.

Figure 26.2 Production possibility frontiers
A movement from A to C would represent economic growth if there were a shift in the production possibility frontier from PPF$_1$ to PPF$_2$. A movement from B to C would represent economic recovery if the production possibility frontier was PPF$_2$.

The causes of economic growth

National output can be increased if there is an increase in the quantity or quality of the inputs to the production process. Output can also be increased if existing inputs are used more efficiently. This can be expressed in terms of a **production function**:

$$\text{Output} = f \text{ (land, labour, capital, technical progress, efficiency)}$$

The remainder of this unit will concentrate on the ways in which the quantity and quality of the factors of production can be increased and on what determines technical progress.

Land

Different countries possess different endowments of land. Land in economics is defined as all natural resources, not just land itself. Some countries, such as Saudi Arabia, have experienced large growth rates almost solely because they are so richly endowed. Without oil, Saudi Arabia today would almost certainly be a poor Third World country. Other countries have

Question 1

Figure 26.3 The output gap, UK

Source: HM Treasury, The Red Book.

(a) Explain what is meant by an output gap, illustrating your answer by referring to 1981 and 1987.
(b) Using a production possibility frontier diagram, explain where the economy was in relation to its productive potential in (i) 2000 and (ii) 2005.
(c) The economy grew relatively fast between 1982 and 1987. To what extent was this economic recovery or economic growth?

received windfalls. The UK, for instance, only started to exploit its oil and gas resources in the mid 1970s. Today oil and gas contribute about 2.7 per cent of GNP. However, most economists argue that the exploitation of raw materials is unlikely to be a significant source of growth in developed economies, although it can be vital in developing economies.

Labour

Increasing the number of workers in an economy should lead to economic growth. Increases in the labour force can result from three factors.

Changes in demography If more young people enter the workforce than leave it, then the size of the workforce will increase. In most western developed countries the population is relatively stable. Indeed, many countries are experiencing falls in the number of young people entering the workforce because of falls in the birth rate from the late 1960s onwards.

Increases in participation rates Nearly all men who wish to work are in the labour force. However, in most Western countries there exists a considerable pool of women who could be brought into the labour force if employment opportunities were present. In the UK, for instance, almost all of the increase in the labour force in the foreseeable future will result from women returning to or starting work.

Immigration A relatively easy way of increasing the labour force is to employ migrant labour. Increasing the size of the labour force may increase output but will not

'Garbage jobs' are holding back the Spanish economy. These are jobs which are short term, offer little security and give few benefits. Of the 900 000 jobs created in the Spanish economy last year, two thirds of them carried contracts of six months or less. Temporary contracts now cover more than 35 per cent of all jobs in Spain compared to an EU average of 12 per cent.

On the plus side, the widespread use of temporary contracts has helped Spain more than halve its official unemployment rate since the 1993 recession. There are now officially 60 per cent more people in work compared to 1993.

But temporary contracts offer little, if any, training. The goal of young people with university degrees is to get a job with a permanent contract, such as a civil service post. This, economists fear, is discouraging young people from being entrepreneurial. Those with a permanent contract don't want to leave their jobs unless it is to take another one offering a permanent contract. This discourages labour mobility and labour flexibility. 'Garbage jobs' have ultimately led to Spain failing to improve its poor labour productivity record compared to the rest of Europe.

Source: adapted from the *Financial Times*, 21.10.2005.

(a) Explain why Spain has an unemployment problem compared to the rest of the euro area and the USA.
(b) Explain three factors which might have caused Spain to grow less fast than it might otherwise have done in the 1990s and 2000s.

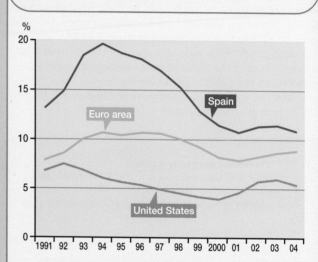

Figure 26.4 *Standardised unemployment rates, % of labour force*

Note: 'Euro area' is the group of EU countries which have adopted the euro as their currency, including Germany, Italy, Spain, France and Ireland but excluding the UK.

Source: adapted from *Economic Outlook*, OECD.

---

necessarily increase economic welfare. One reason is that increased income may have to be shared out amongst more people, causing little or no change in income per person. If women come back to work, they have to give up leisure time to do so. This lessens the increase in economic welfare which they experience. Increasing the quality of labour input is likely to be far more important in the long run.

Labour is not **homogeneous** (i.e. it is not all the same). Workers can be made more productive by education and training. Increases in **human capital** (☞ unit 2) are essential for a number of reasons.

● Workers need to be sufficiently educated to cope with the demands of the existing stock of capital. For instance, it is important for lorry drivers to be able to read, typists to spell and shop assistants to operate tills. These might seem very low grade skills but it requires a considerable educational input to get most of the population up to these elementary levels.
● Workers need to be flexible. On average in the UK, workers are likely to have to change job three times during their lifetime. Increasingly workers are being asked to change roles within existing jobs. Flexibility requires broad general education as well as in-depth knowledge of a particular task.
● Workers need to be able to contribute to change. It is easy to see that scientists and technologists are essential if inventions and new products are to be brought to the market. What is less obvious, but as important, is that every worker can contribute ideas to the improvement of techniques of production. An ability of all workers to take responsibility and solve problems will be increasingly important in the future.

Capital

The stock of capital in the economy needs to increase over time if economic growth is to be sustained. This means that there must be sustained investment in the economy. However, there is not necessarily a correlation between high investment and high growth. Some investment is not growth-related. For instance, investment in new housing or new hospitals is unlikely to create much wealth in the future. Investment can also be wasted if it takes place in industries which fail to sell products. For instance, investment in UK shipbuilding plants during the late 1970s and early 1980s provided a poor rate of return because the shipbuilding industry was in decline. Investment must therefore be targeted at growth industries.

Technological progress

Technological progress increases economic growth in two ways.

● It cuts the average cost of production of a product. For instance, a machine which performed the tasks of a simple scientific calculator was unavailable 100 years ago. 50 years ago, it needed a large room full of expensive equipment to do this. Today calculators are portable and available for a few pounds.
● It creates new products for the market. Without new products, consumers would be less likely to spend increases in their income. Without extra spending, there would be less or no economic growth.

Question 3

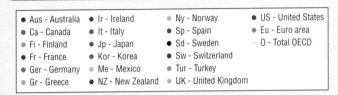

Figure 26.5 *Growth in investment and GDP in selected OECD countries, 1991-2004, annual average*

- Aus - Australia
- Ca - Canada
- Fi - Finland
- Fr - France
- Ger - Germany
- Gr - Greece
- Ir - Ireland
- It - Italy
- Jp - Japan
- Kor - Korea
- Me - Mexico
- NZ - New Zealand
- Ny - Norway
- Sp - Spain
- Sd - Sweden
- Sw - Switzerland
- Tur - Turkey
- UK - United Kingdom
- US - United States
- Eu - Euro area
- O - Total OECD

Source: adapted from OECD, *Economic Outlook*.

(a) What relationship would economic theory suggest exists between investment and economic growth?

(b) To what extent is this relationship shown by the data?

Key terms

Boom - period of time when the economy is growing strongly and is operating around its productive potential.

Business or trade cycle - regular fluctuations in the level of economic activity around the productive potential of the economy. In business cycles, the economy veers from recession, when it is operating well below its productive potential, to booms when it is likely to be at or even above its productive potential.

Economic growth - growth in the productive potential of the economy. It is typically measured by growth in real GDP although this is only a proxy measure because actual GDP can be above or below the productive potential of the economy at a point in time.

Economic recovery - the movement back from where the economy is operating below its productive potential to a point where it is at its productive potential.

Output gap - the difference between the actual level of GDP and the productive potential of the economy. There is a **positive output gap** when actual GDP is above the productive potential of the economy and it is in boom. There is a **negative output gap** when actual GDP is below the productive potential of the economy.

Applied economics

Britain's growth rate

Worries about Britain's growth rate date back over a century. In Edwardian times, for example, it was not difficult to see the economic advance of Germany and France and compare it with the poor economic performance of the UK economy. Britain's poor growth performance persisted in the 1950s, 1960s and 1970s. As Table 26.1 shows, the UK had the lowest average annual rate of growth between 1960 and 1979 of the seven largest industrial economies of the world (the **Group of Seven** or **G7**). By the 1980s and 1990s, however, the UK had ceased to be at the bottom of the growth league. In the 1990s, for the first time, the UK's average rate of growth was above the G7 average, a position which was maintained into the 2000s.

Table 26.1 *Average annual growth in GDP, G7 countries, 1960-2004*

					(%)
	1960-67	1968-73	1974-79	1980-90	1991-04
United States	4.5	3.2	2.4	3.3	3.1
Japan	10.2	8.7	3.6	3.9	1.3
Germany	4.1	4.9	2.3	2.3	1.5
France	5.4	5.5	2.8	2.4	1.8
United Kingdom	3.0	3.4	1.5	2.6	2.4
Italy	5.7	4.5	3.7	2.3	1.4
Canada	5.5	5.4	4.2	2.8	2.8
Average G7	5.0	4.4	2.7	2.8	2.0

Source: adapted from OECD, *Historical Statistics, Economic Outlook*.

Table 26.1 would suggest that over the period 1960-1979, the best performing G7 countries were Japan and the European countries of Germany, France and Italy. Between 1991 and 2004, the position was reversed with the 'Anglo-Saxon' countries of the UK and the USA performing best. Note that Canada throughout the period 1960 to 2004 has performed better than or equal to the G7 average.

All economists agree that the causes of economic growth are complex and that there is no single easy answer to raising a country's trend rate of growth. So what might have caused the relatively poor economic performance of the UK before the 1980s and what might have happened since the 1980s to raise the UK's relative performance? Also, what might have caused countries such as France, Germany, Italy and Japan to performed relatively poorly over the period 1991-2004?

Labour

Education and training Most economists would agree that education and training is one of the key factors, if not the most important factor, in determining long run growth rates. For much of the 20th century, countries such as France and Germany were perceived by some to have better education systems than the UK. Whilst the UK could provide excellence in the education of its top 10 or 20 per cent to the age of 21, it lagged behind some continental countries and the USA in its education of the bottom 80 per cent. In the USA, where standards for children to the age of 18 tend to be fairly low, there is a widespread acceptance that the majority of post-18 year olds will stay on and do some form of college course. The USA still has the highest proportion of 18-24 year olds in full time education of any country in the world. Germany's system of technical and craft education has been seen as a major contributor to its economic success over the past 50 years. Japan has an education system which delivers high standards across the ability range.

In the UK, academic children going through to A levels and university degrees received an education which was as good as if not better than their French, German or US peers. But education for the rest was arguably poor. In the 1960s and 1970s, governments put opportunity and equality at the top of their list of priorities. Comprehensive schools were introduced to give all children a better chance of success whilst the number of university places was considerably increased to give young people more access to higher education. It wasn't till the 1980s that much emphasis was put on the quality of education and lifting standards. The 1980s saw the introduction of the National Curriculum in schools, Ofsted inspections of schools and school league tables. In the 1990s, new national vocational qualifications (NVQs) were introduced, designed to provide qualifications for training in work. Their school or college based equivalent, GNVQs,

were introduced to help those for whom academic A level and GCSE examinations were not suited. The 1990s also saw the introduction of targets into education, for instance for achievement in National Curriculum tests. Targets were intended to raise standards in schools which performed poorly, and to give good schools an incentive to achieve even better results. In 1997, the Labour government under Tony Blair was elected which, for the first time, put education as a top priority in its manifesto. Since 1997, education has been specifically linked by government to the long term performance of the economy. Education spending has been raised as a proportion of GDP and a target of getting 50 per cent of the 18-21 year olds into some form of higher education has been set. It could be argued that the relative improvement of the British educational system compared to other G7 countries has played a part in helping the UK achieve relatively higher growth.

Catching up Why can China grow by 10 per cent per annum whilst the UK barely manages a quarter of that? One suggestion is that the high economic growth rate represents the gains from transferring workers from low productivity agriculture to higher productivity manufacturing and service industries. If a worker can produce £500 per year in output as an agricultural worker but £1 000 working in a factory, then the act of transferring that worker from agriculture to industry will raise the growth rate of the economy. This theory was popular in explaining why the UK performed badly relative to the rest of the EU in the 1950s and 1960s. In 1960-67, for instance, the average proportion of agricultural workers in the total civilian working population of the then Common Market was 18.1 per cent, but was only 4.2 per cent in the UK. By the 1990s, the proportion of workers in agriculture was less than 5 per cent in France and Germany and there was little scope for major transfers of labour out of the primary sector in northern Europe. Hence, this competitive advantage viz a viz the UK has disappeared. However, this theory can still explain why countries like China or Poland, with large amounts of labour in agriculture, can grow at rates several times that of EU countries.

Flexible labour markets In the 1990s, the UK government saw flexible labour markets as key to its **supply side reforms** (☞ unit 38). Labour markets are flexible when it is relatively easy for firms to hire and fire labour, and for workers to move between jobs. Inflexible labour markets create market failure, partly because they tend to lead to unemployment. There are many different aspects to creating flexible labour markets. One is education and training, discussed above. An educated workforce is more attractive to firms and helps workers to change jobs when the need arises. Another aspect is government rules and regulations about employment. Health and safety laws, maximum working hours, minimum wages, minimum holiday entitlements, redundancy regulations and maternity and paternity leave are all examples of government imposed rules which increase the cost of employment to firms and reduce the ability of firms to manage their workforces to suit their production needs.

It is argued that, in EU countries, firms have to comply with too many rules and regulations. They then become reluctant to take on workers, leading to high unemployment and lower growth. In contrast, the UK and the US have fewer regulations and this partly explains their higher growth rates in the 1990s and 2000s. Other aspects of flexible labour markets include pensions and housing. If workers are to move between jobs easily, they must carry with them pension rights. If they lose their pension rights every time they change job, they will be reluctant to move. Difficulty in obtaining housing discourages workers from moving between geographical areas. Part time working is important too. In flexible labour markets, workers should be able to choose how many hours they wish to work and how many jobs they have at any time. If work structures are such that part time working is discouraged, then the skills of many workers at home bringing up children are likely to go unutilised. Equally, there may not be enough full time work in the economy, but flexible labour markets should mean that workers could choose to build up **portfolios** of jobs, making several part time jobs equal to one full time one.

Taxes Another argument put forward is that taxes can have an important impact on growth levels. Before 1979, it could be argued that Britain's tax regime discouraged work, enterprise and investment. For example, the Labour government during 1974-1979 introduced a top marginal tax rate on earned income of 83 per cent. Average tax rates had also been rising since the 1950s as the size of the state expanded and government spending rose. The Conservative government elected in 1979 was committed to lowering the tax burden by lowering levels of government spending. By 1997, when it was defeated at the polls, it had succeeded in limiting government spending to around 40 per cent of GDP, up to 10 per cent less than many of its continental EU rivals. Since then, both the level of government spending as a proportion of GDP and taxation have risen. Increased public spending has been necessary to fund increases in expenditure on health and education. Nevertheless, by 2004, the UK still had relatively low taxes compared to its main EU partners. These relatively low taxes since the 1990s can be argued to be a cause of the UK's higher economic growth.

Lower taxes help in a number of ways. Some economists argue that low taxes encourage workers with no job to enter the labour force, and those with jobs to work harder. This can lead to higher economic

growth. Also, low taxes paid by firms on employing labour encourage firms to employ labour. In France and Germany, social security taxes paid by firms on the labour they employ are relatively high. This discourages them from employing labour, leading to high unemployment. This means that there are large amounts of unemployed scarce resources which could act as a drag on long term growth. Equally, high taxes on labour and profits can discourage inward investment by foreign companies wanting to set up plants in a country. Inward investment doesn't just create jobs and wealth directly. It often acts as a competitive spur to domestic firms which have to compete with the new entrants. Improving efficiency and developing new products in response can raise growth rates.

Table 26.2 Gross fixed capital formation as a percentage of GDP

	Per cent					
	1960-67	1968-73	1974-79	1980-90	1991-99	2000-04
United States	18.1	18.4	18.8	19.1	17.7	18.2
Japan	31.0	34.6	31.8	29.7	28.6	24.8
Germany	25.2	24.4	20.8	22.2	22.0	18.9
France	23.2	24.6	23.6	21.0	18.7	19.2
United Kingdom	17.7	19.1	19.4	18.7	16.7	16.6
Italy	24.9	24.0	24.0	22.4	18.9	19.6
Canada	22.6	22.1	23.5	22.0	19.2	19.8

Source: adapted from OECD, *Historical Statistics*, United Nations Statistics Division.

Capital

Table 26.2 shows that the UK has consistently devoted less of its GDP to investment than other G7 countries. Economic theory would suggest that investment - the addition to the physical capital stock of the country - is essential for economic growth. How can an economy increase its growth rate if it does not increase the amount it is setting aside to increase the production potential of the country? There is a number of possible explanations for why investment and growth rates may or may not be linked.

Quality, not quantity Some economists have argued that it is not the quantity of investment that is important but its direction. The two classic examples used for the UK are Concorde (the supersonic plane) and the nuclear power programme. Large sums of public money were poured into the development of Concorde and the nuclear power programme in the 1960s. Both proved uncommercial. In this view, increasing investment rates without there being the investment opportunities present in the economy would have little or no effect on growth rates. The money would simply be wasted. Moreover, how could investment be increased in an economy? The simplest way would be for government to spend more on investment, either through its own programmes, by investing directly in industry, or through subsidies. Free market economists would then argue that the government is a very poor judge of industries and projects which need further investment. The money would probably be squandered on today's equivalents of Concorde. Only if firms increase investment of their own accord in free markets can growth increase. Even this is no guarantee of success. In the late 1980s and early 1990s, Japanese industry increased its investment because of very low interest rates on borrowed money. In 1986, Japan spent 27.3 per cent of its GDP on investment. In 1990, this peaked at 32.2 per cent. Despite this, the Japanese economy spent much of the 1990s in recession, with an average growth rate of just 1.5 per cent. In retrospect, Japanese companies had clearly overinvested. There was far too much capacity for the levels of production required.

Short-termism In the USA and the UK, banks do not invest in companies. They lend to companies over fairly short time periods, typically up to five years, but many loans (e.g. overdrafts) are repayable on demand. Shares in companies are owned by shareholders, and these shares are traded on stock markets. Stock markets are driven by speculators who are not interested in where a company might be in five or ten years time. They are only interested in the size of the next dividend payment or the price of the share today. In contrast, in Germany and Japan banks own large proportions of industry through shareholdings. The banks are interested in the long term development of companies. Losses this year are less important if the long term future of a company is bright and secure. It is therefore argued that US and UK stock markets lead to short-termism. Firms will only invest if they can make a quick profit to satisfy shareholders who are only interested in the financial performance of the company over, say, 12 months. In Germany and Japan, firms can afford to make long term investment decisions even if these involve poorer short term performance, secure in the knowledge that their shareholders are interested in the long term future of the business.

Supporters of US style capitalism argue that long termism can mask poor investment decisions. When the Japanese economy went into a prolonged period of low or negative growth following the economic bubble of the late 1980s, Japanese companies often failed to take the necessary steps to restructure despite making substantial losses over a lengthy period of time. Without the pressures of shareholders wanting a fast return, they preferred to safeguard the interests of management and workers. This has contributed to the problems of Japanese industry. In France, Germany and Italy, long termism has not prevented them suffering lower economic growth rates than the USA. Indeed, the pressures of globalisation and the single

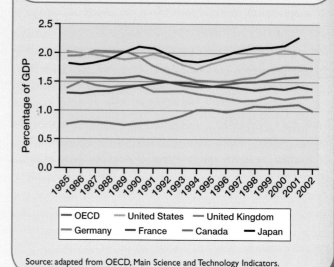

Figure 26.6 Business R&D as a percentage of GDP

Source: adapted from OECD, Main Science and Technology Indicators.

market within the EU are making their firms more short termist. They are finding that their companies are facing the threat of takeover by US or UK companies. One way of fighting this is to increase short term profitability.

Lack of savings The USA and the UK have relatively low savings ratios. Given that over the long term exports roughly equal imports for a country, and the government budget deficit tends to fluctuate around a fixed proportion of GDP, then savings must roughly equal a constant proportion of investment. Higher savings will thus allow higher investment. In the UK, firms have large tax incentives to save through not distributing all their profits to shareholders. This retained profit could be increased through even lower taxation. Or the government could increase its savings by moving to a budget surplus. Individuals could be persuaded to save more again through tax incentives.

Innovation The UK spends a relatively low proportion of its GDP on research and development (R&D). For most of the post-war period, an above average share of that R&D has been devoted to defence research. Hence, some economists argue that R&D spending in total needs to be increased for higher growth, and a larger proportion needs to be spent on civilian projects. The UK's poor R&D record is shown in Figure 26.6. Others argue that it is not so much the quantity that is important as the use to which R&D is put. It is often pointed out that the UK has a good international record in making discoveries and in inventions. However, too many of those have not been taken up by UK businesses. Instead, the ideas have gone overseas and been used by foreign firms as the bases for world-beating products. In this argument, UK firms have been very poor in the past at making a commercial success of R&D.

Catching up Catching up can apply to capital as well as to labour. For instance, a new DVD factory in China is likely to increase labour productivity (output per worker) far more than a new DVD factory in the UK. This is because the workers in China are more likely to have been employed in very low productivity jobs before than in Britain. So, countries like China can import foreign technologies and take huge leaps in productivity, which is then reflected in high economic growth rates. Some economists argue that, in the long run, all countries will arrive at roughly the same output per worker and grow at the same rate. This is because technology is internationally available. Countries can bring their capital stock up to the level of the most productive country in the world. Countries like the USA, however, which has grown at around 2.5 per cent per annum since the Second World War, can't take huge technological leaps like this. It has to create new technologies and new products to sustain its growth.

One argument put forward to explain the US economy's superior performance compared to European countries like France and Germany during the 1990s and 2000s is that its companies have invested much more heavily in IT (information technology). Not only has IT spending as a proportion of GDP been higher, but US companies have integrated IT into their operations much more deeply. The USA has therefore gained a technological advantage over other developed countries which has allowed it to sustain its growth rate whilst many other developed countries have fallen behind.

Privatisation and deregulation Capital may be tied up in relatively unproductive firms or industries. Releasing this capital can increase growth rates. The experience of the 1980s and 1990s in the UK has been that privatisation and deregulation are powerful ways of improving capital productivity. Nationalised industries, such as water, electricity, coal, gas and the railways were inefficient in the 1960s and 1970s. They employed too much capital and too much labour. Privatisation saw output per unit of capital and labour increase substantially as workforces were cut and assets sold off or closed down. The process was painful. In the coal industry, for instance, nearly 200 000 workers lost their jobs between 1980 and

2000. However, in a fast changing economy, failure to move resources between industries leads to inefficiency and slower growth.

Openness to international trade One way of protecting domestic jobs is to erect protectionist barriers against imports. For instance, foreign goods can be kept out by imposing high taxes on imports (called **tariffs** or **customs duties**). It can be argued, though, that protectionism is likely to lead to lower long term economic growth. This is because domestic firms can become insulated from world best practice. There is reduced incentive to invest and innovate if more competitive goods from abroad are kept out of the domestic market.

France and Germany in the 1990s and 2000s have perhaps been more protectionist in their policies than the UK and the USA. Because France and Germany are part of the EU, there is a limit to the amount of protectionism that they can implement compared to other EU countries such as the UK. However, one example of protectionism was the failure of most EU countries to open up their service industries such as banking to foreign competition for much of the 1990s and early 2000s. Equally, countries like France and Germany failed to open up utility markets such as electricity, gas and telecommunications over the same period. Part of the superior performance of the UK and US economies over the period might be due to increased foreign competition in markets other than those traditionally exposed to trade.

Macro-economic management

Some economists argue that recessions do not affect long term growth rates. Growth lost in a recession is made up in the boom which follows. Others argue that the fall in GDP in deep recessions may never be recouped in the subsequent upturn. This is because in a deep recession, labour can become de-skilled, leading to permanently higher unemployment. Capital can also be destroyed as firms cut costs, pulling down factories and throwing away equipment. The UK suffered deeper and longer recessions in the 1970s, 1980s and early 1990s than countries in Europe. This may help account for lower UK growth rates at the time. Equally, the higher growth rate in the UK in the 1990s and 2000s may be because the UK avoided a recession in the middle 1990s and early 2000s, which afflicted European countries.

DataQuestion   Ireland's economic miracle

Ireland has been one of Europe's success stories over the past 30 years. From being one of the European Union's poorest countries, it has now caught up and is among the richer nations of Europe.

Some experts trace Ireland's economic success back to the introduction of free secondary education in the 1960s. Cuts in taxes on businesses in the 1980s and cuts in top rates of income tax on earners provided a boost for business and enterprise. The 1980s also saw an increase in the labour force with the traditional net outflow of labour from Ireland reversing to become a net inflow. Today, an annual 30 000 more workers arrive in Ireland than leave to seek jobs abroad, attracted by a booming job market. Multinational companies were attracted to Ireland from the 1970s onwards by its educated, English speaking workforce and low business taxes. Jobs have been created in manufacturing and service industries, whilst jobs in low productivity agriculture have

been in decline. The enormous productivity gains from these trends have allowed Irish workers to see large pay rises over time without unit labour costs rising too much. Centralised wage agreements have allowed the government to introduce flexible working practices. In exchange for wage moderation, income tax was cut.

Typical of Ireland's success story is Galway. Digital Computers set up a mainframe computer factory in the city in 1971 and became an important employer in the area. Changing patterns of demand saw the factory close in 1994. Since then, Galway has reinvented itself and hosts one of the world's largest clusters of medical device manufacturing. Today there are 28 companies in the city employing 5 000 people. 15 of these are locally owned, many headed by former Digital Computers employees.

Source: adapted from the *Financial Times*, 27.5.2005.

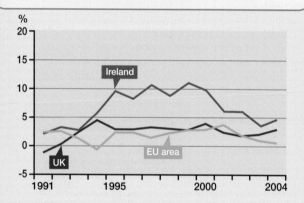

Figure 26.7 Economic growth: annual % change in GDP

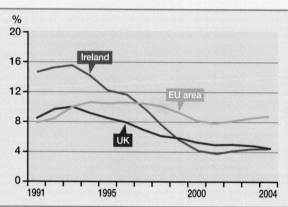

Figure 26.8 Unemployment: standardised measure %

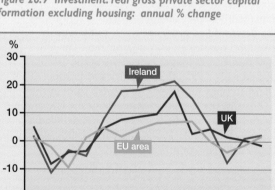

Figure 26.9 Investment: real gross private sector capital formation excluding housing: annual % change

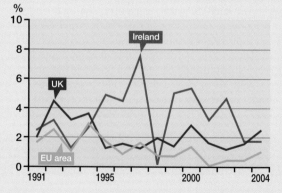

Figure 26.10 Growth in labour productivity in the business sector: annual % change

Note: 'euro area' is the group of EU countries which have adopted the euro as their currency, including Germany, Italy, Spain, France and Ireland but excluding the UK.
Source: adapted from OECD, *Economic Outlook*.

1. (a) Explain what is meant by economic growth.
    (b) Compare the recent growth performance in Ireland with the UK and the whole EU area.

2. Discuss whether higher levels of capital investment can solely account for Ireland's superior economic performance since 1991.

Summary

1. National income is often used as the main indicator of the standard of living in an economy. A rise in GDP per head is used as an indication of economic growth and a rise in living standards.
2. However, there are many other important components of the standard of living, including political freedom, the social and cultural environment, freedom from fear of war and persecution, and the quality of the environment.
3. Economic growth over the past 100 years has transformed the living standards of people in the western world, enabling almost all to escape from absolute poverty.
4. Economic growth is likely to be the only way of removing people in the Third World from absolute poverty.
5. Economic growth has its costs in terms of unwelcome changes in the structure of society.
6. Some believe that future economic growth is unsustainable, partly because of growing pollution and partly because of the exploitation of non-renewable resources.

National income and economic welfare

National income is a measure of the income, output and expenditure of an economy. It is also often used as a measure of the **standard of living**. However, equating national income with living standards is very simplistic because there are many other factors which contribute to the economic welfare of individuals.

Political freedoms We tend to take civil liberties for granted in the UK. But other governments in the world today are totalitarian regimes which rule through fear. In some countries, membership of an opposition party or membership of a trade union can mean death or imprisonment. The freedom to visit friends, to travel and to voice an opinion are likely to be more valuable than owning an extra television or being able to buy another dress.

The social and cultural environment In the UK, we take things such as education for granted. We have some of the world's finest museums and art galleries. We possess a cultural heritage which includes Shakespeare and Constable. The BBC is seen as one of the best broadcasting organisations throughout the world. But we could all too easily live in a cultural desert where the main purpose of television programming might be to sell soap powders and make a profit. Alternatively, the arts could be used as political propaganda rather than exist in their own right.

Freedom from fear of violence If a person doesn't feel safe walking the streets or even at home, then no number of microwave ovens or videos will compensate for this loss. Equally, fears of war, arbitrary arrest, imprisonment or torture make material possessions seem relatively unimportant.

The working environment How long and hard people have to work is vital in evaluating standards of living. One reason why the average worker is far better off today than 100 years ago is because his or her working year is likely to be about half the number of hours of his or her Victorian counterpart's. Equally, the workplace is far safer today than 100 years ago. Industrial accidents were

Question 1

Figure 27.1 Comparison of MDP per capita vs GDP per capita

Source: adapted from Office for National Statistics, Thomson Datastream, CML.

It's official. 1976 was the best on record for the quality of life in Britain, according to an index of economic, social and environmental progress published by the New Economics Foundation, a think-tank. Unlike the standard GDP figure, the measure of domestic progress (MDP) takes into account social and environmental costs, including the damage done by crime, the depletion of natural resources, and pollution such as emissions of greenhouse gases. Britain in the seventies, with less crime, less income inequality, a rise in the national capital stock because of a boom in public sector investment, and lower energy consumption because there were fewer cars and centrally-heated houses, was better-off than today.

Most alternative measures of quality of life seem to show that Britain in the past was better off than today. However, those old enough to remember 1976 might be surprised that this was the best year for Britain's overall affluence. For many, the mid-1970s with record inflation, rising unemployment, strikes and no home computers, mobile phones or DVDs was a rather grey and dismal period. The MDP only captures a very small number of the variables that might go to make up a standard of living index. So perhaps GDP is a better guide after all.

Source: adapted from the *Financial Times*, 16.3.2004.

(a) Why is GDP not the only measure of the standard of living of a country?
(b) What other factors might be included in a measure of the standard of living?
(c) What are the problems identified with the MDP as a measure of the standard of living?

then commonplace and workers received little or no compensation for serious injuries or even death.

The environment Environmental issues are currently at the forefront of people's consciousness. There is an understanding that production activities can damage the environment and that in future we may well have to stop consuming certain products if we are to safeguard the environment.

The growth debate

The rate of economic growth has accelerated historically. Even five hundred years ago, most people would have seen little change in incomes over their lifetimes. In Victorian England, the economy grew at about one per cent per annum. Over the past 60 years, the UK economy has grown at an average of 2.6 per cent per annum.

Table 27.1 *Economic growth rate of £100 over time*

Year	Growth rates				
	1%	2%	3%	5%	10%
0	100	100	100	100	100
5	105	110	116	128	161
10	110	122	130	163	259
25	128	164	203	339	1 084
50	164	269	426	1 147	11 739
75	211	442	891	3 883	127 189
100	271	724	1 870	13 150	1 378 059

Growth at these rates since the end of the Second World War in 1945 has led to undreamt of prosperity for the citizens of the industrialised world. Consider Table 27.1. It shows by how much £100 will grow over time at different rates. At one per cent growth, income will roughly double over the lifetime of an individual. At 2 per cent, it will quadruple over a lifetime. At 3 per cent, it is doubling every twenty five years. At 5 per cent, it only takes about 14 years to double income. At 10 per cent, it only takes about 7 years to double income.

If recent growth rates are a guide to the future, average British workers in 30 years' time will earn in real terms twice what they are earning today. When they are in their seventies, they can expect workers to earn four times as much as their parents did when they were born.

These increases in income have led to the elimination of **absolute poverty** for most citizens in industrialised countries.
- Life expectancy has doubled over the past 300 years and infant mortality rates have plummeted.
- People have enough to eat and drink. What we eat and drink is nearly always fit for human consumption.
- Housing standards have improved immeasurably.
- Nearly everyone can read and write.

Future increases in income are generally desirable. Very few people would prefer to have less income rather than more income in the future (remember economics assumes that people have **infinite wants**). So economic growth has generally been considered to be highly desirable. Moreover, in 2005 only 16 per cent of the world's population lived in 'high income' countries such as the USA, the UK and Japan, with an average annual income per person of $31 000 per year at purchasing power parity prices (☞ unit 25). 38 per cent lived in 'low income' countries with an

The photographs show a modern kitchen and a kitchen at the turn of the century. To what extent do they show that economic growth has been desirable?

average yearly income of just $2 260, not even ten per cent of the average income of high income countries. Many who live in low and middle income countries suffer absolute poverty. It can be argued that the only way to eliminate malnutrition, disease, bad housing and illiteracy in these countries is for there to be real economic growth.

Arguments against growth

Despite the apparent benefits, the goal of economic growth is questioned by some economists and environmentalists.

The falsity of national income statistics One argument is that the increase in national income has been largely fictitious. Three hundred years ago much of the output of the economy was not traded. Women were not on the whole engaged in paid work. Much of the supposed increase in income has come from placing monetary values on what existed already. Much of the increase in income generated by the public sector of the economy comes not from increased production but from increased wages paid to public sector workers who produce the same amount of services. Whilst there is some truth in this, it cannot be denied that material living standards have increased immeasurably over the past three hundred years. People not only consume more goods and services, they have on average far more leisure time.

Negative externalities Another argument is that modern industrialised societies have created large negative **externalities**. For instance, some put forward the view that growth has created a large pool of migrant workers, wandering from job to job in different parts of the country. They become cut off from their roots, separated from their families. The result is alienation and loneliness, particularly of the old, and the collapse of traditional family values. Crime rates soar, divorce rates increase, stress related illnesses become commonplace and more and more has to be spent on picking up the pieces of a society which is no longer content with what it has.

Supporters of this view tend to look back to some past 'golden age', often agricultural, when people lived mainly in villages as parts of large extended families. However, historical evidence suggests that such a rural paradise never existed. Life for many was short and brutish. Drunkenness was always a problem. Family life was claustrophobic and did not allow for individuality. Most people were dead by the age when people today tend to divorce and remarry.

Growth is unsustainable Perhaps the most serious anti-growth argument is that growth is unsustainable. Consider again Table 27.1. If a country like the UK grew at an average 3 per cent per annum then in 25 years' time national income will be twice as large as it is today; in fifty years' time, when an 18 year old student will be retired, it will be over 4 times as large; in 75 years' time, when on current life expectancy figures that student would be dead, it will be nearly 9 times as large; and in 100 years' time it will be nearly 19 times as large. If the average wage in the UK today of a full time employee was £27 000 per annum, then in 100 years' time it will have risen to £800 000 per annum in real terms.

Each extra percent increase in national income uses up **non-renewable resources** such as oil, coal and copper. In the late 1970s, the Club of Rome, a forecasting institute, produced a report called 'The Limits to Growth'. The report claimed that industrialised economies as we know them would collapse. They would be caught between a growth in pollution and a decline in the availability of scarce resources such as oil, coal and timber. Oil was projected to run out in the next century and coal by the year 2400. In the 1980s and 1990s, the world was gripped by reports that people were destroying the ozone layer and raising the world's temperature through the greenhouse effect. The planet cannot support growth rates of even 1 or 2 per cent per year. Growth must stop and the sooner the better.

Economic theory suggests that the future may not be as bleak as this picture makes out. In a market economy, growing scarcity of a resource, such as oil, results in a rise in price. Three things then happen. First, demand and therefore consumption falls - the price mechanism results in conservation. Second, it becomes profitable to explore for new supplies of the resource. Known world oil reserves today are higher than they were in 1973 at the time of the first oil crisis! Third, consumers switch to substitute products whilst producers are encouraged to find new replacement products. After the massive rise in oil prices in 1973-74, the world car makers roughly halved the fuel consumption per mile of the average car over a period of ten years through more efficient engines. Brazil developed cars which ran on fuel made from sugar.

Governments too respond to pressures from scientists and the public. The activities of industry are far more regulated today in the western world than they were 30 years ago. Individual governments, for instance, have introduced strict controls on pollution emissions, regulated disposal of waste and sought to ration scarce resources like water or air through systems of tradable licences (☞ unit 19). Even more impressive has been the willingness of governments to sign international agreements designed to safeguard the environment. For instance, in 1987, 93 governments signed the Montreal Protocol to phase out production of CFC chemicals, a major contributor to the destruction of the ozone layer. Signatories to the 1997 Kyoto Protocol agreed to reduce greenhouse gas emissions by 5.2 per cent from 1990 levels between 2008-2012.

What is worrying, however, is that the market mechanism and governments are frequently slow to act. Governments and markets are not good at responding to pressures which might take decades to build up but only manifest themselves suddenly at the end of that time period. Some scientists have predicted that global warming is now already irreversible. If this is true, the problem that we now face is how to change society to cope with this. There is no clear consensus as to how we could reverse economic growth, consume less, and cope with the coming catastrophe, without creating an economic nightmare with mass starvation.

The anti-growth lobby One point to note is that supporters of the anti-growth lobby tend to be people who are relatively well off. Cutting their consumption by 25 per cent, or producing environmentally friendly alternative technologies, might not create too much hardship for them. However, leaving the mass of people in the Third World today at their present living standards would lead to great inequality. A small minority would continue to live below the absolute poverty line, facing the continual threat of malnutrition. A majority would not have access to services such as education and health care which people in the West take for granted. Not surprisingly, the anti-growth lobby is stronger in the West than in the Third World.

Applied economics

The standard of living in the UK since 1900

GDP is often used as the major economic indicator of welfare. Table 27.2 shows that, on this basis, living standards in the UK rose considerably last century. Between 1900 and 1931 GDP rose 23 per cent and between 1900 and 2004 it rose 626 per cent. Population has increased too, but even when this has been taken into account, the rise in income per person is impressive.

It is possible to chart a multitude of other ways in which it can be shown that the standard of living of the British family has improved. For instance, 14.2 per cent of children in 1900 died before the age of 1. In 2005, the comparable figure was 0.5 per cent. In 1900, the vast majority of children left school at 12. Today all children stay on till the age of 16, whilst 53 per cent of 18 year olds are in full time or part time education or training. In 1900, few people were able to afford proper medical treatment when they fell ill. Today, everyone in the UK has access to the National Health Service.

Table 27.3 illustrates another way in which we are far better off today than a family at the turn of the century. It shows the weekly budget of a manual worker's family in a North Yorkshire iron town, estimated by Lady Bell in her book *At The Works*. The family lived off 7½ home-made loaves of 4lb (1.8kg) each thinly scraped with butter, 4lb (1.8kg) of meat and bacon, weak tea, a quart of milk and no vegetables worth mentioning. In 2003-04, whilst average consumption for five people of bread was only 3.6kg a week, tea 0.16kg and sugar 0.5kg, on the other hand meat consumption was 5.3kg, potato consumption (fresh and frozen) was 4.3kg, and butter, margarine, lard and other oils consumption was 0.9kg. Moreover, today's diet is far more varied and ample with fruit and vegetables apart from potatoes playing a major part. Malnutrition, not uncommon in 1900, is virtually unknown in the UK today.

The budget in Table 27.3 also says a great deal about the very restricted lifestyle of the average family in 1908. Then, a family would consider itself lucky if it could take a day trip to the seaside. In comparison, individuals took an estimated 91 million holidays of one night or more within the UK and 41.2 million holidays abroad in 2003.

In 1908, houses were sparsely furnished. The main form of heating was open coal fires; central heating was virtually unknown. Very few houses were wired for electricity. Table 27.3 shows that the typical house was lighted by oil. All the electrical household gadgets we take for granted, from washing machines to vacuum cleaners to televisions, had not been invented. The 1lb of soap in the 1908 budget would have been used to clean clothes, sinks and floors. Soap powders, liquid detergents and floor cleaners were not available. 'Gold Dust' was the popular name for an exceptionally caustic form of shredded yellow soap notorious for its ability to flay the user's hands. Compare that with the numerous brands of mild soaps available today.

Workers worked long hours, six days a week with few

holidays, whilst at home the housewife faced a life of drudgery with few labour-saving devices. Accidents were frequent and old age, unemployment and sickness were dreaded and even more so the workhouse, the final destination for those with no means to support themselves.

Ecologically, the smoke-stack industries of industrial areas such as London, the Black Country and Manchester created large scale pollution. The smogs which are found in many cities such as Mexico City and Los Angeles today were common occurrences in turn-of-the-century Britain. The urban environment was certainly not clean 100 years ago.

Socially and politically, women, who formed over half the population, were not emancipated. In 1900, they did not have the vote, their place was in the home, they were often regarded as biologically inferior to men, and they were debarred from almost all public positions of influence and authority. In many ways, the standard of living of women has improved more than that of men this century because of the repressive attitude held towards women 100 years ago.

Overall, it would be very difficult to look back on 1900 and see it as some golden age. For the vast majority of those in Britain today, the start of the third millennium is a paradise in comparison. However, whilst there might be little absolute poverty today, it could be argued that there is considerable relative poverty. It could also be argued that the poorest today are probably still worse off than the top 5 per cent of income earners in 1900.

Table 27.2 *GDP, GDP per head and population, 1901-2004*

	GDP (£bn at 2002 prices)	Population (millions)	GDP per head (£ at 2002 prices)
1901	152.8	38.2	4 001
1911	176.1	42.1	4 172
1921	155.8	44.0	3 540
1931	188.4	46.0	4 096
1951	294.8	50.2	5 795
1961	383.0	52.7	7 253
1971	510.7	55.9	9 130
1981	599.0	56.4	10 629
1991	777.4	57.4	13 535
2001	1 027.9	59.1	17 388
2004	1 108.9	59.8	18 613

Note: GDP is at market prices.
Source: adapted from *Social Trends, Annual Abstract of Statistics*, Office for National Statistics.

Family budget in 1908
Income 18s 6d, family of five

	s.	d.
Rent	5	6
Coals	2	6
Insurance	0	4
Clothing	1	7
Meat	1	0
14lb of flour		6
3½ lb of bread meal	0	5
1lb butter	1	4½
Half lb lard	0	1
1lb bacon	0	2½
4 lb sugar	0	9
Half lb tea	0	8
Yeast	0	1
Milk	0	3
1 box Globe polish	0	1
1lb soap	0	3
1 packet Gold Dust	0	1
3 oz tobacco	0	9
7lb potatoes	0	3
Onions	0	1
Matches	0	2
Lamp oil	0	3
Debt	0	2
Total	**18**	**6**

Table 27.3

DataQuestion **Comparative living standards in the UK**

Table 27.4 *Number of abortions, Great Britain*

	1971-72	2003
Abortions	63 400	193 799

Source: adapted from *Social Trends*, Office for National Statistics.

Table 27.5 *Income, prices and population*

	1971	2004
GDP (£bn at current prices)	57.5	1 164.4
Retail Price Index (1971 = 100)	100	907
Population (millions)	55.9	59.8

Source: adapted from *Economic Trends, Annual Abstract of Statistics, Monthly Digest of Statistics*, Office for National Statistics.

Table 27.6 Population[1]

	1971	Millions 2004
Under 18	15.8	13.3
Adults not of pensionable age	31.0	35.4
Pensionable ages[1]	9.1	11.1
Total population	55.9	59.8

1 Pensionable age is 60+ for women and 65+ for men.

Source: adapted from *Annual Abstract of Statistics*, Office for National Statistics.

Table 27.7 Households: by type of household and family

	1971 %	2004 %
One person		
Under state pension age	6	14
Over state pension age	12	15
One family households		
Couple no children	27	29
Couple with children	43	28
Lone parent household	7	10
Other	5	4
Total	100	10.0
All households (millions)	18.6	24.1

Source: adapted from *Social Trends*, Office for National Statistics.

Table 27.8 Real gross weekly earnings of selected workers, £ at 2004 prices

	1971	2004-05
Waiter/waitress	132	127
Caretaker	201	270
Bricklayer/mason	250	404
Carpenter/joiner	257	426
Nurse	179	421
Primary teacher	296	541
Solicitor	439	905
Medical practitioner	631	1 203

Source: adapted from *New Earnings Survey*, *Annual Survey of Hours and Earnings*, Office for National Statistics.

Table 27.9 Percentage of households owning selected consumer durables

	1970-72	1981	2003-2004
Washing machine	65	78	94
Tumble dryer	0	23	57
Microwave	0	0	89
Dishwasher	0	4	31
Television	93	97	98
CD Player	0	0	86
Home computer	0	0	58
Video recorder	0	0	90
Telephone	35	75	92
Internet connection	0	0	49
Mobile phone	0	0	76

Source: adapted from *Social Trends*, *Family Spending*, Office for National Statistics.

Figure 27.2 Mortality: by sex and leading group of causes

Source: adapted from *Social Trends*, Office for National Statistics.

Table 27.10 Employment and unemployment, UK, millions

	1971	2004
Employment		
Males		
full time	13.1	13.7
part time	0.6	1.6
Females		
full time	5.6	7.3
part time	2.8	5.8
Total unemployed[1]	0.75	0.87

1 Claimant count unemployed.

Source: adapted from *Labour Market Trends*, Office for National Statistics; *Economic Trends*, Office for National Statistics.

Table 27.11 Education

	1970-71	2004
Ratio of pupils to teachers in state schools	22.60	17.50
Numbers in state nursery schools (millions)	0.05	0.08
Numbers in all schools (millions)	10.20	9.80
Numbers in higher education (millions)	0.62	2.37
Government spending on education as % of GDP	5.20	5.60

Source: adapted from *Social Trends*, Office for National Statistics.

Table 27.12 Average daily flow of motor vehicles on motorways

	Thousands	
	1971	2003
Vehicles on motorways	28.5	73.2

Source: adapted from *Transport Statistics*, Office for National Statistics.

Figure 27.3 British crime survey offences

Source: adapted from *Social Trends*, Office for National Statistics.

Figure 27.4 Prevalence of adult cigarette smoking: by sex

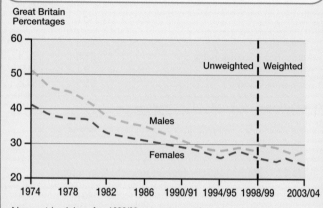

Note: weighted data after 1998/99 to compensate for non-response and to match known population distributions.
Source: adapted from *Social Trends*, Office for National Statistics.

Figure 27.5 Proportion of adults who are obese or overweight: by sex

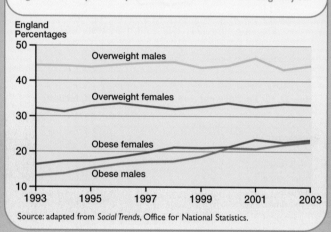

Source: adapted from *Social Trends*, Office for National Statistics.

Figure 27.6 Emissions of selected air pollutants

Source: adapted from *Social Trends*, Office for National Statistics.

Figure 27.7 Environmental impact of households

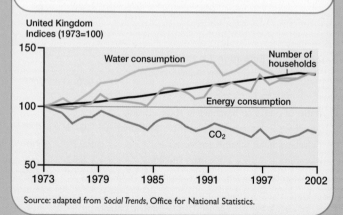

Source: adapted from *Social Trends*, Office for National Statistics.

Figure 27.8 Volume of domestic household expenditure on goods and services

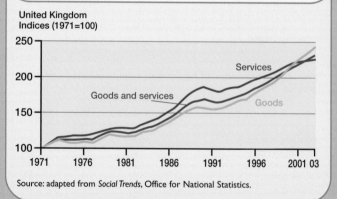

Source: adapted from *Social Trends*, Office for National Statistics.

You have been asked to write a magazine article from an economic perspective comparing the early 1970s and the early 2000s. The focus of the article is a discussion of whether living standards improved in the UK over the period. Construct the article as follows.

1. In your introduction, pick out a small number of key statistics which you feel point out the differences between the two periods.

2. In the main part of the article, compare and contrast the two periods, pointing out how living standards improved and also where it could be argued that the UK was worse off in the early 2000s than in the early 1970s.

3. In the conclusion, discuss whether rising GDP will be sufficient to ensure that the UK is better off in 2020 than in the early 2000s.

28Inflation

Summary

1. Inflation is a general sustained rise in the price level.
2. Inflation is measured by calculating the change in a weighted price index over time. In the UK this index is called the Retail Price Index.
3. A price index only measures inflation for average households. It also cannot take into account changes in the quality and distribution of goods over time.
4. Inflation is generally considered to give rise to economic costs to society. These include shoe-leather and menu costs, psychological and political costs, and costs which arise from the redistribution of income in society. Some economists believe that inflation also results in higher unemployment and lower growth in the long term.
5. Unanticipated inflation tends to give rise to higher economic costs than anticipated inflation.

The meaning of inflation

INFLATION is defined as a sustained general rise in prices. The opposite of inflation - DEFLATION - is a term which can have two meanings. Strictly speaking it is defined as a fall in the PRICE LEVEL. However, it can also be used to describe a slowdown in the rate of growth of output of the economy. This slowdown or recession is often associated with a fall in the **rate of inflation**. Before the Second World War, recessions were also associated with falls in prices and this is the reason why deflation has come to have these two meanings.

A general rise in prices may be quite moderate. CREEPING INFLATION would describe a situation where prices rose a few per cent on average each year. HYPER-INFLATION, on the other hand, describes a situation where inflation levels are very high. There is no exact figure at which inflation becomes hyper-inflation, but inflation of 100 or 200 per cent per annum would be deemed to be hyper-inflation by most economists.

Measuring inflation

The inflation rate is the change in average prices in an economy over a given period of time. The price level is measured in the form of an index (☞ unit 3). So if the price index were 100 today and 110 in one year's time, then the rate of inflation would be 10 per cent.

Calculating a price index is a complicated process. Prices of a representative range of goods and services (a **basket** of goods) need to be recorded on a regular basis. In the UK, there are two widely used measures of the the price level: the RETAIL PRICE INDEX (RPI) and the CONSUMER PRICE INDEX (CPI). In theory, on the same day of the month, surveyors are sent out to record 110 000 prices for a variety of items. Prices are recorded in different areas of the country as well as in different types of retail outlets, such as corner shops and supermarkets. These results are averaged out to find the average price of goods and this figure is converted into **index number form**.

Changes in the price of food are more important than changes in the price of tobacco. This is because a larger proportion of total household income is spent on food than on tobacco. Therefore the figures have to be **weighted** before the final index

can be calculated. For instance, assume that there are only two goods in the economy, food and cars, as shown in Table 28.1. Households spend 75 per cent of their income on food and 25 per cent on cars. There is an increase in the price of food of 8 per cent and of cars of 4 per cent over one year. In a normal average calculation, the 8 per cent and the 4 per cent would be added together and the total divided by 2 to arrive at an average price increase of 6 per cent. But this provides an inaccurate figure because spending on food is more important in the household budget than spending on cars. The figures have to be weighted. Food is given a weight of ¾ (or 0.75 or 750 out of 1 000) and cars a weight of ¼ (or 0.25 or 250 out of 1 000). The average increase in prices is 8 per cent multiplied by ¾

Question I

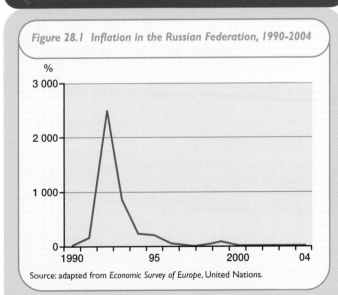

Figure 28.1 Inflation in the Russian Federation, 1990-2004

Source: adapted from *Economic Survey of Europe*, United Nations.

(a) Describe the changes in prices in the Russian Federation shown in the data.
(b) To what extent could the Russian Federation be said to have experienced hyper-inflation during the period shown?

added to 4 per cent multiplied by ¼ (i.e. 6 per cent + 1 per cent). The weighted average is therefore 7 per cent. If the RPI were 100 at the start of the year, it would be 107 at the end of the year. In order to calculate a weighting, it is necessary to find out how money is spent. In the case of the Retail Price Index, the weighting is calculated from the results of the Expenditure and Food Survey. Each year, a few thousand households are asked to record their expenditure for one month. From these figures it is possible to calculate how the average household spends its money. (This average household, of course, does not exist except as a statistical entity.)

Table 28.1

Commodity	Proportion of total spending	Weight	Increase in price	Contribution to increase in RPI
Food	75%	750	8%	6%
Cars	25%	250	4%	1%
Total	100%	1 000		7%

The accuracy of price indices

It is important to realise that any price index is a weighted average. Different rates of inflation can be calculated by changing the weightings in the index. For instance, the Retail Price Index calculates the average price level for the average household in the UK. But it is possible, again using data from the Expenditure and Food Survey, to calculate price indices for pensioner households or one parent households. One major difference between these households and the average household is that they spend a larger proportion of their income on food. So a 10 per cent rise in the price of food compared to a 5 per cent rise in the price of all other items will result in a higher rate of inflation for pensioners and one parent households than for the average household. In fact each individual household will have a different rate of inflation. The Retail Price Index only measures an average rate of inflation for all households across the UK.

The household spending patterns upon which the index is based also change over time. For instance, food was a far more important component of the Retail Price Index 30 years ago than it is today because spending on food was then a higher proportion of total spending. The index cannot indicate changes in the quality of goods. Cars might increase in price because their specifications improve rather than because there has been an inflationary price rise. The weights for the Retail Price Index are changed annually to take account of changes in spending patterns. But this does not get round the fact that the average 'basket' or 'bundle' of goods purchased in 1950 and upon which the RPI for 1950 was calculated was very different from the average bundle of goods purchased in 2005.

The costs of inflation

Inflation is generally considered to be a problem. The higher the rate of inflation the greater the economic cost. There are a number of reasons why this is the case.

Question 2

Table 28.2

Year	Weights			% annual increase in prices	
	Food	All other items	Total	Food	All other items
1	300	700	1 000	10	10
2	250	750	1 000	5	10
3	200	800	1 000	4	6
4	150	850	1 000	3	2
5	125	875	1 000	4	4
6	120	880	1 000	6	4
7	120	880	1 000	5	7
8	110	890	1 000	8	10

Table 28.2 shows the price index weights given to food and to all other items in each of eight years. It also shows the percentage annual increase in prices of those items.
(a) Calculate the rate of inflation (i.e. the percentage increase in prices) in each year 1 to 8.
(b) What would the price index in years 2-8 be if the price index were 100 in year 1?

Shoe-leather costs If prices are stable, consumers and firms come to have some knowledge of what is a fair price for a product and which suppliers are likely to charge less than others. At times of rising prices, consumers and firms will be less clear about what is a reasonable price. This will lead to more 'shopping around', which in itself is a cost.

High rates of inflation are also likely to lead to households and firms holding less cash and more interest bearing deposits. Inflation erodes the value of cash, but since nominal interest rates tend to be higher than with stable prices, the opportunity cost of holding cash tends to be larger, the higher the rate of inflation. Households and firms are then forced to spend more

Question 3

Table 28.3 Index of Retail Prices

	Average annual percentage change					
	1977-81	1982-86	1987-91	1992-96	1997-2000	2001-2004
General index	13.4	5.5	6.5	2.7	2.8	1.9
Pensioner index, two person household	12.8	5.3	5.3	2.8	1.6	1.6

Source: adapted from *Economic Trends Annual Supplement*, Office for National Statistics.

(a) Explain why the change in the General Index of Retail Prices may differ from the change in the Pensioner Index.
(b) A two person pensioner household where the pensioners retired in 1976 receives pensions linked to the General Index of Retail Prices. In which years would it, on average, have seen (i) an increase and (ii) a decrease in its real purchasing power? Explain why this occurs.

time transferring money from one type of account to another or putting cash into an account to maximise the interest paid. This time is a cost.

Menu costs If there is inflation, restaurants have to change their menus to show increased prices. Similarly, shops have to change their price labels and firms have to calculate and issue new price lists. Even more costly are changes to fixed capital, such as vending machines and parking meters, to take account of price increases.

Psychological and political costs Price increases are deeply unpopular. People feel that they are worse off, even if their incomes rise by more than the rate of inflation. High rates of inflation, particularly if they are unexpected, disturb the distribution of income and wealth as we shall discuss below, and therefore profoundly affect the existing social order. Change and revolution in the past have often accompanied periods of high inflation.

Redistributional costs Inflation can redistribute income and wealth between households, firms and the state. This redistribution can occur in a variety of ways. For instance, anybody on a fixed income will suffer. In the UK, many pensioners have received fixed pensions from private company pension schemes which are not adjusted for inflation. If prices double over a five year period, their real income will halve. Any group of workers which fails to be able to negotiate pay increases at least in line with inflation will suffer falls in its real income too.

If **real** interest rates fall as a result of inflation, there will be a transfer of resources from borrowers to lenders. With interest rates at 10 per cent and inflation rates at 20 per cent, a saver will lose 10 per cent of the real value of saving each year whilst a borrower will see a 10 per cent real reduction in the value of debt per annum.

Taxes and government spending may not change in line with inflation. For instance, if the Chancellor fails to increase excise duties on alcohol and tobacco each year in line with inflation, real government revenue will fall whilst drinkers and smokers will be better off in real terms assuming their incomes have risen at least by as much as inflation. Similarly, if the Chancellor fails to increase personal income tax **allowances** (the amount which a worker can earn 'tax free') in line with inflation, then the burden of tax will increase, transferring resources from the taxpayer to the government.

Unemployment and growth Some economists, mainly monetarists, have claimed that inflation creates unemployment and lowers growth. Inflation increases costs of production and creates uncertainty. This lowers the profitability of investment and makes businessmen less willing to take the risk associated with any investment project. Lower investment results in less long term employment and long term growth.

There is also a balance of payments effect. If inflation rises faster in the UK than in other countries, and the value of the pound does not change on foreign currency markets, then

In 2003, the Index of Retail Prices rose by 2.9 per cent and in 2004 by 1.3 per cent. How might the following have been affect by the change?

(a) A pensioner on a fixed income.
(b) A bank deposit saver, given that the rate of interest on a bank deposit saving account was 2.0 per cent in 2003 and 2.5 per cent in 2004.
(c) A worker whose personal income tax allowance was £4 615 between April 2003 and March 2004 and £4 745 between April 2004 and March 2005.
(d) A mother with one child who received £16.05 in child benefit between April 2003 and March 2004, and £16.50 between April 2004 and March 2005.

exports will become less competitive and imports more competitive. The result will be a loss of jobs in the domestic economy and lower growth.

Anticipated and unanticipated inflation

Much inflation is **unanticipated**; households, firms and government are uncertain what the rate of inflation will be in the future. When planning, they therefore have to estimate as best they can the expected rate of inflation. It is unlikely that they will guess correctly and hence their plans will be to some extent frustrated. On the other hand, inflation may be **anticipated**. Inflation may be a constant 5 per cent per year and therefore households, firms and government are able to build in this figure to their plans.

Unanticipated inflation imposes far greater costs than anticipated inflation. If inflation is anticipated, economic agents can take steps to mitigate the effects of inflation. One way of doing this is through INDEXATION. This is where economic variables like wages or taxes are increased in line with inflation. For instance, a union might negotiate a wage agreement with an employer for staged increases over a year of 2 per cent plus the change in the Retail Price Index. The annual changes in social security benefits in the UK are linked to the Retail Price Index. Economists are divided about whether indexation provides a solution to the problem of inflation. On the one hand, it reduces many of the costs of inflation although some costs such as shoe leather costs and menu costs remain. On the other hand, it reduces pressure on government to tackle the problem of inflation directly. Indexation eases the pain of inflation but is not a cure for it.

Moreover, indexation may hinder government attempts to reduce inflation because indexation builds in cost structures, such as wage increases, which reflect past changes in prices. If a government wants to get inflation down to 2 per cent a year, and inflation has just been 10 per cent, it will not be helped in achieving its target if workers are all awarded at least 10 per cent wage increases because of indexation agreements.

Key terms

Consumer Price Index (CPI) - a measure of the price level used across the European Union and used by the Bank of England as its inflation target.

Creeping inflation - small rises in the price level over a long period of time.

Deflation - a fall in the price level.

Headline rate of inflation - the increase in consumer prices including all housing costs. This is the RPI in the UK.

Hyper-inflation - large increases in the price level.

Indexation - adjusting the value of economic variables such as wages or the rate of interest in line with inflation.

Inflation - a general rise in prices.

Price level - the average price of goods and services in the economy.

Retail Price Index (RPI) - a measure of the price level which has been calculated in the UK for over 60 years and is used in a variety of contexts such as by the government to index welfare benefits.

Underlying rate of inflation - the RPIX, the increase in consumer prices excluding changes in mortgage costs, or the RPIY, which also excludes indirect taxes.

Applied economics

The Retail Price Index (RPI)

Measures of inflation

In the UK, there is a wide variety of different measures of inflation. The two most commonly used are the Retail Price Index (RPI) and the Consumer Price Index (CPI).

The Retail Price Index is the traditional measure of the price level in the UK. Apart from informing economists and economics agents such as government or firms of the rate of inflation, it is also used for the indexation of pensions, state benefits and index-linked gilts (a form of long term government borrowing). Trade unions and firms may use the RPI in wage agreements and property companies for calculating increases in leases (rents) on property. Utility regulators, which set prices for firms in industries such as telecommunications and water, may impose restrictions on price increases, or set price falls in terms of the RPI.

There are different measures of the RPI.

- The RPI itself measures the average price of the typical 'basket of goods' bought by the average household. It therefore measures average consumer prices.
- The RPIX excludes mortgage payments from the RPI calculation. This allows policy makers to see how prices are changed without including what can be a volatile and distorting element of the RPI, particularly when house prices are rising particularly fast or are falling.
- The RPIY excludes both mortgage payments and indirect taxes. When a government increases taxes on, say, cigarettes or petrol, these would be included in the RPI. By excluding them, policy makers are able to see how prices in the wider economy are changing.

The RPIX and the RPIY are sometimes referred to as the UNDERLYING RATE OF INFLATION, whilst the RPI is called the HEADLINE RATE OF INFLATION. The RPI is the headline rate because it is the measure which tends to be quoted in newspapers and on television and radio. The RPIX and the RPIY are underlying rates because they give a more reliable measure of trends in inflation over time.

The Consumer Price Index (CPI)

The CPI is a more recent measure of the price level and inflation. It is a measure which was developed by the European Union to be used across all countries in the EU. Before the introduction of the CPI, every country had a slightly different way of measuring the price level. The CPI in the UK before 2003 was called the Harmonised Index of Consumer Prices (HICP), 'harmonised' because it was a common measure across the EU. The CPI has only been calculated in the UK since January 1996, with estimates going back to 1988, and so this limits its use in making historical judgments about inflation. It has been used by the Bank of England to target inflation since 2003, and is therefore now the key indicator for monetary policy, replacing the RPI. However, the RPI is still widely used in other contexts. The two measures will continue to be used side by side in the future and there are no plans to phase out the calculation of the RPI.

Comparing the RPI and CPI

There is a variety of differences between the CPI and the RPI in its calculation. One important difference is that the CPI excludes a number of items relating to housing, whereas these are included in the RPI.

Excluded from the CPI are council tax, mortgage interest payments, house depreciation, buildings insurance, and estate agents' and conveyancing fees. Another important difference is that the CPI uses a different way of calculating the mean value compared to the RPI. The CPI uses a geometric mean whereas the RPI uses an arithmetic mean.

Figure 28.2 shows how annual measures of the RPI, RPIX, RPIY and the CPI have differed since 1989. The CPI tends to be below the RPI for two reasons. One is that for most of the period 1989-2004 housing costs rose at a faster rate than other items. Since the CPI excludes many housing costs, it has tended to be lower. Second, using a geometric mean, as with the CPI, mathematically always produces a lower number than using an arithmetic mean, as with the RPI. On average, this mathematical difference has been 0.5 per cent of inflation over the period 1996-2004.

Calculating the RPI and CPI

The RPI and the CPI are calculated from the same data which is collected through monthly surveys. There are two types of survey carried out.

Prices are recorded in around 150 different areas of the UK. These locations are chosen through a random sampling method and around 30 are changed each year. 110 000 prices are collected per month of a typical 'basket of goods' bought by consumers. Around 650 items are included in the basket. Over time, what is included in the basket is changed to reflect changes in consumer spending. For example, rabbits were taken out of the index in 1955, whilst condoms were added in 1989 and leather settees and laptop computers in 2005.

In addition, a further 10 000 prices are collected centrally each month for items where local sampling would be inappropriate. Prices of goods in catalogues, utility (gas, electricity and telephone) prices, Internet prices, road tolls, and mortgage interest payments are examples.

The typical basket of goods is constructed from another survey, the Expenditure and Food Survey. This survey asks around 7 000 respondent households a year selected at random to keep diaries of what they spend over a fortnight. A spending pattern for the average family can then be worked out. The RPI and CPI are weighted to reflect the importance of different expenditures within the total. So the price of gas carries more weight in the index than the price of processed fruit because households spend more on gas. Figure 28.3 shows how weights have changed between 1962 and 2005. The proportion spent on food in the average budget has been declining over time as incomes have risen (food has a very low positive income elasticity of demand). Travel and leisure and housing and household expenditure, on the other hand, have been rising.

The CPI is based on the average basket of goods bought by all households. The RPI excludes high income households, defined as the top 4 per cent by income of households, and pensioner households which derive at least three quarters of their total income from state pensions and benefits. These two types of household are considered to have atypical spending patterns and so would distort the overall average.

Figure 28.2 Inflation rates

Source: adapted from *Economic Trends*, Office for National Statistics.

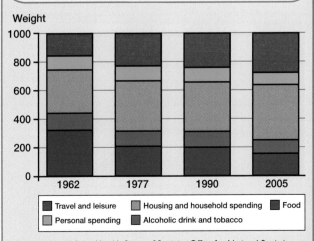

Figure 28.3 Changes in the basket of goods used to calculate the RPI, 1962-2005

Source: adapted from *Monthly Digest of Statistics*, Office for National Statistics.

Inflation

Source: adapted from *Economic Trends*, Office for National Statistics.

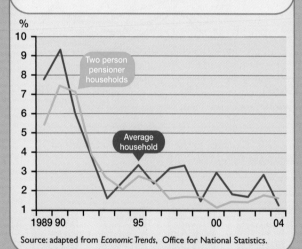

Figure 28.5 **RPI, inflation for different households**

Source: adapted from *Economic Trends*, Office for National Statistics.

1. What is meant by 'inflation'?
2. Explain different ways in which inflation might be measured.
3. How might each of the following have been affected by inflation: (a) a UK pensioner, still alive today, who retired in 1989 with a company pension which remained the same and a state pension which increased in line with changes in the RPI; (b) an ageing UK 'techno-geek' who was 16 in 1989, and who loves everything from computers to mobile phones to cars; (c) a Brazilian food shopper in the early 1990s?

The RPI/CPI

What exactly does the RPI or CPI measure? Each year, items are added to the basket of goods used in the calculation of the index and each year items are removed. You won't find corsets, rabbits or men's cardigans in the RPI index any more but you will find DVDs, mobile phone handsets and frozen chicken nuggets. What's more, when the same item stays in the index, its specification may well change. This isn't true for potatoes, but it is true for, say, cameras. Forty years ago, few cameras had a built in flash. Today, even the cheapest cameras come with flash as a standard feature. Forty years ago, cars didn't come with air conditioning as standard but many do today. As for computers, whose specification became more powerful by the year and month, how can the RPI/CPI hope to reflect such changes?

Does it matter that the basket of goods is constantly changing? The simple answer is yes. By changing the composition of the index, statisticians are not measuring the change in price of a fixed and unchanging basket of goods. Instead, they are attempting to measure changes in prices of how we spend our money. Presumably, we now buy, say, trousers rather than corsets, chicken rather than rabbits, or replica football team shirts rather than cardigans, because we prefer to do so. The amount of satisfaction to be gained from consuming some items rather than others is greater. So changes represent an increase in our living standards, the equivalent of a falling cost of living. As for increases in quality in goods, a failure to take these into account means that we overestimate the price paid for goods over time. When a software company puts additional features into a new computer game, but sells it for the same price as old computer games without these features, prices have effectively fallen but the RPI/CPI won't pick this up.

Inflation in Brazil

Before the conquest of hyper-inflation in Brazil in 1994, both Brazilian retailers and shoppers behaved in ways which seem strange today. Workers would be paid either at the end of the week or the end of the month. With prices going up every day, consumers would rush out with their pay packets and spend as much as they could afford. So retailers became used to sharp peaks in spending at the end of each week and a very large peak at the end of the month. There was little shopping around by consumers because they found it so difficult to keep up with changing prices. They had little or no idea what was a good price and what was expensive on any single shopping expedition. As for retailers, they often made their profit not from sales but from getting free credit. They would receive goods on credit, sell them immediately, but only have to pay in 30 or 60 days time. In the meantime, they could put the money in the bank and earn interest linked to the rate of inflation. In a good month, with inflation of say, 100 per cent, they could double their money.

29 Unemployment

Summary

1. Unemployment is a stock concept, measuring the number of people out of work at a point in time.
2. Unemployment will increase if the number of workers losing jobs is greater than the number of people gaining jobs.
3. The costs of unemployment include financial costs to the unemployed, to taxpayers, and to local and national economies. They also include non-financial costs such as possible increased vandalism or increased suicides.

The measurement of unemployment

Unemployment, the number of people out of work, is measured at a point in time. It is a **stock concept** (☞ unit 45). However, the level of unemployment will change over time. Millions of people seek jobs each year in the UK. Young people leave school, college or university seeking work. Former workers who have taken time out of the workforce, for instance to bring up children, seek to return to work. Workers who have lost their jobs, either because they have resigned or because they have been made redundant, search for new jobs. Equally, millions of workers lose their jobs. They may retire, or leave work to look after children or they may resign or be made redundant from existing jobs.

Unemployment in an economy with a given labour force will rise if the number of workers gaining jobs is less than the number of people losing their jobs. In 2005, for instance, between 197 000 and 230 000 workers a month lost their jobs. However, the numbers gaining jobs were slightly lower per month than the numbers losing jobs. The result was a net rise in unemployment over the year. This flow of workers into or out of the stock of unemployed workers is summarised in Figure 29.1.

Unemployment will also increase if there is a rise in the number of people seeking work but the number of jobs in the economy remains static. During most years in the 1970s and 1980s, there was a rise in the number of school leavers entering the job market as well as more women wanting a job in the UK. It can be argued that at least some of the increase in unemployment in these two decades was a reflection of the inability of the UK economy to provided sufficient new jobs for those extra workers in the labour force.

The costs of unemployment

Long term unemployment is generally considered to be a great social evil. This is perhaps not surprising in view of the following costs of unemployment.

Costs to the unemployed and their dependants The people who are likely to lose the most from unemployment are the unemployed themselves. One obvious cost is the loss of income that could have been earned had the person been in a job. Offset against this is the value of any benefits that the worker might receive and any value placed on the extra leisure time which an unemployed person has at his or her disposal. For most unemployed it is likely that they will be net financial losers.

The costs to the unemployed, however, do not finish there. Evidence suggests that unemployed people and their families suffer in a number of other ways. One simple but very

important problem for them is the stigma of being unemployed. Unemployment is often equated with failure both by the unemployed themselves and by society in general. Many feel degraded by the whole process of signing on, receiving benefit and not being able to support themselves or their families. Studies suggest that the unemployed suffer from a wide range of social problems including above average incidence of stress, marital breakdown, suicide, physical illness and mental instability, and that they have higher death rates.

For the short term unemployed, the costs are relatively low. Many will lose some earnings, although a few who receive large redundancy payments may benefit financially from having lost their job. The social and psychological costs are likely to be limited too.

However, the long term unemployed are likely to be major losers on all counts. The long term unemployed suffer one more cost. Evidence suggests that the longer the period out of work, the less likely it is that the unemployed person will find a job. There are two reasons for this. First, being out of work reduces the human capital of workers. They lose work skills and are not being trained in the latest developments in their occupation. Second, employers use length of time out of work as a crude way of sifting through applicants for a job. For an employer, unemployment is likely to mean that the applicant is, to some

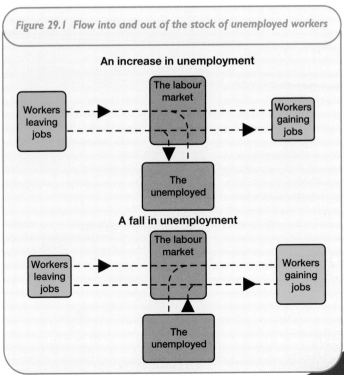

Figure 29.1 Flow into and out of the stock of unemployed workers

An increase in unemployment

Workers leaving jobs → The labour market → Workers gaining jobs → The unemployed

A fall in unemployment

Workers leaving jobs → The labour market → Workers gaining jobs → The unemployed

Question 1

Table 29.1 Unemployment flows, 2005

		Thousands
	Inflow	Outflow
January	200.1	146.5
February	230.2	216.2
March	211.3	214.2
April	197.8	207.0
May	202.3	206.9
June	198.9	209.1
July	216.6	205.5

Source: adapted from *Labour Market Trends*, Office for National Statistics.

(a) In which months did unemployment: (i) increase; and (ii) decrease? Explain your answer.
(b) Explain whether unemployment was higher or lower in July 2005 than in January 2005.
(c) Suggest why the numbers becoming unemployed tend to peak in the winter month of February, fall during the spring and summer, but rise in July.

extent, deskilled. There is a fear that the unemployed worker will not be capable of doing the job after a spell of unemployment. It could show that the worker has personality problems and might be a disruptive employee. It could also be an indication that other employers have turned down the applicant for previous jobs and hence it would be rational to save time and not consider the applicant for this job. The long term unemployed are then in a catch-22 situation. They can't get a job unless they have recent employment experience. But they can't get recent employment experience until they get a job.

Costs to local communities Costs to local communities are more difficult to establish. Some have suggested that unemployment, particularly amongst the young, leads to increased crime, violence on the streets and vandalism. Areas of high unemployment tend to become run down. Shops go out of business. Households have no spare money to look after their properties and their gardens. Increased vandalism further destroys the environment.

Costs to taxpayers The cost to the taxpayer is a heavy one. On the one hand, government has to pay out increased benefits. On the other hand, government loses revenue because these workers would have paid taxes if they had been employed. For instance, they would have paid income tax and National Insurance contributions on their earnings. They would also have paid more in VAT and excise duties because they would have been able to spend more. So taxpayers not only pay more taxes to cover for increased government spending but they also have to pay more because they have to make up the taxes that the unemployed would have paid if they had been in work.

Costs to the economy as a whole Taxpayers paying money to the unemployed is not a loss for the economy as a whole. It is a **transfer payment** which redistributes existing resources within the economy. The actual loss to the whole economy is two-fold. Firstly there is the loss of output which those workers now unemployed could have produced had they been in work. The economy could have produced more goods and services which would then have been available for consumption. Secondly there are the social costs such as increased violence and depression which are borne by the unemployed and the communities in which they live.

Question 2

In a study of 6 000 employed and unemployed workers, a team of academics found that the unemployed had poor psychological health. They were more likely to be depressed, less likely to mix with people in work and had little access to social support networks or to information about jobs. One of the team, Richard Lampard of Warwick University, concluded that unemployment directly increases the risk of marriage break-up, finding that the chances of the marriage of an unemployed person ending in the following year are 70 per cent higher than those of a person who has never been out of work.

The study also found that men in low-paid insecure jobs suffered almost the same level of psychological distress as those who were out of work altogether. It was found that there was a close correlation between perceived job security and psychological well-being. Women were found to be just as distressed by lack of paid work, but less affected by the prospect of an insecure low-paid job.

(a) What problems face the unemployed, according to the article?
(b) Why might these problems give rise to costs not just for the unemployed but also for society as a whole?

Applied economics

Measures of unemployment

In economic theory, the unemployed are defined as those without a job but who are seeking work at current wage rates. Measuring the number of unemployed in an economy, however, is more difficult than economic theory might suggest. There are two basic ways in which unemployment can be calculated.

- Government can undertake a survey of the population to identify the employed and the unemployed. This is the approach taken in countries such as the USA, Japan and Sweden. There is a measure of such unemployment based upon a standard produced by the International Labour Organisation (ILO). In the UK, monthly **ILO unemployment** figures are produced.
- The government can count all those who register as unemployed. In some countries a register of the unemployed is kept by trade unions because unemployment benefit is linked with union membership. In the UK, before 1982, the official monthly unemployment count was based on the numbers who had signed on at Jobcentres. The count was then changed to those who were claiming benefit for being unemployed from the Department of Social Security (DSS). This measure of unemployment is called the **claimant count**.

Unemployment is expressed in two ways. It can be stated as an absolute figure, as millions of workers. Or it can be stated as a relative measure, as a percentage of the workforce, the **unemployment rate**. Expressing it in millions gives a clear indication of the numbers affected by unemployment. Expressing it as percentage is better when the number of workers in the economy is changing. For instance, using absolute figures to compare US unemployment with UK unemployment may not be helpful because there are about five times as many workers in the US as in the UK. Comparing it as a percentage allows a more meaningful comparison to be made. Equally, the size of the workforce is likely to change over time. In 1950 in the UK, there were 23.7 million in the labour force of which 0.4 million were unemployed on a claimant count basis. In 2005, there were 30.0 million in the labour force of which 0.8 million were unemployed. Unemployment was much higher in 2005, but so too was the size of the workforce.

The claimant count

Until 1997, the main measure of UK unemployment was the claimant count. However, the claimant count figure had come under increasing criticism because it was felt to be open to government manipulation. In the 1980s and 1990s, the UK government introduced over 30 different changes to the way in which the claimant count was calculated, most of which served to reduce the numbers officially unemployed. For instance, the change from counting those looking for work at Jobcentres to those receiving benefits led to an estimated 200 000 fall in measured unemployment. Those lost from the unemployment count were mainly women who were looking for work, but were not entitled to claim any benefits. In 1988, 16-17 year olds were no longer able to claim benefit for being unemployed on the grounds that they were all guaranteed a place either in education or on a training scheme if they weren't in work. In 1996, unemployment benefit was cut from 12 months to 6 months, which removed many women from the unemployment register who were then not able to claim other social security payments for being out of work. Not only was the claimant count open to manipulation but it was also not an internationally recognised way of measuring unemployment. Hence, it could not be used to compare UK unemployment levels with those in other countries.

ILO unemployment

In 1998, the newly elected Labour government decided to make the ILO count the main measure of unemployment in the UK. ILO unemployment figures had been collected first on a biannual (once every two years) basis in 1973, and then annually from 1984. In 1993, it became a quarterly count and since 1997 has been monthly. The ILO count is taken from a wider survey of employment called the Labour Force Survey (LFS). 60 000 households, with over 100 000 adults, are surveyed. The questionnaire used covers household size and structure, accommodation details,

Figure 29.2 *ILO and claimant count measures of employment* [1,2]

Millions

ILO

Claimant count

1989 90   95   2000   05

1 Before 1993, ILO figures are estimated. Before 1995, ILO figures are for Great Britain and from 1995 for the UK.
2 Seasonally adjusted.

Source: adapted from *Economic Trends*, Office for National Statistics.

basic demographic characteristics, such as age, sex, marital status and ethnic origin, and economic activity. To be counted as unemployed, an individual has to be without a paid job, be available to start a job within a fortnight and has either looked for work at some time in the previous four weeks or been waiting to start a job already obtained.

ILO unemployment compared to the claimant count

Figure 29.2 shows that ILO unemployment figures differ significantly from claimant count figures. ILO unemployment tends to be above claimant count unemployment in a recovery and boom situation, but in a recession the claimant count figure can be above the ILO measure.

ILO unemployment is likely to be above the claimant count figure because the claimant count excludes a number of key groups of unemployed workers.

- Many female unemployed workers are actively looking for work (and are therefore included in ILO unemployment) but are not entitled to benefits for being unemployed. For instance, they might not have built up sufficient National Insurance contributions to qualify for unemployment benefit, a National Insurance benefit. They may also be living in a household where the husband or partner is earning too high a wage for them to qualify for means tested benefit.
- Older, particularly male, workers in their 50s and 60s may be collecting a pension from their previous employer or be supported financially by their spouse. They are therefore not entitled to benefits but may be actively seeking work.
- Workers are not entitled to register as unemployed with the DSS until they have been out of work for a

number of weeks. However, anyone interviewed for the ILO count who is unemployed and is looking for work is counted as unemployed regardless of how long they have been unemployed.

The claimant count, however, may include some unemployed who would not be included in the ILO count. For instance, those working in the **hidden economy** (☞ unit 25) may claim benefits for being unemployed but actually be in work, usually as a self employed worker.

Both the ILO and claimant counts could be argued to underestimate overall unemployment.

- They do not include part time workers who are actively seeking full time work, for instance.
- Those on government training and work schemes who would prefer to be in proper employment are not included. This particularly affects young workers.
- There are some out of work who are not actively seeking work or receiving benefits for being unemployed but who would take a job if offered. This mainly applies to women bringing up families. Table 29.2 illustrates this point. Between 1993 and 2005, ILO unemployment fell by 1.6 million whilst the total in employment increased by 3.4 million.
- Some unemployed workers have been taken off the unemployment registers by moving them onto sickness and disability benefits. As Figure 29.3 shows, numbers claiming sickness and disability benefits have risen from 0.7 million in 1979 to 2.6 million in 2003. Areas of the country with relatively high unemployment also have relatively high levels of sickness and disability benefit claimants. Some economists argue that all those on sickness and disability benefits should be included amongst the unemployed since all could work given the right working conditions.

However, both measures of unemployment could be argued to overestimate unemployment. Some of those out of work find it almost impossible to get a job. Those with physical and mental disabilities, some ex-criminals or some with no qualifications find the job market very difficult. Some economists would argue that these workers are unemployable and therefore should not be counted as unemployed. A minority of those working in the hidden economy may claim benefits and may declare on surveys that they are out of work and seeking work.

Table 29.2 Employment and unemployment, UK, spring each year, seasonally adjusted

	Total in employment	ILO unemployed
1989	26.7	2.1
1990	26.9	2.0
1991	26.4	2.4
1992	25.6	2.8
1993	25.3	3.0
1994	25.5	2.8
1995	25.7	2.5
1996	26.0	2.3
1997	26.4	2.0
1998	26.7	1.8
1999	27.1	1.8
2000	27.4	1.6
2001	27.7	1.4
2002	27.9	1.5
2003	28.2	1.5
2004	28.4	1.4
2005	28.7	1.4

Source: adapted from *Economic Trends*, Office for National Statistics.

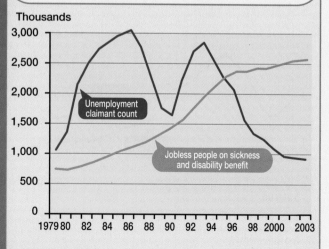

Figure 29.3 Jobless numbers on sickness and disability benefit; unemployment claimant count

Thousands

Unemployment claimant count

Jobless people on sickness and disability benefit

Source: adapted from the Thomson Datastream, DWP, Office for National Statisitcs.

DataQuestion

Unemployment in Wolverhampton

Figure 29.4 Local, County, Regional and National Unemployment Rates

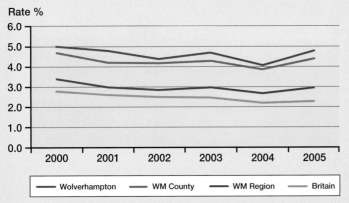

Source: adapted from Wolverhampton City Council, *Monthly Unemployment Briefing*, November 2005.

Table 29.3 Unemployment: claimant count summary, September 2005

	Male		Female		Total	
	Number	Rate	Number	Rate	Number	Rate
Wolverhampton	5 135	6.8	1 762	2.6	6 897	4.8
W'ton travel to work area	9 575	5.8	3 366	2.2	12 941	4.1
W Mids County	51 705	6.4	16 826	2.2	68 531	4.4
W Mids Region	73 258	4.3	24 960	1.6	98 218	3.0
Great Britain	615 016	3.3	227 417	1.3	842 433	2.3

Unemployment rate: unemployment as a % of the working age population.

Source: adapted from Wolverhampton City Council, *Monthly Unemployment Briefing*, November 2005.

Figure 29.5 Wolverhampton unemployment count: age and duration July 2005

	0-3 months	3-6 months	6-12 months	1-2 years	2+ years
18-24	1245	560	350	25	5
25-44	1335	785	600	225	30
45+	540	355	295	130	160

Source: adapted from Wolverhampton City Council, *Monthly Unemployment Briefing*, November 2005

Forty jobs have gone at a Wolverhampton factory after its work was shifted to China, Germany and Bulgaria. Ideal Standard in Bushbury, which has been producing brass taps in the city for 105 years, says it makes business sense to move its manufacturing abroad. The company, which will shed another 30 jobs by the end of the month, is the second city factory this week to make redundancies while taking advantage of cheap labour in other countries. Dunstall-based Turner Powertrain Systems revealed this week that it is cutting 75 jobs and considering farming work out to India.

Source: adapted from the *Express & Star*, 1.10.2005.

Unemployment facts

The proportion of children living in households where no one holds a job is the highest in Europe. This is mainly due to the high number of workless lone-parent households and, as a result, half of all children living with one parent are in income poverty.

Those who are unemployed are more likely to have poor educational qualifications and have been in low paid jobs in the past than those currently in work.

Unemployed people are three times more likely than average to be victims of violent crime. Lone parents, who have above average rates of unemployment, are more than twice as likely as average to be burgled.

Over the past ten years, the chances of a household, where either the head of the household or the spouse is unemployed, having an income below 60 per cent of the average income for all households was between 70 and 80 per cent.

While the total number of jobs in the UK has been rising, the number of jobs in manufacturing, construction and other production industries has been falling.

Two fifths of those making a new claim for Jobseeker's Allowance were last claiming less than six months ago.

Spending on travel by households on low incomes is only one quarter that of households on average incomes.

Source: adapted from New Policy Institute at www.jrf.org.uk.

Table 29.4 Comparisons of selected social statistics

	Wolverhampton	West Midlands	England/GB
Perinatal mortality rate 2001[1], England	13.1	10.0	8.3
Life expectancy at birth 2001-2002, years, England			
Males	74.5	75.4	76
Females	80.1	80.3	80.6
% change in resident population, GB			
1984-1994	- 3.5	+ 1.5	+ 2.5
1994-2004	- 2.5	+ 1.6	+ 3.4
Qualifications, % of residents, 2004			
Degree, NVQ4 or above	18.0	21.1	25.2
No qualifications	22.6	18.7	15.1
Economically active, % of population of working age, 2004			
Males			
Employees	61.8	66.0	65.5
Self employed	9.2	12.0	13.1
Females			
Employees	61.2	64.0	64.4
Self employed	2.2	4.2	4.8
Economically inactive, % of population of working age, 2004			
Wanting a job	5.1	4.6	5.2
Not wanting a job	17.9	12.8	12.5
Job seekers allowance, claimants as % of population of working age, 2004	4.6	3.0	2.4
Employee jobs, % of total, 2004			
Full-time	70.5	68.6	68.1
Part-time	29.5	31.4	31.9
of which			
Manufacturing	19.5	17.9	12.6
Services	74.2	76.3	81.5

1 Number of stillbirths and deaths under one week per thousand live births and stillbirths.

Source: adapted from *nomis, Official Labour Market Statistics*, Office for National Statistics; Wolverhampton City Council, *Statistics*.

One in seven of the working population are claiming incapacity benefit in some parts of Wolverhampton. In the worst-hit areas, 15 per cent of people are off work and claiming because of long-term illness or disability. Numbers vary widely between areas. Over 14 per cent are on incapacity benefit in parts of Bilston and Ettingshall. In affluent Wightwick and Penn, it is just 5 per cent. Wolverhampton South West MP Rob Marris said that 'some of that will be a hangover from our manufacturing heritage'. Wolverhampton North East MP Ken Purchase said: 'At the moment there are many people who could work but are not getting the right kind of support to do it and we have plans to help people back into work.' Nationally, there are 2.7 million people claiming at a cost of £12 billion a year.

Source: adapted from the *Express & Star*, 6.1.2006.

1. Using the data, compare the employment and unemployment situation in Wolverhampton with the West Midlands and Great Britain.
2. Discuss the economic costs that might be created by the redundancies at Ideal Standard and Turner Powertrain Systems to (a) the individuals concerned and their families; (b) the local community in Wolverhampton; (c) taxpayers; (d) the UK economy.

30 The balance of payments

Summary

1. The balance of payments accounts are split into two parts. The current account records payments for the exports and imports of goods and services. The capital account records saving, investment and speculative flows of money.
2. The current account is split into two parts: trade in visibles and trade in invisibles.
3. The balance of payments accounts must always balance. However, component parts of the accounts may be positive or negative. If there is a surplus on the current account, then outflows on the capital account must be greater than inflows.
4. A current account surplus is often seen as a sign of a healthy economy, whilst a current account deficit is seen as a cause for worry. But current account deficits are not necessarily bad as they may be a sign of borrowing which could finance expansion.
5. A current account deficit is most unlikely to be financed by government. The balance of payments deficit and the government deficit are two completely different entities.

The balance of payments

The BALANCE OF PAYMENTS ACCOUNT is a record of all financial dealings over a period of time between economic agents of one country and all other countries. Balance of payments accounts can be split into two components:
● the CURRENT ACCOUNT where payments for the purchase and sale of goods and services are recorded;
● the CAPITAL and FINANCIAL ACCOUNTS where flows of money associated with saving, investment, speculation and currency stabilisation are recorded.
Flows of money into the country are given a positive (+) sign on the accounts. Flows of money out of the country are given a negative (-) sign.

The current account

The current account on the balance of payments is itself split into two components.

Visibles VISIBLES are the trade in goods, from raw materials to semi-manufactured products to manufactured goods. Visible exports are goods which are sold to foreigners. Goods leave the country, whilst payment for these goods goes in the opposite direction. Hence visible exports of, say, cars result in an **inward** flow of money and are recorded with a positive sign on the balance of payments account. Visible imports are goods which are bought by domestic residents from foreigners. Goods come into the country whilst money **flows out**. Hence visible imports of, say, wheat are given a minus sign on the balance of payments. The difference between visible exports and visible imports is known as the BALANCE OF TRADE.

Invisibles INVISIBLES are made up of trade in services, investment income and other payments and receipts. A wide variety of services is traded internationally, including financial services such as banking and insurance, transport services such as shipping and air travel, and tourism. Income results from the loan of factors of production abroad. For instance, a British teacher working in Saudi Arabia and sending back money to his family in England would create an invisible import for Saudi Arabia and an invisible export for Britain. Similarly, a Japanese company repatriating profits made from a factory based in Britain back to Japan would create an invisible import for the UK and an invisible export for Japan. Payments might be in the form of a UK contribution to EU funds and receipts may include EU subsidies to the UK.

The easiest way to distinguish between invisible exports and imports, or invisible **credits** and invisible **debits** as they are known in the official UK balance of payments account, is to consider flows of money rather than flows of services. The British teacher in Saudi Arabia is sending money back to the UK. An inflow of money means that this is classified as an export. The Japanese company repatriating profits is sending money out of the UK. An outflow of money means that this is classified as an import. The difference between invisible exports and invisible imports is known as the BALANCE ON INVISIBLE TRADE or NET INVISIBLES.

The CURRENT BALANCE is the difference between total EXPORTS (visible and invisible) and total IMPORTS. It can also be calculated by adding the balance of trade to the balance on invisible trade.

Question 1

A country has the following international transactions on current account: exports of manufactured goods £20bn; imports of food £10bn; earnings from foreign tourists £5bn; interest, profits and dividends paid to foreigners £4bn; purchase of oil from abroad £8bn; earnings of nationals working overseas which are repatriated £7bn; sale of coal to foreign countries £2bn; payments by foreigners to domestic financial institutions for services rendered £1bn.

(a) Which of these items are: (i) visible exports; (ii) visible imports; (iii) invisible exports; (iv) invisible imports?
(b) Calculate: (i) the balance of trade; (ii) the balance on invisible trade; (iii) the current balance.
(c) How would your answers to (b) be different if it cost the country £3bn to transport its exports (i) in its own ships and (ii) in the ships of other countries?

Current account deficits

The balance of payments account shows all the inflows of money to and the outflows of money from a country. Inflows must equal outflows overall and therefore the balance of payments must always balance. This is no different from a household. All the money going out from a household in spending or saving over a period of time must equal money coming in from earnings, borrowings or running down of savings. If a household spends £60 going out for a meal, the money must have come from somewhere.

However, there can be surpluses or deficits on particular parts of the account. Using the example of the household again, it can spend more than it earns if it borrows money. The same is true of a national economy. It can spend more on goods and services than it earns if it borrows money from overseas. So it can have a CURRENT ACCOUNT DEFICIT, where exports are less than imports, by running a surplus on its capital account. Equally, it can run a CURRENT ACCOUNT SURPLUS, exporting more than it imports, by running a deficit on its capital and financial account. A deficit on the capital account for the UK means that it invests more abroad than foreigners invest in the UK.

Often, the media talk about a 'balance of payments deficit'. Strictly speaking, there can never be a balance of payments deficit because the balance of payments must always balance, i.e. it must always be zero. What the media are, in fact, referring to is either a balance of trade deficit or a current account deficit. Similarly, the term '**trade gap**' is a term used in the media, usually to mean a deficit on the balance of trade in goods.

The size of current account deficits

Current account deficits are generally seen as undesirable and a sign of economic weakness. Conversely, current account surpluses are usually seen as signs of the economic strength of a country. This, though, is a very crude way of analysing the balance of payments. One reason why this is crude is because the size of the current account surplus or deficit is important in deciding its significance. Using the analogy of the household again, if the income of a household is £100 000 per year and its spending over the year is £100 010, it has overspent. But overspending by £10 on an income of £100 000 in one year is of almost no significance. On the other hand, take a household living solely from state benefits. If income is £60 per week, and spending is £70, then this household is likely to be in serious trouble. Unless it has substantial savings to draw on, overspending £10 each week on an income of £60 will soon become unsustainable. Where will the £10 per week come from? If it is from borrowing, then the money must eventually be repaid, eating into a very low income.

This is also the case for a national economy. If the country runs a current account deficit year after year, but this current account deficit is very small in relation to national income over time, then it is of little significance economically. Equally, if a country runs a large deficit over a short period of time, but then follows this with a large surplus over the next period, then it is relatively unimportant. Only if the current account deficit or surplus is large in relation to income and is sustained over a period of time does it really matter.

Large sustained current account deficits

Large sustained current account deficits are usually considered undesirable because they become unsustainable. Deficits on the current account may occur because the government of a country spends excessively on foreign goods and services. Or it could be private firms and individuals which are spending too much, importing far more than they are exporting. Whether it is government or the private sector, the current account deficit has to be financed. Either the level of borrowings abroad is increased or there is a net run down in savings and investments held abroad. Governments and firms can borrow abroad so long as foreign lenders think that they can repay the loans with interest in the future. But if the current account deficit is large and sustained, there usually comes a point when lenders think that the borrowers may **default** on their loans (i.e. not pay them). Lenders then stop lending. At this point, the country is in serious difficulties.

Countries like Poland, Brazil and Uganda in the 1980s, and Thailand and South Korea in the 1990s, have all faced this **credit crunch**, the point at which foreign lenders refuse to lend any more. They are then forced to return their current account to equilibrium. This means cutting down on imports, or exporting more goods which previously might have been sold on the domestic market. Citizens therefore have fewer goods available to them and their consumption and standard of living falls.

If the economy is fundamentally strong, the adjustment will be painful but relatively short, lasting just a few years perhaps. For countries which have very weak economies, the credit crunch can have a negative impact for decades. In sub-Saharan Africa, the credit crunch which occurred in the early 1980s led to Western banks and other agencies refusing to lend significant sums for the next 20 years. This crippled the economies of certain countries and deprived them of foreign funds which could have helped them to grow.

However, large sustained current account deficits may be beneficial to an economy. It depends on its rate of **economic growth** (☞ unit 26). If an economy is growing at 3 per cent per annum, but is running a large current account deficit of 5 per cent of GDP per annum, then it will run into problems. Its foreign debt as a percentage of GDP will grow over time. But if the economy is growing at 10 per cent per annum, and there is a current account deficit of 5 per cent of GDP, accumulated foreign debt as a percentage of GDP is likely to fall. Although foreign debt in absolute terms will be growing, the income of the country available to repay it will be growing even faster. Countries like the USA in the nineteenth century, and South Korea and Malaysia in the late part of the twentieth century, have all run significant current account deficits over a period of time, but they have tended to benefit from this because the money has been used to strengthen their growth potential. Even so, both South Korea and Malaysia were caught up in a credit crunch in the late 1990s when foreign lenders judged that too much had been lent to East Asian economies. High levels of foreign borrowing carry risks for countries even when their economies are highly successful on **measures of national economic performance** (☞ unit 24) such as economic growth, unemployment and inflation.

Question 2

The Czech Republic, since 1990, has been relatively successful in making the transition from being a command economy, where the state dominated every economic decision, to a market economy, where markets are used to allocate a significant proportion of an economy's resources. Over the period 1994-2006, average economic growth in the Czech Republic was an estimated 3%, which was 50% more than that in the euro area (the EU countries which have adopted the euro including France, Germany and Italy).

Inevitably, in opening itself up to other markets, it has sucked in significant levels of imports. Czech consumers have bought cheaper and better quality goods from other countries, whilst Czech businesses have imported raw materials and capital goods from abroad.

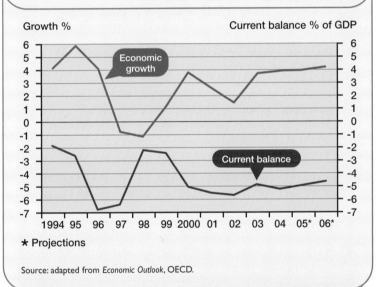

Figure 30.1 Czech Republic: economic growth (%) and current account balance as a percentage of GDP

★ Projections

Source: adapted from *Economic Outlook*, OECD.

(a) Use the data to explain why the Czech Republic has been a success story in the 1990s and 2000s.
(b) Discuss whether its large current account deficit throughout the period are a problem for the Czech Republic.

Large sustained current account surpluses

Some countries run large sustained current account surpluses. By exporting more than they import over a long period of time, these countries increase their net foreign wealth. This has the benefit that the economy then should receive ever increasing amounts of income from that wealth, which can be used to buy more foreign goods and services than would otherwise be the case. This is like a household which consistently saves money. In the long term, it can use the interest on that saving to buy more goods than it would otherwise have been able to afford.

A sustained current account surplus may also make sense if there are long term structural changes occurring. Japan ran large current account surpluses during the last quarter of the twentieth century, consequently building up its net wealth overseas. However, in the first half of the twenty first century, the structure of the Japanese population will change dramatically. From having very few pensioners in proportion to workers, the population will age significantly and there will be a high proportion of pensioners to workers. It could well be that Japan will run down its wealth overseas to pay for the goods and services consumed by non-productive pensioners. Japan could therefore move from having sustained current account surpluses to current account deficits.

Large sustained current account surpluses have their disadvantages though. First, they reduce what is available for consumption now. If the surplus were eliminated, resources used for exports could be diverted to produce goods for domestic consumption. Or the country could increase imports, again increasing the amount available for consumption.

Second, sustained current account surpluses cause friction between countries. If Japan has a current account surplus, the rest of the world must have a deficit. If Japan is a net lender, building up wealth overseas, the rest of the world must be a net borrower, building up debts overseas. Countries which attempt to reduce their current account deficits can only be successful if other countries reduce their current account surpluses. On a microeconomic level, trade unions and firms in deficit countries often accuse firms in surplus countries of 'poaching' jobs. If Japan reduced its trade surplus by reducing exports to the United States, then firms in the United States might be able to fill the gap created by expanding their output.

In practice, the benefits to one country of another country reducing its surplus are likely to be small. If Japan's exports fall, US producers are just as likely to find that other countries like South Korea or the UK fill the market gap as them. When the USA has a large current account deficit and Japan a large surplus, a reduction in the Japanese surplus will improve the current account positions of many countries around the world, not just that of the USA. The benefit of a large reduction in the Japanese surplus to any single country, even to the USA, the largest economy in the world, will be relatively small.

Government deficits and balance of payments deficits

One very common fallacy is to equate current account deficits with government deficits (the PSNCR ☞ unit 36). Most transactions on the balance of payments are made by private individuals and firms. If the country is a net borrower, it is more than likely that this is because private individuals and firms have borrowed more from foreigners than they have lent to foreigners. There is a relationship between government borrowing and the current account deficit but the relationship is complicated, and it could well be the case that the public sector might be in surplus domestically when the current account was in deficit. So the current account deficit is **not** a government deficit in any sense.

Question 3

Figure 30.2 Japan and the USA: current account balances as a percentage of GDP

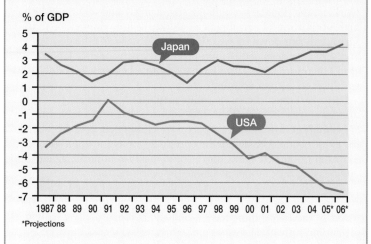

% of GDP

*Projections

Source: adapted from *Economic Outlook*, OECD.

(a) Compare the current account balance of the USA with that of Japan during the late 1980s, 1990s and 2000s.
(b) Discuss the possible benefits and costs to Japan of running a persistent current account surplus.

Key terms

Balance of payments account - a record of all financial dealings over a period of time between economic agents of one country and all other countries.
Balance of trade - visible exports minus visible imports.
Balance on invisible trade or net invisibles - invisible exports minus invisible imports.
Capital and financial accounts - that part of the balance of payments account where flows of savings, investment and currency are recorded.
Current account - that part of the balance of payments account where payments for the purchase and sale of goods and services are recorded.
Current balance - the difference between total exports (visible and invisible) and total imports. It can also be calculated by adding the balance of trade to the balance on invisible trade.
Current account deficit or surplus - a deficit exists when imports are greater than exports; a surplus exists when exports are greater than imports.
Exports - goods and services produced domestically and sold to foreigners. Payments for exports come into the country.
Imports - goods and services purchased from foreign producers. Payments for imports leave the country.
Invisibles - trade in services, transfers of income and other payments or receipts.
Visibles - trade in goods.

Applied economics

The UK current account

The parts of the current account

The Office for National Statistics divides the UK current account into four parts, shown in Table 30.1.

- Trade in goods. Exports of goods minus imports of goods is equal to the balance of trade in goods.
- Trade in services. The main services traded are transport (such as shipping or air transport), travel and tourism, insurance and other financial services, and royalties and licence fees.
- Income. Some countries, such as Pakistan or Egypt, earn substantial amounts from the repatriation of income from nationals working abroad. For the UK, such income is relatively unimportant. Nearly all income in the UK balance of payments accounts relates to UK investments abroad and to foreign investments in the UK (investment income).
- Current transfers. Most current transfers relate to

the UK's membership of the European Union. The UK has to pay part of its tax revenues to the EU, but in return receives payments such as agricultural subsidies or regional grants.

Visibles in the account are the trade in goods. Invisibles are the trade in services, income and current transfers. In terms of relative size, invisibles outweigh visibles. The most important invisible is not trade in services but income. Current transfers are relatively insignificant. The UK's current balance is therefore crucially dependent not just on trade in goods and services, but also on income from foreign investments. Comparing this to a household, it is as if the financial soundness of the household is dependent not just on wage earnings and spending, but also very much on interest and dividends on savings and also on payments of interest on loans.

The current account over time

Since the Second World War, there has been a number of consistent trends on the UK current account.

- The balance of trade in goods has been negative, as can be seen from Figure 30.3. Visible exports have tended to be less than visible imports.
- The overall balance on trade in services, income and current transfers has been positive. Invisible credits have been greater than invisible debits.
- Breaking down invisibles, the balance of trade in services has nearly always been positive - more services have been sold abroad than have been bought from abroad. The balance on income has usually been positive too. Income brought into the country by UK people living abroad and income earned from investments abroad have been greater than income leaving the country. However, the balance on income fluctuates much more from year to year than the balance of trade in services. Current transfers since the 1960s have always been negative. Since joining the EU in 1973, most of the negative balance is due to the UK paying more into EU coffers than receiving in grants.

The size of the current account balances

In the 1950s and 1960s, the current account posed a major problem for the UK. At the time, the value of the pound was fixed against other currencies. In years when the current account went into deficit, currency speculators tended to sell pounds sterling in the hope that the government would be forced to devalue the pound, i.e. make it less valuable against other currencies. So quite small current account deficits as a percentage of GDP, as in 1960 or in 1964, presented large problems for the government of the day.

From the 1970s, the value of the pound was allowed to float, changing from minute to minute on the foreign exchange markets. Figure 30.4 shows that there were two periods when the UK's current account position could have become unsustainable in the long term. In 1973-75 the UK, along with most Western countries, suffered a severe economic shock from a rise in commodity prices, particularly oil prices. Following the Yom Kippur war of November 1973

Table 30.1 The current balance, 2004 (£m)

Trade in goods		
Export of goods	190 859	
Import of goods	249 473	
Balance on trade in goods		- 58 614
Trade in services		
Export of services	99 100	
Import of services	78 911	
Balance of trade in services		20 189
Balance on trade in goods and services		- 38 425
Income		
Credits	139 656	
Debits	113 493	
Balance		26 163
Current transfers		
Credits	12 819	
Debits	23 532	
Balance		- 10 713
Current balance		- 22 975

Source: adapted from The Pink Book, *United Kingdom Balance of Payments*, Office for National Statistics.

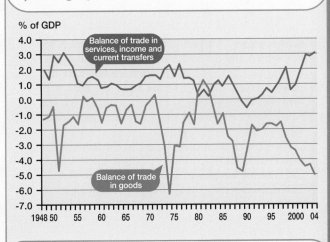

Figure 30.3 The balance of trade in goods, and the balance of trade in services, income and current transfers, as a percentage of GDP

Figure 30.4 The current balance as a percentage of GDP

Source: adapted from www.statistics.gov.uk.

between Egypt and Israel, the members of OPEC (☞ units 2 and 8) chose to restrict supply of oil to the west and as a result its price quadrupled. Import prices roses sharply and the current account approached 4 per cent of GDP in 1974. The UK government was forced to react by cutting domestic spending, which in turn reduced demand for imports. In 1986-89, there was another sharp deterioration in the current account due to the 'Lawson boom', named after the then Chancellor, Nigel Lawson. Fast increases in domestic spending led to sharp increases in imports.

Since the late 1980s, the current account has been consistently in deficit within a range of 0.2 per cent of GDP to 2.7 per cent of GDP. It could be argued that this should pose long term problems for the UK. If the UK is consistently spending more than it is earning abroad, this will lead to a long term build up of debt. Just as households who consistently borrow more and more money should get into financial difficulties, so too should a country.

There are two reasons which might explain why the UK has not encountered problems relating to its persistent current account deficits in the 1990s and 2000s. One is that the deficits are manageable given the economy's average growth rate of between 2.5 and 3.0 per cent over the period. For a household, so long as income is rising faster than debt, there should be no debt problem. Certainly, the financial markets have not shown any particular concern about the UK's current account deficits. Foreign lenders have not refused to lend UK borrowers any more money as they did, for example, to countries such as Mexico, South Korea or Poland when they had debt crises over the past 30 years.

The other reason is that the current account deficit is not the main determinant of the net debt owed by UK citizens, businesses and government to foreigners. The main determinant is changing asset values, such as stock market prices in New York or bond prices in Frankfurt. Since 1990, as Figure 30.8 shows (☞ data question), the net debt of the UK, the difference between what UK households, businesses and government own abroad and what they owe to foreigners, has varied from plus 49 per cent of GDP to minus 150 per cent. Such huge swings are accounted for not by current account deficits but by changes in asset values.

Capital and financial accounts

The capital and financial accounts are the parts of the balance of payments accounts where flows of savings, investment and currency are recorded. The capital account records flows of money associated with the purchase of physical assets such as land. The financial account records flows of money associated with the purchase of paper financial assets such as stocks and shares or international bank loans.

Figure 30.5 Balances of trade in services, total income and current transfers as a percentage of GDP

Source: adapted from www.statistics.gov.uk.

DataQuestion

The trade gap

Trade gap at an all time high

The trade gap has reached an all time record. Never before has the UK seen such a large deficit in our trade in goods. Last year in 2004 it reached 5 per cent of GDP. The last time it approached that level was in 1989 when the economy was in deep trouble as a result of overspending in the 'Lawson boom'. The trade gap in goods far outweighs the surpluses the UK earned last year on its invisibles. The UK's overall current account deficit was 2 per cent of GDP.

The mystery of the UK's investment income

Strange things are happening abroad. According to the latest statistics, the UK earned a net 2.2 per cent of GDP on its net foreign assets. What that means is that the UK earned 2.2 per cent more on the foreign assets owned by UK householders, businesses and government than foreigners earned on UK assets that they owned. But the statistics also show that the value of foreign assets owned by the UK is less than the value of UK assets owned by foreigners. UK households, businesses and government in 2004 owed to foreigners 1.5 times the value of the UK's GDP more than they owned abroad. With these sorts of figures, the UK ought to be paying out more than it receives. Obviously, UK investors are better at making a return on their overseas assets than foreign investors in the UK.

1. Describe the changes in the balance of trade and total investment income shown in the data.
2. What might be the implications for the current account balance of the changes shown in the data?
3. Discuss the extent to which the deterioration in the 'trade gap' in 2004 might have been of economic significance.

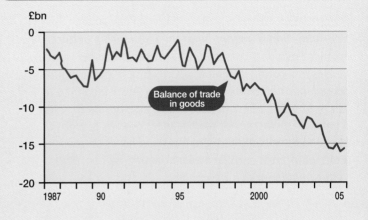

Figure 30.6 Record trade deficit for the UK

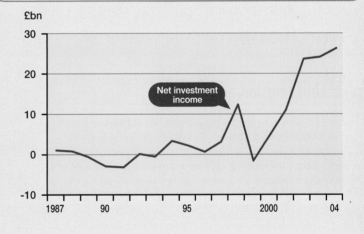

Figure 30.7 Income balance: net investment income

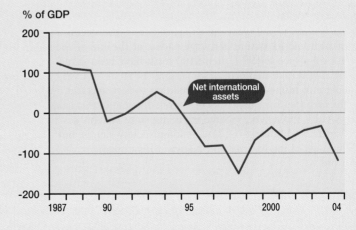

Figure 30.8 UK net international assets as a percentage of GDP

Source: adapted from www.statistics.gov.uk.

3 Consumption and saving

Summary

1. Consumption can be divided into spending on durable goods and non-durable goods.
2. The consumption function shows the relationship between consumption and its determinants, the main one being income.
3. Increases in wealth will lead to an increase in consumption.
4. Expected inflation tends to lead to a rise in saving and a fall in consumption. The effect of households attempting to restore the real value of their stock of savings more than outweighs the effect of households bringing forward their purchases of goods.
5. The rate of interest and the availability of credit particularly affect the consumption of durable goods.
6. A change in the structure of the population will affect both consumption and saving. The greater the proportion of adults aged 35-60 in the population, the higher is likely to be the level of saving.
7. Keynesians hypothesise that consumption is a stable function of current disposable income in the short run.
8. The life cycle hypothesis and the permanent income hypothesis both emphasise that consumption is a stable function of income only in the very long run. In the short run, other factors such as the rate of interest and wealth can have a significant impact upon consumption and savings.

Defining consumption and saving

CONSUMPTION in economics is spending on consumer goods and services over a period of time. Examples are spending on chocolate, hire of videos or buying a car. Consumption can be broken down into a number of different categories. One way of classifying consumption is to distinguish between spending on **goods** and spending on **services**. Another way is to distinguish between spending on DURABLE GOODS and NON-DURABLE GOODS. Durable goods are goods which, although bought at a point in time, continue to provide a stream of services over a period of time. A car, for instance, should last at least 6 years. A television set might last 10 years. Non-durable goods are goods and services which are used up immediately or over a short period of time, like an ice-cream or a packet of soap powder.

SAVING is what is not spent out of income. For instance, if a worker takes home £1 000 in her wage packet at the end of the month, but only spends £900, then £100 must have been saved. The saving might take the form of increasing the stock of cash, or an increase in money in a bank or building society account, or it might take the form of stocks or shares. Income in this case is DISPOSABLE INCOME, income including state benefits such as child benefit and interest on, say, building society shares, but after deductions of income tax and National Insurance contributions.

Consumption and income

There is a number of factors which determine how much a household consumes. The relationship between consumption and these factors is called the CONSUMPTION FUNCTION. The most important determinant of consumption is disposable income. Other factors, discussed in sections below, are far less important but can bring about small but significant changes in the relationship between consumption and income.

Assume that one year a household has an income of £1 000 per month. The next year, due to salary increases, this rises to £1 200 per month. Economic theory predicts that the consumption of the household will rise.

How much it will rise can be measured by the MARGINAL PROPENSITY TO CONSUME (MPC), the proportion of a change in income that is spent:

$$MPC = \frac{\text{Change in consumption}}{\text{Change in income}} = \frac{\Delta C}{\Delta Y}$$

where Y is income, C is consumption and Δ is 'change in'. If the £200 rise in income leads to a £150 rise in consumption, then the marginal propensity to consume would be 0.75 (£150 ÷ £200).

For the economy as a whole, the marginal propensity to consume is likely to be positive (i.e. greater than zero) but less than 1. Any rise in income will lead to more spending but also some saving too. For individuals, the marginal propensity to consume could be more than 1 if money was borrowed to finance spending higher than income.

The AVERAGE PROPENSITY TO CONSUME (or APC) measures the average amount spent on consumption out of total income. For instance, if total disposable income in an economy were £100 billion and consumption were £90 billion, then the average propensity to consume would be 0.9. The formula for the APC is:

$$APC = \frac{\text{Consumption}}{\text{Income}} = \frac{C}{Y}$$

Question 1

Table 31.1

	Consumption	Disposable income
1963	242.4	248.4
1964	250.3	259.4
1973	326.4	341.3
1974	321.9	338.6
1983	372.9	390.2
1984	381.2	404.8
1993	509.2	557.6
1994	524.8	565.7
2003	711.1	730.1
2004	737.0	745.7

£bn at 2002 prices

Source: adapted from *Economic Trends*, *Economic Trends Annual Supplement*, Office for National Statistics.

(a) Using the data, explain the relationship between consumption and disposable income.
(b) (i) Calculate the MPC and the APC for 1964, 1974, 1984, 1994 and 2004.
    (ii) What happened to saving during these years?

Question 2

The number of mortgages being approved fell to its lowest level for more than nine years in November, sending out a strong signal that house prices are set for further falls. The number of loans is an important indicator for consumer spending. Most economists regard a slowdown in consumer spending as a risk to the UK economy over the next year.

Higher house prices lead directly to more consumer spending because people feel wealthier. But Ben Broadbent at Goldman Sachs, the investment bank, argues that consumer spending is more likely to be affected by a slowdown in house turnover than a decline in house prices. He said: 'When you move house, you have to buy a lot of stuff, such as carpets, curtains and fridges. There is already a trend towards slower retail sales and we expect data over the next weeks that will include the Christmas period to reflect this more strongly.'

Consumer spending is also linked to mortgage equity release, when housebuyers take out a larger mortgage than they need to buy a house and then spend the difference. Equally, existing homeowners may remortgage their house, taking on a bigger mortgage and spending the balance. Mortgage equity withdrawal totalled £12.4bn between July and September, down from £13.0bn in the previous quarter.

Source: adapted from the *Financial Times*, 5.1.2005.

(a) Explain three ways in which the housing market can affect consumption levels.

In a rich industrialised economy, the APC is likely to be less than 1 because consumers will also save part of their earnings.

Wealth

The wealth of a household is made up of two parts. **Physical wealth** is made up of items such as houses, cars and furniture. **Monetary wealth** is comprised of items such as cash, money in the bank and building societies, stocks and shares, assurance policies and pension rights.

If the wealth of a household increases, consumption will increase. This is known as the WEALTH EFFECT. There are two important ways in which the wealth of households can change over a short time period.

● A change in the price of houses. If the real price of houses increases considerably over a period of time, as happened in the UK from the mid-1990s to 2004, then households feel able to increase their spending. They do this mainly by borrowing more money secured against the value of their house.
● A change in the value of stocks and shares. Households react to an increase in the real value of a household's portfolio of securities by selling part of the portfolio and spending the proceeds. The value of stocks and shares is determined by many factors. One of these is the rate of interest. If the rate of interest falls, then the value of stocks will rise. So consumption should be stimulated through the wealth effect by a fall in the rate of interest.

Inflation

Inflation, a rise in the general level of prices, has two effects on consumption. First, if households expect prices to be higher in the future they will be tempted to bring forward their purchases. For instance, if households know that the price of cars will go up by 10 per cent the next month, they will attempt to buy their cars now. So expectations of inflation increase consumption and reduce saving.

However, this can be outweighed by the effect of inflation on wealth. Rising inflation tends to erode the real value of money wealth. Households react to this by attempting to restore the real value of their wealth (i.e. they save more). This reduces consumption.

Overall, rising inflation in the UK tends to reduce consumption. The negative effect on consumption caused by the erosion of real wealth more than offsets the positive effect on consumption caused by the bringing forward of purchases.

The rate of interest

Households rarely finance expenditure on **non-durables** such as food or entertainment by borrowing money. However, much of the money to buy **durables** such as cars, furniture, kitchen equipment and hi-fi equipment comes from credit finance. An increase in the rate of interest increases the monthly repayments on these goods. This means that, effectively, the price of the goods has increased. Households react to this by reducing their demand for durables and thus cutting their consumption.

Many households also have borrowed money to buy their houses. Increased interest rates lead to increased mortgage repayments. Again, this will directly cut spending on other items and perhaps, more importantly, discourage households from borrowing more money to finance purchases of consumer durables.

It has already been explained above that a rise in the rate of interest reduces the value of stocks on stock markets and thus reduces the value of household wealth. This in turn leads to a fall in consumption.

their stock of savings to supplement their pensions. So if there is a change in the age composition of households in the economy, there could well be a change in consumption and savings. The more young and old the households, the greater will tend to be the level of consumption.

The determinants of saving

Factors which affect consumption also by definition must affect saving (remember, saving is defined as that part of disposable income which is not consumed). The SAVINGS FUNCTION therefore links income, wealth, inflation, the rate of interest, expectations and the age profile of the population with the level of saving. However, because a typical AVERAGE PROPENSITY TO SAVE (the APS - the ratio of total saving to total income calculated by Saving ÷ Income) is 0.1 to 0.2 in Western European countries, income is far less important in determining saving than it is in determining consumption. Factors other than income are therefore relatively more important. This explains why, in the UK, for instance, the APS has varied from 0.04 to 0.12 between the 1980s and mid-2000s. The MARGINAL PROPENSITY TO SAVE (the proportion that is saved out of a change in income calculated by Change in saving ÷ Change in income) is equally unstable for these reasons.

Question 3

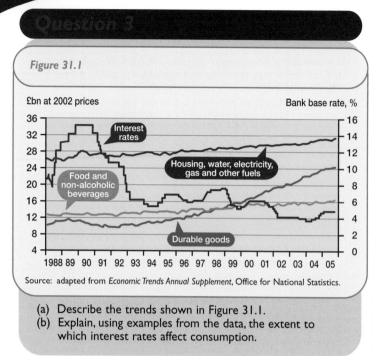

Figure 31.1

£bn at 2002 prices — Bank base rate, %

Labels on graph: Interest rates; Housing, water, electricity, gas and other fuels; Food and non-alcoholic beverages; Durable goods

Source: adapted from *Economic Trends Annual Supplement*, Office for National Statistics.

(a) Describe the trends shown in Figure 31.1.
(b) Explain, using examples from the data, the extent to which interest rates affect consumption.

The availability of credit

The rate of interest determines the price of credit. However, the price of credit is not the only determinant of how much households borrow. Governments in the past have often imposed restrictions on the availability of credit. For instance, they have imposed maximum repayment periods and minimum deposits. Before the deregulation of the mortgage market in the early 1980s in the UK, building societies rationed mortgages. They often operated queueing systems and imposed restrictive limits on the sums that could be borrowed. When these restrictions are abolished, households increase their level of debt and spend the proceeds. Making credit more widely available will increase consumption.

Expectations

Expectations of increases in prices tend to make households bring forward their purchases and thus increase consumption. Expectations of large increases in real incomes will also tend to encourage households to increase spending now by borrowing more. So when the economy is booming, autonomous consumption tends to increase. On the other hand, if households expect economic conditions to become harsher, they will reduce their consumption now. For instance, they might expect an increase in unemployment rates, a rise in taxes or a fall in real wages.

The composition of households

Young people and old people tend to spend a higher proportion of their income than those in middle age. Young people tend to spend all their income and move into debt to finance the setting up of their homes and the bringing up of children. In middle age, the cost of homemaking declines as a proportion of income. With more income available, households often choose to build up their stock of savings in preparation for retirement. When they retire, they will run down

---

Question 4

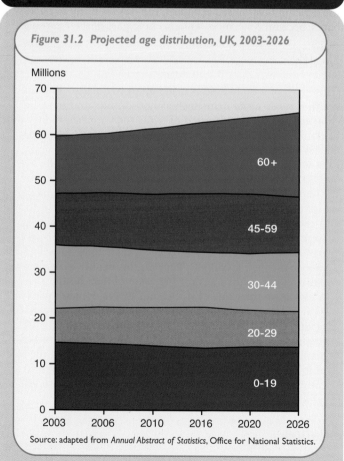

Figure 31.2 Projected age distribution, UK, 2003-2026

Millions

Age groups shown: 60+; 45-59; 30-44; 20-29; 0-19

Years: 2003, 2006, 2010, 2016, 2020, 2026

Source: adapted from *Annual Abstract of Statistics*, Office for National Statistics.

(a) What effects do you think that the changing structure of the population to 2026 is likely to have on consumption and saving?

Confusion sometimes arises between 'saving' and 'savings'. Saving is a **flow** concept which takes place over a period of time. Saving is added to a **stock** of savings fixed at a point in time. A household's stock of savings is the accumulation of past savings. For instance, you might have £100 in the bank. This is your stock of savings. You might then get a job over Christmas and save £20 from that. Your saving over Christmas is £20. Your stock of savings before Christmas was £100 but afterwards it was £120. The savings function explains the relationship between the flow of savings and its determinants. It attempts to explain why you saved £20 over Christmas. It does not explain why you have £100 in the bank already.

The Keynesian consumption function

John Maynard Keynes was one of the greatest economists working in the first half of the twentieth century. He was the founder of modern macro-economics, the subject of much of the rest of this book. It was he who first popularised the idea that consumption was linked to income. 'Keynesian' means that an idea is linked to an idea first put forward by Keynes. Keynesian economists are economists who work within the framework first established by Keynes.

The Keynesian consumption function lays stress upon the relationship between planned current consumption and current disposable income. Other factors, particularly the availability of credit, can have an important impact upon expenditure on consumer durables. However, in the short term at least, income is the most significant factor determining the level of consumption. Changes in wealth and changes in the rate of interest (the two can be interrelated as argued above) have little impact upon short term consumption. This means that the consumption function is relatively stable. It is not subject to frequent large scale shifts.

Keynes himself was worried that increasing prosperity would lead to a stagnant economy. As households became better off, they would spend less and less of their increases in income. Eventually their demand for consumer goods would be completely satiated and without increases in spending, there could be no more increases in income.

The evidence of the past 70 years has proved Keynes wrong. There does not seem to be any indication that households are reducing their MPCs as income increases. However, this view has also led Keynesians to argue that higher income earners have a lower MPC (and therefore save a higher proportion of their income) than low income earners. Therefore, redistributing income from the poor to the rich will lower total consumption. The reverse, taking from the rich to give to the poor, will increase total consumption. But as we shall now see, this too seems to be contradicted not only by the evidence but also by alternative theories of the consumption function.

The life cycle hypothesis

Franco Modigliani and Albert Ando suggested that current consumption is not based upon current income. Rather, households form a view about their likely income over the whole of their lifetimes and base their current spending decisions upon that. For instance, professional workers at the start of their careers in their early 20s may earn as much as manual workers of the same age. But the APC of professional workers is likely to be higher. This is because professional workers expect to earn more in the future and are prepared to

borrow more now to finance consumption. A professional worker will expect, for instance, to buy rather than rent a house. The mortgage she takes out is likely to be at the top end of what banks or building societies will lend. The manual worker, on the other hand, knowing that his earnings are unlikely to increase substantially in the future, will be more cautious. He may be deterred from buying his own home and, if he does, will take out a small rather than large mortgage.

During middle age, households tend to be net savers. They are paying off loans accumulated when they were younger and saving for retirement. During retirement they spend more than they earn, running down their savings.

The permanent income hypothesis

Developed by Milton Friedman, this in many ways develops the insights of the life cycle hypothesis. Friedman argued that households base their spending decisions not on current income but on their PERMANENT INCOME. Broadly speaking, permanent income is average income over a lifetime. Average income over a lifetime can be influenced by a number of factors.
- An increase in wealth will increase the ability of households to spend money (i.e. it will increase their permanent income). Hence a rise in wealth will increase actual consumption over a lifetime.
- An increase in interest rates tends to lower both stock and share prices. This leads to a fall in wealth, a fall in permanent income and a fall in current consumption.
- An increase in interest rates also leads to future incomes being less valuable. One way of explaining this is to remember that a sum of money available in the future is worth less than the same sum available today. Another way is to consider borrowing. If interest rates rise, households will need either to earn more money or cut back on their spending in the future to pay back their loans. Therefore, the real value of their future income (i.e. their permanent income) falls if interest rates rise.
- Unexpected rises in wages will lead to an increase in permanent income.

Friedman argued that the long run APC from permanent income was 1. Households spend all their income over their lifetimes (indeed, Friedman defined permanent income as the income a household could spend without changing its wealth over a lifetime). Hence, the long run APC and the MPC are stable.

In the short run, however, wealth and interest rates change. Measured income also changes and much of this change is unexpected. Income which households receive but did not expect to earn is called transitory income. Initially, transitory income will be saved, as households decide what to do with the money. Then it is incorporated into permanent income. The MPC of the household will depend upon the nature of the extra income. If the extra income is, for instance, a permanent pay rise, the household is likely to spend most of the money. If, however, it is a temporary rise in income, like a £10 000 win on the pools, most of it will be saved and then gradually spent over a much longer period of time. Because the proportion of transitory income to current income changes from month to month, the propensity to consume from current income will vary too. So in the short run, the APC and the MPC are not constant. This contradicts the Keynesian hypothesis that current consumption is a stable function of current income.

Key terms

Average propensity to consume - the proportion of total income spent. It is calculated by C ÷ Y.

Average propensity to save - the proportion of a total income which is saved. It is calculated by S ÷ Y.

Consumption - total expenditure by households on goods and services over a period of time.

Consumption function - the relationship between the consumption of households and the factors which determine it.

Disposable income - household income over a period of time including state benefits, less direct taxes.

Durable goods - goods which are consumed over a long period of time, such as a television set or a car.

Marginal propensity to consume - the proportion of a change in income which is spent. It is calculated by ΔC ÷ ΔY.

Marginal propensity to save - the proportion of a change in income which is saved. It is calculated by ΔS ÷ ΔY.

Non-durable goods - goods which are consumed almost immediately like an ice-cream or a packet of washing powder.

Permanent income - the income a household could spend over its lifetime without reducing the value of its assets. This approximates to the average income of a household over its lifetime.

Savings function - the relationship between the saving of households and the factors which determine it.

Saving (personal) - the portion of households' disposable income which is not spent over a period of time.

Wealth effect - the change in consumption following a change in wealth.

Applied economics

Consumption in the UK

The composition of consumption expenditure

Total real consumption roughly doubled between 1964 and 2004. However, as Figure 31.3 shows, there were significant differences in the rate of growth of the components of expenditure. Real spending on food, for instance, only increased by approximately a half whilst spending on communication, which includes mobile phones, increased 12 fold. Real expenditure on alcoholic drink and tobacco remained constant whilst spending on restaurants and hotels increased 1.5 times. These changes partly reflect a number of different factors. As incomes increase, how consumers choose to spend the extra they earn differs from how they spend their existing income. So they choose not to spend very much extra on food, but quite a lot more on recreation and culture, which is reflected in the different income elasticities of demand for products. Some products, such as mobile phones, were simply not available in 1964. Increased spending reflects a desire to buy into these new technologies. Some changes also reflect changes prices. The price of clothing and footwear has fallen considerably over the past 30 years with globalisation of production. This has arguably led to a significant rise in total spending on clothing and footwear.

Consumption and income

Keynesian theory suggests that income is a major determinant of consumption. The evidence in Figure 31.4 would tend to support this theory. Over the period 1955 to 2004, real households' disposable income rose

3.9 times whilst real consumers' expenditure increased by 3.8 times. Keynesian theory would also suggest that the average propensity to consume declines as incomes rise over time. Figure 31.5 would tend not to support this. The average APC between 1963 and 1969 was 0.94. It fell slightly in the 1970s and 1980s, stabilised in the 1990s but then rose again between 2000-2004. Note that in Figure 31.5 income used to calculate the APC is defined as households disposable income **plus** an adjustment for the net equity of households in pension funds. It is the accounting convention used by the Office for National Statistics (ONS). This produces a slightly lower value of the APC than if only households' disposable income were included. There is considerable fluctuation of the APC, however, around these long term averages. For instance, there was a sharp rise in the APC between 1986 and 1988 during the Lawson boom, and between 1997 and 2004 in the prolonged upswing experienced at the time, whilst the APC fell to less than 0.9 in the two major recessions of 1980-82 and 1990-92. This would suggest that other factors can be important in determining consumption apart from income.

Other determinants of consumption

Economists in the 1960s and early 1970s were fairly confident that the relationship between consumption and income was highly stable. However, from the mid-1970s a number of key variables which can affect consumption were themselves subject to large changes and this had a small but significant effect on the average propensity to consume.

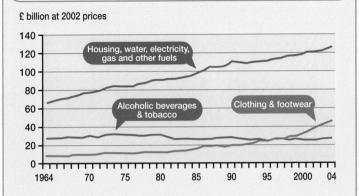

Figure 31.3 Composition of consumer expenditure, 1964-2004

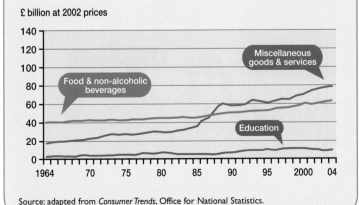

Source: adapted from *Consumer Trends*, Office for National Statistics.

Wealth A sharp appreciation in household wealth was a key feature of most of the 1980s. Figure 31.6 shows that share prices rose considerably between 1980 and 1987. This increase in stock market values was a key element in persuading households to increase their spending in 1986 and 1987. In October 1987, on 'Black Monday', world stock markets crashed and 25 per cent of the value of shares on the London Stock Exchange was wiped out. This helped knock consumer confidence and the subsequent poor performance of share prices was one factor which reduced the average propensity to consume in the late 1980s and early 1990s. Equally, UK stock markets put in a strong performance in the second half of the 1990s, fuelled towards the end by sharp rises in shares of companies related to the Internet. This contributed to strong growth in consumer spending whilst the fall in share prices following the bursting of the 'dot-com' bubble helped subdue consumer spending.

Many households do not own shares but the majority own their home. Again, in the mid-1980s the boom in house prices shown in Figure 31.7 was a major determinant of increased consumer spending during the Lawson boom. Equally, the fall in house prices in the early 1990s played an important role in dampening consumption. The stagnation in house prices which

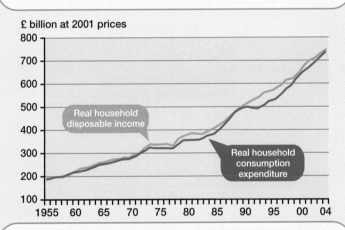

Figure 31.4 Consumption and disposable income, 1955-2004

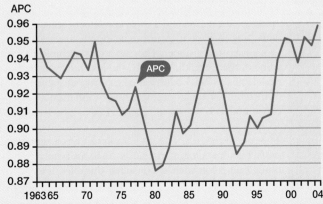

Figure 31.5 The average propensity to consume (APC)

Source: adapted from *Economic Trends Annual Supplement*, Office for National Statistics.

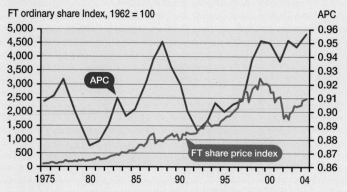

Figure 31.6 London Stock Market prices (FT Ordinary Share Index, 1962=100) and the average propensity to consume

Source: adapted from Economic Trends, Financial Statistics, Office for National Statistics.

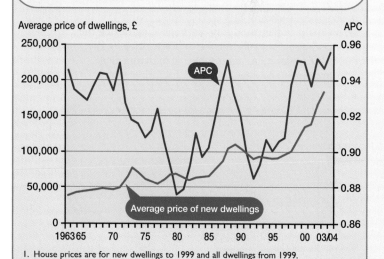

Figure 31.7 Average house prices¹, £ at 2002 prices, and the average propensity to consume

1. House prices are for new dwellings to 1999 and all dwellings from 1999.

Source: adapted from Economic Trends Annual Supplement, Office for National Statistics.

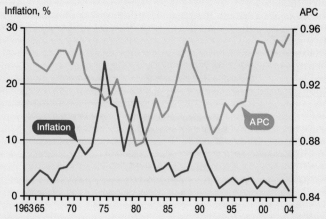

Figure 31.8 Inflation (RPI, % change year on year) and the average propensity to consume

Source: adapted from Economic Trends Annual Supplement, Office for National Statistics.

followed until 1996 helped break growth in consumer spending. Then, with a subsequent boom in house prices which lasted until 2004, there was strong growth in consumer spending.

Inflation Periods of high inflation tend to be marked by a falling APC and vice versa. Following the rise in inflation during the late 1980s, consumers reacted by increasing their savings and reducing the average propensity to consume. They wanted to rebuild the real value of their wealth. Equally, the low inflation of the mid-1990s to 2004 contributed to a rise in spending out of income. The relationship between inflation and consumption is shown in Figure 31.8.

The rate of interest The rate of interest has a significant impact on spending, particularly on items typically bought on credit such as consumer durables. Figure 31.9 shows that during the Lawson boom of 1986-88, relatively low interest rates helped fuel a consumer

spending boom. The raising of bank base rates to 15 per cent in 1988 and the period of high interest rates which followed was the key factor which helped reduce growth in consumer spending and pushed the economy into recession. The reduction of interest rates from 1992 onwards then helped the recovery during the rest of the 1990s. The changes in the rate of interest between 1995 and 2004 were relatively small compared to the changes in the 1980s. A rise in interest rates of 2 per cent does not have the same impact as a rise in interest rates of, say, 8 per cent seen during the 1980s. Therefore, the rises and falls in interest rates from 1995 onwards had an impact on consumer spending but these were relatively small. Certainly, they were not large enough to bring about reductions in total consumer spending.

Interest rates affect consumption in a number of ways. Higher interest rates makes borrowing more expensive and particular hits spending on consumer durables. It also makes it more expensive to buy a house using a mortgage. The rise in interest rates in the late 1980s helped bring about a crash in the housing market, with

Figure 31.9 Interest rates and the change in real consumer expenditure

house prices falling after 1989 in many areas of the country. This affected consumer confidence and reduced willingness to take on further debt. For most of the 1990s, consumers remained cautious about borrowing despite low interest rates. However, the late 1990s saw a sharp growth in spending as consumers became more confident that interest rates would not be driven sharply higher. The early 2000s saw a considerable increase in consumer debt, both to buy houses and finance purchase of goods.

Expectations Expectations can be a crucial determinant of consumption. In the 1980s, the Lawson boom was fuelled by expectations that the economy would grow at fast rates for the foreseeable future. There was much talk at the time about Britain's 'economic miracle'. Unfortunately, the boom was unsustainable. In the subsequent recession, consumers became very pessimistic about the future, particularly since unemployment climbed from 1.5 million in 1989 to 3 million in 1993. In the subsequent recovery, consumers remained cautious about taking on large amounts of new debt, fearing that a recession would recur. It was only in the late 1990s that consumer confidence was restored and this helped increase the rate of growth of consumer spending until 2004.

DataQuestion The determinants of saving

Figure 31.10 The average propensity to save (APS), 1975-2004

Source: adapted from *Economic Trends Annual Supplement*, Office for National Statistics.

You have been asked to write a report for a bank on the determinants of saving in the economy. Use the data here and in the Applied Economics section to construct your report.

- Briefly outline trends in saving and the APS since 1975.
- Briefly outline the main factors which affect saving in the economy.
- Produce a case study of the period 1975 to 2004 to illustrate your discussion.

Summary

1. Investment is the purchase of capital goods which are then used to create other goods and services. This differs from saving, which is the creation of financial obligations.
2. Marginal efficiency of capital theory suggests that investment is inversely related to the price of capital - the rate of interest.
3. Factors which shift the MEC or investment demand schedule include changes in the cost of capital goods, technological change, and changes in expectations or animal spirits.
4. The accelerator theory suggests that investment varies with the rate of change in income.
5. The past and current profitability of industry too may be more important than future rates of return on capital in determining current investment.

A definition of investment

Economists use the word INVESTMENT in a very precise way. Investment is the addition to the **capital stock** of the economy - factories, machines, offices and stocks of materials, used to produce other goods and services.

In everyday language, 'investment' and 'saving' are often used to mean the same thing. For instance, we talk about 'investing in the building society' or 'investing in shares'. For an economist, these two would be examples of saving. For an economist, investment only takes place if real products are created. To give two more examples:

- putting money into a bank account would be saving; the bank buying a computer to handle your account would be investment;
- buying shares in a new company would be saving; buying new machinery to set up a company would be investment.

A distinction can be made between **gross** and **net** investment. The value of the capital stock depreciates over time as it wears

out and is used up. This is called **depreciation** or **capital consumption**. Gross investment measures investment before depreciation, whilst net investment is gross investment less the value of depreciation. Depreciation in recent years in the UK has accounted for about three-quarters of gross investment. So only about one-quarter of gross investment represents an addition to the capital stock of the economy.

Another distinction made is between investment in **physical capital** and in **human capital**. Investment in human capital is investment in the education and training of workers. Investment in physical capital is investment in factories etc.

Investment is made both by the public sector and the private sector. Public sector investment is constrained by complex political considerations. In the rest of this unit, we will consider the determinants of private sector investment in physical capital.

Marginal efficiency of capital theory

Firms invest in order to make a profit. The profitability of investment projects varies. Some will make a high **rate of return**, some will yield a low rate of return and others will result in losses for the company. The rate of return on an investment project is also known as the MARGINAL EFFICIENCY OF CAPITAL (MEC).

At any point in time in the economy as whole, there exists a large number of possible individual investment projects. Table 32.1 shows an economy where there are £4bn of investment projects with an MEC of 20 per cent and above, £8bn with an MEC of 15 per cent and above and so on.

How much of this investment takes place will depend upon the rate of interest in the economy. If the rate of interest is 20 per cent, then firms having to borrow money will make a loss if they undertake any project with an MEC of less than 20 per cent. Hence, planned investment will be £4bn. If, on the other hand,

Question 1

Using the photograph, showing the interior of a UK bank, give examples of: (a) past investment in physical capital; (b) past investment in human capital; (c) saving; (d) capital consumption.

Table 32.1 Planned investment and the marginal efficiency of capital

Marginal efficiency of capital (% per year)	Planned investment (£bn per year)
20	4
15	8
10	12
5	16

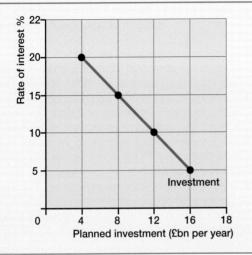

Figure 32.1 The planned investment schedule
A fall in the rate of interest will make more investment projects profitable. Planned investment will rise if the rate of interest falls.

Table 32.2 Average cost of funds (as % of sales) of top spending companies on research and development

	Chemicals	Pharmaceuticals	Engineering	Electronics and electrical equipment
Japan	2.1%	2.8%	2.2%	1.5%
Germany	3.8%	5.1%	2.1%	2.9%
France	5.0%	n.a.	2.5%	2.8%
US	5.9%	9.5%	3.0%	4.2%
UK	5.6%	12.5%	3.1%	5.8%

Source: adapted from DTI, R&D Scoreboard.

The UK's high interest rates in the 1980s and 1990s put British industry at a severe disadvantage. It means that fewer projects are worth taking on because the thresholds for returns are higher. Table 32.2 shows the cost of investment funds measured as a percentage of sales revenues for firms in different industries. In all these industries, the UK has the highest or nearly the highest cost of funds.

Source: adapted from the *Financial Times*.

(a) Explain, using a diagram, why high interest rates may have put British industry at a disadvantage in investment.
(b) During the 1990s and 2000s, UK interest rates have been above those in the rest of the EU. What are the possible implications for UK investment if Britain were to join the euro?

the rate of interest is 5 per cent, then all investment projects with an MEC of 5 per cent or more will be profitable. Hence, planned investment will be £16bn. So the conclusion of marginal efficiency of capital theory is that planned investment in the economy will rise if the rate of interest falls. This relationship, using the figures from Table 32.1, is shown in Figure 32.1.

In our explanation above, the rate of interest was assumed to be the rate of interest at which firms have to borrow money. However, most investment by firms in the UK is financed from RETAINED PROFIT. This is profit which is not used to pay dividends to shareholders or taxes to the government, but is kept back by the firm for its own use. This does not alter the relationship between the rate of interest and investment. Firms which keep back profits have a choice about what to do with the money. They can either invest it or save it. The higher the rate of interest on savings, such as placing the money on loan with banks or other financial institutions, the more attractive saving the money becomes and the less attractive becomes investment. Put another way, the higher the rate of interest, the higher the **opportunity cost** of investment and hence the lower will be the amount of planned investment in the economy.

Factors which shift the planned investment schedule

Cost of capital goods If the price of capital goods rises, then the expected rate of return on investment projects will fall if firms cannot pass on the increase in higher prices. So increases in the price of capital goods, all other things being equal, will reduce planned investment. This is shown by a shift to the left in the planned investment schedule in Figure 32.2.

Technological change Technological change will make new capital equipment more productive than previous equipment. This will raise the rate of return on investment projects, all other things being equal. Hence, technological change such as the introduction of computer aided machinery will raise the level of planned investment at any given rate of interest. This is shown by a shift to the right in the planned investment schedule.

Expectations Businesses have to form views about the future. When calculating the possible rate of return on future

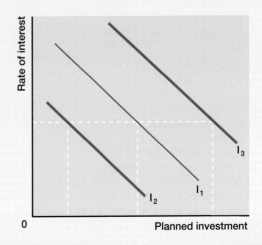

Figure 32.2 Shifts in planned investment
An increase in the cost of planned capital will reduce the rate of return on investment projects. Therefore at any given rate of interest, planned investment will fall. This is shown by a shift to the left in the planned investment schedule. Changes in technology which make capital more productive raise the level of planned investment, shown by a shift to the right of the schedule.

Assume that I_1 in Figure 32.2 shows the planned investment schedule for the UK. Is it more likely to shift to I_2 or I_3 if: (a) there is a rise in the real prices of commercial property; (b) the government announces a billion pound programme to encourage the use of micro-computers in industry; (c) the economy grew much faster than expected last year and forecasts show this set to continue; (d) the price of computers and computer aided tools falls; (e) prices on the New York Stock Exchange crash?

investment, they have to make assumptions about future costs and future revenues. If managers become more pessimistic about the future, they will expect the rate of return on investment projects to fall and hence planned investment will be reduced. If, on the other hand, they become more optimistic their expectations of the rates of return on investment projects will tend to rise. Hence planned investment will rise and this will be shown by a shift to the right in the investment schedule. Keynes called the expectations of businessmen their 'animal spirits'. He believed that expectations were crucial in determining changes in investment, and that these expectations could change suddenly.

Government policy Government can play a crucial role in stimulating private sector investment. This will be discussed in more detail in unit 38.

The accelerator theory

The ACCELERATOR THEORY of investment suggests that the level of planned investment varies with the rate of change of income or output rather than with the rate of interest. To see why this might be the case, consider Table 32.3.

Table 32.3

Year	Annual output £m	Number of machines required	Investment in machines
1	10	10	0
2	10	10	0
3	12	12	2
4	15	15	3
5	15	15	0
6	14	14	0

A firm producing toys needs one machine to produce £1m of output per year. The machines last 20 years and for the purpose of this example we will assume that none of the firm's machines need replacing over the time period being considered (so we are considering net and not gross investment). Initially in year 1 the firm has £10m worth of orders. It already has 10 machines and therefore no investment takes place. In year 2, orders remain unchanged and so again the firm has no need to invest.

However, in year 3 orders increase to £12m. The firm

now needs to invest in another two machines if it is to fulfil orders. Orders increase to £15m in year 4. The firm needs to purchase another 3 machines to increase its capital stock to 15 machines. In year 5, orders remain unchanged at £15m and so investment returns to zero. In year 6, orders decline to £14m. The firm has too much capital stock and therefore does not invest.

In this example investment takes place when there is a change in real spending in the economy. If there is no change in spending, then there is no investment. What is more, the changes in spending lead to much bigger changes in investment. For instance, the increase in spending of 25 per cent in year 4 (from £12m to £15m) resulted in an increase in investment of 50 per cent (from 2 machines to 3 machines). In reality, it should be remembered that about 75 per cent of gross investment is replacement investment which is far less likely than net investment to be affected by changes in income. Even so, the accelerator theory predicts that investment spending in the economy is likely to be more volatile than spending as a whole.

The simplest form of the accelerator theory can be expressed as:

$$I_t = a\ (Y_t - Y_{t-1})$$

where It is investment in time period t, $Y_t - Y_{t-1}$ is the change in real income during year t and a is the accelerator coefficient or CAPITAL-OUTPUT RATIO. The capital-output ratio is the amount of capital needed in the economy to produce a given quantity of goods. So if £10 of capital is needed to produce £2 of goods, then the capital-output ratio is 5. The theory therefore predicts that changes in the level of investment are related to past changes in income.

This accelerator model is very simplistic. There are a number of factors which limit the predictive power of the model.

● The model assumes that the capital-output ratio is constant over time. However, it can change. In the long term, new technology can make capital more productive. In the shorter term, the capital-output ratio is likely to be higher in a recession when there is excess capacity than in a boom.

● Expectations may vary. Businesses may choose not to satisfy extra demand if they believe that the demand will be short lived. There is little point in undertaking new investment if the extra orders will have disappeared within six months. On the other hand, businesses may anticipate higher output. Despite constant income, they may believe that a boom is imminent and invest to be ahead of their rivals.

● Time lags involved are likely to be extremely complicated. Changes in investment are likely to respond to changes in income over several time periods and not just one.

● Firms may have excess capacity (i.e. they can produce more with current levels of capital than they are at present doing). If there is an increase in income, firms will respond not by investing but by bringing back into use capital which has been mothballed or by utilising fully equipment which had been underutilised.

● The capital goods industry will be unable to satisfy a surge in demand. Some investment will therefore either be cancelled or delayed.

Despite these qualifications, evidence suggests that net investment is to some extent linked to past changes in income. However, the link is relatively weak and therefore other influences must be at work to determine investment.

Profits

About 70 per cent of industrial and commercial investment in the UK is financed from retained profit. Some economists argue that many firms do not consider the opportunity cost of investment. They retain profit but rarely consider that it might be better used saved in financial assets. They automatically assume that the money will be spent on investment related to the activities of the firm. The rate of interest is then much less important in determining investment. Investment becomes crucially dependent upon two factors.

● The amount of retained profit available. So the poor investment record of companies in the UK compared to many competitors overseas over the past 50 years may be due to the fact that UK companies pay out a larger percentage of their profits in dividends to their owners. This leaves less for investment.

● The availability of suitable investment projects. If firms do not have suitable investment projects to hand, they will bank the cash or pay it out to shareholders in dividends. New technology or new products can act as a spur to investment on this view.

Question 4

$$I_t = 2 (Y_t - Y_{t-1})$$

(a) In year 0 income was £100m. In subsequent years, it grew by 5 per cent per annum. Calculate the level of investment in years 1 to 5.

(b) Compare what would happen to investment in each year if income grew instead by (i) 10 per cent and (ii) 2.5 per cent.

Key terms

Accelerator theory - the theory that the level of planned investment is related to past changes in income.
Capital-output ratio - the ratio between the amount of capital needed to produce a given quantity of goods and the level of output.
Investment - the addition to the capital stock of the economy.
Marginal efficiency of capital - the rate of return on the last unit of capital employed.
Retained profit - profit kept back by a firm for its own use which is not distributed to shareholders or used to pay taxation.

Applied economics

Investment in the UK

The composition of investment

Gross investment is called **gross fixed capital formation** (GFCF) in UK official statistics. Figure 32.3 shows the composition of investment in 1979 and 2004. Significant changes in this composition are apparent from the data.

● In real terms, investment in housing has risen from £30.9 bn to £38.8 bn. However, as a percentage of total investment, it has fallen one third, from 33 per cent to 22 per cent. Within these totals, there has been a significant fall in public sector housing (mainly council housing), but a rise in private sector housing investment. This reflects changes in government policy. Between 1945 and 1979, government, through local councils, invested heavily in houses for rent. The Conservative governments of 1979-1997, however, reversed the policy. It virtually halted all new building of council houses and introduced a right to buy for council tenants. Its justification was that local councils were highly inefficient in managing their stock of houses. Moreover, everyone should be encouraged to buy their own home. Buying rather than renting helped create a 'property owning democracy' where people had a stake in the economy and were responsible for making decisions about their own homes. With the stock of council houses in decline, households had to turn to the private sector for new housing and this is one of the reasons for the increase in private sector investment in housing. However, there is a debate about whether investment in private sector housing today is large enough. House prices from 1995 onwards more than doubled, most of that reflecting increases in the price of building land rather than increases in the cost of building houses. The number of households is increasing due to factors such as the increase in the number of single elderly people in the population. Also many home buyers would also like to live in larger properties than they can currently afford. Investment in new housing is severely constrained by government planning regulations and green belt laws. It could be argued that investment in housing would be much higher today if planning restrictions were relaxed.

● Investment in 'other machinery and equipment' has roughly trebled compared to an approximate doubling in real GDP. This investment ranges from milking machines to machine lathes to computers and desks.

● Investment in 'other new buildings and structures', has more than doubled, outpacing the percentage growth in

Figure 32.3 *Gross domestic fixed capital formation by type of asset, 1979 and 2004 (£ billion at 2002 prices)*

Other new buildings and structures

Intangible fixed assets

Other new buildings and structures

Transport equipment

£2.9 bn   £2.1 bn   £14.3 bn   £6.2 bn

£13.9 bn   £64.6 bn

£23.4 bn   £57.1 bn

£7.5 bn   £19.2 bn   £3.3 bn   £35.5 bn

Other machinery and equipment

Dwellings, private   Dwellings, public   Dwellings, private

1979
Total investment £94.7 bn (at 2002 prices)
GDP at market prices £620.6 bn

2004
Total investment £181 bn (at 2002 prices)
GDP at market prices £1 108.9 bn

Source: adapted from *Economic Trends Annual Supplement*, *Monthly Digest of Statistics*, Office for National Statistics.

real GDP. This includes new factories and offices.
● Investment in transport equipment has barely changed in real terms, but as a proportion of total investment has nearly halved. This is investment in ships and aircraft.

Table 32.4 shows how the composition of investment has changed by industry. 1989 was an exceptional year for investment. The Lawson boom of 1986-88 had left many firms short of capacity. They had therefore sharply increased their spending on investment. Many firms came to regret this because the economy then went into a deep recession, leaving them with excess capacity. In 1992, real investment spending in the UK was 11 per cent down on its peak 1989 level and by 1996 had barely increased on its 1989 level. Firms were reluctant to invest either because they had continued spare capacity or they feared that the economy would fail to recover. The prolonged period of economic growth of the late 1990s and early 2000s, however, saw investment increase and by 2004 was nearly 40 per cent above its 1989 level.

The pattern of investment spending to some extent reflects trends in output between sectors

Table 32.4 *GDP and gross fixed capital formation by industry*

	£ million, at 2002 prices			% change
	1989	1996	2003	1989-2003
GDP at market prices	767 415	879 679	1 07 4 751	40.0
Total gross fixed capital formation	129 470	131 220	178 993	38.3
of which				
Construction	2 561	1 039	4 594	79.4
Education, health & social work	5 904	6 470	8 748	48.2
Transport, storage & communication	15 222	15 999	21 431	40.8
Investment in dwellings etc.	40 822	31 225	49 520	21.3
Other services	8 448	7 614	10 098	19.5
Public administration & defence	9 946	9 658	10 572	6.3
Distribution, hotels & catering	16 854	15 200	17 382	3.1
Business services & finance	31 813	23 737	28 874	-9.2
Electricity, gas & water supply	5 616	5 200	5 032	-10.4
Agriculture, hunting, forestry and fishing	2 879	3 245	2 505	-13.0
Mining & quarrying	7 276	4 776	4 029	-44.6
Manufacturing	22 388	21 097	12 250	-45.3

Source: adapted from *United Kingdom National Accounts* (Blue Book), Office for National Statistics.

Table 32.5 Determinants of investment

	£ million, at 2002 prices			Per cent
	Private sector investment	Annual change in GDP	Company profits	Interest rate[1]
1979	38.2	16.3	136.9	13.7
1980	43.2	-12.8	129.6	16.3
1981	43.3	-8.8	127.6	13.3
1982	47.4	11.5	140.3	11.9
1983	51.5	21.6	155.6	9.9
1984	58.6	16.3	156.9	9.8
1985	64.4	23.1	166.9	12.2
1986	68.5	26.5	166.3	10.9
1987	79.0	31.7	172.8	9.7
1988	96.2	36.3	180.6	10.1
1989	111.3	16.5	184.1	13.8
1990	114.3	5.7	173.4	14.8
1991	105.2	-10.7	157.3	11.7
1992	100.6	2.2	160.3	9.6
1993	101.0	18.9	175.4	6.0
1994	108.3	35.2	197.4	5.5
1995	117.4	23.8	201.9	6.7
1996	126.3	23.3	215.9	6.0
1997	133.6	27.8	219.3	6.6
1998	150.9	29.4	221.6	7.2
1999	155.5	28.4	214.6	5.3
2000	161.8	39.0	217.1	6.0
2001	165.7	22.4	212.3	5.1
2002	172.6	20.6	227.3	4.0
2003	175.9	26.4	238.3	3.7
2004	190.1	34.0	249.0	4.4

1. London clearing banks, base rate: annual average.

Source: adapted from *Economic Trends Annual Supplement; Monthly Digest of Statistics,* Office for National Statistics.

The determinants of investment

Economic theory suggests that there may be several determinants of private sector investment. The accelerator theory suggests that invest is a function of pays changes in income. Neo-classical theory argues that the rate of interest is the important determinant, whilst other theories point to the current level of profits as significant.

The evidence tends to support the ideas that the level of investment is determined by a number of variables. In Table 32.5, there is some weak correlation between investment and changes in income, profits and the rate of interest. However, these variables tend to move together through the business or trade cycle and so changes in investment may in themselves affect the three variables in the data.

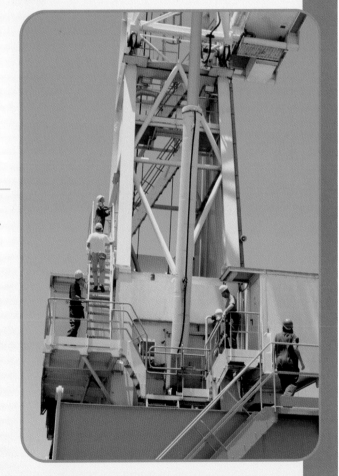

of the economy. Primary industries, including agriculture and mining, have seen their share of output decline between 1989 and 2003. As a consequence, investment in these industries has been relatively static or fallen. Manufacturing output has increased only by a few per cent but real investment in manufacturing has almost halved. Investment by the construction industry has increased by 80 per cent, reflecting particularly an increase in construction of retail and office space. The 50 per cent increase in education, health and social work, investment mainly in new buildings and equipment, reflects growing spending in public services, particularly after the election of the Labour government in 1997.

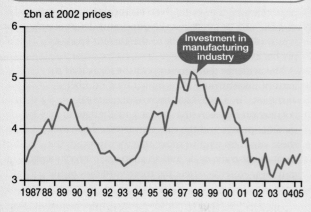

Figure 32.4 Investment by and output of manufacturing industry, and GDP, quarterly (£ billion at 2002 prices)

£bn at 2002 prices — Investment in manufacturing industry

£bn at 2002 prices — Output of manufacturing industry

£bn at 2002 prices — GDP at market prices

Source: adapted from *Economic Trends Annual Supplement, Financial Statistics,* Office for National Statistics.

Figure 32.5 Short term interest rates[1] and investment by manufacturing industry, quarterly

Interest rates, %   Investment, £bn at 2002 prices

Interest rates

Investment in manufacturing industry

1 Average quarterly Treasury bill rate
Source: adapted from *Economic Trends Annual Supplement, Financial Statistics,* Office for National Statistics.

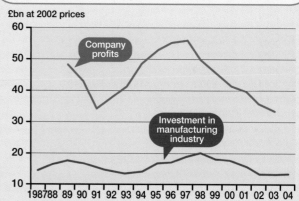

Figure 32.6 Profits of and investment by manufacturing industry, yearly, (£ billion at 2002 prices)

£bn at 2002 prices

Company profits

Investment in manufacturing industry

Source: adapted from *National Income Blue Book, Monthly Digest of Statistics,* Office for National Statistics.

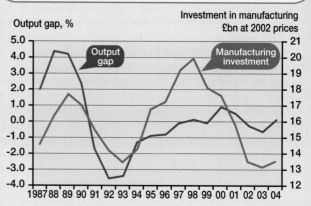

Figure 32.7 The UK output gap[1] and investment by manufacturing industry

Output gap, %   Investment in manufacturing £bn at 2002 prices

Output gap

Manufacturing investment

1 Deviation of actual GDP from trend GDP as a percentage of trend GDP.
Source: adapted from *Monthly Digest of Statistics,* Office for National Statistics; *Economic Outlook,* OECD.

1. Briefly outline the trends in manufacturing investment between 1987 and 2004.
2. Taking each possible determinant of investment (a) explain why economic theory suggests there is a link between the two variables and (b) evaluate whether the evidence from 1987 to 2004 supports the theory.
3. A manufacturing company is reviewing its investment policies. Evaluate which macro-economic variable is the most important variable that it should take into consideration when making an investment decision.

33 Aggregate demand

Summary

1. The aggregate demand curve is downward sloping. It shows the relationship between the price level and equilibrium output in the economy.
2. A movement along the aggregate demand curve shows how equilibrium income will change if there is a change in the price level.
3. A shift in the aggregate demand curve is caused by a change in variables such as consumption and exports at any given price level.
4. Keynesian economists argue that the aggregate demand curve is steep (i.e. changes in the price level have little effect on equilibrium income). Classical economists argue that the aggregate demand curve is much shallower (i.e. increases in the prices will significantly depress the equilibrium level of income).

Aggregate demand

In unit 4, there was a discussion of what determined the demand for an individual product. Demand was defined as the quantity that would be bought at any given price. In this unit, we will consider what determines AGGREGATE demand. 'Aggregate' in economics means a 'total' or 'added up' amount. AGGREGATE DEMAND is the total of all demands or expenditures in the economy at any given price.

It was explained in unit 25 that national expenditure was one of the three ways of calculating national income, usually measured as GDP. National expenditure is made up of four components.

- **Consumption (C).** This is spending by households on goods and services (☞ unit 31).
- **Investment (I).** This is spending by firms on investment goods (☞ unit 32).
- **Government spending (G).** This includes current spending, for instance on wages and salaries. It also includes spending by government on investment goods like new roads or new schools.
- **Exports minus imports (X-M).** Foreigners spend money on goods produced in the DOMESTIC ECONOMY. Hence it is part of national expenditure. However, households, firms and governments also spend money on goods produced abroad. For instance, a UK household might buy a car produced in France. Or a British firm might use components imported from the Far East in a computer which is sold to Germany. These imported goods do not form part of national output and do not contribute to national income. So, because C, I, G and X all include spending on imported goods, imports (M) must be taken away from C + I + G + X to arrive at a figure for national expenditure.

National expenditure (E) can therefore be calculated using the formula:

$$E = C + I + G + X - M$$

The aggregate demand curve

The AGGREGATE DEMAND CURVE shows the relationship between the price level and the level of real expenditure in the economy. Figure 33.1 shows an aggregate demand (AD) curve. The price level is put on the vertical axis whilst real output is put on the horizontal axis.

The **price level** is the average level of prices in the economy.

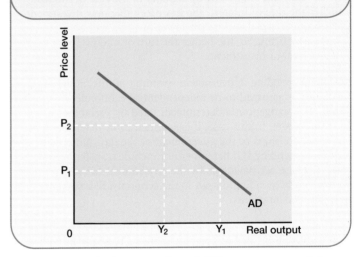

Figure 33.1 The aggregate demand curve
A rise in the price level will lead, via a rise in interest rates, to a fall in the equilibrium level of national income and therefore of national output. Hence the aggregate demand curve is downward sloping.

Governments calculate a number of different measures of the price level. In the UK, for instance, the most widely quoted measure is the **Retail Price Index**, figures for which are published every month and are widely reported in the news. A change in the price level is **inflation** (☞ unit 28).

Real output on the horizontal axis must equal real expenditure and real income. This is because, in the circular flow model of the economy, these are three different ways of measuring the same flow. The aggregate demand curve plots the level of expenditure where the economy would be in an equilibrium position at each price level, all other things being equal.

Demand curves are nearly always downward sloping. Why is the aggregate demand curve the same shape? One simple answer is to consider what happens to a household budget if prices rise. If a household is on a fixed income, then a rise in average prices will mean that they can buy fewer goods and services than before. The higher the price level in the economy, the less they can afford to buy. So it is with the national economy. The higher the price, the less goods and services will be demanded in the whole economy.

A more sophisticated explanation considers what happens to the different components of expenditure when prices rise.

Consumption Consumption expenditure is influenced

by the **rate of interest** in the economy (☞ unit 31). When prices increase, consumers (and firms) need more money to buy the same number of goods and services as before. One way of getting more money is to borrow it and so the demand for borrowed funds will rise. However, if there is a fixed supply of money available for borrowing from banks and building societies, the price of borrowed funds will rise. This price is the rate of interest. A rise in interest rates leads to a fall in consumption, particularly of durable goods such as cars which are commonly bought on credit.

Another way a rise in the price level affects consumption is through the **wealth effect** (☞ unit 31). A rise in the price level leads to the real value of an individual consumer's wealth being lower. For instance, £100 000 at today's prices will be worth less in real terms in a year's time if average prices have increased 20 per cent over the 12 months. A fall in real wealth will result in a fall in consumer spending.

Investment As has just been explained, a rise in prices, all other things being equal, leads to a rise in interest rates in the economy. Investment, according to marginal efficiency of capital theory (☞ unit 32), is affected by changes in the rate of interest. The higher the rate of interest, the less profitable new investment projects become and therefore the fewer projects will be undertaken by firms. So, the higher the rate of interest, the lower will be the level of investment.

Government spending Government spending in this model of the economy is assumed to be independent of economic variables. It is exogenously determined, fixed by variables outside the model. In this case, it is assumed to be determined by the political decisions of the government of the day. Note that government spending (G) here does not include transfer payments. These are payments by the government for which there is no corresponding output in the economy, like welfare benefits or student grants.

Exports and imports A higher price level in the UK means that foreign firms will be able to compete more successfully in the UK economy. For instance, if British shoe manufacturers put up their prices by 20 per cent, whilst foreign shoe manufacturers keep their prices the same, then British shoe manufacturers will become less competitive and more foreign shoes will be imported. Equally, British shoe manufacturers will find it more difficult to export charging higher prices. So a higher UK price level, with price levels in other economies staying the same, will lead to a fall in UK exports.

Hence, aggregate demand falls as prices rise, first, because increases in interest rates reduce consumption and investment and, second, because a loss of international comptitiveness at the new higher prices will reduce exports and increase imports.

Question 1

In 1975, inflation rose to a peak of 24.1 per cent. Real GDP fell in both 1974 and 1975. In 1980, inflation rose to a peak of 18.0 per cent and real GDP fell in 1980 and 1981. In 1990, inflation rose to a peak of 9.5 per cent. GDP fell in 1991 and 1992.

(a) How might economic theory account for this?

Shifts in the AD curve

The aggregate demand (AD) curve shows the relationship between the price level and the equilibrium level of real income and output. A change in the price level results in a **movement along** the AD curve. Higher prices lead to falls in aggregate demand.

Shifts in the aggregate demand curve will occur if there is a change in any other relevant variable apart from the price level. When the AD curve shifts, it shows that there is a change in real output at any given price level. In Figure 33.2, the shift in the AD curve from AD_1 to AD_2 shows that at a price level of P, real output increases from Y_1 to Y_2. There are a number of variables which can lead to a shift of the AD curve. Some of these variables are real variables, such as changes in the willingness of consumers to spend. Others are changes in **monetary variables** such as the rate of interest.

Consumption A number of factors might increase consumption spending at any given level of prices, shifting the AD curve from AD_1 to AD_2 in Figure 33.2. For instance, unemployment may fall, making consumers less afraid that they will lose their jobs and more willing to borrow money to spend on consumer durables. The government might reduce interest rates, again encouraging borrowing for durables. A substantial rise in stock market prices will increase consumer wealth which in turn may lead to an increase in spending. A reduction in the relative numbers of high saving 45-60 year olds in the population will increase the **average propensity to consume** (☞ unit 31) of the whole economy. New technology which creates new consumer products can lead to an increase in consumer spending as households want to buy these new products. A fall in income tax would increase consumers' disposable income, leading to a rise in consumption (☞ unit 31).

Investment One factor which would increase investment spending at any given level of prices, pushing the AD curve from

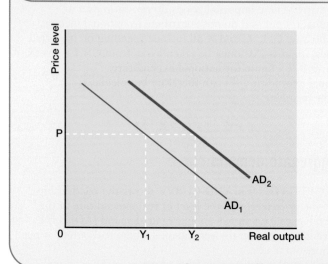

Figure 33.2 A shift in the aggregate demand curve
An increase in consumption, investment, government spending or net exports, given a constant price level, will lead to a shift in the aggregate demand curve from AD_1 to AD_2.

Explain, using a diagram, the likely effect of the following on the aggregate demand curve for the UK.

(a) The increase in real investment expenditure between 2000 and 2005.
(b) The pushing up of interest rates by the government from 7.5 per cent in May 1987 to 15 per cent in October 1989.
(c) The large cuts in taxes in the Lawson Budget of 1987.
(d) The 50 per cent per cent fall in London Stock Market prices (FTSE 100) between December 1999 and January 2003.
(e) The fall in the savings ratio from a peak of 11.5 per cent in 1992 to 4.2 per cent in 2004.
(f) The increase in planned government spending on education and health care by the Labour government 2000-2007.
(g) The more than 25 per cent rise in the average value of the pound against other currencies between 1996 and 2000.

AD_1 to AD_2 in Figure 33.2, would be an increase in business confidence - an increase in 'animal spirits' as John Maynard Keynes once put it. This increase in business confidence could have come about, for instance, because the economy was going into boom. A fall in interest rates ordered by the government would lead to a rise in investment. An increase in company profitability would give firms more retained profit to use for investment. A fall in taxes on profits (corporation tax in the UK) would lead to the rate of return on investment projects rising, leading to a rise in investment.

Government spending A change of government policy might lead to a rise in government spending at any given level of

prices, pushing the AD curve to the right from AD_1 to AD_2 in Figure 33.2.

Exports and imports A fall in the exchange rate of the currency will make exports more competitive and imports less competitive. So exports should rise and imports fall, pushing the AD curve to the right in Figure 33.2. An improvement in the quality of domestically-made goods would again increase domestic competitiveness and increase exports and reduce imports.

The multiplier

If there is an increase in, say, investment of £1, what will be the final increase in national income? John Maynard Keynes argued in his most famous book, *The General Theory of Employment, Interest and Money*, published in 1936, that national income would increase by more than £1 because of the MULTIPLIER EFFECT.

To understand why there might be a multiplier effect, consider what would happen if firms increased spending on new factories by £100m. Firms would pay contractors to build the factories. This £100m would be an increase in aggregate demand. The contractor would use the money in part to pay its workers on the project. The workers would spend the money, on everything from food to holidays. This spending would be an addition to national income. Assume that £10m is spent on food. Food manufacturers would in turn pay their workers who would spend their incomes on a variety of products, increasing national income further. John Maynard Keynes argued that this multiplier effect would increase jobs in the economy. Every job directly created by firms through extra spending would indirectly create other jobs in the economy.

This process can be shown using the **circular flow of income model** (☞ unit 25). Assume that households spend 9/10 ths of their gross income. The other 1/10 th is either saved or paid to the government in the form of taxes. Firms increase their

Figure 33.3 The circular flow of income

Households

Saving, taxes and imports

10 + 9 + 8.1 + ... = 100

Initial investment

Consumption

100 + 90 + 81 + 72.9 ... = 1000

Firms

spending by £100m, money which is used to build new factories. In Figure 33.3, this initial £100m is is shown in stage 1 flowing into firms. The money then flows out again as it is distributed in the form of wages and profits back to households. Households spend the money but remember that there are **withdrawals** of 0.1 of income because of savings and taxes. So only £90m flows back round the economy in stage 2 to firms. Then firms pay £90m back to households in wages and profits. In the third stage, £81m is spent by households with £19 million leaking out of the circular flow. This process carries on with smaller and smaller amounts being added to national income as the money flows round the economy. Eventually, the initial £100m extra government spending leads to a final increase in national income of £1 000m. In this case, the value of the MULTIPLIER is 10.

If leakages from the circular flow in Figure 33.3 had been larger, less of the increase in investment would have continued to flow round the economy. For instance, if leakages had been 0.8 of income, then only £20m (0.2 x £100m) would have flowed round the economy in the second stage. In the third stage, it would have been £4m (0.2 x £20m). The final increase in national income following the initial £100m increase in investment spending would have been £125m.

The multiplier model states that the higher the leakages from the circular flow, the smaller will be the increase in income which continues to flow round the economy at each stage following an initial increase in spending. Hence, the higher the leakages, the smaller the value of the multiplier.

The multiplier effect and increases in government spending and exports

Extra investment spending is only one possible reason why there might be a multiplier effect on aggregate demand. Any increase of the **injections** into the circular flow will lead to a multiple increase in income in the economy. So, an increase in government spending would lead to a multiple increase in income. So too would an increase in export spending.

The shape of the aggregate demand curve

Economists disagree about the shape of the AD curve. **Keynesian economists** argue that the curve is relatively steep, i.e. that changes in the price level have little impact on aggregate demand, as shown in Figure 33.4(a). They argue that increases in the price level have little impact on interest rates. In turn, changes in interest rates have little impact on consumption and investment expenditures. Keynesians argue that the main determinant of consumption is disposable income (☞ unit 31) whilst the main determinants of investment are past changes in income (☞ unit 32). So the link between changes in the price level and aggregate demand is very weak.

Classical economists argue that the link between the price level and aggregate demand is a strong one as shown in Figure 33.4(b). Classical economists are economists who are strongly influenced by the economic theories developed before Keynes. They look back to the nineteenth century when the basics of micro-economics were developed. In particular, they tend to argue that markets usually work efficiently and that labour market failure is relatively unimportant. In this case, they argue that increases in the price level have a strong impact

on interest rates. In turn, changes in interest rates have a considerable impact on consumption and investment. Interest rates are much more important, they argue, in determining expenditure on consumer durables than Keynesian economists would suggest. Also, investment is strongly influenced by interest rates - the **marginal efficiency of capital theory** (☞ unit 32).

Important note

Aggregate demand analysis and aggregate supply analysis outlined in units 33 and 34 are more complex than demand and supply analysis in an individual market. You may already have noticed, for instance, that a change in interest rates could lead to a movement along the aggregate demand curve or lead to a shift in the curve. Similarly, an increase in consumption could lead to a movement along or a shift in the curve. To distinguish between movements along and shifts in the curve it is important to consider what has caused the change in aggregate demand.

If the change has come about because the price level has changed, then there is a movement **along** the AD curve. For instance, a rise in the price level causes a rise in interest rates. This leads to a fall in consumption. This is shown by a movement up the curve.

If, however, interest rates or consumer spending have changed for a different reason than because prices have changed, then there will be a **shift** in the AD curve. A government putting up interest rates at a given price level would lead to a shift in the curve.

Figure 33.4 The responsiveness of equilibrium real output to changes in the price level
Keynesians argue that the AD curve is relatively steep because real output changes little when the price level changes. Classical economists argue that the AD curve is relatively shallow because price changes have a significant effect on real output.

(a)

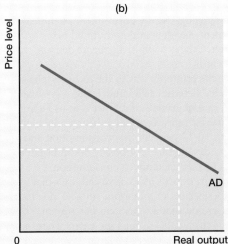

(b)

Key terms

Aggregate - the sum or total.
Aggregate demand - is the total of all demands or expenditures in the economy at any given price.
Aggregate demand curve - shows the relationship between the price level and equilibrium national income. As the price level rises the equilibrium level of national income falls.
Domestic economy - the economy of a single country.

Multiplier - the figure used to multiply a change in autonomous expenditure, such as investment, to find the final change in income. It is the ratio of the final change in income to the initial change in autonomous expenditure.
Multiplier effect - an increase in investment or any other autonomous expenditure will lead to an even greater increase in income.

Applied economics

Aggregate demand 1979-2005

In 1979, a new Conservative government under Margaret Thatcher was elected into office. The economy had been through very difficult times in the 1970s. Imported inflation had been a major problem and trade unions had militantly pushed up wages in an attempt to maintain the real value of their members' earnings. On coming into office, she faced rapidly rising inflation. Partly this was because of a world oil crisis where OPEC was ultimately able to increase the price of oil threefold between 1978 and 1982. Partly it was because wage inflation had taken off again.

Margaret Thatcher was strongly influenced by the relatively new and fashionable monetarist idea that

inflation was solely caused by excessive increases in the money supply. If the money supply increased, this pushed up aggregate demand. Too much money, and so excess demand, chasing too few goods could only lead to increases in prices. To reduce the rate of growth of the money supply, she raised interest rates from 12 per cent in May 1979 to 17 per cent in November 1979 as Figure 33.5 shows. High interest rates of over 10 per cent, which were maintained for four years, depressed both consumption and investment, reducing aggregate demand. The economy went into a major recession, with unemployment climbing from 1.3 million in 1979 to 3.12 million in 1983. As Figure 33.6 shows, a negative output gap of 7 per cent of GDP opened up in 1981. Aggregate demand was far below its trend level.

As interest rates fell, the economy began to recover and aggregate demand began to rise again. Part of the monetarist philosophy was that excessive growth of the money supply was usually caused by excessive government borrowing. So the government attempted to reduce government spending and even raised taxes in 1981. This limited the growth in aggregate demand from 1981 onwards.

Nevertheless, the economy was in the recovery phase of the trade cycle. Between 1983 and 1988, it grew at above its trend rate of growth of 2.5 per cent as Figure 33.6 shows. Interest rates were still at historically high levels, averaging 10-12 per cent, but consumption and investment grew despite this. A housing boom began to develop, which further encouraged consumption.

By 1987, the government had convinced itself that Britain was experiencing an 'economic miracle' due to its economic policies and that a 4 per cent per annum growth rate was sustainable in the long term. There was a substantial tax cutting budget in March 1987 which saw the top rate of income tax fall from 60 per cent to 40 per cent. Lower taxes led to higher disposable income and hence higher consumption. Inflation remained low, so households did not have to increase their savings levels to rebuild the real value of their wealth. The stock market also saw share prices increasing, adding to household's wealth. Unemployment fell sharply, halving from 3 million to 11.2 million between 1986 and 1989. All these factors led to increasing levels of consumer confidence. Households were more willing than before to take out loans and were less willing to save.

By 1988, the economy was operating at 5.5 per cent above its productive potential. Firms sharply increased their investment spending and planned to take advantage of the many profitable opportunities that were now available. In the meantime, importers took advantage of

the UK's inability to satisfy domestic demand and a dangerously high current account deficit was recorded.

In 1988, the government realised that the economy had overheated and that inflation would increase sharply if it did not take action. So it raised interest rates and by late 1989, as Figure 33.5 shows, they stood at 15 per cent, double their lowest 1988 value. This led to a slowdown in consumer spending. The housing market collapsed as borrowers were less willing to take out mortgages to finance new purchases. Existing mortgage borrowers found their mortgage payments increasing sharply, reducing their ability to spend. Lower house prices lowered household wealth and severely dented consumer confidence. So too did rising unemployment, which doubled between 1989 and 1993. Firms cut back their investment spending as they found themselves with too much productive capacity as Figure 33.6 shows. Government spending remained tight although there was some increase in government spending after John Major became Prime Minister in 1989. As for exports, their growth remained subdued because high interest rates kept the value of the pound high. The government also made the policy mistake of taking the pound in the Exchange Rate Mechanism (ERM) of the European Monetary Union (the precursor to the euro and the monetary union) at too high a level. This forced it to keep interest rates high to defend the value of the pound. Britain was forced to leave the ERM by currency speculation in September 1992. By that time, falling levels of aggregate demand meant that GDP was lower than it was in the last quarter of 1988, nearly four years earlier.

Leaving the ERM allowed the government to reduce interest rates rapidly at a time when inflation had fallen to around 2 per cent per annum. The period 1993-2005 was then characterised by above average rates of growth. 1993-1997 can be seen as the recovery from the deep recession of 1990-1992. The period 1997-2005 can be seen as a prolonged period when the economy was

Figure 33.5 Bank base rates and economic growth

Source: adapted from *Economic Trends Annual Supplement.*, Office for National Statistics.

Figure 33.6 The output gap[1]

1 Deviation of actual GDP from potential GDP as a percentage of potential GDP. Positive numbers show actual GDP is above potential GDP, whilst negative numbers show actual GDP is below potential GDP.

Source: adapted from HM Treasury, *Economic Cycles*, 2005 .

growing at roughly its trend rate of growth, as Figure 33.6 would suggest.

The drivers of aggregate demand have fluctuated over the period 1993-2005. On the positive side, consumer spending has tended to increase at a faster rate than growth in aggregate demand overall. Government spending growth was low between 1995 and 2000 before expanding rapidly again. On the other hand, exports were hit by a financial crisis in Asia in 1997 and by a downturn in the Us economy in 2001 made worse by the attacks on World Trade Centre of 9/11. It could be argued that these two events were the major cause of the faltering of the UK economy in 1998 and again in 2002-2003.

DataQuestion

Aggregate demand 2000-2005

Figure 33.7 Real growth in GDP and its components, % change year on year

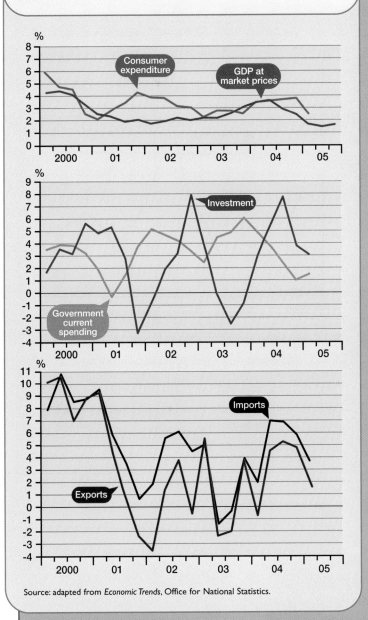

Source: adapted from *Economic Trends*, Office for National Statistics.

Figure 33.8 GDP and its components, 1st quarter 2005

Source: adapted from *Economic Trends*, Office for National Statistics.

Figure 33.9 Short term interest rates

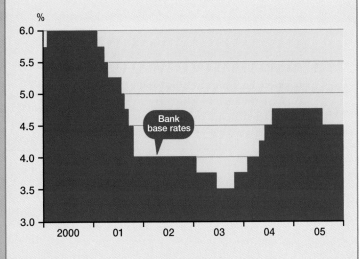

Source: adapted from *Economic Trends*, Office for National Statistics.

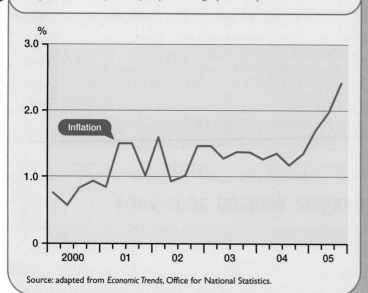

Figure 33.10 Inflation (CPI), % change year on year

Source: adapted from *Economic Trends*, Office for National Statistics.

Figure 33.11 Sterling effective exchange rate, 1990=100

Source: adapted from *Economic Trends*, Office for National Statistics.

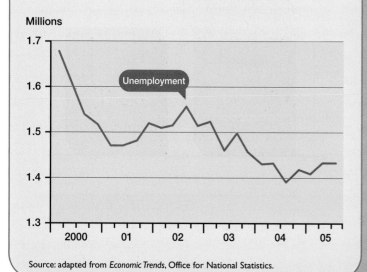

Figure 33.12 Unemployment, ILO measure, millions

Source: adapted from *Economic Trends*, Office for National Statistics.

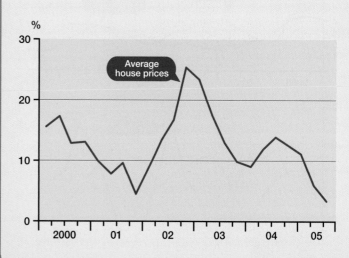

Figure 33.13 Average house prices, % change year on year

Source: adapted from *Economic Trends*, Office for National Statistics.

1. Explain what is meant by 'aggregate demand'.
2. Describe the trend, if any, in aggregate demand and its components between 2000 and 2005.
3. Analyse the factors which contributed to the change in aggregate demand over the period shown in the data.
4. Evaluate the extent to which the mild downturn in the UK economy in 2001-2002 was caused by the international downturn in the world economy which occurred at the time.

34 Aggregate supply

Summary

1. The aggregate supply curve shows the level of output in the whole economy at any given level of average prices.
2. In the short run, it is assumed that the prices of factors of production, such as money wage rates, are constant. Firms will supply extra output if the prices they receive increase. Hence in the short run, the aggregate supply curve is upward sloping.
3. An increase in firms' costs of production will shift the short run aggregate supply curve upwards, whilst a fall in costs will shift it downwards.
4. In the long run, it is assumed that the prices of factors of production are variable but that the productive capacity of the economy is fixed. The long run aggregate supply curve shows the productive capacity of the economy at any given price level.
5. The long run aggregate supply curve shows the productive capacity of the economy in the way that a production possibility frontier or the trend rate of growth shows this productive capacity.
6. Shifts in the long run aggregate supply curve are caused by changes in the quantity or quality of factors of production or the efficiency of their use.
7. In the long run, wage rates may go up or down. Classical economists argue that if wages are perfectly flexible, unemployment will be eliminated by a fall in real wage rates. With full employment in the economy, the long run aggregate supply curve must be vertical at an output level equal to the full employment level of income.
8. Keynesian economists argue that real wages may not fall far enough to eliminate unemployment even in the long run. The long run aggregate supply curve is then horizontal or upward sloping at levels of output below full employment income but becomes vertical at full employment.

The short run aggregate supply curve

In unit 5, it was argued that the supply curve for an industry was upward sloping. If the price of a product increases, firms in the industry are likely to increase their profits by producing and selling more. So the higher the price, the higher the level of output. The supply curve being talked about here is a **micro-economic** supply curve. Is the **macro-economic** supply curve (i.e. the supply curve for the whole economy) the same?

The macro-economic supply curve is called the AGGREGATE SUPPLY CURVE, because it is the sum of all the industry supply curves in the economy. It shows how much output firms wish to supply at each level of prices.

In the short run, the aggregate supply curve is upward sloping. The short run is defined here as the period when money wage rates and the prices of all other factor inputs in the economy are fixed. Assume that firms wish to increase their level of output. In the short run, they are unlikely to take on extra workers. Taking on extra staff is an expensive process. Sacking them if they are no longer needed is likely to be even more costly, not just in direct monetary terms but also in terms of industrial relations within the company. So firms tend to respond to increases in demand in the short run by working their existing labour force more intensively, for instance through overtime.

Firms will need to provide incentives for workers to work harder or longer hours. Overtime, for instance, may be paid at one and a half times the basic rate of pay. Whilst basic pay rates remain constant, earnings will rise and this will tend to put up both the average and marginal costs per unit of output. In many sectors of the economy, where competition is imperfect and where firms have the power to increase their prices, the rise in labour costs will lead to a rise in prices. It only needs prices to rise in some sectors of the economy for the average price level in

the economy to rise. So in the short term, an increase in output by firms is likely to lead to an increase in their costs which in turn will result in some firms raising prices. But the increase in prices is likely to be small because, given constant prices (e.g. wage **rates**) for factor inputs, the increases in costs (e.g. wage **earnings**) are likely to be fairly small too. Therefore the short run aggregate supply curve is relatively price elastic. This is shown in Figure 34.1. An increase in output from Q_1 to Q_2 leads to a moderate rise in the average price level of $P_1 P_2$.

If demand falls in the short run, some firms in the economy will react by cutting their prices to try and stimulate extra orders. But the opportunities to cut prices will be limited. Firms will be reluctant to sack workers and their overheads will remain the same, so their average cost and marginal cost will barely be altered. Again, the aggregate supply curve is relatively price elastic.

Shifts in the short run aggregate supply curve

The SHORT RUN AGGREGATE SUPPLY CURVE shows the

Question 1

Using a short run aggregate supply curve, explain the likely effect on the price level of the following, assuming that the prices of all factor inputs are fixed.
(a) In 1988, output in the UK economy boomed. Real GDP rose by 5 per cent, an increase which has yet to be repeated.
(b) In 1991, there was a recession in the UK economy and output fell. Real GDP declined by 1.5 per cent, the last time in recent economic history a fall occurred.

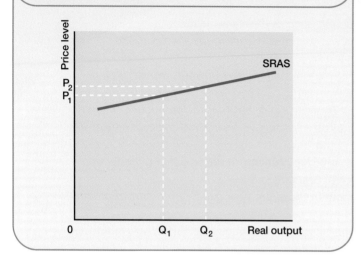

Figure 34.1 The short run aggregate supply curve
The slope of the SRAS line is very shallow because, whilst it is assumed that in the short run wage rates are constant, firms will face some increased costs such as overtime payments when they increase output.

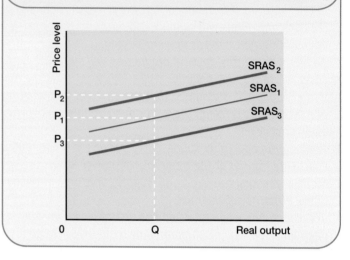

Figure 34.2 Shifts in the short run aggregate supply curve
The short run aggregate supply curve is drawn on the assumption that costs, in particular the wage rate, remain constant. A change in costs is shown by a shift in the curve. For instance, an increase in wage rates would push $SRAS_1$ up to $SRAS_2$ whilst a fall in wages rates would push the curve down to $SRAS_3$.

relationship between aggregate output and the average price level, assuming that money wage rates in the economy are constant. But what if wage rates do change, or some other variable which affects aggregate supply changes? Then, just as in the micro-economic theory of the supply curve, the aggregate supply curve will shift. The following are three examples of SUPPLY SIDE SHOCKS, factors which cause the short run aggregate supply curve to shift.

Wage rates An increase in wage rates will result in firms facing increased costs of production. Some firms will respond by increasing prices. So at any given level of output, a rise in wage rates will lead to a rise in the average price level. This is shown in Figure 34.2 by a shift in the short run aggregate supply curve from $SRAS_1$ to $SRAS_2$.

Raw material prices A general fall in the prices of raw materials will lower industrial costs and will lead to some firms reducing the prices of their products. Hence there will be a shift in the short run aggregate supply curve downwards. This is shown in Figure 34.2 by the shift from $SRAS_1$ to $SRAS_3$.

Taxation An increase in the tax burden on industry will increase costs. Hence the short run aggregate supply schedule will be pushed upwards, for instance from $SRAS_1$ to $SRAS_2$ in Figure 34.2.

The long run aggregate supply curve

In the short run, changes in wage rates or the price of raw materials have an effect on the aggregate supply curve, shifting the SRAS curve up or down. Equally, a rise in real output will lead to a movement along the SRAS curve.

In the long run, however, there is a limit to how much firms can increase their supply. They run into capacity constraints. There is a limit to the amount of labour that can be hired in an economy. Capital equipment is fixed in supply. Labour productivity has been maximised. So it can be argued that in the long run, the aggregate supply curve is fixed at

Using diagrams, show the likely effect of the following on the long run aggregate supply curve.
(a) Real national output in the 2nd quarter of 1992 was the same as in the fourth quarter of 1988 but average prices had increased 27 per cent over the period.
(b) In 2004-2005, the price of crude oil approximately doubled.
(c) Between 2000 and 2004, average money earnings in the UK economy rose by 16.7 per cent.

a given level of real output, whatever the price level. What this means is that the long run aggregate supply curve is vertical on a diagram showing the price level and real output.

Figure 34.3 shows such a vertical LONG RUN AGGREGATE SUPPLY CURVE or LRAS CURVE. The long run aggregate supply curve shows the productive potential of the economy. It shows how much real output can be produced over a period of time with a given level of factor inputs, such as labour and capital equipment, and a given level of efficiency in combining these factor inputs. It can be linked to two other economic concepts.

● The LRAS curve is the level of output associated with production on the production possibility frontier of an economy. In Figure 34.4, any point on the boundary AB is one which shows the level of real output shown by the LRAS curve.
● The LRAS curve is the level of output shown by the trend rate of growth in an economy. In Figure 34.5, the economy is growing along the trend rate of growth of AB. There are short term fluctuations in actual output above and below the trend rate. This shows that actual output can be above or below that given by the long run aggregate supply curve. When actual output is above the trend rate on Figure 34.5 in the short run, and so to the right of the LRAS curve in Figure

Figure 34.3 *The classical long run aggregate supply curve*
Classical economics assumes that in the long run wages and prices are flexible and therefore the LRAS curve is vertical. In the long run, there cannot be any unemployment because the wage rate will be in equilibrium where all workers who want a job (the supply of labour) will be offered a job (the demand for labour). So, whatever the level of prices, output will always be constant at the full employment level of income.

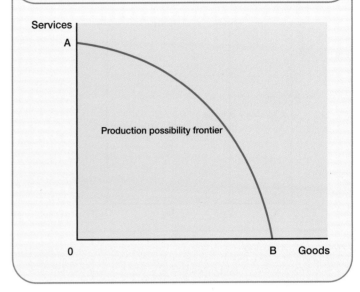

Figure 34.4 *A production possibility frontier*
Any point on the production possibility frontier AB shows the potential output of the economy when all resources are fully utilised. The long run aggregate supply curve also shows the potential output of the economy. At any point in time, if the economy is operating on its long run aggregate supply curve, then it will be operating at one of the points along the production possibility frontier.

34.3, economic forces will act to bring GDP back towards its trend rate of growth. Equally, when it is below its trend rate of growth, and so to the left of the LRAS curve in Figure 34.3, the same but opposite forces will bring it back to that long run position.

Shifts in the long run aggregate supply curve

The long run aggregate supply curve is likely to shift over time. This is because the quantity and quality of economic resources changes over time, as does the way in which they are combined. These changes bring about changes in the productive potential of an economy.

Figure 34.6 shows how a growth in potential output is drawn on an aggregate supply diagram. Assume that the education and skills of the workforce increase. This should lead to labour becoming more productive, in turn leading to an increase in the productive potential of the economy at full employment. The long run aggregate supply curve will then shift from $LRAS_1$ to $LRAS_2$, showing that at a given level of prices, the economy can produce more output. A fall in potential output, caused for instance by a fall in the size of the labour force, would be shown by a leftward shift in the curve, from $LRAS_1$ to $LRAS_3$.

A shift to the right in the LRAS curve shows that there has been economic growth. On a production possibility frontier (PPF) diagram, it would be represented by a movement outwards on the boundary. In Figure 34.5, it would be shown by a movement up along the trend rate of growth line. A shift to the left in the LRAS curve would show that the productive potential of the economy has fallen. On a PPF diagram, the boundary would shift inwards. On a trend rate of growth diagram, there would be a movement along and down the trend rate of growth line.

The long run aggregate supply curve and the labour market

In drawing a vertical long run aggregate supply curve, a number

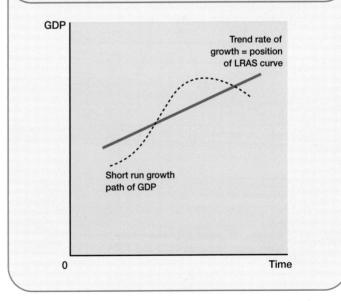

Figure 34.5 *The trend rate of growth for an economy*
At any point in time, the level of output shown by the long run aggregate supply is on the line of the trend rate of growth of output.

of assumptions about the workings of the labour market have been made. When a short run aggregate supply curve is drawn, it is assumed that wage rates are fixed. But what happens in the long run when wage rates might not be fixed but could either increase or decrease? Economists differ about how workers will respond to factors which might change wage rates.

The classical view At one extreme are some classical, monetarist or supply side economists. They argue that the market for labour is like the market for

Figure 34.6 A shift in the long run aggregate supply curve
An increase in the productive potential in the economy pushes the long run aggregate supply curve to the right, for instance from LRAS₁ to LRAS₂. A fall in productive potential, on the other hand, is shown by a shift to the left of the curve, from LRAS₁ to LRAS₃ for instance.

Question 3

Figure 34.7 Output gap estimates

Source: adapted from HM Treasury, *Evidence on the UK economic cycle*, July 2005.

(a) Give six years when the economy was operating on its long run aggregate supply curve, according to the data in Figure 34.7.

(b) GDP at constant prices rose every year between 1972 and 2004 except between 1973 and 1975, 1979 to 1983 and 1990 to 1992. Using a diagram, explain what happened to the long run aggregate supply curve between the six years given in your answer to (a).

(c) The economy experienced deep recessions between 1973 and 1975, 1979 and 1983, and 1990 to 1992. In these recessions, manufacturing suffered particularly badly, with many factories closing, never to reopen again, and some workers became deskilled, resulting in their inability ever to find another job in their working lifetime. Using a diagram, explain what might have happened to the long run aggregate supply curve for the UK economy in these years.

bananas. Excess supply of bananas will bring about a rapid fall in price to clear the market. So too in the labour market. Assume that the economy goes into recession and workers begin to lose their jobs as output falls. Unemployed workers will realise that they will have to accept cuts in pay if they are to get another job. Those in work will know that there is a pool of unemployed workers waiting to take their jobs if they do not show at least restraint in their wage claims. Firms know that they can pick up workers at low rates of pay. Hence in an effort to maximise profitability by minimising costs they will not be prepared to pay their existing workforce such high real wages.

Classical economists differ as to how quickly the labour market clears. Some argue that the labour market takes time to bring about a fall in wages and unemployment. This was the view taken by many during the Great Depression of the 1930s. Their view is based on a theory of ADAPTIVE EXPECTATIONS. This means that expectations of what will happen are based on what has happened in the past. In the short term, workers who are unemployed will hope that the economy will pick up and they will be able to get a job.

Firms will be reluctant to damage relations with existing workers by cutting their wages when, in fact, they could hire new workers at a lower wage rate than that being paid to existing workers. Hence, in the short term, disequilibrium can exist in the labour market. In the longer term, however, unemployed workers will realise that they will never get a job if they stick out for too high a wage. Firms will realise that the new lower level of wages is here to stay and will adopt pay cutting policies. Wages will then fall, bringing the market back to equilibrium.

New Classical economists, in contrast, believe that markets will clear instantaneously. The idea of RATIONAL EXPECTATIONS was developed in the 1970s in America by two economists, Robert Lucus and Thomas Sergeant. They argued that economic agents, such as workers and firms, base their decisions on all the information they have, including current information and predictions of future events. Because they are using all the information they have, they are making their decisions about what to do in a rational way. In the labour market, workers know that long term unemployment can only be solved by accepting wage cuts. Equally, firms know that they can enforce wage cuts when unemployment rises. Therefore, the labour market will clear immediately.

A traditional Keynesian view At the other extreme are some Keynesian economists who argue that unemployment will persist until there is an opposing expansion of demand for labour. They argue that real wages will never fall sufficiently to clear the labour market completely if the market goes into disequilibrium. To understand why real wage rates are unlikely to fall, it is necessary to think clearly about the nature of the labour market in a modern industrialised economy like the UK. In Victorian England, it might have been true that firms hired and fired at will, taking on unemployed workers who were prepared to work for lower wages whilst sacking those who refused to take pay cuts. It might also be true that workers were forced to submit to the iron law of the market place, taking real wage cuts when the demand for labour fell. But conditions are very different in a modern industrialised economy.

● Medium to large employers have little to gain by forcing down wages in the short term. Such action is likely to demotivate the existing workforce and lead to a loss of employee loyalty and goodwill. Employees represent valuable assets of the firm. They have received training and are familiar with working practices. Hiring new labour is a costly process if workers leave because of dissatisfaction with the firm. So such employers are likely to take a long term view of the labour market.

- Trade unions act to protect the interests of their members. Trade union members are almost all in jobs. Therefore they are not particularly concerned with the plight of the unemployed (just as firms are not in business to help alleviate unemployment). Trade unions will naturally not only resist real wage cuts but will press for higher real wages. Can a trade union be said to have achieved its objectives if the workforce of a firm shrinks through natural wastage by a few per cent and those who keep their jobs gain real wage increases?

- If there is minimum wage legislation, then employers of low paid workers will find it difficult if not legally impossible to cut wage rates.

- Benefits for the unemployed discourage workers from taking low paid jobs, preventing employers from offering very low pay when unemployment rises.

- The economy comprises a large number of different labour markets. Labour is immobile geographically in the UK, particularly low paid unskilled workers because of problems with renting low cost housing. Labour is immobile occupationally because of the ever increasing division of labour within the economy and the failure of both firms and government to provide the level of training which would make workers mobile.

According to this view, a modern labour market is inevitably imperfect. Real wage rates may conceivably fall sufficiently in the long run to bring the economy back to full employment but then, as Keynes said, 'in the long run we are all dead'. It is little comfort to a 45 year old made redundant today to know that in 15 years' time the economy will have returned to full employment and he may then have a chance of getting a low paid job.

A moderate Keynesian view New classical economists argue that the labour market adjusts instantaneously. Moderate classical economists argue that it might take a few years. Traditional Keynesians argue that it might take decades. Moderate Keynesians argue that the process might take 5-10 years. According to this view, labour market rigidities are strong. However, in the medium term, employers in the formal sector of the economy will push down real wage rates from what they would otherwise have been. Even if this is only one per cent per year, it amounts to over 5 per cent over a five year period. Moreover, there is a significant small business economy where wages are more flexible. Some of those made unemployed will become self-employed, accepting a lower wage in the process.

The classical and Keynesian long run aggregate supply curves

What happens in the labour market determines the shape of the long run aggregate supply curve. Classical or supply side economists see the labour market as functioning perfectly. Unemployment represents a disequilibrium position in the market. Real wages, the price of labour, will therefore fall until demand exactly equals supply. At this equilibrium point there will be no unemployment. The classical viewpoint therefore argues that in the long run firms will always employ all workers

who wish to work at the equilibrium wage. Similarly, the markets for the other factors of production, land and capital, will be in equilibrium at their full employment level. Hence in the long run firms will supply the maximum potential output of the economy. This is true whatever the level of prices. Therefore the long run aggregate supply curve is vertical and is at the full employment level of output. This is the vertical long run aggregate supply curve shown in Figures 34.3 and 34.8.

Keynesian economists argue that, even if unemployment exists, workers who have got jobs will carry on negotiating and receiving higher pay rises as the economy grows. There will be little tendency for real wages to fall, allowing the labour market to clear (they are **sticky downwards**). Traditional Keynesian economists argue that, even in the long run, the labour market may not clear. Unemployment could be a long run feature of an economy. Three possibilities then present themselves.

- If the economy is in deep recession, an increase in output is unlikely to increase prices. Workers will be too frightened of losing their jobs to negotiate pay rises even if an individual firm is expanding. Here the aggregate supply curve would be horizontal because firms could expand production without experiencing a rise in costs.

- If unemployment is relatively low, workers will be in a position to bid up wages in response to increased demand. Here the aggregate supply curve is upward sloping. The nearer full employment, the more workers will be able to obtain wage increases.

- If the economy is at full employment, firms by definition won't be able to take on any more labour, however much they offer. The economy cannot produce more than its full employment output. Hence at full employment the aggregate supply curve will be vertical.

These three possibilities are shown in Figure 34.8. At levels of output between O and A, mass unemployment exists. The aggregate supply curve is therefore horizontal. Between output levels A and B, the economy is experiencing some unemployment, so the aggregate supply curve is upward sloping.

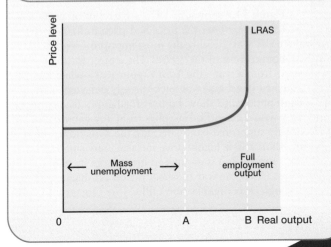

Figure 34.8 The Keynesian long run aggregate supply curve
Traditional Keynesian economists argue that, even in the long run, unemployment may persist because wages don't necessarily fall when unemployment occurs. When there is mass unemployment, output can be increased without any increases in costs and therefore prices. As the economy nears full employment, higher output leads to higher prices. At full employment, the economy cannot produce any more whatever prices firms receive.

Question 4

A survey by analyst IDS claims that an increasing number of companies now have their lowest pay rate set at the level of the minimum wage. The report states that increases in the National Minimum Wage (NMW) have 'had a widespread impact on a broad range of lower paying organisations', with 55 per cent of retail chains now setting their lowest rate of pay at £5.05 an hour, the NMW. This is an increase on last year when the figure was 45 per cent of retail chains.

The National Minimum Wage is also affecting pay structures, with wages rises being given to workers on above the minimum wage when the government raises the actual minimum wage. The IDS survey found that two-thirds of employers in the hotels sector had been directly affected by the latest rise in the NMW.

However, the report said that 'Estimates by economists in the mid-1990s that up to 1.7 million jobs would be lost if a minimum wage were to be introduced now look very wide of the mark.' In fact 'despite NMW increases running ahead of both inflation and average earnings over the past three years, there has been no negative employment effect. Employment in lower paying sectors such as retail, restaurants, hospitality and leisure has been growing.'

In contrast, earlier this month the British Retail Consortium called for a 'fundamental review' of the aims of the NMW, claiming that the proposed increase in October 2006 could lead to around 35 000 jobs losses in the retail sector. It claims that retailers 'simply cannot go on absorbing further increases in their fixed costs - of which labour is one of the biggest.'

Source: adapted from http://news.viewlondon.co.uk.

(a) Explain why a national minimum wage might (i) prevent the labour market from clearing and (ii) lead to a long run aggregate supply curve (LRAS) which is not vertical.
(b) Explain whether the data support the view that in the UK the national minimum wage prevents the LRAS curve from being vertical.

At the full employment level of output, B, the supply curve becomes vertical.

Note that both classical and Keynesian economists agree that at full employment, the long run aggregate supply curve is vertical. Whatever prices are charged, industry cannot increase its output. But Keynesian economists argue that, in the long run, the economy may operate at less than full employment, in which case the aggregate supply curve is horizontal or upward sloping.

Key terms

Adaptive expectations - where decisions are based upon past information.
Aggregate supply curve - the relationship between the average level of prices in the economy and the level of total output.
Long run aggregate supply curve - the aggregate supply curve which assumes that wage rates are variable, both upward and downwards. Classical or supply side economists assume that wage rates are flexible. Keynesian economists assume that wage rates may be 'sticky downwards' and hence the economy may operate at less than full employment even in the long run.
Rational expectations - where decisions are based on current information and anticipated future events.
Short run aggregate supply curve - the upward sloping aggregate supply curve which assumes that money wage rates are fixed.
Supply side shocks - factors such as changes in wage rates or commodity prices which cause the short run aggregate supply curve to shift.

Applied economics

The case of oil

As Figure 34.9 shows, in 1973 a barrel of oil cost $2.83. A year later the price had risen to $10.41. This price rise was possibly the most important world economic event of the 1970s. The trigger for the rise came from a war - the Yom Kippur war - when Egypt attacked Israel and was subsequently defeated. The Arab nations, to show support for Egypt, decreed that they would cut off oil supplies from any country which openly supported Israel. Because the demand for oil in the short run is highly price inelastic, any small fall in the supply of oil is enough to bring large increases in prices. After the war finished, the oil producing nations through their organisation OPEC (the Organisation for

Petroleum Exporting Countries) realised that it was possible to maintain a high price for oil by limiting its supply (i.e. by operating a cartel). Since then OPEC has operated a policy of restricting the supply of oil to the market.

Oil prices rose rather more slowly between 1974 and 1978. But between 1978 and 1982 the average price of a barrel of oil rose from $13.03 to $31.80. Again, a political event was a major factor in triggering the price rise. The Shah of Iran, ruler of an important oil producing country, was deposed by Muslim fundamentalists led by the Ayatollah Khomeini. The revolution plunged Iran into economic chaos and the new rulers, fiercely anti-Western, showed little interest in resuming large scale exports of oil. A small disruption in oil supplies, a situation exploited by OPEC, was again enough to send oil prices spiralling.

In 1990, Iraq invaded Kuwait but was expelled in the Gulf War of 1991. This produced a short lived spike in oil prices but oil prices subsequently fell and by 1998, averaged only $12.21 a barrel. Cutting production quotas enabled OPEC to raise prices again to over $20 a barrel. However, between 2003 and 2005, another boom in oil prices occurred with oil prices at times reaching over $60 a barrel. The main cause of this boom was the relentless increase in demand for oil by fast growing Asian countries, particularly China. Underinvestment by OPEC countries in their oil production facilities over a twenty year period meant that, by 2005, the world oil industry was operating at maximum capacity. Increases in demand could only push prices up.

These three periods of sharp oil price rises all had an important effect on the short run aggregate supply curve of the UK economy. Oil price rises increase the costs of firms. So at any given level of output, firms need to charge higher prices to cover their costs. As a result, the short run aggregate supply curve shifts upwards. The oil price rises of 1973-75 and 1979-81 were a major contributor to the rises in inflation at the time shown in Figure 34.11. Significantly, though, the oil price increase of 2003-2005 had very little impact on inflation. One reason was that the average amount of oil used to generate £1 of GDP was far less in 2005

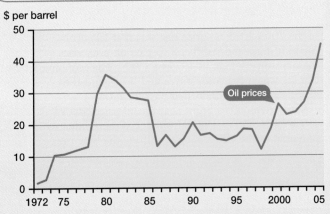

Figure 34.9 Price of oil

Source: adapted from *BP Statistical Review of World Energy*.

Figure 34.10 The effect of steep rises in oil prices on aggregate supply
A large rise in the price of oil will push the short run aggregate supply curve upwards and possibly shift the long run aggregate supply curve to the left.

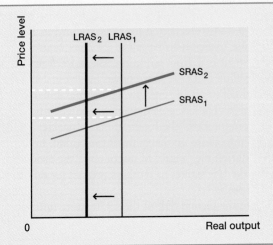

Figure 34.11 Economic growth and inflation (RPI), year on year, in three periods of oil shocks

Source: adapted from *Economic Trends*, Office for National Statistics.

than in 1975 or 1981. Greater energy efficiency and the decline of manufacturing industry were the main reasons for this. Another reason for the small impact of the 2003-2005 oil price rise was that UK firms found it much more difficult to pass on price rises to their customers than in 1975 or 1981. The economic climate was more competitive and firms tended to absorb oil prices rather than pass them on.

Many economists argue that the oil price rises of 1973-75 and 1979-1981 also reduced the productive potential of the UK economy, shifting the long run aggregate supply curve to the left, as shown in Figure 34.10. The rise in oil prices meant that some capital equipment which was oil intensive became uneconomic to run. This equipment was mothballed and then scrapped, leading to a once-and-for-all fall in the amount of capital in the economy. Because the economy was far less oil dependent in 2003-2005, this scrapping of equipment was negligible. Firms had become reluctant to invest in equipment using oil when there were good substitutes because they were afraid of a large rise in oil prices.

DataQuestion

Aggregate supply, 1974-79

Between February 1974 and May 1979, there was a Labour government in the UK. It is often considered to have been a disastrous period for the economy. In 1975, inflation rose to a post-war peak of 24.2 per cent. Unemployment rose from half a million in 1974 to one and half million in 1977. Share prices halved in 1974. The pound fell to an all time low against the dollar in October 1976. The UK government was forced to borrow from the IMF (the International Monetary Fund in late 1976 to shore up the value of the pound. In 1978-79, during the 'winter of discontent', the economy seemed racked by strikes as workers pressed for double digit pay rises.

However, the second half of the 1970s were difficult times for all industrialised economies. Growth rates worldwide fell as economies accommodated the supply-side shock of the first oil crisis in 1973-4. Table 34.1 shows that the growth in real GDP in the UK economy was above its long run trend rate of growth of 2.5 per cent per annum in three of the six years during the period; and although the average yearly growth rate over the six years was only 1.5 per cent, if 1973, a boom year for the economy, were included, the average rate of growth would be 2.3 per cent. Investment spending in the economy remained static, with investment as a percentage of GDP slightly declining. This perhaps reflected a lack of confidence in the future of the economy. Even so, this should be contrasted with the experience of the early 1980s. Investment fell in 1980 and 1981 and did not reach its 1979 levels till 1984.

The 1970s were inflationary times throughout the world. Inflation in the UK accelerated from 7.5 per cent in 1972 to 15.9 per cent in 1974 and 24.1 per cent in 1975. However, the government adopted firm anti-inflationary policies in 1975 and inflation subsequently fell to 8.3 per cent in 1978, before rising again to 13.4 per cent in 1979 as pressure from wages and import prices, including the second round of oil price rises, worsened.

Table 34.1 Selected economic indicators, UK 1974-79

	Real growth in GDP	Gross investment	Inflation (RPI)	Change in import prices	Change in average earnings
	%	% of GDP	%	%	%
1974	-1.5	14.8	15.9	46.2	18.5
1975	-0.6	14.6	24.1	14.1	26.6
1976	2.8	14.4	16.6	22.3	15.9
1977	2.4	13.9	15.9	15.8	8.8
1978	3.2	13.8	8.3	3.8	13.2
1979	2.8	13.8	13.4	6.4	15.2

Source: adapted from *Economic Trends Annual Supplement*, Office for National Statistics.

1. Consider both the passage and the table carefully. Discuss, using diagrams, what happened to aggregate supply in the second half of the 1970s: (a) in the short run and (b) in the long run.

35 Equilibrium output

Summary

1. The economy is in equilibrium when aggregate demand equals aggregate supply.
2. In the classical model, where wages are completely flexible, the economy will be in long run equilibrium at full employment. In the Keynesian model, where wages are sticky downwards, the economy can be in long run equilibrium at less than full employment.
3. In the classical model, a rise in aggregate demand will in the short run lead to an increase in both output and prices, but in the long run the rise will generate only an increase in prices. In the Keynesian model, a rise in aggregate demand will be purely inflationary if the economy is at full employment, but will lead to an increase in output if the economy is below full employment.
4. A rise in long run aggregate supply in the classical model will both increase output and reduce prices. Keynesians would agree with this in general, but would argue that an increase in aggregate supply will have no effect on output or prices if the economy is in a slump.
5. Factors which affect aggregate demand may well affect aggregate supply and vice versa, although this may occur over different time periods. For instance, an increase in investment is likely to increase both aggregate demand and aggregate supply.

Equilibrium output in the short run

Units 33 and 34 outlined theories of aggregate demand and aggregate supply. Both Keynesian and classical economists agree that in the short run the aggregate demand curve is downward sloping whilst the aggregate supply curve is upward sloping. The equilibrium level of output in the short run occurs at the intersection of the aggregate demand and aggregate supply curves. In Figure 35.1, the equilibrium level of income and output is OQ. The equilibrium price level is OP.

Equilibrium output in the long run

The main disagreement amongst economists is about long run equilibrium in the economy. Classical economists argue that in the long run the aggregate supply curve is vertical, as shown in Figure 35.2. Long run equilibrium occurs where the long run aggregate supply curve (LRAS) intersects with the

aggregate demand curve. Hence equilibrium output is OQ and the equilibrium price level is OP. Associated with the long run equilibrium price level is a short run aggregate supply curve (SRAS) which passes through the point where LRAS = AD. The long run aggregate supply curve shows the supply curve for the economy at full employment (☞ unit 34). Hence there can be no unemployment in the long run according to classical economists.

Keynesian economists argue that the long run aggregate supply curve is as shown in Figure 35.3. The economy is at full employment where the LRAS curve is vertical at output OR - a point of agreement with classical economists. However, the economy can be in equilibrium at less than full employment. In Figure 35.3 the equilibrium level of output is OQ where the AD curve cuts the LRAS curve. The key point of disagreement between classical and Keynesian economists is the extent to which workers react to unemployment by accepting real wage cuts.

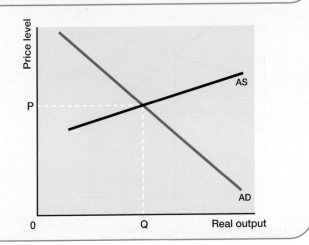

Figure 35.1 Equilibrium output
The equilibrium level of national output is set at the intersection of the aggregate demand and supply curves at OQ. The equilibrium price level is OP.

Figure 35.2 Long run equilibrium in the classical model
Long run equilibrium output is OQ, the full employment level of output, since wages are flexible both downwards as well as upwards.

A rise in aggregate demand

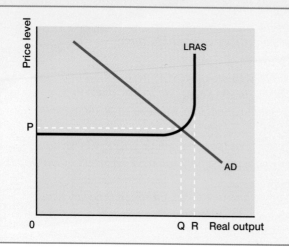

Figure 35.3 Long run equilibrium in the Keynesian model
Long run equilibrium output OQ may be below the full employment level of output OR because real wages may not fall when there is unemployment.

Classical economists argue that a rise in unemployment will lead rapidly to cuts in real wages. These cuts will increase the demand for labour and reduce its supply, returning the economy to full employment quickly and automatically. Economists like Patrick Minford, of the rational expectations school of thought, argue that this short term disequilibrium is corrected so quickly that the short run can be disregarded. Keynesian economists, on the other hand, argue that money wages are sticky downwards. Workers will refuse to take money wage cuts and will fiercely resist cuts in their real wage. The labour market will therefore not clear except perhaps over a very long period of time, so long that it is possibly even not worth considering.

Having outlined a theory of equilibrium output, it is now possible to see what happens if either aggregate demand or aggregate supply changes.

Assume that there is a rise in aggregate demand in the economy with long run aggregate supply initially remaining unchanged. For instance, there may be an increase in the wages of public sector employees paid for by an increase in the money supply, or there may be a fall in the marginal propensity to save and a rise in the marginal propensity to consume. A rise in aggregate demand will push the AD curve to the right. The classical and Keynesian models give different conclusions about the effect of this.

The classical model A rise in aggregate demand, which shifts the aggregate demand curve from AD_1 to AD_2 in Figure 35.4, will move the economy from A to B. There will be a movement along the short run aggregate supply curve. Output will rise from OL to OM and this will be accompanied by a small rise in the price level from ON to OP.

But the economy is now in long run disequilibrium. The full employment level of output is OL, shown by the position of the long run aggregate supply curve. The economy is therefore operating at over-full employment. Firms will find it difficult to recruit labour, buy raw materials and find new offices or factory space. They will respond by bidding up wages and other costs. The short run aggregate supply curve is drawn on the assumption that wage rates and other costs remain constant. So a rise in wage rates will shift the short run aggregate supply curve upwards. Short run equilibrium output will now fall and prices will keep rising. The economy will only return to long run equilibrium when the short run aggregate supply curve has shifted upwards from $SRAS_1$ to $SRAS_2$ so that aggregate demand once again equals long run aggregate supply at C.

The conclusion of the classical model is that increases in aggregate demand will initially increase both prices and output (the movement from A to B in Figure 35.4). Over time prices will continue to rise but output will fall as the economy moves back towards long run equilibrium (the movement from B to C).

Question 1

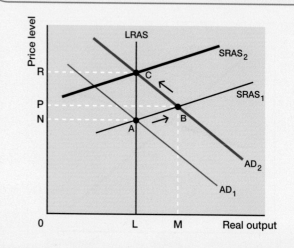

What would be the effect on equilibrium income in the long run if the workers in the photograph were (a) successful and (b) unsuccessful with their demands?

Figure 35.4 The classical model in the short and long run
A rise in aggregate demand shown by a shift to the right in the AD curve will result in a movement along the SRAS curve. Both output and prices will increase. In the long run, the SRAS curve will shift upwards with long run equilibrium being re-established at C. The rise in demand has led only to a rise in the price level.

In the long term an increase in aggregate demand will only lead to an increase in the price level (from A to C). There will be no effect on equilibrium output. So increases in aggregate demand without any change in long run aggregate supply are purely inflationary.

The Keynesian model In the Keynesian model, the long run aggregate supply curve is shaped as in Figure 35.5. Keynesians would agree with classical economists that an increase in aggregate demand from, say, AD_4 to AD_5 will be purely inflationary if the economy is already at full employment at OD.

But if the economy is in deep depression, as was the case in the UK during the early 1930s, an increase in aggregate demand will lead to a rise in output without an increase in prices. The shift in aggregate demand from AD_1 to AD_2 will increase equilibrium output from OA to OB without raising the price level from OP

as there are unused resources available.

The third possibility is that the economy is a little below full employment, for instance at OC in Figure 35.5. Then a rise in aggregate demand from AD_3 to AD_4 will increase both equilibrium output and equilibrium prices.

In the Keynesian model, increases in aggregate demand may or may not be effective in raising equilibrium output. It depends upon whether the economy is below full employment or at full employment.

A rise in long run aggregate supply

A rise in long run aggregate supply means that the potential output of the economy has increased (i.e. there has been genuine economic growth). Rises in long run aggregate supply which are unlikely to shift the aggregate demand curve might occur if, for instance, incentives to work increased or there was a change in technology.

The classical model In the classical model, an increase in long run aggregate supply will lead to both higher output and lower prices. In Figure 35.6 a shift in the aggregate supply curve from $LRAS_1$ to $LRAS_2$ will increase equilibrium output from OL to OM. Equilibrium prices will also fall from ON to OP. Contrast this conclusion with what happens when aggregate demand is increased in the classical model - a rise in prices with no increase in output. It is not surprising that classical economists are so strongly in favour of **supply side policies** (☞ unit 38 - this is why they are often referred to as 'supply side' economists).

The Keynesian model In the Keynesian model, shown in Figure 35.7, an increase in aggregate supply will both increase output and reduce prices if the economy is at full employment. With aggregate demand at AD_1, a shift in the aggregate supply curve from $LRAS_1$ to $LRAS_2$ increases full employment equilibrium output from Y_E to Y_F. If the economy is at slightly less than full employment, with an aggregate demand curve of AD_2, then the shift to the right in the LRAS curve will still be beneficial to the economy, increasing output and reducing prices. But Keynesians disagree with classical economists that supply side measures can

In his Budget of 1981, with unemployment at 3 million and still rising, the Chancellor of the Exchequer, Geoffrey Howe, raised the level of taxes and significantly reduced the budget deficit in order to squeeze inflationary pressures. In a letter to *The Times*, 364 economists protested at what they saw as the perversity of this decision.

(a) Geoffrey Howe was influenced by classical economic thinking. Using a diagram, explain why he believed that his policy (i) would help reduce inflation and (ii) not lead to any increase in unemployment.
(b) The economists who wrote the letter to The Times could broadly be described as Keynesian. Using a diagram, explain why they believed that it was folly to increase taxes at a time when the economy was in the grip of the worst recession since the 1930s.

Figure 35.5 The Keynesian model
If the economy is already at full employment, an increase in aggregate demand in the Keynesian model creates an inflationary gap without increasing output. In a depression, an increase in aggregate demand will increase output but not prices. If the economy is slightly below full employment, an increase in aggregate demand will increase both output and prices.

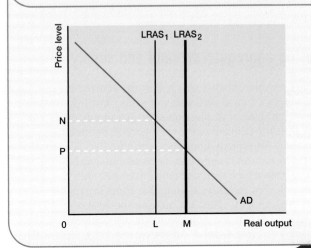

Figure 35.6 An increase in aggregate supply in the classical model
A shift to the right of the LRAS curve will both increase equilibrium output and reduce the price level.

Figure 35.7 An increase in aggregate supply in the Keynesian model
The effect of an increase in long run aggregate supply depends upon the position of the aggregate demand curve. If the economy is at or near full employment, an increase will raise output and lower prices. However, if the economy is in depression at Y_D, an increase in LRAS will have no impact on the economy.

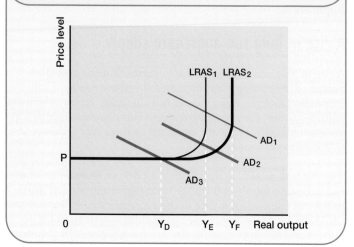

be effective in a depression. If the aggregate demand curve is AD_3, an increase in aggregate supply has no effect on equilibrium output. It remains obstinately stuck at Y_D. Only an increase in aggregate demand will move the economy out of depression.

It is now possible to understand one of the most important controversies in the history of economics. During the 1930s, classical economists argued that the only way to put the millions of unemployed during the Great Depression back to work was to adopt supply side measures - such as cutting unemployment benefits, reducing trade union power and cutting marginal tax rates and government spending. John Maynard Keynes attacked this orthodoxy by suggesting that the depression was caused by a lack of demand and suggesting that it was the government's responsibility to increase the level of aggregate demand. The same debate was replayed in the UK in the early 1980s. This time it was Keynesians who represented orthodoxy. They suggested that the only quick way to get the millions officially unemployed back to work was to expand aggregate demand. In the Budget of 1981, the government did precisely the opposite - it cut its projected budget deficit, reducing aggregate demand and argued that the only way to cure unemployment was to improve the supply side of the economy.

Increasing aggregate demand and supply

In micro-economics, factors which shift the demand curve do **not** shift the supply curve as well and vice versa. For instance, an increase in the costs of production shifts the supply curve but does **not** shift the demand curve for a good (although there will of course be a **movement along** the demand curve as a result). But in macro-economic aggregate demand and aggregate supply analysis, factors which shift one curve may well shift the other curve as well. For instance, assume that firms increase their planned investment. This will increase the level of aggregate demand. But in the long run it will also increase the level of aggregate supply. An increase in investment will

Question 3

In June 1995, a new French government unveiled a stiff budget designed to reduce high unemployment levels by 700 000 and bring down a high budget deficit from 5.7 per cent of GDP to 5.1 per cent of GDP within the fiscal year. The measures included:
- a substantial FF19bn cut in government spending affecting all ministries apart from justice and culture, with defence bearing nearly 50 per cent of the cuts;
- a rise in corporation tax from 33.3 per cent to 36.6 per cent;
- a rise in the standard rate of VAT from 18.6 per cent to 20.6 per cent;
- a 10 per cent rise in wealth tax;
- a 40 per cent cut in employment taxes paid by firms on employment of workers at or near the minimum wage level;
- new programmes targeted particularly at youth in difficulties, offering training, apprenticeship and other policies to bring people into the workforce;
- a rise in the minimum wage by 4 per cent;
- a rise in state pensions by 0.5 per cent;
- measures to stimulate the housing market, particularly focused on lodgings for people on lower incomes.

Using diagrams, explain what effect these measures would have on aggregate supply according to:
(a) classical or supply side economists,
(b) Keynesian economists.

increase the capital stock of the economy. The productive potential of the economy will therefore rise. We can use aggregate demand and supply analysis to show the effects of an increase in investment.

An increase in investment in the classical model will initially shift the aggregate demand curve in Figure 35.8 to the right from

Figure 35.8 An increase in investment expenditure
An increase in investment will increase aggregate demand from AD_1 to AD_2, and is likely to shift the long run aggregate supply curve from $LRAS_1$ to $LRAS_2$. The result is an increase in output and a small fall in prices.

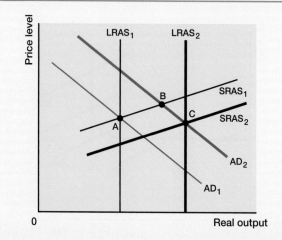

AD_1 to AD_2. There will then be a movement along the short run aggregate supply curve from A to B. There is now long run disequilibrium. How this will be resolved depends upon the speed with which the investment is brought on stream and starts to produce goods and services. Assume that this happens fairly quickly. The long run aggregate supply curve will then shift to the right, say, from $LRAS_1$ to $LRAS_2$. Long run equilibrium will be restored at C. Output has increased and the price level fallen slightly. There will also be a new short run aggregate supply curve, $SRAS_2$. It is below the original short run aggregate supply curve because it is assumed that investment has reduced costs of production.

Not all investment results in increased production. For instance, fitting out a new shop which goes into receivership within a few months will increase aggregate demand but not long run aggregate supply. The long run aggregate supply curve will therefore not shift and the increased investment will only be inflationary. Equally, investment might be poorly directed. The

increase in aggregate demand might be greater than the increase in long run aggregate supply. Here there will be an increase in equilibrium output but there will also be an increase in prices. The extent to which investment increases output and contributes to a lessening of inflationary pressure depends upon the extent to which it gives a high rate of return in the long run.

Using a classical model of the economy, explain the effect of the following on: (i) aggregate demand; (ii) short run aggregate supply; (iii) output and prices in the long run.
(a) A 10 per cent rise in earnings.
(b) An increase in real spending by government on education and training.
(c) An increase in the average long term real rate of interest from 3 per cent to 5 per cent.

Applied economics

Stagflation, 1974-76, 1979-1981 and 1988-1990

In a simple Keynesian model, rising inflation is associated with falling unemployment and vice versa. The experience of the 1950s and 1960s tended to support the hypothesis that there was this trade off between the two variables. However, in 1974-75, 1979-1981 and 1988-90 there were both rising inflation and rising unemployment, as shown in Figure 35.9. This combination of stagnation and inflation came to be called **stagflation**.

The stagflation of the first two of these periods was caused by a large rise in oil prices, an example of an external supply side shock to the economy. The rise had the effect of raising the short run aggregate supply curve (☞ unit 34) from $SRAS_1$ to $SRAS_2$ in Figure 35.10. The economy shifted from A to B. As can be seen from the diagram, prices rose and output fell.

In the first oil crisis, inflation rose from 9.1 per cent in 1973 to 15.9 per cent in 1974 and 24.1 per cent in 1975, before falling back to 16.5 per cent in 1976. Real GDP on the other hand fell by 1.5 per cent in 1974 and 0.8 per cent in 1975, before resuming an upward path in 1976.

In the second oil crisis, inflation rose from 8.3 per cent in 1978 to 13.4 per cent in 1979 and 18.0 per cent in 1980, before falling back again in 1981. Real GDP fell by 2 per cent in 1980 and 1.2 per cent in 1981.

The classical model would suggest that, all other things being equal, the economy would fall back to A from B. Full employment would be restored at the old price level. The above figures indicate that this did not happen. This was because the aggregate demand curve shifted to the right at the same time as the short run

Figure 35.9 *Stagflation: inflation and economic growth, 1973-75, 1979-81, 1989-91*

Source: adapted from *Economic Trends Annual Supplement*, Office for National Statistics.

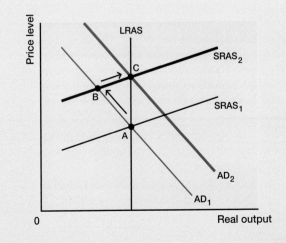

Figure 35.10 *Stagflation caused by supply side shocks*

aggregate supply curve was shifting to the left. This led to continued inflation as output rose from 1976 and again from 1982. The rise in aggregate demand in the first period was partly due to the then Labour government increasing the budget deficit, as well as increases in the money supply (the inflation was **accommodated**). Treasury estimates of the output gap suggest that the economy returned to its long run productive potential, at C in Figure 35.10, in 1978. In the second period, 1979-1981, taxation rose and government spending fell during the downturn in the economy, although the money supply increased again. This difference in fiscal stance is a partial explanation of why the rise in unemployment was lower and the rise in inflation higher in the first period than in the second period. It can be argued that the shift to the right in the aggregate demand curve was greater in the mid-1970s than the early 1980s.

The result was that the economy took much longer to return to the point C on its LRAS curve in this second period. Treasury estimates of the output gap suggest this did not occur until 1986.

The period of stagflation between 1988 and 1990 was different from the two previous periods. This was caused, not by a supply side shock but by a demand side shock. The Conservative government was partly responsible for stoking up an unsustainable boom in 1986-88, called the 'Lawson boom' after Nigel Lawson the Chancellor of the Exchequer at the time. When inflation began to rise, it reacted by raising interest rates from 7.5 per cent in May 1988 to 15 per cent in October 1989 and keeping them at those levels for nearly a year. This, together with a high value of the pound, produced a prolonged recession lasting through to the end of 1992 despite the fact that inflation peaked in the 3rd quarter of 1990. The economy did not return to production on the LRAS curve until 1997.

In all three periods of stagflation, the long run aggregate supply curve was probably still shifting to the right. The productive potential of the economy was increasing despite the actual fall in GDP being recorded. However, some economists argue that these periods of stagflation destroyed some of that productive potential. Capital equipment became redundant through lack of demand and was scrapped. Workers became long term unemployed, deskilled and demotivated, some never to work again. On this argument, stagflation is responsible for slowing down the growth of the productive potential of the economy. So the long run aggregate supply curve shifts less quickly to the right, leading to permanently lower equilibrium output and a higher price level.

DataQuestion

The UK economy, 2005-06

2005 has not been a boom year for the economy. Economic growth has been below trend whilst unemployment has very slightly risen. The housing market has been subdued, with average house price rises of a 'mere' 5 per cent, even if 5 per cent is arguably the right long term rate of growth of house prices. Consumers have not been increasing their spending as much as in previous years, hit by a variety of factors including higher interest rates, higher petrol prices and higher gas and electricity bills.

At the same time, 2005 could have been much worse. Oil prices rising at times to over $60 a barrel, nearly twice the price of 12 months earlier, could have sparked off much higher inflation, as indeed it did in the 1970s. The same rising oil prices and the general steep rise in world commodity prices could have sparked a recession in the world wide economy, causing Britain's exports to slump and sending it too into a recession. Consumers could have taken real fright at deteriorating economic conditions and decided to cut back on their borrowing and increase their saving by considerably reducing their spending. The US economy, with its huge imbalances, could have suddenly gone into recession. It remains extremely vulnerable to overseas lenders which are financing the US current account deficit of over 5 per cent of GDP. If that finance dried up, the value of the dollar would plummet, US imports would shrink and some of those lost US imports would be UK exports.

Dangers remain for 2006. The greatest danger is probably external, from a world recession. But British consumers could cut back on their spending. The government is fortunately in the middle of a large expansion of public spending and has proved reluctant to increase its taxes too much to pay for it. So the government sector should provide a positive boost to GDP. With luck, it will be enough to keep the output gap close to zero and the economy on course.

1. Outline (a) the demand side factors and (b) the supply side factors that influenced the equilibrium level of national output in 2005.
2. Using a diagram, explain why the rise in real national output was low and 'below trend' in 2005.
3. Using a diagram, explain how a recession in the US economy could affect the equilibrium level of real output and the price level of the UK economy.
4. To what extent is it important that the output gap should be 'close to zero' and the economy is kept 'on course'?

36 Fiscal policy

Summary

1. Fiscal policy, the manipulation of government spending, taxation and borrowing, affects aggregate demand.
2. The effect on aggregate demand of a change in government spending or taxation is increased because of the multiplier effect.
3. Classical economists argue that fiscal policy cannot, in the long term, affect the level of output. Hence, it cannot influence unemployment, but can raise inflation.
4. Keynesian economists argue that fiscal policy can affect both output and prices. Hence, fiscal policy can be used to influence both inflation and unemployment.
5. Fiscal policy cannot, as a demand side policy, influence long term economic growth, but it can be used to help an economy out of a recession or reduce demand pressures in a boom.
6. Fiscal policy, through its effect on aggregate demand, can influence imports and the current balance.

Fiscal policy

The UK government has been responsible for between 40 and 50 per cent of national expenditure over the past 20 years. The main areas of public spending are the National Health Service, defence, education and roads. In addition, the government is responsible for transferring large sums of money round the economy through its spending on social security and National Insurance benefits. All of this is financed mainly through taxes, such as income tax and VAT.

In the post-war era, governments have rarely balanced their budgets (i.e. they have rarely planned to match their expenditure with their receipts). In most years, they have run BUDGET DEFICITS, spending more than they receive. As a result, in most years governments have had to borrow money. In the UK, the borrowing of the public sector (central government, local government and other state bodies such as nationalised industries) over a period of time is called the PUBLIC SECTOR NET CASH REQUIREMENT (PSNCR). This was formerly called the Public Sector Borrowing Requirement (PSBR). In two periods, between 1969-70 and 1988-90, the UK government received more revenue than it spent. The normal budget deficit was turned into a BUDGET SURPLUS. There is then a negative PSNCR. A budget surplus allows the government to pay off part of its accumulated debt. This debt, called the NATIONAL DEBT, dates back to the founding of the Bank of England in 1694.

The government has to make decisions about how much to spend, tax and borrow. It also has to decide on the composition of its spending and taxation. Should it spend more on education and less on defence? Should it cut income tax by raising excise duties? These decisions about spending, taxes and borrowing are called the FISCAL POLICY of the government.

There are two key dates in the year for fiscal policy. One is the day of the BUDGET which occurs in March. In the Budget, the Chancellor gives a forecast of government spending and taxation in the coming financial year. Changes in taxation are also announced. The other key date occurs in November or December with the Chancellor's **Pre-Budget Report**. In this report, the Chancellor gives another forecast of government spending and taxation and announces the government's spending plans for the year. The financial year in the UK starts on 6 April and runs until 5 April the following year.

Aggregate demand

Government spending and taxation changes have an effect on aggregate demand. A rise in government spending, with the price

Question 1

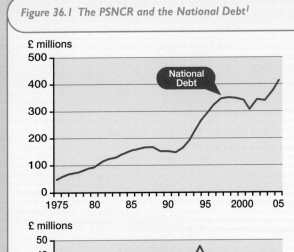

Figure 36.1 The PSNCR and the National Debt[1]

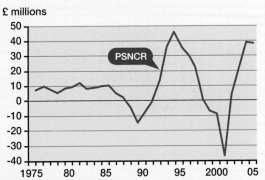

1 Years are financial years, e.g. 1975 is April 1974 to March 1975.
Source: adapted from *Monthly Digest of Statistics*, Office for National Statistics.

(a) (i) What is meant by the PSNCR? (ii) In which years did the government have a budget surplus?
(b) Using examples from the data, explain the link between the PSNCR and the National Debt.
(c) If a government wanted to pay off its National Debt over a number of years, how could it achieve this?

243

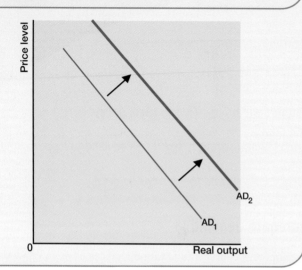

Figure 36.2 Changes in aggregate demand
A cut in taxes will lead to a shift to the right in the aggregate demand curve from AD₁ to AD₂.

Price level

AD₂

AD₁

0   Real output

Question 2

Explain the probable effect the following would have on aggregate demand, all other things being equal:
(a) a rise in income tax rates;
(b) a cut in council tax rates;
(c) a cut in spending on education;
(d) a rise in VAT rates combined with an increase in spending on the NHS.

level constant, will increase aggregate demand, pushing the AD curve to the right as in Figure 36.2.

Equally, a cut in taxes will affect aggregate demand. A cut in taxes on income, such as income tax and National Insurance contributions, will lead to a rise in the disposable income of households. This in turn will lead to a rise in consumption expenditure and hence to a rise in aggregate demand. This rise, because the price level is assumed to remain constant, will shift the AD curve to the right, as in Figure 36.2.

An increase in government spending or a fall in taxes which increases the budget deficit or reduces the budget surplus is known as EXPANSIONARY FISCAL POLICY. Fiscal policy is said to **loosen** as a result. In contrast, a higher budget surplus or lower deficit will lead to a **tightening** of the fiscal stance.

The multiplier

A rise in government spending (G) will not just increase aggregate demand by the value of the increase in G. There will be a multiple increase in aggregate demand. This **multiplier effect** will be larger the smaller the leakages from the circular flow (☞ unit 33).

In a modern economy, where leakages from savings, taxes and imports are a relatively high proportion of national income, multiplier values tend to be small. However, Keynesian economists argue that they can still have a significant effect on output in the economy if the economy is below full employment.

The output gap

Changes in government spending and taxation have an impact on the size of the output gap. In Figure 36.3, the actual path of GDP over time is shown by the red line. Between time period 2 and 3, the economy is going through a downturn or recession with actual GDP below its trend level. There is a negative output gap. Between time period 1 and 2, the economy is in boom, with GDP above its trend level. There is a positive output gap. Through its fiscal policy, however, the government can reduce the impact of the cycle, shown by the blue line. By increasing spending relative to taxation and adopting an expansionary fiscal policy, it can bring the actual level of GDP up closer to the trend level between time periods 2 and 3. By cutting its spending relative to taxation and adopting a tighter fiscal stance, it can bring the actual level of GDP down closer to the trend level between time periods 1 and 2.

Figure 36.3 Fiscal policy and the output gap
Through adjusting its level of spending and taxation, governments can bring the actual level of GDP closer to its trend level. When there is a negative output gap, governments should spend more and tax less. When there is a positive output gap, governments should spend less and tax more.

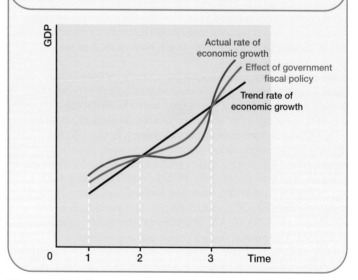

The goals of government policy

In unit 24, it was explained that the government has four major macroeconomic policy goals. These are to achieve full employment with little or no inflation in a high growth economy with an external balance (current account) equilibrium. Fiscal policy affects each of these variables through its impact on aggregate demand.

Fiscal policy can be used to achieve a wide variety of objectives. For example, it can be used to improve standards of health care through increased spending on the health service of a country. It can be used to make incomes less unequal by taxing the better and giving benefits to the less well off. However, when it is used to influence directly the level of aggregate demand it becomes an example of a DEMAND SIDE POLICY or a policy of DEMAND MANAGEMENT. Whether governments deliberately use fiscal policy to influence aggregate demand or not, changes in the balance between government spending and taxation have an effect on the four key objectives

The Labour government which took office in February 1974 barely had a majority in Parliament and therefore was unwilling to increase taxes and cut public expenditure to tackle soaring inflation and a large balance of payments deficit. In November 1974, another general election took place and this time the Labour government secured a workable majority. In the 1975 Budget, it cut planned public expenditure and increased taxes, both by over £1 000 million. Further cuts in public expenditure were announced in 1976. The budget deficit fell from £10 161 million in 1975 to £8 899 million in 1976 and to £5 419 million in 1977. However, the government relaxed its fiscal stance in 1978, and the budget deficit increased to £8 340 million.

(a) What is meant by 'the multiplier'?
(b) Explain, using the concept of the multiplier, the likely effect that the change in fiscal policy between 1974 and 1976 had on national income.
(c) Using a diagram, discuss the impact that the change in the government's fiscal stance in 1978 is likely to have had on prices and output.

of government policy: inflation, unemployment, the rate of economic growth and the balance of payments.

Inflation An increase in government spending or a fall in taxes which leads to a higher budget deficit or lower budget surplus will have a tendency to be inflationary. A higher budget deficit or lower budget surplus leads to an increase in aggregate demand. In Figure 34.4, this is shown by a shift in the aggregate demand curve to the right. This in turn leads to an increase in the price level from P_1 to P_2. So inflation increases.

The extent to which there is an increase in inflation depends on a number of factors. One is the size of the change in government spending or taxation. If the change in the budget deficit or surplus is very small, it will have little impact on the price level. Another factor is the shape of the aggregate supply curve. The short run aggregate supply curve is likely to be

relatively shallow (☞ unit 34) and so an increase in aggregate demand is likely to have a relatively small impact on prices. In the long term, however, the aggregate supply curve could vary from being horizontal to vertical. Classical economists argue that the long run aggregate supply curve (LRAS) is vertical. So, in Figure 36.5, an increase in aggregate demand has a relatively large effect on inflation. In contrast, the Keynesian view suggests that the LRAS curve is L shaped. In Figure 36.6, where the LRAS curve is horizontal, the economy has high levels of unemployment. Any increase in aggregate demand to AD_2 will have no impact on prices. If the level of output rises beyond OB, however, an increase in aggregate demand will lead to increasing inflation. The nearer the level of full employment at OD, the greater will be the rise in inflation from a given rise in government spending or fall in taxes.

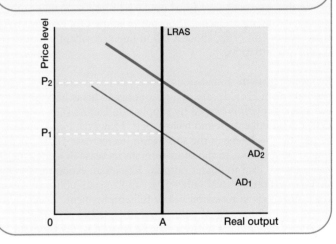

Figure 36.5 The long run classical view
In the long run, classical economists argue that expansionary fiscal policy has no effect on equilibrium output and therefore cannot reduce unemployment. However, it will lead to a higher level of prices.

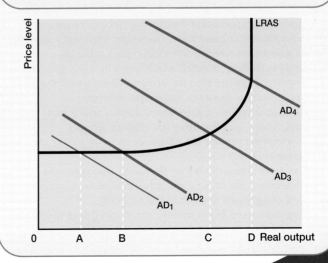

Figure 36.6 The Keynesian view
The effectiveness of fiscal policy depends upon how close the economy is to full employment. At output levels below OB, expansionary fiscal policy can increase output and reduce unemployment without increasing inflation. Between OB and OD, expansionary fiscal policy will increase both output and inflation. At full employment, OD, expansionary fiscal policy will result only in extra inflation.

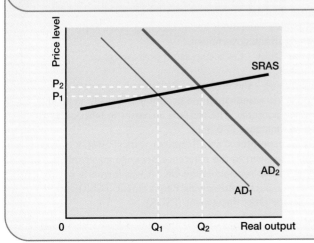

Figure 36.4 Fiscal policy and aggregate demand
A rise in government spending or a cut in taxes will shift the aggregate demand curve to the right from AD_1 to AD_2. In the short run this will be inflationary because the equilibrium price level will rise from P_1 to P_2, but equilibrium output will expand from Q_1 to Q_2.

Unemployment A greater budget deficit or a lower budget surplus will tend to reduce the level of unemployment, at least in the short term. A greater budget deficit will lead to an increase in aggregate demand which, as shown in Figure 36.4, will lead to a higher equilibrium level of output. The higher the level of output the lower is likely to be the level of unemployment.

As with inflation, there is a variety of factors which determines the extent to which unemployment will fall. The smaller the change in government spending and taxation, the less impact it will have on aggregate demand and the labour market. If the long run aggregate supply schedule if vertical, then increases in aggregate demand can only lead to higher inflation and they will have no impact on the level of output and unemployment. In the classical model, shown in Figure 36.5, the economy is in equilibrium at output OA. An increase in the budget deficit might push the level of output beyond OA in the short term because the SRAS is upward sloping, but in the long term it will revert to OA. Hence, in the classical model, demand side fiscal policy cannot be used to alter unemployment levels in the long term. In a Keynesian model, this is also true if the economy is at full employment, at OD in Figure 36.6. But at output levels below this, expansionary fiscal policy will lead to higher output and lower unemployment. If output is below OB, expansionary fiscal policy can bring about a fall in unemployment without any increase in inflation.

Economic growth Expansionary fiscal policy is unlikely to affect the long term growth rate of an economy. This is because economic growth is caused by supply side factors such as investment, education and technology. However, expansionary fiscal policy is likely, in the short term, to increase GDP. As Figure 36.4 shows, in the short term an increase in aggregate demand will lead to higher output. Keynesian economists argue that expansionary fiscal policy is an appropriate policy to use if the economy is in recession below full employment. So in Figure 36.6, expansionary fiscal policy could be used to shift the aggregate demand curve from, say, AD_3 to AD_4. This would then return the economy to operating at full capacity on its production possibility frontier (☞ unit 1). Fiscal policy which

Question 4

Explain, using diagrams, the likely impact of the following on unemployment, inflation, economic growth and the current balance.
(a) The large rises in government spending on health and education between 2003 and 2007 which were not totally matched by increases in taxation.
(b) The virtual freezing of government spending in the early 1980s at a time when tax revenues were rising.

pushes the aggregate demand curve beyond AD_4 would lead to no extra growth in output, but would be highly inflationary. In this situation, the economy would be OVER-HEATING. Classical economists argue that fiscal policy cannot be used to change real output in the long term because the long run aggregate supply curve is vertical. Shifting aggregate demand as in Figure 36.5 has no effect on output.

The balance of payments Expansionary fiscal policy leads to an increase in aggregate demand. This means that domestic consumers and firms will have more income and so will increase their spending on imports. Hence, the current account (exports minus imports ☞ unit 30) position will deteriorate. Tighter fiscal policy, on the other hand, will reduce domestic demand and hence demand for imports will fall. The current account position should then improve. There may be other less important influences on exports and imports. For instance, if domestic demand falls because of tighter fiscal policy, then domestic firms may increase their efforts to find markets for their goods by looking overseas. Equally, a fall in aggregate demand due to tighter fiscal policy should moderate the rate of inflation. British goods will be lower priced than they would otherwise have been. Hence, they will be more competitive against imports and foreigners will find British exports more keenly priced. This should lower imports and raise exports, improving the current account position.

Key terms

Budget - a statement of the spending and income plans of an individual, firm or government. The Budget is the yearly statement on government spending and taxation plans in the UK.
Budget deficit - a deficit which arises because government spending is greater than its receipts. Government therefore has to borrow money to finance the difference.
Budget surplus - a government surplus arising from government spending being less than its receipts. Government can use the difference to repay part of the National Debt.
Demand side policies or demand management - government use of fiscal and other policies to manipulate the level of aggregate demand in the economy.
Expansionary fiscal policy - fiscal policy used to increase aggregate demand.
Fiscal policy - decisions about spending, taxes and borrowing of the government.
National Debt - the accumulated borrowings of government.
Over-heating - the economy over-heats if aggregate demand is increased when the economy is already at its full productive potential. The result is increases in inflation with little or no increase in output.
Public Sector Net Cash Requirement (PSNCR) - the official name given to the difference between government spending and its receipts in the UK. It was formerly known as the Public Sector Borrowing Requirement (PSBR) and Public Sector Debt Repayment (PSDR).

Trade offs

Changing aggregate demand has different effects on the four key macroeconomic variables. The government may not be able to achieve improvements in one with bringing about a deterioration in the other, at least in the short term.

- Expanding the economy to bring it out of recession and reduce unemployment is likely to lead to higher inflation.
- Tightening fiscal policy to reduce inflation is likely to lead to higher unemployment and lower levels of GDP.
- Contracting the domestic economy by tightening fiscal policy to improve the current account situation will also lead to lower inflation, but will increase unemployment.

Fiscal policy therefore needs to be used in conjunction with other policies if the government is to steer the economy towards lower inflation and unemployment, higher growth and a current account equilibrium.

Applied economics

A history of fiscal policy

1950-1975

During the period 1950-75, fiscal policy was probably the most important way in which governments manipulated aggregate demand. During the 1950s, governments learnt to use the 'fiscal levers' with more and more confidence. In a recession, such as in 1958, the government would cut taxes to stimulate spending in the economy. This might also be accompanied by public spending increases, although it was recognised that these would take longer to multiply through the economy than tax cuts. In a boom, when the economy was over-heating, as in 1960, the government would increase taxes and possibly cut public spending.

Borrowing in the economy was mainly controlled through direct controls on banks and building societies, specifying who was allowed to borrow money, or through controls on hire purchase, the most common way of financing the purchase of consumer durables.

In the 1960s, governments began to recognise some of the limitations of fiscal policy. The Labour government of 1964-66 experimented briefly with a National Plan, an attempt to model the economy in terms of the inputs and outputs of each industry. This plan was then to be used to help the government identify where particular industries were failing or creating 'bottlenecks' and might need further investment. This supply side experiment was abandoned as the economy faced yet another sterling crisis, which ultimately ended in the pound being devalued in 1967. Another policy used from 1966 was an incomes policy - government limits on the pay rises that could be given to workers. This supply side measure was designed to lower inflation whilst allowing the economy to grow and enjoy low rates of unemployment.

The last bout of traditional Keynesian demand management came in 1972-73 when the government cut taxes and increased public spending to put the economy into boom. This boom, called the Barber boom (after Anthony Barber, the then Chancellor of the Exchequer), ended disastrously as inflation spun out of control, fuelled by the oil price increases of 1973-74.

1975-1997

The mid-1970s saw a wholesale disillusionment with traditional Keynesian demand management techniques. A classical model of the economy became increasingly accepted as the model for governments to work with. In 1976, the Labour Prime Minister of the day, Jim Callaghan, in addressing his party conference, stated that: 'We used to think that you could just spend your way out of a recession, and increase employment by cutting taxes and boosting government spending. I tell you in all candour that that option no longer exists, and that in so far as it ever did exist, it worked by injecting inflation into the economy.'

The view was taken that cutting taxes produced only a temporary increase in aggregate demand. Unemployment would fall and growth would rise. However, as in the Barber boom, the medium term consequences would be a rise in the inflation rate. To reduce inflation, the government would have to tighten its fiscal stance by raising taxes. Aggregate demand would fall and the economy would return to its equilibrium position but at a higher level of prices and of inflation.

From 1979, when Margaret Thatcher won her first general election, fiscal policy was used for two separate purposes. First, it was used for micro-economic objectives as part of supply side policy for the government (☞ unit 38). For instance, income tax was cut to increase incentives to work. Second, it was used to ensure that monetary targets were met. In particular, it was felt that changes in the PSNCR (known as the PSBR at the time), such as might come about if taxes were cut, would have no effect on aggregate demand if the money for the tax cuts was genuinely borrowed from the non-bank sector. For instance, if the government cut taxes by £1 and financed this by borrowing from the non-bank sector, then there could be no increase in aggregate demand. The taxpayer would have £1 extra to spend but the lender to the government would have £1 less to spend. On this view, increases in the PSNCR completely **crowd-out** other expenditure in the economy resulting in no increase in aggregate demand. They could only work in a Keynesian manner if the increase in the PSNCR was financed through printing the money (the government has the unique power in the economy to print money) and thus increasing the money supply.

During the period of the Lawson boom (1986-89, named after Nigel Lawson, the then Chancellor) and the following recession (1990-92), the government allowed public spending and taxes to change in line with output and employment. So in the boom, the government allowed a large budget surplus to emerge. In the recession, the PSNCR was allowed to grow and by 1993 had reached over 5 per cent of GDP. In 1994-95, the government used active fiscal policy to cut this large deficit, increasing tax rates and introducing new taxes, whilst keeping a tight rein on public spending. On Keynesian assumptions, this put a brake on aggregate demand as it increased during the recovery. On classical assumptions, the tax increases have had no effect on aggregate demand because the accompanying cuts in government borrowing released resources for the private sector to borrow and spend. One of the main reasons why the government felt it was so important to reduce the PSNCR was because of concerns that otherwise the National Debt would grow out of control.

Since 1997
In 1997, a Labour government under Tony Blair was elected and Gordon Brown became Chancellor of the Exchequer. Like previous governments since the mid-1970s, the new government did not believe that fiscal policy should be used to manage aggregate demand. Demand management was left to the Bank of England through its operation of **monetary policy** (☞ unit 37). Instead, fiscal policy was used to achieve a number of objectives such as:
- expanding health and education: government spending was increased to finance an expansion of the provision of merit goods such as health and education (☞ unit 20);
- lessening income inequality: taxes and government spending were used to make the distribution of income less unequal (☞ units 20 and 68-69);
- supply side reforms: rates of tax and government spending programmes were used to improve the performance of the supply side of the economy (☞ unit 38);
- maintaining the possibility of joining the European Monetary Union: one of the criteria for joining was that the UK should have stable public finances, with

annual government borrowing at less than 3 per cent of GDP (☞ unit 95). Note that the way in which the British government measures its annual borrowing and its national debt is different from the measures used by the EU. The British government measure is more flattering to UK public finances than the EU measure.

There was a recognition that changes in government spending and taxation could play a positive role in the trade cycle. In a recession, when the output gap was negative, government spending would increase because of increased welfare benefits to the unemployed. Tax revenues would also fall because households and businesses would have less income and be spending less. Higher government spending and lower tax revenues would increase aggregate demand from what it would otherwise have been and help pull the economy out of recession. Equally, in a boom, when the output gap was positive, government would be raising large amounts of extra tax whilst its spending on welfare benefits would fall. This would dampen growth in aggregate demand, helping to prevent the economy from overheating.

The government was also concerned that the national debt should not increase substantially as a proportion of national income. In 1998, the government therefore announced two new 'fiscal rules'.
- The **golden rule** stated that government would only borrow money to invest over the whole period of a trade cycle. It could increase borrowing to finance current expenditure such as welfare payments or wages in a recession, but this would have to be matched by repayments of debt in a boom. So government spending and taxation could help reduce the size of the fluctuation experienced in a trade cycle by influencing aggregate demand. However, over the whole cycle, net borrowing for this purpose would be zero. The government is allowed, however, to be a net borrower to finance its capital expenditure (i.e. investment), such as the building of new motorways or new hospitals.
- The **public debt rule** stated that the ratio of public debt to national income would be held at a 'stable and prudent' level over the trade cycle at less than 40 per cent of GDP.

Figures 36.10 and 36.11 in the data question show the extent to which the government achieved those objectives up to 2005.

DataQuestion   The budget: March 2005

In his March 2005 Budget, the Chancellor announced a number of changes to both government spending and taxation. For example, free local area bus travel in England would be extended to all people aged 60 and over. A Housing Benefit Reform Fund worth £180 million was launched.

Overall, he predicted that current expenditure in 2005-2006

would increase by £2 billion compared to the estimated amounts for 2004-05. Tax revenues would fall by £3 billion compared to the estimated outturn for 2004-05. Public sector borrowing on current expenditure would therefore rise by £5 billion compared to the previous year's outturn.

Figure 36.7 The output gap

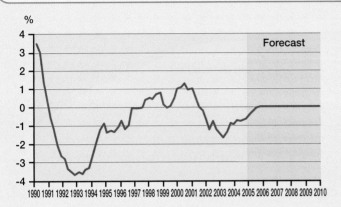

Source: adapted from *Budget 2005: the economy, charts and tables*, HM Treasury.

Figure 36.8 Growth in GDP

Source: adapted from *Budget 2005: Full report*, HM Treasury.

Figure 36.9 Inflation (annual % change in CPI)

Source: adapted from *Budget 2005: Full report*, HM Treasury.

Figure 36.10 Surplus/deficit on government current budget as a percentage of GDP

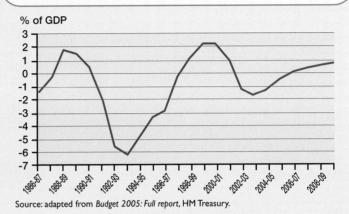

Source: adapted from *Budget 2005: Full report*, HM Treasury.

Figure 36.11 National debt as percentage of GDP

Source: adapted from *Budget 2005: Full report*, HM Treasury.

Figure 36.12 Estimated impact of changes in fiscal policy on GDP

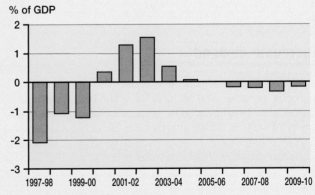

Source: adapted from *Budget 2005: Full report*, HM Treasury.

1. Explain how the Chancellor proposed to change government spending, taxation and government borrowing in the 2005 budget.
2. Figure 36.12 shows how changes in government spending and taxation in one year affected GDP in that year. To what extent did the changes in fiscal policy over the period 1997-2005 help smooth out the effects of the trade cycle?
3. What effect might the changes in total government spending, taxation and government borrowing in the 2005 Budget have had on GDP, unemployment and inflation?
4. To what extent were the Chancellor's plans announced in March 2005 in accordance with the 'fiscal rules'?

Summary

1. Governments can influence the economy through the use of monetary policy - the control of monetary variables such as the rate of interest, the money supply and the volume of credit.

2. Changing interest rates can change the level of aggregate demand through its effect on consumer durables, the housing market, household wealth, saving, investment, exports and imports.

3. A rise in interest rates is likely to reduce inflationary pressures, but lead to lower growth in output and have an adverse effect on unemployment. Exports are likely to fall, but the impact on imports is uncertain and so the overall impact on the current account is likely to vary from economy to economy.

Money and the rate of interest

Governments can, to some extent, control the rate of interest and the amount of money circulating in the economy. It can also affect the amount of borrowing or credit available from financial institutions like banks and building societies. MONETARY POLICY is the manipulation of these monetary variables to achieve its objectives.

The RATE OF INTEREST is the price of money. This is because lenders expect to receive interest if money is supplied for loans to money markets. Equally, if money is demanded for loans from money markets, borrowers expect to have to pay interest on the loans.

At various times in the past, governments have used credit controls, such as restrictions on the amount that can be borrowed on a mortgage or on hire purchase, as the main instrument of monetary policy. Equally, some governments have attempted directly to control the supply of money, the amount of money available for spending and borrowing in the economy. In recent years, the rate of interest has been the key instrument of monetary policy. For instance, both the Bank of England and the Federal Reserve Bank, the central bank of the USA, have used interest rates to achieve their policy objectives.

Aggregate demand

The rate of interest affects the economy through its influence on aggregate demand (AD) (☞ unit 33). The higher the rate of interest, the lower the level of aggregate demand. There is a variety of ways in which interest rates affect the AD curve.

Consumer durables Many consumers buy consumer durables such as furniture, kitchen equipment and cars on credit. The higher the rate of interest, the greater the monthly repayments will have to be for any given sum borrowed. Hence, high interest rates lead to lower sales of durable goods and hence lower consumption expenditure.

The housing market Houses too are typically bought using a mortgage. The lower the rate of interest, the lower the mortgage repayments on a given sum borrowed. This makes houses more affordable. It might encourage people to buy their first house or to move house, either trading up to a more expensive house or trading down to a smaller property. There are three ways in which this increases aggregate demand. First, an increase in demand for all types of housing leads to an increase in the number of new houses being built. New housing is classified as investment in national income accounts. Increased investment leads to increased aggregate demand. Second, moving house stimulates the purchase of consumer durables such as furniture, carpets and kitchens. This increases consumption. Third, moving house may release money which can be spent. A person trading down to a cheaper house will see a release of equity tied up in their home. Those trading up may borrow more than they need for the house purchase and this may be used to buy furniture or perhaps even a new car.

Wealth effects A fall in rates of interest may increase asset prices. For instance, falling interest rates may lead to an increase in demand for housing, which in turn pushes up the price of houses. If house prices rise, all homeowners are better off because their houses have increased in value. This may encourage them to increase their spending. Equally, a fall in interest rates will raise the price of government bonds. Governments issue bonds to finance their borrowing. They are sold to individuals, assurance companies, pension funds and others who receive interest on the money they have loaned to government. Like shares, bonds can go up and down in value. Rises in the price of bonds held by individuals or businesses will increase their financial wealth, which again may have a positive impact on consumer expenditure.

Saving Higher interest rates make saving more attractive compared to spending. The higher the interest rate, the greater the reward for deferring spending to the future and reducing spending now. This may lead to a fall in aggregate demand at the present time.

Investment The lower the rate of interest, the more investment projects become profitable (the marginal efficiency of capital theory ☞ unit 32). Hence the higher the level of investment and aggregate demand. Equally, a rise in consumption which leads to a rise in income will lead, in turn, to a rise in investment (the accelerator theory ☞ unit 32). Firms will need to invest to supply the extra goods and services being demanded by consumers.

The exchange rate A fall in the interest rate is likely to lead to a fall in the value of the domestic currency (its exchange rate, ☞ units 13 and 39). A fall in the value of the pound means that foreigners can now get more pounds for each unit of their currency. However, UK residents have to pay more pounds to get the same number of US dollars or Japanese yen. This in turn means that goods priced in pounds become cheaper for foreigners

Retailers are calling for a further cut in interest rates today after a survey showed another month of weak sales. According to the British Retail Consortium (BRC) survey published today, like-for-like sales, excluding the effect of new stores, were running below last year's levels for a fifth consecutive month. Kevin Hawkins, the BRCs director-general, said: 'Any growth came from heavy discounting, which is not sustainable. The underlying position is still weak and unlikely to improve unless and until there are further cuts in interest rates.' His call was echoed by Geoff Cooper, chief executive officer of Travis Perkins, the builders' merchant and owner of Wickes, that reported falling sales yesterday. 'We don't see consumer confidence or the housing market picking up for the rest of the year', he said.

Source: adapted from the *Financial Times*, 6.9.2005.

(a) Why did (i) Kevin Hawkins and (ii) Geoff Cooper want a cut in interest rates?

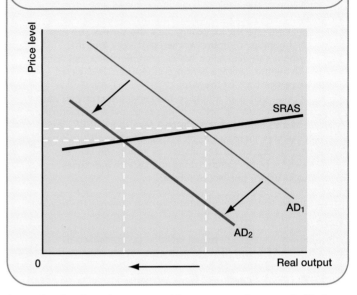

Figure 37.1 A rise in interest rates
A rise in interest rates shifts the aggregate demand curve left from AD₁ to AD₂. This leads to a fall in the price level.

to buy, whilst foreign goods become more expensive for British firms to buy. Cheaper British goods should lead to higher exports as foreigners take advantage of lower prices. In contrast, more expensive foreign goods should lead to fewer imports as British buyers find foreign goods less price competitive. Greater export levels and fewer imports will boost aggregate demand.

Policy objectives

The government has four key macroeconomic policy objectives - to control inflation and unemployment, to maintain a current account equilibrium and to secure high economic growth. Interest rate policy can affect all of these.

Inflation Interest rate policy today is used mainly to control inflation. Figure 37.1 shows a shift to the left in the aggregate demand curve caused by a rise in interest rates. This leads to a lower equilibrium price level.

Higher interest rates in practice rarely lead to the falling prices shown in Figure 37.1. This is because in modern economies aggregate demand tends to increase over time irrespective of government policy. For instance, most workers get pay rises each year, which increases aggregate demand. Profits of companies tend to increase which allows higher dividends to be paid to shareholders. A shift to the right in the aggregate demand curve from AD₁ to AD₂ caused by the annual round of pay rises is shown in Figure 37.2. This leads to a rise in the price level. If the government then increases interest rates, aggregate demand shifts back to the left to AD₃. Prices are then higher than at the start of the year with AD₁ but are not as high as they would otherwise have been. Interest rates have thus moderated the increase in the price level, i.e. they have moderated the inflation rate.

A loosening of monetary policy by lowering interest rates shifts the aggregate demand curve to the right and leads to a higher equilibrium level of prices. Looser monetary policy tends therefore to be inflationary.

Unemployment Tightening monetary policy by raising interest rates will tend to lead to a fall in equilibrium output, as shown in Figure 37.1. Lower output is likely to be associated with

lower levels of employment and hence unemployment is likely to rise. Loosening monetary policy by allowing interest rates to fall, on the other hand, is likely to lead to lower unemployment. Figure 37.1 shows the short run position.

The long run policy implications could be different though. According to classical economists, the long run aggregate supply curve is vertical. Changing the level of interest rates will therefore have no impact on either output or unemployment in the long run. In Figure 37.3, a fall in interest rates pushes the aggregate demand curve to the right but real output remains at OA. However, there is an increase in the price level. For classical economists, then, any fall in unemployment in the short

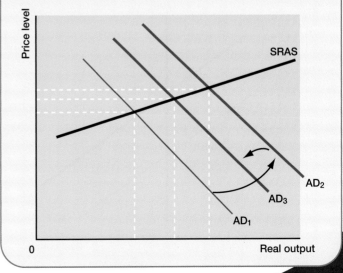

Figure 37.2 A rise in interest rates with increasing aggregate demand
Aggregate demand tends to increase over time. Raising interest rates moderates the increase. Instead of shifting to AD₂, the aggregate demand curve only shifts to AD₃. Inflation is thus lower than it would otherwise have been.

Question 2

In its Minutes for August 2005, the Monetary Policy Committee of the Bank of England explained why it had cut interest rates by 0.25 per cent. Part of the reason was a 'gentle labour market loosening since the turn of the year'. The total number of hours worked per week and the employment rate had fallen whilst unemployment had risen a little. Growth in average earnings of workers had 'eased a little since the start of the year'.

Inflation in prices of inputs to the service sector had 'eased'. In contrast, inflation in prices of inputs to the manufacturing sector were running at their highest level since 1986, due mainly to large increases in oil prices. Despite this bad news from manufacturing, price inflation of goods and services produced by both manufacturing and service industries (output inflation) had 'eased further'.

Source: adapted from Bank of England, Monetary Policy Committee Minutes, August 2005.

(a) Explain the links between inflation (as measured by the RPI or CPI) and (i) wage increases; (ii) costs of materials and other inputs to firms.
(b) Why does an easing of wage increases and material cost increases allow the Bank of England to change interest rates?

Economic growth Economic growth is a long run phenomenon. Shifting the aggregate demand curve is unlikely to have an impact on the position of the long run supply curve. The only possible link is if lower interest rates encourage investment which in turn increases the capital stock of the economy and its productive potential. Monetary policy can, however, be used to influence booms and recessions. In a boom, tighter monetary policy will reduce aggregate demand and thus lower the increase in short run output. In a recession, looser monetary policy may increase aggregate demand and hence increase equilibrium output. Some economists argue that severe recessions depress the long run trend rate of growth. Physical

Question 3

The Bank of England yesterday cut official interest rates by 0.25 per cent for the fourth time since September, citing a 'continuous slowdown' in the UK economy. Ciaràn Barr, senior UK economist at Deutsche Bank in London, said: 'We feel there is more to come. January's data are expected to be on the soft side, with the killer statistic being the first fall in gross domestic product since the second quarter of 1992.' Kate Barker, the Confederation of British Industry's chief economic adviser, said further rate cuts would be needed to ward off an outright recession. 'With continued weak global trends restraining prices in many sectors, inflation pressure is minimal' Ms Barker said.

Source: adapted from the Financial Times, 8.1.1999.

(a) Explain what was happening to the UK economy in late 1998.
(b) How might the 0.25 per cent cut in interest rates have affected (i) output and (ii) inflation?

term caused by a loosening of monetary policy will not be sustained in the long term. Unemployment will revert to its original level.

For Keynesian economists, the impact of loosening monetary policy depends upon how near the economy is to full employment. In Figure 37.4, the nearer the economy is to OA, the full employment level of output, the less impact falling interest rates will have on output and unemployment and the more it will have on inflation.

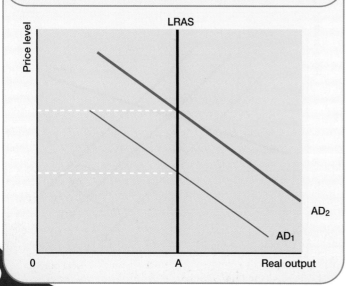

Figure 37.3 Interest rates and the classical long run aggregate supply curve
If the long run aggregate supply curve is vertical, changing interest rates will have no effect on either output or unemployment.

Figure 37.4 Interest rates and the Keynesian long run aggregate supply curve
The nearer to full employment at OA, the less impact a fall in interest rates will have on output and employment and the more on inflation.

Key terms

Bank base rate - the interest rate which a bank sets to determine its borrowing and lending rates. It offers interest rates below its base rate to customers who deposit funds with it, whilst charging interest rates above base rate to borrowers.

Central bank - the financial institution in a country or group of countries typically responsible for the printing and issuing of notes and coins, setting short term interest rates, managing the countries' gold and currency reserves and issuing government debt.

Instrument of policy - an economic variable, such as the rate of interest, income tax rates or government spending on education, which is used to achieve a target of government policy.

Monetary policy - the attempt by government or a central bank to manipulate the money supply, the supply of credit, interest rates or any other monetary variables, to achieve the fulfilment of policy goals such as price stability.

Rate of interest - the price of money, determined by the demand and supply of funds in a money market where there are borrowers and lenders.

Target of policy - an economic goal which the government wishes to achieve, such as low unemployment or high growth.

and human capital are destroyed and the economy starts its recovery from a lower level than would otherwise be the case. These economists would argue that keeping the output gap low throughout the trade cycle leads to a higher long term growth rate than if the output gap is large in successive cycles. Monetary policy can play a part in keeping the economy near to its long run trend rate of growth.

The current balance In the 1950s and 1960s, the UK government used monetary policy to influence the current balance. Higher interest rates lead to lower aggregate demand. This reduces the amount of imports purchased and hence improves the current account position. On the other hand, higher interest rates should also raise the value of the currency (☞ unit 39). A higher value of the pound will make it more difficult for UK firms to export and easier for foreign firms to sell imports to the UK. This will lead to a worsening of the current account position. Which effect is the larger varies from economy to economy and depends upon how sensitive imports are to falls in domestic income (i.e. the value of income elasticity of demand for imports). It also depends upon how sensitive exchange rates are to changes in interest rates and the sensitivity of exports and imports to changes in exchange rates (i.e. the values of price elasticity of demand for exports and imports).

Applied economics

The functions of the central bank in the UK

Since 1997, monetary policy in the UK has been controlled by the Bank of England. This is the CENTRAL BANK of the UK. Central banks tend to have a number of functions.

- They are responsible for the issue of notes and coins. These are sold to the banking system which in turn passes them on to customers as they withdraw cash from their accounts.
- They supervise the financial system, often in conjunction with other bodies specifically set up to regulate distinct parts of the financial system.
- They manage a country's gold and currency reserves. These can be used to influence the level of the exchange rate (☞ unit 39).
- They act as bankers to the government, usually managing the National Debt of the country. They arrange for the issue of new loans to cover current borrowing by a government.
- They act as bankers to the banking system. Usually, they act as lender of last resort. If a bank gets into short term difficulties, not able to raise enough cash to meet demands from its customers, the central bank will supply cash to the banking system to relieve this liquidity shortage.

Targets and instruments

Although the Bank of England is independent of the UK government, its activities are still broadly controlled by government. With regard to monetary policy, the government sets the Bank a TARGET for inflation which it has to achieve. This target was initially set at maintaining inflation, as measured by the RPIX, within a range of 1 to 4 per cent and subsequently modified to 2.5 per cent plus or minus 1 per cent per annum. Today the target is 2.0 per cent plus or minus 1 per cent as measured by the CPI. The Bank of England, therefore, has not been given any targets concerning the other three main macroeconomic policy objectives of government - unemployment, growth and the current account. These are influenced by other policies such as fiscal policy and supply side policies.

Since the mid-1980s, the Bank of England has chosen the rate of interest as its main INSTRUMENT of monetary policy. Each month, it announces whether or not it will change bank base rates. In the 1950s and 1960s, controls on credit (the borrowing of money) were significant instruments of monetary policy as well. In the 1970s and early 1980s, the emphasis shifted to the control of the money supply, the total stock of money in the economy. However, these proved unsatisfactory in an open economy like the UK, where it was increasingly easy for borrowers to gain access to funds abroad and where there was increasing competition between financial institutions.

Bank base rates

BANK BASE RATE is the rate of interest around which the main UK banks fix their lending and borrowing rates. Customers who lend money (i.e. deposit money) with a bank will get a rate of interest less than the base rate. Customers who borrow money will be charged a rate higher than base rates. The difference or spread between borrowing and lending rates is used by the bank to pay its operating costs and provide it with a profit. Each bank can in theory fix its own base rate. However, competitive pressure means that all banks have the same base rate. If one bank had a higher base rate, it would attract more deposits from other banks but would lose customers who wanted to borrow money. It could easily end up with far too much on deposit and too little being lent out. The reverse would be true if a bank set its base rate below that of other banks.

The Bank of England controls base rates through its day to day provision of money to the banking system. In practice, banks in the UK can't decide to have a different base rate from the rate of interest set by the Bank of England, which is technically called the **repo rate**.

Bank base rates are short term rates of interest. They influence other interest rates in other money markets. For instance, building societies are likely to change their interest rates if bank base rates change. If they don't, they face customers moving their business to banks who might offer more competitive deposit or borrowing rates. However, many customers only use banks or only use building societies. Many would not switch their savings from one to the other if a small difference in interest rates appeared. So sometimes building societies will not change their interest rates if the Bank of England changes bank base rates by, say, one quarter of a per cent. There are many other money markets which are even less linked to bank base rates. Credit card rates, for instance, don't tend to change if bank base rates change by 1 or 2 per cent. Long term interest rates

may also not be affected by changes in short term rates of interest. So the Bank of England only has very imperfect control of all the different money markets in the UK.

Factors affecting the decision to change interest rates

The decision as to whether to change interest rates in any one month is taken by the Monetary Policy Committee (MPC). This is a group of 9 people. Five are from the Bank of England, including the Chairperson of the Bank of England. The other four are independent outside experts, mainly professional economists. Inflation is the Bank of England's only target. So the Monetary Policy Committee considers evidence about whether inflationary pressure is increasing, decreasing or remaining stable at the time. If it believes that inflationary pressure is increasing, it is likely to raise interest rates to reduce aggregate demand. If inflationary pressure is weak, it can cut interest rates to boost aggregate demand and allow unemployment to be reduced and output to increase. In coming to any decision, it looks at a wide range of economic indicators.

For instance, it will consider the rate of increase in average earnings. If wages are rising at a faster rate than before, this could be an indication that labour is becoming scarcer in supply. The same could then also be true of goods and services. Equally, faster rising wages could feed through into higher costs for firms. They would then be forced to pass on these costs to customers and so this would be inflationary.

Another indicator is house prices. If house prices are rising fast, it is an indicator that households have money to spend which could spill over into higher demand for goods and services. Higher house prices also add to household wealth and could encourage them to borrow more, which would increase aggregate demand.

The exchange rate is important too. If the exchange rate is falling, it will make British exports more competitive and imports less competitive. This will increase aggregate demand. A rising exchange rate, on the other hand, will tend to reduce aggregate demand.

The output gap is another significant indicator. This measures the difference between the actual level of output and what economists estimate is the potential level of output of the economy. If all factors of production are fully utilised, any increase in aggregate demand will lead to higher inflation.

Problems facing the Monetary Policy Committee

One of the problems facing the Monetary Policy Committee is that economic data for one month is unreliable. If the statisticians say that average earnings increased 0.564 per cent last month, it is almost certain that this is not totally accurate. So the members of the MPC have to make judgments about how plausible are the statistics presented to them.

Another problem is that economists don't agree about exactly how the economy works. Some economists might attach more importance, for instance, to an increase in wage inflation than others. All economists accept that the real world is so complicated that it is often difficult to capture it and portray it in economic theories and models. Finally, the data is often contradictory. Some indicators will suggest an increase in inflationary pressures whilst others will show a decrease. It is less common for most of the economic data to be pointing

in the same direction. This is especially a problem if the Committee is being successful at controlling inflation over a period of time. Then, the output gap is likely to be around zero, with economic resources fully utilised. It is unlikely that one month's figures will show any clear trend. This is very different from a situation where there is, say, a large negative output gap, showing the economy operating at well below its productive potential and with high unemployment. Then it is likely to be clear that interest rates could be cut without fuelling inflation. Equally, if there is a large positive output gap, the situation is unsustainable in the long term and increased inflation is almost inevitable. Then it is clear that interest rates must rise to choke off demand.

DataQuestion — Will the Bank of England cut interest rates today?

The Monetary Policy Committee, meeting today, will have to decide whether to change interest rates. Industry and retailers want to see interest rates cut. They are complaining of a lack of spending in the economy.

On the other hand, the Monetary Policy Committee might feel that inflationary pressures are still too strong to justify a cut in interest rates.

Source: adapted from Bank of England, 9 November 2005.

Figure 37.5 Current CPI inflation projection based on interest rates at 4.5 per cent

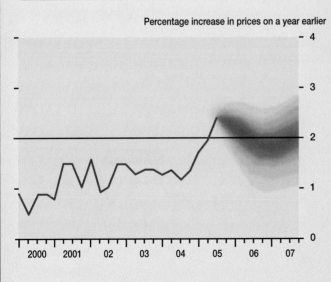

Percentage increase in prices on a year earlier

Source: adapted from Bank of England, *Inflation Report*, November 2005.

Figure 37.6 Bank base rate (%)

Source: adapted from www.statistics.gov.uk.

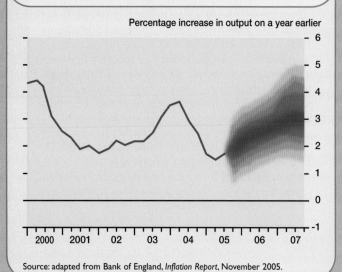

Figure 37.7 *Current projection of real GDP growth based on constant interest rates at 4.5 per cent*

Percentage increase in output on a year earlier

Source: adapted from Bank of England, *Inflation Report*, November 2005.

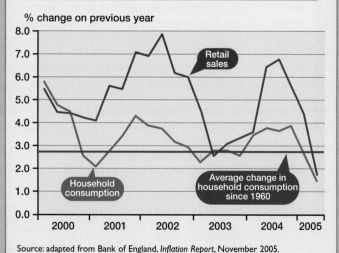

Figure 37.8 *Real household consumption, real retail sales, percentage change on a year earlier*

% change on previous year

Retail sales

Household consumption

Average change in household consumption since 1960

Source: adapted from Bank of England, *Inflation Report*, November 2005.

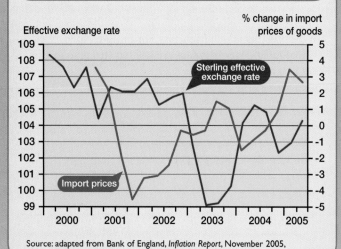

Figure 37.9 *Import prices, goods and services, percentage change on a year earlier; sterling effective exchange rate 1990=100*

Effective exchange rate

% change in import prices of goods

Sterling effective exchange rate

Import prices

Source: adapted from Bank of England, *Inflation Report*, November 2005, www.statistics.gov.uk.

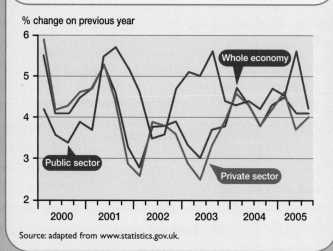

Figure 37.10 *Average earnings growth, including bonuses, percentage change on a year earlier*

% change on previous year

Whole economy

Public sector

Private sector

Source: adapted from www.statistics.gov.uk.

Figure 37.11 *Employment and number of hours worked, percentage change on previous year*

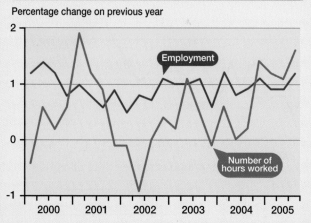

Percentage change on previous year

Employment

Number of hours worked

Source: adapted from Bank of England, *Inflation Report*, November 2005.

1. Outline the trends in inflation between 2000 and 2005.
2. Explain the link between changing interest rates and inflation. Illustrate your answer by looking at the period 2000 to 2005 shown in the data.
3. Assess whether the Bank of England should have raised interest rates, cut them or left them the same in November 2005.
4. Why might the Monetary Policy Committee find it difficult to decide whether or not to change interest rates in any one month?

Summary

1. Supply side policies are designed to increase the average rate of growth of the economy. They may also help reduce inflation and unemployment and improve the current account position.
2. Some economists, called supply side economists, believe that governments should not intervene in the workings of the free market. The government's role, they argue, is to remove restrictions to the operations of individual markets. Keynesian economists believe that governments need to intervene on the supply side to correct market failure.
3. Aggregate supply in the economy can be increased if government intervenes to ensure that labour markets operate more efficiently and if there is an increase in human capital over time.
4. Governments need to encourage firms to invest and take risks if aggregate supply is to increase.
5. Privatisation, deregulation and increased competition can increase aggregate supply.
6. Regional policy and inner city policy can also increase aggregate supply.

Supply side policies

The long run aggregate supply curve shows the productive potential of the economy. At any point in time there is only so much that an economy can produce. Over time, the productive potential of the economy will, hopefully, grow. This can be shown by a shift outwards in the production possibility frontier (☞ unit 1) or by a shift to the right in the long run aggregate supply curve (☞ unit 34).

SUPPLY SIDE POLICIES are government policies designed to increase the rate of economic growth, the rate at which the LRAS curve is shifted to the right. In Figure 38.1, a shift to the right in the LRAS curve increases output from OA to OB. In the UK and the USA, the trend rate of growth for most of the second half of the twentieth century has been around 2.5 per cent. However, average economic growth has been higher in the late 1990s and some economists claim that better supply side policies might have lifted the trend rate of growth for both of these economies. In contrast, the Japanese economy has seen its trend rate of growth fall decade by decade since the 1960s. So long term growth rates are not necessarily a constant. They can be influenced by factors such as government policy.

Supply side policies can also affect other economic variables apart from growth. Figure 38.1 shows that a shift to the right in the LRAS, all other things being equal, leads to a fall in the price level. So supply side policies which succeed in increasing the trend rate of growth of an economy can help to moderate inflation.

Supply side policies also affect unemployment. Economies are constantly changing, with new industries growing and old industries dying. Over time, new technology allows more to be produced with fewer workers. If the economy does not grow fast enough, more workers can lose their jobs in a year than new jobs are created. Unemployment therefore grows. In contrast, fast economic growth is likely to see more new jobs being created than old jobs are lost and so unemployment falls. Faster economic growth in the UK and the US in the second half of the 1990s has been associated in both countries with falling unemployment. There comes a time, as in the UK in the 1950s, when the economy is at full employment and everyone who wants a job is able to get one. Supply side policies can then play a crucial role in ensuring that inflation does not become a problem. They can help keep growth in aggregate supply equal to growth in aggregate demand.

Supply side policies affect the current account too. Increasing aggregate supply allows more goods and services to be available for export and reduces the need to import goods. In practice, effective supply side policies increase the competitiveness of domestic industry in relation to foreign industry. Domestic goods become cheaper or better quality or are of a higher specification than foreign goods. Hence exports rise compared to imports.

Different approaches

Economists agree that government can affect the supply side of the economy. However, they disagree about how this should be done.

Supply side economists Supply side economists come from the same broad school of thought as neo-classical, new classical and

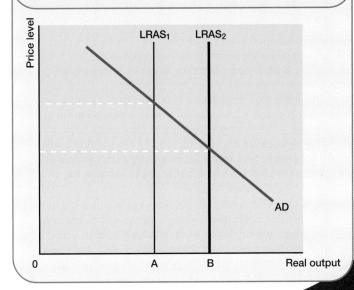

Figure 38.1 Supply side policies
Effective supply side policies push the long run aggregate supply curve to the right. This increases economic growth and reduces inflationary pressures. It may also bring about a reduction in unemployment and lead to higher exports and lower imports.

monetarist economists. They believe that free markets promote economic efficiency and that government intervention in the economy is likely to impair economic efficiency. Government still has a vital role to play in the economy, according to these economists. Government is responsible for creating the environment in which free markets can work. This means eliminating the barriers which exist to the perfect working of markets. SUPPLY SIDE ECONOMICS therefore tends to be the study of how government can intervene using **market orientated** policies.

Keynesian and neo-Keynesian economists Keynesian and neo-Keynesian economists believe that free markets often fail to maximise economic efficiency in the economy. Governments therefore have to correct **market failure** (☞ unit 16). This means intervening in free markets to change the outcome from that which it would otherwise have been.

In the rest of this unit, we will consider these two types of supply side policy - market orientated policies and interventionist policies.

Labour market policies

The level of aggregate supply is determined in part by the quantity of labour supplied to the market and the productivity of that labour. For instance, all other things being equal, an economy with 10 million workers will produce less than an economy with 20 million workers. Equally, an economy where workers have little **human capital** (☞ unit 2) will have a lower output than one where there are high levels of human capital. Classical economists argue that there is a number of ways in which the quantity and quality of labour are restricted because markets are not allowed to work freely.

Trade unions The purpose of a trade union is to organise workers into one bargaining unit. The trade union then becomes a monopsonist, a sole seller of labour, and prevents workers from competing amongst themselves in the job market. Economic theory predicts that if trade unions raise wage rates for their members, then employment and output will be lower in otherwise competitive markets. So classical economists argue that government must intervene to curb the power of trade unions, for instance by reducing their ability to strike.

State welfare benefits Workers are unlikely to take low paid jobs if state benefits are a little below or equal to the pay being offered. Hence, state benefits reduce the level of aggregate supply because more workers remain unemployed. Classical economists argue that the solution is to cut state unemployment benefits to encourage workers to take on low paid jobs. An alternative approach is to give benefits or tax credits to those who take on low paid jobs. For there to be a positive incentive to work, the benefit plus pay must be greater than the benefits the worker would have received had he been out of work.

Minimum wages If there is a minimum wage which is set above the market clearing wage, then unemployment will be created. Minimum wages prevent some workers who would be prepared to work for lower pay from getting jobs. Hence aggregate supply is lowered. Classical economists tend to argue that minimum wages should be abolished.

Marginal tax rates High marginal rates of tax (the rate of tax on the last £1 earned or spent) discourage economic activity. A tax on cigarettes leads to fewer cigarettes being bought. A tax on work (income tax) leads to people working less. A tax on profits (corporation tax) is a disincentive to firms to make profits. Lowering certain taxes will therefore raise the level of economic activity and increase aggregate supply.

Supply side economists believe that the supply of labour is relatively elastic. A reduction in marginal tax rates on income will lead to a significant increase in 'work'. This could mean individuals working longer hours, being more willing to accept promotion, being more geographically mobile, or simply being prepared to join the workforce.

Work is, arguably, an inferior good, whilst leisure, its alternative, is a normal good. The higher an individual's income, the less willing he or she is to work. So a cut in marginal tax rates will have a negative income effect at the margin (i.e. the worker will be less willing to work). However, a cut in marginal tax rates will have a positive substitution effect because the relative price of work to leisure has changed in favour of work (i.e. the worker will be more willing to work).

Supply side economists believe that the substitution effect of a tax cut is more important than the income effect and hence tax cuts increase incentives to work. If cutting marginal income tax rates encourages people to work harder and earn more, then in theory it could be that tax revenues will increase following a tax cut. For instance, if 10 workers, each earning £10 000 a year, pay an average 25 per cent tax, then total tax revenue is £25 000 (10 x £10 000 x 0.25). If a cut in the tax rate to 20 per cent were to make each worker work harder and increase earnings to, say, £15 000, tax revenues would increase to £30 000 (10 x £3 000). This is an example of the LAFFER

Question 1

A number of studies has been completed discussing the link between income tax cuts and incentives to work. For instance, Brown and Dawson (1969) surveyed all the studies published between 1947 and 1968 making links between tax rates and hours worked. They found that high taxation acted as a disincentive to working longer hours for between 5 and 15 per cent of the population. These workers were mainly people who could choose to vary their hours of work relatively easily - the wealthy, rural workers, the middle aged and those without families. On the other hand, a smaller group of people tended to increase their hours of work when taxes were higher. These were typically part of large families, young, less well-off urban dwellers.

In a 1988 study by C V Brown, it was found that the substantial increase in tax allowances in the 1988 Budget only increased the number of hours worked in the economy by 0.5 per cent. The cut in the basic rate of tax had no effect at all on hours worked whilst the massive cut in the top rate of tax from 60 per cent to 40 per cent only had a small effect in stimulating extra hours of work by the rich.

(a) Explain why tax rates might have an effect on incentives to work.
(b) To what extent have tax cuts increased the number of hours worked?
(c) What are the implications of the two studies described in the passage for the shape of the Laffer curve?

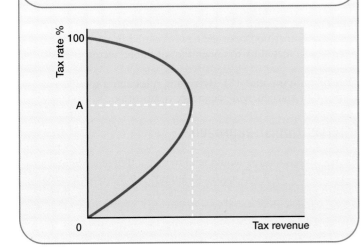

Figure 38.2 The Laffer curve
As tax rates increase, economic activity is discouraged and hence the rate of growth of tax revenues falls. Above OA, an increase in tax rates so discourages economic activity that tax revenues fall.

CURVE effect, named after Professor Arthur Laffer who popularised the idea in the late 1970s. Figure 38.2 shows a Laffer curve, which plots tax revenues against tax rates. As tax rates increase, the rate of growth of tax revenue falls because of the disincentive effects of the tax. OA shows the maximum revenue position of the tax. At tax rates above OA, an increase in the tax rate so discourages economic activity that tax revenues fall.

Poverty and unemployment traps The combination of marginal rates of income tax and withdrawal of benefits can lead to poverty and unemployment traps. The POVERTY or EARNINGS TRAP occurs when a low income working individual or household earns more, for example by gaining promotion, getting a better paid job or working more hours, but the net gain is little or even negative. It occurs because as income increases, welfare benefits are withdrawn. Equally, the individual or household might start to pay tax. For example, if an individual loses 50p in benefits when earning an extra £1, and then pays income tax and National Insurance contributions at 30 per cent, then the net gain from earning the extra £1 is only 20p (£1 - 50p - 30p). The effective marginal rate of tax here is 80 per cent. If the benefit loss were 90p in the pound, the individual would be 20p worse off. The effective marginal rate of tax here would be 120 per cent. The poverty trap is a major disincentive for those working and receiving benefits to work harder or increase their skills. The UNEMPLOYMENT TRAP occurs when an individual is little better off or is even worse off getting a job than staying unemployed because of loss of benefits and taxation. The unemployment trap, where it occurs, is a major disincentive for the unemployed to find work. One solution to both kinds of trap is to lower welfare benefits but this increases poverty. The other solution is to reduce taxes on income and the rate of welfare benefit withdrawal as incomes increase. This is a more expensive solution for the government and the taxpayer.

Taxes on labour Firms will not take on workers if their total wage cost is too high. Part of the total cost is the wages of

workers. However, many countries tax firms for employing labour, often by imposing employer contributions to state social security funds. In the UK, for instance, employers have to pay National Insurance employers' contributions. The higher the tax, the fewer workers will be employed and hence the lower will be the level of aggregate supply.

Reducing the cost of changing jobs In a modern fast-changing economy, workers are likely to be changing jobs on a relatively frequent basis. Some workers will even become **portfolio workers**, having a mix of part-time jobs at any one time rather than a single full time job. If the labour market is such that workers find it difficult to get new jobs when they are made redundant, then unemployment will rise and aggregate supply will fall. So the government must ensure that **barriers to mobility** between jobs are as low as possible. One important barrier to mobility can be pensions. If pension rights are typically provided by individual employers, then a worker who is frequently moving from employer to employer will lose out. Hence, governments should give workers the opportunity to provide for their own pension which they can take with them from job to job. Another problem in the UK has been a lack of geographical mobility due to rigidities in the housing market. If house prices in the south of England are much higher than in the north, then workers will be discouraged from moving from north to south. Equally, if workers are unable to rent houses at an affordable rent in an area, then low paid workers will not be able to move into that area to take up jobs.

In a recent report on the UK economy, the OECD (Organisation for Economic Co-operation and Development) highlighted weaknesses in the UK education and training system that were hindering its growth performance. It was particularly critical of educational provision for less academic students. It said that 'much more could still be done to improve basic literacy and numeracy, thus providing a strong foundation for continued learning'. It also argued that 'continuously improving the relevance and quality of vocational programmes is as important as it is to expand their provision'.

It was worried that the tax and benefits system might discourage individuals from acquiring intermediate skills. It pointed out that, whilst gross earnings of workers with intermediate skills were significantly higher than those of low skilled workers, net income was little different if those workers had children because of tax credits that low skilled, low pay workers can claim. For 16-18 year olds, pilot schemes which have paid teenagers to stay in education appear to have boosted engagement in continued learning. But an alternative might be to increase the very light taxation faced by teenagers taking a job at 16.

Source: adapted from OECD, *Economic Survey of the United Kingdom 2005.*

(a) Using a diagram, explain why the quality of the labour force is so important for the long term growth of the UK economy.
(b) Suggest why improving 'basic literacy and numeracy' might be important for increase the long term human capital stock of the economy.
(c) Explain why taxes and benefits might be a disincentive to acquire skills in the UK.

Education and training Increasing the level of human capital of workers is vital if economies are to develop. Increased levels of education and training will raise the marginal revenue product of workers (i.e. will raise the value of output of workers). This in turn will shift the aggregate supply curve to the right. The value of human capital in the economy is one of the most important determinants of the level of aggregate supply.

The capital market

Increasing the capital stock of the country, such as its factories, offices and roads, will push the aggregate supply curve to the right. According to classical economists, the government has a key role to play in this.

Profitability Firms invest in order to make a profit. The higher the rate of profit, the more investment will take place. Hence, government must create an environment in which firms can make profits for their owners. One way of doing this is by reducing taxes on company profits. Another is to reduce inheritance tax which might be paid by a small business owner when passing on his or her business to a family relative. Another is to reduce taxes on employing workers. Reducing the amount of government red tape, like planning permissions, can also help reduce costs and increase profitability.

Allocating scarce capital resources The government is in a poor position to decide how to allocate resources. It should leave this as much as possible to the private sector. Hence, state owned companies should be **privatised** wherever possible. Government should offer only limited taxpayers' money to subsidise industry. The government should stay well clear of trying to 'back winning companies'.

Increasing the range of sources of capital available to firms Firms can be constrained in their growth if they are unable to gain access to financial capital like bank loans or share capital. Government should therefore encourage the private sector to provide financial capital, particularly to small businesses. They may, for instance, offer tax incentives to individuals putting up share capital for a business.

The goods market

Inefficient production will lead to a lower level of aggregate supply. For instance, if UK car workers produce 50 per cent fewer cars per worker with the same equipment as German workers, then the level of aggregate supply in the UK can obviously be increased if UK labour productivity is raised. The government has a key role to play in increasing efficiency.

Classical economists argue that the most important way of securing increased efficiency is through encouraging **competition**. If firms know that they will go out of business if they do not become efficient, then they have a powerful incentive to become efficient producers. The government can increase competition in the market in a number of ways.

Encouraging free trade (☞ unit 40) Fierce foreign competition results in a domestic industry which has to be efficient in order to survive. The government should therefore liberalise trade, removing tariffs (taxes) and other barriers to imports.

Encouraging small businesses Small businesses can operate in markets where there are no large businesses. Competition here is intense. However, small businesses can operate in markets where there are very large firms. Small businesses then force larger firms to remain cost competitive. Otherwise the larger firms will lose market share.

Privatisation (☞ unit 18) Privatising firms, and in the process creating competition between newly created firms, eliminates the distortions created by the operation of public sector monopolies.

Deregulation (☞ unit 18) Removing rules about who can compete in markets will encourage competition.

Interventionist approaches

Keynesian economists would tend to take a different approach to government policy and aggregate supply. They would tend to focus on issues of where free markets fail. For instance, they would agree with classical economists that a key aspect of government policy must be to increase education and training. However, whereas classical economists would argue that training should be left to individual companies or groups of companies in a local area, Keynesians would argue that training is best organised by government. The state should, for instance, impose levies on firms to finance state organised training placements and schemes.

With regard to investment in physical capital, classical economists would argue that profit should direct the level and pattern of investment. Keynesian economists would argue that if investment is insufficient in the economy, then the government should intervene and, for instance, use taxes to set up state owned companies or subsidise investment by private industry.

In the 1950s and 1960s in the UK, the main supply side

Question 3

Britain's offshore industry has reacted angrily to the UK Chancellor's decision to impose an extra 10 per cent tax on profits from North Sea oil fields. It will raise an estimated £6.5 billion in revenue for the government over the next three years. The UK Offshore Operators Association said that: 'It is almost beyond comprehension that the government has failed to grasp the vulnerability of the industry's future in the UK. His move could not come at a worse time. North Sea activity has recovered remarkably since 2002 when it was last hit by a punitive tax charge.' It went on to say that: 'It will deter investment in new fields and make older fields less attractive for increased recovery. Moreover, the impact will be felt significantly by smaller oil and gas producers. The unexpected tax hit on the industry in 2002 led to a major slump in investor confidence in the North Sea. Exploration and development activity fell to record lows as investment left the North Sea for other less challenging parts of the globe with lower costs.'

Source: adapted from Press Release, United Kingdom Offshore Operators Association, December 2005.

(a) Explain the link between company taxes and North Sea oil exploration and development.
(b) What impact might the 10 per cent extra tax on North Sea oil profits have on long run aggregate supply?

problem was that of regional inequality with the north of England, Scotland and Northern Ireland experiencing higher unemployment rates than the south and the Midlands. The Keynesian policy response was a mixture of offering incentives to firms investing in high unemployment regions and making it difficult for firms to expand in low unemployment regions.

Question 4

Scientific innovation, knowledge transfer, skills, enhancement and transport improvements are main elements of the £100 million spending plan, unveiled today, which is intended to kick-start the north of England's economy.

The Northern Way business plan is an attempt by three northern regional development agencies to tackle the north-south divide in economic performance. The Northern Way has put the output gap between north and south at £30 billion. It calculated this by comparing the Gross Value Added per capita of the three northern regions with the all-England average in the five years 1999-2003.

The £100 million will fund a variety of initiatives to improve the competitiveness of the three regions. For example, £15 million will be spent funding centres of excellence in leadership, innovation and the skills for sustainable communities. £12 million will produce some small but significant transport improvements and develop the case for a new approach to transport investment in the North. £3 million will help establish a new £6.5 million National Industrial Biotechnology Facility in the Tees Valley.

Source: adapted from the *Financial Times* 20.6.2005; Press Release, The Northern Way, 20.6.2005.

(a) Using examples from the passage, explain how assistance from the government might increase aggregate supply.

Key terms

Laffer curve - a curve which shows that at low levels of taxation, tax revenues will increase if tax rates are increased; however, if tax rates are high, then a further rise in rates will reduce total tax revenues because of the disincentive effects of the increase in tax.
Poverty or earnings trap - occurs when an individual is little better off or even worse off when gaining an increase in wages because of the combined effect of increased tax and benefit withdrawal.
Supply side economics - the study of how changes in aggregate supply will affect variables such as national income; in particular, how government micro-economic policy might change aggregate supply through individual markets.
Supply side policies - government policies designed to increase the productive potential of the economy and push the long run aggregate supply curve to the right.
Unemployment trap - occurs when an individual is little better off or even worse off when getting a job after being unemployed because of the combined effect of increased tax and benefit withdrawal.

Applied economics

Supply side policies in the UK

Since 1979, the government has been committed to implementing supply side policies aimed at improving the workings of free markets. A wide range of measures have been introduced which are described below.

The labour market

Trade union power In the 1960s and 1970s, there was a fierce debate about trade union power. It was widely recognised that trade unions, which at their membership peak in 1979 represented half of all UK workers, had considerable power in the workplace at the time. In 1979, the Conservative party under Margaret Thatcher was elected into office with a manifesto pledge to reduce trade union power and make UK industry more flexible and competitive. A number of Acts were passed which effectively made secondary picketing illegal and firms gained the power to sue trade unions involved for damages. Industrial action called by a union now had to be approved by a secret ballot of its membership. Secret ballots were also made compulsory for elections of trade union leaders. Closed shops, places of work where employers agreed that all workers should be trade union members, became more difficult to maintain and enforce. The government also took an extremely hard line with strikes in the public sector, refusing to give in to union demands. The breaking of strikes, such as the miners' strike of 1983-85, increased the confidence of private employers to resist trade union demands. By the mid-1990s, with the loss of over one quarter of their members since 1979, trade unions had become marginalised in many places of work and considerably weakened in others.

The election of a Labour government in 1997 did not reverse this position. In 1999, it passed the Employee Relations Act 1999 which forced employers to recognise the negotiating rights of trade unions if a majority of workers in the workplace voted in favour.

However, whilst this might increase union membership in the long term, it is unlikely in itself to greatly increase union power.

Wage bargaining Supply side economists view collective bargaining as an inflexible way of rewarding workers. They advocate individual pay bargaining with payment systems based on bonuses and performance related pay. By reducing the power of trade unions, the government in the 1980s and early 1990s went some way to breaking collective bargaining. It encouraged employers to move away from national pay bargaining to local pay bargaining. In the public sector, it attempted to move away from national pay agreements to local ones. The Labour government elected in 1979 was more sympathetic to trade unions but made it clear it would not reverse most of the trade union reforms of the 1980s and early 1990s. However, the 1999 Employee Relations Act increased the ability of trade unions to force recognition by employers of their negotiating rights. At the same time, the signing of the Social Chapter influenced some larger firms to set up works councils which involve trade unions. The government is also supporting greater social partnerships between businesses and unions which may also encourage collective bargaining.

State welfare benefits Supply side economists tend to argue that welfare benefits can be a major disincentive to work. The benefit system needs to avoid creating **poverty traps** (where an increase in wages leads to a fall in income for a worker after tax has been paid and benefits withdrawn) and **unemployment traps** (where unemployed workers find that they can receive a higher income from remaining unemployed than by taking low paid jobs). In the 1980s, one solution to this was to cut the real value of benefits for low income households. It was made more difficult to collect unemployment benefits and the unemployed came under much greater pressure to accept jobs that were offered or take up places on training schemes. The Labour government elected in 1997 was committed both to reducing poverty and unemployment. Its main initiative to get round both the unemployment and poverty traps was the Working Families Tax Credit, introduced in 1999, and replaced by the Child Tax Credit and the Working Tax Credit in 2003. These increased the take home pay of low income earners by giving them benefits paid through their earnings. Even so, effective marginal rates of tax for some low paid can still be far more than the 40 per cent top rate of income tax paid by high income earners. With regard to unemployment, some economists argue that much of the fall in unemployment in the 1990s and 2000s occurred simply because the long term unemployed were shifted onto disability and incapacity benefits. In the early 2000s, the government made some attempt to make it more difficult to claim these benefits and to get some

of those already on these benefits onto training schemes or into work. By 2005, however, success had been very limited.

Social legislation Legislation protecting the rights of workers goes back to the nineteenth century when curbs were placed on the employment of children and of women. Over time, workers have gained more and more rights. For example, workers are protected by law from the moment they apply for a job to the time they leave. Holiday entitlements, maternity and paternity leave, sickness, disability, training, health and safety and discrimination are all covered by legislation. In 1997, the UK signed the Social Chapter of the Maastricht Treaty 1992, which gave Brussels the right to introduce regulations covering conditions of employment in the UK. Businesses tend to view regulations as 'red tape' which impairs their competitiveness. However, most other European countries, such as France and Germany, have more onerous regulations and view the UK as being relatively lightly regulated.

Training and education Education and training are recognised by the government as keystones of its supply side policies. Whilst the education of the top 20 or 30 per cent of the population by ability has traditionally been, by international standards, excellent, the education of the rest of the population has tended to be at best mediocre and at worst poor. Since the 1980s, the government has attempted to address these problems in a variety of ways. One has been to take central control of the curriculum in schools, for example through the National Curriculum established in the 1980s and more recently through numeracy and literacy initiatives. Another has been set targets for schools and colleges for student attainment. Another has been through inspection of schools and colleges, such as the work of Ofsted. The idea of competition between schools, and a much greater variety of schools which parents may choose for their children, has been experimented with and remains a central plank of government policy. Successive governments have encouraged more students to stay on in education to 18 and 21. In the mid-2000s training in the UK was the responsibility of a variety of bodies including Regional Development Agencies, Learning and Skills Councils and the Small Business Service.

Much work has been done on providing vocational routes through education, although reform of the vocational framework begun in the 1980s has produced mixed results. This has arguably meant that the educational pathway for less academic students remains poorer than in many of our industrial competitors. Training in the workplace has also come in for continued criticism and lifelong training for workers in the UK, particularly those with low skills, continues to be criticised by international organisations like the OECD.

Marginal tax rates Marginal income tax rates by 1979 were very high. The standard rate of income tax was 33 per cent whilst the highest rate on earned income was 83 per cent. The incoming Conservative government made it a priority to cut these and within ten years the highest marginal income tax rate was 40 per cent, where it has remained since. Income tax cuts were designed in part to increase incentives to work. Incentives to accumulate wealth were given by cuts in both inheritance tax and capital gains tax rates. Employers too have gained with Employers National Insurance contributions falling. The UK has continued to have almost the lowest social security taxes on employers and employees in Europe.

Help to businesses

If aggregate supply is to increase, the private sector needs to expand. Hence, according to supply side economists, the government needs to create an environment in which business can flourish.

Small businesses Small businesses are important in the economy because they provide new jobs and can become the big businesses of tomorrow. Conservative governments between 1979 and 1997 placed particular importance on the development of an 'enterprise culture' and laid the groundwork for many of the policies which are in operation today. Existing small businesses are helped through reduced rates on taxes on profits (corporation tax) and tax allowances for investment. They may be eligible for short term loans in circumstances when a commercial bank would refuse to lend to them. Advice is available from the Small Business Service. Regulation ('red

tape') is often less for small businesses than large businesses. However, the burden of regulation on small businesses is often heavier because they have fewer resources and less expertise to deal with the regulations with which they have to comply. New small businesses can get a variety of help from grants and loans for training.

Innovation and research Since 1997, the government has been keen to promote innovation and research. Tax allowances have traditionally been available to businesses spending on innovation and research. However, there is a variety of programmes which enable some businesses to gain grants for research and development (R&D), and to set up knowledge transfer networks between industry and an academic establishment.

Goods markets

It is argued that competition increases both productive and allocative efficiency. Markets should therefore be made as competitive as possible. Encouraging competition was central to government policy after 1979.

Deregulation and privatisation In the 1980s, the government introduced policies to privatise state owned companies and deregulate markets. Nearly all state owned companies were privatised by the end of the 1990s including British Telecom and the gas industry. Central government departments and local authorities were encouraged to offer such services as waste collection or cleaning to tender rather than employing staff directly to provide the service. Many controls were abolished, such as legal restrictions on pub opening hours and Sunday trading. Since 2000, the government has further increased the involvement of the private sector in providing public sector services. For example, 2004 saw the opening of the UK's first private toll motorway. In the NHS, the government is contracting out operations to private sector health companies. Many new buildings, such as schools and hospitals, are being built and operated by the private sector and the Private Finance Initiative (PFI). The private sector companies are then leasing back the facilities to the state sector for its use. In 2006, the postal letter service was opened up for the first time to serious competition.

Encouragement of international free trade Fierce foreign competition results in a domestic industry which has to be efficient in order to survive. Since 1979, governments have tended to advocate policies of free trade on most issues. For instance, they have been more willing than most other European governments to see greater free trade in agriculture. The UK has also been one of the most welcoming to foreign companies wanting to set up in the UK.

Regional and industrial policy

Before 1979, the main focus of supply side policies was regional and industrial policy. Regional policy aimed to help poorer regions of the UK to attract businesses and create jobs. Industrial policy aimed to help industries which were undergoing difficult trading conditions, such as textiles, shipbuilding, the motor manufacturing industry, coal mining and steel. Since 1999, each region of the UK has a Regional Development Agency (RDA) working to create jobs and improve the competitiveness of the region. The most high profile work of the nine RDAs has been giving grants to incoming foreign companies wanting to set up large showcase manufacturing plants. However, most of their spending is spread amongst a wide range of initiatives, from grants to small start up businesses, to promoting training of workers, to encouraging infrastructure developments such as new roads or airports.

DataQuestion

Lighten taxes

The leading industrial economies need to reform their corporate tax systems by reducing taxes on capital, according to a study by the CD Howe Institute, a Canadian research institute. If they don't, they will fail to overcome Asian countries' advantage in labour costs. 'Heavy taxes on investment discourage businesses from buying the new-vintage capital and latest technologies that improve labour productivity', the study says. 'In the absence of such modernisation, production processes age, businesses fall behind and they have difficulty increasing their employees' incomes... . Lowering taxes on capital investment holds the key to growth.'

The study says that looking at the tax take as a proportion of GDP gives a misleading impression of the burden of corporate tax. A much wider number of variables needs to be considered. Marginal corporate tax rates (the proportion of tax on the last £1 of profit earned) are important. So too are rules on depreciation, stocks, other business expenses, sales taxes, financial transaction taxes and other payments on investments. The study sought to take all these into account in calculating an effective corporate tax rate for 36 countries. The results, shown in Table 38.1, are surprising, with some countries, such as Sweden, where government spends around 60 per cent of GDP, having relatively low effective corporate tax rates. In Sweden, taxes on profits are relatively low because companies are allowed to depreciate the cost of investment very quickly to offset their tax bill. China, on the other hand, has a very high effective tax rate on capital, mainly caused by a 17 per cent value added tax on machinery. This is a surprising result given that the Chinese economy has grown at three times the rate of the average for industrialised countries for the past thirty years.

Countries with low effective tax rates on capital tend to have high levels of inflows of investment capital relative to GDP. Ireland, Hong Kong, Singapore and Sweden have ratios of foreign direct investment (FDI) to GDP of between 8 and 18 per cent. In contrast, the ratio in Germany is just 2.7 per cent and in Canada is 3.8 per cent.

Source: adapted from the *Financial Times*, 20.9.2005.

Table 38.1 Effective tax rates on capital from corporations

	Headline statutory corporate income tax rate %	Average effective tax rate on capital %
China	24.0	45.8
Canada	34.3	39.0
Brazil	34.0	38.5
US	39.2	37.7
Germany	38.4	36.9
Italy	39.4	36.2
Russia	22.0	34.5
Japan	41.9	33.6
France	35.4	33.3
South Korea	27.5	30.8
Spain	35.0	27.3
Netherlands	31.5	25.0
India	33.0	24.3
UK	30.0	21.7
Sweden	28.0	12.1
Hong Kong	17.5	8.1
Singapore	20.0	6.2

1. Explain why having low taxes on profits would be an example of a supply side policy.
2. Using a long run aggregate supply curve diagram, analyse why low corporate taxes might benefit an economy like that of the UK.
3. Discuss whether low corporate taxes could be the main determinant of economic growth.

Summary

1. The value of a currency in a floating exchange rate system is determined by the forces of demand and supply.
2. Governments can influence the value of their currency by changing interest rates and by intervening directly on the foreign exchange markets using their gold and foreign currency reserves.
3. A rise in the value of a currency is likely to reduce exports but increase imports. A fall in the value of a currency is likely to increase exports but reduce imports.
4. Raising the exchange rate is likely to benefit inflation but will tend to reduce output, increase unemployment and lead to a deterioration in the current account. A fall in the exchange rate is likely to increase both inflation and output, reduce unemployment and lead to an improvement in the current account.

Exchange rate systems

The value of currencies like the US dollar, the Japanese yen and Britain's currency, the pound sterling, is determined by the foreign currency markets (☞ unit 13). At any point in time, there are buyers in the market for a currency and there are sellers. The forces of demand and supply then determine the price of the currency.

This system of determining exchange rates is known as a **free or floating exchange rate system**. There have been and still are other types of system. For instance, the value of the pound was fixed against the US dollar between 1946 and 1971. The Bank of England guaranteed to exchange pounds for US dollars at a **fixed exchange rate**. This is an example of a fixed exchange rate system. Before 1914, the world's major currencies were fixed in value in relation to gold. In Europe, before the euro became the official currency of the eurozone, each separate currency was fixed against each other at a specific rate. The value of the French franc could not change against the German deutschmark. Today, the euro itself is allowed to float against other currencies and so its value is determined within a floating exchange rate system.

This unit will consider exchange rate policy within a floating exchange rate system. This is the situation that faced the government in the UK and the European Central Bank which controls the euro at the start of the new millennium.

Influencing the exchange rate

Exchange rate policy tends to be administered by the **central bank** (☞ unit 37) of a country which controls exchange rates and its gold and foreign currency reserves. There are two main ways today in which central banks influence the value of their currency.

Interest rates Increasing domestic interest rates is likely to increase the value of the currency. This is because higher interest rates in, say, the UK, makes depositing money in London more attractive. Savings are attracted into the UK from overseas, whilst UK firms and institutions are less attracted to sending their savings to New York, Tokyo or Paris. Hence the demand for pounds is likely to increase, shown by a shift to the right in the demand curve for pounds, whilst the supply decreases, shown by a shift to the left in the supply curve. This results in a new higher equilibrium price (☞ unit 13).

Use of gold and foreign currency reserves Central banks have traditionally kept gold and foreign currency reserves. These are holdings of gold and foreign currencies which can be used to alter the value of a currency. If the Bank of England wanted to increase the value of the pound, it would sell some of its foreign currency reserves in exchange for pounds. This would increase the demand for the pound and hence raise its price. If it wanted to reduce the value of the pound, it would sell pounds for foreign currency, increasing supply and hence reducing the equilibrium price.

The ability of governments to influence the exchange rate is limited when the currency is floating. The amounts of money being traded each day on foreign exchange markets are so large that a country's foreign currency reserves could be used up within days trying to support a value of the exchange rate which the markets believed was too high. Equally, interest rate differentials between countries have to be substantial to have a significant impact on the value of the currency. Even so, governments can and do intervene to nudge exchange rates in directions which they believe desirable.

How exchange rate movements affect the economy

Exchange rate movements mainly affect the real economy through their effects on exports and imports. A rise or APPRECIATION in the exchange rate will tend to make exports more expensive to foreigners but imports cheaper to domestic customers. A fall or DEPRECIATION in the exchange rate will have the reverse effect, making exports cheaper and imports more expensive.

To understand why, consider a good priced at £100 which is being sold for export to the US by a UK firm. If the exchange rate is £1=$1, the US customer will have to pay $100. If the value of the pound rises to £1=$2, then the US customer will have to pay $200 for it. At the new higher exchange rate, the US customer has to pay more dollars to acquire the same number of pounds as before.

Similarly, consider a good priced at $100 in the US. If the exchange rate is £1=$1, then it will cost a UK customer £100. If the exchange rate rises to £1=$2, the cost to the UK customer will fall to £50.

A rise in the value of the pound will make UK firms less

The pound rose yesterday to its highest level against the dollar since Black Wednesday, the day in September 1992 when the pound was forced out of the Exchange Rate Mechanism. One factor was a report by the Organisation for Economic Co-operation and Development (OECD) which said that the Bank of England would need to increase its interest rates to control inflation. Another factor was reports that Asian central banks have been shifting their foreign exchange rate holdings out of dollars into other currencies such as the pound. Central banks in Japan, China and South Korea in recent years have been selling their own domestic currencies in exchange for US dollars in an attempt to weaken the value of their own currencies.

Source: adapted from the *Financial Times*, 2.12.2004.

(a) Explain why a rise in domestic interest rates by the Bank of England might affect the exchange rate value of the pound.
(b) Explain why the sale of South Korean Won, or Japanese Yen by the South Korean and Japanese central banks for US dollars might affect the value of the Won or the Yen.

---

price competitive internationally. British exporters will find their orders falling as foreign customers switch to other, cheaper sources. In domestic markets, British firms will find that foreign imports are undercutting their prices and gaining market share. Exactly how much EXPORT and IMPORT VOLUMES, the number of goods sold, will change depends upon their price elasticity of demand (☞ unit 8). If the price elasticity of demand for exports is elastic, with a value of, say, 2, then a 10 per cent rise in the price of exports to foreigners will result in a 20 per cent fall in export volumes.

Firms may, however, adopt a different response to an appreciation or depreciation of the currency. They may choose to keep prices to customers in their currency the same. For instance, with the good priced at £100 which is sold to the USA, the British firm could decide to keep the price at $100 when the exchange rate appreciates from £1=$1 to £1=$2. What this means is that the British exporter would then only receive £50 for the good. The British firm would not lose market share as a result, but it would see its profit margins fall. There are two reasons why an exporter might be prepared to accept a lower price for the product in domestic currency terms. First, it may think that the foreign currency movement is temporary. For marketing reasons, it does not want to be constantly changing its foreign currency price every time there is a small change in the exchange rate. Second, it may have been earning **abnormal profit** (☞ unit 17) previously, a higher level of profit than the minimum needed to keep the firm supplying the good.

If firms keep their prices to customers the same in their currencies, then export and import volumes will remain unchanged. However, profitability will have changed. If a currency appreciates in value, exporters will be forced to cut their prices in their own currency to maintain prices in foreign currencies. Their profitability will decline and it will become less attractive to export. Export values will fall too because, although volumes have remained the same, prices in domestic currency terms will have fallen. As for imports, foreign firms importing to the UK that choose to keep their sterling prices the same will see their profits rise. This will

give them a greater incentive to sell into the UK. They might choose, for instance, to advertise more aggressively. Import volumes are therefore likely to rise, increasing import values as a result.

A third alternative is that firms may choose to change their export and import prices but not by as much as the change in the exchange rate. For instance, assume that the value of the pound rises 10 per cent against the US dollar. A UK exporting firm may choose to absorb 6 per cent of the rise by reducing the pound sterling price by 6 per cent and passing on the remaining 4 per cent by raising the dollar price. Profit margins fall and there could be some loss of market share because US customers now face higher prices. But this might be better for the firm than either cutting its sterling price by 10 per cent, eating into its profit margins, or raising US dollar prices by 10 per cent and risking losing substantial market share.

Which type of strategy a firm chooses to use to some extent depends upon the industry in which it operates. For commodity products, like steel, wheat or copper, firms are likely to have little control over their market. They will be forced to pass on price rises or falls to customers as exchange rates change. Firms which can control their markets, like car manufacturers, tend to leave prices unaltered as exchange rates change.

The macroeconomic impact of changes in exchange rates

Exchange rates can be an **instrument** of government policy to achieve policy **goals** or **targets** (☞ unit 37).

Inflation Raising the exchange rate is likely to moderate inflation for two reasons. First, a higher exchange rate will tend

British cheese manufacturers, like most exporters to the USA, are suffering from the recent large rise in the value of the pound against the dollar. It has risen from $1.56 to the pound in November 2002 to $1.79 in December 2003.

Neal's Yard Dairy, a UK seller of high quality cheese, is partially protected because its US customers are less price sensitive than many. Its dollar prices have risen by an average 10 per cent over the past year. 'People go into a shop and spend the same amount on cheese. If the prices have increased, then they buy less', said Jason Hinds, sales manager of Neal's Yard. Exporters of non-niche, commodity cheeses are in for tougher times. Customers buy these purely on price. Stephen Jones, managing director of Summerdale International, a cheese export agency in Taunton, said its global sales could drop from £3m to £2m next year. UK exporters are relieved, though, that they are not in the euro area. The euro has appreciated far more against the US dollar than the pound. Jason Hinds said: 'Our products in the US look cheap compared to cheeses from France or Italy.

Source: adapted from the *Financial Times*, 6.1.2004.

(a) Explain the impact that the rise in the value of the pound against the dollar in 2003 had on UK cheese exporters.
(b) Why might the rise in the value of the euro against the dollar have given British cheese exporters a competitive advantage?

to lead to a fall in import prices, which then feeds through to lower domestic prices. As explained above, some importers will choose to keep their foreign currency prices the same in order to increase their profit margins. But other importers will cut their foreign currency prices. The extent to which a rise in the exchange rate leads to a fall in domestic prices depends upon what proportion of importers choose to cut prices.

Second a higher exchange rate will lead to a fall in aggregate demand. Exports will fall and imports will rise as explained above. The fall in aggregate demand then leads to a fall in inflation. The extent to which aggregate demand falls depends upon the price elasticity of demand for exports and imports. The higher the price elasticities, the greater will be the change in export and import volumes to changes in prices brought about by the exchange rate movement.

The reverse occurs when there is a depreciation of the exchange rate. Import prices will tend to rise, feeding through to higher domestic inflation. Aggregate demand will rise as exports become more price competitive and imports less price competitive. As a result, inflation will tend to increase.

Economic growth Changing the exchange rate may have an impact on long term growth rates. A higher exchange rate which discourages exports and encourages imports may lead to lower domestic investment, and vice versa for a lower exchange rate. However, the main impact of a changing exchange rate will be felt on short run output. A rise in the exchange rate will dampen output in the short term because exports fall and imports rise, leading to a fall in aggregate demand. A fall in the exchange rate will lead to rising exports and falling imports, raising aggregate demand and thus equilibrium output.

Unemployment A rise in the exchange rate will tend to increase unemployment. This is because an exchange rate rise will tend to lower aggregate demand and thus equilibrium output. A fall in the exchange rate will tend to reduce unemployment. Changes in unemployment will be felt unequally in different sectors of the economy. In those industries which export a significant proportion of output, or where imports are important, there will tend to be larger changes in employment and unemployment as a result of exchange rate changes. In industries, particularly some service industries, where little is exported or imported, changes in the exchange rate will have little effect on employment and unemployment.

The current balance A rise in the exchange rate is likely to lead to a deterioration in the current balance. A rise in the exchange rate will lead to lower exports as they become less price competitive. The volume of imports is likely to rise leading to higher import values. So the current account position (exports minus imports) is likely to deteriorate. On the other hand, a fall in the exchange rate is likely to lead to an improvement in the current balance. Exports are likely to rise, but imports fall.

Question 3

In 2003 and 2004, the Japanese central bank spent an estimated £150bn buying up US dollars with Japanese yen to depress the value of the yen against the dollar. This was part of a much longer period of intervention in foreign currency markets going back to 1991, all designed to lower the yen:US$ exchange rate. The Japanese economy in the early 2000s was in a weak state having spent much of the previous decade either in recession or experiencing low growth. The Japanese central bank wanted to support the recovery of the Japanese economy with a low exchange rate.

However, since March 2004 intervention has stopped. One possible reason is that the Japanese central bank has become concerned about the recent boom in commodity prices. Japan is a major importer of commodities such as oil, having few natural resources itself. The lower the value of the yen, the higher the cost of imported commodities for Japanese manufacturers. Imported inflation poses a threat both to the competitiveness and profitability of Japanese companies and to the economy as a whole.

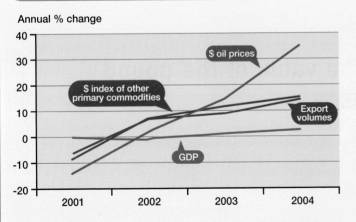

Figure 39.1 *Japan, annual percentage growth in export volumes and GDP; $ oil prices and $ index of all other primary commodities*

Source: adapted from OECD, *Economic Outlook*; *The Times*, 29.3.2004; www.dailyfx.com, May 2005.

(a) Explain how Japan's central bank used its intervention in foreign currency markets as an instrument of policy to improve the performance of the Japanese economy.
(b) Using Figure 39.1, discuss the extent to which this intervention was successful in achieving its aims.

Key terms

Appreciation or depreciation of a currency - a rise or fall in the value of a currency when the currency is floating and market forces determine its value.
Export and import volumes - the number of exports and imports. In statistics, they are usually expressed in index number form. They can be calculated by dividing the value of total exports or imports by their average price.

Applied economics

UK government policy

Since September 1992, the UK government has chosen not use the exchange rate as an instrument of policy. Instead, it has allowed the pound to float freely on the foreign exchange markets. So it has not used either interest rates or its foreign currency reserves to affect the price of sterling.

This policy has been very much influenced by the experience during the period 1990-92. In 1990, the Conservative government with John Major as Chancellor of the Exchequer decided to join the Exchange Rate Mechanism (ERM) of the European Monetary Union (EMU). This was a mechanism designed to stabilise the value of European exchange rates prior to the creation of a single currency, the euro. Any single ERM currency was fixed in value against other currencies within the ERM within a band. For instance, the French franc was fixed against the German deutschmark within a 2.5 per cent band. So the French franc could appreciate or depreciate in value against the deutschmark but within very narrow limits.

The British government's main economic concern since 1988 had been combating inflation, which had risen from 4 per cent in 1987 to 10 per cent in 1990. It decided to enter the ERM at a high value for the pound. This put pressure on import prices and prevented a future fall in the exchange rate from reigniting inflation. Between 1990 and September 1992, it used its foreign currency reserves to keep the value of the pound within its band against other European currencies. More importantly, it was forced

to keep interest rates high. By 1991, inflation was falling rapidly but the economy was in a deep recession. The government wanted to ease monetary policy by cutting interest rates, but was prevented from cutting them as much as they wanted because high interest rates were needed to keep the value of the pound high. In September 1992, the pound came under fierce selling pressure. Despite using an estimated £30 billion in foreign currency reserves buying up pounds to keep its value within its band, speculation continued against the pound. On Black Wednesday, September 15, the government was forced to abandon its membership of the ERM. The pound rapidly fell 15 per cent in value.

This illustrates the problem that governments face when attempting to defend a value for the currency. Speculative flows of money are so large that it can be difficult for a government to prevent the markets from driving the currency up or down in value.

Since 1992, the UK government has chosen not to defend any particular value of the pound. However, the United Kingdom periodically reviews whether or not to join the single European currency. If it does join, it will have to peg the pound against the euro and it, together with the European Central Bank, will have to defend that value for a period of time. Under current arrangements the pound would eventually be abolished and the euro would become the UK's currency. Once the pound has disappeared, exchange rate policy will no longer be the responsibility of the UK government. It will pass to the European Central Bank.

DataQuestion

The value of the pound

In October 1990, the British government fixed the value of the pound against a basket of European currencies which would eventually become the euro. It fixed the value at a deliberately high value because it wanted to reduce inflation within the economy. The high value of the pound meant that exports became less competitive whilst imports became more competitive. However, less than two years later, in September 1992, the government was forced to take the UK out of the Exchange Rate Mechanism (ERM). Free market forces now determined the value of the pound, pushing it quickly down by over 15 per cent.

In 1996, free market forces pushed up the average value of the pound rose again, eventually reaching a high in

2000. The 30 per cent rise from its low in 1996 to its high in 2000 severely limited export growth, whilst imports rose substantially. The value of the pound then eased from its 2000 high.

These movements of the effective exchange rate, the average value of the pound against other currencies, masked individual movements. For example, whilst the average value of the pound fell between 2000 and 2004, the value of the pound against the dollar rose significantly. This meant that whilst UK exporters in general benefited from currency movements over this period, UK exporters to the US suffered.

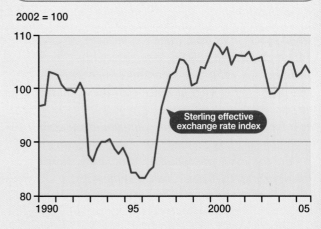

Figure 39.4 Selected exchange rates

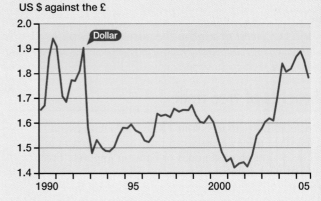

Figure 39.2 *Export and import volumes, trade in goods, seasonally adjusted, 2002=100*

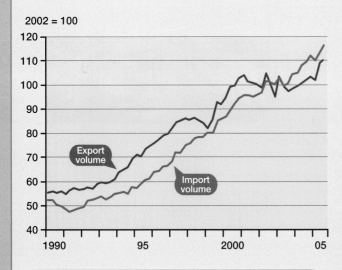

Figure 39.3 *Export and import prices, trade in goods, not seasonally adjusted, 2002=100*

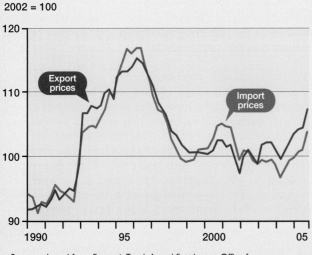

Source: adapted from *Economic Trends Annual Supplement*, Office for National Statistics.

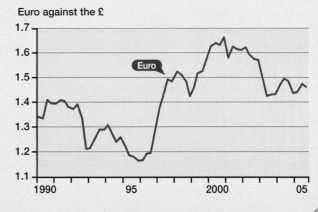

1. Using the data in Figure 39.4, describe briefly what happened to the value of the pound between 1990 and 2005. Support your description with statistics.
2. Explain how the fall in the effective exchange rate of the pound between 2000 and 2005 might have affected (a) export and import volumes; (b) average export and import prices; (c) the profitability of UK exporting firms.
3. What impact on the economic performance of the UK might the fall in the effective exchange rate of the pound have had between 2000 and 2005?

Summary

1. Although the gains from trade can be large, all countries choose to adopt protectionist policies to some extent.
2. Tariffs, quotas, voluntary export agreements and safety standards are some of the many ways in which countries limit free trade in goods and services.
3. The infant industry argument is one argument used to justify protectionism. It is claimed that young industries need protection if they are to survive the competition of larger, more established industries in other countries. When the industry has grown sufficiently, barriers can be removed.
4. It is claimed that protectionism can save jobs. However, there is a great danger that the erection of barriers for this purpose will lead to retaliation by other trading nations, resulting in an overall welfare loss.
5. Protection against dumping will only lead to a gain in long run welfare for a nation if the dumping is predatory.
6. One valid argument in favour of protectionist policies is if the importing country is a monopsonist. The imposition of tariffs will lead to a fall in the price of imports, leading to a gain in welfare for the nation at the expense of foreign suppliers and an improvement in the terms of trade.

The benefits of free trade

Economists today tend to favour FREE TRADE between countries. Free trade occurs when there are no barriers to trade, such as taxes on imported goods or bans on imports. Free trade is beneficial for a number of reasons.

Specialisation The theory of **comparative advantage** (☞ unit 14) shows that world output can be increased if countries specialise in what they are relatively best at producing. It makes little point, for instance, for the UK to grow bananas given its climate when they can be grown much more cheaply in Latin America. Equally, it makes little sense for Barbados to manufacture motor vehicles given the size of the island, the relatively small population, the small domestic market and its geographical location.

Economies of scale Trade allows economies of scale to be maximised and thus costs reduced. Economies of scale are a source of comparative advantage. Small countries can buy in goods and services which are produced in bulk in other countries, whilst themselves specialising in producing and exporting goods where they have developed economies of scale.

Choice Trade allows consumers the choice of what to buy from the whole world, and not just from what is produced domestically. Consumer welfare is thus increased because some consumers at least will prefer to buy foreign goods rather than domestic goods.

Innovation Free trade implies competition. A lack of free trade often leads to domestic markets being dominated by a few firms who avoid competition amongst themselves. Competition provides a powerful incentive to innovate. Not only are new goods and services being put onto the market, but firms are also competing to find production methods which cut costs and improve the quality and reliability of goods. A few firms are at the forefront of innovation in their industries. In a competitive market, however, other firms copy this innovation to remain competitive. The few countries in the world which for political reasons have chosen to isolate themselves from trade and attempt to be self-sufficient, like North Korea, have found that over time their economies have tended to stagnate. On their own, they simply do not have the resources or the incentives to keep up with the pace of innovation in the outside world.

Free trade, though, produces winners and losers. Firms which fail to innovate will go out of business. Their owners and their workers may therefore oppose free trade. Countries and firms which are particularly successful may see large rises in their incomes at the expense of less competitive nations and firms. Concerns may then be expressed about how some firms are able to charge high prices or earn high profits at the expense of consumers in other countries. Environmentalists worry that low prices in, say, the UK may be gained at the expense of the destruction of the environment in, say, Brazil. Some worry about the complexity of the world trading system, and are concerned that it is too large for any single institution like a government to control if necessary. Certainly, events like the Asian crisis of 1998, when a number of countries such as South Korea and Indonesia suffered large falls in their GDP due to a banking crisis, show that crises in one country can have a considerable impact in other countries because of the world trading system.

Globalisation

In the 1990s, the growing integration of world economies was given the name of GLOBALISATION. One thousand years ago, most goods and services were produced and sold within a very restricted area within a country. The industrial revolution of the 18th and 19th centuries helped increase the size of markets and many markets became national rather than regional in size. At the end of the 20th century, many markets became truly international.

Globalisation has already yielded enormous benefits to consumers by bringing down the cost of products.

Manufactured goods in particular have tended to fall in price over the past decade. Typically, either their production has shifted to cheap labour countries, particular in the Far East, or technology has eliminated the need for large quantities of expensive labour in Europe, the USA or Japan and labour inputs have been considerably reduced.

However, globalisation has come in for fierce criticism from a variety of groups. Workers in richer industrialised countries whose jobs are threatened by low cost imports often argue that the competition is 'unfair' because it is based on cheap labour operating in conditions which might be unacceptable in the West. Environmentalists argue that world capitalism is destroying the environment in poor countries. Anti-capitalist groups and many Western charities working in the Third World argue that the West is exploiting cheap labour and harming the development of poor countries.

Inevitably, globalisation has created costs both in rich developed countries and in poor developing countries. However, there have also been considerable benefits. For example, China could not have made the economic progress that it has done, with GDP growing at around 10 per cent per annum, without the ability to export goods and import raw materials and technology. Pro-globalisation economists argue that the only way that poorer countries around the world will achieve the

Question 1

Figure 40.1 Domestic demand and supply

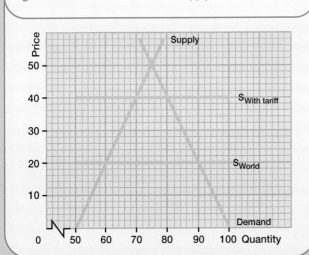

Figure 40.1 shows the domestic demand and supply curves for a good.
(a) What is the equilibrium price and quantity demanded and supplied domestically?
(b) The country starts to trade internationally. The international price for the product shown is 20. The country can import any amount at this price. What is:
(i) the new level of demand; (ii) the new level of domestic supply; (iii) the quantity imported?
(c) The government, alarmed at the loss of jobs in the industry, imposes a tariff of 20 per unit. By how much will: (i) domestic demand fall; (ii) domestic supply rise; (iii) imports fall?
(d) What would happen if the government imposed a tariff of 40 per unit?

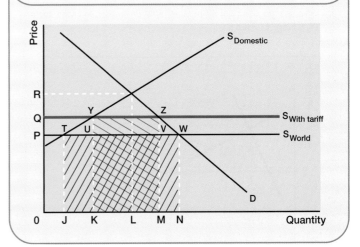

Figure 40.2 Tariffs
If the world price of a good is OP, a tariff of PQ will shift the supply curve upwards from S$_{World}$ to S$_{With\ tariff}$. Domestic consumption will fall by MN whilst domestic production will rise by JK. Imports will fall from JN to KM.

living standards enjoyed by First World citizens is by full integration into a free market world trading system. Nevertheless, countries often choose for a variety of reasons to restrict trade.

Methods of protection

There is a large number of ways in which a country may choose to erect TRADE BARRIERS.

Tariffs A TARIFF is a tax on imported goods. It is sometimes called an IMPORT DUTY or a CUSTOMS DUTY. Tariffs can be used by governments to raise revenue to finance expenditure. However, they are most often used in a deliberate attempt to restrict imports. A tariff, by imposing a tax on a good, is likely to raise its final price to the consumer (although occasionally a foreign supplier will absorb all the tariff to prevent this from happening). A rise in the price of the good will lead to a fall in demand and the volume of imports will fall. A tariff should also help domestic producers. Some consumers will switch consumption from imported goods to domestically produced substitutes following the imposition of a tariff. For instance, if the UK imposed a tariff on sugar cane imports, British produced sugar beet would become more competitive and demand for it would rise.

This is shown in Figure 40.2. D is the domestic demand for a good. S$_{Domestic}$ is the domestic supply curve of the product. With no foreign trade, equilibrium output would occur where domestic demand and supply were equal at OL. However, with foreign trade, world producers are assumed to be prepared to supply any amount of the product at a price of OP. Consumers will now buy imported goods because the world price OP is below the domestic price of OR. Domestic supply will fall back along the supply curve to OJ. Demand for the good will rise to ON. Imports must be JN if demand is ON and domestic supply is OJ.

Now assume that the government of the country imposes a tariff of PQ per unit. The price to domestic consumers will rise to OQ. Domestic producers will not pay

Figure 40.3 Quotas

If the world price of a good is £8, the introduction of a quota of 3 million units will reduce supply and raise the domestic price to £10. Domestic consumption will fall from 10 million units to 6 million units whilst domestic production will rise from 2 million units to 3 million units. Importers of the 3 million units subject to quota will make a windfall gain. Before the imposition of the quota they could only get a price of £8 per unit. After the imposition of the quota they can charge £10 per unit.

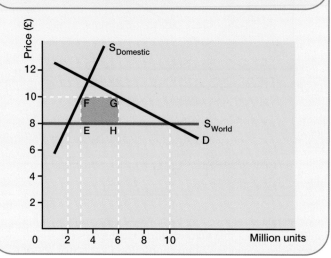

Question 2

President George Bush has decided to abandon the tariffs he put in place 20 months ago on steel imports. The import tariffs of between 8 and 30 per cent were designed to protect the US steel industry and steel jobs from fierce foreign competition. The US industry had argued that it needed protection to give it time to restructure, make investments and reduce costs in order to remain competitive against foreign imports.

The EU and Japan took the US to the World Trade Organisation (WTO) which ruled the tariffs illegal. The EU responded to the WTO judgment by threatening to impose tariffs on up to $2.2 billion worth of exports from the United States if the tariffs were not withdrawn immediately. The tariffs would have been placed on EU imports of orange juice and citrus products from Florida, motor cycles, farm machinery, textiles, shoes and other products.

US steel executives have said they feel betrayed by the repeal. Unions and the industry plan to organise a 'strong and negative response'. On the other hand, US steel customers, such as US car and car component manufacturers, were quietly relieved that tariffs were being removed since they had added to their costs.

Source: adapted from the *Washington Post*, 1.12.2003.

(a) Explain, using the example of the US steel industry, what is meant by a 'tariff'.
(b) Analyse, using a diagram, why US steel manufacturers were in favour of tariffs whilst US steel customers were against the tariffs.
(c) Who would have benefited and who would have suffered if the US government had decided to maintain tariffs on steel imports in December 2003?

the tariff. Therefore they find it profitable to expand production to OK. Higher prices cause demand to fall to OM. Hence imports will only be KM. Expenditure on imports will fall from JTWN (price JT times quantity bought JN) to KYZM. Of that area KYZM, KUVM will be the revenue gained by foreign firms. The rest, UYZV, is the tax collected on the imports and will therefore go to the government.

Quotas A QUOTA is a physical limit on the quantity of a good imported. It is an example of a **physical control**. Imposing a limit on the quantity of goods imported into a country will increase the share of the market available for domestic producers. However, it will also raise the price of the protected product.

This is shown in Figure 40.3. The world supply price of a product is £8. Domestic demand shown by the demand curve D is 10 million units. Of that, 2 million is produced domestically. The remaining 8 million is imported. Now assume that a quota of 3 million units is imposed on imports. Because output is now 4 million units less than it would otherwise have been, price will rise to £10. Domestic production will rise to 3 million units. Domestic consumption is 6 million units. The rise in price has led to a reduction in demand of 4 million units. It should be noted that quotas, unlike tariffs, can lead to gains by importers. It is true in Figure 40.3 that foreign firms have lost orders for 4 million units. But those firms which have managed to retain orders have gained. They used to sell their units for £8. They can now get £10. This is a windfall gain for them, shown on the diagram by the rectangle EFGH.

Other restrictions There is considerable number of other trade barriers which countries can erect against foreign imports. In the 1970s and 1980s, there was widespread use of **Voluntary Export Agreements**. These are a type of quota which is enforced by importers. For instance, the UK had an agreement with Japanese car manufacturers that they should not take more than 10 per cent of the UK car market. Another widespread barrier is non-competitive purchasing by governments. They are major buyers of goods and services and most governments around the world have a policy of buying only from domestic producers even if this means paying higher prices. Meeting different safety standards can lead to higher costs of production for importers. Simple tactics like lengthy delays at customs posts can also deter imports.

Arguments used to justify protection

The theory of comparative advantage states that there are major welfare gains to be made from free trade in international markets. However, protectionism has always been widespread. What arguments can be put forward to justify protectionist policies?

The infant industry argument This is one of the oldest arguments in favour of protection. Industries just starting up may well face much higher costs than foreign competitors. Partly this is because there may be large economies of scale in the industry. A new low volume producer will find it impossible to compete on price against an established foreign high volume producer. Once it is sufficiently large, tariff barriers can be removed and the industry exposed to the full heat of foreign competition. There may also be a learning curve. It takes some

Chinese shoe manufacturers have increased their exports to the European Union by almost 700 per cent since trade restrictions were abolished in January. European shoe manufacturers have called for immediate action to stop the flood of shoes onto the market. Adolfo Urso, deputy Italian industry minister, has urged the EU Commission to 'intervene urgently' to defend Italy's shoe industry. 'It's a red alert for the import of shoes from China. The situation is dramatic for this vital component of the Made in Italy export sector' he said. 'Italy is ready to do battle in Europe to ensure commercial rules are respected' said Rossano Soldini, president of the Italian shoemaking association. He said that the industry could lose up to 40 000 of 101 000 jobs this year if China's import boom continued.

A spokesperson for Peter Mandelson, EU trade commissioner, said Brussels would look into industry complaints of dumping 'as a matter of urgency'. 'If products were exported at below the cost of production, we would not hesitate to take action', she said. This would probably mean the imposition of anti-dumping duties on imports of Chinese shoes.

Source: adapted from the *Financial Times*, 9.7.2005.

(a) What is meant by (a) 'dumping' and (b) 'duties on imports'?
(b) Discuss why European shoe manufacturers are arguing that duties should be imposed on Chinese shoes.
(c) To what extent would Europe gain from the imposition of duties on Chinese shoes?

time for managers and workers in a new industry to establish efficient operational and working practices. Only by protecting the new industry can it compete until the 'learning' benefits come through.

Some countries, such as Japan, have successfully developed infant industries behind high trade barriers. It is also true that many countries such as the UK have financial systems which tend to take a short view of investment. It is difficult, if not impossible, to find backers for projects which might only become profitable in 10 or even 5 years' time.

However, infant industries in general have not grown successfully behind trade barriers. One problem is that government needs to be able to identify those infant industries which will grow successfully. Governments have a poor record of picking such 'winners'. Second, industries protected by trade barriers lack the competitive pressure to become efficient. Infant industries all too often grow up to be lame duck industries. They only carry on operating because they have become skilled at lobbying government to maintain high trade barriers. Third, it is usually more efficient to use other policy weapons if a government genuinely wishes to encourage the development of a new industry. Specific subsidies, training grants, tax concessions, or even the creation of state enterprises, are likely to be better ways of creating new industries.

Job protection Another argument with a very long history is the idea that protectionism can create or at least preserve jobs. During the 1970s, the share of the UK car market taken by domestic car manufacturers shrank drastically. It would have been possible to erect trade barriers against foreign imported cars to preserve jobs in the motor car industry. However, there

are two major problems with this policy. Firstly, although the policy may benefit manufacturers and their workers, consumers are likely to have less choice and pay higher prices. Much of the gain for producers is an internal transfer of resources from domestic consumers. Moreover, foreign countries could retaliate by imposing trade restrictions on exports, leading to a loss of jobs in the domestic economy. If they do, then all countries participating in the trade war will suffer. Production will be switched from lower cost to higher cost producers, resulting in a loss of welfare for consumers. The gains from trade resulting from comparative advantage will be lost.

Dumping DUMPING can be defined in a number of ways. Broadly speaking it is the sale of goods below their cost of production, whether marginal cost, average total cost, or average variable cost. Foreign firms may sell products 'at a loss' for a variety of reasons.

- They may have produced the goods and failed to find a market for them, so they are dumped on one country in a distress sale.
- In the short run, a firm may have excess capacity. It will then sell at a price below average total cost so long as that price at least covers its variable cost.
- Low prices could represent a more serious long term threat to domestic industry. A foreign producer may deliberately price at a loss to drive domestic producers out of business. Once it has achieved this, it can increase prices and enjoy monopoly profits.

Goals of long term domination by a foreign producer might justify trade barriers, although it might be more efficient to subsidise domestic industries. It is more difficult to say whether short term distress dumping leads to a loss of domestic welfare. On the one hand, domestic producers and their workers may suffer a loss of profits and wages. The impact on employment should be limited if dumping is only a short term phenomenon. On the other hand, consumers gain by being able to buy cheap goods, even if only for a limited period.

Cheap labour Countries which have plentiful sources of cheap labour are often accused of 'unfair competition'. High labour cost countries find it difficult if not impossible to compete against products from these countries and there is pressure from threatened industries to raise trade barriers. However, cheap labour is a source of comparative advantage for an economy. There is a misallocation of resources if domestic consumers are forced to buy from high wage domestic industries rather than low wage foreign industries. Resources which are used in high cost protected industries could be used elsewhere in the economy to produce products for which the country does have a comparative advantage in production.

The terms of trade One argument in favour of tariffs for which an economic case can be made is the optimal tariff argument. In Figure 40.2 it was assumed that a country could import any amount at a given price because it was a relatively small buyer on the world market. However, if a country imports a significant proportion of world production, then it is likely to face an upward sloping supply curve. The more it buys, the higher the price per unit it will have to pay. At the extreme, the country may be a **monopsonist** (i.e. the sole buyer of a product).

If the country faces an upward sloping supply curve, the marginal cost of buying an extra unit will not only be the cost of the extra unit but also the extra cost of

Question 4

Researchers in Thailand, India and Australia claim that excessively strict hygiene standards are increasingly being used to block food imports from developing countries. The world's leading 10 food producers are all developing countries and the main markets are the European Union, the USA and Japan. Food scares are one problem. For example, the UN Food and Agriculture Organisation reported recently that one third of global meat exports were threatened by outbreaks of bird flu and mad cow disease. 'If current bans were extended to the end of the year, trade worth up to $10 billion would be lost', it added. A World Bank study found that trade in cereals and nuts would increase by $12 billion if all 15 importing countries adopted the international Codex standards for aflatoxin contamination, which is produced by a cancer-linked mould, than if they all abided by tougher EU requirements.

Source: adapted from the *Financial Times*, 6.4.2004.

(a) According to the article, what justification is often given for blocking imports of food into the EU, the USA and Japan?
(b) Why might EU farmers benefit from such bans?
(c) Explain who are likely to be net losers from these bans.

buying all other units. For instance, a country buys 10 units at £1. If it buys an eleventh unit, the price rises to £11. The cost of the eleventh unit is therefore £11 plus 10 x £1 - a total of £21. The decision to buy the eleventh unit will be made by individual producers and consumers. The cost to them of the eleventh unit is just £11 - the other £10 extra is borne by the producers and consumers who bought the other 10 units.

Therefore the marginal cost to the economy as a whole of buying an extra unit of imports is greater than the marginal cost to the individual. But it is the individual which makes the decision about whether to buy or not. If the marginal cost of purchase is lower for the individual than for the economy as a whole, more imports will be bought than if the individual had to pay the whole cost of purchase (i.e. the cost including the increased price of previously purchased units). This would suggest that a tariff which increased prices to the point where the cost to the individual purchaser was equal to the cost borne by society as a whole of that decision would increase economic welfare.

Imposition of a tariff will reduce demand for imported goods, and this in turn will lead to a fall in the price of imported goods (☞ unit 11 - a tariff is an indirect, ad valorem or specific tax which shifts the supply curve for imported goods to the left, resulting in a fall in equilibrium price received by suppliers). Hence the terms of trade (the ratio between export prices and import prices ☞ unit 14) will rise in favour of the importing country. The importing country will be able to buy goods more cheaply. But it is important to remember that this gain will be at

the expense of the exporting country. If, for instance, the UK imposed a tariff on tea, the price of tea might fall. The UK will gain but only at the expense of India and Sri Lanka. Also, if the exporting country retaliates by imposing its own tariffs, both countries could be worse off than before.

Other arguments A number of other arguments are put forward in favour of trade barriers. It is sometimes argued that a country needs a particular domestic industry for defence purposes. A country may wish to preserve a particular way of life, such as preventing depopulation of remote rural areas heavily dependent upon a particular agricultural product. It may be felt that some imports are too dangerous to be sold domestically. 'Danger' could range from unsafe electrical products, to toxic waste to drugs. Alternatively, a country may decide that it is too dependent upon one industry. Some small Third World countries depend crucially upon one cash crop such as cocoa, bananas or sugar cane for their economic well being. These commodities are subject to large fluctuations in price on world markets. Falls in price can give rise to large falls in living standards in these economies. Diversifying, even if the newly established industries are uneconomic by world standards, could provide a valuable insurance policy against commodity price fluctuations. Trade barriers are one means of sheltering these industries from foreign competition.

In all of this, however, it is important to question whether trade barriers are the best means of achieving the desired objective. Economists tend to argue that other policies, such as subsidising industries, are likely to be more efficient than trade protection.

Key terms

Dumping - the sale of goods at less than cost price by foreign producers in the domestic market.
Free trade - international trade conducted without the existence of barriers to trade, such as tariffs or quotas.
Globalisation - the integration of the world's economies into a single international market rather than many local or national markets.
Tariff, import duty or customs duty - a tax on imported goods which has the effect of raising the domestic price of imports and thus restricting demand for them.
Trade barriers - any measure which artificially restricts international trade.
Quota - a physical limit on the quantity of an imported group.

WTO and protectionism

Economic theory suggests that free trade is likely to benefit countries. By allowing each country to specialise, production will take place in locations which enjoy a comparative advantage. World trade expanded in the 19th century. As Figure 40.4 shows, though, the first half of the twentieth century saw a fall in trade. This was partly caused by the economic disruption of two world wars. The Great Depression of the 1930s also led countries to adopt deeply protectionist policies. Governments mistakenly believed that by keeping foreign goods out, they could save domestic jobs. In practice, all countries adopted the same mix of measures. World trade collapsed, jobs were lost in export industries and consumers were left having to pay higher prices to inefficient domestic producers when before they could buy goods from overseas at cheaper prices.

After the Second World War, there was a general recognition that these protectionist policies had been self-defeating. The Bretton Woods system of exchange rates banned competitive devaluations, whilst 23 countries in 1947 signed the General Agreement on Tariffs and Trade (GATT). Under GATT rules, member countries were not allowed to increase the degree of protection given to their domestic producers. Also, under the **most-favoured nation** clause of the agreement, a country which offered a cut in tariffs to one country had to offer the same terms to all member countries.

GATT rules prevented protection increasing, but did nothing to reduce protectionism. For this reason, GATT, and its successor organisation, the WTO (World Trade Organisation), have, over the years, organised a series of negotiations (called 'rounds') aimed at reducing tariffs and quotas. By the end of the Tokyo round of negotiations in 1979, the average tariff on industrial goods had fallen to 4.7 per cent. Between 1986 and 1994 an eighth round of negotiations, the Uruguay Round, was successfully completed. In this round, unlike previous rounds, agreements were made not just on trade of manufactures, but also agriculture and services.

● In agriculture, non-tariffs barriers, such as quotas, were dismantled and replaced by tariffs. This was intended to make the level of protectionism more transparent.
● In manufactures, the single most important agreement was dismantling protectionist barriers in textiles and garments from 2005. This has led to a substantial increase in exports, particularly from China, since then.
● In services, copyright and royalty fee agreements were tightened up, and a start made in opening up highly protected services industries such as finance and telecommunications.

The various trade rounds have been a powerful influence in expanding trade in the post-war period. Figure 40.5 shows that world exports of goods rose nearly four times as fast as world production of goods between 1950 and 2004. Trade in manufactured goods has risen even faster, at over seven times the rate of world production of goods.

The Doha round, 1999-2006

The current round of talks, the Doha round, the 9th since 1945, was launched in 1999 and completed in 2006. It covered a variety of areas.
● In agriculture, Third World countries, Australia and

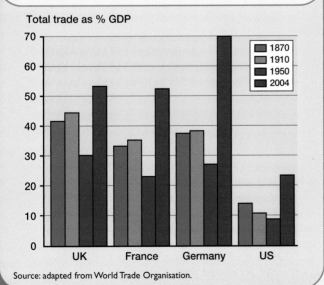

Figure 40.4 *Total trade as % of GDP, selected countries, 1870 - 2004*

Total trade as % GDP

Source: adapted from World Trade Organisation.

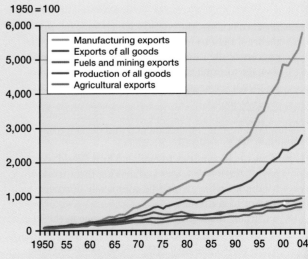

Figure 40.5 *World exports and production of goods, volume, 1950 = 100*

1950 = 100

Source: adapted from World Trade Organisation.

New Zealand wanted substantial cuts in tariffs on imports to the highly protectionist US and EU markets. They also wanted an end to all export subsidies from the US and the EU. Export subsidies were used to dump unsold US and EU produce onto world markets, but were seriously damaging to agricultural producers in Third World countries.

- In manufacturing, further reductions in tariff barriers were negotiated.
- In services, access to markets was the key issue. In many service markets, non-tariff barriers, such as limiting the ability of foreign companies to bid for government contracts, were key to restricting trade. Forcing open markets would increase trade.
- First World countries were particularly concerned to tighten up intellectual property rights in the face of widespread piracy, whilst Third World countries wanted their rights over plant derived compounds and traditional knowledge and folklore protected.
- There was agreement to tighten up the role of the WTO in settling trade disputes.

World Trade Organisation

The World Trade Organisation, set up in 1995, has two main functions.

- It encourages countries to lower protectionist barriers and thus increase trade flows between countries. It does this mainly through the various rounds of talks, the Doha round being the latest, which have occurred since the Second World War.
- It is responsible for ensuring that countries act according to the various trade agreements they have signed. Any country or group of countries can file a complaint with the WTO against the competitive practices of another country. The WTO attempts to resolve most complaints through negotiations between the two parties. Ultimately, though, the complaint can go to a panel of experts (effectively an international court), and this panel will deliver a judgment. Either side can then appeal against the judgment. However, ultimately they must accept the WTO ruling. If they reject the ruling, the country which wins the ruling has the legal right to impose trade sanctions against the exports of the losing country to impose the same damage to trade that it is suffering. When this has occurred, the losing country has quickly gone back to the negotiating table.

The WTO has come in for fierce criticism from the anti-globalisation, environmental and development lobbies. They argue that the WTO:

- allows rich countries to exploit Third World workers, paying them low wages and making them work in conditions which would be completely unacceptable in developed countries;
- is causing an environmental catastrophe in the Third World as rich countries plunder the national resources of the planet and give very little in return to poor countries;

- forces poor countries to lower their barriers to trade whilst rich countries keep their barriers in place;
- is destroying native cultures and ways of life, and is replacing it with a shallow, materialistic American life-style;
- is leading to the impoverishment of Third World countries whose economies are exploited by the rich countries of the world because free trade allows rich countries to force down prices of goods made in the Third World, whilst allowing their own technology-rich products to go up in price;
- gives ownership of the rules of the world trading system to a few rich countries and their multinational companies and strips power from poor countries and their citizens.

However, much of this criticism of the WTO is arguably unjustified because the WTO does not have the power to destroy cultures or force a Vietnamese worker to work for £1 a week. The WTO is there to encourage countries to negotiate rules of trade, which include mechanisms for ensuring that those rules are enforceable. It does have a pro-free trade bias but it cannot force poor countries to enter internationally binding agreements. Ultimately, the WTO is an organisation which helps develop freer trade between nations. The criticisms of the WTO are, in fact, first criticisms of free trade itself, the power of the market mechanism which does give richer countries more influence than poorer countries because they have more spending 'votes', and second the globalisation of culture.

The benefits and costs of free trade

Whether free trade is desirable is an issue which is fiercely debated. The main beneficiaries of free trade are consumers.

- They are able to buy goods and services at lower prices because they can source many of their purchases ultimately from anywhere in the world.
- They are given much greater choice of product.
- Quality and innovation is encouraged because consumers will tend to buy goods which are better quality or are more innovative at any given price.

For example, UK consumers today can buy a much greater range of clothes than they could 50 years ago. Prices of garments have fallen as trade barriers have been dismantled.

Economies, and therefore their citizens, also arguably benefit from free trade. Over the past 50 years, a large number of economic studies have found a correlation between openness to trade and economic growth. Poor countries which have become rich over the past 50 years, have tended to be export orientated economies, such as South Korea, Singapore and Hong Kong. China's economic growth miracle since the mid-1970s would not have been possible without access to Western markets, finance and technology. Countries which have limited their trade, for whatever reason, such as Cuba or North Korea, have performed poorly.

Third World workers employed in export industries at low rates of pay are 'exploited' in the sense that similar jobs in First World countries would carry higher rates of pay. But, they wouldn't accept these jobs if there were better alternatives. Being paid £1 a day to work in a Chinese factory is better than being paid 50p a day to work on a farm which might be the next best alternative. Equally, the job in China wouldn't exist if wages were just as high as in, say, the UK. China would not have a competitive advantage compared to the UK if wages were as high. On this argument, free trade and globalisation creates jobs in poor countries and those jobs are typically at least as well paid if not better paid than other similar jobs in the economy.

Free trade imposes costs, however. In the short term, reducing trade barriers can lead to unemployment in industries which are now exposed to foreign competition. Industries which are most likely to suffer from international competition are often those which lobby the hardest to retain protectionist barriers. In the long term, the market mechanism should lead to resources being redeployed. Workers find new jobs. But inevitably some will be losers, for instance because the new jobs are paid less well than the old ones. In the UK coal mining industry, for example, jobs were lost in the 1980s and 1990s as cheap labour, imported coal was substituted for high wage, domestically produced coal. Most UK coal miners made redundant who gained another job were forced to accept lower wages in their new job.

Greater trade which leads to greater output also implies greater use of natural resources. If the construction industry worldwide grows, for example, then more trees will be cut down to feed the industry. If more people can afford a car, then demand for oil will increase. This will lead to environmental damage in the Third World if production is uncontrolled. But free trade and protecting the environment can go together if governments round the world have the right safeguards in place. The problem is often that Third World governments do not place sufficient value on protecting their environment, whilst First World governments, firms and consumers will buy raw materials whether or not they have been produced in an environmentally friendly way.

As for damage to culture and ways of life, Coca-Cola has a mission to put its products within hands' reach of every consumer on the planet. So, unless governments ban Coca-Cola, globalisation will indeed mean that this part of American 'culture' will be exported across the world. But it is a two way process. In the UK, 'British culture' now includes Italian pizzas, Chinese acupuncture, Australian soap operas and 'ethnic' clothes. Trade has always brought with it new ideas and different ways of living which have become incorporated into local culture. Anti-globalisation protesters tend to see these changes in a negative way, but they can also be seen as positive, because they enrich different cultures.

DataQuestion

Abolition of trade restrictions in the world clothing and textiles industry

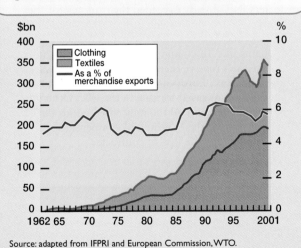

Figure 40.6 Global textiles and clothing exports

Legend:
- Clothing
- Textiles
- As a % of merchandise exports

Source: adapted from IFPRI and European Commission, WTO.

The end of textile quotas

As part of the Uruguay world trade round, all restrictions on trade in textiles were to be abolished from 1 January 2005. The main importers are the USA and Canada and the European Union. The main exporters are Third World countries such as China and Bangladesh. An explosion of trade is expected as domestic producers in the main importing countries lose their markets to cheaper textile products from overseas. However, because China only joined the Word Trade Organisation in 2004, it was forced to negotiate an agreement which allowed other countries temporarily to reimpose quotas on its exports until 2008.

The abolition of quotas worldwide will lead to a shakeout in the textile and garment industries. However, this will be an ongoing process. 'Clothing and textiles is the first manufacturing activity industrialising economies get into', says Sheila Page of Britain's Overseas Development Institute. 'It is also the first they get out of as they grow more prosperous.' Chinese workers won't stay on Third World wages forever. With very fast economic growth, their wages will rise faster than poorer performing countries. In the process, they will lose some of their competitive advantage in textiles.

Winners and losers

The end of trade restrictions on textiles in January 2005 will create winners and losers. The winners will be the most competitive producers in the world, which will almost certainly include firms in China and Pakistan. The other winners will be consumers in Western countries who are able to buy clothes at much cheaper prices. Quotas have inflated clothing prices by creating scarcity and 'rents', price premiums that act as taxes on trade. The annual cost to US consumers has been put at $70 billion and has fallen hardest on poor families which spend a relatively large share of income on clothing. Each job saved in the US textile industry by quotas is estimated to have cost consumers an average of $170 000 a year. Once quotas are lifted, poor developing countries will be able to expand their sales by an estimated $40 billion a year, creating 27 million jobs. This is 35 times the number of jobs that will be lost in rich nations.

Losers will include firms in North America and the EU and their employees who will no longer be competitive in the world market. 770 000 jobs are likely to go. In the EU, where 2.7 million people work in clothing and textiles, it is estimated that 15 per cent of UK textile workers will lose their jobs and 13 per cent of German workers. However, some Third World countries will also suffer. Under the quota regime, many countries were able to develop export industries, selling up to their quota limits. With free trade, the least efficient of these will lose out to the most efficient countries such as China. Countries like Mauritius with higher wages compared to China could be casualties. So too could countries like Bangladesh where, although wages are low, the industry is less efficient than competitors like China. In Bangladesh, the industry employs an estimated 3 million people and generates more than three quarters of the country's exports. Losing just 20 per cent of that to China would be a national disaster.

Source: adapted from the *Financial Times* 19.7.2004.

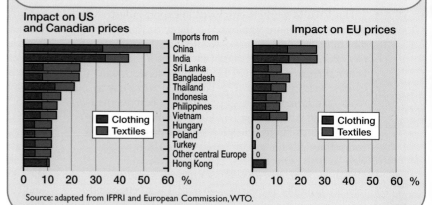

Figure 40.7 Estimated impact of pre-2005 quotas in raising the price of clothing and textiles from producing countries in US/Canada and the EU

Impact on US and Canadian prices

Impact on EU prices

Imports from: China, India, Sri Lanka, Bangladesh, Thailand, Indonesia, Philippines, Vietnam, Hungary, Poland, Turkey, Other central Europe, Hong Kong

Clothing / Textiles

Source: adapted from IFPRI and European Commission, WTO.

Fast fashion

UK retailers are moving production from China to Eastern Europe, Turkey and India as customers' appetites for 'fast fashion' forces a fundamental rethink of supply chains.

If price were the only factor, China would win hands down. According to AT Kearney, a consultancy, a typical blouse costs £6.50 to manufacture in China against £7 in Eastern Europe, £8 in Turkey and £10 in the UK. But stores like Primark, Zara, H&M and New Look have stolen a march on their rivals by getting the latest fashion look onto their rails faster than their competitors. It takes 22 days by water to reach the UK from China, while products from Turkey can take as little as five days to arrive. Twenty years ago, more traditional retailers would buy stock 18 months in advance. Today, a retailer might pick out six key trends for the coming season. But if one or two of those really take off, it will need to be able to get extra stock of these into its stores quickly. It could equally be that the retailer hasn't spotted a key trend in advance anyway. Fast manufacture and delivery could mean the difference between a good season and a disappointing season's sales.

Source: adapted from the *Financial Times* 30.8.2005.

EU quota fiasco

Following a flood of textile imports from China, the EU forced the Chinese to agree to the short term reimposition of quotas on imports from 12 July 2005. However, on many items, Chinese exporters had already exceeded their quotas for the year by this date. The result is that an estimated 80 million trousers, pullovers and bras are now stuck in European ports. Supermarket chains like Tesco and Asda have ordered and paid for the goods but can't receive them because they are over quota. Peter Mandelson, European trade commissioner, has proposed that they are released for sale in the EU. Otherwise, he said, 'are we going to send all the unlicensed goods back to China? Who will pay for this? Who will compensate importers and retailers for the loss of contracts?'

Source: adapted from the *Financial Times*, 31.8.2005.

1. Using a diagram, explain how the textile quotas in operation before 2005 (a) created 'price premiums that act as taxes on trade'; (b) cost US consumers an estimated $70 billion annually; (c) saved jobs in high cost countries like the USA and the UK; (d) cost low price countries '$40 billion a year' in lost sales and led to 27 million fewer jobs in these economies.
2. Discuss who would gain most and lose most from the EU reimposition of textile quotas on imports from China.
3. To what extent is China (a) now and (b) in twenty years' time likely to be the most competitive country in the world producing textiles?

41 Command economies

Summary

1. The function of any economic system is to resolve the basic economic problem.
2. In a command economy, the state allocates resources through a planning mechanism. Some goods and services are provided free at the point of consumption. Others are sold, although goods may be rationed if the price is below the market clearing price.
3. Command economies have mainly been associated with the former communist regimes of Eastern Europe and the Soviet Union, although Britain during the Second World War was run very much as a command economy.
4. The command economies of Eastern Europe, whilst possibly reducing inequalities in society, had relatively low economic growth rates over the past 20 years. Choice and economic freedom were limited whilst their environmental record was very poor.

Economic systems

The function of an economy is to resolve the basic **economic problem** - resources are scarce but wants are infinite (☞ unit 1). Resources therefore need to be allocated. This allocation has three dimensions:
- **what** is to be produced;
- **how** is it to be produced;
- **for whom** it is to be produced.

An ECONOMIC SYSTEM is a complex network of individuals, organisations and institutions and their social and legal interrelationships. The function of an economic system is to resolve the basic economic problem. Within an economic system there will be various 'actors'.
- Individuals. They are consumers and producers. They may own factors of production which they supply for production purposes.
- Groups. Firms, trade unions, political parties, families and charities are just some of the groups which might exist in an economic system.
- Government. Government might range from a group of elders in a village, to a local authority, to a national or international parliament. One key role of government is to exercise power. It establishes or influences the relationships between groups, for instance through the passing of laws.

Relationships between groups can be regulated by law. In many cases, however, they are regulated by custom - traditional ways of organisation which are accepted by participants within the economic system.

Command economies

In a free market economy (☞ unit 42), economic decision making is decentralised. Millions of economic agents individually make decisions about how resources are allocated. In contrast, in a COMMAND ECONOMY (or PLANNED ECONOMY) resources are allocated by government through a planning process. There are a number of key characteristics of a pure command economy.

The main actors There are three main types of actors within a planned economy - the planners (the government), consumers and workers.

Motivation Consumers, workers and government are all assumed to be selfless, co-operating together to work for the common good. This is in marked contrast with most economic agents in a market economy who are assumed to be motivated only by their own self-interest.

Public ownership All factors of production apart from labour are owned by the state (although labour services can be directed by the state). There is no private property.

Planning Resources are allocated through a planning process. At its most extreme, this means that the state will direct labour into jobs as well as directing consumers what to consume, although it is more likely that they will direct producers what to produce, thus determining the choice of goods available to consumers.

The first command economy was created in the Soviet Union (The Soviet Union was dissolved in 1990 to form Russia and a number of other countries such as Georgia) in the 1920s and 1930s. China and countries in Eastern Europe became command economies in the 1950s. A number of Third World countries such as Vietnam and Cuba also adopted planning models. Today, there are relatively few command economies as most have transformed themselves into mixed economies (☞ unit 43). The few that remain, including North Korea and Cuba, have performed poorly in recent years. Their problems have been made worse by various trade embargoes imposed on their exports and imports.

The planning process

Allocating resources through a planning mechanism is a complex operation. Planners have to decide what is to be produced. They have to decide, for instance, how many pairs of shoes, how much alcohol or how many tanks are to be manufactured. They then have to decide how it is to be made. They must decide what techniques of production are to be used and which factors of production are to be employed. Finally decisions about distribution have to be made - which consumers will receive what goods and services.

Planners tend to make use of **input-output analysis** when drawing up their plans. This is a method of charting the flows of resources in an economy. For instance, with a given technology, planners know how many workers, how much iron, how much coal etc. is needed to produce 1 tonne of steel. So they can work out what resources are needed if the economy is to produce, say, 20 million tonnes of steel. Having allocated so many tonnes of coal to steel production, planners now need to work out how many inputs are needed to produce the coal. A complex chart of the economy then arises showing how the factors of production (the inputs) are to be distributed to produce a given quantity of output. Most planned economies have used a mixture of 5, 10 or 15 year plans to outline the growth of their economies in the long term, whilst preparing yearly plans to cover short term planning.

Planning and forecasting is notoriously difficult. Accurate forecasting to produce maximum output assumes that planners know the most efficient way to produce goods and services (i.e. that they have available to them an efficient **production function** for each industry ☞ unit 1). Planners must have accurate statistics about the current state of the economy. There are also many variables which are beyond the control of forecasters. The weather is one important factor which can lead to severe misallocation in the economy.

In practice, planning is so complicated that some choices at least are left to individuals. In all command economies today, workers receive wages. They are then free to choose within limits how to spend this money. Some goods and services, such as education and health care, may be provided free of charge to citizens. Others, such as housing, may need to be paid for but there is no free market in the product. Housing is allocated by the state and it is not possible to choose which house to occupy. However, some goods are available for purchase, such as food or clothing.

Ideology and the command economy

Command economies came to be associated with communist (or Marxist) regimes. However, there is no reason why other types of political system should not be associated with a planned economy. Many Third World countries have issued 5 year plans, although they were usually 'indicative' plans because they have relied upon free market forces to deliver much of the output.

Question 1

The Belarus tractor factory was a typical example of production in the former Soviet Union. It was allocated supplies of raw materials by the state, and in return manufactured approximately 100 000 tractors a year. It was the sole manufacturer of a particular class of tractor in the country and the sole supplier of these tractors to state farms. Nearly 25 per cent of the factory's output was exported to other Comecon countries. The management estimated that, at current prices, it could sell twice as many tractors as it produced if there were a free market in tractors.

(a) Why was the Belarus tractor factory a 'typical example of production' in a centrally planned economy?

During the Second World War, the British economy was run very much as a planned economy. Government directed resources and issued output targets to factories. Consumer choice was restricted through a system of rationing.

Moreover, it has been argued that underlying market economies are a complex network of command economies. A firm is a small command economy. With a given number of inputs the firm has to allocate those resources to produce a given quantity of outputs. As in a command economy, firms have to plan how to use those resources and face exactly the same questions of **what** to produce, **how** to produce and **for whom** to produce as a state. The largest firms in the world today, such as Shell, Toyota or Microsoft, have larger outputs than many small developing countries. So even supposedly 'free markets' have an element of planning.

Because communist regimes have tended to organise their economies under command structures, planned economies have tended to be associated with greater equality than under market systems. But again, this need not be the case. Governments could just as well plan to distribute resources in an extremely unequal fashion if they so wished, as is the case in many Third World countries.

The allocation of resources

The planning process determines the allocation of resources within a command economy. However, in practice consumers are given money to spend freely on a limited range of goods and services. There is therefore a type of market mechanism operating in the sale of these products. In a free market, resources are allocated by price. Price rises to the point where demand equals supply. Only those with money can afford to buy the goods. In a planned economy, planners may decide to limit prices so that goods are within the price range of all consumers. For instance, planners may set maximum prices for food or clothing. Experience shows, however, that low prices often result in excess demand. Everyone can afford to buy meat, for instance, but there is insufficient meat in the shops to satisfy consumer demand. There are therefore shortages and resources are usually allocated via a queueing system. When a consignment of goods arrives in a shop, a queue will develop. Those at the front of the queue will be able to buy the goods. Those at the back will be turned away empty-handed.

An evaluation of command economies

Choice In a planned economy, individuals have relatively little choice. As workers, they may be allocated jobs in particular occupations or in particular geographical areas. They may be restricted in their ability to change jobs by state requirements. As consumers, they will have little say about what is provided directly by the state, particularly in non-traded services such as education, health, public transport and housing. What is provided for purchase in shops is likely to be limited. There is no mechanism by which firms compete with each other to provide different types of the same good (what would be called brands in a free enterprise economy). So consumers are offered only one make of car, one make of cooker, one type of soap powder, etc.

Subsidies on many essential items such as food and clothing are likely to lead to shortages. Queueing is endemic in many planned economies. Moreover, what is available can often be of

Question 2

In the 1980s, retail prices were determined centrally in the former Soviet Union. Essentials, such as bread and meat, were very cheap; shop prices of bakery products, sugar and vegetable oil were last changed in 1955. To travel any distance by metro, bus or trolleybus in Moscow cost only 5 kopecs (5p). Housing rent normally cost only 3 per cent of income. Low prices meant long queues and often poor quality goods. This led to large secondary and black markets. Anything more than the essentials of life, such as furniture and many articles of clothing, were very expensive and often in short supply. A typical car owner would, for instance, have saved up for seven to eight years to buy a car. However, the system threw up absurdities. For instance, in 1984 the Soviet Union, with a population of 275m, produced 740m pairs of shoes. Yet many of these were unsaleable. There were shortages of shoes in various parts of the Soviet Union and sports shoes and sandals commanded premium prices on the black market.

(a) How are resources allocated in a command economy? Illustrate your answer with examples from the data.

poor quality. In a planned economy, it is difficult to provide sufficient incentives for enterprises and individual workers to produce good quality products. Production targets are often set in volume terms or in value terms. A factory may be told to produce 10 000 cookers. But it is not penalised if these cookers are of poor quality. They will be delivered to state shops which in turn will receive instructions to sell them to consumers.

Income and growth Economic history suggests that, if a country has a relatively low GDP per head, both planned systems and free market systems will deliver comparable rates of economic growth. However, the experience in the 1970s and 1980s in Eastern Europe was that planned economies consistently failed to match the growth performance of free enterprise and mixed economies. This was perhaps not surprising. As economies grow, they become more complex. The more complex the economy, the more difficult it is to plan the allocation of resources efficiently. Large firms (remember that a firm in itself is like a planned economy) in free enterprise economies have faced similar problems. They can experience **diseconomies of scale** (i.e. larger size leading to higher average costs of production) because their management structures fail to keep production efficient. Many large firms have responded by decentralising decision making. Parts of the business may become 'profit centres', responsible for attaining profit targets set by headquarters. In some firms, individual production units may even compete with each other for business.

It is not only the problems that arise from inadequate planning that can lead to low economic growth in command economies. There is also little individual incentive for enterprise and innovation. If a firm exceeds its targets for this year, its only 'reward' will be an increased target for the following year, which it might find impossible to achieve. If there are very heavy taxes on high incomes, there is little point in individuals working hard within the state sector. If there is no possibility of ownership of the means of production, there is no incentive for individuals to take risks, establishing new enterprises to do something better than existing firms in the market. There is every incentive for individuals to minimise the amount of effort they put into their

official work. They are unlikely to lose their jobs, nor will they lose income (although they may be arrested for anti-state activities - which might act as a deterrent). This contrasts with the considerable energy that the same individuals might put into their jobs in unofficial markets. There might be a thriving black market, for instance. Or the state may allow people to rent small private plots for production of food.

The distribution of income Planners may choose any particular distribution of resources within a planned economy. In practice, command economies were associated with socialist or Marxist governments committed to a degree of equality of income. Hence planners set high priorities on providing all citizens with a minimum standard of living. They achieved this through subsidising essential goods, such as food, and providing other essential services, such as health care free of charge.

Equally, there is considerable evidence to suggest that those in power (e.g. members of the Communist Party) used the planning system to their own advantage. For instance, special shops have been set up where a privileged few can purchase a much wider variety of goods than is generally available and without queuing. Housing allocation, or placements at university, have been biased in favour of Party members. Indeed, this is what capitalist, neo-classical economists would predict. Those in power are using that power to maximise their own utility. They are not the disinterested, selfless individuals that the model assumes.

Risk Karl Marx dreamt of creating a society in which each would receive according to their need. A family of four would have a bigger house than a family of two. A sick person would receive medical care. Those no longer able to work would still receive an income. So the risks associated with ill health, injury at work, old age and redundancy would be considerably reduced. Communist planned economies, to some extent, achieved this reduction in risk for the individual. However, it can be argued that removing risk also removes incentives to work and create wealth. If, for instance, a worker knows that

Question 3

In the early 1990s, the former Soviet Union was in the throes of an ecological crisis, compared with which most other global pollution problems paled into insignificance. For instance, the huge Aral Sea, once the world's fourth largest inland water, effectively ceased to exist. It had turned into two shrunken salt-poisoned pools in the desert, thanks to the effects of massive and thoughtless irrigation schemes. In Belarus, one-quarter of all the arable land has been destroyed by the fall-out from the Chernobyl nuclear disaster - contaminated with Caesium 137.

'The most serious problem is in fact the economic system', said academician Mr Alexei Yablokov. 'All the decision making comes from the centre - from the government, the ministries, and the Communist Party'. 'The central committee of the party decides what sort of factory is built where. All the ministries are full of people with the old thinking - more and more production, whatever the price. Their aim is not human happiness, but more production.'

(a) What ecological problems are highlighted in the passage?
(b) Why might such problems be created in a centrally planned economy?

he will never be made redundant, then there may be little incentive for him to do his job well. If an enterprise knows that it will always be able to sell its produce because consumers have no choice about what to buy, then it has no incentive to produce high quality goods or to be innovative.

The environment One of the problems with a market economy is that individual producers base their production decisions on **private** rather than **social** costs (☞ unit 19), thus creating negative externalities. However, the environmental record of command economies in the past is arguably worse than those of market economies. The problem is that planners have been far more interested in securing increased output than in reducing damage to the environment. If environmental objectives are not written into plans, then it is inevitable that damage will be caused to the environment by industrial production.

Political and social costs Command economies can only work if there is a centralised bureaucracy devising and implementing plans. They leave little room for individual freedom. Perhaps not surprisingly, the former command economies of Eastern

Europe and the economy of China were police states, where the political rights of citizens were, to a very great extent, taken away. Whether a pure command economy could operate within a political democracy is debatable.

Key terms

Command or planned economy - an economic system where government, through a planning process, allocates resources in society.
Economic system - a complex network of individuals, organisations and institutions and their social and legal interrelationships.

Applied economics

Central planning in the Soviet Union

The Soviet economy from the 1930s to the late 1980s was the country whose economic system perhaps came closest to the model of a command economy. Overall decisions about economic priorities were taken by the highest political body in the Soviet Union, the Politburo, the central committee of the Communist Party. It would decide whether more resources should be devoted to, say, defence, housing or agriculture. Its decisions would then have to be implemented by the Council of Ministers, who would decide how this could be achieved with the help of **Gosplan**, the State Planning Committee. Gosplan was the major planning body. It constructed input-output matrices for the whole of the Soviet economy and worked out production targets for each region and each industry. Over 20 000 products or groups of products needed to be structured into its plan. Yearly plans were made within the context of successive **five year plans**, the first of which was announced by Stalin in 1928. The five year plan was an attempt to plan the economy in the medium term, because a year was really too short for the achievement of longer term goals.

Production plans would then be communicated to 40 different ministries which, working with Regional Planning Commissions in each Republic of the Soviet Union, would send out orders to hundreds of thousands of production units across the country. At each stage, those lower down the hierarchy had the right to challenge the orders sent to it. Almost invariably, they would be challenged if it was felt that the orders could not be fulfilled. If the challenge was accepted, the plan

would have to be modified. There was no need for production units to communicate between themselves. If goods were poor quality, for instance, shops would complain not to the manufacturer but to the planners at the next stage in the hierarchy.

The system arguably worked reasonably well in the 1930s and 1940s. It is true that the transition from a market economy in the 1920s to a command economy in the 1930s was marked by political oppression on a scale which possibly even dwarfed the horrors of Nazi Germany, but this was more a political struggle than an economic necessity. However, by the 1960s the Soviet economy was getting far too large to manage centrally and large diseconomies of scale were emerging.

One key factor became apparent. The incentives within the system discouraged efficient production. For those with a job from which they would be unlikely to be sacked because the right to work was guaranteed, there was an incentive to devote little energy to the official job and take a job on the side to supplement earnings. For managers, the key to success was to negotiate for as many raw material and labour inputs as possible and have as low a production target as possible. Hoarding raw materials too was essential in an economy where supplies were variable. That way, production managers could easily reach and even exceed their production targets.

By the 1980s, many in the Soviet Union felt that if their economy was to be dynamic, it should not be planned centrally. Hence, economic reform to transform the economy into a market economy was begun.

The Cuban economy

Figure 41.1 Real growth in GDP

Source: adapted from *Background briefing on Cuba*, Canadian Foundation for the Americas; www.cubagob.cu.

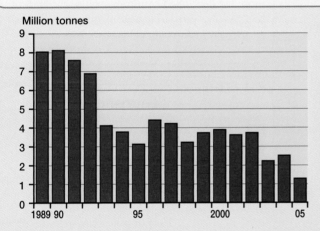

Figure 41.2 Cuban sugar production

Source: adapted from *Background briefing on Cuba*, Canadian Foundation for the Americas; www.cubagob.cu.

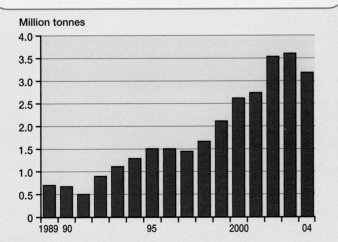

Figure 41.3 Crude oil extraction

Source: adapted from *Background briefing on Cuba*, Canadian Foundation for the Americas; www.cubagob.cu; *International Energy Annual*, Energy Information Administration.

The Cuban economy

Cuba has been run along socialist lines since a revolution brought Fidel Castro, the country's President, to power in 1958. Today, most key industries are owned by the state. The exceptions are some of those industries which Cuba is heavily reliant on for export earnings such as the tourist industry. There is free, universal healthcare, education and other social services. Other essential goods and services, such as food, clothes and petrol, are subsidised by the state but are rationed.

Economic restructuring

During the 1960s and 1970s, sugar was the most important industry in Cuba. With the demise of the Soviet link in the early 1990s and low world sugar prices since then, sugar production has fallen as Figure 41.2 shows. Cuba has been forced to develop other existing industries and diversify.

Tobacco has for over a century been an important export earner. Havana cigars are world-renowned and, in the second half of the 1990s, tobacco growing has been extended by the state to practically every province on the island. The number of cigar factories has risen from 17 to 44 during that time and production rose from 100 million cigars in 1998 to 150 million in 2004.

The most important developments, though, have occurred with the help of overseas investors, first allowed to invest in Cuban industry in 1990. Figure 41.4, for instance, shows that both steel and nickel production has risen in the second half of the 1990s with considerable help from mainly Canadian companies. Crude oil and gas production have risen, as shown in Figure 41.3 with the help of mainly European oil companies.

The fastest growing industry has been tourism as shown in Figure 41.5. In 1990, there were 12 000 hotel rooms, often of poor quality. This had risen to 44 000 in 2005, with a considerable improvement in quality. The number of tourists rose from 0.5 million in 1993 to 2.1 million in 2005 and is projected to increase to 5 million in 2010.

Figure 41.4 Nickel and steel production

Nickel (thousand tonnes)   Steel (Million tonnes)

Source: adapted from *The Cuban economy in mid-1997*, J Perez-Lopez; www.cubasource.org.

Figure 41.5 Tourism: number of visitors and gross revenues

Million   Revenue $ million

Source: adapted from www.cartedecuba.org; *Survival Story: Cuba's economy in the post-Soviet decade*, Philip Peters, Lexington Institute; www.cubagob.cu.

Black markets

Black markets are now an important feature of Cuban life since the breakdown of trade with the former Soviet Union. Most Cubans say the subsidised food and consumer goods provided by the state rationing system each month do not even come close to feeding an average family. The wide availability of US dollars in Cuba has encouraged the development of black markets in everything from meat to washing powder to repairs.

The welfare state

The Cuban government since 1958 has attempted to reduce inequalities in society and give everyone a minimum standard of living. A welfare state has been created which provides everyone with free access to education and health care. The result is that Cuba comes out very well compared to most of Latin America on certain indicators and matches those for developed countries such as the USA or the UK. For instance, adult literacy in 2003 was 97 per cent, whilst life expectancy was 77.

Tourism

Cuba's Tourism Ministry has issued instructions to workers in the tourist industry that they should mingle as little as possible with foreign tourists. They have been prohibited from accepted personal gifts and going to events in the homes or embassies of foreigners without written permission. The action is the latest in a series of attempts by the government to tighten state control in Cuba.

Unemployment

Cuba has a population of 11.4 million. Since the 1960s, the State has ensured that there has been virtually no unemployment, with today's unemployment being 2 per cent, lower than that of the UK. However, the restructuring of the economy in the wake of the collapse of trade with the former Soviet Union in the late 1980s and early 1990s put this commitment under immense strain. Under regulations which came into effect in 1994, workers made redundant were assigned to other available jobs or to strategic social or economic tasks. If no new job was found immediately, unemployed workers had the right to receive one month's full pay and 60 per cent of their previous salary thereafter.

Self-employment was only re-legalised in 1993. In 1994 the government allowed small businesses to be set up in selected parts of the economy such as the restaurant trade. However, it was made illegal for anyone to employ another person unless they were a family member. Labour market reforms remain fragile. In 2004, for example, the government withdrew permission for self-employment in 40 trades.

The dollar connection

In the 1980s, there was a growing trend for emigre families in the USA to send US dollars to their families back home in Cuba. These dollars were then spent on the black market. Following the collapse of trade with the former Soviet Union, Cuba legalised the use of dollars in 1993. Cubans were now allowed to spend their US dollars on food, clothes and consumer items such as televisions at special newly opened state stores. The Cuban government was forced to open dollar shops for two reasons. First, it needed dollars to finance imports of essentials which were then sold at a subsidised peso price to Cubans. Second, the alternative would have been to use the police to enforce a ban on all black market activity. The government would have received no dollar earnings from this. GDP would have fallen as less was being produced.

In 2004, the economy took a battering from a variety of factors including large rises in imported oil prices, poor harvests and a severe hurricane. Part of the government response was to make the use of US dollars illegal. Individuals and businesses wanting to spend US dollars had to convert them into a form of money called 'convertible Cuban pesos' or 'CUCs'. 1 CUC was equal to 1 US$. These became the only legal tender in former dollar only stores. Prices at dollar stores were raised and a 10 per cent tax was imposed on converting dollars into CUCs. The effect of both of these measures was to reduce the purchasing power of US dollars held by Cuban citizens and divert dollars into the reserves of the Cuban central bank. More importantly, it showed how far away the Cuban economy was still from adopting a free market approach where the forces of demand and supply would determine prices, such as the foreign exchange price of the currency, in the economy.

The Soviet and US connection

Following the Revolution in Cuba in 1958, the former Soviet Union supported the Cuban economy financially by buying exports from them at preferential prices. In the late 1980s, 85 per cent of Cuba's exports went to the USSR. Cuba also received direct aid from the USSR. The collapse of the Soviet Union in the early 1990s brought this special relationship to an end and Cuban exports plummeted causing a major recession in the economy. Acute shortages of essential items like petrol, which previously had been sold to Cuba at subsidised prices, became common. The Cuban economy has still to recover from this crisis. For example, GDP in 2005 was still lower than it was in 1989.

Cuba's economic problems have been made far worse by the economic embargo that the USA imposed on the island in the 1960s. It is illegal for US companies to trade with or own assets in Cuba. The embargo has limited specialisation, raised costs and lowered export revenues. Cuba's poor economic performance is arguably as much to do with the US embargo as it is with internal economic mismanagement arising from the workings of the country's command economy.

The development dilemma

Tourism shows the problems that the Cuban government has in maintaining control over the economy. Foreign companies control key assets in the economy in the form of hotels and associated leisure facilities. They also employ labour, although they are only able to do this via a Cuban intermediary company. Development of the industry is crucially dependent on foreign investment and also the state of the world economy. If tourists choose to stay at home, for instance, Cuba will suffer. In 2005, an estimated 41 per cent of Cuba's export earnings came from tourism. Many of the 160 000 self-employed and small business owners are linked to tourism, including restaurant owners and artisans. Growth of tourism will increase their numbers and provide greater opportunities for work in the private sector. Tourism also brings in US dollars, some of which filter through to the workers associated with the industry. In 2005, it was estimated that over 50 per cent of the population lived in households with access to dollars, either through tourism or from remittances from family working abroad. Households with dollars can buy goods unavailable to other households. Inequalities are therefore widened without the state being able to prevent this.

Source adapted from www.cybercuba.com; havanajournal, *The Globe and Mail*, 26.2.2005.

1. (a) What is meant by a 'command economy'?
   (b) Why might Cuba be described as a command economy? Illustrate your answer with examples from the data.
2. Why does the growth of small business and foreign investment threaten the existence of the command economy in Cuba?
3. Discuss whether a lifting of the US trade embargo on Cuba would make it easier or more difficult for the Cuban government to retain a planning model for its economy.

42 Market economies

Summary

1. In a free market economy, resources are allocated through the spending decisions of millions of different consumers and producers.
2. Resource allocation occurs through the market mechanism. The market determines what is to be produced, how it is to be produced and for whom production is to take place.
3. Government must exist to supply public goods, maintain a sound currency, provide a legal framework within which markets can operate, and prevent the creation of monopolies in markets.
4. Free markets necessarily involve inequalities in society because incentives are needed to make markets work.
5. Free markets provide choice and there are incentives to innovate and for economies to grow.

Characteristics of the system

A MARKET ECONOMY (also called a FREE ENTERPRISE ECONOMY or a CAPITALIST ECONOMY) is an economic system which resolves the basic economic problem mainly through the market mechanism. There is a number of key characteristics of the system.

The main actors The four main types of actors within the system are consumers, producers, owners of private property (land and capital) and government.

Motivation In a pure market economy, consumers, producers and property owners are motivated by pure self-interest. Their decisions are based upon private gain. Consumers aim to maximise their individual welfare or utility. Producers aim to maximise profit. The owners of the factors of production aim to maximise their wages, rents, interest and profits.

Government on the other hand is assumed to be motivated by considerations of the good of the community and not by self-interest. It seeks to maximise social welfare.

Private ownership Nearly all factors of production within the economy are owned mainly by private individuals and organisations. Government has a duty to uphold the rights of citizens to own property. This it does mainly through the legal system.

Free enterprise Owners of the factors of production as well as producers of goods and services have the right to buy and sell what they own through the market mechanism. Government places few limits on what can be bought and sold. Workers can work for whom they want. Homeowners can sell their houses if they so wish. People are free to set up their own businesses. Consumers are free to use their money to buy whatever is offered for sale. Producers are free to sell whatever they wish to sell.

Competition Competition will exist if economic units are free to allocate their resources as they wish. Producers will have to compete for the spending 'votes' of consumers. Workers will have to compete for the spending 'votes' of their employers. Those wishing to borrow money will have to compete with everyone else who wishes to borrow.

Decentralised decision making Because individual economic agents are free to choose how they wish to allocate resources, decision making within a market economy is decentralised. There is no single body which allocates resources within the economy. Rather, the allocation of resources is the result of countless decisions by individual economic agents. This is Adam Smith's **invisible hand** of the market. He argued that, although economic actors pursued their own self interest, the result would be an allocation of resources in the economy which would be in the interests of society as a whole.

The market mechanism

Any type of economic system must be capable of allocating resources. In particular, it must be able to provide a mechanism for deciding **what**, **how** and **for whom** production will take place. How are resources allocated under a market mechanism?

What is to be produced? In a pure free market, it is the consumer which determines the allocation of resources. Consumers are **sovereign**. Each consumer has a certain amount of money to spend and each £1 is like a spending vote. Consumers cast their spending votes when they purchase goods and services. Firms receive these spending votes and this in turn enables them to buy the factors of production needed to produce goods and services. How firms cast their spending votes on factors of production in turn will determine how much income each individual consumer has to spend. What happens if consumers want to change the composition of the bundle of goods that they are currently buying? Say, for instance, they decide they want to buy more clothes but buy fewer package holidays. The increase in demand for clothes initially will increase the price of clothes. Clothing manufacturers will consequently earn abnormal profit (☞ unit 17), profit over and above what is normal in the industry. They will respond to this by increasing production of clothes. New firms too will set themselves up, attracted by the high profit levels. Supply will

Question 1

In 1993, Nigel Lawson, a former Chancellor of the Exchequer, gave a speech at the British Association's annual conference. In the speech, he said: 'Throughout the western world ... capitalism has appeared to be in the ascendant and socialism in retreat.' One reason for this was that: 'the rational decisions needed to make a modern economy even halfway efficient can be taken only by a multiplicity of decision-makers armed with the knowledge provided by a myriad of market prices.' A key characteristic of the system is self interest. 'A regard for one's self-interest is a prominent feature in the make-up of almost all mankind. It is not the only feature, but it is a uniquely powerful one. The characteristic of market capitalism is not that it alone is based on the idea of channelling self-interest for the greater good - not that there is anything wrong with that. It is rather that it is a unique mechanism for doing so directly, with the least interposition of government.'

Capitalism also possesses key moral features. 'The family, which looms large in the scheme of market capitalism, is not only the foundation of a stable society, but an important bulwark against tyranny - as is of course the institution of private property, the more widely spread the better. Another key feature of market capitalism is the private sector, non-monopolistic firm. Capitalism is sometimes portrayed as an unattractive competitive jungle, where the values of co-operation are lost in a free-for-all. What this overlooks is that the private sector firm itself provides a model of effective co-operation.'

As for inequality, 'absolute equality, even in the sense in which it is theoretically attainable, must of necessity lead to misery. If there is to be no greater reward for work or saving or effort of any kind than is meted out to those who decline to work or save or make any effort, then remarkably little work, saving or effort will be undertaken. If two people are working at the same job, with equal skill, and one chooses to work overtime while the other does not, failure to pay the former more would be seen as not merely self-defeating but grossly inequitable.' Government has an important role to play here. 'Just as the sensible successful businessman who seeks to help those less fortunate will do so not by changing the way he runs his business but by applying part of his personal wealth to philanthropy, so the wise government will best help the poor not by interfering with the market but by creating a well-designed social security safety net alongside it.'

(a) Identify from the passage the main characteristics of a market economy.
(b) Why, according to Nigel Lawson, does the pursuit of self interest and the existence of inequality in society lead to greater efficiency in the economy?

thus expand as will the degree of competition in the industry. This will force down prices to a level where clothing manufacturers are making a high enough profit to stop some going out of business, but a low enough profit to prevent new suppliers from being attracted into the industry. In the package holiday business, the fall in demand will result in a price war. Profitability will fall. Some firms may even make losses. As a result, firms will scale back the number of holidays offered and some firms may even go bankrupt. This will continue until package holiday firms once again can earn a sufficiently high level of profit to prevent firms leaving the industry.

Changes in the goods market will then be reflected in the

factor markets. Demand for workers, buildings, machines, raw materials etc. will rise in the clothing industry, but fall in the package holiday industry. There will thus be a transfer of resources from one industry to the other.

Notice the key role of profits in this mechanism. Profits act as a signal for what is to be produced. If firms are earning abnormal profits, it is a signal that consumers wish to buy more of a product. If firms are earning insufficient profits or even losses, it must be a signal that consumers wish to see a fall in production in that industry.

How is it to be produced? Producers are in competition with each other. All other things being equal, consumers will buy from the producer which offers the lowest price. So producers must produce at lowest cost if they are to survive in the market place. This then determines how goods are produced. Firms will adopt the lowest cost technique of production. Hence, free markets result in **productive efficiency** (☞ unit 16).

For whom? Consumers spend money. The amount of money they can spend is determined by their wealth and by their income. In a free market economy, this is determined by ownership of the factors of production. Workers receive income from sale of their labour, owners of land receive rents, etc. Those with high incomes and wealth are therefore able to buy large amounts of goods and services. Those with low incomes and little wealth can only buy a few goods and services. In a market economy, the wealthy gain a disproportionate share of what is produced. The poor receive relatively little.

The role of government

Government has a number of key roles in a market economy.
- Some goods will not be provided by the market mechanism. Examples are defence, the judiciary and the police force. These are known as **public goods**

Question 2

Bargain hunters were out in force yesterday as a growing number of retailers opened their doors on Boxing Day, heralding the start of the sales season. At Selfridges in Oxford Street, the store rang up 5 000 transactions between 9.00 a.m. and 10. a.m., with designer handbags being the first five items rung through the tills.

Germans are flocking to have their loved ones cremated in the Czech Republic. Hearses from as far away as Berlin are carrying German corpses over the border where cremation services are offered for less than a third of German prices.

Novartis, the Swiss drug company, has developed Coartem, the first artemisinin combination therapy (ACT) to tackle malaria. ACTs are the most effective treatment for the disease. Sales of Coartem are low, though, because at $2.50 per adult treatment, it is still 10-20 times more expensive than other malaria drugs.

Source: adapted from the *Financial Times*, 27.12.2005.

(a) Explain, using the data to illustrate your answer, how resources are allocated in a market economy.

(☞ unit 20). The government therefore has to provide these and raise taxes to pay for them.

- The government is responsible for the issue of money and for the maintenance of its value. In a market economy, the government has a duty to maintain stable prices.

- The government needs to ensure an adequate legal framework for the allocation and enforcement of property rights. It is pointless having a system based upon individual self-interest if citizens are unable to defend what they have gained. For instance, owners of private property need to be protected from the possibility of theft. There need to be laws about contracts of purchase and sale. It must be illegal willfully to destroy other people's property.

- It is equally important that property rights of any value are allocated to an economic unit in society. If they are not, they will treated as a **free good** (a good unlimited in supply) and over-consumed. The atmosphere is one example of an economic resource which in the past has been owned by no one. Producers and consumers have polluted the atmosphere. This would not be important if it weren't for the fact that we now recognise that such pollution can have an adverse impact upon economic units. At worst, it is predicted that the greenhouse effect and the destruction of the ozone layer will wipe out most life on this planet. Contrast this with the care that people show with their own private property.

- Markets may malfunction for other reasons. In particular, firms or trade unions may seek to gain control over individual markets. Governments therefore need to have powers to break up monopolies, prevent practices which restrict free trade and control the activities of trade unions.

The role of government is vital in a market economy. Without government, there would be anarchy. But in a free market economy, the presumption is that government should intervene as little as possible. Government regulation should be the minimum necessary to secure the orderly working of the market economy. Government spending should be confined to the provision of public goods.

Question 3

Political 'democracy' that takes half of personal incomes to spend on welfare, or industrial services which give voters as taxpayers little say and less escape, can be as oppressive as communist socialism. Government cannot be depended on to redress market failure. Its electoral short-termism, its ignorance or indifference to individual preference, its vulnerability to pressure groups and its corruption create government failure that is worse than market failure because it is less corrigible. The common people are best empowered by the market. Government should concentrate on the irreducible minimum of goods and services that cannot be supplied in the market. Optimal size of government is unattainable. But it is better to risk having too little government than too much.

(a) Explain what, according to the article, should be the role of government in an economy.
(b) What arguments can be put forward to justify this position?

An evaluation of free market economies

Choice In a rich free enterprise economy, consumers will be faced with a wide range of choice. Firms will compete with each other either on price if a good is homogeneous, or on a wider range of factors such as quality if the good is non-homogeneous. However, choice is not available to all. Those with high incomes will have a great deal of choice. Those on low incomes will have little. It matters little to low income families, for instance, if there are 100 types of luxury car on the market, or if it is possible to take cruises on even more luxurious liners. In a planned economy, consumers may find it impossible to spend all their income because goods which are priced within the reach of everyone are not in the shops. In a free enterprise economy, there may be plenty of goods in the shops, but they may be out of the price range of the poorest in society.

Quality and innovation One advantage claimed of a free market economy is that there are strong incentives built into the system to innovate and produce high quality goods. Companies which fail to do both are likely to be driven out of business by more efficient firms. However, this assumes that there is consumer sovereignty in the market. In practice, markets tend to be oligopolistic in structure, dominated by a few large producers which manipulate the market through advertising and other forms of marketing in order to exploit the consumer. So whilst choice and innovation are greater than under planned systems, the advantages of free market economies may not be as great as it might at first seem.

Economic growth In a free market economy, there may be considerable dynamism. However, some free market economies have grown at a considerably faster rate than other free market economies. Many mixed economies too have grown at comparable if not higher rates to the USA. So free markets are not necessarily the key to high economic growth.

Distribution of income and wealth In a pure free market economy, resources are allocated to those with spending power. Individuals with no source of income can pay the ultimate penalty for their economic failure - they die, perhaps from starvation or cold or disease. This fear of economic failure and its price is a major incentive within the free market system for people to take jobs, however poorly paid. One problem with this mechanism is that there are many groups in society who are likely to have little or no income through no fault of their own. The handicapped, orphaned or abandoned children and old people are examples. Free market economists point out that there is a mechanism by which such people can find support - charity. Individuals who earn money can give freely to charities which then provide for the needs of the least well off in society, or individuals can look after their aged relatives, their neighbours and their children within the local neighbourhood community. In practice, it is unlikely that individuals would give enough to charities, or that the better off would provide accommodation for tramps in their homes to fulfil this role. In a free market economy, there is no link whatsoever between need and the allocation of resources. The unemployed can starve, the sick can die for lack of medical treatment, and the homeless can freeze to death on the streets. Income is allocated to those with wealth, whether it is physical, financial or human wealth.

Question 4

Socialism captured the imagination because it offered an enticing conception of social and economic progress. It promised not just a great increase in material wealth, but a world where income would not depend primarily on individuals' arbitrary endowments of financial and genetic capital. It also talked sense about freedom - which can be measured only by the choices individuals have the power to exercise. The range of choice is profoundly influenced by a person's economic means.

Capitalism, whilst offering forever increasing economic output, gives no commitment to increased equality. Quite the contrary: incentives are regarded as an essential motor of growth, and they require inequality. But the commitment to inequality means that poverty will never be eradicated. It will be institutionalised. Once a minimum standard of living is attained, people feel poor if they have less than their neighbours. If a trip to the Asteroids becomes a typical weekend jaunt in the 21st or 22nd century, those who cannot afford extra-terrestrial travel will be considered poor. And they will not be comforted by the thought that they are better off than the poor of 2006.

(a) Assess the criticisms made in the extract of a capitalist economic system.
(b) What are the causes and nature of poverty in a free market economy?

Risk Individuals take great care to reduce the economic risk which lies at the heart of any free market economy. They can overcome the problem of risk by insuring themselves. They take out health insurance. They buy life insurance contracts which pay out to dependants if they should die. Unemployment and sickness can also be insured against. To cope with the problem of old age, individuals ensure that they have pension contracts. However, only a percentage of the population have enough foresight or the income to insure themselves adequately. This then means that many in a free market economy become poor, perhaps unable to support themselves, or die through lack of medical attention.

Key terms

Free market economy, or free enterprise economy or capitalist economy - an economic system which resolves the basic economic problem through the market mechanism.

Applied economics

The UK - a free market economy?

In 1979, before the radical government of Margaret Thatcher took power, the UK was quite clearly a mixed economy. Many of the leading industries in the country, such as gas, electricity, telecommunications and the railways were in state control. The government was spending about 45 per cent of the country's income, a very similar proportion to other mixed economies such as France and West Germany. Education and health were both provided by the state along with a wide variety of services from libraries to parks to roads. There was widespread control of the labour market, with minimum wages in many industries and conditions of employment of workers regulated by law.

The changes implemented in the 1980s transformed the shape of the UK economy. The privatisation programme led to large amounts of state assets being sold off to the private sector. The list was long but included car companies (the Rover Group and Jaguar), steel firms (British Steel), energy companies (British Petroleum, British Gas, the electricity companies, British Coal), water companies (the water boards) and telecommunications (BT). The role of the state was cut

as public spending programmes axed services. Where the government felt that it could not privatise the service, it attempted to introduce competition into the public sector. For instance, private firms were encouraged to bid for public sector contracts. In the health service, a competitive internal market was established.

Moreover, a wide range of reforms was instituted to reduce regulation and imperfections in markets. In the labour market, trade unions lost the power to act as monopoly suppliers of labour. Rules and regulations in various financial markets were removed to encourage greater competition. In the bus industry, firms were allowed to compete freely on national and local routes.

The spirit of 'Thatcherism' was to release the energies of entrepreneurs in society, to encourage people to work hard and take risks. The successful had to be rewarded and hence marginal rates of income tax were cut, particularly for high earners. On the other hand, those who avoided work should be penalised and hence benefits such as unemployment benefit were cut. The result was an increase in inequality in society.

Arguably, the aim of the Thatcher revolution was to

transform the UK's mixed economy into a free market economy. The reforms were not deep enough to achieve this. Health, for instance, continued to be provided by the state unlike, say, in the USA. Welfare benefits were also much more generous than in the USA. On the other hand, a divide had been created between the 'social model' welfare states of Continental Europe and the 'Anglo-Saxon' model of the UK which was becoming more like that of the USA.

When a Labour government was elected in 1997, it stated that it did not intend to raise the proportion of national income spent by the state in the long term. Government spending was tightly controlled with the result that large budget surpluses emerged. However, the government had already stated that improving education was a priority which necessitated increases in spending. It also came under increasing pressure from the electorate to improve the National Health Service. In 2000, the government announced that it would raise its health spending as a percentage of GDP to the average for the EU by 2008. This meant taking spending on health from 6.8 per cent of GDP in 2000 (of which 1 per cent was spending on private health care) to a possible 8 or 9 per cent by 2008.

Large increases in spending on health and education have, in part, helped push up government spending as a percentage of GDP from a low of 37.5 per cent in 2000 to an estimated 44.8 per cent in 2006, as can be seen in Figure 42.1. (Note that the percentages in Figure 42.1 are ones calculated by the OECD, the international forecasting organisation, and that the UK government calculates its government spending as a percentage of GDP in a different way which gives a

Figure 42.1 *Government spending as a percentage of GDP[1]*

1 Figures for 2004 and 2005 were estimates.
Source: adapted from OECD, *Economic Outlook*.

different outcome). This was still below the eurozone average but considerably above that of the USA. As such, the UK remains a mixed economy with far more similarities to other EU mixed economies than to the more free market USA.

DataQuestion

The US economy

Table 42.1 *Income distribution and purchasing power parity estimates of GNP*

	Date of estimate of income distribution	% share of national income							PPP estimates of GNP per capita US$, 2004
		Lowest 10%	Lowest 20%	Second quintile	Third quintile	Fourth quintile	Highest 20%	Highest 10%	
United States	2000	1.9	5.4	10.7	15.7	22.4	45.8	29.9	39 710
UK	1999	2.1	6.1	11.4	16.0	22.5	44.0	28.5	31 460
Germany	2000	2.8	8.5	13.7	17.8	23.1	36.9	22.1	27 950
France	1995	3.2	7.2	12.6	17.2	22.8	40.2	25.1	29 320
Sweden	2000	3.6	9.1	14.0	17.6	22.7	36.6	22.2	29 770

Source: adapted from the World Bank, *World Development Indicators*.

Face of America that destroys its Land of Free myth

Until a year ago, my image of the United States was of a wealthy, classless, melting-pot society whose values were embodied in the tough, free-thinking rebel usually portrayed by John Wayne. That image took a knock during seven days in Arkansas last summer and crumbled this week in Texas.

There is certainly money. In Houston, mirror-glass skyscrapers soar confidently over immaculate parks. In its fabulously wealthy River Oaks suburb, colonnaded million-dollar mansions exceed the dreams of avarice. But look again and you see another face of America. Shacks and shanty settlements strung out along the highways. Second-hand cars at a half or even a third of British prices. Wal-Mart supermarkets where a pair of jeans costs a fiver.

At first, it strikes you as a land of bargains. Then you talk to ordinary Americans and realise that the prices match the wages and the wages, in many cases, are desperately low. One of our coach drivers earned a wretched £4,500 a year - below the official poverty level. The average American family of four earns barely £10,000 and to reach that level, both partners invariably work. In the Land of the Free there is no free lunch. If you can work, you do.

If that sounds fine in theory, what it means in practice is that both our coach drivers in Houston were women, one middle-aged, the other well into her 60s. It means that a woman hotel executive I met in Brownsville returned to work two weeks after giving birth and thought her employers generous for paying her salary during her absence. It means that employees accept two weeks' annual holiday as the norm. It means that a word like 'welfare' which has a friendly, benevolent ring to European ears, is regarded in the States as the work of the devil. Welfare and free health care would sap the American spirit, so the story goes.

The education system is a problem too for Americans. America has recognised the appalling state of its educational system and is making much of its latest drive to improve schools and recruit better teachers. But there is little talk of producing educated people for their own sake. The motivation, as always, is hard cash and the need to be more competitive against the better-educated Japanese and Europeans. The campaign for better schools seems to overlook the most important point, that a good education produces thoughtful, innovative people who are prepared to break the mould and try something new. And maybe that is deliberate. For in its present state of intellectual awareness, America is happy to swallow myths that we Europeans laughed out years ago.

They call it the Land of the Free yet small-town sheriffs and corporate bosses hold powers that feudal lords would have envied. They boast their classlessness yet have created a society far more formal and unmixed than our own. And they still foster the belief that any backwoods kid can make it to president, blithely ignoring the fact that every president in living memory has been very wealthy indeed. You can still make your way to the top in America but it means climbing over rather more backs than Britons might find comfortable.

The woman hotel executive in Brownsville epitomised the thrusting, go-getting face that America likes to project. Back at work a fortnight after childbirth and every inch the liberated ambitious female. How does she do it? Simple. She has a live-in Mexican maid on £25 a week and God knows how she looks her in the eyes on pay day.

Source: *Express and Star.*

Table 42.2 Real growth of GDP							
					Annual growth in real GDP, %		
	USA	Germany	Japan	UK	France	Italy	Canada
1960-67	4.5	4.1	10.2	3.0	5.4	5.7	5.5
1968-73	3.2	4.9	8.7	3.4	5.5	4.5	5.4
1974-79	2.4	2.3	3.6	1.5	2.8	3.7	4.2
1980-89	2.5	1.8	4.0	2.4	2.2	2.4	3.1
1990-99	3.0	2.2	1.7	2.1	1.7	1.5	2.4
2000-05	2.9	1.1	1.3	2.6	1.9	1.0	3.0
1960-2005	3.1	2.7	4.8	2.5	3.1	3.0	3.8

Source: adapted from OECD, *Historical Statistics, Economic Outlook.*

1. Using the USA as an example, explain how resources are allocated in a free market economy.
2. (a) To what extent are incomes unequal in the USA?
   (b) Are inequalities in income desirable in a free market economy?
3. Discuss what might be the advantages and disadvantages to an individual of migrating to work in the USA from the UK.

43 Mixed economies

Summary

1. In a mixed economy, a significant amount of resources are allocated both by government through the planning mechanism, and by the private sector through the market mechanism.
2. The degree of mixing is a controversial issue. Some economists believe that too much government spending reduces incentives and lowers economic growth, whilst others argue that governments must prevent large inequalities arising in society and that high taxation does not necessarily lead to low growth.

Mixed economies

A MIXED ECONOMY, as the name implies, is a mixture of a planned economy and a free enterprise economy. In practice, no **pure** planned economies or free enterprise economies exist in the world. They are **paradigm models** (☞ unit 45). What we call free enterprise economies are economies where most resources are allocated by the market mechanism. What are called planned economies are economies where most resources are allocated by the planning process. Mixed economies are economies where the balance between allocation by the market mechanism and allocation by the planning process is much more equal.

Characteristics

A mixed economy possesses a number of characteristics.

The main actors The four main types of actor within the system are consumers, producers, factor owners and government.

Motivation In the private sector of the economy, consumers, producers and factor owners are assumed to be motivated by pure self-interest. The public sector, however, is motivated by considerations of the 'good' of the community.

Ownership The factors of production are partly owned by private individuals and organisations, but the state also owns a significant proportion.

Competition In the private sector of the economy there is competition. In the state sector, however, resources will be allocated through the planning mechanism. This implies that consumers are offered choice of goods and services within the private sector of the economy but little or no choice within the public sector.

Government Government has a number of important functions. One is to regulate the economic activities of the private sector of the economy. It needs, for instance, to ensure that competition exists and that property laws are upheld. Another function is to provide not just public goods but also **merit goods** (☞ unit 20), like education and health care. These may be provided directly by the state, or provision may be contracted out to private firms but still paid for out of tax revenues. The state may also choose to own key sectors of the economy, such as the railways, postal services and electricity industries. Many of these will be **natural monopolies** (☞ unit 18).

The degree of mixing

There is considerable controversy about the degree of mixing that should take place in a mixed economy. In 2004, 57.1 per cent of GDP was accounted for by public spending in Sweden compared to 46.9 per cent in Germany, 44.1 per cent in the UK and 36.0 per cent in the free market economy of the USA.

In Sweden, there is much greater government spending per capita than, say, in the USA. This means that in Sweden compared to the USA all citizens have access to medical care free at the point of consumption, there are generous state pensions, automatic retraining for those made unemployed and free child care for all working mothers. However, there is a cost. Taxes in Sweden are much higher than in the USA. The fundamental issues concern the following.

- To what extent should the state ensure that all its citizens enjoy a minimum standard of living? For instance, should the state provide insurance for those who become unemployed? Should it in effect guarantee them a job by training longer term unemployed workers until they succeed in obtaining work? Do citizens have a right to free medical care?
- To what extent should there be inequalities in society? The degree of inequality in an economy like Sweden is far less than in the USA. Inequality in the UK increased in the 1980s as both taxes and government spending were cut as a proportion of GDP. Inequality decreased when this trend was reversed in the 1990s and 2000s.
- To what extent should citizens be free to choose how to spend their money? In Sweden, the effective tax burden is nearly 60 per cent, leaving little more than 40 per cent of income for individuals and companies to choose how to spend. In Sweden, free child care for mothers is provided whether an individual wants it or not.
- To what extent are incentives needed to ensure continued high growth? Until the late 1980s, the top rate of income tax in Sweden was 72 per cent, with the ordinary worker paying between 40 and 50 per cent. Tax reforms in the late 1980s switched the burden of tax from income tax, reducing it to 30 per cent for 85 per cent of workers, but extending the 30 per cent VAT rate to a much wider range of goods and services. The top marginal rate of income tax at 56.5 per cent in 2005 was still much higher, though, than the 35 per cent in the USA. Supply side economists would argue that higher rates of tax discourage incentives to work and take risks and that this will lead to lower economic growth (☞ unit 38).
- To what extent is government an efficient provider of goods and services compared to the private sector?

Mixed economies can be judged on the above issues. They could also be evaluated according to their environmental impact.

Question 1

From your knowledge of the UK economy, explain to what extent it possesses the characteristics of a mixed economy.

Mixed economies have a better record on the environment than command economies. Indeed, the Scandinavian mixed economies are in the forefront of implementing measures to protect the environment from industrial activity.

Question 2

The degree of mixing between public and private sectors in the UK has changed over time. In the post-war period, government spending reached a high of 49.9 per cent of GDP in 1975-76, partly due to a severe recession at the time. The pro-free market government of Margaret Thatcher from 1979 saw government spending fall to 39.4 per cent of GDP in 1988-89 before rising again in the recession of 1989-1992 and then falling as the economy recovered in the rest of the decade. From 2000, the Labour government under Tony Blair made a policy shift to increase public spending, particularly on the health service, to improve the standard of public sector services. The proportion of GDP devoted to public spending consequently began to rise again.

Figure 43.1 *Government spending as a percentage of GDP[12]*

1 Government spending is Total Managed Expenditure.
2 Years are fiscal years. So, for instance, 1970 is the fiscal year 1970-71.

Source: adapted from HM Treasury, *Pre-Budget Report December 2005*

(a) Suggest the possible economic consequences of the shift in resources between the public and private sectors shown in Figure 43.1.

Key terms

Mixed economy - an economy where both the free market mechanism and the government planning process allocate significant proportions of total resources.

Applied economics

Sweden

In 1932, the Swedish Democratic Party gained power and created a model of a mixed economy which has been the envy of left wing economists ever since. The Swedish economy lies at one extreme of the mixed economy model. Public spending as a proportion of GDP peaked in the post-war period in 1993 at the height of a recession at 73 per cent. In the early 2000s, it stabilised between 57 and 58 per cent as Figure 43.2 shows. The public sector in Sweden has, over the past 50 years, devoted a larger proportion of GDP to government spending than in any other OECD country. In 2004, as Figure 43.3 shows, government expenditure was 57.1 per cent of GDP, more than half as much again as that of the USA and one third more than in the UK.

Government spending as a percentage of GDP has changed over time. In the early 1970s, it stood at around 45 per cent. However, two factors caused it to soar. First, there was continued upward pressure on public spending which the Swedish government found hard to resist. Second, the two oil shocks of 1974-5 and 1979-80 led to recessions throughout the Western World with sharp rises in unemployment. Unlike many countries, Sweden adopted Keynesian demand management policies to reduce unemployment. It increased public spending to create jobs. Large sums of money were also spent on job creation schemes and retraining for the unemployed. During the 1970s and 1980s, when other economies were experiencing very high levels of unemployment, the Swedish government was successful in maintaining low unemployment at between 2-3 per cent.

Increased government spending had to be financed and Sweden became one of the most highly taxed economies in the world. In 1991, a voter backlash saw the election for the first time since the 1930s of a right wing government. At the time, the economy was beginning to go into recession. The government refused to increase public spending to a level which would have kept unemployment relatively low. The result was a quadrupling of unemployment. Government spending as a proportion of GDP still rose to 72 per cent in 1993, partly because of rises in welfare and training expenditure on the unemployment and partly because GDP itself fell in each year between 1991 and 1993. However, the government was committed to rolling back the state, cutting spending programmes and reducing the tax burden. The rest of the 1990s saw a tight control of public spending which, combined with rising GDP, led to successive falls in government spending as a proportion of GDP.

Even so, in the first half of the 2000s, Sweden still had the highest proportion of government spending as a proportion of GDP amongst industrialised countries. Its welfare state was extremely generous. The old, the young and the poor receive a mix of benefits which looks lavish in comparison with spending in, say, the USA or

the UK. Women, for instance, are entitled to free creche care for their children if they go out to work. This encourages Swedish women to continue with their careers full time when they have children. Equally, high taxes mean that one person working households do not have the disposable income of their English or US counterparts. To maintain a high standard of living, women have to go out to work.

Critics of the Swedish model say that high taxes have reduced incentives to work and led to a flight of capital from the country. Swedish companies have been forced out of business because of high costs or have relocated outside the country. Foreign companies have been discouraged from investing in Sweden. In 1970, Sweden

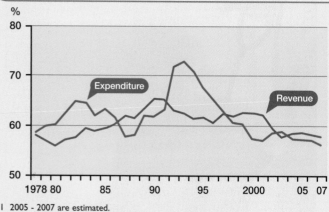

Figure 43.2 Sweden: public expenditure and revenue as a percentage of GDP[1]

1 2005 - 2007 are estimated.
Source: adapted from OECD, *Economic Outlook*.

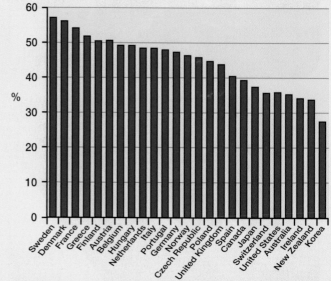

Figure 43.3 Government spending as a percentage of GDP, 2004

Source: adapted from OECD, *Economic Outlook*.

had the third highest GNP per capita in the world measured at purchasing power parity rates. By 1998, it had slipped to 27th. However, after coming out of recession in 1994, Sweden's growth rate was comparable to the average for industrialised countries. This improved economic performance led to Sweden moving up to 13th in the world in terms of GDP per capita at PPP rates. The Swedish government has become much more sensitive to the needs of business and has adopted policies which attempt to encourage investment in the country. At the same time, there is no desire by the majority of Swedish voters to dismantle their welfare state. Sweden is likely to remain at one extreme of the mixed economy model.

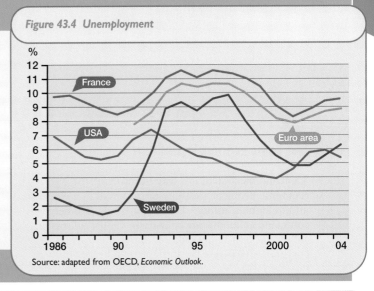

Figure 43.4 Unemployment

Source: adapted from OECD, *Economic Outlook.*

DataQuestion

France

The French welfare state

France has a large welfare state. Education, from nursery provision to universities, is paid for by the state. Health care is funded through a complicated system of insurance schemes paid for mainly by employers. However, the state provides a safety net for anyone who is not in an insurance scheme, particularly the poor and the elderly. Local government is a major landlord, offering homes for rent at affordable prices. Home ownership, at less than 50 per cent, is not considered particularly desirable in France.

There is also a state pension scheme which offers pensions of 50 per cent of salary for workers who have paid 37½ years contributions. Critics say it is too generous to meet the demands of a rapidly ageing population. The scheme is a cash management system. This means that contributions by workers today into the scheme are used to pay today's pensions. There are no funds of savings stored up in the scheme to pay future pensioners. With the number of workers to pensioners rapidly declining, pension contributions will have to rise sharply from workers to fund the scheme. The French government has long recognised the problem but has failed to address it. Changing the scheme would be very unpopular amongst both pensioners and future pensioners. However, it would like to see French workers taking out more private pension schemes and saving for their retirement. If benefits in the state scheme have to be cut, this would soften the blow for at least some French workers.

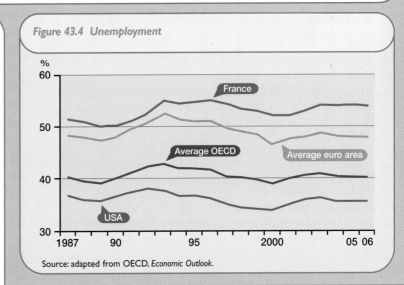

Figure 43.4 Unemployment

Source: adapted from OECD, *Economic Outlook.*

Riots

In Autumn 2005, there was serious rioting in Paris and other French cities by young, disaffected youths from ethnic minorities. At the heart of the problem was very high unemployment amongst this particular group, and the fact that members of ethnic minorities who are relatively poor tend to live in what are effectively ghetto suburbs of large cities. The response of the French authorities was to increase funding to deal with the perceived problems of poverty, lack of education and lack of jobs for these young people. Critics, however, argued that the typical French response of throwing public money at a problem when it became a serious political issue was inappropriate. Part of the reason why unemployment was so high, they argued, was because taxes were so high. This discouraged enterprise, inward investment and employment. Drastically cutting the size of the French public sector would create jobs and reduce unemployment.

1. 'France is a mixed economy.' Explain what this means, illustrating your answer with examples from the data.

2. To what extent could reducing the size of the public sector ensure less inequality in society and greater opportunities for all French citizens?

Applied economics

The basic economic problem

An economic system is a way of resolving the basic economic problem - scarcity of resources in a world of infinite human wants. The Soviet Union had been a command economy since the early 1930s, following collectivisation of agriculture. Eastern European countries and China became command economies in the late 1940s and early 1950s following communist takeover of their governments. However, China from 1978 and countries of the former Soviet Union and Eastern Europe from the start of the 1990s began the process of transformation back from command economies to more market-orientated economies. How can an economy move from being a planned economy to, say, a mixed economy and what costs will be involved in the transition phase?

Output

The process of transformation for most Eastern Europe countries began in 1990, although Poland and the former Soviet Union began restructuring in the late 1980s. As Figure 44.1 shows, the early 1990s saw a fall in output as measured by GDP. The average fall was nearly 30 per cent. This is much larger than, say, the UK or the USA experienced during the Great Depression of the 1930s. In the prolonged UK recession of 1990-92, which saw a doubling of unemployment to 3 million, output fell by 2.7 per cent between the second quarter of 1990 and the third quarter of 1992. So the fall in output in Eastern Europe was on a scale unseen in Western Europe and the USA.

This average masked very different figures for different countries. The group of countries which performed best were the 8 countries which joined the European Union in 2004. On average, their GDP was 25.6 per cent higher in 2004 than in 1989 as Figure 44.2 shows. The countries which became independent from the Soviet Union, and formed the Commonwealth of Independent States (CIS), performed worst.

It is almost inevitable that a transition from a command structure to a market structure will initially reduce output. In a command structure, it was central planners who decided what, how, where and by whom goods were to be produced and who was to receive those goods. In a market economy, those decisions are made by customers and firms. So, in a command economy, the planners may decide that 500 000 cars will be made a year, in two models, all in the same

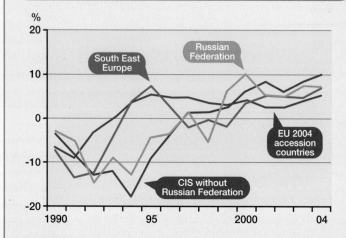

Figure 44.1 Economic growth in transition economies[1]: annual % change in real GDP

1. For names of countries in different regional groupings, see Figure 44.2.

Source: adapted from *Economic Survey of Europe*, United Nations; http://unstats.un.org/unsd/snaama/dnllist.asp.

plant. Only cars made in the country can be sold in that country. In a market economy, some consumers may decide they prefer imported cars even though they are more expensive. If the former domestic producer can now only sell 300 000 cars a year, it will need fewer workers, fewer raw materials and need to replace less equipment. This will have knock on (or multiplier) effects throughout the economy. Total output will fall as resources lie unemployed. Until new firms spring up or existing firms expand, GDP will remain below what it was before.

In China, the transition has been much more

Figure 44.2 Index of real GDP: 2004 compared to 1989

Real GDP 2004 (1989 = 100)

1. China	380.5
2. Poland	141.7
3. Albania	130.1
4. Estonia	129.1
5. Slovenia	125.1
6. Slovakia	120.9
7. Hungary	119.8
8. Uzbekistan	119.5
9. Czech Republic	113.7
10. Belarus	113.4
11. Kazakhstan	102.4
12. Armenia	101.5
13. Romania	100.8
14. Latvia	95.5
15. Croatia	94.7
16. Lithuania	93.2
17. Bulgaria	92.0
18. Turkmenistan	90.2
19. Kyrgyzstan	84.2
20. Macedonia	83.5
21. Russian Federation	82.5
22. Azerbaijan	77.3
23. Ukraine	58.8
24. Serbia and Montenegro	53.7
25. Tajikstan	52.8
26. Moldova	44.6
27. Georgia	41.5

EU 2004 accession countries
Czech Republic
Estonia
Hungary
Latvia
Lithuania
Poland
Slovakia
Slovenia

South East Europe
Albania
Bulgaria
Croatia
Romania
Serbia and Montenegro
Macedonia

Commonwealth of Independent States (CIS)
Armenia
Azerbaijan
Belarus
Georgia
Kazakhstan
Kyrgyzstan
Moldova
Tajikstan
Turkmenistan
Ukraine
Uzbekistan

Russian Federation

China

Source: adapted from *Economic Survey of Europe*, United Nations; http://unstats.un.org/unsd/snaama/dnllist.asp.

Figure 44.3 The informal economy in transition economies, % of GDP, 2002-2003

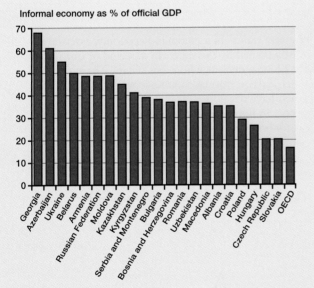

Informal economy as % of official GDP

Note: Actual output of the economy official = GDP + output of informal economy.
Source: adapted from *Economic Survey of Europe*, United Nations.

prolonged, spanning the period from 1978 to today. Initially, economic reform was confined to relatively small geographical areas on the eastern coast of China and in particular the province of Guangdong, next to Hong Kong. As a result, there was not the large falls in output that Eastern Europe and the former Soviet Union suffered in the early 1990s as Figure 44.1 shows. However, arguably, China has achieved less of a transformation today to a market economy than, say, Poland or even the Russian Federation despite the fact that it has grown at such a fast rate.

The data in Figures 44.1 and 44.2 should be treated with some caution. Transition tends to bring about a large rise in the size of the informal economy (☞ unit 25). Figure 44.3, for example, shows that Georgia, which suffered the largest fall in official GDP over the period 1989-2004, also had the largest informal economy amongst former Eastern bloc countries in 2003. Informal economies also exist in developed countries like the UK. The average size of the informal economy in OECD developed countries in 2003 was 15 per cent of GDP.

Unemployment

The large falls in output shown in parts of Figures 44.1 and 44.2 cannot but have led to sharp rises in unemployment. When Eastern European countries were command economies, one of their strengths was that the economies were managed to ensure almost zero unemployment. The move to a market system led to a large shake-out of labour. First, many enterprises have gone out of business. Factories and plant have been closed and their workers made unemployed. Second, enterprises have been forced to become more efficient, especially if they are now competing in sectors of the economy subject to competition from imports of Western firms. Efficiency is easily gained by shedding labour and making the remaining workforce work harder and more productively.

Figure 44.4 shows the year on year changes in employment in the formal sector of the economy. When employment falls, either workers become unemployed or they gain jobs in the informal sector. The pattern of employment reflects what happened to GDP. In the early 1990s, when restructuring was at its peak, there was a considerable loss of jobs in all transition economies. By the mid-1990s, employment was rising and unemployment falling in the 8 countries which were to join the EU in 2004. However, employment continued to fall in many other countries. By 2004, employment in the formal sector was still below its 1989 level in almost every country and unemployment was higher.

Inflation

When countries were command economies, goods fell into four categories. Some goods, such as health, education and possibly housing were free to citizens. Others, such as food, rail travel or books, were subsidised and sold below cost. Some goods were sold at the market clearing prices. Finally, some were unobtainable, such as most goods produced abroad. In the early transition phase, countries tended to remove subsidies from basic items such as food and fuel which in turn led to large rises in average prices. To compensate workers, wages were often allowed to rise substantially, which in turn led to increases in costs and further increases in prices by producers. Governments and central banks accommodated these large rises in prices by printing money, rather than maintaining tight monetary policies. They did this because running tight monetary policies would have led to even greater unemployment and falls in GDP.

Many transition economies suffered bouts of hyperinflation as a result, as Figure 44.5 shows. In the second half of the 1990s, countries tended to run more restrictive monetary policies, bringing inflation down but accepting the deflationary consequences of this on their economies. By 2004, all transition countries had annual inflation rates below 20 per cent, with the EU 2004 accession countries being the best performing with average inflation below 5 per cent.

Factors affecting performance

Transition economies have differed widely in their performance. At one extreme, China has been growing at approximately 10 per cent per year for over 25 years since it started its transition process. On the other hand, Georgia's official GDP in 2004 was less than half what it was in 1989. A number of factors have influenced the performance of these economies.

War One problem for a number of transition economies has been war, either external or civil war. A war leads to destruction of resources and a disruption of normal production. Prolonged war can be devastating, leading to a large shift in the production possibility frontier to the left. Serbia, for example, in its first war with its neighbours in the former Yugoslavia, saw GDP fall by 59 per cent by 1993 compared of its 1989 level. In its war with Kosovo in 1999, GDP fell 18 per cent. Georgia suffered civil war which devastated its economy.

Property rights In a command economy, assets are mostly owned by the state. In a period of transition, it can become unclear who owns what. Those economies which have performed best have tended to be those which have developed clear rules about property rights. In poorly performing countries, it is often not clear who owns an asset. Firms can be privatised, for example, only to be renationalised on technicalities. A firm may buy land, build a factory on it and then find

Figure 44.4 *Employment in transition economies*

Annual % change

CIS without Russian Federation

EU 2004 accession countries

Russian Federation

South East Europe

Key	2004 as % of 1989
EU 2004 accession countries	-16.5
South East Europe	-28.1
Russian Federation	-10.9
CIS without Russian Federation	-7.3

Source: adapted from *Economic Survey of Europe*, United Nations.

Figure 44.5 *Inflation in transition economies*

| ● EU 2004 accession countries | ● Russian Federation | ● South East Europe | ○ CIS without Russian Federation |

Source: adapted from *Economic Survey of Europe*, United Nations.

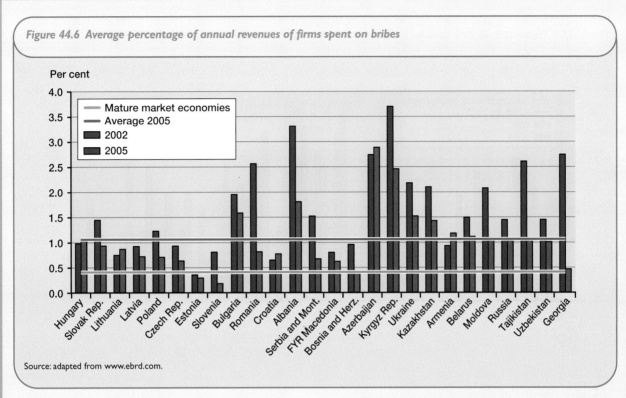

Figure 44.6 Average percentage of annual revenues of firms spent on bribes

Source: adapted from www.ebrd.com.

it loses control of the factory because another party is able to seize ownership of the land.

Privatisation Privatisation is the sale of state owned assets to the private sector. In a mixed economy (☞ unit 43), the private sector typically produces 50 per cent of more of GDP. So moving from a command economy to a mixed economy necessitates the sale or transfer of state owned assets to the private sector. Some countries such as Poland and the Czech Republic have been successful in making this transfer. Others, including the Russian Federation and China, have been less successful. In Russia, much of the oil industry which was privatised was renationalised. In China, much of heavy industry is still state owned. The problem with state owned enterprises is that they tend to be less efficient than privatised ones, with higher costs and less investment. The reason why governments are often reluctant to privatise is because it lessens their control over the economy and its resources, and because privatisation is typically associated with making workers redundant and closing down factories and plants.

Access to finance In a healthy economy, all sizes of firms have access to finance in different parts of a country. In transition economies, small firms, including start ups, and those away from the capital city often experience difficulties in getting finance. By comparison, inefficient, large state owned enterprises may have relatively easy access to finance. This slows growth because firms which have the potential for greater efficiency and faster growth are unable to

operate or finance expansion because of lack of funds whereas firms which are less efficient and will not grow have access to those funds.

Bribery and corruption Bribery and corruption are a major problem in many transition countries including China. Bribery and corruption were typically part of life in command economies. Because resources were often rationed by bureaucrats rather than the market, paying bureaucrats for favours created quasi markets for goods and services. Bureaucrats had considerable incentives to accepts bribes because often their wages were very low. Equally, at the top, corruption enabled senior government members to accumulate large fortunes. This is an example of government failure. Power enables government members and officials effectively to extract rents from economic activities. They can enjoy a higher standard of living by rent-seeking activities than through promoting efficient government and a growing economy. Figure 44.6 shows the percentage of annual revenues of firms which are spent on bribes in different countries. Note that bribes are also a feature of some mature market economies.

Regulatory framework In the UK, firms complain about the amount of 'red tape' with which they have to comply. In transition economies, such red tape is typically much worse, both because it is more impenetrable and also because much has little economic or social value. Heavy regulations also make it much easier for bribery and corruption to flourish. Figure 44.7 compares the amount of time that senior

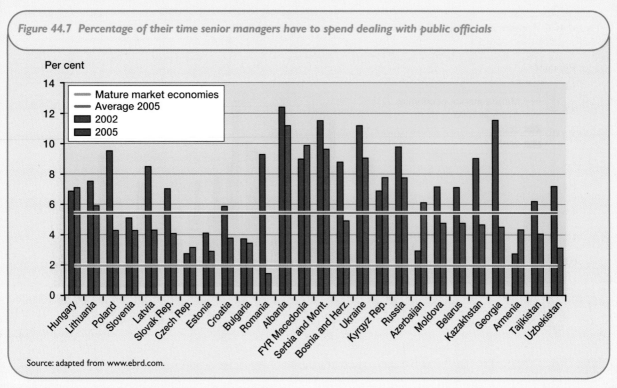

Figure 44.7 *Percentage of their time senior managers have to spend dealing with public officials*

Source: adapted from www.ebrd.com.

managers have to spend dealing with public officials, an indication of the amount of red tape in an economy.

Competition Neo-classical economics suggests that competition increases efficiency. In transition countries, firms which are most efficient in terms of lowest cost (productive efficiency) and which are growing fastest tend to be in markets where they face competition. This could either be domestic competition from other firms in the country, or international competition. Where there are still state firms, they often have a degree of monopoly power which protects their inefficiency.

Openness to trade and foreign investment Transition economies which have become most open to trade and to foreign investment have tended to grow the fastest. China, for example, could not have grown at such a fast rate without competing in export markets and enjoying large inflows of foreign investment. Figure 44.8 shows that productivity (output per worker) in transition economies is highest in foreign owned firms and lowest in state-owned firms.

Macroeconomic stability Macroeconomic stability, such as low inflation and a manageable current account position, helps firms plan and grow. Macroeconomic instability, such as hyperinflation, or a drying up of export credit because of a foreign exchange crisis, severely disrupts the ability of firms to plan and finance production and sales.

Taxation and government support Taxes, government

Figure 44.8 *Productivity in different types of firm in transition economies compared to state owned firms[1], 2004*

1. For example, productivity in privatised firms was 10% above productivity of state owned firms.
Source: adapted from www.ebrd.com.

spending and support for business can play a crucial role. Some transition economies have adopted low taxes on business to attract foreign investment. Estonia, for example, has seen rapid growth on the back of low taxation, partly because it has managed to attract jobs away from high tax Finland which is geographically very close. In China, the start of China's high growth back in the late 1970s and 1980s occurred in Guangdong Province which benefited from relatively low taxation compared to the rest of China.

Government support for business, such as providing low cost loans, can be important too.

EU membership By 2006, eight former command economies in Eastern Europe had joined the EU. All eight have been among the best performing transition countries. EU membership confers three important advantages. First, the EU will only accept new members if their laws and institutions conform to EU standards. This gives applicant countries a strong incentive to make necessary reforms. Second, EU

membership opens their economies up to competition. Typically, their cheap labour gives them a competitive advantage in exports. Domestic firms competing against imports have to raise their product standards and their productivity to survive. Third, the EU will give regional aid and these countries are likely to benefit from the Common Agricultural Policy. Applying for and then gaining EU membership can therefore bring considerable gains for transition countries.

The Czech Republic is one of the EU 2004 accession countries which joined the EU in 2004.

DataQuestion

China

Table 44.1 Governance indicators[1], 2004

	Voice and accountability	Political stability	Government effectiveness	Regulatory quality	Rule of law	Control of corruption
Bulgaria	65.0	51.5	54.8	69.5	55.1	56.2
China	7.30	46.6	60.1	35.0	40.6	39.9
Czech Republic	81.1	73.8	71.6	81.8	69.6	58.7
Kazakhstan	13.6	45.6	29.8	18.2	17.4	9.9
Russian Federation	25.7	21.8	48.1	30.5	29.5	29.1
UK	94.2	71.4	94.2	94.1	93.7	94.6

1. 'Percentile rank' is the percentage of countries that rate below the selected country, e.g. 25% would indicate that 25 per cent of countries worldwide are worse, and therefore 75% are better. The lower the percentile rank, the worse is the country on an indicator.

Voice and accountability (including civil liberties, political and human rights, free and fair elections)
Political Stability and absence of violence (including threat of political unrest, likelihood of coup d'etats, domestic violence and terrorism)
Government effectiveness (including quality of public service provision and the bureaucracy, competence and independence of civil servants)

Regulatory quality (including incidence of market-unfriendly policies such as price controls, inadequate bank supervision and excessive regulation)
Rule of law (including the incidence of crime, the effectiveness and predictability of the judiciary, and the enforceability of contracts)
Control of corruption (the exercise of public power for private gain)

Source: adapted from World Bank.

Figure 44.9 Annual percentage growth in real GDP, the UK and five selected transition countries

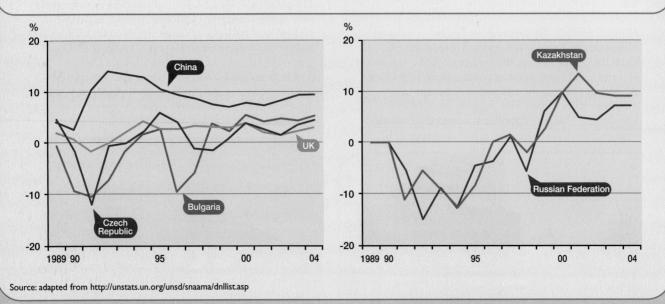

Source: adapted from http://unstats.un.org/unsd/snaama/dnllist.asp

The legacy of China's command economy past is still very much with it. In 2002, 41 per cent of industrial output (which includes industries from coal to steel to television sets) was still produced by state owned enterprises. This is despite the fact that economic reform was first started in 1978.

Source: adapted from www.economist.com, 9.2.2004.

China still has room to make vast gains in GDP. Between 1993 and 2000, more than 60 per cent of all financial credit, such as loans, went to inefficient state enterprises. The private sector, because it lacked finance, accounted for only between 15 and 27 per cent of total Chinese investment during this period. Yet the private sector created 56 per cent of all new jobs. Foreign direct investment (investment by foreign companies in existing Chinese companies or setting up new factories and premises) was around 5 per cent of GDP in the 1990s. Yet in 2002, foreign owned companies accounted for 50 per cent of all Chinese exports and 29 per cent of industrial output.

Source: adapted from the *Financial Times*, 13.4.2005.

1. Countries such as China, Bulgaria and Kazakhstan have moved from being a command economy toward a mixed economy in recent years. Explain the difference between the two economic systems.

2. Using the data in Figure 44.9, suggest which countries have benefited most and least from economic change since 1989.

3. To what extent can China be said to have made a full transition to a market economy?

45 Economic methodology

Summary

1. Economics is generally classified as a social science.
2. It uses the scientific method as the basis of its investigation.
3. Economics is the study of how groups of individuals make decisions about the allocation of scarce resources.
4. Economists build models and theories to explain economic interactions.
5. Positive economics deals with statements of 'fact' which can either be refuted or not refuted. Normative economics deals with value judgments, often in the context of policy recommendations.
6. Models and theories are simplifications of reality.
7. A good model is one which yields powerful conclusions, is elegant and internally consistent.
8. In addition, a good positive model is one which explains past and present events, can predict future events, is universally applicable and has realistic assumptions.
9. A good positive model must be capable of being refuted whilst a good normative model is one which sets out an ideal or paradigm state of affairs.
10. Models can be distinguished according to whether they are static or dynamic models, equilibrium or disequilibrium models, partial or general models, or micro-economic or macro-economic models.

What is a science?

There are many sciences covering a wide field of knowledge. What links them all is a particular method of work or enquiry called the SCIENTIFIC METHOD. The scientific method at its most basic is relatively easy to understand. A scientist:

- postulates a THEORY - the scientist puts forward a hypothesis which is capable of refutation (e.g. the earth travels round the sun, the earth is flat, a light body will fall at the same speed as a heavy body);

- gathers evidence to either support the theory or refute it - astronomical observation gives evidence to support the theory that the earth travels round the sun; on the other hand, data refutes the idea that the earth is flat; gathering evidence may be done through **controlled experiments**;

- accepts, modifies or refutes the theory - the earth does travel round the sun; a light body will fall at the same speed as a heavy body although it will only do so under certain conditions; the earth is not flat.

Theories which gain universal acceptance are often called LAWS. Hence we have the law of gravity, Boyle's law, and in economics the laws of demand and supply.

Economics - the science

Some sciences, such as physics or chemistry, are sometimes called 'hard sciences'. This term doesn't refer to the fact that physics is more difficult than a science such as biology! It refers to the fact that it is relatively easy to apply the scientific method to the study of these subjects. In physics much of the work can take place in laboratories. Observations can be made with some degree of certainty. Control groups can be established. It then becomes relatively easy to accept or refute a particular hypothesis.

This is all much more difficult in social sciences such as economics, sociology, politics and anthropology. In economics it is usually not possible to set up experiments to test hypotheses. It is not possible to establish control groups or to conduct experiments in environments which enable one factor to be varied whilst other factors are kept constant. The economist has to gather data in the ordinary everyday world where many variables are changing over any given time period. It then becomes difficult to decide whether the evidence supports or refutes particular hypotheses. Economists sometimes come to very different conclusions when considering a particular set of data as their interpretations may vary. For example, an unemployment rate of 12 per cent in the North region compared to a national average of 8 per cent may indicate a failure of government policy to help this area.

Question 1

Table 45.1

Year	Change in households' final consumption expenditure, £bn at 2002 prices	Change in households' disposable income, £bn at 2002 prices	Bank base rate (%)	Change in house prices (%)
1997	19.9	21.2	6.56	7.8
1998	22.8	5.8	7.24	7.5
1999	26.4	19.6	5.34	13.1
2000	28.4	30.4	5.97	9.8
2001	19.8	27.9	5.13	11.1
2002	23.2	11.8	4.00	13.7
2003	17.7	19.9	3.69	21.3
2004	26.0	15.7	4.38	15.8

Source: adapted from *Economic Trends, Financial Statistics, Housing Statistics*, Office for National Statistics.

(a) Economists suggest that changes in consumer spending vary with changes in the incomes of consumers (their personal disposable income), interest rates (such as banks' interest rates) and changes in the personal wealth of consumers. Does the evidence in Table 45.1 support or refute this hypothesis?

Others may conclude that policy had been a success as unemployment may have been far greater without the use of policy.

It is sometimes argued that economics cannot be a science because it studies human behaviour and human behaviour cannot be reduced to scientific laws. There is an element of truth in this. It is very difficult to understand and predict the behaviour of individuals. However, nearly all economics is based on the study of the behaviour of groups of individuals. The behaviour of groups is often far more predictable than that of individuals. Moreover, we tend to judge a science on its ability to establish laws which are certain and unequivocal. But even in a hard science such as physics, it has become established that some laws can only be stated in terms of probabilities. In economics, much analysis is couched in terms of 'it is likely that' or 'this may possibly happen'. Economists use this type of language because they know they have insufficient data to make firm predictions. In part it is because other variables may change at the same time, altering the course of events. But it is also used because economists know that human behaviour, whilst broadly predictable, is not predictable to the last £1 spent or to the nearest 1 penny of income.

Theories and models

The terms 'theory' and MODEL are often used interchangeably. There is no exact distinction to be made between the two. However, an economic theory is generally expressed in looser terms than a model. For instance, 'consumption is dependent upon income' might be an economic theory.
'$C_t = 567 + 0.852Y_t$,' where 567 is a constant, C_t is current consumption and Y_t current income would be an economic model. Theories can often be expressed in words. But economic models, because they require greater precision in their specification, are often expressed in mathematical terms.

The purpose of modelling

Why are theories and models so useful in a science? The universe is a complex place. There is an infinite number of interactions happening at any moment in time. Somehow we all have to make sense of what is going on. For instance, we assume that if we put our hand into a flame, we will get burnt. If we see a large hole in the ground in front of us we assume that we will fall into it if we carry on going in that direction. One of the reasons why we construct theories or models is because we want to know why something is as it is. Some people are fascinated by questions such as 'Why do we fall downwards and not upwards?' or 'Why can birds fly?'. But more importantly we use theories and models all the time in deciding how to act. We keep away from fires to prevent getting burnt. We avoid holes in the ground because we don't want to take a tumble.

Positive and normative models

These two uses of models - to investigate the world as it is and to use the model as a basis for decision making - lead us to distinguish between two types of economic model.
POSITIVE MODELS and positive economics deal with objective or scientific explanations of the economy. For instance, the model of price determination which states that a rise in price will lead to a fall in the quantity demanded is a positive model. It is capable of refutation. It is argued by some economists that positive models are value free.

NORMATIVE MODELS and normative economics attempt to describe what ought to be. A normative statement is one which contains a value judgement. A normative model sets a standard by which reality can be judged. For instance, 'The government has a duty to protect the incomes of everybody in society, not just the well-off' would be a normative statement. It contains a value judgement about the role of government.

For some, the study of economics is fascinating in itself. Studying and constructing positive models is reward enough. But most who study economics are principally interested in the subject because of its normative aspects. They want to know how society can be changed - 'Should society help the poor and disadvantaged?', 'How best might pollution be dealt with?'.

Academic economics has a long tradition of the study of positive economics. But 'political economy', the normative study of economics, has an equally long tradition going back to Adam Smith. In fact it is difficult to separate the two. To know how best to help raise the living standards of the poor (normative economics) we need to know how the economy operates and why people are poor.

Some economists argue that positive economics cannot be distinguished from normative economics because positive economics is subtly value laden. Why, for instance, did economists become so much more interested in the role of the entrepreneur (the risk-taking small businessman) during the 1980s? Much of the answer must be because Margaret Thatcher and Ronald Reagan made such important claims about the benefits of entrepreneurial activity for an economy.

In practice, all economists make value judgements. But many

Question 2

From Lord Fraser of Carmyllie and Mr Robert Mabro

Sir, The time has come to re-establish a Department of Energy led by a cabinet minister. The department was abolished at a time when world oil was in excess supply, and energy security concerns were dampened by a feeling of abundance. The UK was a net exporter.

The energy situation is radically different today. The UK will become an oil-importing country at a time of high oil prices. Subsidies for research and development are going to be required and the government will have to determine who should be helped and on which scale.

Downing Street has too much on its plate to be able to deal effectively with these complex issues. The Treasury is about taxes, and the Department of Environment is about an important aspect of energy but not about energy as such. The energy problems facing us need more resources for research and policymaking than are now available to the ever-shrinking energy division of the Department of Trade and Industry.

Fraser of Carmyllie, House of Lords
Robert Mabro, Emeritus Director, Oxford Institute for Energy Studies

(a) Explain which are the positive statements and which are the normative statements in this letter to the *Financial Times*, 13 December 2005.

economists argue that 'good' economics distinguishes between positive and normative aspects. Value judgements are exposed so that we can see whether the analysis can lead to different conclusions if different value judgements are made.

Simplification

One criticism made of economics is that economic theories and models are 'unrealistic'. This is true, but it is equally true of Newton's law of gravity, Einstein's Theory of Relativity or any theory or model. This is because any theory or model has to be a simplification of reality if it is to be useful. Imagine, for instance, using a map which described an area perfectly. To do this it would need to be a full scale reproduction of the entire area which would give no practical advantage. Alternatively, drop a feather and a cannon ball from the top of the leaning tower of Pisa. You will find that both don't descend at the same speed, as one law in physics would predict, because that law assumes that factors such as air resistance and friction don't exist.

If a model is to be useful it has to be simple. The extent of simplification depends upon its use. If you wanted to go from London to Tokyo by air, it wouldn't be very helpful to have maps which were on the scale of your local A to Z. On the other hand, if you wanted to visit a friend in a nearby town it wouldn't be very helpful to have a map of the world with you. The local A to Z is very much more detailed (i.e. closer to reality) than a world map but this does not necessarily make it more useful or make it a 'better' model.

Simplification implies that some factors have been included in the model and some have been omitted. It could even be the case that some factors have been distorted to emphasise particular points in a model. For instance, on a road map of the UK, the cartographer will almost certainly not have attempted to name every small hamlet or to show the geological formation of the area. On the other hand, he or she will have marked in roads and motorways which will appear several miles wide according to the scale of the map. There is a number of reasons why this occurs.

- Models are constructed in an attempt to present a clear and simple explanation of reality. Trying to include weather and geological information on a large scale road map would make it much more difficult for the motorist to see how to get from A to B. On the other hand, distorting reality by making roads very wide is extremely helpful to a motorist studying a map because it is much easier to read thick lines than thin lines.
- Models must assume that explanations for much of what is contained in the model lie elsewhere. For instance, a model which explains that consumption varies with income doesn't explain what determines income itself.
- The creator of a model may not be interested in a particular aspect of reality (which is an example of how normative values can be superimposed on supposedly positive models). The cartographer, for instance, preparing an ordinary road map is not interested in the geology of an area.
- The model may be constructed deliberately to distort and mislead. For instance, employers might choose to use a model which predicts that minimum wages always increase unemployment, whilst trade unions might construct a different model which showed that minimum wages increased employment.

Models may also omit variables because the author does not believe them to be of importance. This may be a correct premise. On the other hand, it may be false, leading to the model being poorer than it might otherwise be. For instance, few would criticise a weather model which omits the UK rate of inflation from among its variables. On the other hand, a weather model of the UK which omits wind speed is unlikely to perform well.

In conclusion, all subject disciplines simplify and select from a mass of data. This process seems to cause little concern in sciences such as physics and chemistry. However, it is unfortunate for economists that many critics of the subject seem to think that simplification in economics shows that economists have little or no understanding of economic matters. Nothing could be further from the truth!

'Good' models

Many of the units in this book are devoted to one economic model or another. Which of these models are 'good' models? A number of criteria can be used to judge a model.

One important criterion by which a positive economic model may be judged is the extent to which it accurately **explains reality**. Reality exists in three different time periods: **the past, the present and the future**. A very powerful model, such as the model of price determination, is able to explain what happened in the past, explain what is happening today and predict what will happen in the future. Price theory provided an explanation of why the rise in oil prices during the 1970s led to a fall in world wide demand for oil. Today it helps us understand why a restriction in the supply of oil by OPEC leads to a price rise. We can predict with confidence that as world oil reserves, all other things being equal, diminish over the next 300 years, the price of oil will rise.

The simple Keynesian theory of income determination, however, is not such a good theory. It explains relatively well the workings of the UK economy in the 1950s and 1960s but only gives a partial insight into how the economy performed in the 1970s and 1980s. This is because the simple Keynesian model ignores both changes in the money supply and supply side shocks - reasonable simplifying assumptions in the 1950s and 1960s but very misleading in the context of economic events in the 1970s and 1980s.

Macro-economic computer models of the economy, such as the Treasury model, the Bank of England model or the National Institute of Economic and Social Research (NIESR) model, are judged mainly on their ability to predict the future. They are specifically called '**forecasting models**'. It could be that the best predictor of next year's rate of inflation is this year's rainfall in the Sahara desert. A model which incorporated this would be a good model if we were solely interested in its ability to forecast but it would be a poor model if we wished to understand the causes of inflation in the UK.

There is a number of economic models which are claimed to be good predictors but are not based on **realistic assumptions**. An example is the neo-classical theory of the firm. In the real world there are virtually no industries which conform to the assumptions of either perfect competition or pure monopoly yet these theories are widely taught and discussed. One justification is that although the assumptions are unrealistic the models provide very powerful and clear predictions about the extremes of behaviour of firms. If we know how firms behave at either end of the spectrum of competition then we can predict how firms will behave between these two extremes. Unfortunately these justifications have no logical or empirical validity. It could be argued that the models of perfect competition and monopoly give us little help in understanding the behaviour of firms in the real world, which is why there are so many alternative theories of the firm.

Positive models must be capable of refutation. A good model will be one where it is possible to gather data and perhaps perform controlled experiments to refute or support the model.

Normative models need to be judged on different criteria. A normative model does not claim to mirror reality. It attempts to provide a guide as to what is desirable or to be recommended. The neo-classical theory of the firm provides such a **paradigm**. By making a number of assumptions, it is possible to show that efficiency will be maximised in an economy where all firms are perfectly competitive. Increasing the degree of competition in industry then becomes an ideal or a goal to be aimed for. Monopoly, on the other hand, is shown to diminish welfare. Therefore the policy goal should be to break up monopolies.

Ultimately it is impossible to judge between competing normative theories. It is impossible to prove or disprove a statement such as 'Citizens should not be economically dependent upon the state'. However, it is possible to expose false reasoning within a normative model. In the 1950s, Lipsey and Lancaster, for instance, proved that greater competition might lead to a loss of welfare in the economy if at least one industry in the economy was not perfectly competitive. This 'theory of the second best' rebutted the general assumption prevalent at the time (and indeed still prevalent amongst certain economists and politicians) that greater competition was always good whilst greater monopoly was always bad.

All models need to be judged on the grounds of internal consistency, and elegance. **Internal consistency** simply means that the logic in the argument is correct and that no mistakes have been made with any mathematics used. An **elegant** model is one which is as simple and as lucid as possible.

Finally, models need to be judged on their power. Price theory is a very **powerful** model. With few assumptions and a minimum of logic, it can be used to explain important events across time and between countries. Aggregate demand and aggregate supply analysis similarly is a powerful model which can show the effects of a variety of demand side and supply side shocks on the price level and output.

Realism and models

It is often said that some economic models are poor because they are not 'realistic'. However, before coming to this conclusion about any particular theory, it is important to consider what is the purpose of the theory.

- The model may be used to predict future events. In this case, it is unimportant if the assumptions or workings of the model are realistic. The value of the model should only be judged in terms of its predictive power.
- The model may be used to analyse the workings of a **group** of individuals. The fact that some individuals behave in a different way to that predicted by the model which attempts to say how groups work on the whole does not make the model unrealistic.
  - The model may be used to explain the **workings** of a market or an economy. The detail may be realistic even if the overall predictive power of the model is relatively

Question 3

Table 45.2

	Investment[1] (£bn at 2002)	Bank base rate[2] (%)	Change in national income[3] (£bn at 2002 prices)
1997	84.4	6.56	27.8
1998	100.0	7.24	29.5
1999	103.5	5.34	28.5
2000	108.2	5.97	39.0
2001	109.8	5.13	22.4
2002	110.2	4.00	20.6
2003	107.7	3.69	26.4
2004	111.4	4.38	34.0

1 Business investment.
2 Bank base rate.
3 GDP at market prices.

Source: adapted from *Economic Trends Annual Supplement*, *Financial Statistics*, Office for National Statistics.

To what extent does the data show that (a) the accelerator model (investment in one year is determined by the change in national income in the previous year) and (b) the marginal efficiency of investment model (that investment is determined by the rate of interest) are 'good' models of investment behaviour?

weak. In this case, the fact that the predictions of the model are unrealistic is not particularly important.
- The model may be **normative**, used to describe what ought to be rather than what is. In this case, realism is obviously not an important criterion.
- The model may be very **simple**. With a few assumptions, the model may come to powerful but simplified conclusions. The fact that predictions are not accurate to the nearest 0.1 per cent does not mean that the model is unrealistic.

Forms of expression

There is a variety of ways in which models can be expressed.

Verbally A model can be expressed in words. 'Consumption increases when disposable income increases' would be an example. The advantage of using words is that models can be made accessible to a wide variety of readers. On the other hand, the use of jargon, such as 'disposable income', can be a barrier to the non-economist. Words can also be imprecise. In the above statement, we don't know the extent to which the increase is proportional.

Algebraically Over the past fifty years there has been an explosion in the use of algebra in academic economics. It enables relationships to be set down very precisely but is often totally incomprehensible to the non-specialist. It also presumes that economic relationships are precise. Many economists argue the contrary - that economic relationships, whilst consistent, cannot be expressed so accurately.

Question 4

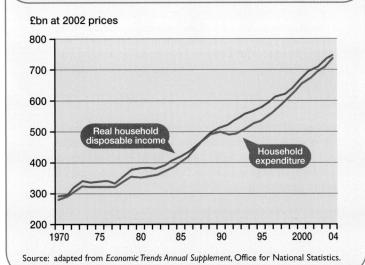

Figure 45.1 Real household expenditure and household disposable income at 2002 prices

£bn at 2002 prices

Source: adapted from *Economic Trends Annual Supplement*, Office for National Statistics.

Look at the diagram.
(a)   To what extent does it show that there is a positive correlation between consumers' expenditure and their income?
(b)   How might you express the relationship between consumers' expenditure and income (i) verbally and (ii) algebraically?

Graphically   The use of graphs has a long history in economics. It provides a convenient shorthand, encapsulating what would otherwise take many words to explain. Graphs, however, have their limitations. For instance, the fact that they can only be used in two dimensions with any ease limits the number of variables that can be used in a model.

Statistically   Statistics are essential for economists if they are to verify hypotheses. They encourage precision, but as with algebra, they can be difficult for the non-specialist to understand and can give a misleading impression of accuracy in economics. **Econometrics**, the empirical testing of economic theories using statistical data, is an important branch of economics.

Exogenous and endogenous variables

Economic models are built with two types of variables. EXOGENOUS VARIABLES are variables whose value is determined outside the model. For instance, in the simple Keynesian model of income determination, investment, government expenditure and exports are exogenous variables. Their values are constant whatever the change in other variables in the model unless it is assumed otherwise. The value of exogenous variables therefore cannot be calculated within the model.
     ENDOGENOUS VARIABLES are variables whose value is determined within the model. For instance, in the simple

Keynesian model of income determination both consumption and income are endogenous variables. Their value is determined by variables such as income within the consumption function equation. The value of endogenous variables will change if other variables within the model change too.

Static and dynamic

A DYNAMIC model is one which contains time as one of its variables. A STATIC model is one which contains no time element within the model. Nearly all the models explained in this book are static models. For instance, neither the theory of perfect competition nor the Keynesian theory of income determination contain a time variable. Static models can be used to compare two different situations, a technique called **comparative static analysis**. In the theory of perfect competition, it is common to compare one equilibrium situation with another equilibrium situation. For instance, a short run equilibrium position may be compared to the long run equilibrium position. A time element may even be implicitly assumed within the model - it is assumed that the movement from one equilibrium position to another in perfect competition will take place over a period of time rather than instantly at a point in time. However, the model does not explain the path which the industry or the firm will take in the move from one equilibrium position to another. It merely assumes a 'before' and 'after' situation.
     The cobweb theorem and the accelerator theory are the only two dynamic models explained in this book. The cobweb theorem, for instance, explicitly charts the movement over time of a market in a disequilibrium state.
     Dynamic models are in one sense more 'realistic' than static models. Time is a very important variable in the real world. However, as we have already argued, greater realism is not always a desirable characteristic in a model. Dynamic models in economics are more complex and difficult to work with than static models and their predictions are not necessarily more powerful. For instance, if we wish to know how much revenue a government will raise by increasing taxes on beer, all we need is a static price model comparing the equilibrium situation before and after the imposition of the tax. There is no need to know the exact path that the market takes to get from one equilibrium position to another. Dynamic models are not therefore 'better' or 'worse' than static models - that judgement depends upon the use to which a model is to be put.

Equilibrium and disequilibrium models

Equilibrium is a central feature of all the models studied in this book. In economics, EQUILIBRIUM can be described as a point where expectations are being realised and where no plans are being frustrated. For instance, in the Keynesian model of national income determination, equilibrium national income is the point where planned expenditure equals actual income. In neo-classical price theory the cobweb theory is a disequilibrium model because it charts the behaviour of the market as planned demand and supply differ from actual demand and supply. All static models are equilibrium models because they deal with equilibrium positions.
     An equilibrium position may be stable. If there is a movement away from equilibrium for some reason, there will be an in-built tendency for equilibrium to be restored. If the equilibrium point is unstable, there

will be no tendency to move towards an equilibrium point once disequilibrium has been established.

It is easy to make the incorrect assumption that the market (or whatever is being studied) will always return to an equilibrium position; or that the equilibrium point is somehow the optimal or most desirable position. Neither is necessarily true even if economists tend to believe that knowing where is the equilibrium point is helpful in explaining economic events and in making policy recommendations.

Partial and general models

Just as there is no clear distinction between theories and models, so too there is no clear dividing line between a partial and a general model. A GENERAL MODEL can be said to be one which contains a large number of variables. For instance, a model which includes all markets in the economy is a general model. A PARTIAL MODEL is one which contains relatively few variables. A model of the oil market or the demand for money would be partial models.

A partial model will be one in which most variables are assumed to be in the category of CETERIS PARIBUS. Ceteris paribus is Latin for 'all other things being equal' or 'all other things remaining the same'. It is a very powerful simplifying device which enables economists to explain clearly how an economy works. For instance, in neo-classical price theory ceteris paribus is used constantly. When the effect of a change in price on demand is analysed we assume that incomes, the prices of all other goods, and tastes remain the same. In the Keynesian multiplier model, it is assumed that government spending, exports, the marginal propensity to consume etc. do not change when analysing the effect of a change in investment on national income.

A general model may be realistic because it contains more variables. But again it is not necessarily better than a partial model. If we wish to study the effects of a rise in indirect taxes

Question 5

Consider the following economic models and explain whether they are static or dynamic, equilibrium or disequilibrium, partial or general, and macro-economic or micro-economic models: (a) the model of demand, supply and price determination in the goods market; (b) the cobweb theorem; (c) the model of perfect competition; (d) the aggregate demand and supply model of income determination; (e) the accelerator model of investment.

on the car industry, it is much simpler and easier to use a partial model of price determination than to use a general model. The general model may provide marginally more information but the extra information is unlikely to be worth the time and effort needed to generate it.

Macro-economics and micro-economics

A macro-economic model is one which models the economy as a whole. It deals with economic relationships at the level of all participants in the economy. A micro-economic model, on the other hand, deals with the economic behaviour of individuals or groups within society. For instance, the study of the spending decisions of individual consumers or consumers within a particular market such as the market for cars (demand theory) would be micro-economics. The study of consumption patterns for the whole economy (the consumption function) would be an example of macro-economics. The study of the determination of wage rates (wage theory) would be micro-economics. The study of the overall level of wages in the economy (part of national income accounting) would be macro-economics.

Key terms

Ceteris paribus - the assumption that all other variables within the model remain constant whilst one change is being considered.
Endogenous variables - variables whose value is determined within the model being used.
Equilibrium - the point where what is expected or planned is equal to what is realised or actually happens.
Exogenous variables - variables whose value is determined outside the model under consideration.
Law - a theory or model which has been verified by empirical evidence.
Normative economics - the study and presentation of policy prescriptions involving value judgements about the way in which scarce resources are allocated.
Partial and general models - a partial model is one with few variables whilst a general model has many.
Positive economics - the scientific or objective study of the allocation of resources.
Static and dynamic models - a static model is one where time is not a variable. In a dynamic model, time is a variable explicit in the model.
The scientific method - a method which subjects theories or hypotheses to falsification by empirical evidence.
Theory or model - a hypothesis which is capable of refutation by empirical evidence.

Applied economics

Positive and normative economics

The *Financial Times* devoted its lead editorial to the subject of 'Disruption at the heart of the online revolution' on 12 November 2005. Its subject was the rapid evolution of online technologies from operating systems to search engines to data sharing to online telephony.

The leader writer introduces the article by making a number of positive statements about 'disruptive technologies', defined as ones that 'destroy old business models by providing products more cheaply and efficiently'. Microsoft, which makes 'the software that powers personal computers and much of the Internet' is now threatened by disruptive technologies. The first paragraph ends with a normative statement, a value judgment on the part of the leader writer, that this 'should be a cause for rejoicing in a market economy'.

The leader writer goes on to explain, using positive statements, how Microsoft came to have a dominant position in the information technology world and how that position is being challenged by companies such as Google, Adobe, Skype and RSS. The leader writer then makes a normative judgment, that Microsoft is responding to these challenges 'with characteristic focus'. A number of positive statements follow about how Microsoft is responding to the threat posed by these other companies and technologies.

The leader writer then points out that this is the 'same challenge that other industries have already faced' because of the Internet revolution. A normative statement follows, that 'the most important' common element of that challenge is the 'empowerment of the customer'.

In the final paragraph, the leader writer makes the normative statement that 'adapting to a world being remade by the disruptive influence of the Internet is tough'. However, this is 'a story as old as capitalism', reflecting 'an economic system that rewards successful innovation and sweeps away the casualties'. This is an example of 'the process known as creative destruction', a positive statement. The leader writer ends by saying that: 'Technological change leaves no business model unscathed, as Microsoft has belatedly discovered at the heart of the most disruptive technology of our era.' That Microsoft has 'belatedly' discovered its shortcomings and that the Internet is the 'most' disruptive technology of our era are both value judgements. However, many would agree with the writer that Microsoft faces the loss of its monopoly position in its sector of the computing software market because of these new developments.

DataQuestion — The Common Agricultural Policy (CAP)

CAP

In 2005, there were difficult negotiations about the EU budget between member countries. The British Prime Minister, Tony Blair, wanted to reopen a deal made in 2002 about the Common Agricultural Policy which set CAP budgets to 2014. He, in turn, came under intense pressure to give up the 'British Rebate', an annual refund to the UK first negotiated in the 1980s to compensate the UK for its low level of subsidies from the CAP budget. The ten, mainly Eastern European, countries which joined in the EU in 2004 wanted a larger slice of EU spending than proposed. France and Ireland, both major beneficiaries of CAP subsidies, strongly defended the deal made in 2002.

Over the page are two contributions to this debate, one from Bertie Ahern, the Irish Prime Minister who was against further CAP reform, the other from Tony Blair's Press Spokesperson, who argued for CAP reform.

We must stand by the Common Agricultural Policy

In an article written for the *Financial Times*, Bertie Ahern, the Irish Prime Minister, argued for maintaining the CAP deal made in 2002. His comments included the following.

The defeat of the European Union's proposed constitution in the French and Dutch referendums has led to a renewed debate on the way forward for Europe. As part of this debate, the Common Agricultural Policy has in recent months been the subject of much criticism, with repeated calls for further reform.

2003 saw a radical reform of CAP, decoupling 'subsidies' from production. This reform is in its first year of implementation. It would be both unfair and unwise to ask farmers to accept another radical reform now. Farmers, like other business people, need a reasonable degree of stability in the policy environment in which they operate. However, there is more at stake. To try to overturn an agreement reached unanimously by the European Council as recently as October 2002 would be to send the wrong signal to Europe's people. The public needs to see a Europe that stands by its agreements.

There are other issues too. Reform would mean that European agricultural production would fall rapidly. The food supply gap would be filled by imports from, for example, South America and Australia, which can produce at prices below European levels. Europe's food supplies could, once again, become vulnerable. Reform would also result in serious damage to the social and economic fabric of rural areas across Europe. As for the scale of subsidies, the Organisation for Economic Co-operation and Development (OECD) has estimated that transfers to agriculture from both consumers and taxpayers amount to $103bn (£58bn) in the EU and $92bn (£52bn) in the USA, or 1.32 per cent of GDP for the EU and 0.92 per cent for the US. There is therefore broad comparability of support.

Calls for radical CAP reform are misplaced and outdated; they are based on a misunderstanding of the role of the CAP in European society and the world economy. They are also based on a false premise about the relative cost of the CAP.

Source: adapted from the *Financial Times*, 26.9.2005.

Briefing from the Prime Minister's Official Spokesperson on the Common Agricultural Policy

Our policy all along has been to get rid of subsidies for crops because we believe that this was a distorted way in which to support the rural economy. Therefore what we have always argued for was a managed process of change in which you maintain sustainable livelihoods in the countryside but didn't do so at the expense of distorting world trade. That was why we always argued for fundamental reform of CAP and we recognised that there had been some progress in that direction but we are arguing for more.

We are still in a situation where some 80 per cent of the existing budget is directed towards the original 15 member states, and that does not allow the spending to be prioritised towards providing the infrastructure support that accession countries need. Therefore we still have a distorted system.

There should be a policy of managed change which would include more efficient farming and viable, sustainable rural communities. You cannot have a situation where we go into another decade with 40 per cent of the EU budget being spent on 5 per cent of the population.

Source: adapted from The Office of the Prime Minister, www.number-10.gov.uk/output/page7762.asp.

1. Explain the difference between positive and normative statements. Give at least six examples from the views of Bertie Ahern and Tony Blair.
2. Evaluate the case for and against reform of the CAP using the arguments put forward in the data.

Study skills

When you start your AS/A Level course, you should try to evaluate whether or not your study and organisational skills are effective. For instance:
- are you always present and on time for classes or lectures?
- do you always hand work in on time?
- is work done to the best of your ability?
- do you work in a suitable environment?
- do you leave time to plan and evaluate your work?
- do you participate in all learning activities in a way which helps you to learn?
- do you listen to advice and act on constructive comments about your work?

Having good study skills does not necessarily mean that work is done well in advance, or that the room where you work at home is tidy. Some students are very organised in what might at first seem chaotic situations. For instance, they might always write their essays close to the time they have to be handed in. Or their study room might look an incredible mess. However, if you work best under pressure of deadlines, and you know what is where in the mess of your room, then it could be argued that in fact you are an organised student!

In class

The core of your study is likely to take place in the classroom or lecture room. Not only will you spend a considerable proportion of your studying time in class, but what you do in the classroom and the instructions you receive there will influence what you do outside. Effective classroom skills are therefore essential. They include the following.

Attending classes regularly and on time Good organisational skills involve attending all lessons unless there are serious reasons for absence. They also involve arranging doctor's and dentist's appointments, driving lessons or holidays outside class time so that work is not missed.

Always being attentive It is important to be attentive at all times and engage in the activities being presented. Participation in class also helps other students to learn.

Making clear and concise notes during lessons Notes can act as a record of what has been said. Taking notes whilst the teacher/lecturer is talking is a form of active learning. It can help some students to focus on what is being said and identify what they don't understand. For other students, though, note taking can get in the way of understanding what the teacher or lecturer is saying. They may prefer to read handouts or notes given out by the teacher or lecturer. You have to decide what is best for you.

Asking questions of the teacher or lecturer It is unlikely that all students will understand everything that goes on in a lesson. Asking questions helps to fill in these gaps. It is also very important to keep you focussed on the lesson. If you are thinking about what you do and don't understand, you will inevitably be participating in that lesson. Formulating questions is also important for developing oral skills, which will be essential in the world outside of school or college.

Participating in classroom discussions Classroom discussions enable you to practice important key learning skills. Some students find they want to contribute more than others. Remember though that in a discussion, listening is as important as talking. All participants must respect the contributions of others. There must be a balance between communication and listening.

Preparing for the next lesson Many schools and colleges issue their students with homework diaries, or encourage them to buy one. They are a useful tool for planning and organising work. They help you to remember what you have to do and structure your out of class activities.

Planning outside the class

Planning is an essential part of good study skills. By keeping a diary, for instance, students can see at a glance what needs to be done and when. They can then mentally allocate time slots for completion of the work. For work which is not structured by the teacher or lecturer, such as coursework or revision, students need to construct a plan. Typically, this will show dates and the work to be done on or by a particular date. It may also show times during the day when work is to be done. Some students find it helpful to discipline themselves by the clock. So they plan to start, say, revision at 9.00 each morning, have a ten minute break each hour on the hour, break for lunch at 1.00, etc.

It may also be helpful to construct precise plans for day to day work outside the classroom. When you start on your AS/A level course, for instance, it might be useful to plan meticulously when you are going to complete work during the first month. This will ensure that work gets done and you have set out on your course with good work habits. Hopefully, you will then be able to relax your planning because you will have got into a sound routine for completing work.

Planning tends to increase in importance:
- the longer the task to be completed:
- the less structure is given by your school or college for its completion.

Organising time

Every student has different preferences about organising time. Some of the key issues are as follows.

Time during the week You have to decide when you want to complete your work during the week. There are likely to be conflicting claims on your time. For instance, you may have a part time job which takes priority at certain times of the week. You may have family or social commitments. You may decide that you will never work on Friday or Saturday nights (except in emergencies!). There are no right or wrong times to study. However, it is essential to build in enough time during the week to study. AS/A level examinations have been developed on the assumption that you are studying full time for 1 to 2 years.

Time during the day Some people work best in the morning, some in the afternoon and some at night. You should know whether you are a 'morning person' or otherwise. Try to work at times of day when you are most likely to learn effectively.

Breaks Breaks are essential to maintain concentration. How frequent and how long your breaks need to be varies from one individual to another. You need to find out what works best for you. Try to be as disciplined as possible in your approach to breaks. It is all too easy for the break to extend itself over the whole period when you planned to work. Get to know what is most likely to stop you from getting back to work. For instance, if you start watching television during your break, do you find that you only go back to work at the end of the programme?

Variety Some students like variety in what they do. So during an hour's work session, they may do a little on three pieces of work. Others find that they cannot cope with such short blocks of time and would rather concentrate on just one piece of work. Longer pieces of work, such as essays or coursework, may need to be broken down and completed in several different work sessions anyway.

Networking and resources

It is important that students make use of all the resources that are available to them. Here are some suggestions about how to find help when completing work.

The textbook Using a textbook effectively will help students to achieve the highest possible marks for their work. Remember that the textbook is there to help you understand a topic. The relevant section should be read before you attempt a piece of work and you are likely to want to refer to the textbook as you write. You may wish to consult a number of textbooks if, for example, you do not understand a particular area in one book.

The library Schools and colleges will have libraries, perhaps even in the classroom or lecture room, of books and other materials which can be borrowed. Reading around a topic is an essential part of preparing any work such as an essay. Libraries will also hopefully carry daily quality newspapers. Economics is about the real world. AS/A level Economics students should be aware of the major economic issues of the day and be able to discuss them.

The Internet The Internet can be very useful in the learning process. It is most perhaps useful when students are able to use the same site repeatedly. They know what is on the site and how to navigate around it. There may be more difficulties, however, when searching for general information. This requires skill in using search engines to find appropriate sites which can often take time. The Internet is likely to be very useful to students working on their own in Economics when researching coursework.

Ask the teacher/lecturer Make full use of your teacher or lecturer as a resource. If you are stuck on a piece of homework, for instance, ask the teacher or lecturer

to help you out. If you frequently need help, it is a good idea to start the homework well in advance of the date it needs to be handed in, so that you can contact the teacher or lecturer.

Network with fellow students Students may find networking with friends helpful. If they have a problem, they can call a friend or see them in school or college. Students who prefer to work in this way should be aware of which students in their teaching group are most likely to give helpful advice. Networking is a valuable tool in the learning process both to the person who receives the help and the person who gives it.

Parents, business people, etc. Parents, family members, friends or contacts in the business community may all be sources of help in different situations and for different pieces of work.

The work environment

Your work environment needs to be chosen to maximise learning. Students often work either in a library or study area, or at home in their own room. What is there about these work places which makes them effective?

Availability Your work place should be available to you when you want to study. If you like to complete as much work as possible at school or college, and work hard between time-tabled lessons, then the library might be an excellent environment for you. You may prefer to complete homework in your own home. Your bedroom may be the only place where you are guaranteed that you can work uninterrupted. Not only must a place be available but so too must the resources. If you are undertaking research, for instance, you may have to work in a library or at a computer terminal.

Music, television and noise Some students find it easy to concentrate in the midst of chaos. They like distractions and find it easier to work if they know they can also listen to music, stroke the dog or have a conversation. Many students find distractions impossible to cope with. To work effectively, they need relative peace and quiet. They might or might not like background music.

Alone or in groups Some students find that working in a group is ineffective. One person may start talking about a non-work issue and work is then never resumed. They therefore prefer to work alone. However, other students who can avoid such distractions find working in groups highly effective. It means they can instantly network with others when they have a problem.

Furniture Furniture can be very important in studying. Some students prefer to read in an armchair and write at a desk. You may find it easier to create work spaces where particular types of work can be done. Make sure that the chair you sit in is comfortable and doesn't give you back problems.

Lighting Experiment with lighting to reduce eye strain. If you find studying makes you tired very quickly, one reason might be inadequate lighting. You can also use lighting to create a mood which encourages you to study.

Movement Your work environment should allow you to move around if you wish. When trying to memorise something, for instance, some students may prefer to walk around, whereas others may prefer to sit.

Preparing for tests and examinations

Different students prepare effectively for tests or examinations in a variety of different ways. You have to find out what is most effective for you. Different methods may also be useful in different circumstances. For instance, you may want to spend most time memorising information for an essay-based examination, but for a multiple-choice examination you may want to spend most time practising past questions.

Written notes Many students use notes in their revision. Notes are useful records of what has been learned either because the student has made them and therefore hopefully can understand them, or because they have been given by the teacher or lecturer and show what material is likely to occur in the examination.

Good note taking is a skilled art. Notes are meant to be a precis, a shortening of what, for instance, might be found in a textbook. So it is important to develop a style of writing notes which does shorten material.
- Miss out common words like 'the' and 'a' which do not affect the meaning.
- Abbreviate words. For example, write 'gov' for 'government', 'C' for consumption, or 'P' for price.

Notes should be clearly laid out using headings and subheadings. Ideally, headings and subheadings should be colour coded to make them easier to skim read. The headings should provide a story in themselves which prompts you to remember the material contained underneath each heading. Highlight key terms within the notes. Star, circle or underline important points.

Some students like to work from notes written on A4 paper. Other students like to transfer notes onto small cards where there is less on each card. Whichever method you use, make sure that the notes are logically ordered and can be referred to instantly.

When memorising material from notes, some students find it helpful to think of the layout of individual pages. This then prompts memory recall of what is on the page.

The textbook Some students dislike revising from notes and prefer to use a textbook. They may find it easier, for instance, to read printed material rather than their own handwriting. They may want to use material collected together rather than a series of handouts or loose pages. Also, notes may be incomplete in places.

Some students rely on both notes and textbooks for revision. Revising from a textbook involves the same skills as revising from notes. The textbook will have chapter or unit headings, and headings and subheadings within these. These provide the skeleton on which the detail should be hung.

Pictures and visual presentations Some students find pictures particularly helpful when revising. Examples of commonly used visual presentations include mind maps, flow charts and family trees, which are illustrated in Figures 46.1 to 46.3. These illustrations summarise the main points in unit 4,

The Demand Curve, of this book. Visual presentations work through helping the student see a topic laid out. Places on the page can be visualised and connections clearly identified.

Oral methods Some students like to be 'tested' by another person on a topic to see if they have learnt the material. Repeating words or phrases can be helpful. So too can devising word associations and mnemonics. A word association is linking one word with another. For instance, you may be particularly interested in football, and decide to remember the main components of aggregate demand (consumption, investment, government spending and exports minus imports) by assigning each term to the name of a football club. Remember the football clubs and you remember the components. Alternatively, you may make up a mnemonic, a rhyme or phrase usually associated with the first letter of each word. For instance, you could have Clobber In Gap Extremely Important OR Chelsea In Goal Excitement Incident for consumption, investment, government spending, exports and imports.

Active learning Some students find it difficult just to sit and memorise material. They need to be doing something to help them remember.
- One way is to construct a set of notes, or a mind map. Once written out, the notes may be of little use, but it is in the doing that the learning has taken place.
- You may want to practice past examination questions. Multiple choice question papers, for instance, are best revised for in this way. If you practice essay questions, it is often more useful to spend scarce time writing out essay plans for a wide variety of questions than answering a few essays in detail.
- You may use published materials which give short answer questions on a topic such as 'Define economies of scale', or 'List the costs of unemployment'.
- Some students practice past homework tasks which they have been set and then compare their results with their first marked attempt.

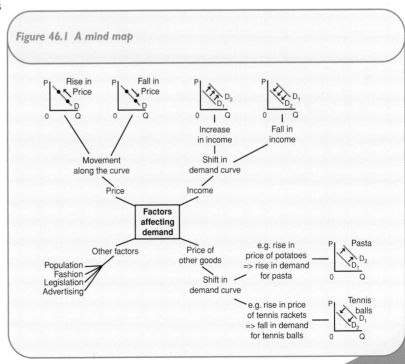

Figure 46.1 A mind map

Figure 46.2 Flow charts

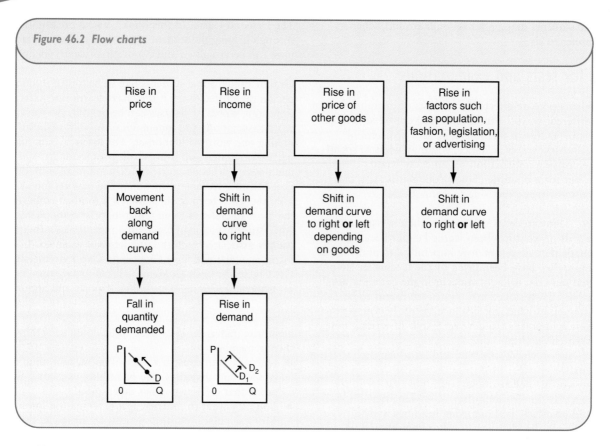

Figure 46.3 A family tree

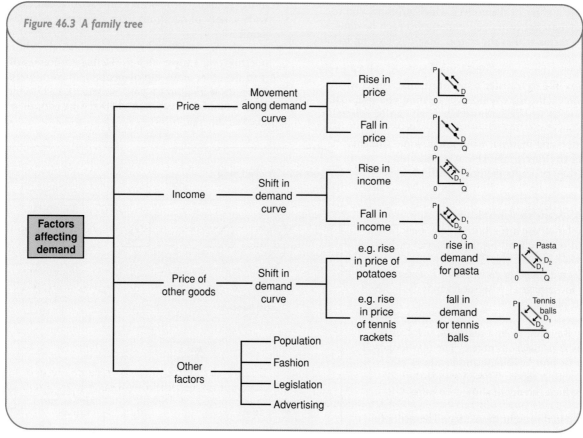

Assessment criteria

Specifications are drawn up and papers are set to test a range of assessment criteria. These are qualities and skills which a candidate must demonstrate to the examiners to gain marks in any form of assessment. In Economics at AS/A level, these assessment criteria are grouped into four areas.

Demonstration of knowledge and understanding of the specified subject content **Knowledge and understanding** requires candidates to show that they can recognise economic concepts and terms and be able to define or explain them. For instance, *Explain what is meant by economies of scale* asks for a definition of economies of scale (knowledge) and a good answer is likely to give examples to demonstrate clear understanding of the term. Knowledge and understanding are also present when economic theories are used. For instance, knowledge is required when drawing a demand and supply diagram. Has the candidate correctly identified the axes? Is the demand curve downward sloping? Is the supply curve upward sloping? Is the candidate using proper conventions by clearly labelling the axes and the demand and supply curves? Another example would be the link between interest rates and inflation. Does a candidate show knowledge of the chain of causality between a change in interest rates, a change in aggregate demand and a change in the equilibrium price level of the economy?

Application of knowledge and critical understanding to economic problems and issues arising from both familiar and unfamiliar situations Knowledge is essential for any economist, but the knowledge must be **applied** to economic problems to be of use. For instance, being able to define economies of scale is of little use if economies of scale at work in motor vehicle manufacturing cannot be recognised. Application is the skill of being able to use knowledge in a wide variety of contexts. Some of these contexts will be familiar. For instance, you might have studied leisure industries during your course and in the examination a question is set on economies of scale in leisure industries. The context may, however, be unfamiliar. For instance, you may have studied the environment as part your course. In the examination, a question on pollution permits in the USA may be set. Pollution permits is part of expected knowledge and understanding but the USA may be an unfamiliar context. Another example of application would be using mathematical formulae to work out answers to problems. Calculating a value for price elasticity of demand is application.

Analyse economic problems and issues **Analysis** is the process of breaking down information into relevant parts and then using this to understand a problem or issue. A simple piece of analysis, for instance, would be to identify a trend from a set of unemployment figures on a graph. The graph might be accompanied by a passage which contains information about why unemployment might be falling. The skill of analysis is needed to link the trend with its causes. Analysis would also be required if a candidate were asked to identify possible government policies to tackle unemployment. The candidate might have to select which policies from a list might be appropriate and justify why these policies might be effective.

Evaluate economic arguments and evidence, making informed judgements **Evaluation** requires candidates to make conclusions and argue which courses of action might be most appropriate in a situation. If a government wanted to reduce unemployment today, which would be the most effective policies for it to pursue? If global warming is to be stopped, what are the most important actions which consumers and firms must take? It is relatively easy to make a simple judgement. At this level, though, examiners expect candidates to be able to justify their answers. It is this justification which tends to carry most marks. To do this, candidates must weigh up the evidence presented to them and judge which is important and which is not. They must consider whether the information presented is reliable and whether or not it is complete enough to come to a decision. If it is not, what other information is required to come to a definitive conclusion? Candidates must also distinguish between fact and opinion.

Candidates are also assessed in Economics AS/A level on the **quality of written communication**. Candidates must:
- select and use a form and style of writing appropriate to purpose and complex subject matter. For instance, candidates must be able to write an essay, or a short answer to a question;
- organise relevant information clearly and coherently, using specialist vocabulary when appropriate. So candidates must, for instance, be able to write in paragraphs and they must be able to use terms like price elasticity or the current balance when these are required;
- ensure writing is legible, and spelling, grammar and punctuation are accurate, so that meaning is clear. Candidates must therefore write clearly, construct proper sentences and spell correctly.

Command, directive or key words

Questions typically start off with command or key words. These words indicate which skills are required when answering the question. It is important for candidates to respond in an appropriate manner. For instance, if candidates are asked to evaluate a problem, but only show knowledge and understanding, then they will lose most of the marks for that question. Command words can be grouped according to what skills will be required in an answer.

Knowledge and understanding

- Define - to give the exact meaning of a term or concept using words or mathematical symbols whose meaning is already understood by the reader, e.g. *Define what is meant by economies of scale*.
- Describe - to give an account of something, e.g. *Describe the costs of inflation*.
- Give - to state or say, e.g. *Give two examples of goods in which Saudi Arabia has a comparative advantage in production*.

- How - to present an account of something, e.g. *How does the government raise taxes?*
- Identify - to single out from other information, e.g. *Identify three factors which cause inflation.*
- Illustrate - to use examples to explain a point, e.g. *Illustrate the way in which monopolists keep out competitors from their markets.*
- List - to state in the briefest form, e.g. *List three factors which affect the demand for a product.*
- Outline - to give a short description of the main aspects or features, e.g. *Outline the arguments used by Greenpeace against genetically modified (GM) crops.*
- State - to give or say, e.g. *State three factors which affect elasticity of supply.*
- Summarise - to bring out the main points from a more complex set of data, e.g. *Summarise the main arguments in favour of government intervention.*
- What - to clarify a point, e.g. *What are the main characteristics of a perfectly competitive industry?*

Application

- Apply - use knowledge of economics to understand a situation, issue or problem, e.g. *Apply the theory of perfect competition to the market for potatoes.*
- Calculate - use mathematics to work out an answer, e.g. *Calculate the price elasticity of demand if price increases from £3 to £4.*
- Distinguish between - identify the characteristics which make two or more ideas, concepts, issues, etc. different, e.g. *Distinguish between price elasticity of demand and income elasticity of demand.*
- Explain - making clear. It is often useful to define terms and give examples in an explanation, e.g. *Explain how prices are determined in a free market.*
- Suggest - give possible reasons or ideas. These must be plausible but not necessarily correct. 'Suggest' may require candidates to analyse a problem and not just apply economic problems, e.g. *Suggest reasons why the firm did not put up its prices.*

Analysis

- Analyse - to break down into constituent parts in order to be able to understand an issue or problem. Analysis involves recognising what is important, and relating to knowledge and understanding of economics where necessary, e.g. *Analyse the reasons for the firm investing in new machinery.*
- Compare and contrast - to show the similarities and differences between two or more ideas or problems, e.g. *Compare and contrast the performance of the UK and Chinese economies over the past ten years.*
- Examine - to break down an issue or problem to understand it, e.g. *Examine the problems facing the UK economy today.*
- Investigate - to look for evidence to explain and analyse, e.g. *Investigate why the government chose to cut interest rates in May.*

Evaluation

- Assess - to analyse an economic issue or problem and then to weigh up the relative importance of different strands, e.g. *Assess the impact of high interest rates on the UK economy.*
- Comment on - invites the candidate to make their judgements based upon evidence which they have presented, e.g. *Comment on why the Bank of England thought it necessary to raise interest rates in June.*
- Critically analyse - to analyse an issue or problem and then to weigh up the relative importance of part of this analysis, e.g. *Critically analyse the problems facing the industry today.*
- Do you think - invites candidates to put forward their own opinions about an issue or problem. However, the marks will always be awarded for the quality of the arguments put forward and not for any individual opinions, e.g. *Do you think the government should have allowed the motorway to be built?*
- Discuss - to compare a number of possible views about an issue or problem and to weigh up their relative importance. A conclusion is essential, e.g. *Discuss the advantages and disadvantages of fixing rents in the housing market.*
- Evaluate - like discuss, to compare a number of possible views about an issue or problem and weigh up their relative importance. A final judgement is essential, e.g. *Evaluate the policies available to government to reduce unemployment.*
- To what extent - invites candidates to explain and analyse and then to comment upon the relative importance of arguments, e.g. *To what extent should the government rely upon interest rates to control inflation?*

Levels of response

Questions which test the higher order skills of analysis and evaluation are likely to be marked using a levels of response mark scheme. Rather than giving candidates a mark or several marks for a point made or an argument developed within an answer, the answer is marked holistically (as a whole). It is then compared to descriptions of what answers might look like in terms of the skills displayed. The answer is then put within a level. This level will have a range of marks which the examiner can award depending upon whether it is a good answer within that level or not.

For instance, a levels mark scheme might have three levels and 12 marks are awarded. The level descriptors are as follows.

Level 1

One or more reasons given, but little development of points. The answer lacks coherence and there is no valid analysis or evaluation. 1-3 marks

Level 2

Several reasons given with reasonable analysis. Arguments are expressed with some confidence and coherence. Evaluation, though, is weakly supported by evidence. 4-8 marks

Level 3

A good coverage of the main reasons. Sound analysis with clear links between the issues raised. Arguments for and against have been evaluated and a conclusion reached. 9-12 marks

Mark schemes are available from the awarding bodies. You should become familiar with the levels of response mark schemes used by examiners on the papers you will sit. To gain a mark in the highest level, candidates typically have to give evidence of all four main skills of knowledge, application, analysis and evaluation.

Multiple choice questions

Some awarding bodies use multiple choice questions as a form of assessment. They are used mainly to test lower order skills of knowledge and application. They are also a convenient way of testing breadth. A data response question or an essay is likely to cover only one topic. If there is choice, candidates may be encouraged only to revise part of the course in the hope that they will still be able to answer a full set of questions. A multiple choice test covers the whole course and therefore penalises candidates who are selective in their revision.

Success at multiple choice questions involves being thoroughly familiar with the basics of economics. It also requires skill in answering multiple choice questions, just as essays requires essay writing skills. Practice on questions is therefore very important. Using past question papers from the awarding body can also be very helpful. Not only will it help you familiarise yourself with the style of multiple choice question being used, but past questions may be reused on new papers.

There are two ways in which candidates are likely to get to a correct answer on a multiple choice question.
- Knowing the correct answer.
- Eliminating the wrong answers.
Candidates should make full use of the laws of probability. If the correct answer is not obvious, but two out of four responses can be eliminated, the chances of getting the answer right are improved from 1 in 4 for guessing to 1 in 2. Taken over a whole paper, a strategy of eliminating wrong answers can significantly improve marks.

Some multiple choice tests require candidates not just to give an answer from A to D but also to justify their answers. The written explanation should be short and to the point.

In an examination, do not spend more than the allotted time on any single question but pass over it. For instance, if there are 30 questions to be answered in 30 minutes, there is on average just 1 minute per question. Don't spend 10 minutes working out question 5. Come back at the end to the questions which you have missed out. If you have nearly run out of time, always make sure that there is an answer to every question. You will then have some chance rather than no chance to gain marks. Some candidates prefer to draw a line through incorrect responses (i.e. wrong answers) within a question and visibly isolate the correct answer.

Data response questions

Data response questions are used to test a candidate's ability to apply their knowledge and understanding to familiar or unfamiliar data. They usually also require candidates to display skills of analysis and evaluation as well.

The data presented may be verbal or in numerical form, or a mixture of both. Candidates often find data in verbal form easier to understand and interpret. However, in practice, examiners construct questions so that there is little or no difference in outcome in marks between questions which contain mainly verbal data and those which contain mainly numerical data.

Some awarding bodies only use real data, such as newspaper extracts or statistics from government sources. Others also use hypothetical or imaginary data - data which has been made up by the examiner. In some areas of Economics, it is difficult to obtain real data. Exact figures for price elasticity of demand is one example. Therefore some examiners prefer to use imaginary data for questions.

There is a number of ways in which candidates can improve their performance on data response questions in examinations.
- Read through the material thoroughly.
- Use highlighter pens to mark what you think are important words or passages.
- Highlight the key words in a question.
- Think carefully about what each question is asking of you. In particular, think about the skills you are required to display in a question.
- If there are any numerical calculations, show all your workings carefully. You may get marks for the workings even if you fail to get the final answer correct.
- Have a clear understanding of how long each answer should be. For instance, assume there are 60 marks overall, with the first two questions being awarded 5 marks each, the third question carrying 10 marks, the fourth carrying 15 marks and the last 25 marks. The first question should be roughly one fifth the length of the last question and should take only $5/60$ of the time to complete. Many candidates write too much on questions which carry few marks and too little on questions which carry many marks.
- Be aware of what economic concepts and theories the question is testing.
- Some candidates find it helpful to prepare plans for longer answers.
- Make sure you don't run out of time. It is usually better to abandon one part and move onto the next if you are running out of time rather than attempting to create the perfect answer on that part.
- Last parts of data response questions may expect candidates to write for around 20 minutes. These questions then become small essays and the techniques for writing essays outlined below need to be applied to them.

Sometimes, it is appropriate to use a diagram in a data response question. Some questions, in fact, specifically ask for a diagram to be drawn. There are some easy rules to remember when drawing diagrams.
- Examiners will expect to see standard diagrams which are found in any Economics textbook.
- When drawing diagrams, make sure they are large enough to be read.
- Diagrams are easier to read and look much better if they are drawn with a ruler where appropriate.
- Always label the axes and the lines or curves.
- Always refer to and explain the diagram in your written answer.

Essays

Essays are often used to test higher order skills of analysis and evaluation, although there are likely to be marks for knowledge and application in the mark scheme too. Typically, candidates are expected to write for 35 to 45 minutes on an essay title which is likely to be split into two separate but linked parts. Essay writing is a skill which needs to be practised and learnt. It requires putting together (or

synthesising) a number of ideas to form one complete answer. Essays are likely to be marked using levels of response mark schemes.

Candidates can improve their essay writing skills if they can learn the following techniques.

● Before you start writing, have a clear understanding of what the question is asking. In particular, identify the skills which will be required from you to write a successful essay by looking at the command words. Identify too the areas of economics of relevance to the essay. Some candidates also find it useful to highlight the key words in an essay title to focus them on what the question is asking. For instance, take the following question: *Evaluate the policies which a government might adopt to deal with the problem of youth unemployment.* The key words here are *Evaluate, government policies* and *youth unemployment.* Evaluate means that you will have to compare the effectiveness of different types of government policy. You will be expected to argue that some might be more useful than others in order to gain the maximum number of marks. Government policies to deal with unemployment is the main area of economic knowledge. However, especially important is the word *youth*. Your answer must focus on *youth* unemployment if it is to get the higher marks.

● Some candidates find it useful to write out an **essay plan**. This is a brief synopsis of what you will write. It allows you to jot points down and to see how they can be organised to form a coherent whole. Often candidates start their answer and add points to their plan as they go along because writing triggers their memories. This is good practice, but always check that your new points will not unbalance the structure of your answer. Adding new material after you have written your conclusion, for instance, may gain you extra marks but it is unlikely to help you get the highest marks.

● Paragraph your essay properly. Remember that a paragraph should contain material on one idea or one group of ideas. A useful technique to use is to see a paragraph as an opening sentence which makes a point, and the rest of the paragraph as an explanation or elaboration of that point.

● Include diagrams wherever they are appropriate. Advice about the effective use of diagrams is given above.

● Write a concluding paragraph. This is especially important if you are answering an evaluation question. The conclusion gives you the opportunity to draw your points together and to weigh up the arguments put forward.

● With two part questions, ensure that you have allocated your time effectively between the two parts. Don't spend too much time on the first half of the question. It is particularly important to work out how long to spend on each part if the two parts carry very unequal mark weighting.

● Essays are continuous pieces of prose. They should not include bullet points, lists, subheadings, etc.

● Spot the story. Many essay questions are set because they cover a topical issue. Recognising what this topical issue is should help you decide what to stress in your essay. Knowledge of the issue will also give you additional material to introduce into the essay.

● Adapt your material to suit what is required. Don't write out an answer to an essay question you have already answered in class and memorised and which is similar to the essay question set. Equally, don't write 'everything I know about' one or two key words in the essay title. For instance, answering a question about the costs of inflation by

writing at length about the causes of inflation is likely to be an inappropriate answer.

● Remember there are likely to be marks for quality of language in the mark scheme. Write in a simple and clear style and pay attention to your spelling.

Coursework

You may be required to write a piece of coursework. You are likely to be given extensive help in doing this by your teacher or lecturer.

Planning One key issue in coursework for the student is time management. Coursework is likely to be carried out over a period of time. It is important that deadlines are not missed because they are weeks or months ahead before the coursework is due to be handed in. It is also important that all work is not left to the end when there may not be enough time to complete it. Planning is therefore very important. Your teacher or lecturer is likely to help you in this, setting goals and helping you to complete the coursework well within the time limit required.

Following specification instructions The examination specification will give detailed instructions about how topics should be chosen, how the coursework should be written up and how marks will be awarded. You should always keep a copy of this with your work. Awarding bodies also publish specification support materials for teachers and lecturers. These too will contain information about coursework which should be made available to you. High marks are usually gained by following what examiners have told candidates to do.

Choice of topic Your first task will be to decide upon a topic to research. This should be an investigation into an economic problem or issue. The choice of topic is vital for two reasons. First, the student must be able to obtain primary and/or secondary data on the topic. Secondary data is data and information which have already been collected by someone else. It is likely to be the main source if not the sole source of data for the investigation. It might, for instance, include newspaper articles, government statistics, or material from web sites on the Internet. Primary data is data which have been collected directly by the student and do not come from another source. The results of a questionnaire conducted by the student would be an example. Primary data may not be available for the chosen topic. Primary data may also be of poor quality, for example from a poorly conducted survey. So primary data should only be included when it is reliable and relevant to the chosen topic.

Choice of topic is also important because it will determine whether the candidate can display all the skills required by the examination. This will include both analysis and evaluation. The key is to phrase the coursework title as a problem or issue. 'Is the package tour industry an oligopoly?' may not be a suitable title. It does not give candidates sufficient scope to display skills of evaluation. A title which asked whether the UK or EU competition authorities should allow a merger which is currently being proposed between package tour companies is a more suitable title. Candidates will be able to explore the issue, including commenting on the oligopolistic nature of the package tour industry. They will then have to use this analysis to evaluate a policy decision. This is precisely what economists working for the competition authorities would, of course, also be doing.

Collecting information Collecting information is likely to take time although the Internet is now increasingly reducing this. For example, a newspaper search may have taken a number of sessions in a library but may now be carried out in the session using a search engine and a site. Gathering statistical information from government publications such as *Economic Trends Annual Supplement* and converting it into a form which is useful in your chosen assignment may take longer. However, the Internet may be equally time consuming. You may have to sift through large amounts of irrelevant information to find something of value.

If you undertake any primary research, you should have a clear understanding of the techniques you are using and what makes them valid as evidence. For instance, if you construct a questionnaire, you should be aware of the issues involved in setting appropriate questions. You should also understand the size and nature of the sample needed to give valid results. Data are likely to be collected from the following sources:

- books, including textbooks;
- newspapers;
- magazines;
- specialist trade journals;
- advertising literature;
- government statistical publications including *Monthly Digest of Statistics, Economic Trends* and *Economic Trends Annual Supplement, Annual Abstract of Statistics, Social Trends, Regional Trends, Environmental Statistics* and *Transport Statistics*;
- websites on the Internet.

When collecting information, seek the help of others where possible. For instance, if you use a library, ask the librarian for help in finding material. If you use the Internet, make sure that you understand how best to use a search engine.

Collecting information is time consuming and challenging. Don't underestimate the difficulty of this part of the task.

Structuring the report The awarding body will give clear guidance on how the report should be laid out and what should be included. For instance, awarding bodies may recommend that there should be:

- a contents page;
- an introduction outlining the economic issue or problem to be investigated, framed in the form of either an hypothesis to be tested or a question requiring further investigation;
- a brief outline of economic concepts and theories relevant to the issue or problem, in some cases involving reference to existing literature;
- a brief outline of the technique(s) to be used to collect the relevant data;
- a presentation of the findings related to the hypothesis or the question posed;
- an evaluation of the findings and method of research, with recommendations where appropriate;
- a bibliography of sources.

When writing your report, remember that you are writing about economic theory and presenting the evidence you have collected to arrive at a set of conclusions. It is important to avoid writing everything you can find from textbooks about certain economic theories, or forgetting that the purpose of collecting evidence is to evaluate problems or issues.

Report writing

Students may be required to write a report. The style of a report is different from that of an essay.

- It should begin with a section showing who the report is for, who has written it, the date it was written and the title. If the report is written under examination conditions, this may all be omitted.
- It should be broken down into a number of sections. Each section should address a particular issue. A heading should start each section to help the reader see the structure of the report. In most reports, sections are numbered in sequence.
- A section may be broken down into sub-sections, each with their own headings and their own numbers. For instance, section 3 of the report may have two sub-sections, 3.1 and 3.2.
- The report must be written in complete sentences and not in note form. However, unlike in an essay, it is acceptable to use bullet points to further structure the report.
- Use diagrams wherever appropriate. Diagrams must be part of the argument used in the report. It is important that the reader understands why they have been included.

A report will require you to draw conclusions and make judgements, i.e. show that you can evaluate an issue or problem. The evaluation can be presented at the end of the report, or it can be included in each section of the report. If it is included in each section, a conclusion or summary still needs to be written at the end to bring together what has been said earlier.

The report should also highlight missing information that would have been useful or, perhaps, was essential, to come to reasoned conclusions or recommendations. The reliability or accuracy of the information provided could also be questioned.

If the report is written in examination conditions, as with a data response question, take time at the start to read through the data given. Highlight key ideas or data. It may not be necessary to understand all the data before you start writing as this may waste important time which may be needed to write the report. However, it is important to understand what is required of you before you start writing.

Constructing a plan is essential. A report is a complex piece of writing. Identify the main headings of your report and jot down the main points which you are likely to include under each heading. You may add to your plan as you write your report if you think of new points. In an examination, you are unlikely to have the time to write a number of drafts of the report. However, outside the examination room, it would be useful to produce several drafts.